D1135102

THE ANNALS
OF
AMERICA

THE ANNALS OF AMERICA

Volume 1
1493 - 1754

Discovering a New World

ENCYCLOPÆDIA BRITANNICA, INC.

Chicago London Toronto Geneva Sydney Tokyo Manila Johannesburg Seoul

The editors wish to express their gratitude for permission to reprint material from the following sources:

Harvard University Press for Selection 93, from *A Brief Narrative of the Case and Trial of John Peter Zenger*, by James Alexander, ed. by Stanley Nider Katz, Cambridge, Mass.: Harvard University Press, Copyright 1963 by the President and Fellows of Harvard College.

Alfred A. Knopf for Selection 13, from *Of Plymouth Plantation*, by William Bradford, ed. by Samuel Eliot Morison, Copyright 1952 by Alfred A. Knopf, Inc.

Charles Scribner's Sons for Selection 98, from *American Christianity, An Historical Interpretation with Representative Documents*, ed. by H. Shelton Smith, Robert T. Handy, and Lefferts A. Loetscher, Vol. I.

Staff for Volumes 1-18

CODED SOURCES IN THIS VOLUME

Force

Tracts and Other Papers, Relating Principally to the Origin, Settlement, and Progress of the Colonies in North America, from the Discovery of the Country to the Year 1776. Edited by Peter Force. In 4 vols. Washington, 1836-1846.

Hazard

Historical Collections; Consisting of State Papers, and Other Authentic Documents; Intended as Materials for An History of the United States of America. Edited by Ebenezer Hazard. In 2 vols. Philadelphia, 1792-1794.

Hening

The Statutes at Large; Being a Collection of all Laws of Virginia, from the first Session of the Legislature in the year 1619. Edited by William W. Hening. In 13 vols. covering the years 1619 to 1792. New York and Philadelphia, 1819-1823.

MHSC

Collections, Massachusetts Historical Society. Cambridge and Boston, 1795 et seq.

OSL

Old South Leaflets. Published by the Directors of the Old South Work, Old South Meeting House. In 8 vols. (Documents 1-200). Boston, n.d.

Pickering

The Statutes at Large [of Great Britain]. Volumes 1-46 edited by Danby Pickering. Cambridge (England), various dates.

Poore

The Federal and State Constitutions, Colonial Charters, and Other Organic Laws of the United States. Edited by B. P. Poore. In 2 vols. Washington, 1877.

Sparks

The Works of Benjamin Franklin, etc., etc. Edited by Jared Sparks. In 10 vols. Boston, 1836-1840.

Thorpe

The Federal and State Constitutions, Colonial Charters, and Other Organic Laws of the States, Territories, and Colonies now or Heretofore Forming the United States of America. Edited by Francis N. Thorpe. In 7 vols. Washington, 1909.

Works
[of Benjamin Franklin]

The Complete Works in Philosophy, Politics, and Morals of the Late Dr. Benjamin Franklin, now First collected and Arranged, with Memoirs of his Early Life, written by Himself. 2nd edition in 3 vols. London, n.d.

Contents

On Corporal Punishment
On the Killing of Slaves

1661

1666

1674 - 1677

1675

1676

1677

1682

1684

1754

DISCOVERING A NEW WORLD
In Pictures

Following Columbus' discovery the Spanish quickly expanded their
influence in the West Indies, Florida, and Central America.
Reports of the riches of Spain's empire attracted others to the
New World, first as marauders, then as colonists.

The engravings of Theodore de Bry and others gave Europeans their
first detailed impression of the "salvages" of North America.

As Spain's power declined after the defeat of her Armada in
1588, other European countries, notably France and England,
planted colonial settlements in North America, the first
permanent one at Jamestown in Virginia.

Several new colonies, such as Pennsylvania and Carolina,
were established during the 17th century by emigrants
from Europe and migrants from the already established colonies, while
French explorers and traders penetrated the Mississippi Valley.

New England 351-359

By the 18th century New England was prospering from commerce
and fishing. The intellectual climate was marked by
religious discussion — and disputation.

The Southern Colonies 389-393

Virginia, Maryland, and Carolina were largely dominated
by their economies, which were based on cash crops — mainly
tobacco and rice — cultivated by slave labor.

Rival Colonial Empires 447-453

The expansion of the French, British, and Spanish colonial empires
in North America brought the three European nations into increasing
conflict during the first half of the 18th century.

The Middle Colonies 509-517

Pennsylvania was notable for the diversity of its population,
mainly made up of small-holders and craftsmen, and was
in marked contrast to New York, whose commercial and
landowning structure was aristocratic.

1493

1.

CHRISTOPHER COLUMBUS: Discovery of the New World

The story of America's "discovery" by Christopher Columbus is familiar to every schoolboy, yet neither Columbus nor any of his crew realized what it was they had discovered. On the first of his four voyages to the New World, Columbus led a flotilla of three ships, the Niña, the Pinta, and his flagship, the Santa Maria, departing from Palos, Spain, in the summer of 1492, and arriving in the Bahamas in October. Land was sighted for the first time at dawn on October 12 — hence the modern Columbus Day. The expedition touched at such Caribbean islands as San Salvador, Cuba, and Española (Santo Domingo), and Columbus, convinced that he had discovered "the Indies," established trading posts and returned to Spain to announce his success, and to organize a larger expedition. He stopped at Lisbon on his way home, and from there sent a description of the lands and people he had seen to Lord Raphael Sanchez, treasurer of Aragon and one of his patrons. In the letter, dated March 14, 1493, Columbus referred to the natives he had found as "Indians," believing, as he did until his death, that he had reached the eastern shores of Asia.

Source: *Select Letters of Christopher Columbus, etc., etc.*, R. H. Major, ed., London, 1847, pp. 1-17.

KNOWING that it will afford you pleasure to learn that I have brought my undertaking to a successful termination, I have decided upon writing you this letter to acquaint you with all the events which have occurred in my voyage, and the discoveries which have resulted from it. Thirty-three days after my departure from [Gomera] I reached the Indian Sea, where I discovered many islands, thickly peopled, of which I took possession without resistance in the name of our most illustrious monarch, by public proclamation and with unfurled banners. To the first of these islands, which is called by the Indians Guanahani, I gave the name of the blessed Savior (San Salvador), relying upon whose protection I had reached this as well as the other islands; to each of these I also gave a name, ordering that one should be called Santa Maria de la Concepcion, another Fernandina, the third Isabella, the fourth Juana [Cuba], and so with all the rest. . . .

As soon as we arrived at that, which as I have said was named Juana, I proceeded along its coast a short distance westward and found it to be so large and apparently without termination that I could not suppose it to be an island, but the continental province of Cathay. Seeing, however, no towns or populous places on the seacoast, but only a few detached houses and cottages, with whose inhabitants I was unable to communicate because they fled as soon as they saw us, I went further on, thinking that in my progress I should certainly find some city or village.

At length, after proceeding a great way and finding that nothing new presented itself and that the line of coast was leading us northward (which I wished to avoid because it was winter, and it was my intention to move southward, and because, moreover, the winds were contrary), I resolved not to attempt any further progress but rather to turn back and retrace my course to a certain bay that I had observed, and from which I afterward dispatched two of our men to ascertain whether there were a king or any cities in that province. These men reconnoitered the country for three days and found a most numerous population and great numbers of houses, though small and built without any regard to order; with which information they returned to us. In the meantime I had learned from some Indians whom I had seized that that country was certainly an island, and therefore I sailed toward the east, coasting to the distance of 322 miles, which brought us to the extremity of it; from this point I saw lying eastward another island, 54 miles distant from Juana, to which I gave the name of Española [Hispaniola]. I went thither and steered my course eastward as I had done at Juana, even to the distance of 564 miles along the north coast. . . .

In that island also, which I have before said we named Española, there are mountains of very great size and beauty, vast plains, groves, and very fruitful fields, admirably adapted for tillage, pasture, and habitation. The convenience and excellence of the harbors in this island and the abundance of the rivers, so indispensable to the health of man, surpass anything that would be believed by one who had not seen it. The trees, herbage, and fruits of Española are very different from those of Juana, and, moreover, it abounds in various kinds of spices, gold, and other metals.

The inhabitants of both sexes in this island, and in all the others which I have seen or of which I have received information, go always naked as they were born, with the exception of some of the women, who use the covering of a leaf or small bough or an apron of cotton which they prepare for that purpose. None of them, as I have already said, are possessed of any iron, neither have they weapons, being unacquainted with and indeed incompetent to use them, not from any deformity of body (for they are well formed) but because they are timid and full of fear. They carry, however, in lieu of arms, canes dried in the sun, on the ends of which they fix heads of dried wood sharpened to a point, and even these they dare not use habitually; for it has often occurred when I have sent two or three of my men to any of the villages to speak with the natives, that they have come out in a disorderly troop and have fled in such haste at the approach of our men that the fathers forsook their children and the children their fathers. This timidity did not arise from any loss or injury that they had received from us; for, on the contrary, I gave to all I approached whatever articles I had about me, such as cloth and many other things, taking nothing of theirs in return; but they are naturally timid and fearful.

As soon, however, as they see that they are safe and have laid aside all fear, they are very simple and honest and exceedingly liberal with all they have; none of them refusing anything he may possess when he is asked for it, but, on the contrary, inviting us to ask them. They exhibit great love toward all others in preference to themselves. They also give objects of great value for trifles, and content themselves with very little or nothing in return. I, however, forbade that these trifles and articles of no value (such as pieces of dishes, plates, and glass, keys, and leather straps) should be given to them, although if they could obtain them, they imagined themselves to be possessed of the most beautiful trinkets in the world. It even happened that a sailor received for a leather strap as much gold as was worth three golden nobles, and for things of more trifling value offered by our men, especially newly coined blancas or any gold coins, the Indians would give whatever the seller required; as, for instance, an ounce and a half or two ounces of gold, or thirty or forty pounds of cotton, with which commodity they were already acquainted. Thus they bartered, like idiots, cotton and gold for fragments of bows, glasses, bottles, and jars, which I forbade as being unjust, and myself gave them many beautiful and acceptable articles which I had brought with me, taking nothing from them in return. I did this in order that I might the more easily conciliate them, that they might be led to become Christians and be inclined to entertain a regard for the King and Queen, our Princes, and all Spaniards, and that I might induce them to take an interest in seeking out and collecting and delivering to us such things as they possessed in abundance, but which we greatly needed. They practise no kind of idolatry, but have a firm belief that all strength and power, and indeed all good things, are in heaven, and that I had descended from thence with these ships and sailors, and under this impression was I received after they had thrown aside their fears. Nor are they slow or stupid, but of very clear understanding; and those men who have crossed to the neighboring islands give an admirable description of everything they observed; but they never saw any people clothed nor any ships like ours.

On my arrival at that sea, I had taken

Courtesy, Reference Department, New York Public Library

Facsimile of the earliest reproduction of the landing of Columbus, in Dati, "Narrative of Columbus," 1493

some Indians by force from the first island that I came to, in order that they might learn our language and communicate to us what they knew respecting the country; which plan succeeded excellently and was a great advantage to us, for in a short time, either by gestures and signs or by words, we were enabled to understand each other. These men are still traveling with me, and although they have been with us now a long time, they continue to entertain the idea that I have descended from heaven; and on our arrival at any new place they published this, crying out immediately with a loud voice to the other Indians, "Come, come and look upon beings of a celestial race"; upon which both women and men, children and adults, young men and old, when they got rid of the fear they at first entertained, would come out in throngs, crowding the roads to see us, some bringing food, others drink, with astonishing affection and kindness.

Each of these islands has a great number of canoes, built of solid wood, narrow and not unlike our double-banked boats in length and shape, but swifter in their motion; they steer them only by the oar. These canoes are of various sizes, but the greater number are constructed with eighteen banks of oars, and with these they cross to the other islands, which are of countless number, to carry on traffic with the people. I saw some of these canoes that held as many as seventy-eight rowers. In all these islands there is no difference of physiognomy, of manners, or of language, but they all clearly understand each other, a circumstance very propitious for the realization of what I conceive to be the principal wish of our most serene King, namely, the conversion of these people to the holy faith of Christ, to which indeed, as far as I can judge, they are very favorable and well-disposed. I said before that I went 322 miles in a direct line from west to east, along the coast of the island of Juana, judging by which voyage, and the length of the passage, I can assert that it is larger than England and Scotland united; for independent of the said 322 miles there are in the western part of the island two provinces which I did not visit; one of these is called by the Indians Anam, and its inhabitants are born with tails. . . .

But the extent of Española is greater than all Spain from Catalonia to Fontarabia, which is easily proved, because one of its four sides which I myself coasted in a direct line, from west to east, measures 540 miles. This island is to be regarded with special interest and not to be slighted; for although as I have said I took possession of all these islands in the name of our invincible King, and the government of them is unreservedly committed to His Said Majesty, yet there was one large town in Española of which especially I took possession, situated in a remarkably favorable spot and in every way convenient for the purposes of gain and commerce. To this town I gave the name of Navidad del Señor, and ordered a fortress to be built there, which must by this time be completed, in which I left as many men as I thought necessary, with all sorts of arms and enough provisions for more than a year. I also left them one caravel and skillful workmen, both in shipbuilding and other arts, and engaged the favor and friendship of the king of the island in their behalf, to a degree that would not be believed, for these people are so amiable and friendly that even the king took a pride in calling me his brother. But supposing their feelings should become changed and they should wish to injure those who have remained in the fortress, they could not do so, for they have no arms, they go naked, and are moreover too cowardly; so that those who hold the said fortress can easily keep the whole island in check, without any pressing danger to themselves, provided they do not transgress the directions and regulations which I have given them.

As far as I have learned, every man throughout these islands is united to but one wife, with the exception of the kings and princes, who are allowed to have twenty. The women seem to work more than the men. I could not clearly understand whether the people possess any private property, for I observed that one man had the charge of distributing various things to the rest, but especially meat and provisions and the like. I did not find, as some of us had expected, any cannibals among them, but, on the contrary, men of great deference and kindness. Neither are they black, like the Ethiopians; their hair is smooth and straight, for they do not dwell where the rays of the sun strike most vividly and the sun has intense power there, the distance from the equinoctial line being, it appears, but six-and-twenty degrees. On the tops of the mountains the cold is very great, but the effect of this upon the Indians is lessened by their being accustomed to the climate and by their frequently indulging in the use of very hot meats and drinks.

Thus, as I have already said, I saw no cannibals, nor did I hear of any, except in a certain island called Charis, which is the second from Española on the side toward India, where dwell a people who are considered by the neighboring islanders as most ferocious; and these feed upon human flesh. The same people have many kinds of canoes in which they cross to all the surrounding islands and rob and plunder wherever they can; they are not different from the other islanders, except that they wear their hair long, like women, and make use of the bows and javelins of cane, with sharpened spearpoints fixed on the thickest end, which I have before described, and therefore they are looked upon as ferocious and regarded by the other Indians with unbounded fear; but I think no more of them than of the rest. These are the men who form unions with certain women, who dwell alone in the island Matenin, which lies next to Española on the side toward India; these latter employ themselves in no labor suitable to their own sex, for they use bows and javelins as I have already described their paramours as doing, and for defensive armor have plates of brass, of which metal they possess great abundance. They assure me that there is another island larger than Española, whose inhabitants have no hair, and which abounds in gold more than any of the rest. I bring with me individuals of this island and of the others that I have seen, who are proofs of the facts which I state.

Finally, to compress into few words the entire summary of my voyage and speedy return and of the advantages derivable therefrom, I promise, that with a little assistance afforded me by our most invincible sovereigns, I will procure them as much gold as they need, as great a quantity of spices, of cotton, and of mastic (which is only found in Chios), and as many men for the service of the navy as Their Majesties may require. I promise also rhubarb and other sorts of drugs, which I am persuaded the men whom I have left in the aforesaid

fortress have found already and will continue to find; for I myself have tarried nowhere longer than I was compelled to do by the winds, except in the city of Navidad, while I provided for the building of the fortress and took the necessary precautions for the perfect security of the men I left there.

Although all I have related may appear to be wonderful and unheard of, yet the results of my voyage would have been more astonishing if I had had at my disposal such ships as I required. But these great and marvelous results are not to be attributed to any merit of mine but to the holy Christian faith and to the piety and religion of our sovereigns; for that which the unaided intellect of man could not compass, the Spirit of God has granted to human exertions, for God is wont to hear the prayers of His servants who love His precepts even to the performance of apparent impossibilities. Thus it has happened to me in the present instance, who have accomplished a task to which the powers of mortal men had never hitherto attained; for if there have been those who have anywhere written or spoken of these islands, they have done so with doubts and conjectures, and no one has ever asserted that he has seen them, on which account their writings have been looked upon as little else than fables.

Therefore, let the King and Queen, our Princes, and their most happy kingdoms, and all the other provinces of Christendom render thanks to our Lord and Savior Jesus Christ, who has granted us so great a victory and such prosperity. Let processions be made and sacred feasts be held and the temples be adorned with festive boughs. Let Christ rejoice on earth, as He rejoices in heaven in the prospect of the salvation of the souls of so many nations hitherto lost. Let us also rejoice, as well on account of the exaltation of our faith as on account of the increase of our temporal prosperity, of which not only Spain but all Christendom will be partakers.

1564 - 1565

2.

John Sparke: The Attractions of Florida

Following Christopher Columbus' discovery and exploration of the West Indies, Europeans soon became aware of the potential commercial value of the new products of the region — and also of the profits to be made in the slave trade that Columbus had established. Adventurous men such as the English admiral, John Hawkins, led trading ventures that often began with a stop on the coast of Guinea to capture Negro slaves. Hawkins embarked on his second voyage to the West Indies in 1564. After exchanging his cargo of slaves for the rich produce of the islands, he went on to explore the Florida coast. One of the men who accompanied Hawkins on this expedition, John Sparke, wrote an account of it, Principal Navigations, etc., *in 1589, part of which is reprinted here. Sparke's description of the tobacco and potatoes found in Florida is noteworthy, for it first acquainted Englishmen with these plants.*

Source: *The Hawkins' Voyages, etc., etc.,* Clements R. Markham, ed., London, 1878, pp. 8-64.

Master John Hawkins, with the *Jesus of Lubek,* a ship of 700; and the *Salomon,* a ship of 140; the *Tiger,* a bark of 50; and the *Swallow,* of 30 tons; being all well furnished with men to the number of 170, as also with ordinance and victual requisite for such a voyage departed out of Plymouth the 18th day of October, in the year of our Lord 1564, with a prosperous wind. . . .

[Hawkins sailed to Africa and from there to the West Indies, reaching Dominica on March 9, 1565. He visited a number of the islands, arriving at the Isle of Pines on June 16.]

Thus the 17th of June we departed and the 20th fell with the west end of Cuba, called Cape St. Anthony, where for the space of three days we doubled along till we came beyond the shoals, which are twenty leagues beyond St. Anthony. And the ordinary breeze taking us which is the northeast wind, put us the twenty-four from the shore, and therefore we went to the northwest to fetch wind, and also to the coast of Florida to have the help of the current, which was judged to have set to the eastward. So the 29th we found ourselves in 27°, and in the soundings of Florida, where we kept ourselves the space of four days, sailing along the coast as near as we could, in ten or twelve fathom water, having all the while no sight of land. . . .

In ranging this coast along, the captain found it to be all an island and, therefore, it is all lowland and very scant of fresh water, but the country was marvelously sweet, with both marsh and meadow ground and goodly woods among. There they found sorrel to grow as abundantly as grass, and near their houses were great store of maize and millet and grapes of great bigness, but of taste much like our English grapes. Also deer great plenty, which came upon the sands before them. Their houses are not many together, for in one house a hundred of them do lodge; they being made much like a great barn and in strength not inferior to ours, for it has stanchions and rafters of whole trees and covered with palmito leaves, having no place divided but one small room for their king and queen. In the middle of this house is a hearth where they make great fires all night, and upon certain pieces of wood hewn in for the bowing of their backs, and another place made high for their heads, they lie upon the same which they put one by another all along the walls on both sides.

In their houses they remain only in the nights, and in the day they desire the fields, where they dress their meat and make provision for victuals, which they provide only for a meal from hand to mouth. There is one thing to be marveled at, for the making of their fire, and not only they but also the Negroes do the same, which is made only by two sticks, rubbing them one against another, and this they may do in any place they come where they find sticks sufficient for the purpose.

In their apparel the men only use deerskins, wherewith some only cover their privy members, othersome use the same as garments to cover them before and behind; which skins are painted, some yellow and red, some black and russet, and every man according to his own fancy. They do not omit to paint their bodies also with curious knots, or antique work, as every man in his own fancy devises, which painting, to have it continue the better, they use with a thorn to prick their flesh and dent in the same, whereby the painting may have better hold. In their wars they use a slighter color of painting their faces, thereby to make themselves show the more fierce; which, after their wars ended, they wash away again.

In their wars they use bows and arrows, whereof their bows are made of a kind of yew, but blacker than ours, but many passing the strength of the Negroes or Indians, for it is not greatly inferior to ours. Their arrows also of a great length, but yet of reeds like other Indians, but varying in two points both for length, and also for nocks and feathers, which the other lack, whereby they shoot very steady. The heads of the same are vipers' teeth, bones of fishes, flintstones, piked points of knives, which having gotten of the Frenchmen, broke the same, and put the points of them in their arrows heads. Some of them have their heads of silver; othersome that have want of these put in a kind of hardwood, notched, which pierces as far as any of the rest.

In their fight, being in the woods, they use a marvelous policy for their own safeguard, which is by clasping a tree in their arms, and yet shooting notwithstanding. This policy they used with the Frenchmen in their fight, whereby it appears that they are people of some policy. And although they are called by the Spaniards "gentetriste," that is to say, sad people, meaning thereby that they are not men of capacity, yet have the Frenchmen found them so witty in their answers that by the captain's own report, a counselor with us could not give a more profound reason.

The women also in their apparel use painted skins but most of them gowns of moss, somewhat longer than our moss, which they sew together . . . and make the same surplice, wearing their hair down to their shoulders, like the Indians. . . .

The Floridians, when they travel, have a kind of herb dried [tobacco], which, with a cane and an earthen cup in the end, with fire, and the dried herbs put together, do suck through the cane the smoke thereof, which smoke satisfies their hunger; and therewith they live four or five days without meat or drink; and this all the Frenchmen used for this purpose. Yet do they hold opinion withal, that it causes water and phlegm to void from their stomachs.

The commodities of this land are more than are yet known to any man; for besides the land itself whereof there is more than any king Christian is able to inhabit, it flourishes with meadow, pasture ground, with woods of cedar and cypress, and other sorts, as better cannot be in the world. They have for apothecary herbs, trees, roots, and gum, great store, as liquid storax, turpentine, gum, myrrh, and frankincense, with many others, whereof I know not the names. Colors, both red, black, yellow, and russet, very perfect, wherewith they paint their bodies, and deer skins which they wear about them, that with water it neither fades away, nor alters color.

Gold and silver they want not; for at the Frenchmen first coming thither, they had the same offered them for little or nothing, for they received for a hatchet two pound weight of gold, because they knew not the estimation thereof. But the soldiers, being greedy of the same, did take it from them, giving them nothing for it; the which, they perceiving, that both the Frenchmen did greatly esteem it and also did rigorously deal with them, at last would not be known they had any more, neither dared they wear the same for fear of being taken away; so that saving at their first coming, they could get none of them. And how they came by this gold and silver, the Frenchmen knew not as yet, but by guess, who having traveled to the southwest of the cape, having found the same dangerous, by means of sandy banks, as we also have found the

same, and there finding masts which were wrecks of Spaniards coming from Mexico, judged that they had gotten treasure by them. For it is most true that diverse wrecks have been made of Spaniards having much treasure. For the Frenchmen having traveled to the capeward 150 miles did find the Spaniards with the Floridians, which they brought afterward to their fort, whereof one being in a caravel coming from the Indias, was cast away fourteen years ago, and the other twelve years, whose fellows some escaped, othersome were slain by the inhabitants.

It seems they had estimation of their gold and silver, for it is wrought flat and graven, which they wear about their necks; othersome made round like a pancake, with a hole in the middle to bolster up their breasts withal, because they think it a deformity to have great breasts. As for mines either of gold or silver, the Frenchmen can hear of none they have upon the island, but of copper, whereof as yet also they have not made the proof, because they were but few men. But it is not unlike but that in the mainland, where are high hills, may be gold and silver as well as in Mexico, because it is all one mainland. The Frenchmen obtained pearls of them of great bigness, but they were black by means of roasting of them, for they do not fish for them as the Spaniards do, but for their meat; for the Spaniards used to keep daily a fishing some 200 or 300 Indians, some of them that be of choice 1,000. And their order is to go in canoes, or rather great pinnaces, with thirty men in a piece, whereof the one half, or most part be divers, the rest do open the same for the pearls; for it is not suffered that they should use dragging, for that would bring them out of estimation, and mar the beads of them. The oysters which have the smallest sort of pearls are found in seven or eight fathom water, but the greatest in eleven or twelve fathoms.

The Floridians have pieces of unicorns'

horns, which they wear about their necks, whereof the Frenchmen obtained many pieces. Of those unicorns they have many, for that they do affirm it to be a beast with one horn, which coming to the river to drink, puts the same into the water before she drinks. Of these unicorns there is of our company, that having gotten the same of the Frenchmen, brought home thereof to show. It is therefore to be presupposed that there are more commodities, as well as that, which for want of time and people sufficient to inhabit the same, cannot yet come to light; but I trust God will reveal the same before it be long, to the great profit of them that shall take it in hand.

Of beasts in this country, besides, deer, foxes, hares, polecats, cunnies [rabbits], ownces [lynx], leopards, I am not able certainly to say; but it is thought that there are lions and tigers as well as unicorns, lions especially, if it be true that it is said of the enmity between them and the unicorns. For there is no beast but has his enemy, as the cunny, the polecat; a sheep, the wolf; the elephant, the rhinoceros; and so of other beasts the like; insomuch, that whereas the one is the other cannot be missing. And seeing I have made mention of the beasts of this country, it shall not be from my purpose to speak also of the venomous beasts, as crocodiles, whereof there is a great abundance; adders of great bigness, whereof our men killed some of a yard and a half long. . . . On these adders the Frenchmen did feed to no little admiration of us, and affirmed the same to be a delicate meat. And [their] captain . . . saw also a serpent with three heads and four feet, of the bigness of a great spaniel, which for want of a harquebus he dared not attempt to slay.

Of the fish also they have in the river, pike, roche [striped bass], salmon, trout, and diverse other small fishes, and of a great fish, some of the length of a man and longer, being of bigness accordingly, having a snout much like a sword of a yard long. There be also of sea fishes, which we saw coming along the coast flying, which are of the bigness of a smelt, the biggest sort whereof have four wings, but the other have but two. Of these we saw coming out of Guinea, a hundred in a company, which being chased by the giltheads, otherwise called the bonitos, do to avoid them the better take their flight out of the water, but yet are they not able to fly far because of the drying of their wings, which serve them not to fly but when they are moist, and, therefore, when they can fly no farther, fall into the water, and having wet their wings take a new flight again. . . .

There is a sea fowl, also, that chases this flying fish as well as the bonito; for as the flying fish takes her flight, so does this fowl pursue to take her, which to behold is a greater pleasure than hawking, for both the flights are as pleasant, and also more often than 100 times; for the fowl can fly no way but one or other lights in her paws, the number of them are so abundant. There is an innumerable young fry of these flying fishes, which commonly keep about the ship, and are not so big as butterflies, and yet by flying do avoid the unsatiableness of the bonito. Of the bigger sort of these fishes, we took many, which both night and day flew into the sails of our ship; and there was not one of them which was not worth a bonito; for being put upon a hook drabbling in the water, the bonito would leap thereat, and so was taken. Also, took many with a white cloth made fast to a hook, which being tied so short in the water that it might leap out, and, in the greedy bonito thinking it to be a flying fish, leaps thereat and is deceived. We took also dolphins, which are of very goodly color and proportion to behold, and no less delicate in taste.

Fowls also there be many, both upon land and upon sea. But concerning them on the land I am not able to name them, because my abode was there so short. But for the fowl of fresh rivers, these two I noted to be the chief; whereof the flamingo is one, having all red feathers and long red legs like a heron, a neck according to the bill red, whereof the upper nebu hangs an inch over the nether. And an egripte [egret], which is all white as the swan, with legs like to a heronshaw, and of bigness accordingly, but it has in her tail feathers of so fine a plume that it passes the estridge [ostrich] his feather. Of sea fowl above all other not common in England, I noted the pelican, which is feigned to be the lovingest bird that is, which rather than her young should want, will spare her heart blood out of her belly. . . .

Here I have declared the estate of Florida and the commodities therein to this day known, which although it may seem unto some, by the means that the plenty of gold and silver is not so abundant as in other places, that the cost bestowed upon the same will not be able to quit the charges. Yet am I of the opinion that by that which I have seen in other islands of the Indians, where such increase of cattell [livestock] has been that, of twelve head of beasts in twenty-five years, did in the hides of them raise £1,000 yearly profit . . . the increase of cattell only would raise profit sufficient for the same; for we may consider if so small a portion did raise so much gains in such a short time, what would a greater do in many years. And surely I may this affirm, that the ground of the Indians for the breed of cattell is not in any point to be compared to this of Florida, which all the year long is so green, as any time in the summer with us; which surely is not to be marveled at, seeing the country stands in so watery a climate; for, once a day without fail, they have a shower of rain, which, by means of the country itself which is dry and more fervent hot than ours, does make all things to flourish therein. And because there is not the thing we all seek for, being rather desirous of present gains, I do therefore affirm

the attempt thereof to be more requisite for a prince, who is of power able to go through with the same, rather than for any subject.

From thence we departed the 28th of July upon our voyage homeward, having there all things as might be most convenient for our purpose, and took leave of the Frenchmen that there still remained, who with diligence determined to make great speed after, as they could. Thus by means of contrary winds oftentimes, we prolonged our voyage in such manner that victuals scanted with us, so that we were diverse (or rather the most part) in despair of ever coming home, had not God of His goodness better provided for us than our deserving. In which state of great misery, we were provoked to call upon Him by fervent prayer, which moved Him to hear us; so that we had a prosperous wind, which did set us so far short, as to be upon the bank of Newfoundland . . . and sounded, thereupon finding ground at 130 fathoms, being that day somewhat becalmed, and took a great number of fresh codfish, which greatly relieved us.

And very glad thereof, the next day departing, by lingering little gales for the space of four or five days, at the which we saw a couple of French ships and had so much fish as would serve us plentifully for all the rest of the way, the captain paying for the same both gold and silver, to the just value thereof, unto the chief owners of the said ships, which they not looking for anything at all, were glad in themselves to meet with such good entertainment at sea as they had at our hands. After which departure from them, with a good, large wind, the 20th of September we came to Padstow in Cornwall, God be thanked, in safety, with the loss of twenty persons in all the voyage and profitable to the venturers of the said voyage, as also to the whole Realm, in bringing home both gold, silver, pearls, and other jewels great store. His name . . . be praised forevermore. Amen.

1602

3.

JOHN BRERETON: An Account of New England

Bartholomew Gosnold and Bartholomew Gilbert, sailing from Falmouth, England, visited the southeastern New England coast in the summer of 1602 for the purpose of finding out what chances there were for profitable trading in that region. They probably chose this locality because it had not before been explored by English sailors, and because they sailed without a license from Sir Walter Raleigh, to whom had been granted the exclusive right of English trade with that part of the world. Had they succeeded in returning undetected to England, nobody today would know anything about the details of their voyage. A sudden drop in the price of sassafras showed Raleigh that something was wrong, and investigation soon brought their cargo to light. As some men prominent in the court circle had taken shares in the Gosnold-Gilbert venture, a compromise was arranged to avoid public scandal, and Raleigh allowed the report to go out that he had authorized the voyage. The following account of the voyage, written by John Brereton and addressed to Raleigh, was published for circulation among those who it was hoped might subscribe toward the cost of equipping another expedition to the same locality. The book, A Brief and True Relation of the Discovery of the North Part of Virginia, etc., etc., *is the earliest English account relating to New England.*

Source: *Sailors Narratives of Voyages Along the New England Coast, 1524-1624,* Boston, 1905, pp. 33-50.

Honorable sir,

Being earnestly requested by a dear friend to put down in writing some true relation of our late performed voyage to the north parts of Virginia, at length I resolved to satisfy his request, who also emboldened me to direct the same to your honorable consideration, to whom, indeed, of duty it pertains.

May it please Your Lordship, therefore, to understand that upon the 26th of March, 1602, being Friday, we went from Falmouth, being in all thirty-two persons, in a small bark of Dartmouth, called the "Concord," holding a course for the north part of Virginia; and although by chance the wind favored us not at first as we wished but enforced us so far to the southward, as we fell with St. Marie, one of the islands of the Azores (which was not much out of our way); yet holding our course directly from thence, we made our journey shorter (than hitherto accustomed) by the better part of a thousand leagues, yet were we longer in our passage than we expected; which happened, for that our bark being weak, we were loath to press her with much sail. Also, our sailors being few, and they none of the best, we bear (except in fair weather) but low sail; besides, our going upon an unknown coast, made us not overbold to stand in with the shore, but in open weather; which caused us to be certain days in sounding, before we discovered the coast, the weather being by chance somewhat foggy.

But on Friday, the 14th of May, early in the morning, we made the land — being full of fair trees, the land somewhat low, certain hummocks or hills lying into the land, the shore full of white sand but very stony or rocky. And, standing fair along by the shore, about twelve o'clock of the same day we came to an anchor, where six Indians in a Basque shallop with mast and sail, an iron grapple, and a kettle of copper came boldly aboard us, one of them appareled with a waistcoat and breeches of black serge, made after our sea fashion, hose and shoes on his feet. All the rest (saving one that had a pair of breeches of blue cloth) were all naked. These people are of tall stature, broad and grim visage, of a black swart complexion, their eyebrows painted white; their weapons are bows and arrows. It seemed by some words and signs they made that some Basques or [some] Saint-Jean-de-Luz have fished or traded in this place, being in the latitude of 43°.

But riding here in no very good harbor and withal doubting the weather, about three o'clock the same day in the afternoon we weighed. . . .

From this place we sailed round about this headland almost all the points of the compass, the shore very bold; but as no coast is free from dangers, so I am persuaded this is as free as any — the land somewhat low, full of goodly woods, but in some places plain. At length we were come among many fair islands, which we had partly discerned at our first landing, all lying within a league or two one of another and the outermost not above six or seven leagues from the mainland. . . .

But, not to cloy you with particular rehearsal of such things as God and nature have bestowed on these places, in comparison whereof the most fertile part of all England is (of itself) but barren; we went in our light horseman [gig] from this island to the mainland, right against this island some two leagues off, where, coming ashore, we stood a while like men ravished at the beauty and delicacy of this sweet soil. For besides diverse clear lakes of fresh water (whereof we saw no end), meadows very large and full of green grass, even the most woody places (I speak only of such as I saw) do grow so distinct and apart, one tree from another, upon green, grassy ground somewhat higher than the plains, as if nature would show herself above her power artificial.

Hard by we espied seven Indians, and, coming up to them, at first they expressed some fear, but, being emboldened by our courteous usage and some trifles which we gave them, they followed us to a neck of land, which we imagined had been severed from the mainland. But, finding it otherwise, we perceived a broad harbor or river's mouth which ran up into the mainland; but because the day was far spent we were forced to return to the island from whence we came, leaving the discovery of this harbor for a time of better leisure. Of the goodness of which harbor, as also of many others thereabouts, there is small doubt, considering that all the islands, as also the mainland (where we were), is all rocky grounds and broken lands.

Now, the next day, we determined to fortify ourselves in the little plot of ground in the middle of the lake above mentioned, where we built a house and covered it with sedge, which grew about this lake in great abundance; in building whereof we spent three weeks and more. But the second day after our coming from the mainland we espied nine canoes or boats with fifty Indians in them coming toward us from this part of the mainland, where we, two days before, landed. And being loath they should discover our fortification, we went out on the seaside to meet them; and, coming somewhat near them, they all sat down upon the stones, calling aloud to us (as we rightly guessed) to do the like a little distance from them. Having sat a while in this order, Captain Gosnold willed me to go unto them to see what countenance they would make; but as soon as I came up unto them, one of them, to whom I had given a knife, two days before in the mainland, knew me (whom I also very well remembered) and, smiling upon me, spoke somewhat unto their lord or captain, which sat in the midst of them, who presently rose up and took a large beaver skin from one that stood about him and gave it unto me, which I requited for that time the best I could.

But I, pointing toward Captain Gosnold, made signs unto him that he was our captain and desirous to be his friend and enter league with him, which (as I perceived) he understood and made signs of joy. Whereupon Captain Gosnold with the rest of his company, being twenty in all, came up unto them and after many signs of gratulations (Captain Gosnold presenting their l[ord] with certain trifles which they wondered at and highly esteemed), we became very great friends and sent for meat aboard our shallop and gave them such meats as we had then ready dressed, whereof they misliked nothing but our mustard, whereat they made many a sour face.

While we were thus merry, one of them had conveyed a target of ours into one of their canoes, which we suffered only to try whether they were in subjection to this

l[ord], to whom we made signs (by showing him another of the same likeness and pointing to the canoe) what one of his company had done; who suddenly expressed some fear and, speaking angrily to one about him (as we perceived by his countenance), caused it presently to be brought back again. So the rest of the day we spent in trading with them for furs, which are .beavers, lucerns, martens, otters, wildcat skins, very large and deep fur, black foxes, cony skins of the color of our hares but somewhat less, deerskins very large, sealskins, and other beasts' skins to us unknown.

They have also great store of copper, some very red and some of a paler color; none of them but have chains, earrings, or collars of this metal. They head some of their arrows herewith much like our broad arrowheads, very workmanly made. Their chains are many hollow pieces cemented together, each piece of the bigness of one of our reeds, a finger in length, ten or twelve of them together on a string, which they wear about their necks. . . .

They strike fire in this manner: everyone carries about him in a purse of tewed leather a mineral stone (which I take to be their copper), and, with a flat emery stone (wherewith glaziers cut glass and cutlers glaze blades) tied fast to the end of a little stick, gently he strikes upon the mineral stone; and within a stroke or two a spark falls upon a piece of touchwood (much like our sponge in England) and with the least spark he makes a fire presently.

We had also of their flax, wherewith they make many strings and cords, but it is not so bright of color as ours in England. I am persuaded they have great store growing upon the mainland, as also mines and many other rich commodities, which we, wanting both time and means, could not possibly discover.

Thus they continued with us three days, every night retiring themselves to the farthermost part of our island, two or three miles from our fort. But the fourth day they returned to the mainland; pointing five or six times to the sun and once to the mainland, which we understood that within five or six days they would come from the mainland to us again. But, being in their canoes a little from the shore, they made huge cries and shouts of joy unto us, and we, with our trumpet and cornet and casting up our caps into the air, made them the best farewell we could. Yet six or seven of them remained with us behind, bearing us company every day into the woods, and helped us to cut and carry our sassafras, and some of them lay aboard our ship.

These people, as they are exceeding courteous, gentle of disposition, and well-conditioned, excelling all others that we have seen, so for shape of body and lovely favor I think they excel all the people of America — of stature much higher than we; of complexion or color much like a dark olive; their eyebrows and hair black, which they wear long, tied up behind in knots, whereon they prick feathers of fowls in fashion of a crownet. Some of them are black, thin-bearded. They make beards of the hair of beasts, and one of them offered a beard of their making to one of our sailors for his that grew on his face, which, because it was of a red color, they judged to be none of his own. They are quick-eyed and steadfast in their looks; fearless of others' harms, as intending none themselves; some of the meaner sort given to filching, which the very name of savages (not weighing their ignorance in good or evil) may easily excuse. Their garments are of deerskins, and some of them wear furs round and close about their necks. They pronounce our language with great facility, for one of them one day sitting by me, upon occasion I spoke smiling to him these words: "How now (sirrah) are you so saucy with my tobacco?" Which words (without any further repetition) he suddenly

spoke so plain and distinctly as if he had been a long scholar in the language. Many other such trials we had which are here needless to repeat.

Their women (such as we saw), which were but three in all, were but low of stature, their eyebrows, hair, apparel, and manner of wearing like to the men, fat and very well favored, and much delighted in our company. The men are very dutiful toward them. And truly, the wholesomeness and temperature of this climate does not only argue this people to be answerable to this description but also of a perfect constitution of body — active, strong, healthful, and very witty, as the sundry toys of their's cunningly wrought may easily witness.

For the agreeing of this climate with us (I speak of myself, and so I may justly do for the rest of our company) that we found our health and strength all the while we remained there so to renew and increase as, notwithstanding our diet and lodging was none of the best, yet not one of our company (God be thanked) felt the least grudging or inclination to any disease or sickness but were much fatter and in better health than when we went out of England.

But after our bark had taken in so much sassafras, cedar, furs, skins, and other commodities as were thought convenient, some of our company that had promised Captain Gosnold to stay, having nothing but a saving voyage in their minds, made our company of inhabitants (which was small enough before) much smaller; so as Captain Gosnold, seeing his whole strength to consist but of twelve men, and they but meanly provided, determined to return for England, leaving this island (which he called Elizabeth's Island) with as many true sorrowful eyes as were before desirous to see it. So the 18th of June, being Friday, we weighed; and with indifferent fair wind and weather came to anchor the 23rd of July, being also Friday (in all, bare five weeks), before Exmouth.

1606

4.

First Charter of Virginia

All of the attempts by English adventurers to establish colonies in America during the sixteenth century failed, usually because of a lack of capital. However, interest in such ventures continued unabated, and the Crown, concerned to further the cause of Protestantism as well as to increase Britain's trade, determined to lend more active support. Reports of several exploratory expeditions in the early 1600s led two groups of merchants to petition the Crown in 1605 for a patent to Virginia — to the territory extending from South Carolina to Maine and "from sea to sea." The Charter of Virginia was issued jointly to the two companies, the London and the Plymouth, on April 10, 1606. The Plymouth Company's venture on the Maine coast was not successful, but the London Company, more adequately planned and financed, was able in 1607 to establish the first permanent English colony in America at Jamestown, Virginia.

Source: Hazard, I, pp. 50-58.

JAMES, BY THE GRACE OF GOD, King of England, Scotland, France, and Ireland, Defender of the Faith, etc.: Whereas Our loving and well-disposed subjects, Sir Thomas Gates, and Sir George Somers, Knights, Richard Hackluit, Clerk, Prebendary of Westminister, and Edward-Maria Wingfield, Thomas Hanham, and Ralegh Gilbert, Esquires William Parker, and George Popham, Gentlemen, and diverse others of Our loving subjects, have been humble suitors unto Us, that We would vouchsafe unto them Our license, to make habitation, plantation, and to deduce a colony of sundry of Our people into that part of America commonly called Virginia, and other parts and territories in America, either appertaining unto Us, or which are not now actually possessed by any Christian prince or people, situate, lying, and being all along the seacoasts, between 34° of northerly latitude from the equinoctial line, and 45° of the same latitude, and in the mainland between the same 34° and 45°, and the islands thereunto adjacent or within 100 miles of the coast thereof;

And to that end, and for the more speedy accomplishment of their said intended plantation and habitation there, are desirous to divide themselves into two several colonies and companies; the one consisting of certain knights, gentlemen, merchants, and other adventurers of our City of London and elsewhere, which are, and from time to time shall be, joined unto them, which do desire to begin their plantation and habitation in some fit and convenient place, between 34° and 41° of the said latitude, along the coasts of Virginia and the coasts of America aforesaid. And the other consisting of sundry knights, gentlemen, merchants, and other adventurers, of our cities of Bristol and Exeter, and of our town of Plymouth, and of other places, which do join themselves unto that colony, which do desire to begin their plantation and habitation in some fit and convenient place, between 38° and 45° of the said latitude, all along the said coasts of Virginia and America, as that coast lies.

We, greatly commending, and graciously accepting of, their desires for the furtherance of so noble a work, which may, by the providence of Almighty God, hereafter tend to the glory of His Divine Majesty, in propagating of Christian religion to such people as yet live in darkness and miserable ignorance of the true knowledge and worship of God, and may in time bring the infidels and savages living in those parts to human civility and to a settled and quiet government, do, by these Our letters patent, graciously accept of, and agree to, their humble and well-intended desires.

And do therefore, for Us, Our Heirs, and Successors, grant and agree, that the said Sir Thomas Gates, Sir George Somers, Richard Hackluit, and Edward-Maria Wingfield, Adventurers of and for our City of London, and all such others, as are, or shall be, joined unto them of that colony, shall be called the first colony; and they shall and may begin their said first plantation and habitation at any place upon the said coast of Virginia or America, where they shall think fit and convenient, between the said 34° and 41° of the said latitude; and that they shall have all the lands, woods, soils, grounds, havens, ports, rivers,

mines, minerals, marshes, waters, fishings, commodities, and hereditaments, whatsoever, from the said first seat of their plantation and habitation by the space of 50 miles of English statute measure, all along the said coast of Virginia and America, toward the west and southwest, as the coast lies, with all the islands within 100 miles directly over against the same seacoast; and also all the lands, soils, grounds, havens, ports, rivers, mines, minerals, woods, waters, marshes, fishings, commodities, and hereditaments, whatsoever, from the said place of their first plantation and habitation for the space of 50 English miles, all along the said coasts of Virginia and America, toward east and northeast, or toward the north, as the coast lies, together with all the islands within 100 miles, directly over against the said seacoast; and also all the lands, woods, soils, grounds, havens, ports, rivers, mines, minerals, marshes, waters, fishings, commodities, and hereditaments, whatsoever, from the same 50 miles every way on the seacoast, directly into the mainland by the space of 100 English miles; and shall and may inhabit and remain there; and shall and may also build and fortify within any the same for their better safeguard and defense, according to their best discretion and the discretion of the council of that colony; and that no other of our subjects shall be permitted or suffered to plant or inhabit behind, or on the backside of them, toward the mainland, without the express license or consent of the council of the colony, thereunto in writing first had and obtained.

And We do likewise, for Us, Our Heirs, and Successors, by these presents, grant and agree, that the said Thomas Hanham, and Ralegh Gilbert, William Parker, and George Popham, and all others of the town of Plymouth in the County of Devon, or elsewhere, which are, or shall be, joined unto them of that colony, shall be called the second colony; and that they shall and may begin their said plantation and seat of their first abode and habitation at any place upon the said coast of Virginia and America, where they shall think fit and convenient, between 38° of the said latitude, and 45° of the same latitude. . . .

Provided always, and Our will and pleasure herein is, that the plantation and habitation of such of the said colonies, as shall last plant themselves, as aforesaid, shall not be made within 200 English miles of the other of them, that first began to make their plantation, as aforesaid.

And We do also ordain, establish, and agree, for Us, Our Heirs, and Successors, that each of the said colonies shall have a council, which shall govern and order all matters and causes, which shall arise, grow, or happen, to or within the same several colonies, according to such laws, ordinances, and instructions, as shall be, in that behalf, given and signed with Our hand or sign manual, and pass under the privy seal of Our Realm of England; each of which councils shall consist of thirteen persons, to be ordained, made, and removed, from time to time, according as shall be directed and comprised in the same instructions. . . .

And that also there shall be a council, established here in England, which shall, in like manner, consist of thirteen persons, to be, for that purpose, appointed by Us, Our Heirs, and Successors, which shall be called Our Council of Virginia; and shall from time to time, have the superior managing and direction, only of and for all matters that shall or may concern the government, as well of the said several colonies, as of and for any other part or place, within the aforesaid precincts of 34° and 45° abovementioned; which council shall, in like manner, have a seal, for matters concerning the council or colonies, with the like arms and portraiture, as aforesaid, with this inscription engraved round about on the one side — *Sigillum Regis Magnae Britanniae, Franciae, & Hiberniae;* and round about on

the other side — *Pro Concilio suo Virginiae* [For his council of Virginia].

And moreover, We do grant and agree, for Us, Our Heirs, and Successors, that the said several councils of and for the said several colonies, shall and lawfully may, by virtue hereof, from time to time, without any interruption of Us, Our Heirs, or Successors, give and take order, to dig, mine, and search for all manner of mines of gold, silver, and copper, as well within any part of their said several colonies, as of the said mainlands on the backside of the same colonies; and to have and enjoy the gold, silver, and copper, to be gotten thereof, to the use and benefit of the same colonies, and the plantations thereof; yielding therefore to Us, Our Heirs, and Successors, the fifth part only of all the same gold and silver, and the fifteenth part of all the same copper, so to be gotten or had, as is aforesaid, without any other manner of profit or account, to be given or yielded to Us, Our Heirs, or Successors, for or in respect of the same.

And that they shall, or lawfully may, establish and cause to be made a coin, to pass current there between the people of those several colonies, for the more ease of trade and bargaining between and among them and the natives there, of such metal, and in such manner and form, as the said several councils there shall limit and appoint. . . .

Also We do, for Us, Our Heirs, and Successors, declare, by these presents, that all and every of the persons being Our subjects, which shall dwell and inhabit within every or any of the said several colonies and plantations, and every of their children, which shall happen to be born within any of the limits and precincts of the said several colonies and plantations, shall have and enjoy all liberties, franchises, and immunities, within any of our other dominions, to all intents and purposes, as if they had been abiding and born, within this Our Realm of England, or any of Our said dominions. . . .

5.

On the Value of Colonies to England

During the first years of the seventeenth century, English merchants and commercial planners came to believe that colonization of the New World could bring immense prosperity to England by supplying English manufacturers with raw materials and providing a new market for finished products. The following tract, proposing the establishment of public companies to sponsor colonization attempts, is attributed variously to Richard Hakluyt, a London lawyer and economic planner, and to Sir John Popham. According to some historians, the document was written shortly before King James I granted the royal charter for the colony of Virginia on April 10, 1606. However, the original copy of the selection bears the date January 5, 1607.

Source: *The Genesis of the United States,* Alexander Brown, ed., Boston, 1891, Vol. I, pp. 36-42: "Reasons for Raising a Fund."

REASONS OR MOTIVES for the raising of a public stock to be employed for the peopling and discovering of such countries as may be found most convenient for the supply of those defects which this Realm of England most requires:

1. All kingdoms are maintained by rents or trade, but especially by the latter, which in maritime places flourishes the most by means of navigation.

2. The Realm of England is an island impossible to be otherwise fortified than by strong ships and able mariners, and is secluded from all corners with those of the main continent; therefore, fit abundance of vessels should be prepared to export and import merchandise.

3. The furniture of shipping consists in masts, cordage, pitch, tar, resin, and that of which England is by nature unprovided; at this present time it enjoys them only by the favor of a foreign country.

4. The life of shipping rests in the number of able mariners and worthy captains,

which cannot be maintained without assurance of reward of honorable means to be employed for their adventures.

5. Private sources are cold comforts to adventurers and have ever been found fatal to all enterprises hitherto undertaken by the English because of delays, jealousies, and unwillingness to back that project which did not succeed the first time.

6. The example of the Hollanders is very [germane], for a main backing or stock has effected marvelous matters in trade and navigation in a few years.

7. It is honorable for a state to back an exploit by a public [corporation] rather than a private monopoly.

8. Where colonies are founded for a public-weal, they may continue in better obedience and become more industrious than where private men are absolute backers of a voyage. Men of better behavior and quality will engage themselves in a public service, which carries more reputation with it, than a private, which is for the most part

ignominious in the end, because it is presumed to aim at a profit and is subject to rivalry, fraud, and envy, and when it is at the greatest height of fortune can hardly be tolerated because of the jealousy of the state.

9. The manifest decay of shipping and mariners and of many borough and port towns and harbors cannot be relieved by private increase nor amended otherwise than by a voluntary consent of many purses of the public.

10. It is publicly known that trade with our neighbor countries is beginning to be of small request, the game seldom answering the merchants' adventure, and foreign states either have already or at this present time are preparing to enrich themselves with wool and cloth of their own which they heretofore borrowed of us, which purpose of theirs is now being achieved in France, as it already has been done in Spain and Italy. Therefore, we must, of necessity, forgo our great showing if we do not wish to prepare a place fit for the vent of our wares and so set our mariners to work, who daily run to serve foreign nations for want of employment and cannot be restrained by any law when necessity forces them to serve in the hire of a stranger rather than to serve at home.

11. That realm is more complete and wealthy which either has the sufficiency to serve itself, or can find the means to export its natural commodities, than if it has occasion necessarily to import, for, consequently, it must ensue that by public consent a colony transported into a good and plentiful climate able to furnish our wants, our moneys, and wares, that now run into the hands of our adversaries or cold friends, shall pass unto our friends and natural kinsmen and from them likewise we shall receive such things as shall be most available to our necessities. This intercourse of trade may rather be called a homebred traffic than a foreign exchange.

12. Foreign nations yearly attempt discoveries in strange coasts, moved thereunto by the policy of the state which affects that gain most which is gotten either without any trick of their neighbor, or at best by the smallest advantage that may turn unto them by their trade.

13. Experience teaches us that it is dangerous to our state to enterprise a discovery and not to proceed therein even to the very sifting of it to the utmost. For not only disreputation grows thereby but disability and weak power reveals our own idleness and want of counsel to manage our enterprises, as if the glorious state of ours were rather broached by the virtue of our ancestry than of our own worthiness.

14. The want of our fresh and present supply of our discoveries has in a manner taken away the title which the law of nations gives us unto the coast first found out by our industry, forasmuch as whatsoever a man relinquishes may be claimed by the next finder as his own property. Neither is it sufficient to set foot in a country but to possess and hold it, in defense of an invading force (for want whereof) the king of Denmark intends to a northwest voyage (as it is reported). It is also reported that the French intend to inhabit Virginia, which they may safely achieve if their second voyage proves strong and there does not languish for want of sufficient and timely supplies, which cannot be had but by the means of a large contribution.

The circumstances necessary to back a colony sent out are these:

1. Reputation and opinion of the enterprise.

2. A competent sum of money raised beforehand to supply all accidents, that distrust hereby may be wrought in all foreign states that attempt to do anything in prejudice of our colonies, because they be well assured that where there is not a public purse, and a common consent to prosecute

an action, it is but hopeless to hope of advantage to be gotten without revenge.

3. As ——— are most apt to make a conquest, so are public-weals fitter to hold what is gotten and, by industry, more skillful to enrich it.

4. It is probable that if the whole state be engaged in these adventures it will be not a hard matter when apparent growth of profit is laid to persuade every county according to the proportion of bigness and ability to build barks and ships of a competent size and to maintain them, when gentlemen's youngest sons and other such men of quality may be employed.

5. Also it imports much that no man be suffered to venture more than he may be deemed able to spare out of his own wealth, or if he goes in person, he would idly spend at home, lest such men enter into a rage of repentance, and thereby discourage others and scandalize the enterprise.

The money to be raised to the use and purposes aforesaid:

1. Ought not to be levied of those things which may hinder the Commonwealth to enjoy the necessities of food and apparel, but shall rather advance them to the needy.

2. It shall not be raised without moderation and ease to the payer, neither shall anything be demanded from any man without present assurance of gain and hope of future profit.

3. It shall not be raised upon the sweat of the poor, or industry of the husbandman, artificer, or tradesman.

4. It is not to be levied to a private intent.

But it is to be raised:

1. Upon the immoderate gains of those that contrary to law abuse the poor; but in such sort that for every sum paid, the payer shall gain fourfold.

2. That they upon whom the main charge of payment shall lie may be greater gainers than the merchant adventurer.

3. That the whole state shall be interested in the benefit of it.

4. That the superfluous waste may be avoided of which the poor most want.

5. The merchandise increasing thereby, the Realm shall be enriched yearly many thousands of pounds, and the King's levy and customs increased.

6. That at the least, £200,000 yearly may be saved in the Realm which now is consumed to the displeasure of God and the hurt of the people.

Also, it is reason that the King's Majesty have as well part of the money so raised, either to adventure or otherwise dispose of at His Highness' good pleasure:

1. In respect of his royal assent to be given to an act of Parliament enabling commissioners to gather the monies aforesaid.

2. Privileges and license to transport a colony or colonies are to be obtained at the King's hands; neither is it reason that His Highness' prerogative should be valued at nothing.

3. That the King's Majesty will be engaged in honor, the rather to assist and to protect the project.

4. It would savor too much of affectation of a popular state to levy monies without imparting some convenient portion to His Majesty.

5. That portion ought not to be so small, that it should seem to undervalue the King's greatness and favor.

Westward the course of empire takes its way;
The four first acts already past,
A fifth shall close the drama with the day:
Time's noblest offspring is the last.
GEORGE BERKELEY

1607 - 1614

6.

John Smith: Starving Time in Virginia

In December 1606, the Virginia Company sent three ships to Virginia with 144 colonists, only 105 of whom actually disembarked at Jamestown the following May. Among them was Captain John Smith, a soldier-adventurer and promoter of the company, who became its chief historian. He had an especially resourceful spirit in many a dark day, and he saved the colony from starvation during the winter of 1608-1609 by obtaining corn from the Indians he had befriended. On an expedition to discover the source of the Chickahominy River, Captain Smith was captured by the Indians and was to be executed. As the controversial legend holds, Pocahontas saved his life by throwing herself upon him and entreating her father, Powhatan, to spare Smith. Smith's Generall Historie of Virginia, *an indispensable — though at times unreliable — work, is reprinted here in part. The selection deals with the events of 1607-1614 and is actually a series of reports or accounts by various persons with interpolations by Smith himself. Thus, part of the narrative covers an interval when he had returned temporarily to England.*

Source: *Works 1608-1631*, Edward Arber, ed., Birmingham, England, 1884, pp. 391-401, 497-516.

1607. Being thus left to our fortunes, it fortuned that within ten days scarce ten among us could either go or well stand, such extreme weakness and sickness oppressed us. And thereat none need marvel if they consider the cause and reason, which was this.

While the ships stayed, our allowance was somewhat bettered by a daily proportion of biscuits, which the sailors would pilfer to sell, give, or exchange with us for money, sassafras, furs, or love. But when they departed, there remained neither tavern, beer, house, nor place of relief, but the common kettle. Had we been as free from all sins as gluttony and drunkenness, we might have been canonized for saints; but our president [Wingfield] would never have been admitted for engrossing to his private [use] oatmeal, sack, aquavitae, beef, eggs, or what not, but the kettle; that indeed he allowed equally to be distributed, and that was half a pint of wheat, and as much barley boiled with water for a man a day, and this having fried some twenty-six weeks in the ship's hold, contained as many worms as grains; so that we might truly call it rather so much bran than corn, our drink was water, our lodgings castles in the air.

With this lodging and diet, our extreme toil in bearing and planting palisades so strained and bruised us, and our continual labor in the extremity of the heat had so weakened us, as were cause sufficient to have made us as miserable in our native country, or any other place in the world.

From May to September, those that escaped lived upon sturgeon, and sea crabs. Fifty in this time we buried, the rest seeing the president's projects to escape these miseries in our pinnace by flight (who all this time had neither felt want nor sickness) so moved our dead spirits, as we deposed him, and established Ratcliffe in his place (Gosnoll being dead), Kendall deposed. Smith newly recovered, Martin and Ratcliffe was by his care preserved and relieved, and the most of the soldiers recovered with the skillful diligence of Master Thomas Wolton, our chirurgeon [surgeon] general.

But now was all our provision spent, the sturgeon gone, all helps abandoned, each hour expecting the fury of the savages; when God, the Patron of all good endeavors in that desperate extremity so changed the hearts of the savages that they brought such plenty of their fruits and provision as no man wanted.

And now where some affirmed it was ill done of the Council to send forth men so badly provided, this incontradictable reason will show them plainly they are too ill advised to nourish such ill conceits. First, the fault of our going was our own; what could be thought fitting or necessary we had; but what we should find, or want, or where we should be, we were all ignorant, and supposing to make our passage in two months, with victual to live and the advantage of the spring to work. We were at sea five months, where we both spent our victual and lost the opportunity of the time and season to plant, by the unskillful presumption of our ignorant transporters, that understood not at all what they undertook. . . .

And now, the winter approaching, the rivers became so covered with swans, geese, ducks, and cranes that we daily feasted with good bread, Virginia peas, pumpions [pumpkins], and putchamins [persimmons], fish, fowl, and diverse sorts of wild beasts as fat as we could eat them; so that none of our tuftaffety humorists desired to go for England.

But our comedies never endured long without a tragedy; some idle exceptions being muttered against Captain Smith for not discovering the head of the Chickahamania [Chickahominy] River, and taxed by the Council to be too slow in so worthy an attempt. The next voyage he proceeded so far that with much labor by cutting of trees asunder he made his passage; but when his barge could pass no farther, he left her in a broad bay out of danger of shot, commanding none should go ashore till his return. Himself, with two English and two savages, went up higher in a canoe; but he was not long absent but his men went ashore, whose want of government gave both occasion and opportunity to the savages to surprise one George Cassen, whom they slew, and much failed not to have cut off the boat and all the rest.

Smith, little dreaming of that accident, being got to the marshes at the river's head, twenty miles in the desert, had his two men slain (as is supposed) sleeping by the canoe, while himself, by fowling, sought them victual. Finding he was beset with 200 savages, two of them he slew still defending himself with the aid of a savage, his guide, whom he bound to his arm with his garters, and used him as a buckler, yet he was shot in his thigh a little, and had many arrows that stuck in his clothes; but no great hurt, till at last they took him prisoner. When this news came to Jamestown, much was their sorrow for his loss, few expecting what ensued.

Six or seven weeks those barbarians kept him prisoner, many strange triumphs and conjurations they made of him, yet he so demeaned himself among them as he not only diverted them from surprising the fort but procured his own liberty, and got himself and his company such estimation among them that those savages admired him more than their own *quiyouckosucks* [gods].

The manner how they used and delivered him is as follows:

The savages, having drawn from George Cassen whether Captain Smith was gone, prosecuting that opportunity, they followed him with 300 bowmen, conducted by the king of Pamaunkee, who, in divisions, searching the turnings of the river, found Robinson and Emry by the far side. Those they shot full of arrows and slew. Then finding the captain . . . yet, dared they not come to him till, being near dead with cold, he threw away his arms. Then . . . they drew him forth and led him to the fire, where his men were slain. Diligently, they chafed his benumbed limbs.

He demanding for their captain, they showed him Opechancanough, king of Pamaunkee, to whom he gave a round, ivory double compass dial. Much they marveled at the playing of the fly and needle, which they could see so plainly and yet not touch it because of the glass that covered them. But when he demonstrated by that globe-like jewel the roundness of the earth and skies, the sphere of the sun, moon, and stars, and how the sun did chase the night round about the world continually; the greatness of the land and sea, the diversity of nations, variety of complexions, and how we were to them antipodes, and many other suchlike matters, they all stood as amazed with admiration. Notwithstanding, within an hour after they tied him to a tree, and as many as could stand about him prepared to shoot him; but the king, holding up the compass in his hand, they all laid down their bows and arrows, and in a triumphant manner led him to [the town of] Orapaks, where he was after their manner kindly feasted and well used.

Their order in conducting him was thus:

Drawing themselves all in file, the king in the middle had all their pieces and swords borne before him. Captain Smith was led after him by three great savages, holding him fast by each arm; and on each side, six went in file with their arrows nocked. But arriving at the town (which was but only thirty or forty hunting houses made of mats, which they remove as they please, as we our tents), all the women and children staring to behold him, the soldiers first, all in file and on each flank, officers . . . to see them keep their orders. A good time they continued this exercise, and then cast themselves in a ring, dancing in such several postures, and singing and yelling out such hellish notes and screeches; being strangely painted, everyone his quiver of arrows, and at his back a club; on his arm a fox or an otter's skin . . . their heads and shoulders painted red . . . which scarletlike color made an exceeding handsome show; his bow in his hand, and the skin of a bird with her wings abroad dried, tied on his head, a piece of copper, a white shell, a long feather, with a small rattle growing at the tails of their snakes tied to it, or some suchlike toy.

All this while, Smith and the king stood in the middle, guarded, as before is said; and after three dances they all departed. Smith they conducted to a longhouse, where thirty or forty tall fellows did guard him; and ere long more bread and venison was brought him than would have served twenty men. I think his stomach at that time was not very good; what he left they put in baskets and tied over his head. About midnight they set the meat again before him, all this time not one of them would eat a bite with him, till the next morning they brought him as much more; and then did they eat all the old, and reserved the new as they had done the other, which made him think they would fat him to eat him. Yet in this desperate estate to defend him from the cold, one . . . brought him

Capt. John Smith, detail from a 1616 engraving of
his map of New England by Simon van de Passe

his gown, in requital of some beads and
toys Smith had given him at his first arrival
in Virginia.

Two days after, a man would have slain
him (but that the guard prevented it) for
the death of his son, to whom they conducted him to recover the poor man then
breathing his last. Smith told them that at
Jamestown he had a water would do it, if
they would let him fetch it, but they would
not permit that; but made all the preparations they could to assault Jamestown craving his advice; and for recompense he
should have life, liberty, land, and women.
In part of a tablebook he wrote his mind to
them at the Fort, what was intended, how
they should follow that direction to affright
the messengers, and without fail send him
such things as he wrote for and an inventory with them. The difficulty and danger, he
told the savages, of the mines, great guns,
and other engines exceedingly affrighted
them, yet according to his request they
went to Jamestown in as bitter weather as
could be of frost and snow, and within
three days returned with an answer.

But when they came to Jamestown, seeing men sally out as he had told them they
would, they fled; yet in the night they came
again to the same place where he had told
them they should receive an answer, and
such things as he had promised them;
which they found accordingly, and with
which they returned with no small expedition, to the wonder of them all that heard
it, that he could either divine, or the paper
could speak. . . .

Not long after, early in the morning, a
great fire was made in a longhouse, and a
mat spread on the one side, as on the other;
on the one they caused him to sit, and all
the guard went out of the house, and presently came skipping in a great grim fellow,
all painted over with coal, mingled with oil,
and many snakes' and weasels' skins stuffed
with moss, and all their tails tied together,
so as they met on the crown of his head in
a tassel; and round about the tassel was as a
coronet of feathers, the skins hanging round
about his head, back, and shoulders, and in
a manner covered his face; with a hellish
voice, and a rattle in his hand. With most
strange gestures and passions he began his
invocation, and environed the fire with a
circle of meal; which done, three more
suchlike devils came rushing in with the like
antic tricks, painted half black, half red; but
all their eyes were painted white, and some
red strokes like Mutchato's along their
cheeks. Round about him those fiends
danced a pretty while, and then came in
three more as ugly as the rest, with red eyes
and white strokes over their black faces. At
last they all sat down right against him;
three of them on the one hand of the chief
priest, and three on the other.

Then all with their rattles began a song,
which ended, the chief priest laid down five
wheat corns. Then straining his arms and
hands with such violence that he sweat, and
his veins swelled, he began a short oration;
at the conclusion they all gave a short
groan, and then laid down three grains

more. After that, began their song again, then another oration, ever laying down so many corns as before, till they had twice encircled the fire. That done, they took a bunch of little sticks prepared for that purpose, continuing still their devotion, and at the end of every song and oration, they laid down a stick between the divisions of corn. Till night, neither he nor they did either eat or drink; and then they feasted merrily, with the best provisions they could make.

Three days they used this ceremony; the meaning whereof they told him was to know if he intended them well or no. The circle of meal signified their country, the circles of corn, the bounds of the sea, and the sticks, his country. They imagined the world to be flat and round, like a trencher; and they in the middle.

After this they brought him a bag of gunpowder, which they carefully preserved till the next spring, to plant as they did their corn, because they would be acquainted with the nature of that seed.

Opitchapam, the king's brother, invited him to his house, where, with as many platters of bread, fowl, and wild beasts as did environ him, he bid him welcome; but not any of them would eat a bite with him, but put up remainder in baskets.

At his return to Opechancanough's, all the king's women and their children flocked about him for their parts; as a due by custom, to be merry with such fragments. . . .

1608. At last they brought him to Meronocomoco, where was Powhatan, their emperor. Here more than 200 of those grim courtiers stood wondering at him, as he had been a monster; till Powhatan and his train had put themselves in their greatest braveries. Before a fire upon a seat like a bedstead, he sat covered with a great robe made of raccoon skins, and all the tails hanging by. On either hand did sit a young wench of sixteen or eighteen years, and along on each side the house, two rows of

Ætatis suæ 21. Aº 1616.

Courtesy, National Portrait Gallery, Smithsonian Institution

Pocahontas, portrait painted in London in 1616 by an unknown artist

men, and behind them as many women, with all their heads and shoulders painted red, many of their heads bedecked with the white down of birds, but everyone with something, and a great chain of white beads about their necks. At his entrance before the king, all the people gave a great shout. The queen of Appamatuck was appointed to bring him water to wash his hands, and another brought him a bunch of feathers instead of a towel to dry them.

Having feasted him after their best barbarous manner they could, a long consultation was held, but the conclusion was: two great stones were brought before Powhatan; then as many as could laid hands on him, dragged him to them, and thereon laid his head, and being ready with their clubs to beat out his brains, Pocahontas, the king's dearest daughter, when no entreaty could prevail, got his head in her arms, and laid her own upon his to save his from death. Whereat the emperor was contented he should live to make him hatchets, and her bells, beads, and copper; for they thought him as well of all occupations as themselves.

For the king himself will make his own robes, shoes, bows, arrows, pots; plant, hunt, or do anything so well as the rest. . . .

Two days after, Powhatan having disguised himself in the most fearful manner he could, caused Captain Smith to be brought forth to a great house in the woods, and thereupon a mat by the fire, to be left alone. Not long after, from behind a mat that divided the house, was made the most doleful noise he ever heard; then Powhatan, more like a devil than a man, with some 200 more as black as himself, came unto him and told him now they were friends, and presently he should go to Jamestown to send him two great guns and a grindstone, for which he would give him the country of Capahowosick, and forever esteem him as his son Nantaquoud. . . .

1609. The day before Captain Smith returned for England with the ships, Captain Davis arrived in a small pinnace, with some sixteen proper men more. To these were added a company from Jamestown, under the command of Captain John Sickelmore, alias Ratcliffe, to inhabit Point Comfort. Captain Martin and Captain West, having lost their boats and near half their men among the savages, were returned to Jamestown; for the savages no sooner understood Smith was gone but they all revolted, and did spoil and murder all they encountered.

Now we were all constrained to live only on that Smith had only for his own company, for the rest had consumed their proportions. And now they had twenty residents with all their appurtenances. Master Piercie, our new president, was so sick he could neither go nor stand. But ere all was consumed, Captain West and Captain Sickelmore, each with a small ship and thirty or forty men well appointed, sought abroad to trade. Sickelmore, upon the confidence of Powhatan, with about thirty others as careless as himself, were all slain; only Jeffrey Shortridge escaped; and Pocahontas, the

king's daughter, saved a boy called Henry Spilman, that lived many years after, by her means, among the Patawomekes. Powhatan still, as he found means, cut off their boats, denied them trade; so that Captain West set sail for England.

Now we all found the loss of Captain Smith; yea, his greatest maligners could now curse his loss. As for corn provision and contribution from the savages, we had nothing but mortal wounds, with clubs and arrows. As for our hogs, hens, goats, sheep, horses, or what lived, our commanders, officers, and savages daily consumed them; some small proportions sometimes we tasted, till all was devoured. Then swords, arms, pieces, or anything we traded with the savages, whose cruel fingers were so oft imbrued in our blood, that what by their cruelty, our governor's indiscretion, and the loss of our ships, of 500 within six months after Captain Smith's departure there remained not past 60 men, women, and children — most miserable and poor creatures. And those were preserved for the most part by roots, herbs, acorns, walnuts, berries, now and then a little fish. They that had starch in these extremities made no small use of it; yea, even the very skins of our horses.

Nay, so great was our famine that a savage we slew and buried, the poorer sort took him up again and ate him; and so did diverse one another boiled and stewed with roots and herbs. And one among the rest did kill his wife, powdered [salted] her, and had eaten part of her before it was known; for which he was executed, as he well deserved. Now, whether she was better roasted, boiled, or carbonadoed [broiled], I know not; but of such a dish as powdered wife I never heard.

This was that time, which still to this day, we called the starving time. It were too vile to say, and scarce to be believed, what we endured; but the occasion was our own for want of providence, industry, and government, and not the barrenness and defect of the country, as is generally supposed. For till then in three years, for the numbers were landed us, we had never from England provision sufficient for six months, though it seemed by the bills of lading sufficient was sent us, such a glutton is the sea, and such good fellows the mariners. We as little tasted of the great proportion sent us as they of our want and miseries, yet, notwithstanding, they ever overswayed and ruled the business, though we endured all that is said, and chiefly lived on what this good country naturally afforded. Yet had we been even in Paradise itself with these governors, it would not have been much better with us; yet there was among us, who, had they had the government as Captain Smith appointed, but that they could not maintain it, would surely have kept us from those extremities of miseries. This in ten days more would have supplanted us all with death.

Engraving of George Percy, [Piercie] governor of the Jamestown colony during the "starving time"

1610. But God, that would not this country should be unplanted, sent Sir Thomas Gates and Sir George Sommers with 150 people most happily preserved by the Bermudas to preserve us. Strange it is to say how miraculously they were preserved in a leaking ship. . . .

1611. In the beginning of September 1611, he [Sir Thomas Dale] set sail, and arrived where he intended to build his new town. Within ten or twelve days he had environed it with a pale, and in honor of our noble Prince Henry called it Henrico. The next work he did was building at each corner of the town a high, commanding watchhouse, a church, and storehouses; which finished, he began to think upon convenient houses for himself and men, which, with all possible speed he could, he effected, to the great content of his company and all the colony.

This town is situated upon a neck of a plain rising land, three parts environed with the main river; the neck of land, well impaled, makes it like an isle. It has three streets of well-framed houses, a handsome church, and the foundation of a better laid (to be built of brick), besides storehouses, watchhouses, and suchlike. Upon the verge of the river there are five houses, wherein live the honester sort of people, as farmers in England, and they keep continual sentinel for the town's security. About two miles from the town, into the mainland, is another pale, nearly two miles in length, from river to river, guarded with several commanders, with a good quantity of corn-ground impaled, sufficiently secured to maintain more than I suppose will come this three years.

On the other side of the river, for the security of the town, is intended to be impaled for the security of our hogs, about two miles and a half, by the name of Hope in Faith, and Coxendale, secured by five of our manner of forts, which are but palisades, called Charity Fort, Mount Malado (a guesthouse [hospital] for sick people), a high seat and wholesome air, Elisabeth Fort, and Fort Patience. And here has Master Whitaker chosen his parsonage, impaled a fair-framed parsonage, and 100 acres called Rocke Hall, but these are not half finished.

About Christmas following, in this same year 1611, in regard of the injury done us by them of Appamatuck, Sir Thomas Dale, without the loss of any except some few savages, took it and their corn, being but five miles by land from Henrico; and considering how commodious it might be for us, resolved to possess and plant it, and at the instant called it the New Bermudas, whereunto he has laid out and annexed . . . many miles of champion and woodland ground. . . .

In the nether hundred he first began to plant; for there is the most corn-ground, and with a pale of two miles, cut over from river to river, whereby we have secured eight English miles in compass. Upon which circuit, within half a mile of each other, are many fair houses already built; besides particular men's houses near to the number of fifty. Rochdale, by a cross pale almost four miles long, is also planted with houses along the pale, in which hundred our hogs and cattle have [a] twenty-mile circuit to graze in securely. The building of the city is referred till our harvest be in, which he intends to make a retreat against any foreign enemy.

About fifty miles from these is Jamestown, upon a fertile peninsula, which, although formerly scandaled for an unhealthful air, we find it as healthful as any other part of the country. It has two rows of houses of framed timber, and some of them two stories and a garret higher; three large storehouses joined together in length; and he has newly strongly impaled the town. This isle, and much ground about it, is much inhabited. To Kecoughtan we ac-counted it forty miles, where they live well with half that allowance the rest have from the store, because of the extraordinary quantity of fish, fowl and deer. . . .

1612. Since, there was a ship laden with provision and forty men; and another since then with the like number and provision, to stay twelve months in the country, with Captain Argall, which was sent not long after. After he had recreated and refreshed his company, he was sent to the River Patawomeke to trade for corn, the savages about us having small quarter, but friends and foes as they found advantage and opportunity. But to conclude our peace, thus it happened. Captain Argall, having entered into a great acquaintance with Japazaws, an old friend of Captain Smith's, and so to all our nation, ever since he discovered the country, heard by him there was Pocahontas, whom Captain Smith's *Relations* entitles the nonpareil of Virginia. And though she had been many times a preserver of him and the whole colony, yet till this accident she was never seen at Jamestown since his departure.

1613. Being at Patawomeke, as it seems, thinking herself unknown, was easily by her friend Japazaws persuaded to go abroad with him and his wife to see the ship; for Captain Argall had promised him a copper kettle to bring her but to him, promising no way to hurt her but keep her till they could conclude a peace with her father. The savage, for this copper kettle, would have done anything, it seemed by the *Relations.* For though she had seen and been in many ships, yet he caused his wife to feign how desirous she was to see one, that he offered to beat her for her importunity, till she wept. But at last he told her if Pocahontas would go with her, he was content; and thus they betrayed the poor innocent Pocahontas aboard, where they were all kindly feasted in the cabin. Japazaws treading oft on the captain's foot to remember he had done his part.

The captain, when he saw his time, persuaded Pocahontas to the gunroom, feigning to have some conference with Japazaws, which was only that she should not perceive he was any way guilty of her captivity. So sending for her again, he told her before her friends she must go with him and compound peace between her country and us before she ever should see Powhatan. Whereat, [Japazaws] and his wife began to howl and cry as fast as Pocahontas; that upon the captain's fair persuasions, by degrees pacifying herself, and Japazaws and his wife with the kettle and other toys, went merrily on shore, and she to Jamestown. A messenger forthwith was sent to her father, that his daughter Pocahontas he loved so dearly, he must ransom with our men, swords, pieces, tools, etc., he treacherously had stolen.

This unwelcome news much troubled Powhatan, because he loved both his daughter and our commodities well, yet it was three months after ere he returned us any answer; then by the persuasion of the Council, he returned seven of our men, with each of them an unserviceable musket, and sent us word that when we would deliver his daughter, he would make us satisfaction for all injuries done us, and give 500 bushels of corn, and forever be friends with us. That he sent, we received in part of payment, and returned him this answer: That his daughter should be well used; but we could not believe the rest of our arms were either lost or stolen from him, and, therefore, till he sent them, we would keep his daughter.

This answer, it seemed, much displeased him, for we heard no more from him for a long time after; when with Captain Argall's ship, and some other vessels belonging to the colony, Sir Thomas Dale, with 150 men well appointed, went up into his own river, to his chief habitation, with his daughter. With many scornful bravados they affronted us, proudly demanding why we came thither. Our reply was we had brought his daughter, and to receive the ransom for her that was promised, or to have it perforce. They, nothing dismayed thereat, told us we were welcome if we came to fight, for they were provided for us; but advised us, if we loved our lives, to retire, else they would use us as they had done Captain Ratcliffe. We told them we would presently have a better answer; but we were no sooner within shot of the shore than they let fly their arrows among us in the ship.

Being thus justly provoked, we presently manned our boats, went on shore, burned all their houses, and spoiled all they had we could find; and so the next day proceeded higher up the river, where they demanded why we burned their houses. And we, why they shot at us. They replied it was some straggling savage, with many other excuses, they intended no hurt, but were our friends. We told them we came not to hurt them but visit them as friends also. Upon this we concluded a peace, and forthwith they dispatched messengers to Powhatan, whose answer, they told us, we must expect four-and-twenty hours ere the messengers could return. Then they told us our men had run away for fear we would hang them, yet Powhatan's men were run after them. As for our swords and pieces, they should be brought us the next day, which was only but to delay time, for the next day they came not.

Then we went higher, to a house of Powhatan's called Matchot, where we saw about 400 men well appointed. Here they dared us to come on shore, which we did. No show of fear they made at all, nor offered to resist our landing, but walking boldly up and down among us, demanded to confer with our captain, of his coming in that manner, and to have truce till they could but once more send to their king to

Thomas West, 3rd Lord De La Warr, leader of settlers whose arrival saved the Jamestown colony from extinction

presence of Powhatan, but they spoke with Opechancanough his brother and successor. He promised to do the best he could to Powhatan, all might be well. So it being April, and time to prepare our ground and set our corn, we returned to Jamestown, promising the forbearance of their performing their promise till the next harvest.

1614. Long before this, Master John Rolfe, an honest gentleman and of good behavior, had been in love with Pocahontas, and she with him; which thing, at that instant, I made known to Sir Thomas Dale by a letter from him, wherein he entreated his advice, and she acquainted her brother with it, which resolution Sir Thomas Dale well approved. The bruit of this marriage came soon to the knowledge of Powhatan, a thing acceptable to him, as appeared by his sudden consent, for within ten days he sent Opachisco, an old uncle of hers, and two of his sons to see the manner of the marriage, and to do in that behalf what they were requested, for the confirmation thereof, as his deputy; which was accordingly done about the first of April. And ever since we have had friendly trade and commerce, as well with Powhatan himself as all his subjects.

Besides this, by the means of Powhatan, we became in league with our next neighbors, the Chickahamanias [Chickahominies], a lusty and a daring people, free of themselves. These people, so soon as they heard of our peace with Powhatan, sent two messengers with presents to Sir Thomas Dale and offered them his service, excusing all former injuries. Hereafter they would ever be King James's subjects, and relinquish the name of Chickahamania, to be called Tassautessus, as they call us, and Sir Thomas Dale [to be] their governor, as the king's deputy. Only they desired to be governed by their own laws, which is eight of their elders as his substitutes. This offer he kindly

know his pleasure, which if it were not agreeable to their expectation, then they would fight with us, and defend their own as they could. Which was but only to defer the time, to carry away their provision. Yet we promised them truce till the next day at noon, and then, if they would fight with us, they should know when we would begin by our drums and trumpets.

Upon this promise, two of Powhatan's sons came into us to see their sister; at whose sight, seeing her well, though they heard to the contrary, they much rejoiced, promising they would persuade her father to redeem her, and forever be friends with us. And upon this, the two brethren went aboard with us; and we sent Master John Rolfe and Master Sparkes to Powhatan to acquaint him with the business. Kindly they were entertained, but not admitted to the accepted, and appointed the day he would come to visit them.

When the appointed day came, Sir Thomas Dale and Captain Argall, with fifty men well appointed, went to Chickahamania, where we found the people expecting our coming. They used us kindly, and the next morning sat in council to conclude their peace upon these conditions:

First, they should forever be called Englishmen, and be true subjects to King James and his deputies.

Second, neither to kill nor detain any of our men nor livestock but bring them home.

Third, to be always ready to furnish us with 300 men against the Spaniards or any.

Fourth, they shall not enter our towns, but send word they are new Englishmen.

Fifth, that every fighting man, at the beginning of harvest, shall bring to our store two bushels of corn, for tribute, for which they shall receive so many hatchets.

Last, the eight chief men should see all this performed, or receive the punishment themselves. For their diligence they should have a red coat, a copper chain, and King James's picture, and be accounted his nobleman.

All this they concluded with a general assent and a great shout to confirm it. Then one of the old men began an oration, bending his speech first to the old men, then to the young, and then to the women and children to make them understand how strictly they were to observe these conditions, and we would defend them from the fury of Powhatan, or any enemy whatsoever, and furnish them with copper, beads, and hatchets. But all this was rather for fear Powhatan and we, being so linked together, would bring them again to his subjection; the which to prevent, they did rather choose to be protected by us than tormented by him, whom they held a tyrant. And thus we returned again to Jamestown.

When our people were fed out of the common store and labored jointly together, glad was he who could slip from his labor, or slumber over his task he cared not how; nay, the most honest among them would hardly take so much true pains in a week as now for themselves they will do in a day. Neither cared they for the increase, presuming that howsoever the harvest prospered, the general store must maintain them, so that we reaped not so much corn from the labors of thirty as now three or four do provide for themselves. To prevent which, Sir Thomas Dale has allotted every man three acres of clear ground, in the nature of farms, except the Bermudas, who are exempted, but for one month's service in the year, which must neither be in seed-time nor harvest; for which doing, no other duty they pay to the store but two barrels and a half of corn.

From all those farmers (whereof the first was William Spence, an honest, valiant, and an industrious man, and has continued from 1607 to this present) from those is expected such a contribution to the store, as we shall neither want for ourselves, nor to entertain our supplies. For the rest, they are to work eleven months for the store, and have one month only allowed them to get provision to keep them for twelve, except two bushels of corn they have out of the store. If those can live so, why should any fear starving? And it were much better to deny them passage that would not, ere they come, be content to engage themselves to those conditions; for only from the slothful and idle drones, and none else, have sprung the manifold imputations Virginia innocently has undergone; and therefore I would deter such from coming here that cannot well brook labor, except they will undergo much punishment and penury, if they escape the scurvy. But for the industrious, there is reward sufficient, and if any think there is nothing but bread, I refer you to [Smith's] *Relations* that discovered the country first.

1609

7.

WILLIAM SYMONDS: Britain's Claim to a New World Empire Justified

Throughout most of the sixteenth century, Britain had little interest in colonial ventures in the New World — and few resources to sustain them, if she would. As the century wore on, however, the vast wealth being acquired by Spain and Portugal in the newly discovered territories became more and more evident, and Britain began to look toward the west with envious eyes. Central and South America occupied most of the efforts of the two Latin nations, but the Atlantic coast of North America remained largely unsettled. It was to this area that Britain, after her defeat of the Spanish Armada in 1588, began to send her ships. England's efforts at colonization were prompted by a number of different reasons. Her population was growing, but commerce and manufacturing were lagging and there was increasing unemployment; there was a widespread desire for new sources of raw materials and new outlets for foreign trade; there was the age-old hope of finding a passage to India; and last but not least, there was the need to extend the Protestant sphere, as against the encroachments of Catholic France, Portugal, and Spain. The Church of England thus was as anxious to promote colonization as was the Crown, and many churchmen gave vocal support to the government's enterprises in this regard. Such a one was the Reverend William Symonds, who preached a sermon at "White-Chappel" in London, on April 25, 1609. A portion of the sermon, which was directed to prospective settlers in Virginia, appears below.

Source: *Virginia, A Sermon Preached at White-Chappel, etc., etc.,* London, 1609.

TO THE RIGHT, NOBLE, AND WORTHY advancers of the standard of Christ among the gentiles, the Adventurers for the plantation of Virginia, William Symonds prayeth that nations may bless them and be blessed by them. . . .

This land was of old time offered to our kings. Our late Sovereign Queen Elizabeth (whose story hath no peer among princes of her sex), being a pure virgin, found it, set foot in it, and called it Virginia. Our most sacred Sovereign, in whom is the spirit of his great ancestor Constantine, the pacifier of the world and planter of the Gospel in places most remote, desireth to present this land a pure virgin to Christ. Such as do manage the expedition are careful to carry thither no traitors, nor Papists that depend on the Great Whore. Lord, finish this good work Thou hast begun; and marry this land, a pure virgin, to Thy kingly son Christ Jesus; so shall Thy name be magnified; and we shall have a virgin or maiden Britain, a comfortable addition to our Great Britain. . . .

> *For the Lord had said unto Abraham, get thee out of thy country, and from thy kindred, and from thy father's house, unto the land that I will show thee.*
> *And I will make of thee a great nation, and will bless thee, and make thy name great, and thou shalt be a blessing.*
> *I will bless them also that bless thee, and curse them that curse thee, and in thee shall all the families of the earth be blessed.* . . .
> Gen. 12:1-3

In [this] story . . . are these two points: First, the vocation of Abraham, in these three verses, and then his obedience unto this heavenly calling, in the fourth verse. His vocation hath first the commandment of the Lord, and then the reasons and arguments by which God doth induce him thereunto. The commandment is to take a journey, in which we must consider the places from whence and whither he was to go. The place from whence is not described cosmographically, but morally, containing three important reasons, in all good sort, to rest him where he was. The first is his *country,* which was pleasant and fruitful; the second, his *kindred,* which was holy and blessed; the third, *his father's house,* which was loving and rich. Hence must he go and leave them all behind if they would not go with him. The place whither he must go is also very generally noted out; namely, the place which God would show him, a place utterly unknown unto him, so that from thence he had no argument to quicken him to that voyage. . . .

The reason why God will have His to fill the earth is because the Lord would have His works to be known. Now, in diverse countries God hath His diverse works of herbs and trees and beasts and fishes and fowls and serpents, etc., which (if the people of God come not there) cannot praise the Creator. When David saith, "All Thy works praise Thee, O God, and Thy saints bless Thee; they show the glory of Thy kingdom and speak of Thy power," the implication is manifest that His saints must be witnesses of all His works, in all climates; for else they cannot bless Him in all His works. Another reason is that one that hath the knowledge of the fear of God should communicate it to others. . . . Neither can there be any doubt but that the Lord that called Abraham into another country doth also, by the same holy hand, call you to go and carry the Gospel to a nation that never heard of Christ. . . .

Seeing that, thanks be to God, we are thronged with multitudes; the Lord of Hosts Himself hath given us the calling of His children to seek for room and place to dwell in. And here might we have proceeded to the next point were it not for one scruple which some that think themselves to be very wise do cast in our way; which is this, in effect: The country, they say, is possessed by owners that rule and govern it in their own right. Then with what conscience and equity can we offer to thrust them, by violence, out of their inheritances?

For answer to this objection, first, it is plain that the objector supposeth it not lawful to invade the territories of other princes by force of sword. This proposition, I confess, I never was willing to examine, considering my vocation is private. . . . And because myself am but weak-eyed in so great a mystery — Come forth ye great princes and monarchs of Assyria, Persia, Media, Greece, and Rome, with your gravest counselors, and answer for your facts in conquering and subduing nations. For your stories, that were wont to be read with singular admiration of your fortitude, your wisdom, your magnificence, and your great justice, are now arraigned and must be found guilty, that through your sides an action of truer honor than ever you attempted may be wounded. . . . Sure I am persuaded that, at the only naming of so mighty monarchs and holy conquerors, our objectors, out of their modesty, will, with some distinction, qualify their proposition and say that it is not lawful by force to invade the territories of other princes that are in quiet possession, in some sort and in some cases. . . . And if our objector be descended of the noble Saxons' blood, let him take heed lest, while he cast a stone at us, he wounds his father, that first brought him in his loins from foreign parts into this happy life. . . .

We see that, where God giveth a due vocation to spread abroad and inhabit the earth, neither the love of the country, be it never so fruitful; the love of kindred, be they never so noble and holy; the love of a man's father's house, be the family never so kind, so rich, so numbersome; no, nor the largeness of possession ought to be any impediment to keep us from obedience. . . .

I am not ignorant that many are not willing to go abroad and spread the Gospel in this most honorable and Christian voyage of the plantation of Virginia. Their reasons are diverse according to their wits. One saith, England is a sweet country. True indeed, and the God of glory be blessed, that, whereas the country was as wild a forest, but nothing so fruitful as Virginia, and the people in their nakedness did arm themselves in a coat armor of wood, fetching their curets and polderns [shoulder armor] from a painter's shop, by the civil care of conquerors and planters it is now become a very paradise in comparison of that it was. . . .

But look seriously into the land, and see whether there be not just cause, if not a necessity, to seek abroad. The people, blessed be God, do swarm in the land, as young bees in a hive in June; insomuch that there is very hardly room for one man to live by another. The mightier, like old strong bees, thrust the weaker, as younger, out of their hives. Lords of manors convert townships, in which were a hundred or two hundred communicants, to a shepherd and his dog. The true laboring husbandman that sustaineth the prince by the plow; who was wont to feed many poor, to set many people on work, and pay twice as much subsidy and fifteenths to the King for his proportion of earth as his landlord did for ten times as much; that was wont to furnish the church with saints, the musters with able persons to fight for their sovereign; is now in many places turned laborer, and can hardly escape the statute of rogues and vagrants.

The gentleman hath gotten most of the tillage in his hand; he hath rotten sheep to sell at Michaelmas, his summer-fed oxen at Easter; asking no better price for hay than his beasts, to keep that till spring that they got at grass. By these means he can keep his corn till the people starve, always provided that the poor husbandmen which are left and the clothier must buy their feed and wool at such a rate that shall wear them out in a very few years. And were it not that the honest and Christian merchant doth often help, who putteth all his estate upon the providence of God, which they call venturing, to bring corn into the land, for which he hath many a bitter curse of the cursed cornmongers, we should find an extreme famine in the midst of our greatest plenty.

The rich shopkeeper hath the good, honest, poor laborer at such advantage that he can grind his face when he pleaseth. The poor metalman worketh his bones out, and swelteth himself in the fire, yet, for all his labor, having charge of wife and children, he can hardly keep himself from the almsbox. Always provided that his masters, to whom he worketh, will give never a penny toward his living; but they can tell of their own knowledge that, if the poor man were a good husband, he might live well; for he receiveth much money in the year at their hands, very near four pence for every six pennyworth of work. . . . Many such sweets are in England, which I know not how better to interpret than to say the strong old bees do beat out the younger, to swarm and hive themselves elsewhere. . . .

The land, by the constant report of all that have seen it, is a good land, with the fruitfulness whereof and pleasure of the climate, the plenty of fish and fowl, England, our mistress, cannot compare, no, not when she is in her greatest pride. . . .

Let us . . . go to the place that God will show us to possess in peace and plenty, a land more like the Garden of Eden, which the Lord planted, than any part else of all the earth. . . .

If a man leaves his country at God's commandment, the blessing of the Lord shall ever wait upon him to feed his body and sanctify his soul. The truth is that none do so shine in piety as those that fear God and are out of their country. We never read of such a blessing of men, with constancy and deliverance, in their own country as we find of some abroad. . . . Where did Daniel show his constancy in prayer and found deliverance from the lion's den but among the gentiles? Stand fast, then, in the faith, and you shall see the blessings of God redoubled upon you more, being in a strange country, than you were able to discern at home. . . .

Out of these arguments, by which God enticed Abraham to go out of his country, such as go to a Christian plantation may gather many blessed lessons. God will make him a great nation. Then must Abraham's posterity keep them to themselves. They may not marry nor give in marriage to the heathen that are uncircumcised. And this is so plain that out of this foundation arose the law of marriage among themselves. The

breaking of this rule may break the neck of all good success of this voyage, whereas, by keeping the fear of God, the planters in short time, by the blessing of God, may grow into a nation formidable to all the enemies of Christ and be the praise of that part of the world, for so strong a hand to be joined with the people here that fear God. . . .

Whereas God doth promise to bless him in his journey, as He did indeed, giving him the gift of a prophet to teach, of a priest to pray, of a king to rule, of plenty in his temporal estate, and joy in seeing Christ the Savior of his soul; here may such as transplant at God's commandment be assured of that promise of God — I will not leave thee, nor forsake thee; but, as God saith to Joshua — As I was with Moses so will I be with thee — so God saith to them — As I was with Abraham, so will I be with you. I will bless you, to wit, with the blessings of this life and of the Kingdom of Heaven.

But further, if you will have Abraham's blessing, you must do your diligence to walk in those ways by which the Lord doth give His blessings. You must not with idleness enforce God to work miracles of mercy on the willfully sinful. You must be diligent to hear the word of God; reverent in believing and receiving of it; fruitful in the Christian practice of it, that the blessing of God may come upon you. God can raise children unto Abraham of the very stones, and cast you away if you cast Him off.

In that the Lord doth promise Abraham to make him a great name, know that it is a blessed thing to be well spoken of This will God bring upon the obedient. But if you disobey, you will but make the ears of them to tingle that hear of you. And as we are in continual expectation of some honorable effect, if you continue in the faith, so will you bring a confusion upon yourselves and a shame upon your nation, if you stick not fast to God and His blessed commandments.

1616

8.

John Smith: Encouragement of Settlers in New England

Some of the most desired seventeenth-century luxuries — silk, spices, dates, figs — were obtained from the Orient and elsewhere only with great difficulty and expense. Tales of the rich produce found in the New World raised hopes that such commodities could be secured there easily and profitably. But interest decreased when more realistic reports became known. Still, a number of men continued colonization efforts, promoting the less glamorous products of the region, such as furs, timber, and fish. Captain John Smith, the hero of the first successful colony at Jamestown, conducted an exploration party along the New England coast in 1614. As a result of that venture, he wrote the tract, A Description of New England *(1616). The portion reprinted here is in praise of the available resources there.*

Source: Force, II: "A Description of New England, etc., etc."

THE GROUND IS SO FERTILE that doubtless it is capable of producing any grain, fruits, or seeds you will sow or plant, but it may be that not every kind of plant will grow to such a perfection of delicacy. Some tender plants may not live because the summer is not very hot and the winter is colder in those parts near the sea than we find at the same latitude in Europe or Asia. Yet, I made a garden upon the top of a rocky island in 43°30′N, four leagues from the mainland, in May, that grew so well that it provided us salads in June and July.

All sorts of cattle may be bred here and fed in the islands or peninsulas, safely for nothing. In the interim, until they begin to increase, if need be (observing the seasons) I would undertake to have enough corn for 300 men from the savages for a few trifles; and if the savages should be hostile (as it is most certain they are), thirty or forty good men will be sufficient to bring them all to subjection. If they understand what they do, a provision can be made whereby 200 can be employed nine months of the year in making merchantable fish, until the rest provide other necessities, fit to furnish us with other commodities.

In March, April, May, and half of June, cod is here in abundance; in May, June, July, and August, mullet and sturgeon, whose roe makes caviar, and puttargo [botargo]. If any desire them, I have taken many herring out of the bellies of cods and some I caught in nets. The savages compare their store in the sea to the hairs of their heads, and surely there is an incredible abundance upon this coast. In the end of August, and in September, October, and November, you have cod again to make corfish [salt fish] or Poor John; each hundred cod is as good as two or three hundred in Newfoundland. Half the labor of hooking, splitting, and turning is saved, and you may have your fish at whatever market you will before they can have any in Newfoundland, where their fishing is chiefly in June and July, whereas it is here in March, April, May, September, October, and November, as I said. So that by reason of this plantation, the merchants may have freight both to export and to sell at home, yielding an advantage worth consideration.

Your corfish you may in like manner transport as you see fit, to serve the ports in Portugal (as Lisbon, Avers, and Porta Port [Oporto], and diverse others), or what market you please, before your islanders return, they being tied to the season in the open sea. You having a double season, and fishing before your doors, may sleep every night on shore with good cheer and what fires you will, or when you please with your wives and families. The islanders must remain on their ships in the main ocean.

The mullets here are in such abundance that you may take them in nets, sometimes by the hundreds, where at Cape Blank they hook them, and they are only a foot and a half in length. I have often measured these at two, three, or four feet. Some men have found many salmon up the rivers, as they have passed. Here the air is so temperate that salmon may be well preserved at any time. Young savage boys and girls, or any others, not being idlers, may turn, carry, and return fish, without either shame or any great pain. He is very idle who is past twelve years of age and cannot do very much; and she is very old who cannot spin a thread to make engines [traps] to catch them.

For their [i.e., the settlers'] transportation, the ships that go to fish may transport the first, who for their passage will spare the charge of double manning their ships, which they must do in Newfoundland to get their freight; but one-third of that company is only fit to serve a stage, carry a barrow, and turn Poor John, notwithstanding, they must have meat, drink, clothes, and passage, as well as the rest. Now all I desire is but this — that those who will voluntarily send shipping should make here the best choice they can, or accept such as are presented to them, to serve them at that rate.

Their ships returning home, they should leave such things with me (with the value of what they should receive coming home), as provisions and necessary tools, arms, bedding and apparel, salt, hooks, nets, lines, and suchlike as they can spare of the remainings. Until the next return these persons will keep their boats and do for them many other profitable offices.

I must have men of ability to teach them their duties, and a company fit for soldiers to be ready upon occasion because of the abuses against the poor savages, and the liberty with which the French and others deal with them as they please. These disorders will be hard to reform, and the longer the worse. Such order might be taken with facility if every port town or city observes but this order, and with free power converts the benefits of their freights to what advantage they please and increases their numbers as they see occasion. Whoever are able to subsist of themselves may begin new towns in New England in memory of their old towns. This freedom is confined but to the necessity of the general good, and the event (with God's help) might produce an honest, a noble, and a profitable emulation.

Salt upon salt may assuredly be made, if not first in ponds, at least, until they be provided, this may be used. Then the ships may transport cattle, horses, goats, coarse cloth, and such commodities as we want. When these things arrive, the ships can re-

John Smith's map of New England drawn in 1614. Engraving by De Passe reprinted in "Mercantor's Atlas," 1637

turn with a freight of fish, so if the sailors go for wages it matters not. It is hard if this return does not defray the charges, but care must be had that they arrive in spring, or else provision must be made for them against the winter.

Certain red berries called alkermes, worth 10s. a pound, but which have been sold for 30s. or 40s. a pound, may yearly be gathered in good quantities.

Muskrat may be raised for profit and is well worth the labor. Six or seven thousand beavers, otters, martens, black foxes, and furs of value may be had a year, and if the trade of the French were prevented, many more. This year, 25,000 were brought from those northern parts into France. We may have as good a part of the trade as the French, if we take good measures.

Of mines of gold, silver, and copper, and the probabilities of lead, crystal, and alum, I could say much if stories were good assurances. It is true I made many trials accord-

ing to those instructions I had, which persuade me that I need not despair, and that there are metals in the country. But I am no alchemist, nor will promise more than I know. Who will undertake the rectifying of an iron forge if those that buy meat, drink, coals, ore, and all necessities at a dear rate do profit? Where all these things are to be had for the taking up, in my opinion one cannot lose.

There is plenty of all kinds of woods, and all other provisions for the nourishing of man's life. If those that build ships and boats buy wood at as great a price as it is in England, Spain, France, Italy, and Holland, they will live well by their trade, when all that is required to take those necessities, without any other tax, is labor. There is no hazard and they will do much better. And what commodity in Europe decays more than wood?

For the goodness of the ground, let us take it fertile, or barren, or as it is, seeing it is certain it bears fruits to nourish and feed man and beast, as well as England. The same for the sea, whose several sorts of fishes I have related.

Thus, seeing that all good provisions for man's sustenance may with facility be had by a little extraordinary labor until more has been transported; and that all necessities for shipping can be had but for the labor; to which may be added the assistance of the savages which may be easily had if they be discreetly handled in their kinds, toward fishing, planting, and destroying woods — what gains might be raised if this were followed may easily be conjectured. (When there are but once men to fill your storehouses, dwelling there, you may serve all Europe better and far cheaper than can the Iceland fishermen, or those of Holland, Cape Blank, or Newfoundland, who must be at much more charge than you.)

Two thousand pounds will fit out one ship of 200 and one of 100 tons. If they both have freight of dry fish and go to Spain and sell it at 10s. a quintal, commonly going for 15s. or 20s. (especially when it comes first to the market), this amounts to £3,000 or £4,000 — but say at 10s., which is the lowest, allowing the rest for waste — it amounts at that rate to £2,000, which is the whole charge of your two ships and their equipage. The return of the money, and the freight of the ship for the vintage, or any other voyage, is clear gain . . . besides the beavers and other commodities. And that you may have at home within six months, if God please but to send on ordinary passage.

Then saving half this charge by your ships not staying, your victuals, oversupply of men, and wages, with the freight of things necessary for the planters, the salt being made there . . . if nothing were to be expected but this, it might equal your Hollanders' gains, if not exceed them. They return but wood, pitch, tar, and such gross

commodities: you return wines, oils, fruits, silks, and such straight commodities as you please to provide by your factors, against such times as your ships arrive with them. This would increase our shipping and sailors, and employ and encourage a great part of our idlers and others that want employment, fitting their qualities at home where they are ashamed to do what they would do abroad. If they could but once taste the sweet fruits of their own labors, doubtless many thousands would be advised by good discipline to take more pleasure in honest industry than in their humors of dissolute idleness. . . .

The most northern part I was at was the Bay of Penobscot, which is — east, west, north, and south — more than ten leagues. But such were my occasions, I was constrained to be satisfied by those [persons] I found in the Bay, that the river ran far up into the land and was well inhabited with many people, but they were away from their habitations, either fishing among the isles or hunting the lakes and woods for deer and beavers. The Bay is full of islands, of one, two, six, eight, or ten miles in length, which divide it into many fair and excellent harbors. . . .

And then the country of the Massachusetts, which is the paradise of all those parts. Here are many isles all planted with corn, groves, mulberries, savage gardens, and good harbors. The coast is, for the most part, high clay and sand cliffs. The seacoast as you pass shows you all along large cornfields and great troops of wellproportioned people. . . .

We found the people in those parts very kind but in their fury no less valiant. Upon a quarrel we had with one of them, he along with three others crossed the harbor of Quonahassit to certain rocks whereby we must pass. There they let fly their arrows for our shot, until we were out of range.

1619

9.

John Pory: The Work of a Colonial Legislature

Governor George Yeardley, his council, and twenty-two representatives — two from each of eleven settlements — met at Jamestown, July 30, 1619, to establish a new government for Virginia. This body, the first representative assembly in the colonies, repealed the harsh laws enforced by Sir Thomas Dale during his 1611-1616 tenure as marshal of Virginia, and replaced them with statutes based on English common law. The new House of Burgesses did not immediately achieve the status of an independent legislature. The governor and English patent company could still veto its acts and formulate policy without its approval; but the pattern for future representative governmental bodies had been drawn. The historic assembly opened with a prayer and then appointed John Pory as speaker. He also acted as secretary to the meeting and set down the following report.

Source: *Collections of the New-York Historical Society*, 2nd series, Vol. III, New York, 1857, Pt. 1, pp. 335-358: "Proceedings of the First Assembly of Virginia, 1619."

THE MOST CONVENIENT PLACE we could find to sit in was the choir of the church, where Sir George Yeardley, the governor, being set down in his accustomed place, those of the Council of Estate sat next him on both hands, except only the secretary, then appointed speaker, who sat right before him. John Twine, clerk of the General Assembly being placed next the speaker, and Thomas Pierse, the sergeant, standing at the bar to be ready for any service the Assembly should command him. But, forasmuch as men's affairs do little prosper where God's service is neglected, all the burgesses took their places in the choir, till a prayer was said by Mr. Bucke, the minister, that it would please God to guide and sanctify all our proceedings to His own glory, and the good of this plantation.

Prayer being ended, to the intent that as we had begun at God Almighty so we might proceed w[ith] awful and due respect toward his lieutenant, our most gracious and dread sovereign, all the burgesses were entreated to retire themselves into the body of the church; which being done, before they were fully admitted, they were called in order and by name, and so every man (none staggering at it) took the oath of supremacy, and then entered the Assembly. At Captain Warde, the speaker took exception, as at one that without any commission or authority had seated himself either upon the company's and then his plantation could not be lawful, or on Captain Martin's land, and so he was but a limb or member of him, and so there could be but two burgesses for all. So Captain Warde was commanded to absent himself till such time as the Assembly had agreed what was fit for him to do. After much debate they resolved on this order following:

> At the reading of the names of the burgesses, exception was taken against Captain Warde, as having planted here in Virginia, without any authority or commission from the Treasurer, Council, and Company in England. But considering he had been at so great charge and pains to augment this colony, and had adventured his own person in the action, and since that time had brought home a good quantity of fish to relieve the colony by way of trade . . . the Assembly was contented to admit of him and his lieutenant as members of their body and burgesses into their society. Provided that the said Captain Warde with all expedition, that is to say, between this and the next General Assembly (all lawful impediments excepted), should procure from the Treasurer, Council, and Company in England a commission lawfully to establish and plant himself and his company, as the chiefs of other plantations have done . . . having given his consent and undertaken to perform the same, was together with his lieutenant by voices of the whole Assembly first admitted to take the oath of supremacy and then to make up their number, and to sit among them. . . .

These committees thus appointed, we broke up the first forenoon's Assembly.

After dinner, the governor and those that were not of the committees sat a second time; while the said committees were employed in the perusal of those two books. And whereas the speaker had propounded four several objects for the Assembly to consider on; namely, first the Great Charter of orders, laws, and privileges; second, which of the instructions given by the Council in England to My Lord La Warre, Captain Argall, or Sir George Yeardley might conveniently put on the habit of

laws; third, what laws might issue out of the private concept of any of the burgesses or any other of the colony; and, lastly, what petitions were fit to be sent home for England. It pleased the governor, for expedition's sake, to have the second object of the four to be examined and prepared by himself and the noncommittees; wherein, after having spent some three hours' conference, the two committees brought in their opinions concerning the two former books (the second of which begins at these words of the Charter: "And forasmuch as our intent is to establish one equal and uniform kind of government over all Virginia, etc.," which the whole Assembly, because it was late, deferred to treat of till the next morning.

Saturday, July 31

The next day, therefore, out of the opinions of the said committees, it was agreed these petitions ensuing should be framed to be presented to the Treasurer, Council, and Company in England. Upon the committee's perusal of the first book, the General Assembly do become most humble suitors to their Lords, and to the rest of that honorable Council and renowned Company, that albeit they have been pleased to allot unto the governor, to themselves, together with the Council of Estate here and to the officers of incorporations, certain large portions of land to be laid out with the limits of the same; yet they would vouchsafe, also, that such grounds as heretofore had been granted by patent to the ancient planters by former governors, that had from the Company received commission so to do, might not now, after so much labor and cost, and so many years habitation be taken from them. And to the end that no man might do or suffer any wrong in this kind, that they would favor us so much (if they mean to grant this our petition) as to send us notice, what commission or authority for granting of lands they have given to each particular governor in times past. . . .

At the same time there remaining no further scruple in the minds of the Assembly touching the said Great Charter of laws, orders, and privileges, the speaker put the same to the question; and so it had both the general assent and the applause of the whole Assembly; who as they professed themselves in the first place, most submissively thankful to Almighty God, therefore, so they commanded the speaker to return (as now he does) their due and humble thanks to the Treasurer, Council, and Company for so many privileges and favors, as well in their own names as in the names of the whole colony whom they represented.

This being dispatched, we fell once more to debating of such instructions given by the Council, in England, to several governors as might be converted into laws, the last whereof was the establishment of the price of tobacco, namely: of the best at 3s., and of the second at 18d. the pound.

At the reading of this, the Assembly thought good to send for Mr. Abraham Persey, the cape merchant, to publish this instruction to him, and to demand of him if he knew any impediment why it might not be admitted of? His answer was that he had not as yet received any such order from the Adventurers of the Magazine [Company] in England. And notwithstanding he saw the authority was good, yet was he unwilling to yield till such time as the governor and Assembly had laid their commandment upon him [which was done]. . . .

By this present General Assembly *be it enacted* that no injury or oppression be wrought by the English against the Indians whereby the present peace might be disturbed and ancient quarrels might be revived. *And further be it ordained* that the Chicohomini [Chickahominy] are not to be excepted out of this law, until either that such order come out of England or that they do provoke us by some new injury.

Against idleness, gaming, and drunkenness, and excess in apparel, the Assembly has enacted as follows:

First, in detestation of idleness, *be it enacted* that if any man be found to live as an idler, or runagate, though a freedman, it shall be lawful for that incorporation or plantation to which he belongs, to appoint him a master to serve for wages till he show apparent signs of amendment.

Against gaming at dice and cards *be it ordained* by this present Assembly that the winner or winners shall lose all his or their winnings, and both winners and losers shall forfeit 10s. a man, one 10s. whereof to go to the discoverer, and the rest to charitable and pious uses in the incorporation where the fault is committed.

Against drunkenness *be it also decreed* that if any private person be found culpable thereof, for the first time he is to be reproved privately by the minister; the second time publicly; the third time to tie in bolts twelve hours in the house of the provost marshal, and to pay his fee; and if he still continue in that vice, to undergo such severe punishment as the governor and Council of Estate shall think fit to be inflicted on him.

But if any officer offend in this crime, the first time he shall receive a reproof from the governor; the second time he shall openly be reproved in the church by the minister; and the third time he shall first be committed and then degraded; provided it be understood that the governor has always power to restore him, when he shall in his discretion think fit.

Against excess in apparel, that every man be assessed in the church for all public contributions, if he be unmarried, according to his own apparel; if he be married, according to his own and his wife's, or either of their apparel.

As touching the instructions of drawing some of the better disposed of the Indians to converse with our people, and to live and labor among them, the Assembly, who know well their dispositions, think it fit to enjoin at least to counsel those of the colony, neither utterly to reject them nor yet to draw them to come in.

But in case they will of themselves come voluntarily to places well peopled, there to do service in killing of deer, fishing, beating of corn, and other works, that then five or six may be admitted into every such place, and no more — and that with the consent of the governor; provided that good guard in the night be kept upon them, for generally (though some among many prove good) they are a most treacherous people, and quickly gone when they have done a villainy. And it were fit a house were built for them to lodge in apart by themselves, and lone inhabitants by no means to entertain them.

Be it enacted by this present Assembly that for laying a surer foundation of the conversion of the Indians to Christian religion, each town, city, borough, and particular plantation do obtain unto themselves, by just means, a certain number of the natives' children to be educated by them in true religion and a civil course of life; of which children the most towardly boys in wit and graces of nature to be brought up by them in the first elements of literature, so as to be fitted for the college intended for them; that from thence they may be sent to that work of conversion.

As touching the business of planting corn, this present Assembly does ordain that year by year all and every householder and householders have in store for every servant he or they shall keep, and also for his or their own persons, whether they have any servants or no, one spare barrel of corn to be delivered out yearly either upon sale or exchange as need shall require; for the neglect of which duty he shall be subject to the censure of the governor and Council of Estate; provided always, that for the first year of every new man this law shall not be of force.

About the plantation of mulberry trees, *be it enacted* that every man, as he is seated

upon his division, do for seven years together every year plant and maintain in growth six mulberry trees at the least, and as many more as he shall think convenient. . . .

For hemp, also, both English and Indian, and for English flax and aniseeds, we do require and enjoin all householders of this colony that have any of those seeds to make trial thereof the next season.

Moreover, *be it enacted* by this present Assembly that every householder do yearly plant and maintain ten vines, until they have attained to the art and experience of dressing a vineyard, either by their own industry or by the instruction of some *vigneron*. And that upon what penalty soever the governor and Council of Estate shall think fit to impose upon the neglecters of this act.

Be it also enacted that all necessary tradesmen, or so many as need shall require, such as are come over since the departure of Sir Thomas Dale, or that shall hereafter come, shall work at their trades for any other man, each one being paid according to the quality of his trade and work, to be estimated, if he shall not be contented, by the governor and officers of the place where he works.

Be it further ordained by this General Assembly, and we do by these presents enact, that all contracts made in England between the owners of land and their tenants and servants which they shall send hither may be caused to be duly performed, and that the offenders be punished as the governor and Council of Estate shall think just and convenient.

Be it established also by this present Assembly that no crafty nor advantageous means be suffered to be put in practice for the enticing away the tenants or servants of any particular plantation from the place where they are seated. And that it shall be the duty of the governor and Council of Estate most severely to punish both the seducers and the seduced, and to return these latter into their former places.

Be it further enacted that the orders for the Magazine lately made be exactly kept, and that the Magazine be preserved from wrong and sinister practices, and that according to the orders of court in England, all tobacco and sassafras to be brought by the planters to the cape merchant, till such time as all the goods be taken off their hands at the prices agreed on. . . .

And the General Assembly by voices concluded . . . the acceptance and observation . . . of the instruction . . . to Sir Geo. Yeardley, next preceding the same.

Provided first that the cape merchant do accept of the tobacco of all and every the planters here in Virginia, either for goods or upon bills of exchange at 3s. the pound the best, and 18d. the second sort; provided, also, that the bills be duly paid in England. Provided, in the third place, that if any other besides the Magazine have at any time any necessary commodity which the Magazine does want, it shall and may be lawful for any of the colony to buy the said necessary commodity of the said party, but upon the terms of the Magazine, viz.: allowing no more gain than twenty-five in the hundred, and that with the leave of the governor. Provided, lastly, that it may be lawful for the governor to give leave to any mariner or any other person that shall have any such necessary commodity, wanting to the Magazine to carry home for England so much tobacco, or other natural commodities of the country as his customers shall pay him for the said necessary commodity or commodities.

And to the end we may not only persuade and incite men but enforce them also thoroughly and loyally to cure their tobacco before they bring it to the Magazine, *be it enacted*, and by these presents we do enact, that if upon the judgment of four sufficient men of any incorporation where the Magazine shall reside (having first taken their oaths to give true sentence, two whereof to be chosen by the cape merchant and two by

the incorporation) any tobacco whatsoever shall not prove vendable at the second price, that it shall there immediately be burned before the owner's face. Hitherto such laws as were drawn out of the instructions. . . .

Wednesday, August 4

This day (by reason of extreme heat, both past and likely to ensue, and by that means of the alteration of the healths of diverse of the General Assembly) the governor, who himself also was not well, resolved should be the last of this first session. So in the morning, the speaker (as he was required by the Assembly) read over all the laws and orders that had formerly passed the House, to give the same yet one review more and to see whether there were anything to be amended, or that might be excepted against. This being done, the third sort of laws . . . were read over and thoroughly discussed; which together with the former did now pass the last and final consent of the General Assembly.

A third sort of laws, such as may issue out of every man's private conceit.

It shall be free for every man to trade with the Indians, servants only excepted, upon pain of whipping, unless the master will redeem it off with the payment of an angel [about 10s.], one-fourth part whereof to go to the provost marshal, one-fourth part to the discoverer, and the other moiety to the public uses of the incorporation.

That no man do sell or give any of the greater howes [hounds] to the Indians, or any English dog of quality, as a mastiff, greyhound, bloodhound, land or water spaniel, or any other dog or bitch whatsoever of the English race, upon pain of forfeiting £5 sterling to the public uses of the incorporation where he dwells.

That no man do sell or give any Indians any piece, shot, or powder, or any other arms, offensive or defensive, upon pain of being held a traitor to the colony, and of being hanged so soon as the fact is proved, without all redemption.

That no man may go above twenty miles from his dwelling place, nor upon any voyage whatsoever shall be absent from thence for the space of seven days together, without first having made the governor or commander of the same place acquainted therewith, upon pain of paying 20s. to the public uses of the same incorporation, where the party delinquent dwells.

That no man shall purposely go to any Indian towns, habitations, or places of resort without leave from the governor or commander of that place where he lives, upon pain of paying 40s. to public uses as aforesaid.

That no man living in this colony but shall between this and the 1st of January next ensuing come or send to the Secretary of Estate, to enter his own and all his servants names, and for what term, or upon what conditions they are to serve, upon penalty of paying 40s. to the said Secretary of Estate.

Also, whatsoever masters or people do come over to this plantation, that within one month of their arrival (notice being first given them of this very law) they shall likewise resort to the Secretary of Estate, and shall certify him upon what terms or conditions they be come hither, to the end that he may record their grants and commissions, and for how long time, and upon what conditions their servants (in case they have any) are to serve them, and that upon pain of the penalty next above mentioned.

All ministers in the colony shall once a year, namely, in the month of March, bring to the Secretary of Estate a true account of all christenings, burials, and marriages, upon pain, if they fail, to be censured for their negligence by the governor and Council of Estate. Likewise, where there be no ministers, that the commanders of that place do supply the same duty.

No man without leave from the governor shall kill any neat [domesticated] cattle whatsoever, young or old, especially kine [cows], heifers, or cow calves, and shall be careful to preserve their steers and oxen, and to bring them to the plow, and such profitable uses, and without having obtained leave as aforesaid, shall not kill them upon penalty of forfeiting the value of the beast so killed.

Whosoever shall take any of his neighbors' boats, oars, or canoes without leave from the owner shall be held and esteemed as a felon, and so proceeded against. Also he that shall take away by violence or stealth any canoes or other things from the Indians shall make valuable restitution to the said Indians; and shall forfeit, if he be a freeholder £5; if a servant, £40, or endure a whipping. And anything under the value of 13d. shall be accounted petty larceny.

All ministers shall duly read divine service and exercise their ministerial function according to the ecclesiastical laws and orders of the Church of England, and every Sunday in the afternoon shall catechize such as are not yet ripe to come to the communion. And whosoever of them shall be found negligent or faulty in this kind shall be subject to the censure of the governor and Council of Estate.

The ministers and churchwardens shall seek to present all ungodly disorders; the committees whereof, if upon good admonitions and mild reproof they will not forbear the said scandalous offenses, as suspicions of whoredomes, dishonest company-keeping with women and suchlike, they are to be presented and punished accordingly.

If any person, after two warnings, do not amend his or her life, in point of evident suspicion of incontinency, or of the commission of any other enormous sins, that then he or she be presented by the churchwardens, and suspended for a time from the church by the minister. In which interim, if the same person do not amend and humbly submit him or herself to the church, he is then fully to be excommunicated, and soon after a writ or warrant to be sent from the governor for the apprehending of his person and seizing on all his goods; provided always that all the ministers do meet once a quarter, namely at the feast of St. Michael the Archangel, of the Nativity of our Savior, of the Annunciation of the Blessed Virgin, and about midsummer, at James City, or any other place where the governor shall reside, to determine whom it is fit to excommunicate, and that they first present their opinion to the governor ere they proceed to the act of excommunication.

For reformation of swearing, every freeman and master of a family, after thrice admonition, shall give 5s., or the value upon present demand, to the use of the church where he dwells; and every servant, after the like admonition, except his master discharge the fine, shall be subject to whipping; provided that the payment of the fine notwithstanding the said servant shall acknowledge his fault publicly in the church.

No man whatsoever, coming by water from above, as from Henrico, Charles City, or any place from the westward of James City, and being bound for Kiccowtan, or any other part on this side the same, shall presume to pass by, either by day or by night, without touching first here at James City, to know whether the governor will command him any service. And the like shall they perform that come from Kiccowtanward, or from any place between this and that, to go upward, upon pain of forfeiting £10 sterling a time to the governor; provided that if a servant having had instructions from his master to observe this law do notwithstanding transgress the same, that then the said servant shall be punished at the governor's discretion; otherwise that the master himself shall undergo the foresaid penalty.

No man shall have trade into the bay, either in shallop, pinnace, or ship, without the governor's license; and without putting in security that neither himself nor his company shall force or wrong the Indians, upon pain, that doing otherwise, they shall be censured at their return by the governor and Council of Estate.

All persons whatsoever upon the Sabbath days shall frequent divine service and sermons both forenoon and afternoon; and all such as bear arms shall bring their pieces, swords, powder, and shot. And everyone that shall transgress this law shall forfeit 3s. a time to the use of the church, all lawful and necessary impediments excepted. But if a servant in this case shall willfully neglect his master's command, he shall suffer bodily punishment.

No maid or woman servant, either now resident in the colony or hereafter to come, shall contract herself in marriage without either the consent of her parents or of her master or mistress or of the magistrate and minister of the place both together. And whatsoever minister shall marry or contract any such persons without some of the foresaid consents shall be subject to the severe censure of the governor and Council of Estate.

Be it enacted by this present Assembly that whatsoever servant has heretofore, or shall hereafter, contract himself in England, either by way of indenture or otherwise, to serve any master here in Virginia, and shall afterward, against his said former contract, depart from his master without leave, or being once embarked shall abandon the ship he is appointed to come in, and so being left behind, shall put himself into the service of any other man that will bring hither; that then at the same servant's arrival here, he shall first serve out his time with that master that brought him hither, and afterward also shall serve out his time with his former master, according to his covenant.

Here end the laws.

Columbus bearing Christ to the New World, from world map by Juan de la Cosa, 1500

THE ERA OF SPANISH ADVANTAGE

European acquaintance with Asian opulence during the Crusades stimulated a desire for Oriental spices and other goods, but Christians in the West had to buy these new luxuries from hated Muslim middlemen or send expensive camel caravans far overland to China. At the same time, new developments in shipbuilding and navigation made possible long-distance voyages in the open seas. Thus it became possible for Europeans to dream of ignoring Muslim traders by sailing direct to China or India to bring back valuable cargoes of merchandise. Europeans also saw an opportunity to export Christianity, and perhaps to regain in the East some of the influence Christianity had lost in the West since the spread of Islam in the 8th century.

These desires, for both material and spiritual gain, motivated Columbus to seek a new route to the "Indies," as all Asia east of Suez was called. After landing in the Bahamas, and unaware that his calculations were drastically short of the true distance around the world, Columbus confidently called the natives "Indians."

Courtesy, Metropolitan Museum of Art; gift of J. Pierpont Morgan

Discovery of a New World

Since most geographers disagreed with Columbus' estimates of distance, he had difficulty finding royal backers. Finally Isabella of Spain provided him with three ships. After initial reports seemed to indicate success, Henry VII of England, who had turned down Columbus, supported John Cabot's search for a more northerly route to the Indies.

(Above) Christopher Columbus; (left) 1493 woodcut from book announcing Columbus' discoveries; (below) his patron, Queen Isabella of Spain

El Patrimonio Nacional

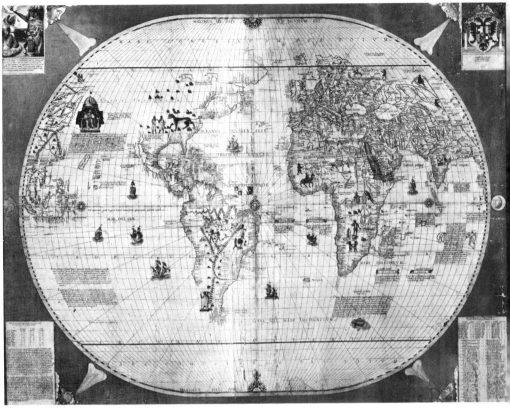

(Above) Sebastian Cabot's world map, 1544;
(below) detail showing North America; (right)
Sebastian Cabot

The Conquest of Mexico

The riches of Hispaniola and the West Indies were soon eclipsed by the discovery and conquest of Mexico (1519-1521) by Hernando Cortes. To the south, Balboa's crossing of the Isthmus of Panama led to Pizarro's conquest of Peru and the Incas.

MUTECZUMA
Rex ultimus Mexicanorum

Hernando Cortes

Mexico City, from Ramusio's "Navigationi et Viaggi," 1557

los finados

el dios de las aguas

el dios de los truanes

French watercolors of Montezuma meeting the Spaniards and the massacre of Mexican nobles

View of Mexico City from Montanus' "New World," 1671

El Adelantado Hernando de Soto

Spanish Colonization

While the search for emerald cities continued to carry Spanish explorers like De Soto and Coronado on rambling expeditions into the present South and Southwest, the methodical process of settlement and conversion to Christianity continued in Mexico throughout the 16th century.

Although their treatment of the Indians was often brutal, many converts were made through an effective dual system of military government and Catholic missionaries that introduced Spanish civilization decades before the English arrived at Jamestown.

De Soto in Florida, by Theodore de Bry

Two missionaries meeting a native king and his three wives

Bartolome de las Casas (1474-1566) missionary leader, opposed enslaving Indians

Fighting Indians in Florida, from Montanus' "New World," 1671

View of Santo Domingo, Hispaniola, by Montanus

Plundering Spanish Riches

Although the Spanish remained the dominant power in the New World during the 16th century, after about 1550 new challengers began to appear. England and France, jealous of Spain but also weaker, began to allow their sea captains to make piratical raids on Spain's treasure ships and on her colonies.

French pirates looting a Spanish settlement; engraving by Theodore de Bry

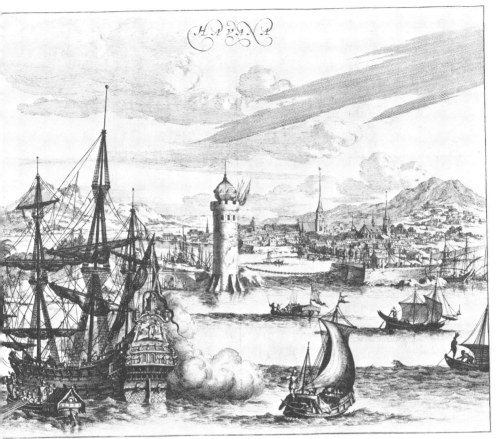

Havana, c. 1671, somewhat romanticized

Sir John Hawkins

S.ʳ Walter Ralegh's Conqueſt of the City of S.ᵗ Joſeph in the Isle of Trinidade?

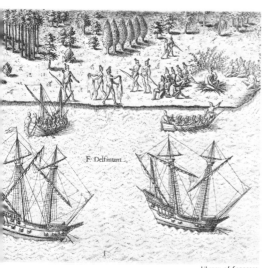

Challenging Spanish Dominion

Florida was the site of the earliest North American settlements, but the first settlers were French, not Spanish. In 1564 a band of Huguenots seeking religious freedom established a colony near modern Jacksonville. The Spanish in 1565 ended this threat to their sovereignty, killing all the Huguenots, "not as Frenchmen, but as Lutherans." The first permanent settlement, St. Augustine, founded by the Spanish in 1565, was nearly destroyed in 1586 by the increasingly venturesome British.

Library of Congress

French, under Jean Ribault, land in Florida, 1562

Library of Congress

Frenchmen aiding Indian allies in intertribal war; engraving by Theodore de Bry

The French Fort Caroline was never as elaborate as shown in this 1671 engraving
Library of Congress

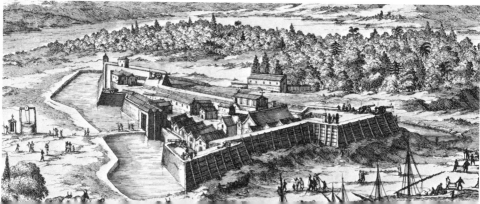

Two views of the Spanish settlement at St. Augustine: (above) earliest known view, from the Mestes map, possibly as early as 1570

Sir Francis Drake's fleet plundered Spanish settlements

Drake, in 1591

Raleigh and his captain, Grenville

The Roanoke Settlement

The first English attempt at settlement was Sir Walter Raleigh's colony on Roanoke Island, off present North Carolina. Raleigh, who never saw America himself, financed a group of about 100 settlers in 1585. They were replaced in 1587 by another 100 men, women, and children, who by 1591 had disappeared without a trace.

(Right) Map of Raleigh's Virginia; (below) Roanoke, after a drawing by John White

1620

10.

The Apprenticeship of Orphans

Settlement of the colonies of New York, Pennsylvania, Maryland, North Carolina, and Virginia promised financial reward to both individual investors and charter companies, but such colonies required large numbers of laborers to settle the land and produce crops for export. Accordingly, various methods of attracting contract laborers, indentured servants, and apprenticed workers were employed; probably half of all immigrants to colonies south of New England came under contract. The following selection is a petition by the leaders of Virginia to the parent Virginia Company of London, reporting on the employment of apprenticed children in the colony and requesting the importation of more groups in the future. The rules and rewards outlined in the company's proceedings on January 31, 1620, are typical of such arrangements.

Source: *Abstract of the Proceedings of the Virginia Company of London, 1619-1624, etc., etc.,*
R. A. Brock, ed., Richmond, 1887, Vol. I, pp. 39-42.

Whereas, the number of one hundred children . . . were the last spring sent and transported by the Virginia Company from the City of London unto Virginia, and toward the charge for the transportation and appareling of the same one hundred children a collection of the sum of £500 was made of diverse well and godly disposed persons, charitably minded toward the plantation in Virginia, dwelling within the City of London and suburbs thereof, and thereupon the said £500 was paid unto the said Company for the purpose aforesaid. And, thereupon, for the good of the same children, and in consideration of the premises, it is fully concluded, ordered, and decreed by and at a general Quarter Court, this day held by the Treasurer, Council, and Company of Virginia, that every of the same children which are now living at the charges, and by the provision of the said Virginia Company, shall be educated and brought up in some good trade and profession, whereby they may be enabled to get their living and maintain themselves when they shall attain their several ages of four-and-twenty years, or be out of their apprenticeships, which shall endure at the least seven years if they so long live.

And, further, that every of the same children — that is to say, the boys at their ages of one-and-twenty years or upward, and the maids or girls at their age of one-and-twenty years, or day of marriage, which shall first happen, shall have freely given and allotted unto them fifty acres of land apiece in Virginia, aforesaid, within the limits of the English plantation, the said acres to be appointed according to the statute *de terris mesurandis* [of the land to be measured] in England, and that in convenient place or places to hold in fee simple by socage tenure to every of them and their heirs forever, freely at the rent of 12*d.* by the year, in full of all rents or other payment or service due unto the Lord, therefore to be rendered or done.

If the lord mayor, aldermen, and Common Council shall not be satisfied with the Company's reasons (who desire that some of themselves may be admitted to allege them), that it is better for the former children to have the same conditions with these latter, the Company will let it pass for this time, yet, with this protestation, that as it is not beneficial to the children, so it is the extreme wrong and prejudice of the whole plantation.

And, whereas, also, it is intended and fully resolved that this next spring the number of one hundred children more . . . shall be sent and transported by the said Virginia Company out of the City of London unto Virginia, aforesaid, and that toward the charge of transporting and appareling the same children, the like collection of £500, of men godly and charitably disposed toward the said plantation, which do reside within the said city and the suburbs thereof, is to be made, and, upon collecting thereof, the same shall be paid to the Virginia Company for the purpose aforesaid. Now, therefore, for the good of the same children, and in consideration of the premises, it is fully concluded and ordered and decreed at a great and general Quarter Court, this day held by the Treasurer, Council, and Company of Virginia, that the said hundred children last mentioned shall be sent at the Virginia Company's charge, and during their voyage shall have their provision sweet and

good and well appareled, and all other things necessary for the voyage; and that every of the same children shall be there placed apprentices with honest and good masters — that is to say, the boys for the term of seven years or more, so as their apprenticeships may expire at their several ages of one-and-twenty years or upward, and the maids or girls for the term of seven years, or until they shall attain their several ages of one-and-twenty years, or be married, to be by the same masters during that time educated and brought up in some good crafts, trades, or husbandry, whereby they may be enabled to get their living and maintain themselves when they shall attain their several ages or be out of their apprenticeships; and during their apprenticeships shall have all things provided for them as shall be fit and requisite, as meat, drink, apparel, and other necessaries.

And, further, that at the expiration of their several apprenticeships, every of the said children shall have freely given unto them and provided for them, at the said Company's charge, provision of corn for victuals for one whole year, and shall also have a house ready built to dwell in, and be placed as a tenant in some convenient place upon so much land as they can manage; and shall have one cow and as much corn as he or she will plant, and 40*s.* to apparel them, or apparel to that value; and shall also have convenient weapons, munition, and armor for defense, and necessary implements and utensils for household, and sufficient working tools and instruments for their trades, labor, and husbandry in such sort as other tenants are provided for.

Moreover, that every of the said children last mentioned, which shall have thus served their apprenticeships and be placed and provided for as aforesaid, shall be tied to be tenants or farmers in manner and form aforesaid for the space of seven years after their apprenticeships ended, and during that time of their labor and pains therein they shall have half of all the increase, profit, and benefit that shall arise, grow, and increase by the management thereof, as well the fruits of the earth, the increased of the cattle as otherwise, and the other moiety thereof, to go and remain to the owners of the land, in lieu and satisfaction of a rent to be paid for the same land so by them to be occupied; and that at the expiration of the same last seven years every of the said children to be at liberty either to continue tenants or farmers of the Company upon the same lands, if they will, at the same rates and in the manner aforesaid, or else provide for themselves elsewhere.

And, lastly, that either of the same children, at the end of the last seven years, shall have moreover five-and-twenty acres of land, to be given and allotted to them in some convenient place or places within the English plantations in Virginia aforesaid, to hold in fee simple by socage tenure to every of them and their heirs forever freely, for the rent of *6d.* for every five-and-twenty acres by way of quit rent in lieu of all services in regard of the tenure. All which premises we, the said Treasurer, Council, and Company, do order and decree, and faithfully promise shall be justly and truly performed toward the said children according to the true intent and meaning thereof.

11.

JOHN ROBINSON: Spiritual Advice to Pilgrim Planters

The Plymouth Pilgrims were Puritans of East Anglia who, in 1609, removed from England to Leyden, Holland, where they formed an English Separatist Church. After about ten years, owing to unsettled conditions in Holland, they decided to go to America, and secured a land-patent from the Virginia Company in England. Prior to the Pilgrims' departure in August 1620, their minister, the Reverend John Robinson, wrote a letter of instruction and encouragement to them. This letter has especial significance in that the last paragraph, urging the little company to establish a civil order and to employ wisdom in selecting and obeying their magistrates, is thought to have inspired the Mayflower Compact. In William Bradford's account of the Pilgrims' voyage, he particularly noted Robinson's letters, in which, Bradford said, "the tender love and godly care of a true pastor appears."

Source: *The Journal of the Pilgrims at Plymouth in New England, in 1620, etc., etc.,* George B. Cheever, ed., 2nd edition, New York, 1849, pp. 18-22.

Loving and Christian Friends:

I do heartily and in the Lord salute you all, as being they with whom I am present in my best affection, and most earnest longings after you, though I be constrained for a while to be bodily absent from you. I say constrained, God knowing how willingly and much rather than otherwise I would have borne my part with you in this first brunt, were I not by strong necessity held back for the present. Make account of me in the meanwhile, as of a man divided in myself with great pain, and as (natural bonds set aside) having my better part with you. And though I doubt not but in your godly wisdoms you both foresee and resolve upon that which concerns your present state and condition, both severally and jointly, yet have I thought but my duty to add some further spur of provocation unto them who run already, if not because you need it, yet because I owe it in love and duty.

And first, as we are daily tŏ renew our repentance with our God, especially for our sins known, and generally for our unknown trespasses, so does the Lord call us in a singular manner upon occasions of such difficulty and danger as lie upon you, to a both more narrow search and careful reformation of our ways in his sight, lest He, calling to remembrance our sins forgotten by us or unrepented of, take advantage against us, and in judgment leave us for the same to be swallowed up in one danger or other; whereas on the contrary, sin being taken away by earnest repentance and the pardon thereof from the Lord, sealed up into a man's conscience by his spirit, great shall be his security and peace in all dangers, sweet his comforts in all distresses, with happy deliverance from all evil, whether in life or in death.

Now next after this heavenly peace with God and our own consciences, we are carefully to provide for peace with all men what in us lies, especially with our associates, and for that end watchfulness must be had, that we neither at all in ourselves do give, no, nor easily take offense being given by others. Woe be unto the world for offenses, for though it be necessary (considering the malice of Satan and man's corruption) that offenses come, yet woe unto the man or woman either by whom the offense comes, says Christ (Matt. 18:7). And if offenses in the unseasonable use of things in themselves indifferent be more to be feared than death itself, as the Apostle teaches (I Cor. 9:15), how much more in things sim-

ply evil, in which neither honor of God nor love of man is thought worthy to be regarded.

Neither yet is it sufficient that we keep ourselves by the grace of God from giving offense, except withal we be armed against the taking of it when given by others. For how imperfect and lame is the work of grace in that person, who wants charity to cover a multitude of offenses, as the Scriptures speak. Neither are you to be exhorted to this grace only upon the common grounds of Christianity, which are, that persons ready to take offense, either want charity to cover offenses, or wisdom duly to weigh human frailty; or lastly are gross, though close hypocrites, as Christ our Lord teaches (Matt. 7:1-3), as indeed in mine own experience, few or none have been found who sooner give offense, than such as easily take it; neither have they ever proved sound and profitable members in societies, who have nourished in themselves that touchy humor. But besides these, there are diverse special motives provoking you above others to great care and conscience this way. As first, you are many of you strangers, as to the persons, so to the infirmities one of another, and so stand in need of more watchfulness this way, lest when such things fall out in men and women as you suspected not, you be inordinately affected with them; which does require at your hands much wisdom and charity for the covering and preventing of incident offenses that way. And lastly, your intended course of civil community will minister continual occasion of offense, and will be as fuel for that fire, except you diligently quench it with brotherly forbearance. And if taking of offense causelessly or easily at men's doings be so carefully to be avoided, how much more heed is to be taken that we take not offense at God himself, which yet we certainly do so oft as we do murmur at His providence in our crosses, or bear impatiently such afflictions as wherewith He pleases to visit us. Store we up, therefore, patience against the evil day, without which we take offense at the Lord himself in His holy and just works.

A fourth thing there is carefully to be provided for, to wit, that with your common employments you join common affections truly bent upon the general good, avoiding as a deadly plague of your both common and special comfort all retiredness of mind for proper advantage, and all singularly affected any manner of way; let every man repress in himself and the whole body in each person, as so many rebels against the common good, all private respects of men's selves, not sorting with the general convenience. And as men are careful not to have a new house shaken with any violence before it be well settled and the parts firmly knit, so be you, I beseech you, brethren, much more careful, that the house of God which you are and are to be, be not shaken with unnecessary novelties or other oppositions at the first settling thereof.

Lastly, whereas you are to become a body politic, using among yourselves civil government, and are not furnished with any persons of special eminence above the rest, to be chosen by you into office of government, let your wisdom and godliness appear, not only in choosing such persons as do entirely love, and will diligently promote the common good, but also in yielding unto them all due honor and obedience in their lawful administrations, not beholding in them the ordinariness of their persons, but God's ordinance for your good;

nor being like unto the foolish multitude, who more honor the gay coat than either the virtuous mind of the man or glorious ordinance of the Lord. But you know better things: that the image of the Lord's power and authority which the magistrate bears is honorable in all persons, be they ever so mean. And this duty you both may the more willingly, and ought the more conscionably, to perform because you are, at least for the present, to have only them for your ordinary governors, which yourselves shall choose for that work.

Sundry other things of importance I could put you in mind of and of those before mentioned in more words, but I will not so far wrong your godly minds as to think you heedless of these things, there being also diverse among you so well able to admonish both themselves and others of what concerns them. These few things, therefore, and the same in few words I do earnestly commend unto your care and conscience, joining therewith my daily incessant prayers unto the Lord, that He who has made the heavens and the earth, the sea and all rivers of waters, and whose providence is over all His works, especially over all His dear children for good, would so guide and guard you in your ways, as inwardly by His Spirit, so outwardly by the hand of His power, as that both you and we also, for and with you, may have after matter of praising His name all the days of your and our lives.

Fare you well in Him in whom you trust, and in whom I rest.

—————◆—————

First make thy will.
    ANON., opening of "official" guide to voyagers to the New World in the late sixteenth century

12.

The Mayflower Compact

The voyagers on the Mayflower *were carried by wind and wave to a point — within the curve of the present Cape Cod — that was north of the Virginia Company's jurisdiction. Finding themselves thus outside the authority of their original patent, and hoping to arrest mutinous talk among some of the passengers, a compact was drawn up and signed by forty-one men aboard the ship, on November 11, 1620. By the terms of this, the so-called Mayflower Compact, the Pilgrims agreed to govern themselves until they could arrange for a charter of their own; they were never able to arrange for such a charter, and the Compact remained in force until their colony at Plymouth was absorbed in that of Massachusetts Bay in 1691. In fact, however, the Virginia.Charter had been amended earlier in 1620 so as to allow for greater local autonomy, and had the Pilgrims landed at their original destination, they could still have formed their own government, as long as it was consonant with the laws of England. The original Compact has been lost, and historians are forced to rely for its wording on* Mourt's Relation *(1622), which is the earliest source of the text reprinted here.*

Source: *The Journal of the Pilgrims at Plymouth in New England, in 1620, etc., etc.,*
George B. Cheever, ed., 2nd edition, New York, 1849, pp. 30-31.

THIS DAY, before we came to harbor, observing some not well affected to unity and concord, but gave some appearance of faction, it was thought good there should be an association and agreement that we should combine together in one body, and to submit to such government and governors as we should by common consent agree to make and choose, and set our hands to this that follows word for word.

In the name of God, Amen. We whose names are underwritten, the loyal subjects of our dread sovereign lord, King James, by the grace of God, of Great Britain, France, and Ireland, King, Defender of the Faith, etc.

Having undertaken for the glory of God, and advancement of the Christian faith and honor of our king and country, a voyage to plant the first colony in the northern parts of Virginia, do by these present, solemnly and mutually, in the presence of God and one of another, covenant and combine ourselves together into a civil body politic, for our better ordering and preservation and furtherance of the ends aforesaid; and by virtue hereof to enact, constitute, and frame such just and equal laws, ordinances, acts, constitutions, offices from time to time as shall be thought most meet and convenient for the general good of the colony; unto which we promise all due submission and obedience. In witness whereof we have hereunder subscribed our names, Cape Cod, 11th of November, in the year of the reign of our sovereign lord, King James, of England, France, and Ireland 18, and of Scotland 54. Anno Domini 1620.

1620 - 1644

13.

WILLIAM BRADFORD: Of Plymouth Plantation

William Bradford was the contemporary historian of a very small colony. About 100 persons reached Plymouth in the Mayflower *in December 1620; thirty years later, at the completion of Governor Bradford's narrative, in 1650, the Plymouth colony still had fewer than 1,000 inhabitants. Book I of the narrative was completed about 1630 and chronicles the events up to the landing at Plymouth. The remainder of the history was written between 1646 and 1651. The manuscript went at Bradford's death to his nephew, who loaned it to several of his contemporaries; it disappeared from the colonies during the Revolutionary War and finally came to light in 1855 in the library of the Bishop of London. Through the efforts of numerous diplomats and historians, the original text was finally returned to America in 1897. It is now on view in the State House, Boston. The portions of the* Journal *reprinted here are taken from Samuel Eliot Morison's carefully edited version of the manuscript, published in 1963.*

Source: *Of Plymouth Plantation 1620-1647*, Samuel Eliot Morison, ed., New York, 1963, pp. 23-334.

THEY CHOSE, or rather confirmed, Mr. John Carver (a man godly and well approved among them) their governor for that year. And after they had provided a place for their goods, or common store (which were long in unlading for want of boats, foulness of the winter weather, and sickness of diverse kinds), and begun some small cottages for their habitation, as time would admit, they met and consulted of laws and orders, both for their civil and military government as the necessity of their condition did re-quire, still adding thereunto as urgent occasion in several times and as cases did require.

In these hard and difficult beginnings they found some discontents and murmurings arise among some, and mutinous speeches and carriages in other; but they were soon quelled and overcome by the wisdom, patience, and just and equal carriage of things by the governor and better part, which clave faithfully together in the main.

The patent of Plymouth Colony issued to John Pierce in 1621

THE STARVING TIME

BUT THAT WHICH WAS MOST SAD and lamentable was that in two or three months' time half of their company died, especially in January and February, being the depth of winter, and wanting houses and other comforts; being infected with the scurvy and other diseases which this long voyage and their inaccommodate condition had brought upon them. So as there died sometimes two or three of a day in the aforesaid time, that of one hundred and odd persons, scarce fifty remained. And of these, in the time of most distress, there were but six or seven sound persons who to their great commendations, be it spoken, spared no pains night or day, but with abundance of toil and hazard of their own health fetched them wood, made them fires, dressed them meat, made their beds, washed their loathsome clothes, clothed and unclothed them. In a word, did all the homely and necessary offices for them which dainty and queasy stomachs cannot endure to hear named; and all this willingly and cheerfully, without any grudging in the least, showing herein their true

love unto their friends and brethren; a rare example and worthy to be remembered. Two of these seven were Mr. William Brewster, their reverend elder, and Myles Standish, their captain and military commander, unto whom myself and many others were much beholden in our low and sick condition. And yet the Lord so upheld these persons as in this general calamity they were not at all infected either with sickness or lameness. And what I have said of these I may say of many others who died in this general visitation, and others yet living; that while they had health, yea, or any strength continuing, they were not wanting to any that had need of them. And I doubt not but their recompense is with the Lord. . . .

INDIAN RELATIONS

ALL THIS WHILE the Indians came skulking about them, and would sometimes show themselves aloof off, but when any approached near them, they would run away; and once they stole away their tools where they had been at work and were gone to dinner. But about the 16th of March, a certain Indian came boldly among them and spoke to them in broken English, which they could well understand but marveled at. At length they understood by discourse with him that he was not of these parts but belonged to the eastern parts where some English ships came to fish, with whom he was acquainted and could name sundry of them by their names, among whom he had got his language. He became profitable to them in acquainting them with many things concerning the state of the country in the east parts where he lived, which was afterward profitable unto them; as also of the people here, of their names, number and strength, of their situation and distance from this place, and who was chief among them. His name was Samoset. He told them also of another Indian whose name was Squanto, a native of this place, who had been in England and could speak better English than himself.

Being, after some time of entertainment and gifts dismissed, a while after he came again, and five more with him, and they brought again all the tools that were stolen away before, and made way for the coming of their great sachem, called Massasoit, who, about four or five days after, came with the chief of his friends and other attendants, with the aforesaid Squanto; [and] with whom, after friendly entertainment and some gifts given him, they made a peace with him (which has now continued this twenty-four years) in these terms:

1. That neither he nor any of his should injure or do hurt to any of their people.
2. That if any of his did hurt to any of theirs, he should send the offender that they might punish him.
3. That if anything were taken away from any of theirs, he should cause it to be restored; and they should do the like to his.
4. If any did unjustly war against him, they would aid him; if any did war against them, he should aid them.
5. He should send to his neighbors confederates to certify them of this that they might not wrong them, but might be likewise comprised in the conditions of peace.
6. That when their men came to them, they should leave their bows and arrows behind them.

After these things, he returned to his place called Sowams, some forty miles from this place, but Squanto continued with them and was their interpreter and was a special instrument sent of God for their good beyond their expectation. He directed them how to set their corn, where to take fish, and to procure other commodities, and was also their pilot to bring them to unknown places for their profit, and never left them till he died. . . .

The spring now approaching, it pleased God the mortality began to cease among them, and the sick and lame recovered apace, which put, as it were, new life into them, though they had borne their sad affliction with much patience and contentedness as I think any people could do. But it was the Lord which upheld them and had beforehand prepared them, many having long borne the yoke, yea, from their youth. Many other smaller matters I omit, sundry of them having been already published in a journal made by one of the company, and some other passages of journeys and relations already published, to which I refer those that are willing to know them more particularly.

And being now come to the 25th of March, I shall begin the year 1621.

MAYFLOWER DEPARTS AND CORN PLANTED

THEY NOW BEGAN to dispatch the ship away which brought them over, which lay till about this time, or the beginning of April. The reason on their part why she stayed so long was the necessity and danger that lay upon them; for it was well toward the end of December before she could land anything here, or they able to receive anything ashore.

Afterward, the 14th of January, the house which they had made for a general rendezvous by casualty fell afire, and some were fain to retire aboard for shelter; then the sickness began to fall sore among them, and the weather so bad as they could not make much sooner any dispatch. Again, the governor and chief of them, seeing so many die and fall down sick daily, thought it no wisdom to send away the ship, their condition considered and the danger they stood in from the Indians, till they could procure some shelter; and therefore thought it better to draw some more charge upon themselves and friends than hazard all. The master and seamen likewise, though before they hasted the passengers ashore to be gone, now many of their men being dead, and of the ablest of them (as is before noted), and of the rest many lay sick and weak; the master dared not put to sea till he saw his men begin to recover, and the heart of winter over.

Afterward they (as many as were able) began to plant their corn, in which service Squanto stood them in great stead, showing them both the manner how to set it and after how to dress and tend it; also he told them, except they got fish and set with it in these old grounds, it would come to nothing. And he showed them that in the middle of April they should have store enough come up the brook by which they began to build, and taught them how to take it, and where to get other provisions necessary for them. All which they found true by trial and experience. Some English seed they sowed, as wheat and peas, but it came not to good, either by the badness of the seed or lateness of the season or both, or some other defect.

BRADFORD SUCCEEDS CARVER; CIVIL MARRIAGE

IN THIS MONTH OF APRIL, while they were busy about their seed, their governor (Mr. John Carver) came out of the field very sick, it being a hot day. He complained greatly of his head and lay down, and within a few hours his senses failed, so as he never spoke more till he died, which was within a few days after; whose death was much lamented and caused great heaviness among them, as there was cause. He was buried in the best manner they could, with some volleys of shot by all that bore arms. And his wife, being a weak woman, died within five or six weeks after him.

Shortly after, William Bradford was cho-sen governor in his stead, and being not recovered of his illness, in which he had been near the point of death, Isaac Allerton was chosen to be an assistant unto him who, by renewed election every year, continued sundry years together. Which I here note once for all.

May 12 was the first marriage in this place which, according to the laudable custom of the Low Countries, in which they had lived, was thought most requisite to be performed by the magistrate, as being a civil thing, upon which many questions about inheritances do depend, with other things most proper to their cognizance and most consonant to the Scriptures (Ruth 4) and nowhere found in the Gospel to be laid on the ministers as a part of their office. "This decree or law about marriage was published by the States of the Low Countries Anno 1590. That those of any religion (after lawful and open publication) coming before the magistrates in the Town, or State house, were to be orderly (by them) married one to another" (Petit's *History*, fol. 1029). And this practice has continued among not only them but has been followed by all the famous churches of Christ in these parts to this time — Anno 1646.

INDIAN DIPLOMACY

HAVING IN SOME SORT ordered their business at home, it was thought meet to send some abroad to see their new friend Massasoit, and to bestow upon him some gratuity to bind him the faster unto them; as also that hereby they might view the country and see in what manner he lived, what strength he had about him, and how the ways were to his place, if at any time they should have occasion. So the 2nd of July they sent Mr. Edward Winslow and Mr. Hopkins, with the aforesaid Squanto for their guide, who gave him a suit of clothes and a horseman's coat with some other small things, which were kindly accepted; but they found but short commons and came both weary and hungry home; for the Indians used then to have nothing so much corn as they have since the English have stored them with their hoes, and seen their industry in breaking up new grounds therewith.

They found his place to be forty miles from hence, the soil good and the people not many, being dead and abundantly wasted in the late great mortality which fell in all these parts about three years before the coming of the English, wherein thousands of them died. They not being able to bury one another, their skulls and bones were found in many places lying still above the ground where their houses and dwellings had been, a very sad spectacle to behold. But they brought word that the Narragansetts lived but on the other side of that great bay, and were a strong people and many in number, living compact together, and had not been at all touched with this wasting plague.

About the latter end of this month, one John Billington lost himself in the woods, and wandered up and down some five days, living on berries and what he could find. At length he [came] on an Indian plantation twenty miles south of this place, called Manomet. They conveyed him farther off, to Nauset among those people that had before set upon the English when they were coasting while the ship lay at the Cape, as is before noted. But the governor caused him to be inquired for among the Indians, and at length Massasoit sent word where he was, and the governor sent a shallop for him and had him delivered. Those people also came and made their peace; and they gave full satisfaction to those whose corn they had found and taken when they were at Cape Cod.

Thus their peace and acquaintance was pretty well established with the natives about them. . . .

FIRST THANKSGIVING

THEY BEGAN NOW to gather in the small harvest they had, and to fit up their houses and dwellings against winter, being all well recovered in health and strength and had all things in good plenty. For as some were thus employed in affairs abroad, others were exercised in fishing, about cod and bass and other fish, of which they took good store, of which every family had their portion. All the summer there was no want; and now began to come in store of fowl, as winter approached, of which this place did abound when they came first (but afterward decreased by degrees). And besides waterfowl there was great store of wild turkeys, of which they took many, besides venison, etc. Besides they had about a peck of meal a week to a person, or now since harvest, Indian corn to that proportion. Which made many afterward write so largely of their plenty here to their friends in England, which were not feigned but true reports.

ARRIVAL OF THE *FORTUNE*

IN NOVEMBER, about that time twelvemonth that [they] themselves came, there came in a small ship [the *Fortune*] to them unexpected or looked for, in which came Mr. Cushman . . . and with him thirty-five persons to remain and live in the plantation; which did not a little rejoice them. And they, when they came ashore, and found all well and saw plenty of victuals in every house, were no less glad; for most of them were lusty young men, and many of them wild enough, who little considered whither or about what they went till they came into the harbor at Cape Cod and there saw nothing but a naked and barren place. They then began to think what should become of them if the people here were dead or cut off by the Indians. They began to consult (upon some speeches that some of the seamen had cast out) to take the sails from the yard lest the ship should get away and leave them there. But the master, hearing of it, gave them good words and told them if anything but well should have befallen the people here, he hoped he had victuals enough to carry them to Virginia; and while he had a bit they should have their part, which gave them good satisfaction.

So they were all landed; but there was not so much as biscuit-cake or any other victuals for them, neither had they any bedding but some sorry things they had in their cabins; nor pot or pan to dress any meat in; nor overmany clothes, for many of them had brushed away their coats and cloaks at Plymouth as they came. But there was sent over some Birching Lane suits in the ship, out of which they were supplied. The plantation was glad of this addition of strength, but could have wished that many of them had been of better condition, and all of them better furnished with provisions. But that could not now be helped. . . .

NARRAGANSETT CHALLENGE

SOON AFTER THIS SHIP'S DEPARTURE, that great people of the Narragansetts, in a braving manner, sent a messenger unto them with a bundle of arrows tied about with a great snakeskin, which their interpreters told them was a threatening and a challenge. Upon which the governor, with the advice of others, sent them a round answer that if they had rather have war than peace, they might begin when they would; they had done them no wrong, neither did they fear them or should they find them unprovided; and by another messenger sent the snakeskin back with bullets in it. But they would not receive it, but sent it back again. But these things I do but mention because they are more at large already put forth in print by Mr. Winslow at the request of some friends. And it is like the reason was their own ambition who (since the death of so many of the Indians) thought to domi-

neer and lord it over the rest, and conceived the English would be a bar in their way, and saw that Massasoit took shelter already under their wings.

But this made them the more carefully to look to themselves, so as they agreed to enclose their dwellings with a good strong pale, and make flankers in convenient places with gates to shut, which were every night locked, and a watch kept; and when need required, there was also warding in the daytime. And the company was, by the captain's and the governor's advice, divided into four squadrons, and everyone had their quarter appointed them unto which they were to repair upon any sudden alarm. And if there should be any cry of fire, a company were appointed for a guard, with muskets, while others quenched the same, to prevent Indian treachery. This was accomplished very cheerfully, and the town impaled round by the beginning of March, in which every family had a pretty garden plot secured.

And herewith I shall end this year. Only I shall remember one passage more, rather of mirth than of weight. On the day called Christmas Day, the governor called them out to work as was used. But the most of this new company excused themselves and said it went against their consciences to work on that day. So the governor told them that if they made it matter of conscience, he would spare them till they were better informed; so he led away the rest and left them. But when they came home at noon from their work, he found them in the street at play, openly; some pitching the bar, and some at stool-ball and suchlike sports. So he went to them and took away their implements and told them that was against his conscience that they should play and others work. If they made the keeping of it matter of devotion, let them keep their houses; but there should be no gaming or reveling in the streets. Since which time nothing has been attempted that way, at least openly. . . .

THE FORT BUILT; VISITORS FROM VIRGINIA RECEIVED

THIS SUMMER THEY BUILT A FORT with good timber, both strong and comely, which was of good defense, made with a flat roof and battlements, on which their ordnance were mounted, and where they kept constant watch, especially in time of danger. It served them also for a meetinghouse and was fitted accordingly for that use. It was a great work for them in this weakness and time of wants, but the danger of the time required it; and both the continual rumors of the fears from the Indians here, especially the Narragansetts, and also the hearing of that great massacre in Virginia, made all hands willing to dispatch the same.

Now the welcome time of harvest approached, in which all had their hungry bellies filled. But it arose but to a little, in comparison of a full year's supply; partly because they were not yet well acquainted with the manner of Indian corn (and they had no other), also their many other employments; but chiefly their weakness for want of food, to tend it as they should have done. Also, much was stolen both by night and day before it became scarce eatable, and much more afterward. And though many were well whipped when they were taken for a few ears of corn, yet hunger made others, whom conscience did not restrain, to venture. So as it well appeared that famine must still ensue, the next year also if not some way prevented, or supply should fail, to which they dared not trust. Markets there were none to go to, but only the Indians, and they had no trading commodities.

Behold, now, another Providence of God. A ship comes into the harbor, one Captain Jones being chief therein. They were set out by some merchants to discover all the harbors between this and Virginia and the shoals of Cape Cod, and to trade along the coast where they could. This ship had store of English beads (which were then good trade) and some knives; but would sell none but at dear rates and also a good quantity together. Yet they were glad of the occasion and fain to buy at any rate; they were fain to give after the rate of cento per cento [100 percent], if not more; and yet pay away coat-beaver at 3s. per pound, which in a few years after yielded 20s. By this means they were fitted again to trade for beaver and other things, and intended to buy what corn they could. . . .

After these things, in February a messenger came from John Sanders, who was left chief over Mr. Weston's men in the Bay of Massachusetts, who brought a letter showing the great wants they were fallen into; and he would have borrowed a hogshead of corn of the Indians but they would lend him none. He desired advice whether he might not take it from them by force to succor his men till he came from the eastward whither he was going. The governor and rest dissuaded him by all means from it, for it might so exasperate the Indians as might endanger their safety, and all of us might smart for it; for they had already heard how they had so wronged the Indians by stealing their corn, etc., as they were much incensed against them. Yea, so base were some of their own company as they went and told the Indians that their governor was purposed to come and take their corn by force. The which, with other things, made them enter into a conspiracy against the English, of which more in the next. Herewith I end this year.

SAD STRAITS OF WESTON'S MEN AND THE GREAT INDIAN CONSPIRACY

IT MAY BE THOUGHT STRANGE that these people should fall to these extremities in so short a time, being left competently provided when the ship left them, and had an ambition by that moiety of corn that was got by trade, besides much they got of the Indians where they lived, by one means and other. It must needs be their great disorder, for they spent excessively while they had or could get it; and, it may be, wasted part away among the Indians; for he that was their chief was taxed by some among them for keeping Indian women, how truly I know not. And after they began to come into wants, many sold away their clothes and bed coverings; others (so base were they) became servants to the Indians, and would cut them wood and fetch them water for a capful of corn; others fell to plain stealing, both night and day, from the Indians, of which they grievously complained. In the end, they came to that misery that some starved and died with cold and hunger. One, in gathering shellfish, was so weak as he stuck fast in the mud and was found dead in the place. At last most of them left their dwellings and scattered up and down in the woods and by the watersides, where they could find peanuts and clams, here six and there ten. . . .

This was the end of these, that sometime boasted of their strength (being all able, lusty men) and what they would do and bring to pass in comparison of the people here, who had many women and children and weak ones among them; and said at their first arrival, when they saw the wants here, that they would take another course and not to fall into such a condition as this simple people were come to. But a man's way is not in his own power; God can make the weak to stand. Let him also that standeth take heed lest he fall. . . .

END OF THE "COMMON COURSE AND CONDITION"

ALL THIS WHILE no supply was heard of, neither knew they when they might expect any. So they began to think how they might raise as much corn as they could and obtain a better crop than they had done, that they might not still thus languish in misery. At length, after much debate of things, the governor (with the advice of the chief among them) gave way that they should set corn, every man for his own particular, and in that regard trust to themselves; in all other things to go on in the general way as before. And so [was] assigned to every family a parcel of land, according to the proportion of their number, for that end, only for present use (but made no division for inheritance), and ranged all boys and youth under some family. This had very good success, for it made all hands very industrious, so as much more corn was planted than otherwise would have been by any means the governor or any other could use, and saved him a great deal of trouble and gave far better content. The women now went willingly into the field, and took their little ones with them to set corn, which before would allege weakness and inability, whom to have compelled would have been thought great tyranny and oppression.

The experience that was had in this common course and condition, tried sundry years and that among godly and sober men, may well evince the vanity of that conceit of Plato's and other ancients applauded by some of later times — that the taking away of property and bringing in community into a commonwealth would make them happy and flourishing, as if they were wiser than God. For this community (so far as it was) was found to breed much confusion and discontent and retard much employment that would have been to their benefit and comfort. For the young men that were most able and fit for labor and service did repine that they should spend their time and strength to work for other men's wives and children without any recompense. The strong, or man of parts, had no more in division of victuals and clothes than he that was weak and not able to do a quarter the other could; this was thought injustice. The aged and graver men to be ranked and equalized in labors and victuals, clothes, etc., with the meaner and younger sort thought it some indignity and disrespect unto them. And for men's wives to be commanded to do service for other men, as dressing their meat, washing their clothes, etc., they deemed it a kind of slavery; neither could many husbands well brook it. Upon the point all being to have alike, and all to do alike, they thought themselves in the like condition and one as good as another; and so, if it did not cut off those relations that God has set among men, yet it did at least much diminish and take off the mutual respects that should be preserved among them. And it would have been worse if they had been men of another condition. Let none object this is men's corruption, and nothing to the course itself. I answer, seeing all men have this corruption in them, God in His wisdom saw another course fitter for them.

SHORT RATIONS

BUT TO RETURN. After this course [was] settled, and by that their corn was planted, all their victuals were spent, and they were only to rest on God's Providence, at night, not many times knowing where to have a bit of anything the next day. And so, as one well observed, had need to pray that God would give them their daily bread, above all people in the world. Yet they bore these wants with great patience and alacrity of spirit, and that for so long a time as for the most part of two years. . . .

But alas! These, when they had maize (that is, Indian corn) they thought it as good as a feast and wanted not only for five days together, but sometime two or three months together, and neither had bread nor any kind of corn. . . .

They having but one boat left and she not overwell fitted, they were divided into several companies, six or seven to a gang or company, and so went out with a net they had bought to take bass and suchlike fish by course, every company knowing their turn. No sooner was the boat discharged of what she brought but the next company took her and went out with her. Neither did they return till they had caught something, though it were five or six days before, for they knew there was nothing at home, and to go home empty would be a great discouragement to the rest. Yea, they strive who should do best. If she stayed long or got little, then all went to seeking of shellfish, which at low water they dug out of the sands. And this was their living in the summertime, till God sent them better; and in winter they were helped with peanuts and fowl. Also in the summer they got now and then a deer, for one or two of the fittest was appointed to range the woods for that end, and what was got that way was divided among them. . . .

THE *ANNE* AND *LITTLE JAMES*

ABOUT FOURTEEN DAYS AFTER, came in this ship, called the *Anne*, whereof Mr. William Peirce was master; and about a week or ten days after, came in the pinnace which, in foul weather, they lost at sea — a fine, new vessel of about forty-four ton [the *Little James*], which the company had built to stay in the country. They brought about sixty persons for the general, some of them being very useful persons and became good members to the body; and some were the wives and children of such as were here already. And some were so bad as they were fain to be at charge to send them home again the next year. Also, besides these, there came a company that did not belong to the general body but came on their particular [on their own] and were to have lands assigned them and be for themselves, yet to be subject to the general government; which caused some difference and disturbance among them, as will after appear. . . .

MORE SEMISTARVATION

THESE PASSENGERS, when they saw their low and poor condition ashore, were much daunted and dismayed, and according to their diverse humors were diversely affected. Some wished themselves in England again; others fell a-weeping, fancying their own misery in what they saw now in others; othersome pitying the distress they saw their friends had been long in and still were under. In a word, all were full of sadness. Only some of their old friends rejoiced to see them, and that it was no worse with them, for they could not expect it should be better, and now hoped they should enjoy better days together. And truly it was no marvel they should be thus affected, for they were in a very low condition; many were ragged in apparel and some little better than half-naked, though some that were well stored before were well enough in this regard. But for food they were all alike, save some that had got a few peas of the ship that was last here. The best dish they could present their friends with was a lobster or a piece of fish without bread or anything else but a cup of fair spring water. And the long continuance of this diet, and their labors abroad, had something abated the freshness of their former complexion; but God gave them health and strength in a good measure, and showed them by experience the truth of that word, "That man liveth not by bread only, but by every word that proceedeth out of the mouth of the Lord doth a man live" (Deut. 8:3). . . .

I may not here omit how, notwithstand-[ing] all their great pains and industry and the great hopes of a large crop, the Lord seemed to blast and take away the same, and to threaten further and more sore famine unto them. By a great drought which continued from the third week in May till about the middle of July, without any rain and with great heat for the most part, insomuch as the corn began to wither away

though it was set with fish, the moisture whereof helped it much. Yet at length it began to languish sore, and some of the drier grounds were parched like withered hay, part whereof was never recovered. Upon which they set apart a solemn day of humiliation to seek the Lord by humble and fervent prayer in this great distress. And He was pleased to give them a gracious and speedy answer, both to their own and the Indians' admiration that lived among them. For all the morning and greatest part of the day, it was clear weather and very hot, and not a cloud or any sign of rain to be seen; yet toward evening it began to overcast, and shortly after to rain with such sweet and gentle showers as gave them cause of rejoicing and blessing God. It came without either wind or thunder or any violence, and by degrees in that abundance as that the earth was thoroughly wet and soaked and therewith; which did so apparently revive and quicken the decayed corn and other fruits, as was wonderful to see, and made the Indians astonished to behold. And afterward the Lord sent them such seasonable showers, with interchange of fair warm weather as, through His blessing, caused a fruitful and liberal harvest, to their no small comfort and rejoicing. For which mercy, in time convenient, they also set apart a day of thanksgiving.

On the other hand, the old planters were afraid that their corn, when it was ripe, should be imparted to the newcomers, whose provisions which they brought with them they feared would fall short before the year went about, as indeed it did. They came to the governor and besought him that as it was before agreed that they should set corn for their particular (and accordingly they had taken extraordinary pains thereabout) that they might freely enjoy the same; and they would not have a bit of the victuals now come, but wait till harvest for their own and let the newcomers enjoy what they had brought. They would have none of it except they could purchase any of it of them by bargain or exchange. Their request was granted them, for it gave both sides good content; for the newcomers were as much afraid that the hungry planters would have eaten up the provisions brought, and they should have fallen into the like condition.

This ship was in a short time laden with clapboard by the help of many hands. Also they sent in her all the beaver and other furs they had, and Mr. Winslow was sent over with her to inform of all things and procure such things as were thought needful for their present condition. By this time harvest was come, and instead of famine now God gave them plenty, and the face of things was changed, to the rejoicing of the hearts of many, for which they blessed God. And the effect of their particular planting was well seen, for all had, one way and other, pretty well to bring the year about; and some of the abler sort and more industrious had to spare, and sell to others; so as any general want or famine has not been among them since to this day.

AGREEMENT WITH NEWCOMERS

THOSE THAT CAME on their particular looked for greater matters than they found or could attain unto, about building great houses and such pleasant situations for them as themselves had fancied; as if they would be great men and rich all of a sudden. But they proved castles in the air. These were the conditions agreed on between the colony and them.

1. That the governor, in the name and with the consent of the company, does in all love and friendship receive and embrace them, and is to allot them competent places for habitations within the town. And promises to show them all such other courtesies as shall be reasonable for them to desire or us to perform.

2. That they on their parts be subject to all such laws and orders as are already made, or hereafter shall be, for the public good.

3. That they be freed and exempt from the general employments of the said company (which their present condition of community requires) except common defense and such other employments as tend to the perpetual good of the colony.

4. Toward the maintenance of government and public officers of the said colony, every male above the age of sixteen years shall pay a bushel of Indian wheat, or the worth of it, into the common store.

5. That, according to the agreement the merchants made with them before they came, they are to be wholly debarred from all trade with the Indians, for all sorts of furs and suchlike commodities, till the time of the communality be ended. . . .

[POLITICS IN PLYMOUTH]

THE TIME OF NEW ELECTION of their officers for this year [1624] being come, and the number of their people increased, and their troubles and occasions therewith, the governor desired them to change the persons, as well as renew the election, and also to add more assistants to the governor for help and counsel and the better carrying on of affairs. Showing that it was necessary it should be so, if it was any honor or benefit, it was fit others should be made partakers of it; if it was a burden (as doubtless it was) it was but equal others should help to bear it, and that this was the end of annual elections. The issue was that as before there was but one assistant, they now chose five, giving the governor a double voice; and afterward they increased them to seven, which course has continued to this day. . . .

Some of those that still remained here on their particular began privately to nourish a faction; and being privy to a strong faction that was among the Adventurers in England, on whom sundry of them did depend. By their private whispering they drew some of the weaker sort of the company to their side, and so filled them with discontent as nothing would satisfy them except they might be suffered to be in their particular also; and made great offers, so they might be freed from the general. The governor, consulting with the ablest of the general body what was best to be done herein, it was resolved to permit them so to do upon equal conditions. The conditions were the same in effect with the former before related, only some more added, as that they should be bound here to remain till the general partnership was ended. And also that they should pay into the store the one-half of all such goods and commodities as they should anywise raise above their food, in consideration of what charge had been laid out for them, with some suchlike things. This liberty granted, soon stopped this gap; for there were but a few that undertook this course when it came to, and they were as soon weary of it. For the other had persuaded them and Mr. Weston together that there would never come more supply to the general body, but the Particulars had such friends as would carry all, and do for them I know not what.

WINSLOW BRINGS CATTLE AND LETTERS

SHORTLY AFTER, Mr. Winslow came over and brought a pretty good supply, and the ship came on fishing — a thing fatal to this plantation. He brought three heifers and a bull, the first beginning of any cattle of that kind in the land, with some clothing and other necessaries, as will further appear; but withal the report of a strong faction among the Adventurers against them, and especially against the coming of the rest from Leyden, and with what difficulty this supply was

procured, and how, by their strong and long opposition, business was so retarded as not only they were now fallen too late for the fishing season but the best men were taken up of the fishermen in the West Country; and he was forced to take such a master and company for that employment as he could procure upon the present. . . .

OBJECTIONS OF THE "PARTICULARS" ANSWERED

WITH [A] . . . LETTER written by Mr. Sherley, there were sent sundry objections concerning which he thus wrote: "These are the chief objections which they that are now returned make against you and the country; I pray you consider them, and answer them by the first conveniency." These objections were made by some of those that came over on their particular and were returned home, as is before mentioned, and were of the same suit with those that this other letter mentions. I shall here set them down, with the answers then made unto them, and sent over at the return of this ship; which did so confound the objectors as some confessed their fault, and others denied what they had said and ate their words; and some others of them have since come over again and here lived to convince themselves sufficiently, both in their own and other men's judgments.

First objection was diversity about religion. *Answer:* We know no such matter, for here was never any controversy or opposition, either public or private (to our knowledge) since we came. *Second obj.:* Neglect of family duties on the Lord's Day. *Ans.:* We allow no such thing, but blame it in ourselves and others, and they that thus report it should have showed their Christian love the more if they had in love told the offenders of it, rather than thus to reproach them behind their backs. But (to say no more) we wish themselves had given better example.

Third obj.: Want of both the sacraments. *Ans.:* The more is our grief that our pastor is kept from us, by whom we might enjoy them; for we used to have the Lord's Supper every Sabbath, and baptism as often as there was occasion of children to baptize.

Fourth obj.: Children not catechized nor taught to read. *Ans.:* Neither is true, for diverse take pains with their own as they can. Indeed, we have no common school for want of a fit person, or hitherto means to maintain one, though we desire now to begin.

Fifth obj.: Many of the Particular members of the plantation will not work for the general. *Ans.:* This also is not wholly true, for though some do it not willingly, and others not honestly, yet all do it; and he that does worst gets his own food and something besides. But we will not excuse them, but labor to reform them the best we can; or else to quit the plantation of them.

Sixth obj.: The water is not wholesome. *Ans.:* If they mean not so wholesome as the good beer and wine in London (which they so dearly love), we will not dispute with them; but else for water it is as good as any in the world (for aught we know) and it is wholesome enough to us that can be content therewith.

Seventh obj.: The ground is barren and does bear no grass. *Ans.:* It is here, as in all places, some better and some worse; and if they well consider their woods in England, they shall not find such grass in them as in their fields and meadows. The cattle find grass, for they are as fat as need be; we wish we had but one for every hundred that here is grass to keep. Indeed, this objection, as some other, are ridiculous to all here which see and know the contrary.

Eighth obj.: The fish will not take salt to keep sweet. *Ans.:* This is as true as that which was written that there is scarce a fowl to be seen or a fish to be taken. Things likely to be true in a country where so many sail of ships come yearly a-fishing?

They might as well say there can no ale or beer in London be kept from souring.

Ninth obj.: Many of them are thievish and steal one from another. *Ans.:* Would London had been free from that crime, then we should not have been troubled with these here. It is well known sundry have smarted well for it, and so are the rest like to do, if they be taken.

Tenth obj.: The country is annoyed with foxes and wolves. *Ans.:* So are many other good countries, too; but poison, traps, and other such means will help to destroy them.

Eleventh obj.: The Dutch are planted near Hudson Bay and are likely to overthrow the trade. *Ans.:* They will come and plant in these parts, also, if we and others do not but go home and leave it to them. We rather commend them than condemn them for it.

Twelfth obj.: The people are much annoyed with mosquitos. *Ans.:* They are too delicate and unfit to begin new plantations and colonies that cannot endure the biting of a mosquito. We would wish such to keep at home till at least they be mosquito-proof. Yet this place is as free as any, and experience teaches that the more the land is tilled and the woods cut down, the fewer there will be, and in the end scarce any at all. . . .

CORN AND ALLOTMENTS OF LAND

THESE THINGS PREMISED, I shall now prosecute the proceedings and affairs here. And before I come to other things, I must speak a word of their planting this year. They having found the benefit of their last year's harvest, and setting corn for their particular, having thereby with a great deal of patience overcome hunger and famine. . . .

They began now highly to prize corn as more precious than silver, and those that had some to spare began to trade one with another for small things, by the quart, pottle [two quarts], and peck, etc.; for money they had none, and if any had, corn was preferred before it. That they might, therefore, increase their tillage to better advantage, they made suit to the governor to have some portion of land given them for continuance and not by yearly lot. For by that means, that which the more industrious had brought into good culture (by much pains) one year, came to leave it the next, and often another might enjoy it; so as the dressing of their lands were the more slighted over and to less profit. Which being well considered, their request was granted. And to every person was given only one acre of land, to them and theirs, as near the town as might be; and they had no more till the seven years were expired. The reason was that they might be kept close together, both for more safety and defense, and the better improvement of the general employments. . . .

NEW DEAL WITH THE ADVENTURERS AND WITHIN THE COLONY

At the usual season of the coming of ships, Mr. Allerton returned and brought some useful goods with him, according to the order given him. For upon his commission he took up £200 which he now got at 30 percent. The which goods they got safely home and well conditioned, which was much to the comfort and content of the plantation. He declared unto them also how with much ado and no small trouble he had made a composition with the Adventurers, by the help of sundry of their faithful friends there, who had also taken much pains thereabout. The agreement or bargain he had brought a draft of, with a list of their names thereto annexed, drawn by the best counsel of law they could get, to make it firm. The heads whereof I shall here insert:

To All Christian People, Greetings, etc.

Whereas at a meeting the 26th of October last past, diverse and sundry persons, whose names to the one part of these presents are subscribed in a schedule hereunto annexed, Adventurers to New Plymouth in New England in America were contented and agreed, in consideration of the sum of £1,800 sterling to be paid (in manner and form following) to sell and make sale of all and every the stocks, shares, lands, merchandise, and chattels whatsoever to the said Adventurers, and other their fellow Adventurers, to New Plymouth aforesaid, any way accruing or belonging to the generality of the said Adventurers aforesaid; as well by reason of any sum or sums of money or merchandise at anytime heretofore adventured or disbursed by them, or otherwise howsoever.

For the better expression and setting forth of which said agreement, the parties to these presents subscribing, do for themselves severally, and as much as in them is, grant, bargain, alien, sell, and transfer all and every the said shares, goods, lands, merchandise, and chattels to them belonging as aforesaid, unto Isaac Allerton, one of the planters resident at Plymouth aforesaid, assigned, and sent over as agent for the rest of the planters there. And to such other planters at Plymouth aforesaid as the said Isaac, his heirs, or assigns, at his or their arrival, shall by writing or otherwise think fit to join or partake in the premises, their heirs, and assigns, in as large, ample, and beneficial manner and form to all intents and purposes, as the said subscribing Adventurers here could or may do, or perform. All which stocks, shares, lands, etc., to the said Adventurers in severality allotted, apportioned, or any way belonging, the said Adventurers do warrant and defend unto the said Isaac Allerton, his heirs, and assigns, against them, their heirs, and assigns, by these presents. And therefore the said Isaac Allerton does, for him, his heirs, and assigns, covenant, promise, and grant to and with the Adventurers whose names are hereunto subscribed, their heirs, etc., well and truly to pay, or cause to be paid unto the said Adventurers, or five of them which were at that meeting aforesaid nominated and deputed; viz.,

John Pocock, John Beauchamp, Robert Keane, Edward Bass, and James Sherley, merchants, their heirs, etc., to and for the use of the generality of them, the sum of £1,800 of lawful money of England, at the place appointed for the receipts of money, on the west side of the Royal Exchange in London; by £200 yearly, and every year on the feast of St. Michael, the first payment to be made Anno 1628, etc.

Also, the said Isaac is to endeavor to procure and obtain from the planters of New Plymouth aforesaid, security, by several obligations or writings obligatory, to make payment of the said sum of £1,800 in form aforesaid, according to the true meaning of these presents. In testimony whereof to this part of these presents, remaining with the said Isaac Allerton, the said subscribing Adventurers have set to their names, etc. And to the other part remaining with the said Adventurers, the said Isaac Allerton has subscribed his name, the 15 November, Anno 1626, in the second year of His Majesty's reign.

This agreement was very well liked and approved by all the plantation, and consented unto, though they knew not well how to raise the payment and discharge their other engagements and supply the yearly wants of the plantation, seeing they were forced for their necessities to take up money or goods at so high interests. Yet they undertook it, and seven or eight of the chief of the place became jointly bound for the payment of this £1,800 in the behalf of the rest, at the several days. In which they ran a great adventure, as their present state stood, having many other heavy burdens already upon them, and all things in an uncertain condition among them. So the next return it was absolutely confirmed on both sides, and the bargain fairly engrossed in parchment and in many things put into better form, by the advice of the most learned counsel they could get. And lest any forfeiture should fall on the whole for nonpayment at any of the days, it ran thus: to forfeit 30s. a week if they missed the time, and was concluded

under their hands and seals, as may be seen at large by the deed itself.

Now though they had some untoward persons mixed among them from the first, which came out of England, and more afterward by some of the Adventurers, as friendship or other affections led them — though sundry were gone, some for Virginia and some to other places — yet diverse were still mingled among them, about whom the governor and council with other of their chief friends had serious consideration how to settle things in regard of this new bargain or purchase made, in respect of the distribution of things both for the present and future.

For the present, except peace and union were preserved, they should be able to do nothing, but endanger to overthrow all now that other ties and bonds were taken away. Therefore they resolved, for sundry reasons, to take in all among them that were either heads of families, or single young men that were of ability and free (and able to govern themselves with meet discretion, and their affairs, so as to be helpful in the commonwealth) into this partnership or purchase.

First, they considered that they had need of men and strength, both for defense and carrying on of businesses. Second, most of them had borne their parts in former miseries and wants with them, and therefore in some sort but equal to partake in a better condition if the Lord be pleased to give it. But chiefly they saw not how peace would be preserved without so doing, but danger and great disturbance might grow to their great hurt and prejudice otherwise. Yet they resolved to keep such a mean in distribution of lands, and other courses, as should not hinder their growth in others coming to them.

So they called the company together and conferred with them, and came to this conclusion, that the trade should be managed as before to help to pay the debts, and all such persons as were above named should be reputed and enrolled for purchasers; single freemen to have a single share, and every father of a family to be allowed to purchase so many shares as he had persons in his family, that is to say, one for himself and one for his wife; and for every child that he had living with him, one. As for servants, they had none but what either their masters should give them out of theirs or their deservings should obtain from the company afterward.

Thus all were to be cast into single shares according to the order abovesaid; and so everyone was to pay his part according to his proportion toward the purchase and all other debts, what the profit of the trade would not reach to; viz., a single man for a single share, a master of a family for so many as he had. This gave all good content. . . .

ARRIVALS FROM LEYDEN AND HEAVY EXPENSES

MR. ALLERTON safely arriving in England and delivering his letters to their friends there and acquainting them with his instructions, found good acceptance with them, and they were very forward and willing to join with them in the partnership of trade and in the charge to send over the Leyden people, a company whereof were already come out of Holland, and prepared to come over, and so were sent away before Mr. Allerton could be ready to come. They had passage with the ships that came to Salem that brought over many godly persons to begin the plantations and churches of Christ there and in the Bay of Massachusetts. So their long stay and keeping back was recompensed by the Lord to their friends here with a double blessing, in that they not only enjoyed them now beyond their late expectation (when all their hopes seemed to be cut off) but with them many more godly friends and Christian brethren as the beginning of a larger harvest unto the Lord. In

the increase of His churches and people in these parts, to the admiration of many, and almost wonder of the world, that of so small beginnings so great things should ensue, as time after manifested. And that here should be a resting place for so many of the Lord's people, when so sharp a scourge came upon their own nation. But it was the Lord's doing, and it ought to be marvelous in our eyes. . . .

That I may handle things together, I have put these two companies that came from Leyden in this place. Though they came at two different times, yet they both came out of England this year [1629]. The former company, being thirty-five persons, were shipped in May and arrived here about August. The latter were shipped in the beginning of March and arrived here the latter end of May 1630. . . .

Their charge as Mr. Allerton brought it in afterward on account came to above £500, besides their fetching hither from Salem and the Bay where they and their goods were landed; viz., their transportation from Holland to England and their charges lying there and passages hither, with clothing provided for them. For I find by account for the one company, 125 yards of kersey, 127 ellons [old measure equal to 45 inches] of linen cloth, shoes 66 pair, with many other particulars. The charge of the other company is reckoned on the several families; some £50, some £40, and some £30, and so more or less as their number and expenses were. And besides all this charge, their friends and brethren here were to provide corn and other provisions for them till they could reap a crop, which was long before; those that came in May were thus maintained upward of sixteen or eighteen months before they had any harvest of their own, and the other by proportion. And all they could do in the meantime was to get some housing and prepare grounds to plant on, against the season. And this charge of maintaining them all this while was little less than the former sum. These things I note more particularly, for sundry regards.

First, to show a rare example herein of brotherly love and Christian care in performing their promises and covenants to their brethren, to, and in a sort beyond, their power, that they should venture so desperately to engage themselves to accomplish this thing and bear it so cheerfully; for they never demanded, much less had any repayment of all these great sums thus disbursed.

Second, it must needs be that there was more than of man in these achievements that should thus readily stir up the hearts of such able friends to join in partnership with them in such a case, and cleave so faithfully to them as these did, in so great adventures. And the more because the most of them never saw their faces to this day, there being neither kindred, alliance, or other acquaintance or relations between any of them than has been before mentioned. It must needs be therefore the special work and hand of God.

Third, that these poor people here in a wilderness should notwithstanding be enabled in time to repay all these engagements, and many more unjustly brought upon them through the unfaithfulness of some and many other great losses which they sustained; which will be made manifest, if the Lord be pleased to give life and time. In the meantime I cannot but admire His ways and works toward His servants, and humbly desire to bless His holy name for His great mercies hitherto.

The Leyden people being thus come over, and sundry of the generality seeing and hearing how great the charge was like to be that was that way to be expended, they began to murmur and repine at it, notwithstanding the burden lay on other men's shoulders, especially at the paying of the three bushels of corn a year, according to the former agreement, when the trade was let for the six years aforesaid. But to give them content herein also it was promised them that if they could do it in the time without it, they would never demand it of them, which gave them good content. And indeed it never was paid, as will appear by the sequel. . . .

BILLINGTON HANGED

This year [1630] John Billington the elder, one that came over with the first, was arraigned, and both by grand and petty jury found guilty of willful murder, by plain and notorious evidence. And was for the same accordingly executed. This, as it was the first execution among them, so was it a matter of great sadness unto them. They used all due means about his trial and took the advice of Mr. Winthrop and other [of] the ablest gentlemen in the Bay of Massachusetts, that were then newly come over, who concurred with them that he ought to die, and the land to be purged from blood. He and some of his had been often punished for miscarriages before, being one of the profanest families among them; they came from London, and I know not by what friends shuffled into their company. His fact was that he waylaid a young man, one John Newcomen, about a former quarrel and shot him with a gun, whereof he died. . . .

MR. ROGER WILLIAMS

Mr. Roger Williams, a man godly and zealous, having many precious parts but very unsettled in judgment, came over first to the Massachusetts; but upon some discontent left that place and came hither, where he was friendly entertained according to their poor ability, and exercised his gifts among them and after some time was admitted a member of the church; and his teaching well approved, for the benefit whereof I still bless God and am thankful to him even for his sharpest admonitions and reproofs so far as they agreed with truth. He this year began to fall into some strange opinions, and from opinion to practice, which caused some controversy between the church and him. And in the end [there was] some discontent on his part, by occasion whereof he left them something abruptly. Yet afterward sued for his dismission to the church of Salem, which was granted, with some caution to them concerning him and what care they ought to have of him. But he soon fell into more things there, both to their and the government's trouble and disturbance. I shall not need to name particulars; they are too well known now to all, though for a time the church here went under some hard censure by his occasion from some that afterward smarted themselves. But he is to be pitied and prayed for; and so I shall leave the matter and desire the Lord to show him his errors and reduce him into the way of truth and give him a settled judgment and constancy in the same, for I hope he belongs to the Lord, and that He will show him mercy. . . .

THE PEQUOT WAR

[1637] IN THE FORE PART of this year, the Pequots fell openly upon the English at Connecticut, in the lower parts of the river, and slew sundry of them as they were at work in the fields, both men and women, to the great terror of the rest, and went away in great pride and triumph, with many high threats. They also assaulted a fort at the river's mouth, though strong and well-defended; and though they did not there prevail, yet it struck them with much fear and astonishment to see their bold attempts in the face of danger; which made them in all places to stand upon their guard and to prepare for resistance, and earnestly to solicit their friends and confederates in the Bay of Massachusetts to send them speedy aid, for they looked for more forc-

ible assaults. Mr. Vane, being then governor, wrote from their General Court to them here to join with them in this war; to which they were cordially willing, but took opportunity to write to them about some former things, as well as present, considerable hereabout. . . .

In the meantime, the Pequots, especially in the winter before, sought to make peace with the Narragansetts, and used very pernicious arguments to move them thereunto — as that the English were strangers and began to overspread their country, and would deprive them thereof in time, if they were suffered to grow and increase; and if the Narragansetts did assist the English to subdue them, they did but make way for their own overthrow, for if they were rooted out, the English would soon take occasion to subjugate them; and if they would hearken to them they should not need to fear the strength of the English, for they would not come to open battle with them but fire their houses, kill their cattle, and lie in ambush for them as they went abroad upon their occasions; and all this they might easily do without any or little danger to themselves. The which course being held, they well saw the English could not long subsist but they would either be starved with hunger or be forced to forsake the country. With many the like things, insomuch that the Narragansetts were once wavering and were half-minded to have made peace with them, and joined against the English.

But again, when they considered how much wrong they had received from the Pequots, and what an opportunity they now had by the help of the English to right themselves, revenge was so sweet unto them as it prevailed above all the rest, so as they resolved to join with the English against them, and did.

The Court here agreed forthwith to send fifty men at their own charge; and with as much speed as possibly they could, got them armed and had made them ready under sufficient leaders, and provided a bark to carry them provisions and tend upon them for all occasions. But when they were ready to march, with a supply from the Bay, they had word to stay, for the enemy was as good as vanquished and there would be no need.

I shall not take upon me exactly to describe their proceedings in these things, because I expect it will be fully done by themselves who best know the carriage and circumstances of things. I shall therefore but touch them in general. From Connecticut, who were most sensible of the hurt sustained and the present danger, they set out a party of men, and another party met them from the Bay, at Narragansetts, who were to join with them. The Narragansetts were earnest to be gone before the English were well rested and refreshed, especially some of them which came last. It should seem their desire was to come upon the enemy suddenly and undiscovered. There was a bark of this place, newly put in there, which was come from Connecticut, who did encourage them to lay hold of the Indians' forwardness, and to show as great forwardness as they, for it would encourage them, and expedition might prove to their great advantage. So they went on, and so ordered their march as the Indians brought them to a fort of the enemy's (in which most of their chief men were) before day. They approached the same with great silence and surrounded it both with English and Indians, that they might not break out; and so assaulted them with great courage, shooting among them, and entered the fort with all speed.

And those that first entered found sharp resistance from the enemy, who both shot at and grappled with them; others ran into their houses and brought out fire and set them on fire, which soon took in their mat; and standing close together, with the wind all was quickly on a flame, and thereby more were burned to death than were otherwise slain. It burned their bowstrings and

made them unserviceable; those that escaped the fire were slain with the sword, some hewed to pieces, others run through with their rapiers, so they were quickly dispatched and very few escaped. It was conceived they thus destroyed about 400 at this time. It was a fearful sight to see them thus frying in the fire and the streams of blood quenching the same, and horrible was the stink and scent thereof; but the victory seemed a sweet sacrifice, and they gave the praise thereof to God, who had wrought so wonderfully for them, thus to enclose their enemies in their hands and give them so speedy a victory over so proud and insulting an enemy.

The Narragansett Indians all this while stood round about, but aloof from all danger and left the whole execution to the English, except it were the stopping of any that broke away. They were insulting over their enemies in this, their ruin and misery, when they saw them dancing in the flames, calling them by a word in their own language, signifying "O brave Pequots!" which they used familiarly among themselves in their own praise in songs of triumph after their victories. After this service was thus happily accomplished, they marched to the waterside where they met with some of their vessels, by which they refreshed with victuals and other necessaries. But in their march the rest of the Pequots drew into a body and accosted them, thinking to have some advantage against them by reason of a neck of land. But when they saw the English prepare for them, they kept aloof, so as they neither did hurt nor could receive any.

After their refreshing, they repaired together for further counsel and directions, and they resolved to pursue their victory and follow the war against the rest. But the Narragansett Indians, most of them, forsook them, and such of them as they had with them for guides or otherwise, they found them very cold and backward in the business, either out of envy, or that they saw the English would make more profit of the victory than they were willing they should; or else deprive them of such advantage as themselves desired, by having them become tributaries unto them, or the like. . . .

That I may make an end of this matter, this Sassacus (the Pequots' chief sachem) being fled to the Mohawks, they cut off his head, with some other of the chief of them, whether to satisfy the English or rather the Narragansetts (who, as I have since heard, hired them to do it) or for their own advantage, I well know not; but thus this war took end. The rest of the Pequots were wholly driven from their place, and some of them submitted themselves to the Narragansetts and lived under them. Others of them betook themselves to the Mohegans under Uncas, their sachem, with the approbation of the English of Connecticut, under whose protection Uncas lived; and he and his men had been faithful to them in this war and done them very good service. But this did so vex the Narragansetts, that they had not the whole sway over them, as they have never ceased plotting and contriving how to bring them under; and because they cannot attain their ends, because of the English who have protected them, they have sought to raise a general conspiracy against the English, as will appear in another place. . . .

WICKEDNESS BREAKS FORTH

MARVELOUS IT MAY BE to see and consider how some kind of wickedness did grow and break forth here, in a land where the same was so much witnessed against and so narrowly looked unto, and severely punished when it was known, as in no place more, or so much, that I have known or heard of; insomuch that they have been somewhat censured even by moderate and good men for their severity in punishments. And yet all this could not suppress the breaking out of sundry notorious sins (as this year

[1642], besides other, gives us too many sad precedents and instances), especially drunkenness and uncleanness. Not only incontinency between persons unmarried, for which many both men and women have been punished sharply enough, but some married persons also. But that which is worse, even sodomy and buggery (things fearful to name) have broken forth in this land oftener than once.

I say it may justly be marveled at and cause us to fear and tremble at the consideration of our corrupt natures, which are so hardly bridled, subdued, and mortified; nay, cannot by any other means but the powerful work and grace of God's Spirit. But (besides this) one reason may be that the devil may carry a greater spite against the churches of Christ and the Gospel here, by how much the more they endeavor to preserve holiness and purity among them and strictly punish the contrary when it arises either in church or commonwealth; that he might cast a blemish and stain upon them in the eyes of [the] world, who use to be rash in judgment. I would rather think thus, than that Satan has more power in these heathen lands, as some have thought, than in more Christian nations, especially over God's servants in them.

Another reason may be that it may be in this case as it is with waters when their streams are stopped or dammed up. When they get passage they flow with more violence and make more noise and disturbance than when they are suffered to run quietly in their own channels; so wickedness being here more stopped by strict laws, and the same more nearly looked unto so as it cannot run in a common road of liberty as it would and is inclined, it searches everywhere and at last breaks out where it gets vent.

A third reason may be, here (as I am verily persuaded) is not more evils in this kind, nor nothing near so many by proportion as in other places; but they are here more discovered and seen and made public by due search, inquisition, and due punishment; for the churches look narrowly to their members, and the magistrates over all, more strictly than in other places. Besides, here the people are but few in comparison of other places which are full and populous and lie hid, as it were, in a wood or thicket and many horrible evils by that means are never seen nor known; whereas here they are, as it were, brought into the light and set in the plain field, or rather on a hill, made conspicuous to the view of all. . . .

THE NEW ENGLAND CONFEDERATION AND THE NARRAGANSETTS

BY REASON OF THE PLOTTINGS of the Narragansetts ever since the Pequots' war, the Indians were drawn into a general conspiracy against the English in all parts, as was in part discovered the year before; and now made more plain and evident by many discoveries and free confessions of sundry Indians upon several occasions from diverse places, concurring in one, with such other concurring circumstances as gave them sufficiently to understand the truth thereof; and to think of means how to prevent the same and secure themselves, which made them enter into this more near union and confederation following.

These were the articles of agreement in the union and confederation which they now first entered into. And in this, their first meeting held at Boston the day and year abovesaid, among other things they had this matter of great consequence to consider on:

The Narragansetts, after the subduing of the Pequots, thought to have ruled over all the Indians about them. But the English, especially those of Connecticut, holding correspondency and friendship with Uncas, sachem of the Mohegan Indians which lived

near them (as the Massachusetts had done with the Narragansetts), and he had been faithful to them in the Pequot war, they were engaged to support him in his just liberties and were contented that such of the surviving Pequots as had submitted to him should remain with him and quietly under his protection. This did much increase his power and augment his greatness, which the Narragansetts could not endure to see. But Miantonomo, their chief sachem, an ambitious and politic man, sought privately and by treachery, according to the Indian manner, to make him away by hiring some to kill him. Sometime they assayed to poison him; that not taking, then in the nighttime to knock him on the head in his house or secretly to shoot him, and suchlike attempts. But none of these taking effect, he made open war upon him (though it was against the covenants both between the English and them, as also between themselves and a plain breach of the same). He came suddenly upon him with 900 or 1,000 men, never denouncing any war before. The other's power at that present was not above half so many, but it pleased God to give Uncas the victory and he slew many of his men and wounded many more; but the chief of all was, he took Miantonomo prisoner.

And seeing he was a great man, and the Narragansetts a potent people and would seek revenge, he would do nothing in the case without the advice of the English, so he, by the help and direction of those of Connecticut, kept him prisoner till this meeting of the commissioners. The commissioners weighed the cause and passages as they were clearly represented and sufficiently evidenced between Uncas and Miantonomo; and the things being duly considered, the commissioners apparently saw that Uncas could not be safe while Miantonomo lived; but either by secret treachery or open force, his life would be still in danger. Wherefore they thought he might justly put such a false and bloodthirsty enemy to death; but in his own jurisdiction, not in the English plantations. And they advised in the manner of his death all mercy and moderation should be shown, contrary to the practice of the Indians, who exercise tortures and cruelty. And Uncas having hitherto shown himself a friend to the English, and in this craving their advice, if the Narragansett Indians or others shall unjustly assault Uncas for this execution, upon notice and request the English promise to assist and protect him as far as they may against such violence.

This was the issue of this business. The reasons and passages hereof are more at large to be seen in the acts and records of this meeting of the commissioners. And Uncas followed this advice and accordingly executed him in a very fair manner according as they advised, with due respect to his honor and greatness. . . .

PROPOSAL TO REMOVE TO NAUSET

Mr. Edward Winslow was chosen governor this year [1644].

Many having left this place (as is before noted) by reason of the straitness and barrenness of the same and their finding of better accommodations elsewhere more suitable to their ends and minds, and sundry others still upon every occasion desiring their dismissions, the church began seriously to think whether it were not better jointly to remove to some other place than to be thus weakened and as it were insensibly dissolved. Many meetings and much consultation were held hereabout, and diverse were men's minds and opinions. Some were still for staying together in this place, alleging men might here live if they would be content with their condition, and that it was not for want or necessity so much that they removed as for the enriching of themselves.

Others were resolute upon removal and so signified that here they could not stay; but if the church did not remove, they must. Insomuch as many were swayed, rather than there should be a dissolution, to condescend to a removal if a fit place could be found that might more conveniently and comfortably receive the whole, with such accession of others as might come to them for their better strength and subsistence, and some suchlike cautions and limitations.

So as, with the aforesaid provisos, the greater part consented to a removal to a place called Nauset, which had been superficially viewed and the goodwill of the purchasers to whom it belonged obtained, with some addition thereto from the Court. But now they began to see their error that they had given away already the best and most commodious places to others, and now wanted themselves. For this place was about fifty miles from hence, and at an outside of the country remote from all society; also that it would prove so strait as it would not be competent to receive the whole body, much less be capable of any addition or increase; so as, at least in a short time, they should be worse there than they are now here. The which with sundry other like considerations and inconveniences made them change their resolutions. But such as were before resolved upon removal took advantage of this agreement and went on, notwithstanding; neither could the rest hinder them, they having made some beginning.

And thus was this poor church left, like an ancient mother grown old and forsaken of her children, though not in their affections yet in regard of their bodily presence and personal helpfulness; her ancient members being most of them worn away by death, and these of later time being like children translated into other families, and she like a widow left only to trust in God. Thus, she that had made many rich became herself poor.

1624 - 1656

14.

Toleration in the Early Colonies

Many of the early settlers in America came here to escape religious persecution at home. Nevertheless, once they were established in the new land, they often set up standards of worship that smacked of the intolerance they had fled. For example, in the year of their arrival, 1624, the settlers of New Netherland attempted to enforce the Reformed Church doctrines of encouraging "true religion," and suppressing "heresy," by drafting a regulation restricting public worship to the orthodox. The "freedom of conscience" granted to all permitted freedom of worship in the privacy of the family, but not in public. The New England settlers on Long Island received permission from the New Netherland government in 1641 to practise their Congregationalist and Presbyterian forms of worship, which shared with the Reformed Church a common Calvinist heritage. However, the arrival of Quakers and other dissenters in their midst spurred the New Netherland Council to issue a new ordinance in 1656, once again restricting the forms of public worship. Similarly, the inhabitants of Pascataquacke, Gorgeana, and Wells in the proprietary province of Maine, who established a township and governmental authority of 1649, declared in an ordinance of October 16 that all men of good character within the province might form an autonomous Christian church, but by implication forbade this to the unorthodox. Maryland's practice of religious toleration was on the whole contrary to the custom of the time. The Toleration Act, passed in 1649 under the guidance of the colonial proprietor, Lord Baltimore, was designed to safeguard the ruling Roman Catholic minority from charges of intolerance and to safeguard their rights from the Protestant majority. However, even here there were difficulties. The Protestants gained control of the Maryland government in 1654 and rescinded those portions of the Toleration Act that gave protection to Catholics; but when Lord Baltimore regained control of the colony, the Act of 1649 was revived.

Source: Manuscript in the Henry E. Huntington Library. *Laws and Ordinances of New Netherland 1638-1674*, E. B. O'Callaghan, ed., Albany, 1868, p. 27.
Proceedings and Acts of the General Assembly of Maryland, January 1637/8-September 1664, William H. Browne, ed., Vol. I, Baltimore, 1883, pp. 244-247.
Province and Court Records of Maine, Portland, 1928, Vol. I, p. 136.
Ecclesiastical Records, State of New York, Albany, 1901, Vol. I, pp. 343-344.

I.

Regulations for Colonists in New Amsterdam

[THE COLONISTS] shall practise no other form of divine worship within their territory than that of the Reformed religion as presently practised here in this country, and, in so doing, by their Christian life and conduct, lead the Indians and other blind people to the knowledge of God and of His Word, without, however, persecuting anyone because of his faith, but leaving to everyone the freedom of his conscience. But, if anyone among them or within their jurisdiction should wantonly revile or blaspheme the name of God or of our Savior Jesus Christ, he shall be punished by the commander and his council according to the circumstances.

II.

New Netherland Freedoms and Privileges

Whereas a considerable number of respectable Englishmen, with their clergyman, have applied to us for permission to settle here and to reside under us, and requested that some articles might be offered to them, we have therefore resolved to communicate the following articles to them:

1. They shall be bound to take the oath of allegiance to the Noble Lords States General and the West India Company, under whose protection they will reside.

2. They shall enjoy free exercise of religion.

III.

Maryland Toleration Act

FORASMUCH as in a well-governed and Christian commonwealth, matters concerning religion and the honor of God ought in the first place to be taken into serious consideration and endeavored to be settled, *be it therefore ordered and enacted,* by the Right Honorable Cecilius, Lord Baron of Baltimore, Absolute Lord and Proprietary of this province, with the advice and consent of this General Assembly, that whatsoever person or persons within this province and the islands thereunto belonging shall henceforth blaspheme God, that is, curse Him, or deny our Savior Jesus Christ to be the Son of God, or shall deny the Holy Trinity — the Father, Son, and Holy Ghost — or the Godhead or any of the said three Persons of the Trinity or the unity of the Godhead, or shall use or utter any reproachful speeches, words, or language concerning the said Holy Trinity, or any of the said three Persons thereof, shall be punished with death and confiscation or forfeiture of all his or her lands and goods to the Lord Proprietary and his heirs.

And be it also enacted, by the authority and with the advice and assent aforesaid, that whatsoever person or persons shall from henceforth use or utter any reproachful words or speeches concerning the Blessed Virgin Mary, the Mother of Our Savior, or the holy apostles or evangelists or any of them, shall in such case for the first offense forfeit to the said Lord Proprietary and his heirs, Lords, and Proprietaries of this province the sum of £5 sterling or the value thereof to be levied on the goods and chattels of every such person so offending, but in case such offender or offenders shall not then have goods and chattels sufficient for the satisfying of such a forfeiture, or that the same be not otherwise speedily satisfied, that then such offender or offenders shall be publicly whipped and be imprisoned during the pleasure of the Lord Proprietary or the lieutenant or chief governor of this province for the time being. And that every such offender or offenders for the second offense forfeit £10 sterling or the value thereof to be levied as aforesaid, or in case such offender or offenders shall not then have goods and chattels within this province sufficient for that purpose, then to be publicly and severely whipped and imprisoned as before is expressed. And that every person or persons before mentioned offending herein the third time, shall for such third offense forfeit all his lands and goods and be forever banished and expelled out of this province.

And be it also further enacted, by the same authority, advice, and assent, that whatsoever person or persons shall from henceforth upon any occasion of offense or otherwise in a reproachful manner or way declare, call, or denominate any person or persons whatsoever inhabiting, residing, trading, or commercing within this province or within any of the ports, harbors, creeks, or havens to the same belonging, a heretic, schismatic, idolator, Puritan, independent, Presbyterian, popish priest, Jesuit, Jesuited papist, Lutheran, Calvinist, Anabaptist, Brownist, Antinomian, Barrowist, Roundhead, Separatist, or any other name or term in a reproachful manner relating to matter of religion, shall for every such offense forfeit and lose the sum of 10s. or the value thereof to be levied on the goods and chattels of every such offender and offenders, the one half thereof to be forfeited and paid unto the person and persons of whom such reproachful words are or shall be spoken or uttered, and the other half thereof to the Lord Proprietary and his heirs, Lords, and Proprietaries of this province. But if such person or persons who shall at any time utter or speak any such reproachful words or language shall not have goods or chattels sufficient and overt within this province to be taken to satisfy the penalty aforesaid, or that the same be not speedily satisfied, that then the person or persons so offending shall be publicly whipped, and shall suffer imprisonment without bail or mainprise until he, she, or they, respectively, shall satisfy the party so offended or grieved by such reproachful language, by asking him or her,

respectively, forgiveness publicly for such offense before the magistrate or chief officer or officers of the town or place where such offense shall be given.

And be it further likewise enacted, by the authority and consent aforesaid, that every person and persons within this province that shall at any time hereafter profane the Sabbath or Lord's Day called Sunday, by frequent swearing, drunkenness, or by any uncivil or disorderly recreation, or by working on that day when absolute necessity does not require it, shall for every such first offense forfeit 2s. 6d., or the value thereof, and for the second offense 5s. or the value thereof, and for the third offense and so for every time he shall offend in like manner afterward, 10s., or the value thereof. And in case such offender and offenders shall not have sufficient goods or chattels within this province to satisfy any of the said penalties respectively hereby imposed for profaning the Sabbath or Lord's Day called Sunday as aforesaid, that in every such case the party so offending shall for the first and second offense in that kind be imprisoned till he or she shall publicly in open court before the chief commander, judge, or magistrate of that county, town, or precinct where such offense shall be committed acknowledge the scandal and offense he has in that respect given against God and the good and civil government of this province, and for the third offense and for every time thereafter shall also be publicly whipped.

And whereas the enforcing of the conscience in matters of religion has frequently fallen out to be of dangerous consequence in those commonwealths where it has been practised, and for the more quiet and peaceable government of this province, and the better to preserve mutual love and amity among the inhabitants thereof, be it, therefore, also by the Lord Proprietary, with the advice and consent of this assembly, ordained and enacted (except as in this present act is before declared and set forth) that no person or persons whatsoever within this province, or the islands, ports, harbors, creeks, or havens thereunto belonging, professing to believe in Jesus Christ, shall from henceforth be in any way troubled, molested, or discountenanced for or in respect of his or her religion, nor in the free exercise thereof within this province or the islands thereunto belonging, nor in any way compelled to the belief or exercise of any other religion against his or her consent, so as they be not unfaithful to the Lord Proprietary, or molest or conspire against the civil government established or to be established in this province under him or his heirs.

And that all and every person and persons that shall presume contrary to this act and the true intent and meaning thereof directly or indirectly either in person or estate willfully to wrong, disturb, trouble, or molest any person whatsoever within this province professing to believe in Jesus Christ for, or in respect of, his or her religion or the free exercise thereof, within this province other than is provided for in this act, that such person or persons so offending shall be compelled to pay treble damages to the party so wronged or molested, and for every such offense shall also forfeit 20s. in money or the value thereof, half thereof for the use of the Lord Proprietary, and his heirs, Lords, and Proprietaries of this province, and the other half for the use of the party so wronged or molested as aforesaid. Or if the party so offending shall refuse or be unable to recompense the party so wronged, or to satisfy such fine or forfeiture, then such offender shall be severely punished by public whipping and imprisonment, during the pleasure of the Lord Proprietary, or his lieutenant or chief governor of this province, for the time being without bail or mainprise.

And be it further also enacted, by the authority and consent aforesaid, that the sheriff or other officer or officers from time to time to be appointed and authorized for that purpose, of the county, town, or precinct where every particular offense in this present act contained shall happen at any time to be committed and whereupon there is hereby a forfeiture, fine, or penalty imposed, shall from time to time distrain and seize the goods and estate of every such person so offending as aforesaid against this present act or any part thereof, and sell the same or any part thereof for the full satisfaction of such forfeiture, fine, or penalty as aforesaid, restoring unto the party so offending the remainder or overplus of the said goods or estate after such satisfaction so made as aforesaid.

The freemen have assented.

THOMAS HATTON

Enacted by the Governor William Stone.

IV.

Maine Township Order on Religious Liberty

IT IS ORDERED [by] this Court and power thereof: That all good people within the jurisdiction of this province who are out of a church way and orthodox in judgment and not scandalous in life shall have full liberty to gather themselves into a church estate, provided they do it in a Christian way, with the due observation of the rules of Christ revealed in His Word.

And every church has free liberty of election and ordination of all her officers from time to time, provided they are able, pious, and orthodox.

V.

New Netherland Restrictions on Religious Meetings

THE DIRECTOR GENERAL and council have been credibly informed that not only conventicles and meetings have been held here and there in this province but also that unqualified persons presume in such meetings to act as teachers, in interpreting and expounding God's Holy Word, without ecclesiastical or secular authority. This is contrary to the general rules, political and ecclesiastical, of our fatherland; and, besides, such gatherings lead to trouble, heresies, and schisms.

Therefore, to prevent this, the director general and council strictly forbid all such public or private conventicles and meetings except the usual and authorized ones, where God's Word, according to the Reformed and established custom, is preached and taught in meetings held for the religious service of the Reformed Church, conformably to the Synod of Dort, which is to be followed here, as in the fatherland, and in the other Reformed churches of Europe; under a fine of £100 Flemish, to be paid by all who, in such public or private meetings, except at the usual authorized gatherings on Sundays or other days, presume to exercise, without due qualification, the duties of a preacher, reader, or chorister; and each man or woman, married or unmarried,

who is found at such a meeting, shall pay a fine of £25 Flemish.

The director general and council, however, do not hereby intend to force the consciences of any, to the prejudice of formerly given patents, or to forbid the preaching of God's Holy Word, the use of family prayers, and divine services in the family; but only all public and private conventicles and gatherings, be they in public or private houses, except the already mentioned usual and authorized religious services of the Reformed.

And that this order may be the better observed, and nobody plead ignorance thereof, the director general and council direct and charge their fiscal, and the inferior magistrates and schouts [bailiffs], to publish the same everywhere in this province, and to prosecute transgressors; inasmuch as we have so decreed this, for the honor of God, the advancement of the Reformed services, and the quiet, unity, and welfare of the country generally.

1628

15.

JONAS MICHAËLIUS: Attempts to Christianize the Indians

The success of the Dutch colonies in America led the Reformed Church to assign an ordained pastor, Jonas Michaëlius, to establish the first Dutch Reformed Church in America. Prior to Michaëlius' arrival at New Amsterdam in 1628, the needs of the Dutch community had been served by two lay workers, Bastien Krol and Jan Huyghens, who acted as "comforters of the sick" and conducted religious meetings. In the following letter of August 11, 1628, Michaëlius described his duties in America to Adrian Smoutius, a pastor in Holland.

Source: A. Eekhof, *Jonas Michaëlius, Founder of the Church in New Netherland,* Leyden, 1926, pp. 129-135.

OUR COMING HERE was agreeable to all, and I hope, by the grace of the Lord, that my service will not be unfruitful. The people, for the most part, are rather rough and unrestrained, but I find in almost all of them both love and respect toward me — two things with which hitherto the Lord has everywhere graciously blessed my labors, and which, in our calling, as Your Reverence well knows and experiences, are especially desirable in order to make our ministry fruitful.

From the beginning we established a form of a church, and, as Brother Bastien Krol very seldom comes down from Fort Orange because the directorship of that fort and the trade there is entrusted to him, it has been thought best to choose two elders

for my assistance and for the proper consideration of all such ecclesiastical matters as might occur, intending the coming year, if the Lord permit, to let one of them retire and to choose another in his place from a double number first lawfully proposed to the congregation. One of those whom we have now chosen is the Honorable Director himself, and the other is the storekeeper of the Company, Jan Huyghens, his brother-in-law, persons of very good fame as far as I have been able to learn at that time, both having formerly held office in the church, the one as deacon and the other as elder, respectively, in the Dutch and French churches at Wesel.

At the first administration of the Lord's Supper which was observed, not without great joy and comfort to many, we had fully fifty communicants, Walloons and Dutch, a number of whom made their first confession of faith before us, and others exhibited their church certificates. Others had forgotten to bring their certificates with them, not thinking that a church would be formed and established here; and some who brought them had lost them, unfortunately, in a general conflagration, but they were admitted upon the satisfactory testimony of others to whom this was known and also upon their daily good deportment, since one cannot observe strictly all the usual formalities in making a beginning under such circumstances. . . .

I keep myself as far as practicable within the pale of my calling, wherein I find myself sufficiently occupied. And, although our small consistory embraces at the most, when Brother Krol is down here, not more than four persons, all of whom, myself alone excepted, have also public business to attend to, I still hope to separate carefully the ecclesiastical from the civil matters which occur, so that each one may be occupied with his own subject. And though many things are *mixti generis,* and political and ecclesiastical persons can greatly assist each other, nevertheless, the matters and offices, proceeding together, must not be mixed but kept separate, in order to prevent all confusion and disorder. As the council of this place consists of good people who are, however, for the most part simple and have little experience in public affairs, I should have little objection to serve them in any difficult or dubious affair with good advice, provided I considered myself capable and my advice should be asked. . . .

In my opinion it would be seemly that the Honorable Directors should furnish this place with plainer and more precise instructions to the rulers, that they may distinctly know how to conduct themselves in all possible public difficulties and events, and also that I should some time have here all such

Acta Synodalia as have been adopted in the synods of Holland, both the special ones of our quarter and those which are provincial and national, in relation to ecclesiastical difficulties, or at least such of them as in the judgment of the Honorable Brethren at Amsterdam would be most likely to be of service to us here. . . .

As to the natives of this country, I find them entirely savage and wild, strangers to all decency, yea, uncivil and stupid as garden stakes, proficient in all wickedness and ungodliness, devilish men who serve nobody but the devil, that is, the spirit which in their language they call Menetto [Manitou], under which title they comprehend everything that is subtle and crafty and beyond human skill and power. They have so much witchcraft, divination, sorcery, and wicked arts that they can hardly be held in by any bands or locks. They are as thievish and treacherous as they are tall, and in cruelty they are altogether inhuman, more than barbarous, far exceeding the Africans. . . .

How these people can best be led to the true knowledge of God and of the Mediator Christ is hard to say. I cannot myself wonder enough who it is that has imposed so much upon Your Reverence and many others in the fatherland concerning the docility of this people and their good nature, the proper *principia religionis* [principles of religion] and *vestigia legis naturae* [vestiges of natural law] which are said to be among them, in whom I have as yet been able to discover hardly a single good point, except that they do not speak so jeeringly and so scoffingly of the godlike and glorious majesty of their Creator as the Africans dare to do. But it may be because they have not such a certain knowledge of Him, or none at all. If we speak to them of God, it appears to them like a dream, and we are compelled to speak of Him, not under the name of Menetto, whom they know and serve, for that would be blasphemy, but of one great, yea, most high Sackiema [sachem], by which name they, having no king, call those who have the command over several hundred among them, who by our people are called Sackemakers; and, as they hear it, some begin to mutter and shake their heads, as if it were a silly fable, and others, in order to get out of the difficulty with honor and friendship, will say Orith, that is good. Now, by what means are we to prepare this people for salvation? . . .

Shall we then leave the parents as they are and begin with the children, who are still young. Let it be so. But they ought in youth to be separated from their parents, yea, from their whole nation. For, without this, they would forthwith be as much accustomed as their elders to the heathenish tricks and deviltries which of itself are kneaded in their hearts by nature by a just judgment of God, so that having once, by habit, obtained deep root, they would, with great difficulty, be brought away from it. But this separation is hard to effect, for the parents have a strong affection for their children and are very loath to part with them, and when this happens, as has already been proved, the parents are never fully contented, but take them away stealthily, or induce them to run away.

Nevertheless, we must proceed in this direction, although it would be attended with some expense, to obtain the children by means of presents and promises, with the gratitude and consent of the parents, in order to place them under the instruction of some experienced and godly schoolmaster, where they may be instructed, not only to speak, read, and write our language but especially in the fundaments of our Christian religion, and where, besides, they will see nothing but good examples of virtuous living. But they must sometimes speak their native tongue among themselves in order not to forget it, as being evidently a principal means of spreading the knowledge of religion through the whole nation. . . .

Perchance God may finally have mercy upon them, that the fullness of the heathen may be gradually brought in and the salvation of our God may be here also seen among these wild and savage men. I hope to keep a watchful eye on these people and to learn as much as possible of their language and to seek better opportunities for their instruction than hitherto it has been possible to find.

As to what concerns myself and my household affairs: I find myself through the loss of my good and helpful partner very much hindered and distressed, for my two little daughters are still small; maidservants are not to be had here, at least none whom they can advise me to take, and the Angola slavewomen are thievish, lazy, and useless trash. The young man whom I took with me I discharged after Whitsuntide, for the reason that I could not employ him out-of-doors at any agricultural work, and indoors he was a burden to me instead of an assistance. He is now elsewhere at service among the farmers.

The promise which the Honorable Directors of the Company had made me of some morgens or acres of land for me to support myself, instead of a free table, which otherwise was due to me, is quite void and useless. For Their Honors well knew that there are no horses, cows, or laborers to be obtained here for money. Everyone is short of these things and wants more. I should not mind the expense if the opportunity only offered itself, for the sake of our own comfort, although there were no profit in it (the Honorable Directors nevertheless remaining indebted to me for as much as the value of a free table), for supplies of butter, milk, etc., cannot be obtained here, though it is indeed sold at a very high price, for those who bring it in or order it are jealous of each other. So I shall be compelled to pass through the winter without butter and other necessities, which the ships do not bring with them to be sold here.

1629

16.

Francis Higginson: On the Riches of New England

Most of the first colonists in New England were firmly convinced that their removal to the New World had been ordained by Divine Providence; indeed, had it not been for this faith, many of the Puritans would probably have returned to the more civilized life they had left behind. However, their enthusiasm was not shared by the Puritans who remained in England. The latter looked with disfavor on the "barren desert," as they were wont to call it, of the New World, and often harshly criticized the way of life it engendered. In response to such criticisms, American Puritans like the Reverend Francis Higginson of Salem wrote in the colonies' defense. Here, where the fruits of the earth abounded, Higginson declared, was the true City of God on earth. His pamphlet, New England's Plantation or A Short and True Description of the Commodities of that Country, *was sent to England in August 1629, and was published by the London Company — which wanted settlers — in 1630.*

Source: *Chronicles of the First Planters of the Colony of Massachusetts Bay, from 1623 to 1636,* Alexander Young, ed., Boston, 1846, pp. 242-259.

LETTING PASS our voyage by sea, we will now begin our discourse on the shore of New England. And because the life and welfare of every creature here below, and the commodiousness of the country whereas such creatures live, do by the most wise ordering of God's providence, depend, next unto himself, upon the temperature and disposition of the four elements, earth, water, air, and fire (for as of the mixture of all these all sublunary things are composed, so by the more or less enjoyment of the wholesome temper and convenient use of these consists the only well-being both of

man and beast in a more or less comfortable measure in all countries under the heavens). Therefore, I will endeavor to show you what New England is by the consideration of each of these apart, and truly endeavor, by God's help, to report nothing but the naked truth, and that both to tell you of the discommodities as well as of the commodities; though as the idle proverb is, "Travelers may lie by authority," and so may take too much sinful liberty that way, yet I may say of myself, as once Nehemiah did in another case, "Shall such a man as I lie?" No, verily; it becomes not a preacher of truth to be a writer of falsehood in any degree; and, therefore, I have been careful to report nothing of New England but what I have partly seen with my own eyes, and partly heard and inquired from the mouths of very honest and religious persons, who, by living in the country a good space of time, have had experience and knowledge of the state thereof, and whose testimonies I do believe as myself.

FIRST, THEREFORE, OF THE EARTH OF NEW ENGLAND AND ALL THE APPURTENANCES THEREOF

IT IS A LAND of diverse and sundry sorts all about Massachusetts Bay, and at Charles River is as fat black earth as can be seen anywhere, and in other places you have a clay soil; in other gravel; in other sandy, as it is all about our plantation at Salem, for so our town is now named.

The form of the earth here, in the superficies of it, is neither too flat in the plains nor too high in hills, but partakes of both in a mediocrity, and fit for pasture, or for plow, or meadow ground, as men please to employ it. Though all the country be, as it were, a thick wood for the general, yet in diverse places there is much ground cleared by the Indians, and especially about the plantation; and I am told that about three miles from us a man may stand on a little hilly place and see diverse thousands of acres of ground as good as need to be, and not a tree in the same.

It is thought here is good clay to make brick and tiles and earthen pots, as need to be. At this instant we are setting a brick kiln on work to make bricks and tiles for the building of our houses. For stone, here is plenty of slates at the Isle of Slate in Massachusetts Bay, and limestone, freestone, and smoothstone, and ironstone, and marblestone, also, in such store that we have great rocks of it, and a harbor hard by.

Our plantation is from thence called Marble Harbor.

Of minerals there has yet been but little trial made, yet we are not without great hope of being furnished in that soil.

The fertility of the soil is to be admired at, as appears in the abundance of grass that grows everywhere, both very thick, very long, and very high in diverse places; but it grows very wildly, with a great stalk and a broad and ranker blade, because it never had been eaten with [grazed by] cattle, nor mowed with a scythe, and seldom trampled on by foot. It is scarce to be believed how our kine [cows] and goats, horses and hogs do thrive and prosper here and like well of this country.

In our plantation we have already a quart of milk for a penny; but the abundant increase of corn proves this country to be a wonderment. Thirty, forty, fifty, sixty are ordinary here. Yea, Joseph's increase in Egypt is outstripped here with us. Our planters hope to have more than a hundredfold this year, and all this while I am within compass. What will you say of two hundredfold and upward?

It is almost incredible what great gain some of our English planters have had by our Indian corn. Credible persons have assured me, and the party himself avouched the truth of it to me, that of the setting of thirteen gallons of corn he has had increase of it fifty-two hogsheads, every hogshead holding seven bushels of London measure, and every bushel was by him sold and trusted to the Indians for so much beaver as was worth 18s. And so of this thirteen gallons of corn, which was worth 6s. 8d., he made about £327 of it the year following, as by reckoning will appear, where you may see how God blesses husbandry in this land.

There is not such great and plentiful ears of corn, I suppose, anywhere else to be found but in this country, being also of variety of colors, as red, blue, and yellow, etc.; and of one corn there springs 400 or

500. I have sent you many ears of diverse colors that you might see the truth of it.

Little children here by setting of corn may earn much more than their own maintenance.

They have tried our English corn at New Plymouth plantation, so that all our several grains will grow here very well, and have a fitting soil for their nature.

Our governor has store of green peas growing in his garden as good as ever I ate in England.

This country abounds naturally with store of roots of great variety and good to eat. Our turnips, parsnips, and carrots are here both bigger and sweeter than is ordinarily to be found in England. Here are also store of pumpkins, cucumbers, and other things of that nature which I know not. Also diverse excellent potherbs grow abundantly among the grass, as strawberry leaves in all places of the country, and plenty of strawberries in their time, and pennyroyal, winter savory, sorrel, brooklime, liverwort, chervil, and watercresses; also leeks and onions are ordinary, and diverse physical herbs. Here are also abundance of other sweet herbs delightful to the smell, whose names we know not, and plenty of single damask roses very sweet; and two kinds of herbs that bear two kinds of flowers very sweet, which they say are as good to make cordage or cloth as any hemp or flax we have.

Excellent vines are here up and down in the woods. Our governor has already planted a vineyard with great hope to increase.

Also, mulberries, plums, raspberries, currants, chestnuts, filberts, walnuts, smallnuts, hurtleberries, and haws of whitethorn near as good as our cherries in England; they grow in plenty here.

For wood there is no better in the world, I think, here being four sorts of oak differing both in the leaf, timber, and color, all excellent good. There [are] also good ash, elm, willow, birch, beech, sassafras, juniper, cypress, cedar, spruce, pines, and fir that will yield abundance of turpentine, pitch, tar, masts, and other materials for building both of ships and houses. Also here are store of sumac trees, that are good for dyeing and tanning of leather; likewise such trees yield a precious gum called white benjamin [benzoin] that they say is excellent for perfumes. Also here be diverse roots and berries wherewith the Indians dye excellent holding colors that no rain nor washing can alter. Also, we have materials to make soap ashes and saltpeter in abundance.

For beasts there are some bears, and they say some lions also, for they have been seen at Cape Anne. Also, here are several sorts of deer, some whereof bring three or four young ones at once, which is not ordinary in England. Also, wolves, foxes, beavers, otters, martens, great wildcats, and a great beast called a molke [moose] as big as an ox. I have seen the skins of all these beasts since I came to this plantation, excepting lions. Also here are great store of squirrels, some greater and some smaller and lesser; there are some of the lesser sort, they tell me, that by a certain skin will fly from tree to tree though they stand far distant.

OF THE WATERS OF NEW ENGLAND WITH THE THINGS BELONGING TO THE SAME

NEW ENGLAND has water enough, both salt and fresh. The greatest sea in the world, the Atlantic Sea, runs all along the coast thereof. There are abundance of islands along the shore, some full of wood and mast to feed swine; and others clear of wood, and fruitful to bear corn. Also we have store of excellent harbors for ships, as at Cape Anne, and at Massachusetts Bay, and at Salem, and at many other places; and they are the better because for strangers there is a very difficult and dangerous passage into them, but unto such as are well acquainted with them, they are easy and safe enough.

The abundance of sea fish [is] almost beyond believing; and sure I should scarce have believed it except I had seen it with my own eyes. I saw great store of whales and grampuses, and such abundance of mackerels that it would astonish one to behold; likewise codfish [in] abundance on the coast, and in their season are plentifully taken. There is a fish called a bass, a most sweet and wholesome fish as ever I did eat. It is altogether as good as our fresh salmon, and the season of their coming was begun when we came first to New England in June, and so continued about three months' space. Of this fish our fishers may take many hundreds together, which I have seen lying on the shore, to my admiration. Yea, their nets ordinarily take more than they are able to haul to land, and for want of boats and men they are constrained to let a many go after they have taken them, and yet sometimes they fill two boats at a time with them.

And besides bass, we take plenty of skate and thornback, and abundance of lobsters; and the least boy in the plantation may both catch and eat what he will of them. For my own part I was soon cloyed with them, they were so great, and fat, and luscious. I have seen some myself that have weighed sixteen pounds, but others have had diverse times so great lobsters as have weighed twenty-five pounds, as they assured me. Also, here, is abundance of herring, turbot, sturgeon, cusks, haddocks, mullets, eels, crabs, mussels, and oysters.

Besides, there is probability that the country is of an excellent temper for the making of salt; for, since our coming, our fishermen have brought home very good salt which they found candied [caked] by the standing of the seawater and the heat of the sun upon a rock by the seashore. And in diverse salt marshes that some have gone through they have found some salt in some places crushing under their feet and cleaving to their shoes.

And as for fresh water, the country is full of dainty springs and some great rivers, and some lesser brooks; and at Massachusetts Bay they dug wells and found water at three feet deep in most places. And near Salem they have as fine clear water as we can desire, and we may dig wells and find water where we list.

Thus we see both land and sea abound with store of blessings for the comfortable sustenance of man's life in New England.

OF THE AIR OF NEW ENGLAND WITH THE TEMPER AND CREATURES IN IT

THE TEMPER OF THE AIR of New England is one special thing that commends this place. Experience does manifest that there is hardly a more healthful place to be found in the world that agrees better with our English bodies. Many that have been weak and sickly in old England, by coming hither, have been thoroughly healed and grown healthful and strong. For here is an extraordinary clear and dry air that is of a most healing nature to all such as are of a cold, melancholy, phlegmatic, rheumatic temper of body.

None can more truly speak hereof by their own experience than myself. My friends that knew me can well tell how very sickly I have been and continually in physic, being much troubled with a tormenting pain through an extraordinary weakness of my stomach, and abundance of melancholic humors. But since I came hither on this voyage, I thank God I have had perfect health, and freed from pain and vomiting, having a stomach to digest the hardest and coarsest fare, who before could not eat finest meat; and whereas my stomach could only digest and did require such drink as was both strong and stale, now I can and do oftentimes drink New England water very well. And I that have not gone without a cap for many years together, neither dared leave off the same, have now cast away my cap, and do wear none at all in the daytime. And whereas beforetime I clothed myself with double clothes and thick waistcoats to keep me warm, even in the summertime, I do now go as thin clad as any, only wearing a light stuff cassock upon my shirt, and stuff breeches of one thickness without linings.

Besides, I have one of my children that was formerly most lamentably handled with sore breaking out of both his hands and feet of the king's evil [scrofula], but since he came hither he is very well ever he was, and there is hope of perfect recovery shortly, even by the very wholesomeness of the air, altering, digesting, and drying up the cold and crude humors of the body. And, therefore, I think it is a wise course for all cold complexions to come to take physic in New England, for a sup of New England's air is better than a whole draft of old England's ale.

In the summertime, in the midst of July and August, it is a good deal hotter than in old England; and in winter, January and February are much colder, as they say; but the spring and autumn are of a middle temper.

Fowls of the air are plentiful here, and of all sorts as we have in England, as far as I can learn, and a great many of strange fowls which we know not. While I was writing these things, one of our men brought home an eagle which he had killed in the wood; they say they are good meat. Also, here are many kinds of excellent hawks, both sea hawks and land hawks; and myself walking in the woods with another in company sprung a partridge so big that through the heaviness of his body could fly but a little way. They that have killed them say they are as big as our hens. Here are likewise abundance of turkeys often killed in the woods, far greater than our English turkeys, and exceeding fat, sweet, and fleshy; for here they have abundance of feeding all the year long, as strawberries (in summer all places are full of them) and all manner of berries and fruits. In the wintertime I have seen flocks of pigeons, and have eaten of them. They do fly from tree to tree as other birds do, which our pigeons will not do in England. They are of all colors as ours are, but their wings and tails are far longer, and, therefore, it is likely they fly swifter to escape the terrible hawks in this country. In wintertime this country does abound with wild geese, wild ducks, and other seafowl, that a great part of winter the planters have eaten nothing but roast meat of diverse fowls which they have killed.

Thus you have heard of the earth, water, and air of New England; now it may be you expect something to be said of the fire proportionable to the rest of the elements.

Indeed, I think New England may boast of this element more than of all the rest, for, though it be here somewhat cold in the winter, yet here we have plenty of fire to warm us, and that a great deal cheaper than they sell billets and faggots in London. Nay, all Europe is not able to afford to make so great fires as New England. A poor servant here that is to possess but fifty acres of land may afford to give more wood for timber and fire as good as the world yields than many noblemen in England can afford to do. Here is good living for those that love good fires. And although New England [has] no tallow to make candles of, yet by the abundance of the fish thereof, it can afford oil for lamps. Yea, our pine trees that are the most plentiful of all wood . . . allow us plenty of candles which are very useful in a house, and they are such candles as the Indians commonly use, having no other; and they are nothing else but the wood of the pine tree cloven into two little slices something thin, which are so full of the moisture of turpentine and pitch that they burn as clear as a torch. I have sent you some of them.

17.

First Charter of Massachusetts

The Massachusetts Bay Company was incorporated as a commercial venture in 1629 and immediately set out for the settlement at Salem. However, the position of the Puritan directors of the company was becoming insecure in England, and they decided to remove to America the next year (1630), taking with them to what is now Boston 1,000 settlers and their charter. This migration was by far the largest of its kind up to that time. By taking their charter with them — a maneuver that was unprecedented and that was also of uncertain legality — the directors made it practically impossible for any unsympathetic investors remaining in England to exert control over the company. What is more, the presence of the charter in the colony itself fostered from the beginning a feeling of independence of English rule that was typical of Massachusetts until the Revolution. Portions of the charter of March 4, 1629, which remained in effect until Massachusetts became a royal colony in 1684, are reprinted below.

Source: Hazard, I, pp. 239-255.

CHARLES, BY THE GRACE OF GOD, King of England . . . to all to whom this presence shall come, Greetings.

Whereas our most dear and royal father, King James, of blessed memory, by His Highness' letters patent, bearing date at Westminster the 3rd day of November, in the eighteenth year of his reign, has given and granted unto the Council established at Plymouth, in the County of Devon, for the planting, ruling, ordering, and governing of New England in America, and to their successors and assigns forever, all that part of America lying and being in breadth from 40° north latitude . . . to 48° of the said north latitude inclusive and in length of and within all the breadth aforesaid throughout the mainlands from sea to sea . . . provided always that the said islands or any the premises by the said letters patent intended and meant to be granted were not then actually possessed or inhabited by any other Christian prince or state. . . .

And whereas the said Council . . . have by their deed, indented under their common seal bearing date the 19th day of March last past in the third year of Our reign, given, granted . . . and confirmed to Sir Henry Rosewell, Sir John Young, knights; Thomas Southcott, John Humfrey, John Endecott, and Simon Whetcombe, their heirs and assigns and associates forever, all that part of New England in America aforesaid which lies and extends between a great river there, commonly called Mono-mack, alias Merrimac, and a certain other river there, called Charles River, being in the bottom of a certain bay there, commonly called Massachusetts, alias Mattachusetts, alias Massatusetts Bay, and also all and singular those lands and hereditaments whatsoever . . . and all jurisdictions, rights, royalties, liberties, freedoms, immunities, privileges, franchises, preeminences, and commodities whatsoever which they, the said Council . . . then had or might use, exercise, or enjoy in or within the said lands and premises by the said indenture mentioned to be given, granted, bargained, sold, enfeoffed, and confirmed, or in or within any part or parcel thereof . . . yielding and paying therefore unto Us, Our Heirs, and Successors the fiftieth part of the ore of gold and silver which shall, from time to time and at all times hereafter, happen to be found, gotten, had, and obtained in any of the said lands . . . Now know ye that We, at the humble suit and petition of the said Sir Henry Rosewell [*et al.*] and of others whom they have associated unto them, have, for diverse good causes and considerations, . . . granted and confirmed all the said part of New England in America lying and extending between the bounds and limits in the said recited indenture expressed. . . .

And forasmuch as the good and prosperous success of the plantation of the said parts of New England . . . cannot but chiefly depend next under the blessing of Almighty God and the support of Our Royal Authority upon the good government of the same, to the end that the affairs and businesses which, from time to time, shall happen and arise concerning the said lands and the plantation of the same may be the better managed and ordered, We have further . . . granted and confirmed . . . unto Our said trusty and well-beloved subjects Sir Henry Rosewell [*et al.*] and all such others as shall hereafter be admitted and made free of the Company and Society hereafter mentioned, shall, from time to time and at all times forever hereafter, be . . . one body corporate and politic in fact and name, by the name of the governor and Company of the Massachusetts Bay in New England, and them by the name of the governor and Company of the Massachusetts Bay in New England, one body politic and corporate, in deed, fact, and name; We do . . . confirm . . . that they and their successors shall have perpetual succession, and

that they and their successors shall and may be capable and enabled as well to implead and to be impleaded, and to prosecute, demand, and answer and be answered unto in all and singular suits, causes, quarrels, and actions of what kind or nature soever. And also to have, take, possess, acquire, and purchase any lands, tenements, or hereditaments or any goods or chattels, and the same to lease, grant, demise, alien, bargain, sell, and dispose of, as other Our liege people of this Our Realm of England, or any other corporation or body politic of the same may lawfully do.

And, further, that the said governor and Company . . . may have forever one common seal to be used in all causes and occasions of the said Company, and the same seal may alter, change, break, and new make, from time to time, at their pleasures. And Our will and pleasure is . . . that from henceforth forever there shall be one governor, one deputy governor, and eighteen assistants of the same Company, to be from time to time constituted, elected, and chosen out of the freemen of the said Company, for the time being, in such manner and form as hereafter . . . is expressed, which said officers shall apply themselves to take care for the best disposing and ordering of the general business and affairs of, for, and concerning the said lands and premises . . . and the government of the people there.

And for the better execution of Our royal pleasure and grant in this behalf, We do . . . nominate . . . Our well-beloved the said Matthew Cradock to be the first and present governor of the said Company, and the said Thomas Goffe to be deputy governor . . . Sir Richard Saltonstall, Isaack Johnson, Samuell Aldersey, John Ven, John Humfrey, John Endecott, Simon Whetcombe, Increase Noell, Richard Pery, Nathaniell Wright, Samuell Vassall, Theophilus Eaton, Thomas Adams, Thomas Hutchins, John Browne, George Foxcrofte, William Vassall, and William Pinchion to be the present assistants of the said Company, to continue in the said several offices, respectively, for such time and in such manner as in and by this presence is hereafter declared and appointed.

And, further, We will . . . that the governor of the said Company, for the time being, or in his absence by occasion of sickness or otherwise, the deputy governor, for the time being, shall have authority . . . to give order for the assembling of the said Company and calling them together to consult and advise of the business and affairs of the said Company and . . . shall or may, once every month, or oftener, at their pleasures, assemble and hold and keep a court or assembly of themselves for the better ordering and directing of their affairs. And that any seven or more persons of the assistants, together with the governor or deputy governor, so assembled, shall be said, taken, held, and reputed to be, and shall be, a full and sufficient court or assembly of the said Company for the handling, ordering, and, dispatching of all such business . . . as shall from time to time happen . . . and that there shall or may be held and kept by the governor, or deputy governor, of the said Company and seven or more of the said assistants, for the time being, upon every last Wednesday in Hilary, Easter, Trinity, and Michas Terms, respectively forever, one great general and solemn assembly, which four general assemblies shall be styled and called the four Great and General Courts of the said Company; in all and every . . . General Courts so assembled, We do . . . give and grant to the said governor and Company . . . that the governor . . . and such of the assistants and freemen of the said Company as shall be present . . . whereof the governor or deputy governor and six of the assistants, at the least to be seven, shall have full power and authority to choose, nominate, and appoint such and so many others as they shall think fit, and that shall be willing to accept the same,

to be free of the said Company and body, and them into the same to admit; and to elect and constitute such officers as they shall think fit and requisite for the ordering, managing, and dispatching of the affairs of the said governor and Company . . . and to make laws and ordinances for the good and welfare of the said Company . . . and the people inhabiting and to inhabit the same . . . so as such laws and ordinances be not contrary or repugnant to the laws and statutes of this Our Realm of England.

And Our will and pleasure is . . . that yearly, once in the year, forever hereafter, namely, the last Wednesday in Easter Term yearly, the governor, deputy governor, and assistants of the said Company and all other officers of the said Company shall be in the General Court or assembly . . . newly chosen for the year ensuing. . . . And if it shall happen the present governor, deputy governor, and assistants . . . or any other of the officers to be appointed for the said Company to die or to be removed from his or their several offices or places before the said general day of election (whom We do hereby declare for any misdemeanor or defect to be removable by the governor, deputy governor, assistants, and Company, or such greater part of them in any of the public courts to be assembled as is aforesaid) that then, and in every such case, it shall and may be lawful to and for the governor, [etc.,] to proceed to a new election of one or more others of their Company in the room or place, rooms or places of such officer or officers so dying or removed. . . . Provided, also . . . that . . . [they] take their corporal oaths for the due and faithful performance of their duties in their several offices and places. . . .

And We do further . . . give and grant to the said governor and Company . . . that it shall be lawful and free for them and their assigns . . . to take, lead, carry, and transport, for and into their voyages and for and toward the said plantation in New England, all such and so many of Our loving subjects, or any other strangers that will become Our loving subjects, and live under Our allegiance, as shall willingly accompany them in the same voyages and plantation. . . . That they and every of them shall be free and quit from all taxes, subsidies, and customs in New England for the like space of seven years, and from all taxes and impositions for the space of twenty-one years, upon all goods and merchandises at any time or times hereafter, either upon importation thither or exportation from thence into Our Realm of England, or into any other Our dominions by the said governor and Company. . . .

And, further, Our will and pleasure is . . . that all and every the subjects of Us . . . which shall go to and inhabit within the said lands and premises hereby mentioned to be granted and every of their children which shall happen to be born there, or on the seas in going thither or returning from thence, shall have and enjoy all liberties and immunities of free and natural subjects within any of the dominions of Us. . . .

And We do . . . grant . . . that it shall and may be lawful to and for the governor or deputy governor, [etc.,] to make, ordain, and establish all manner of wholesome and reasonable orders, laws, statutes, and ordinances, directions, and instructions not contrary to the laws of this Our Realm of England . . . as also for the disposing and or-dering of the elections of such of the said officers as shall be annual and of such others as shall be to succeed in case of death or removal, and ministering the said oaths to the new elected officers, and for impositions of lawful fines, mulcts, imprisonment, or other lawful correction, according to the course of other corporations in this Our Realm of England; and for the directing, ruling, and disposing of all other matters and things whereby Our said people, inhabitants there, may be so religiously, peaceably, and civilly governed, as their good life and orderly conversation may win and incite the natives of country to the knowledge and obedience of the only true God and Savior of mankind, and the Christian faith, which in Our royal intention and the adventurers' free profession, is the principal end of this plantation. . . .

And We do, further, for Us . . . give and grant to the said governor and Company . . . that it shall and may be lawful to and for the chief commanders, governors, and officers of the said Company, for the time being, who shall be resident in the said part of New England in America . . . for their special defense and safety, to encounter, expulse, repel, and resist by force of arms, as well by sea as by land and by all fitting ways and means whatsoever, all such person and persons as shall at any time hereafter attempt or enterprise the destruction, invasion, detriment, or annoyance to the said plantation or inhabitants.

18.

Rights and Privileges of Patroons

The Charter of Freedoms and Exemptions for New Netherland was granted by the Dutch West India Company on June 7, 1629. It provided for the perpetual proprietorship of vast estates, called patroonships, to those members of the Company founding settlements of fifty or more persons on land purchased from the Indians. In return for a pledge of loyalty to the Company, patroons were given complete jurisdiction over their territory. Under the terms of this Charter, a handful of patroons quickly took control of most of the Hudson River valley, the choicest portion of New Netherland. However, disputes within the Company and difficulties with the Indians doomed the system, so that by 1680 only two of the original grants remained in force. The colony itself passed under British control in 1664.

Source: E. B. O'Callaghan, *History of New Netherland; or, New York Under the Dutch*, New York, 1846, pp. 112-120.

ALL SUCH SHALL BE acknowledged patroons of New Netherland who shall, within the space of four years next after they have given notice to any of the chambers of the Company here, or to the commander or council there, undertake to plant a colony there of fifty souls, upward of fifteen years old; one-fourth part within one year, and within three years after the sending of the first, making together four years, the remainder, to the full number of fifty persons, to be shipped from hence, on pain, in case of willful neglect, of being deprived of the privileges obtained; but it is to be observed that the Company reserve the island of the Manhattes [Manhattan] to themselves.

They shall, from the time they make known the situation of the places where they propose to settle colonies, have the preference to all others of the absolute property of such lands as they have there chosen, but, in case the situation should not afterward please them, or that they should have been mistaken as to the quality of the land, they may, after remonstrating concerning the same to the commander and council there, be at liberty to choose another place.

The patroons, by virtue of their power, shall and may be permitted, at such places as they shall settle their colonies, to extend their limits four miles along the shore, that is, on one side of a navigable river, or two miles on each side of a river, and so far into the country as the situation of the occupiers will permit; provided and conditioned that the Company keep to themselves the lands lying and remaining between the limits of colonies, to dispose thereof, when and at such time as they shall think proper, in such manner that no person shall be allowed to come within seven or eight miles of them without their consent, unless the situation of the land thereabout were such that the commander and council, for good reasons, should order otherwise; always observing that the first occupiers are not to be prejudiced in the right they have obtained, other than, unless the service of the Company should require it, for the building of fortifications or something of that sort; remaining, moreover, the command of each bay, river, or island of the first-settled colony, under the supreme jurisdiction of their High Mightinesses the States General and the Company. But that, on the next colonies being settled on the same river or island, they may, in conjunction with the first, appoint one or more council in order to consider what may be necessary for the prosperity of the colonies on the said river and island.

They shall forever possess and enjoy all the lands lying within the aforesaid limits . . . and, in case any one should in time prosper so much as to found one or more cities, he shall have power and authority to establish officers and magistrates there and to make use of the title of his colony, according to his pleasure and to the quality of the persons. . . .

The patroons and colonists shall be privileged to send their people and effects thither in ships belonging to the Company, provided they take the oath and pay to the Company for bringing over the people. . . .

Inasmuch as it is intended to people the island of the Manhattes first, all fruits and wares that are produced on the lands situate[d] on the North River and lying thereabout shall, for the present, be brought there before they may be sent elsewhere; excepting such as are from their nature unnecessary there, or such as cannot, without great loss to the owner thereof be brought there; in which case the owners thereof shall be obliged to give timely notice in writing of the difficulty attending the same to the Company here, or the commander and council there, that the same may be remedied as the necessity thereof shall be found to require.

All the patroons of colonies in New Netherland and of colonies on the island of Manhattes shall be at liberty to sail and traffic all along the coast from Florida to Terra Neuf, provided that they do again return with all such goods as they shall get in trade to the island of Manhattes and pay 5 percent for recognition to the Company, in order, if possible, that, after the necessary inventory of the goods shipped be taken, the same may be sent hither. . . .

In case the ships of the patroons, in going to or coming from or sailing on the coast from Florida to Terra Neuf and no farther without our grant, should overpower any of the prizes of the enemy, they shall be obliged to bring, or cause to be brought, such prize to the college of the place from whence they sailed out, in order to be rewarded by them; the Company shall keep the one-third part thereof, and the remaining two-thirds shall belong to them, in consideration of the cost and risk they have been at, all according to the orders of the Company.

It shall be also free for the aforesaid patroons to traffic and trade all along the coast of New Netherland and places circumjacent, with such goods as are consumed there, and receive in return for them all sorts of merchandise that may be had there, except beavers, otters, minks, and all sorts of peltry, which trade the Company reserve to themselves. . . .

The Company promises the colonists of the patroons that they shall be free from customs, taxes, excise, imposts, or any other contributions for the space of ten years; and, after the expiration of the said ten years at the highest, such customs as the goods are taxable with here for the present.

They will not take from the service of the patroons any of their colonists, either man or woman, son or daughter, manservant or maidservant; and, though any of them should desire the same, they will not receive them, much less permit them to leave their patroons and enter into the service of another, unless on consent obtained from their patroons in writing; and this for and during so many years as they are bound to their patroons; after the expiration whereof, it shall be in the power of the patroons to send hither all such colonists as will not continue in their service and until then shall not enjoy their liberty. And all such colonists as shall leave the service of his patroon and enter into the service of another or shall, contrary to his contract, leave his service, we promise to do everything in our power to apprehend and deliver the same into the hands of his patroon, or attorney, that he may be proceeded against. . . .

In regard to such private persons as on their own account, or others in the service of their masters here (not enjoying the same privileges as the patroons), shall be inclined to go thither and settle, they shall, with the approbation of the director and council there, be at liberty to take up as much land, and take possession thereof, as they shall be able properly to improve and shall enjoy the same in full property either for themselves or masters.

They shall have free liberty of hunting and fowling, as well by water as by land, generally, and in public and private woods and rivers, about their colonies, according to the orders of the director and council.

Whosoever, whether colonists of patroons for their patroons or free persons for themselves or other particulars for their masters, shall discover any shores, bays, or other fit places for erecting fisheries or the making of salt ponds, they may take possession thereof and begin to work on them in their own absolute property, to the exclusion of all others. . . .

In case any of the colonists should, by his industry and diligence, discover any minerals, precious stones, crystals, marbles, or suchlike or any pearl fishery, the same shall be and remain the property of the patroon or patroons of such colony; giving and ordering the discoverer such premium as the patroon shall beforehand have stipulated with such colonists by contract. And the patroons shall be exempt from all recognition to the Company for the term of eight years and pay only for freight to bring them over, 2 percent, and after the expiration of the aforesaid eight years, for recognition and freight, the one-eighth part of what the same may be worth.

The Company will take all the colonists, as well free as those that are in service, under their protection and the same, against all outlandish and inlandish wars and powers, with the forces they have there, as much as lies in their power, defend.

Whosoever shall settle any colony out of the limits of the Manhattes Island shall be obliged to satisfy the Indians for the land they shall settle upon, and they may extend or enlarge the limits of their colonies if they settle a proportionate number of colonists thereon.

The patroons and colonists shall in particular, and in the speediest manner, endeavor to find out ways and means whereby they may support a minister and schoolmaster, that thus the service of God and zeal for religion may not grow cool and be neglected among them; and that they do, for the first, procure a comforter of the sick there.

The colonies that shall happen to lie on the respective rivers or islands (that is to say, each river or island for itself) shall be at liberty to appoint a deputy, who shall give information to the commander and council of that Western quarter, of all things relating to his colony, and who are to further matters relating thereto, of which deputies there shall be one altered, or changed, in every two years; and all colonies shall be obliged, at least once in every twelve months, to make exact report of their colony and lands thereabout to the commander and council there, in order to be transmitted hither.

The colonists shall not be permitted to make any woolen, linen, or cotton cloth, nor weave any other stuffs there, on pain of being banished, and as perjurers to be arbitrarily punished.

The Company will use their endeavors to supply the colonists with as many blacks as they conveniently can, on the conditions hereafter to be made; in such manner, however, that they shall not be bound to do it for a longer time than they shall think proper.

1630

19.

JOHN COTTON: The Divine Right to Occupy the Land

The compelling desire of the Puritans to leave their homeland was matched by a need to justify their action. Before departing from Southampton in 1630, John Winthrop and his followers heard a sermon by the Reverend John Cotton that may have given courage to any who doubted their mission. The sermon, God's Promise to His Plantation, *was based on II Samuel 7:10, and Cotton emphasized the parallel between the Puritans and God's chosen people, preaching that it was God's will that they should inhabit all the world. The sermon, a portion of which follows, was the first printed work of Cotton and bears the same relation to the Massachusetts Bay Colony as does John Robinson's farewell sermon to the colony at Plymouth. Cotton later joined his compatriots in New England.*

Source: OSL 53.

Moreover I will appoint a place for my people Israel, and I will plant them, that they may dwell in a place of their own, and move no more [II Sam. 7:10]. . . .

The placing of a people in this or that country is from the appointment of the Lord. . . .

Quest. Wherein doth this work of God stand in appointing a place for a people?

Answ. First, when God espies or discovers a land for a people, as in Ezek. 20:6: "He brought them into a land that He had espied for them." And, that is, when either He gives them to discover it themselves, or hears of it discovered by others, and fitting them.

Second, after He hath espied it, when He carrieth them along to it, so that they plainly see a providence of God leading them from one country to another, as in Ex. 19:4: "You have seen how I have borne you as on eagles' wings, and brought you unto Myself." So that though they met with many difficulties, yet He carried them high above them all, like an eagle, flying over seas and rocks, and all hindrances.

Third, when He makes room for a people to dwell there, as in Ps. 80:9: "Thou preparedst room for them. . . ."

Now, God makes room for a people three ways: First, when He casts out the enemies of a people before them by lawful war with the inhabitants, which God calls them unto, as in Ps. 44:2: "Thou didst drive out the heathen before them." But this course of warring against others and driving them out without provocation depends upon special commission from God, or else it is not imitable.

Second, when He gives a foreign people favor in the eyes of any native people to come and sit down with them, either by way of purchase, as Abraham did obtain the field of Machpelah; or else when they give it in courtesy, as Pharaoh did the land of Goshen unto the sons of Jacob.

Third, when He makes a country, though not altogether void of inhabitants, yet void in that place where they reside. Where there is a vacant place, there is liberty for the sons of Adam or Noah to come and inhabit, though they neither buy it nor ask their leaves. . . . So that it is free from that common grant for any to take possession of vacant countries. Indeed, no nation is to drive out another without special commission from Heaven, such as the Israelites had, unless the natives do unjustly wrong them, and will not recompense the wrongs done in a peaceable fort [way]. And then they may right themselves by lawful war and subdue the country unto themselves. . . .

This may teach us all, where we now dwell or where after we may dwell: Be sure you look at every place appointed to you from the hand of God. We may not rush into any place and never say to God, "By Your leave." But we must discern how God appoints us this place. There is poor comfort in sitting down in any place that you cannot say, "This place is appointed me of God." Canst thou say that God spied out this place for thee, and there hath settled thee above all hindrances? Didst thou find that God made room for thee either by lawful descent, or purchase, or gift, or other warrantable right? Why, then, this is the place God hath appointed thee; here He hath made room for thee, He hath placed thee in Rehoboth, in a peaceable place. This we must discern or else we are but intruders upon God. And when we do withal discern that God giveth us these outward blessings from His love in Christ, and maketh comfortable provision as well for

our soul as for our bodies by the means of grace, then do we enjoy our present possession as well by gracious promise as by the common, and just, and bountiful providence of the Lord. Or, if a man do remove, he must see that God hath espied out such a country for him. . . .

Quest. But how shall I know whether God hath appointed me such a place, if I be well where I am, what may warrant my removal?

Answ. There be four or five good things, for procurement of any of which I may remove. Second, there be some evil things, for avoiding of any of which we may transplant ourselves. Third, if withal we find some special providence of God concurring in either of both concerning ourselves, and applying general grounds of removal to our personal estate.

First, we may remove for the gaining of knowledge. . . .

Second, some remove and travail for merchandise and gainsake: "Daily bread may be sought from far" (Prov. 31:14). . . .

Third, to plant a colony, that is, a company that agree together to remove out of their own country, and settle a city or commonwealth elsewhere. Of such a colony, we read in Acts 16:12, which God blessed and prospered exceedingly, and made it a glorious church. . . .

Fourth, God alloweth a man to remove when he may employ his talents and gift better elsewhere, especially when where he is, he is not bound by any special engagement. . . .

Fifth, for the liberty of the ordinances. . . . This case was of seasonable use to our fathers in the days of Queen Mary, who removed to France and Germany in the beginning of her reign, upon proclamation of alteration of religion, before any persecution began. . . . There be evils to be avoided that may warrant removal: First, when some grievous sins overspread a country that threaten desolation. . . . Second, if men be overburdened with debts and miseries. . . . Third, in case of persecution. . . . As these general cases, where any of them do fall out, do warrant removal in general; so there be some special providences or particular cases which may give warrant unto such or such a person to transplant himself, and which apply the former general grounds to particular persons; first, if sovereign authority command and encourage such plantations by giving way to subjects to transplant themselves and set up a new commonwealth. This is a lawful and expedient case for such particular persons as be designed and sent; Matt. 8:9: "And for such as they who are sent have power to command." Second, when some special providence of God leads a man unto such a course.

20.

JOHN WINTHROP: A Model of Christian Charity

One of the most distinguished members of the Massachusetts Bay Colony was the Puritan, John Winthrop, who left England with his followers in four ships on March 22, 1630, and, after a delay of several weeks in Yarborough, arrived in Salem on June 12. Winthrop had given much thought, not only to his personal decision to leave England but also to the goals, both religious and political, that he felt should be pursued by the Puritans in their new community. Before debarking from his flagship, the Arabella, *he wrote a statement of the principles that he thought the colony should incorporate into its organization. Entitled "A Modell of Christian Charity," it is one of the best expressions of the ideals of the Puritan Commonwealth in America.*

Source: *Winthrop Papers,* The Massachusetts Historical Society, 1931, Vol. II, pp. 282-295.

GOD ALMIGHTY, in His most holy and wise providence, has so disposed of the condition of mankind, as in all times some must be rich; some poor; some high and eminent in power and dignity; others mean and in subjection.

The Reason Hereof: first, to hold conformity with the rest of His works, being delighted to show forth the glory of His wisdom in the variety and difference of the creatures and the glory of His power, in ordering all these differences for the preservation and good of the whole; and the glory of His greatness in that, as it is the glory of princes to have many officers, so this Great King will have many stewards, counting Himself more honored in dispensing His gifts to man by man than if He did it by His own immediate hand.

Second, that He might have the more occasion to manifest the work of His spirit; first, upon the wicked in moderating and restraining them, so that the rich and mighty should not eat up the poor, nor the poor and despised rise up against their superiors and shake off their yoke; second, in the regenerate in exercising His graces in them, as in the great ones their love, mercy, gentleness, temperance, etc.; in the poor and inferior sort, their faith, patience, obedience, etc.

Third, that every man might have need of others, and from hence they might be all knit more nearly together in the bond of brotherly affection. From hence it appears plainly that no man is made more honorable than another or more wealthy, etc., out of any particular or singular respect to himself, but for the glory of his Creator and the common good of the creature, man. Therefore, God still reserves the property of these gifts to Himself, as [in] Ezek. 16:17; He there calls wealth His gold and His silver, etc; [in] Prov. 3:9 He claims their service as His due: "Honor the Lord with thy riches," etc. All men are thus (by Divine Providence) ranked into two sorts, rich and poor; under the first are included all men such as are able to live comfortably by their own means duly improved; and all others are poor according to the former distribution.

There are two rules whereby we are to walk one toward another: *justice and mercy.* These are always distinguished in their act and in their object, yet may they both concur in the same subject in each respect, as sometimes there may be an occasion of showing mercy to a rich man in some sudden danger of distress; and also doing of mere justice to a poor man in regard of some particular contract, etc. There is likewise a double law by which we are regulated in our conversation one toward another: in both the former respects, the law of nature and the law of grace, or the moral law or the law of the gospel (we may omit the law of justice as not properly belonging to this purpose otherwise than it may fall into consideration in some particular case). By the first of these laws, man . . . is commanded to love his neighbor as himself. Upon this ground stands all the precepts of the moral law which concerns our dealings with men. To apply this to the works of mercy, this law requires two things: first,

that every man afford his help to another in every want or distress; second, that he perform this out of the same affection which makes him careful of his own good, according to that of our Savior, (Matt. 7:12) "Whatsoever ye would that men should do to you. . . ."

The law of grace or the gospel has some difference from the former as in these respects: First, the law of nature was given to man in the estate of innocence; the law of the gospel in the estate of regeneracy. Second, the law of nature propounds one man to another, as the same flesh and image of God, the law of gospel as a brother in Christ also, and in the communion of the same spirit, and so teaches us to put a difference between Christians and others. . . . The law of nature could give no rules for dealing with enemies, for all are considered as friends in the state of innocence, but the gospel commands love to an enemy. . . . "If thine enemy hunger, feed him; love your enemies; do good to them that hate you" (Matt. 5:44).

This law of the gospel propounds, likewise, a difference of seasons and occasions. There is a time when a Christian must sell all and give to the poor as they did in the apostles' times. There is a time also when Christians (though they give not all yet) must give beyond their ability. . . . Likewise, community of perils calls for extraordinary liberality and so does community in some special service for the Church. Lastly, when there is no other means whereby our Christian brother may be relieved in this distress, we must help him beyond our ability, rather than tempt God in putting him upon help by miraculous or extraordinary means.

This duty of mercy is exercised in . . . giving, lending, and forgiving.

Question: What rule shall a man observe in giving in respect to the measure?

Answer: If the time and occasion be ordinary, he is to give out of his abundance — let him lay aside, as God has blessed him. If the time and occasion be extraordinary, he must be ruled by them. . . . Then a man cannot likely do too much, especially if he may leave himself and his family under . . . means of comfortable subsistence.

Objection: A man must lay up for posterity; the fathers lay up for posterity and children, and he is worse than an infidel that provides not for his own.

Answer: For the first, it is plain that the statement is made by way of comparison and must be meant for the ordinary and usual course of fathers and cannot extend to times and occasions extraordinary, for in another place the apostle speaks against those who walk inordinately, and it is without question that he is worse than an infidel who through his own sloth and voluptuousness shall neglect to provide for his family.

Objection: "The wise man's eyes are in his head," says Solomon (Eccles. 2:14), "and foreseeth the plague," therefore we must forecast and lay up against evil times when he or his may stand in need of all he can gather.

Answer: Solomon uses this very argument to persuade to liberality. Eccles. 2:1: "Cast thy bread upon the waters . . . for thou knowest not what evil may come upon the land"; Luke 16: "Make you friends of the riches of iniquity." You will ask how this shall be? Very well. First, he that gives to the poor lends to the Lord, who will repay him even in this life and a hundredfold to him or his. The righteous man is ever merciful and lends, and his seed enjoy the blessing; and besides we know what advantage it will be to us in the day of accounting, when many such witnesses shall stand forth for us to witness the improvement of our talent. And I would know of those who plead so much for laying up for time to come, whether they hold Matt. 16:19 to be gospel: "Lay not up for yourselves treasures upon earth." If they acknowledge it, what extent will they allow it? If only to those primitive times, let them consider the reason whereupon our Savior grounds it. The

first is that treasures are subject to the moth, rust, and the thief; the second is that they will steal away the heart; where the treasure is, there will the heart be also.

The reasons are of like force at all times; therefore, the exhortation must be general and perpetual, which applies always in respect of the love and affection for riches and in regard to the things themselves, when any special service for the church or particular distress of our brother call for the use of riches; otherwise it is not only lawful but necessary to lay up as Joseph did, to have ready upon such occasions as the Lord (whose stewards we are) shall call for them from us.

Christ gave us an instance of the first, when He sent His disciples for the ass and bade them answer the owner thus: "The Lord hath need of him" (Matt. 21:2-3). . . . The Lord expects that when He is pleased to call for anything we have, our own interest must stand aside till His turn is served. For the other instance, we need look no further than John 1: "He who hath this world's goods and seeth his brother in need, and shuts up his compassion from him, how dwelleth the love of God in him?" Which comes punctually to this conclusion: If your brother is in want and you can help him, you can have no doubt as to what you should do. If you love God you must help him.

Question: What rule must we observe in lending?

Answer: You must observe whether your brother has present or probable or possible means of repaying you, or if none of these, you must give to him according to his necessity, rather than lend to him as he asks. If he has present means of repaying, you are to look at him not as the recipient of mercy but by way of commerce, wherein you are to walk by the rule of justice. But if his means of repaying you are only probable or possible, then he is an object of mercy and you must lend to him though there is danger of losing it. Deut. 15:7: "If any of thy brethren be poor . . . thou shalt lend him sufficient." That men might not shift off this duty because of the apparent hazard, he tells them that though the Year of Jubilee were at hand (when he must remit it, if he could not repay it before), yet he must lend, and that cheerfully. Deut. 15:7-11: "It may not grieve thee to give him," and because some might object, why so I should impoverish myself and my family, he adds: "With all thy work." Matt. 3:42: "From him that would borrow of thee turn not away."

Question: What rule must we observe in forgiving?

Answer: Whether you lend by way of commerce or in mercy. If he has nothing to repay, you must forgive him (unless you have a surety or a lawful pledge). Every seventh year the creditor was to quit that which he lent to his brother if his brother was as poor as he appeared. . . . In all these and like cases Christ gave a general rule in Matt. 7:22: "Whatsoever ye would that men should do to you, do ye the same to them also."

Question: What rule must we observe and walk by in the case of a community of peril?

Answer: The same as before, but with more enlargement toward others and less respect toward ourselves and our own right. Hence, in the primitive church they sold all and had all things in common, nor did any man say that what he possessed was his own. Likewise, in their return from captivity, because the work was great for the restoring of the church and the danger of enemies was common to all, Nehemiah exhorted the Jews to liberality and readiness in remitting their debts to their brethren, and disposed liberally of his own goods to those that wanted, standing not upon what was due him, which he might have demanded of them. Some of our forefathers did the same in times of persecution in England, and so did many of the faithful in other churches,

and so we keep an honorable remembrance of them.

It is also to be observed both in the Scriptures and later stories of the church, that those who have been most bountiful to the poor saints — especially in . . . extraordinary times and occasions — God has left highly commended to posterity. . . . Observe again that the Scripture gives no caution to restrain any from being overliberal in this way, but recommends all men to the liberal and cheerful practice hereof by the sweetest promises. . . . Isa. 58:10:

If thou pour out thy soul to the hungry, then shall thy light spring out in darkness, and the Lord shall guide thee continually, and satisfy thy soul in drought, and make fat thy bones; thou shalt be like a watered garden, and they shall be of thee that shall build the old waste places.

On the contrary, most heavy curses are laid upon those who are illiberal toward the Lord and His people. . . .

Having already set forth the practice of mercy according to the rule of God's law, it will be useful to lay open the grounds of it; also being the other part of the Commandment, and that is the affection from which this exercise of mercy must arise. The apostle tells us that this love is the fulfilling of the law (Rom. 13:10). Not that it is enough to love our brother and no more. . . . Just as, when we bid a man to make the clock strike, he does not lay his hand on the hammer, which is the immediate instrument of the sound, but sets to work the first manner or main wheel, knowing that it will certainly produce the sound which he intends, so the way to draw men to the works of mercy is not by force of argument on the goodness or necessity of the work, for though this course may persuade a rational mind to some present act of mercy (as is frequent in experience), yet it cannot work the habit of mercy into a soul so that it will be prompt on all occasions to produce the same effect except by framing the affections of love in the heart, which will as natively bring forth mercy as any cause produces an effect.

The definition which the Scripture gives us of love is this: love is the bond of perfection (Col. 3:14). First, it is a bond, or ligament. Second, it makes the work perfect. There is no body that does not consist of parts, and that which knits these parts together gives the body its perfection, because it makes each part so contiguous to the others that they mutually participate with each other, both in strength and infirmity, in pleasure and in pain. To instance the most perfect of all bodies: Christ and His church make one body. The several parts of this body considered apart before they were united were as disproportionate and as much disordered as so many contrary qualities or elements, but when Christ came and by His spirit and love knit all these parts to Himself and to each other, it became the most perfect and best proportioned body in the world. . . .

For patterns we have first our Savior, who out of His goodwill and in obedience to His Father became a part of this body, and, being knit with it in the bond of love, found such a native sensitivity to our infirmities and sorrows that He willingly yielded Himself to death to ease the infirmities of the rest of His body and so heal their sorrows. From like sympathy of parts did the apostles and many thousands of saints lay down their lives for Christ again, as we may see in the members of this body among themselves, and as we shall find in the history of the church in all ages: the sweet sympathy of affections in the members of this body, one toward another, their cheerfulness in serving and suffering together. How liberal they were without repining, harborers without grudging, helpful without reproaching, and all from this, that they had fervent love among them, which only makes the practice of mercy constant and easy.

The next consideration is how this love comes to be wrought. Adam in his first estate was a perfect model of mankind in all their generations, and in him this love was perfected. . . . But Adam rent himself from his Creator, rent all his posterity also one from another; whence it comes that every man is born with this principle in him, to love and seek himself only. And thus a man continues till Christ comes and takes possession of his soul, and infuses another principle — love to God and our brother. . . .

The third consideration concerns the exercise of this love, which is twofold — inward or outward. The outward has been handled in the former preface of this discourse; for unfolding the other we must take . . . that maxim of philosophy, *simile simili gaudet*, or, like will to like. . . . The ground of love is a recognition of some resemblance in the things loved to that which affects it. This is the reason why the Lord loves the creature to the extent that it has any of His image in it; He loves His elect because they are like Himself; He beholds them in His Beloved Son. So a mother loves her child, because she thoroughly conceives a resemblance of herself in it. Thus is between the members of Christ. Each discerns by the work of the spirit his own image and resemblance in another, and therefore cannot but love him as he loves himself. . . .

If any shall object that it is not possible that love should be bred or upheld without hope of requital, it is granted. But that is not our cause, for this love is always under reward; it never gives but always receives with advantage. . . . Among members of the same body, love and affection are reciprocal in a most equal and sweet kind of commerce. . . . In regard to the pleasure and content that the exercise of love carries with it, we may see in the natural body that the mouth receives and minces the food which serves to nourish all the other parts of the body, yet it has no cause to complain. For first, the other parts send back by secret passages a due proportion of the same nourishment in a better form for the strengthening and comforting of the mouth. Second, the labor of the mouth is accompanied by pleasure and content which far exceed the pains it takes, so it is all a labor of love.

Among Christians, the party loving reaps love again, as was shown before, which the soul covets more than all the wealth in the world. Nothing yields more pleasure and content to the soul than when it finds that which it may love fervently, for to love and be loved is the soul's paradise, both here and in heaven. In the state of wedlock there are many comforts to bear out the troubles of that condition, but let those who have tried the most say whether there is any sweetness . . . comparable to the exercise of mutual love. . . .

Now to make some application of this discourse to the situation which gave the occasion of writing it. Herein are four things to be propounded: the persons, the work, the end, the means.

First, for the persons, we are a company professing ourselves fellow members of Christ. . . . Though we are absent from each other by many miles, and have our employments at far distance, we ought to account ourselves knitted together by this bond of love, and live in the exercise of it, if we would have the comfort of our being in Christ. This was common in the practice of Christians in former times; they used to love any of their own religion even before they were acquainted with them.

Second, the work we have in hand is by mutual consent with a special overruling Providence, with a more than ordinary mandate from the churches of Christ to seek out a place to live and associate under a due form of government both civil and ecclesiastical. In such cases as this the care of the public must hold sway over all private interests. To this not only conscience

but mere civil policy binds us, for it is a true rule that private estates cannot exist to the detriment of the public.

Third, the end is to improve our lives to do more service to the Lord and to comfort and increase the body of Christ of which we are members, so that ourselves and our posterity may be better preserved from the common corruptions of this evil world in order to serve the Lord and work out our salvation under the power and purity of His holy ordinances.

Fourth, the means whereby this must be effected are twofold. First, since the work and end we aim at are extraordinary, we must not content ourselves with usual ordinary means. Whatsoever we did or ought to have done when we lived in England, we must do that and more also wherever we go. That which most people in their churches only profess as a truth, we must bring into familiar and constant practice. We must love our brothers without pretense; we must love one another with a pure heart and fervently; we must bear one another's burdens; we must not look only on our own things but also on the things of our brethren. Nor must we think that the Lord will bear with such failings at our hands as He does from those among whom we have lived, for three reasons: (1) Because of the closer bonds of marriage between the Lord and us, wherein He has taken us to be His own in a most strict manner, which makes Him more jealous of our love and obedience, just as He told the people of Israel, "You only have I known of all the families of the Earth; therefore will I punish you for your transgressions" (Amos 3:2); (2) Because the Lord will be sanctified in those who come near Him. We know that there were many who corrupted the service of the Lord, some setting up altars to other gods before Him, others offering both strange fires and sacrifices; yet no fire came from heaven, or other sudden judgment upon them. . .; (3) When God gives a special commission He wants it strictly observed in every article. . . .

Thus stands the case between God and us. We are entered into covenant with Him for this work. We have taken out a commission. The Lord has given us leave to draw our own articles; we have promised to base our actions on these ends, and we have asked Him for favor and blessing. Now if the Lord shall please to hear us, and bring us in peace to the place we desire, then He has ratified this covenant and sealed our commission, and will expect strict performance of the articles contained in it. But if we neglect to observe these articles, which are the ends we have propounded, and — dissembling with our God — shall embrace this present world and prosecute our carnal intentions, seeking great things for ourselves and our posterity, the Lord will surely break out in wrath against us and be revenged of such a perjured people, and He will make us know the price of the breach of such a covenant.

Now the only way to avoid this shipwreck and to provide for our posterity is to follow the counsel of Micah: to do justly, to love mercy, to walk humbly with our God. For this end, we must be knit together in this work as one man; we must hold each other in brotherly affection; we must be willing to rid ourselves of our excesses to supply others' necessities; we must uphold a familiar commerce together in all meekness, gentleness, patience, and liberality. We must delight in each other, make others' conditions our own and rejoice together, mourn together, labor and suffer together, always having before our eyes our commission and common work, our community as members of the same body.

So shall we keep the unity of the spirit in the bond of peace. The Lord will be our God and delight to dwell among us as His own people. He will command a blessing on us in all our ways, so that we shall see

much more of His wisdom, power, goodness, and truth than we have formerly known. We shall find that the God of Israel is among us, and ten of us shall be able to resist a thousand of our enemies. The Lord will make our name a praise and glory, so that men shall say of succeeding plantations: "The Lord make it like that of New England." For we must consider that we shall be like a City upon a Hill; the eyes of all people are on us.

If we deal falsely with our God in this work we have undertaken and so cause Him to withdraw His present help from us, we shall be made a story and a byword throughout the world; we shall open the mouths of enemies to speak evil of the ways of God and all believers in God; we shall shame the faces of many of God's worthy servants and cause their prayers to be turned into curses upon us, till we are forced out of the new land where we are going.

Now to end this discourse with the exhortation of Moses, that faithful servant of the Lord, in his last farewell to Israel (Deut. 30):

Beloved, there is now set before us life and good, death and evil, in that we are commanded this day to love the Lord our God, and to love one another; to walk in His ways and to keep His commandments and His ordinance, and His laws, and the articles of our covenant with Him, that we may live and be multiplied, and that the Lord our God may bless us in the land whither we go to possess it. But if our hearts shall turn away so that we will not obey, but shall be seduced and worship other gods, our pleasures and profits, and serve them; it is propounded unto us this day, we shall surely perish out of the good land whither we pass over this vast sea to possess it. Therefore, let us choose life that we and our seed may live; by obeying His voice, and cleaving to Him, for He is our life and our prosperity.

21.

Two Songs of the Colonists

A good example of the early native ballad, "Forefathers' Song," which dates from around 1630, has interest as a straightforward, unromanticized account of life in the English colonies in America. A note in the Massachusetts Historical Collection says that the song was first recorded in 1785 "from the lips of an old lady at the advanced period of ninety-six." "We Gather Together" was originally a Dutch rather than an English song, and the general modern impression that it has been sung as America's Thanksgiving Hymn for three centuries may be incorrect, since it was probably not translated into English until the First World War. Nevertheless, the song is now America's Thanksgiving Hymn, and it was sung by the first Dutch settlers in America, who thereby expressed their hope for a better life in the new land, as well as their gratitude for God's bounty already enjoyed. It was first published in Holland, in Dutch, around 1630.

❧ FOREFATHERS' SONG

New England's annoyances you that would know them,
Pray ponder these verses which briefly doth show them.
The place where we live is a wilderness wood,
Where grass is much wanting that's fruitful and good:
Our mountains and hills and our valleys below,
Being commonly covered with ice and with snow;
And when the north-west wind with violence blows,
Then every man pulls his cap over his nose:
But if any's so hardy and will it withstand,
He forfeits a finger, a foot or a hand.

But when the Spring opens we then take the hoe,
And make the ground ready to plant and to sow;
Our corn being planted and seed being sown,
The worms destroy much before it is grown;
And when it is growing, some spoil there is made
By birds and by squirrels that pluck up the blade;
And when it is come to full corn in the ear,
It is often destroyed by raccoon and by deer.

And now our garments begin to grow thin,
And wool is much wanted to card and to spin;
If we can get a garment to cover without,
Our other in-garments are clout upon clout:
Our clothes we brought with us are apt to be torn,
They need to be clouted soon after they're worn,
But clouting our garments they hinder us nothing,
Clouts double are warmer than single whole clothing.

If fresh meat be wanting to fill up our dish,
We have carrots and turnips as much as we wish:
And if there's a mind for a delicate dish
We repair to the clam-banks, and there we catch fish.
Instead of pottage and puddings and custards and pies,
Our pumpkins and parsnips are common supplies;
We have pumpkins at morning and pumpkins at noon,
If it was not for pumpkins we should be undone!
If barley be wanting to make into malt,
We must be contented, and think it no fault;
For we can make liquor to sweeten our lips,
Of pumpkins and parsnips and walnut-tree chips. . . .

Now while some are going let others be coming,
For while liquor's boiling it must have a scumming;
But I will not blame them, for birds of a feather
By seeking their fellows are flocking together.
But you whom the Lord intends hither to bring,
Forsake not the honey for fear of the sting;
But bring both a quiet and contented mind,
And all needful blessings you surely will find.

WE GATHER TOGETHER

We gather together to ask the Lord's blessing,
He chastens and hastens His will to make known.
The wicked oppressing now cease to be distressing,
Sing praises to His name for He forgets not His own.

Beside us to guide us our God with us joining,
Ordaining, maintaining His kingdom divine.
So from the beginning the fighting we were winning,
Thou Lord wast at our side and all the glory be Thine.

We all do extol Thee, Thou leader triumphant,
And pray that Thou still our defender wilt be.
Let thy congregation escape all tribulation,
Thy name be ever praised in glory, Lord make us free.

1631

22.

Thomas Dudley: Hardships in Massachusetts Bay Colony

Deputy governor and later governor of the Massachusetts Bay Colony, Thomas Dudley was a representative of the narrower and stricter Puritanism that has often been contrasted to the more moderate spirit of John Winthrop. Dudley, who had been a steward to the Earl of Lincoln, addressed the following account of the colony's early days to Bridget, Countess of Lincoln. The letter, written between March 12 and 28, 1631, has been described as "the most interesting as well as authentic document in our [New England's] early annals."

Source: *Chronicles of the First Planters of the Colony of Massachusetts Bay, from 1623 to 1636,* Alexander Young, ed., Boston, 1846, pp. 303-340.

Madam,

Your letters (which are not common nor cheap), following me hither into New England and bringing with them renewed testimonies of the accustomed favors you honored me with in the old, have drawn from me this narrative retribution, which (in respect of your proper interest in some persons of great note among us) was the thankfullest present I had to send over the seas. Therefore, I humbly entreat Your Honor this be accepted as payment from him, who neither has nor is any more than Your Honor's old thankful servant,

THOMAS DUDLEY

Boston in New England,
March 12, 1631.

For the satisfaction of Your Honor and some friends, and for use of such as shall hereafter intend to increase our plantation in New England, I have, in the throng of domestic and not altogether free from public business, thought fit to commit to memory our present condition, and what has befallen us since our arrival here; which I will do shortly, after my usual manner, and must do rudely, having yet no table nor other room to write in than by the fireside upon my knee, in this sharp winter; to which my family must have leave to resort, though they break good manners, and make me many times forget what I would say and say what I would not. . . .

Now, concerning the English that are planted here, I find that about the year 1620 certain English set out from Leyden in Holland intending their course for Hudson's River, the mouth whereof lies south of the river of the Pecoates, but arises, as I am informed, northward in about 43°, and so a good part of it within the compass of our patent. These, being much weather-beaten and wearied with seeking the river, after a most tedious voyage arrived at length in a small bay lying northeast from Cape Cod, where, landing about the month of December, by the favor of a calm winter such as was never seen here since, began to build their dwellings in that place which is now called New Plymouth. . . . After much sickness, famine, poverty, and great mortality (through all which God, by an unwonted providence, carried them), they are now grown up to a people, healthful, wealthy, politic, and religious. Such things does the Lord for those that wait for His mercies. These of Plymouth came with patents from King James and have since obtained others from our sovereign, King Charles, having a governor and council of their own.

There was about the same time one Mr. Weston, an English merchant, who sent diverse men to plant and trade, who sat down by the river of Wesaguscus [Weymouth]. But these coming not for so good ends as those of Plymouth sped not so well, for the most of them dying and languishing away, they who survived were rescued by those of Plymouth out of the hands of Chickatalbott and his Indians, who oppressed these weak English, and intended to have destroyed them, and the Plymotheans also.

Also, since, one Captain Wollaston, with some thirty with him, came near to the same place and built on a hill which he named Mount Wollaston, but being not supplied with renewed provisions they vanished away as the former did. Also, diverse merchants of Bristol and some other places have yearly for these eight years or thereabouts sent ships hither at the fishing times to trade for beaver, where their factors, dishonestly for their gains, have furnished the Indians with guns, swords, powder, and shot.

Touching the plantation which we here have begun, it fell out thus. About the year 1627, some friends being together in Lincolnshire, fell into some discourse about New England and the planting of the gospel there. And after some deliberation, we imparted our reasons by letters and messages to some in London and the west country, where it was likewise deliberately thought upon; and at length, with often negotiation so ripened, that in the year 1628 we procured a patent from His Majesty for our planting between the Massachusetts Bay and Charles River on the south and the river of Merrimac on the north and three miles on either side of those rivers and bay, as also for the government of those who did or should inhabit within that compass. And the same year we sent Mr. John Endecott and some with him to begin a plantation and to strengthen such as he should find there, which we sent thither from Dorchester and some places adjoining; from whom the same year receiving hopeful news, the next year, 1629, we sent diverse ships over with about 300 people, and some cows, goats, and horses, many of which arrived safely.

These, by their too large commendations of the country and the commodities thereof, invited us so strongly to go on that Mr. Winthrop of Suffolk (who was well known in his own country and well approved here for his piety, liberality, wisdom, and gravity) coming in to us, we came to such resolution that in April 1630 we set sail from old England with four good ships. And in May following, eight more followed, two having gone before in February and March, and two more following in June and August, besides another set out by a private merchant. These seventeen ships arrived all safe in New England, for the increase of the plantation here, this year 1630; but made a long, a troublesome, and a costly voyage being all windbound long in England, and hindered with contrary winds after they set sail and so scattered with mists and tempests that few of them arrived together.

Our four ships, which set out in April,

arrived here in June and July, where we found the colony in a sad and unexpected condition, above eighty of them being dead the winter before, and many of those alive, weak and sick. All the corn and bread among them all hardly sufficient to feed them a fortnight, insomuch that the remainder of 180 servants we had the two years before sent over, coming to us for victuals to sustain them, we found ourselves wholly unable to feed them by reason that the provisions shipped for them were taken out of the ship they were put in, and they who were trusted to ship them in another failed us and left them behind. Whereupon necessity enforced us, to our extreme loss, to give them all liberty, who had cost us about £16 or £20 a person furnishing and sending over.

But bearing these things as we might, we began to consult of the place of our sitting down, for Salem, where we landed, pleased us not. And to that purpose some were sent to the Bay to search up the rivers for a convenient place; who, upon their return, reported to have found a good place upon Mystic; but some other of us seconding these to approve or dislike of their judgment, we found a place [we liked] better, three leagues up Charles River. And thereupon unshipped our goods into other vessels and with much cost and labor brought them in July to Charlestown. But there, receiving advertisements by some of the late arrived ships from London and Amsterdam of some French preparations against us (many of our people brought with us being sick of fevers and the scurvy and we thereby unable to carry up our ordnance and baggage so far), we were forced to change counsel and for our present shelter to plant dispersedly, some at Charlestown which stands on the north side of the mouth of Charles River; some on the south side thereof, which place we named Boston (as we intended to have done the place we first resolved on); some of us upon Mystic, which we named Medford; some of us westward on Charles River, four miles from Charlestown, which place we named Watertown; others of us, two miles from Boston, in a place we named Rocksbury; others upon the river of Saugus, between Salem and Charlestown; and the western men, four miles south from Boston, at a place we named Dorchester.

This dispersion troubled some of us, but help it we could not, wanting ability to remove to any place fit to build a town upon, and the time too short to deliberate any longer lest the winter should surprise us before we had built our houses. The best counsel we could find out was to build a fort to retire to, in some convenient place, if any enemy pressed us thereunto, after we should have fortified ourselves against the injuries of wet and cold. So ceasing to consult further for that time, they who had health to labor fell to building, wherein many were interrupted with sickness and many died weekly, yea, almost daily, among whom were Mrs. Pynchon, Mrs. Coddington, Mrs. Phillips, and Mrs. Alcock, a sister of [The Rev. Thomas] Hooker's.

Insomuch that the ships being now upon their return, some for England, some for Ireland, there was, as I take it, not much less than a hundred (some think many more), partly out of dislike of our government which restrained and punished their excesses, and partly through fear of famine, not seeing other means than by their labor to feed themselves, which returned back again. And glad were we so to be rid of them. Others, also, afterward, hearing of men of their own disposition, which were planted at Piscataqua, went from us to them, whereby, though our numbers were lessened, yet we accounted ourselves nothing weakened by their removal. Before the departure of the ships we contracted with Mr. Peirce, master of the *Lion* of Bristol, to return to us with all speed with fresh supplies of victuals, and gave him directions accordingly. With this ship returned Mr. Revell, one of the five undertakers here for the joint stock of the company, and Mr. Vassall, one of the assistants, and his family, and also Mr. Bright, a minister sent hither the year before.

The ships being gone, victuals wasting, and mortality increasing, we held diverse fasts in our several congregations, but the Lord would not yet be deprecated; for about the beginning of September died Mr. Gager, a right godly man, a skillful surgeon, and one of the deacons of our congregation; and Mr. Higginson, one of the ministers of Salem, a zealous and a profitable preacher — this of a consumption, that of a fever. And on the 30th of September died Mr. Johnson, another of the five undertakers (the lady Arbella, his wife, being dead a month before). This gentleman was a prime man among us, having the best estate of any, zealous for religion, and the greatest furtherer of this plantation. He made a most godly end, dying willingly, professing his life better spent in promoting this plantation than it could have been any other way. He left to us a loss greater than the most conceived. Within a month after, died Mr. Rossiter, another of our assistants, a godly man and of a good estate, which still weakened us more; so that there now were left of the five undertakers but the governor, Sir Richard Saltonstall, and myself, and seven other of the assistants. And of the people who came over with us from the time of their setting sail from England in April 1630 until December following, there died by estimation about 200 at the least. So low has the Lord brought us!

Well, yet they who survived were not discouraged, but bearing God's corrections with humility and trusting in His mercies, and considering how after a lower ebb, He had raised up our neighbors at Plymouth, we began again in December to consult about a fit place to build a town upon, leaving all thoughts of a fort, because upon any invasion we were necessarily to lose our houses when we should retire thereinto. So after diverse meetings at Boston, Rocksbury, and Watertown, on the 28th of December, we grew to this resolution — to bind all the assistants (Mr. Endecott and Mr. Sharpe excepted, which last purposes to return by the next ships into England) to build houses at a place a mile east from Watertown, near Charles River, the next spring, and to winter there the next year, that so by our examples and by removing the ordnance and munition thither, all who were able might be drawn thither, and such as shall come to us hereafter to their advantage be compelled so to do. And so, if God would, a fortified town might there grow up, the place fitting reasonably well thereto.

I should before have mentioned how both the English and Indian corn being at 10s. a strike [bushel], and beaver being valued at 6s. a pound, we made laws to restrain the selling of corn to the Indians, and to leave the price of beaver at liberty, which was presently sold for 10s. and 20s. a pound. I should also have remembered how half of our cows and almost all our mares and goats sent us out of England died at sea in their passage hither, and that those intended to be sent us out of Ireland were not sent at all; all which, together with the loss of our six months' building, occasioned by our intended removal to a town to be fortified, weakened our estates, especially the estates of the undertakers, who were £3,000 or £4,000 engaged in the joint stock which was now not above so many hundreds. Yet many of us labored to bear it as comfortably as we could, remembering the end of our coming hither and knowing the power of God, Who can support and raise us again, and uses to bring His servants low, that the meek may be made glorious by deliverance.

In the end of this December departed from us the ship *Handmaid* of London, by which we sent away one Thomas Morton, a proud, insolent man who has lived here diverse years and had been an attorney in the west countries while he lived in England. Multitude of complaints we received against him for injuries done by him both to the English and Indians, and among others, for shooting hail-shot at a troop of Indians for not bringing a canoe unto him to cross a river withal, whereby he hurt one and shot through the garments of another. For the satisfaction of the Indians wherein, and that it might appear to them and to the English that we meant to do justice impartially, we caused his hands to be bound behind him and set his feet in the bilboes, and burned his house to the ground — all in the sight of the Indians — and so kept him prisoner till we sent him for England, whither we sent him for that My Lord Chief Justice there so required that he might punish him capitally for fouler misdemeanors there perpetrated, as we were informed.

I have no leisure to review and insert things forgotten, but out of due time and order must set them down as they come to memory. About the end of October, this year 1630, I joined with the governor and Mr. Maverick in sending out our pinnace to the Narragansetts to trade for corn and to supply our wants. But after the pinnace had doubled Cape Cod, she put into the next harbor she found, and there, meeting with Indians who showed their willingness to truck, she made her voyage there and brought us 100 bushels of corn at about 4s. a bushel, which helped us somewhat. From the coast where they traded they saw a very large island, four leagues to the east, which the Indians commended as a fruitful place full of good vines and free from sharp frosts, having only one entrance into it, by a navigable river, inhabited by a few Indians, which for a trifle would leave the island if the English would set them upon the mainland. But the pinnace, having no direction for discovery, returned without sailing to it,

which in two hours they might have done. Upon this coast they found store of vines full of grapes dead ripe, the season being past; whither we purpose to send the next year sooner, to make some small quantity of wine, if God enable us, the vines growing thin with us and we not having any leisure to plant vineyards.

But now having some leisure to discourse of the motives for other men's coming to this place or their abstaining from it, after my brief manner I say this: that if any come hither to plant for worldly ends that can live well at home, he commits an error of which he will soon repent him. But if for spiritual and that no particular obstacle hinder his removal, he may find here what may well content him: viz., materials to build, fuel to burn, ground to plant, seas and rivers to fish in, a pure air to breathe in, good water to drink till wine or beer can be made, which, together with the cows, hogs, and goats brought hither already, may suffice for food. . . . As for fowl and venison, they are dainties here as well as in England. . . . Clothes and bedding they must bring them with them till time and industry produce them here. In a word, we yet enjoy little to be envied but endure much to be pitied in the sickness and mortality of our people. . . .

Also, to increase the heap of our sorrows, we received advertisement by letters from our friends in England and by the reports of those who came hither in this ship to abide with us (who were about twenty-six) that they who went discontentedly from us the last year, out of their evil affections toward us, have raised many false and scandalous reports against us, affirming us to be Brownists in religion and ill affected to our state at home; and that these vile reports have won credit with some who formerly wished us well. But we do desire, and cannot but hope, that wise and impartial men will at length consider that such malcontents have ever pursued this manner of casting dirt to make others seem as foul as themselves, and that our godly friends, to whom we have been known, will not easily believe that we are so soon turned from the profession we so long have made in our native country.

And for our further clearing, I truly affirm that I know no one person who came over with us the last year to be altered in his judgment and affection, either in ecclesiastical or civil respects, since our coming hither. But we do continue to pray daily for our sovereign lord the King, the Queen, the Prince, the royal blood, the council, and whole state as duty binds us to do and reason persuades others to believe; for how ungodly and unthankful should we be if we should not thus do, who come hither by virtue of His Majesty's letters patent, and under his gracious protection, under which shelter we hope to live safely and from whose kingdom and subjects we now have received and hereafter expect relief. Let our friends, therefore, give no credit to such malicious aspersions, but be more ready to answer for us than we hear they have been. We are not like those which have dispensations to lie, but as we were free enough in old England to turn our insides outward, sometimes to our disadvantage, very unlike is it that now (being *procul a fulmine* [far from the power]) we should be so unlike ourselves; let, therefore, this be sufficient for us to say and others to hear in this matter.

Among others who died about this time was Mr. Robert Welden, whom, in the time of his sickness, we had chosen to be Captain of a Hundred Foot; but before he took possession of his place he died the 16th of this February, and was buried as a soldier with three volleys of shot. Upon the 22nd of February we held a general day of thanksgiving throughout the whole colony for the safe arrival of the ship which came last with our provisions.

About this time we apprehended one Robert Wright, who had been sometime a linen draper in Newgate Market and after that a brewer on the Bankside and on Thames Street. This man, we lately understood, had made an escape in London from those who came to his house to apprehend him for clipping the King's coin. . . . Upon his examination he confessed the fact and his escape, but affirmed he had the King's pardon for it under the broad seal, which, he yet not being able to prove, and one to whom he was known charging him with untruth in some of his answers, we therefore committed him to prison to be sent by the next ship to England.

Likewise, we were lately informed that one Mr. Gardiner, who arrived here a month before us, and who passed here for a knight by the name of Sir Christopher Gardiner, all this while was no knight, but instead thereof had two wives now living in a house at London, one of which came about September last from Paris in France (where her husband had left her years before) to London, where she had heard her husband had married a second wife, and whom, by inquiring, she found out. And they both, condoling each other's estate, wrote both their letters to the governor (by Mr. Peirce, who had conference with both the women in the presence of Mr. Allerton of Plymouth), his first wife desiring his return and conversion; his second, his destruction for his foul abuse and for robbing her of her estate, of a part whereof she sent an inventory hither comprising therein many rich jewels, much plate, and costly linen. This man had in his family (and yet has) a gentlewoman whom he called his kinswoman and whom one of his wives in her letter names Mary Grover, affirming her to be a known harlot, whose sending back into old England she also desired, together with her husband.

Shortly after this intelligence, we sent to the house of the said Gardiner (which was seven miles from us) to apprehend him and his woman with a purpose to send them both to London to his wives there. But the man, who having heard some rumor from some who came in the ship that letters were come to the governor requiring justice against him, was readily prepared for flight so soon as he should see any crossing the river likely to apprehend him, which he accordingly performed; for he, dwelling alone, easily discerned such who were sent to take him half a mile before they approached his house. And with his piece on his neck went his way, as most men think, northward, hoping to find some English there like to himself. But likely enough it is, which way soever he went he will lose himself in the woods and be stopped with some rivers in his passing, notwithstanding his compass in his pocket, and so with hunger and cold will perish before he find the place he seeks.

His woman was brought unto us and confessed her name, and that her mother dwells eight miles from Boirdly in Salopshire [Shropshire], and that Gardiner's father dwells in or near Gloucester and was (as she said) brother to Stephen Gardiner, bishop of Winchester, and did disinherit his son for his twenty-six years' absence in his travels in France, Italy, Germany, and Turkey; that he had (as he told her) married a wife in his travels from whom he was divorced, and the woman long since dead; that both herself and Gardiner were Catholics till of late, but were now Protestants; that she takes him to be a knight, but never heard where he was knighted. The woman was impenitent and close, confessing no more than was wrested from her by her own contradictions, so we have taken order to send her to the two wives in old England to search her further.

Upon the 8th of March, from after it was fair daylight until about eight o'clock in the forenoon, there flew over all the towns in our plantations so many flocks of doves, each flock containing many thousands, and some so many that they obscured the light, that it passes credit, if but the truth should be written; and the thing was the more strange because I scarce remember to have seen ten doves since I came into the country. They were all turtles, as appeared by diverse of them we killed flying, somewhat bigger than those of Europe, and they flew from the northeast to the southwest; but what it portends I know not.

The ship now waits but for wind, which when it blows there are ready to go aboard therein for England Sir Richard Saltonstall, Mr. Sharpe, Mr. Coddington, and many others, the most whereof purpose to return to us again, if God will. In the meantime we are left a people poor and contemptible, yet such as trust in God and are contented with our condition, being well assured that He will not fail us nor forsake us. . . .

I thought to have ended before, but the stay of the ship and my desire to inform Your Honor of all I can has caused this addition; and everyone having warning to prepare for the ship's departure tomorrow, I am now, this 28th of March, 1631, sealing my letters.

You must obey this, now, for a law — that "he that will not work shall not eat."

JOHN SMITH, *The Generall Historie of Virginia,* 1624

1632

23.

THOMAS MORTON: On Puritan Intolerance

Lively Merry Mount, established in present-day Quincy by the raucous Englishman, Thomas Morton, in 1625, was veritable anathema to the strict Pilgrim Massachusetts settlements. "Having more craft than honesty," as William Bradford described him, Morton was a source of ammunition and supplies for the dreaded enemies of the Pilgrim settlements, the Indians. The Pilgrims despised him not only for his trade with the Indians and his wild festivities at Merry Mount, but also for his vitriolic attacks on every aspect of their way of life. The Pilgrims finally dispatched Miles Standish to subdue the settlement. Morton was returned to England, but his account of early New England in the New English Canaan, *published in London in 1632, caused much consternation among the colonists. The following selection is taken from this work.*

Source: *New English Canaan; or, New Canaan, Containing An Abstract of New England* [London], Printed by Charles Green, 1632, pp. 70-123.

RELIGIOUS PRACTICES OF THE SEPARATISTS

THE CHURCH OF THE SEPARATISTS is governed by pastors, elders, and deacons; and there is not any of these (though he be but a cow keeper) but is allowed to exercise his gifts in the public assembly on the Lord's Day; so as he does not make use of any notes for the help of his memory; for such things, they say, smell of lamp oil [study], and there must be no such unsavory perfume admitted to come into the congregation.

These are all public preachers. There is among these people a deaconess made of the sisters that uses her gifts at home in an assembly of her sex, by way of repetition or exhortation: such is their practice.

The pastor (before he is allowed of) must disclaim his former calling to the ministry as heretical and take a new calling after their fantastical inventions; and then he is admitted to be their pastor.

The manner of disclaiming is to renounce his calling with bitter execrations for the time that he has heretofore lived in it; and after his new election, there is great joy conceived at his commission.

And their pastors have this preeminence above the civil magistrate: He must first consider of the complaint made against a member, and if he be disposed to give the party complained of an admonition, there is no more to be said; if not, he delivers him over to the magistrate to deal with him in a course of justice, according to their practice in cases of that nature.

Of these pastors I have not known many; some I have observed, together with their carriage in New Canaan, and can inform you what opinion has been conceived of their conditions in the particular. There is one who (as they give it out there that think they speak it to advance his worth) has been expected to exercise his gifts in an assembly, that stayed his coming, in the midst of his journey falls into a fit (which they term a zealous meditation) and was four miles past the place appointed before he came to himself, or did remember whereabouts he went. And how much these things are different from the actions of crazed men, I leave to any indifferent man to judge; and if I should say they are all much alike, they that have seen and heard what [such men] have done will not condemn me altogether.

Now forasmuch as by the practice of their church every elder or deacon may preach, it is not amiss to discover their practice in that particular, before I part with them.

It has been an old saying, and a true, what is bred in the bone will not out of the flesh, nor the stepping into the pulpit that can make the person fit for the employment. The unfitness of the person undertaking to be the messenger has brought a blemish upon the message, as in the time of Louis XI, king of France, who (having advanced his barber to [a] place of honor and graced him with eminent titles) made him so presumptuous to undertake an embassage to treat with foreign princes of civil affairs.

But what was the issue? He behaved himself unworthily (yet as well as his breeding would give him leave) [so] that both the messenger and the message were despised; and had not he (being discovered) conveyed himself out of their territories, they had made him pay for his barbarous presumption.

Socrates says, *loquere ut te videam* [speak that I may see you]. If a man observe these people in the exercise of their gifts, he may thereby discern the tincture of their proper calling: the ass's ears will peep through the lion's hide. I am sorry they cannot discern their own infirmities. I will deal fairly with them; for I will draw their pictures *cap a pé* [head to toe], that you may discern them plainly from head to foot in their postures that so much bewitch (as I may speak with modesty) these illiterate people to be so fantastical, to take Jonas' task upon them without sufficient warrant.

One steps up like the minister of justice with the balance only, not the sword for fear of affrighting his auditory [audience]. He points at a text, and handles it as evenly as he can, and teaches the auditory that the thing he has to deliver must be well weighed, for it is a very precious thing, yet much more precious than gold or pearl; and he will teach them the means how to weigh things of that excellent worth; that a man would suppose he and his audience were to part stakes by the scale; and the like distribution they have used about a bag pudding.

Another (of a more cutting disposition) steps in his stead; and he takes a text, which he divides into many parts (to speak truly) as many as he list. The fag end of it he pares away, as a superfluous remnant.

He puts his auditory in comfort that he will make a garment for them and teach them how they shall put it on, and encourages them to be in love with it, for it is of such a fashion as does best become a Christian man. He will assure them that it shall be armor, proof against all assaults of Satan. This garment (says he) is not composed as the garments made by a carnal man, that are sewed with a hot needle and a burning thread; but it is a garment that shall outlast all the garments; and (if they will make use of it as he shall direct them) they shall be able (like St. George) to terrify the great dragon error and defend truth — which error, with her wide chops, would devour; whose mouth shall be filled with the shreds and parings which he continually gapes for under the cutting board.

A third supplies the room, and in the exercise of his gifts begins with a text that is drawn out of a fountain that has in it no dregs of popery. This shall prove unto you (says he) the cup of repentance; it is not like unto the cup of the Whore of Babylon, who will make men drunk with the dregs thereof; it is filled up to the brim with comfortable juice, and will prove a comfortable cordial to a sick soul (says he). And he handles the matter as if he dealt by the pint and the quart with nick and froth [false-bottom glass and all head].

Another (a very learned man indeed) goes another way to work with his auditory and exhorts them to walk upright, in the way of their calling, and not (like carnal men) tread awry. And if they should fail in the performance of that duty, yet they should seek for amendment while it was time, and tells them it would be too late to seek for help when the shop windows were shut up; and pricks them forward with a friendly admonition not to place their delight in worldly pleasures, which will not last, but in time will come to an end.

But so to handle the matter that they may be found to wax better and better, and then they shall be doubly rewarded for their work; and so closes the matter in a comfortable manner.

But stay: here is one stepped up in haste, and (being not minded to hold his auditory in expectation of any long discourse) he takes a text, and (for brevity's sake) divides it into one part, and then runs so fast afore with the matter that his auditory cannot follow him. Doubtless his father was some Irish footman; by his speed it seems so. And it may be at the hour of death (the son being present) did participate of his fa-

ther's nature (according to Pythagoras), and the virtue of his father's nimble feet (being infused into his brains) might make his tongue outrun his wit.

Well, if you mark it, these are special gifts indeed, which the vulgar people are so taken with that here is no persuading them that it is so ridiculous.

This is the means (O, the means) that they pursue; this that comes without premeditation; this is the superlative; and he that does not approve of this, they say, is a very reprobate.

Many unwarrantable tenets they have likewise, some of which being come to my knowledge I will here set down, one whereof being in public practice maintained is more notorious than the rest. I will, therefore, begin with that and convince them of manifest error by the maintenance of it, which is this:

1. That it is the magistrate's office absolutely (and not the minister's) to join the people in lawful matrimony. And for this they vouch the history of Ruth, saying Boaz was married to Ruth in presence of the elders of the people. Herein they mistake the scope of the text.

2. That it is a relic of popery to make use of a ring in marriage, and that it is a diabolical circle for the devil to dance in.

3. That the purifications used for women after delivery is not to be used.

4. That no child shall be baptized whose parents are not received into their church first.

5. That no person shall be admitted to the sacrament of the Lord's Supper that is without [the church].

6. That the Book of Common Prayer is an idol, and all that use it, idolators.

7. That every man is bound to believe a professor upon his bare affirmation only, before a Protestant upon oath.

8. That no person has any right to God's creatures, but God's children only who are

themselves, and that all others are but usurpers of the creatures.

9. And that for the general good of their church and commonwealth, they are to neglect father, mother, and all friendship.

10. Much ado they keep about their church discipline, as if that were the most essential part of their religion. Tithes are banished from thence, all except the tithe of mint and cumin.

11. They differ from us something in the creed, too, for if they get the goods of one that is without [the church] into their hands, he shall be kept without remedy for any satisfaction; and they believe that this is not cosenage [fraud].

12. And, last, they differ from us in the manner of praying; for they wink when they pray, because they think themselves so perfect on the highway to heaven that they can find it blindfold: so do not I. . . .

SIR CHRISTOPHER GARDINER

SIR CHRISTOPHER GARDINER (a knight that had been a traveler, born by sea and land, a good, judicious gentleman in mathematics and other sciences useful for plantations, chemistry, etc., and also being a practical engineer) came into those parts, intending discovery.

But the Separatists love not those good parts when they proceed from a carnal man (as they call every good Protestant); in short time [they] had found the means to pick a quarrel with him. The means is that they pursue to obtain what they aim at — the word is there the means.

So that when they find any man like to prove an enemy to their church and state, then straight the means must be used for defense. The first precept in their politics is to defame the man at whom they aim, and then he is a holy Israelite, in their opinions, who can spread that fame broadest, like butter upon a loaf; no matter how thin, it will serve for a veil; and then this man (whom they have thus depraved) is a spotted, unclean leper; he must out lest he pollute the land and them that are clean.

If this be one of their gifts, then Machiavelli had as good gifts as they. Let them raise a scandal on any, though ever so innocent; yet they know it is never wiped clean out; the stained mark remains, which has been well observed by one in these words of his:

Stick candles 'gainst a virgin wall's
     white back:
If they'll not burn, yet at the least
     they'll black.

And thus they dealt with Sir Christopher, and plotted by all the ways and means they could to overthrow his undertakings in those parts.

And therefore I cannot choose but conclude that these Separatists have special gifts, for they are given to envy and malice extremely.

The knowledge of their defamation could not please the gentleman well, when it came to his ear, which would cause him to make some reply (as they supposed) to take exceptions at . . . and this would be a means, they thought, to blow the coal, and so to kindle a brand that might fire him out of the country, too, and send him after mine host of Ma-re-Mount.

They took occasion (some of them) to come to his house when he was gone up into the country; and (finding he was from home) so went to work, that they left him neither house nor habitation, nor servant, nor anything to help him if he should return; but of that they had no hope (as they gave it out) for he was gone (as they affirmed) to lead a savage life, and for that cause took no company with him; and they, having considered of the matter, thought it not fit that any such man should live in so remote a place within the compass of their patent. So they fired the place and carried away the persons and goods.

Sir Christopher was gone with a guide (a savage) into the inland parts for discovery, but, before he . . . returned, he met with a savage that told the guide [that] Sir Christopher would be killed; Master Temperwell (who had now found out matter against him) would have him dead or alive. This he related, and would have the gentleman not to go to the place appointed because of the danger that was supposed.

But Sir Christopher was nothing dismayed; he would [go] on, whatsoever come of it, and so met with the savages, and between them was a terrible skirmish; but they had the worst of it, and he escaped well enough.

The guide was glad of it and learned of his fellows that they were promised a great reward for what they should do in this employment.

Which thing (when Sir Christopher understood) he gave thanks to God; and after (upon this occasion, to solace himself) in his tablebook, he composed this sonnet, which I have here inserted for a memorial.

THE SONNET

Wolves in sheep's clothing, why will ye
Think to deceive God that doth see
Your simulated certainty?
For my part I do wish you could
Your own infirmities behold,
For then you would not be so bold.
Like Sophists why will you dispute
With wisdom so, you do confute
None but yourselves: for shame be mute
Lest great Jehovah with his power
Do come upon you in an hour
When you least think, and you devour.

This sonnet the gentleman composed as a testimony of his love toward them that were so ill affected toward him; from whom they might have received much good if they had been so wise to have embraced him in a loving fashion.

But they despise the help that shall come from a carnal man (as they termed him) who (after his return from those designs) finding how they had used him with such disrespect, took ship and disposed of himself for England, and discovered their practices in those parts toward His Majesty's true-hearted subjects, which they made weary of their abode in those parts.

It were better to be of no church, than to be bitter for any.

WILLIAM PENN

1633

24.

John Eliot: A College Proposed for Massachusetts Bay

The religious zeal of the Massachusetts Bay Puritans was matched by their concern for the education of their youth, and after arriving in the New World they very soon began to discuss plans for establishing a school of higher learning, where their sons might prepare for the ministry and the other professions. One of the earliest recorded expressions of this concern is a letter written in 1633 by John Eliot to Sir Simonds D'Ewes, in England. In the letter, reprinted here, Eliot, known for his missionary work among the Indians, made a plea for funds that, had they been forthcoming, might have secured for D'Ewes the honor that later fell to John Harvard.

Source: Manuscript in the British Museum.

I EARNESTLY DESIRE that God will move your heart for the sake of the commonwealth, and also for the sake of learning (which I know you love and will be ready to further; indeed, we want a store of men to further that, for if we do not nourish learning, both church and commonwealth will sink). Because I am on this point, I beseech you to let me be bold enough to make one motion, for the furtherance of learning among us.

God has bestowed upon you a bountiful blessing, and if you should please to employ one mite of that great wealth which God has given, to erect a school of learning — a college — among us, you would be doing a glorious work, acceptable to God and man, and the commemoration of the first founder of the means of learning would perpetuate your name and honor among us.

Now, because my proposition may seem to require great costs, I will be bold to propose a way that will make it attainable with little.

First, there are no improved lands and revenues at present to maintain such a work. All the charge is the building of such a place as may be fit for such a purpose. And such learned men as are here and may come must, of their own proper charge, frequent those places at fit seasons, for the exercising of learning; and such young men as may be trained must bear their own costs.

We only want a convenient house. Now,

the bare building of a house big enough for our young beginnings will be done with little cost. I doubt not that if you should set apart but £ 500 for that work it would be a sufficient beginning and would make convenient housing for the many years. Nay, £ 400 or £ 300 would do pretty well. And you would have this privilege: You should not need to send beforehand (if you should come) to build a house for your habitation for that would be ready to give you complete comfort. . . .

For a library, and a place for the exercise of learning, it is my earnest desire and prayer that God would stir up the hearts of some well-wishers to learning to make such a beginning. Indeed, sir, I know of no one in every way more fitting than yourself. I beseech you, therefore, to consider it and to do that which may comfort us. A library is

the first project, and then a college. I know from our experience that we shall most need convenient chambers to entertain students, and a little room, which, I fear, will hold all of our first stock of books; then as they increase we may enlarge the room.

In our young beginnings, men lack funds for such buildings, and, therefore, public exercises of learning have not yet begun, though we have many learned men, both gentlemen and ministers. But if we had a suitable place we could have debates and lectures not only in divinity but in other arts and sciences and also in law, which is very important for the welfare of our commonwealth.

Now I will say no more, but will pray that the Lord will move your heart (which I hope is already moved) to be the first founder of so glorious a work as this.

1633 - 1639

25.

John Winthrop: Life Among the Puritans

Of the original leaders of the Massachusetts Bay Colony, the first was John Winthrop, appointed governor in 1629 and many times reelected to that position. His Journal is an invaluable account of the colony between 1630 and 1649. He gives us a first-hand view of the attempt by the colony to build "a city upon a hill." Winthrop, convinced that this attempt to carve a life out of the wilderness was a great experiment, never doubted that the colony's affairs were guided by the hand of God. The Journal was begun before Winthrop arrived in Boston and was never revised by him, yet it treats of both great and small concerns in prose that, despite the fact that it was hastily written, has been called "excellent, grave, and measured." Part of the Journal was published in 1790 in Hartford; it first appeared as a whole in 1826. The selection reprinted here deals with the period between 1633 and 1639.

Source: *The History of New England from 1630 to 1649*, James Savage, ed., Boston, 1826, Vol. II, pp. 116-317.

1633. The scarcity of workmen had caused them to raise their wages to an excessive rate, so as a carpenter would have 3s. the day, a laborer 2s. 6d. etc., and accordingly those who had commodities to sell advanced their prices sometime double to that they cost in England, so as it grew to a general complaint, which the court, taking knowledge of, as also of some further evils which were springing out of the excessive rates of wages, they made an order that carpenters, masons, etc., should take but 2s. the day, and laborers but 18d., and that no commodity should be sold at above 4d. in the shilling more than it cost for ready money in England; oil, wine, etc., and cheese, in regard of the hazard of bringing, etc., excepted.

The evils which were springing, etc., were: (1) Many spent much time idly, etc., because they could get as much in four days as would keep them a week. (2) They spent much in tobacco and strong waters, etc., which was a great waste to the commonwealth, which, by reason of so many foreign [scarce] commodities expended, could not have subsisted to this time, but that it was supplied by the cattle and corn, which were sold to newcomers at very dear rates, viz.; corn at 6s. the bushel, a cow at £20 — yea, some at £24, some £26 — a mare at £35, a ewe goat at £3 or £4;

and yet many cattle were every year brought out of England, and some from Virginia. Soon after order was taken for prices of commodities, viz., not to exceed the rate of 4*d.* in the shilling above the price in England, except cheese and liquors, etc. . . .

1634. Order was taken for ministering an oath to all housekeepers and sojourners, being twenty years of age and not freemen, and for making a survey of the houses and lands of all freemen.

Notice being sent out [of] the General Court to be held the 14th day of . . . May, the freemen deputed two of each town to meet and consider of such matters as they were to take order in at the same General Court; who, having met, desired a sight of the patent, and, conceiving thereby that all their laws should be made at the General Court, repaired to the governor to advise with him about it, and about the abrogating of some orders formerly made, as for killing of swine in corn, etc. He told them that, when the patent was granted, the number of freemen was supposed to be (as in like corporations) so few as they might well join in making laws; but now they were grown to so great a body as it was not possible for them to make or execute laws, but they must choose others for that purpose. And that howsoever it would be necessary hereafter to have a select company to intend [do] that work, yet for the present they were not furnished with a sufficient number of men qualified for such a business, neither could the commonwealth bear the loss of time of so many as must intend [do] it. Yet this they might do at present, viz., they might, at the General Court, make an order that, once in the year, a certain number should be appointed (upon summons from the governor) to revise all laws, etc., and to reform what they found amiss therein; but not to make any new laws but prefer their grievances to the Court of Assistants; and

that no assessment should be laid upon the country without the consent of such a committee, nor any lands disposed of . . .

1635. Mr. Vane and Mr. Peter, finding some distraction in the commonwealth arising from some difference in judgment, and withal some alienation of affection among the magistrates and some other persons of quality, and that hereby factions began to grow among the people, some adhering more to the old governor, Mr. Winthrop, and others to the late governor, Mr. Dudley — the former carrying matters with more lenity, and the latter with more severity — they procured a meeting, at Boston, of the governor, deputy, Mr. Cotton, Mr. Hooker, Mr. Wilson . . . Mr. Winthrop, Mr. Dudley, and themselves; where, after the Lord had been sought, Mr. Vane declared the occasion of this meeting (as is before noted) and the fruit aimed at, viz., a more firm and friendly uniting of minds, etc., especially of the said Mr. Dudley and Mr. Winthrop, as those upon whom the weight of the affairs did lie, etc., and therefore desired all present to take up a resolution to deal freely and openly with the parties, and they each with other, that nothing might be left in their breasts, which might break out to any jar or difference hereafter (which they promised to do).

Then Mr. Winthrop spoke to this effect: that when it pleased Mr. Vane to acquaint him with what he had observed, of the dispositions of men's minds inclining to the said faction, etc., it was very strange to him, professing solemnly that he knew not of any breach between his brother Dudley and himself, since they were reconciled long since, neither did he suspect any alienation of affection in him or others from himself, save that, of late, he had observed that some newcomers had estranged themselves from him, since they went to dwell at Newtown; and so desired all the company that, if they had seen anything amiss in his government or otherwise, they would deal freely and faithfully with him. And for his part he promised to take it in good part, and would endeavor, by God's grace, to amend it.

Then Mr. Dudley spoke to this effect: that for his part he came thither a mere patient, not with any intent to charge his brother Winthrop with anything; for though there had been formerly some differences and breaches between them, yet they had been healed, and, for his part, he was not willing to renew them again; and so left it to others to utter their own complaints.

Whereupon the governor, Mr. Haynes, spoke to this effect: that Mr. Winthrop and himself had been always in good terms, etc.; therefore, he was loath to give any offense to him; and he hoped that, considering what the end of this meeting was, he would take it in good part, if he did deal openly and freely, as his manner ever was. Then he spoke of one or two passages, wherein he conceived that [he] dealt too remissly in point of justice. To which Mr. Winthrop answered that his speeches and carriage had been in part mistaken; but withal professed that it was his judgment that, in the infancy of plantations, justice should be administered with more lenity than in a settled state, because people were then more apt to transgress, partly of ignorance of new laws and orders, partly through oppression of business and other straits; but, if it might be made clear to him that it was an error, he would be ready to take up a stricter course.

Then the ministers were desired to consider of the question by the next morning, and to set down a rule in the case. The next morning they delivered their several reasons, which all sorted [served] to this conclusion: that strict discipline, both in criminal offenses and in martial affairs, was more needful in plantations than in a settled state, as tending to the honor and safety of

the gospel. Whereupon Mr. Winthrop acknowledged that he was convinced that he had failed in overmuch lenity and remissness, and would endeavor (by God's assistance) to take a more strict course hereafter. Whereupon there was a renewal of love among them, and articles drawn to this effect:

1. That there should be more strictness used in civil government and military discipline.

2. That the magistrates should (as far as might be) ripen their consultations beforehand, that their vote in public might bear (as the voice of God).

3. That, in meetings out of Court, the magistrates should not discuss the business of parties in their presence, nor deliver their opinions, etc.

4. That trivial things, etc., should be ended [ordered] in towns, etc.

5. If differences fall out among them in public meetings, they shall observe these rules. . . .

6. The magistrates shall be more familiar and open each to other, and more frequent in visitations, and shall, in tenderness and love, admonish one another (without reserving any secret grudge), and shall avoid all jealousies and suspicions, each seeking the honor of another, and all, of the Court, not opening the nakedness of one another to private persons; in all things seeking the safety and credit of the gospel.

7. To honor the governor in submitting to him the main direction and ordering the business of the Court.

8. One assistant shall not seem to gratify any man in undoing or crossing another's proceedings, without due advice with him. . . .

10. All contempts against the Court, or any of the magistrates, shall be specially noted and punished; and the magistrates shall appear more solemnly in public, with attendance, apparel, and open notice of their entrance into the Court. . . .

For preventing the loss of time and drunkenness, which sometimes happened by people's running to the ships, and the excessive prices of commodities, it was ordered that one in each town should buy for all, etc., and should retain [return] the same within twenty days at five per hundred, if any came to buy in that time. But this took no good effect; for most of the people would not buy, except they might buy for themselves; and the merchants appointed could not disburse so much money, etc.; and the seamen were much discontented, yet some of them brought their goods on shore and sold them there. . . .

1636. The General Court began. When any matter about these new opinions was mentioned, the Court was divided; yet the greater number far were sound. They questioned the proceeding against Mr. Wilson, for his speech in the last Court, but could not fasten upon such as had prejudiced him, etc.; but, by the vote of the greater party, his speech was approved, and declared to have been a seasonable advice and no charge or accusation.

The ministers, being called to give advice about the authority of the Court in things concerning the churches, etc., did all agree of these two things: First, that no member of the Court ought to be publicly questioned by a church for any speech in the Court, without the license of the Court. The reason was because the Court may have sufficient reason that may excuse the sin, which yet may not be fit to acquaint the church with, being a secret of state. The second thing was that, in all such heresies or errors of any church members as are manifest and dangerous to the state, the Court may proceed without tarrying for the church; but if the opinions be doubtful, etc., they are first to refer them to the church, etc.

At this Court, when Mr. Wheelwright was to be questioned for a sermon, which

seemed to tend to sedition, etc., near all the church of Boston presented a petition to the Court for two things: (1) That as freemen they might be present in cases of judicature; (2) That the Court would declare, if they might deal in cases of conscience before the church, etc. This was taken as a groundless and presumptuous act, especially at this season, and was rejected with this answer: That the Court had never used to proceed judicially, but it was openly; but for matter of consultation and preparation in causes, they might and would be private.

One Stephen Greensmith, for saying that all the ministers, except A.B.C., did teach a covenant of works, was censured to acknowledge his fault in every church, and fined £40.

Mr. Wheelwright, one of the members of Boston, preaching at the last fast, inveighed against all that walked in a covenant of works, as he described it to be, viz., such as maintain sanctification as an evidence of justification, etc., and called them antichrists, and stirred up the people against them with much bitterness and vehemency. For this he was called into the Court, and his sermon being produced, he justified it, and confessed he did mean all that walk in such a way. Whereupon the elders of the rest of the churches were called and asked whether they, in their ministry, did walk in such a way. They all acknowledged they did. So, after much debate, the Court adjudged him guilty of sedition, and also of contempt, for that the Court had appointed the fast as a means of reconciliation of the differences, etc., and he purposely set himself to kindle and increase them. . . .

1637. There was great hope, that the late General Assembly would have had some good effect in pacifying the troubles and dissensions about matters of religion; but it fell out otherwise. For though Mr. Wheelwright and those of his party had been clearly confuted and confounded in the Assembly, yet they persisted in their opinions, and were as busy in nourishing contentions (the principal of them) as before. Whereupon the General Court, being assembled in the 2nd of the 9th month, and finding, upon consultation, that two so opposite parties could not contain [continue] in the same body without apparent hazard of ruin to the whole, agreed to send away some of the principal. And for this a fair opportunity was offered by the remonstrance or petition which they proffered to the Court the 9th of the 1st month, wherein they affirm Mr. Wheelwright to be innocent, and that the Court had condemned the truth of Christ, with diverse other scandalous and seditious speeches . . . subscribed by more than sixty of that faction, whereof one William Aspinwall, being one, and he that drew the said petition being then sent as a deputy for Boston, was for the same dismissed, and after called to the Court and disfranchised and banished.

John Coggeshall was another deputy, who, though his hand were not to the petition, yet, professing himself to approve of it, etc., was also dismissed, and after disfranchised. Then the Court sent warrant to Boston to send other deputies in their room; but they intended to have sent the same men again; but Mr. Cotton, coming among them, dissuaded them with much ado. Then the Court sent for Mr. Wheelwright, and, he persisting to justify his sermon, and his whole practice and opinions, and refusing to leave either the place or his public exercisings, he was disfranchised and banished. Upon which he appealed to the King, but neither called witnesses, nor desired any act to be made of it. The Court told him that an appeal did not lie; for by the King's grant we had power to hear and determine without any reservation, etc. So he relinquished his appeal, and the Court gave him leave to go to his house, upon his promise that, if he were not gone out of

our jurisdiction within fourteen days, he would render himself to one of the magistrates.

The Court also sent for Mrs. Hutchinson, and charged her with diverse matters, as her keeping two public lectures every week in her house, whereto sixty or eighty persons did usually resort, and for reproaching most of the ministers (viz., all except Mr. Cotton) for not preaching a covenant of free grace, and that they had not the seal of the Spirit, nor were able ministers of the New Testament; which were clearly proved against her, though she sought to shift it off. And, after many speeches to and fro, at last she was so full as she could not contain, but vented her revelations; among which this was one, that she had it revealed to her that she should come into New England, and should here be persecuted [presented], and that God would ruin us and our posterity, and the whole state, for the same. So the Court proceeded and banished her; but, because it was winter, they committed her to a private house, where she was well provided, and her own friends and the elders permitted to go to her, but none else.

The Court called also Captain Underhill, and some five or six more of the principal, whose hands were to the said petition; and because they stood to justify it, they were disfranchised, and such as had public places were put from them.

The Court also ordered that the rest, who had subscribed the petition (and would not acknowledge their fault, and which near twenty of them did) and some others, who had been chief stirrers in these contentions, etc., should be disarmed. This troubled some of them very much, especially because they were to bring them in themselves; but at last, when they saw no remedy, they obeyed. . . .

1639. At a General Court held at Boston, great complaint was made of the oppression used in the country in sale of foreign commodities; and Mr. Robert Keaine, who kept a shop in Boston, was notoriously above others observed and complained of; and, being convented, he was charged with many particulars; in some, for taking above 6d. in the shilling profit; in some above 8d.; and, in some small things, above two for one; And being hereof convict (as appears by the records), he was fined £200, which came thus to pass: The deputies considered apart of his fine, and set it at £200; the magistrates agreed but to £100. So, the Court being divided, at length it was agreed that his fine should be £200, but he should pay but £100, and the other should be respited to the further consideration of the next General Court. By this means the magistrates and deputies were brought to an accord, which otherwise had not been likely, and so much trouble might have grown and the offender escaped censure. For the cry of the country was so great against oppression, and some of the elders and magistrates had declared such detestation of the corrupt practice of this man (which was the more observable, because he was wealthy and sold dearer than most other tradesmen, and for that he was of ill report for the like covetous practice in England, that incensed the deputies very much against him).

And sure [indeed] the course was very evil, special circumstances considered: (1) he being an ancient professor of the gospel; (2) a man of eminent parts; (3) wealthy, and having but one child; (4) having come over for conscience sake, and for the advancement of the gospel here; (5) having been formerly dealt with and admonished, both by private friends and also by some of the magistrates and elders, and having promised reformation; being a member of a church and commonwealth now in their infancy, and under the curious observation of all churches and civil states in the world. These added much aggravation to his sin in the judgment of all men of understanding. Yet most of the magistrates (though they dis-

Massachusetts Historical Society
First entry in John Winthrop's "Journal," March 1630

cerned of the offense clothed with all these circumstances) would have been more moderate in their censure: (1) Because there was no law in force to limit or direct men in point of profit in their trade. (2) Because it is the common practice, in all countries, for men to make use of advantages for raising the prices of their commodities. (3) Because (though he were chiefly aimed at, yet) he was not alone in this fault. (4) Because all men through the country, in sale of cattle, corn, labor, etc., were guilty of the like excess in prices. (5) Because a certain rule could not be found out for an equal rate between buyer and seller, though much labor had been bestowed in it, and diverse laws had been made, which, upon experience, were repealed as being neither safe nor equal. Lastly, and especially, because the law of God appoints no other punishment but double restitution; and, in some cases, as where the offender freely confesses, and brings his offering, only half added to the principal.

After the Court had censured him, the church of Boston called him also in question, where (as before he had done in the Court) he did, with tears, acknowledge and bewail his covetous and corrupt heart, yet making some excuse for many of the particulars, which were charged upon him, as partly by pretense of ignorance of the true price of some wares, and chiefly by being misled by some false principles, as: (1) That, if a man lost in one commodity, he might help himself in the price of another. (2) That if, through want of skill or other occasion [otherwise], his commodity cost him more than the price of the market in England, he might then sell it for more than the price of the market in New England, etc. These things gave occasion to Mr. Cotton, in his public exercise the next lecture day, to lay open the error of such false principles, and to give some rules of direction in the case.

Some false principles were these:

1. That a man might sell as dear as he can, and buy as cheap as he can.

2. If a man lose by casualty of sea, etc., in some of his commodities, he may raise the price of the rest.

3. That he may sell as he bought, though he paid too dear, etc., and though the commodity be fallen, etc.

4. That, as a man may take the advantage of his own skill or ability, so he may of another's ignorance or necessity.

5. Where one gives time for payment, he is to take like recompense of one as of another.

The rules for trading were these:

1. A man may not sell above the current price, i.e., such a price as is usual in the time and place, and as another (who knows the worth of the commodity) would give

for it, if he had occasion to use it; as that is called current money, which every man will take, etc.

2. When a man loses in his commodity for want of skill, etc., he must look at it as his own fault or cross, and therefore must not lay it upon another.

3. Where a man loses by casualty of sea, or, etc., it is a loss cast upon himself by Providence, and he may not ease himself of it by casting it upon another; for so a man should seem to provide against all providences, etc., that he should never lose; but where there is a scarcity of the commodity, there men may raise their price; for now it is a hand of God upon the commodity, and not the person.

4. A man may not ask any more for his commodity than his selling price, as Ephron to Abraham, the land is worth thus much.

The cause being debated by the church, some were earnest to have him excommunicated; but the most thought an admonition would be sufficient. Mr. Cotton opened the causes, which required excommunication, out of that in I Cor. 5:11. The point now in question was, whether these actions did declare him to be such a covetous person, etc. Upon which he showed that it is neither the habit of covetousness (which is in every man in some degree) nor simply the act, that declares a man to be such, but when it appears, that a man sins against his conscience, or the very light of nature, and when it appears in a man's whole conversation. But Mr. Keaine did not appear to be such, but rather upon an error in his judgment, being led by false principles; and, beside, he is otherwise liberal, as in his hospitality, and in church communion, etc. So, in the end, the church consented to an admonition.

German woodcut of American Indians, c. 1505

NORTH AMERICAN INDIANS

Reports concerning the native population were often as fanciful as the pictures on this page. The reality was a wide variety of Indian tribes and societies, with differing modes of life and languages, and no single attitude toward the white man.

Imaginary view of the American Southwest painted by Jan Mostaert in the 16th century

Florida Indians

French artist Jacques Le Moyne came to Florida in 1564 with the short-lived Huguenot colony. One of the few to escape massacre by the Spanish in 1565, he made his way to London. There, after his death in 1588, the Flemish engraver Theodore de Bry obtained Le Moyne's paintings of Florida Indians and published them in 1591.

The Indians on these pages were members of the eastern Timucua tribe in northeast Florida: (below) a typical fortified village with guardhouses at the entrance and the chief's house in the center; OPPOSITE PAGE: (above) Indians using animal skins as a disguise for deer hunting; (below) Indians tilling the soil with hoes made of fish bones

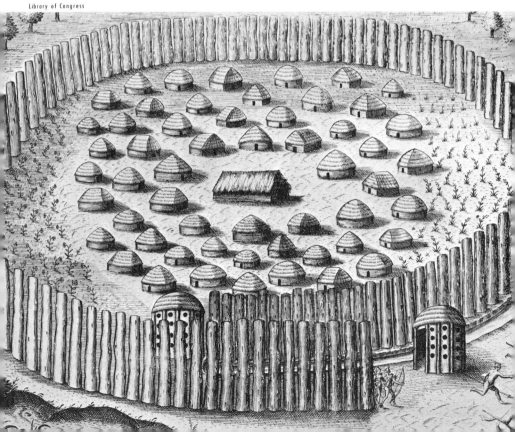

Von jhrer Hirschjacht. XXV.

DJe Jndianer brauchen eine solche Geschicklichkeyt/Hirsche zu
fangen/dergleichen wir zuvor nie gesehen. Die Häute der allergrössesten Hirsche/so
sie jemals gefangen/legen sie so geschicklich an Leib/daß sie das Theil/so dem Hirsch
am Kopff gestanden/auch vber jhren Kopff ziehen/damit sie durch die Augenlöcher/
gleich als durch eine Larven/sehen können/ Wann sie sich nun also angethan/gehen
sie so nahe/als jnen möglich/zun Hirschen/so sich im geringsten dafür nicht scheuwen)
zu/doch daß sie der Zeit warnemmen/zu welcher die Hirsche ans Wasser zu trincken kommen/
be sie nachmals leichtlich mit Bogen/sampt den Pfeilen/so sie in den Händen haben/schiessen kön-
diewcil jrer in diesem Lande sehr viel sind. Damit sie aber im schiessen/am lincken Arme/durch die
nen deß Bogens/nie verletzt werden/verwaren sie denselben mit einer Rinden von eim Baum/
sie die Natur vnterwiesen. Die Hirschhäute aber/welche sie jnen abziehen/können sie ohne
Stahel/nur mit Muscheln/so artig bereyten/daß es zu verwundern/Vnd ich halte dar-
für/daß niemand in gantz Europa zu finden sey/der diese Häute
kunstreicherer weise zu bereyten/als
eben sie.

G iij Wie sie

Le Moyne's drawings of life in the Florida Indian villages were based in part on stories the Indians told the French. (Above) Indians taking crops to a public granary where all crops were stored; everyone was free to take supplies from there as needed; (right) Indians claimed their gold supply came from the bottom of mountain streams and was removed by using hollow reeds; (below left) alligators were a constant threat to the Indians who killed them by driving 10-foot poles down their throats and beating them with clubs; (below right) young Indian braves training for a variety of sporting contests to demonstrate their strength and skill

Virginia Indians

Group of Indians seated around a fire, possibly a thanksgiving celebration

English artist John White was among the first group of settlers on Roanoke Island in 1585. While there, he made a series of at least 75 watercolors portraying Indians, wildlife, fish, and plants. These paintings, also engraved and published in London in 1590 by Theodore de Bry, received wide circulation and were frequently reprinted or copied.

(Left) Indian priest; (center) Indian woman and baby of Pomeiooc; (right) Indian elder or chief

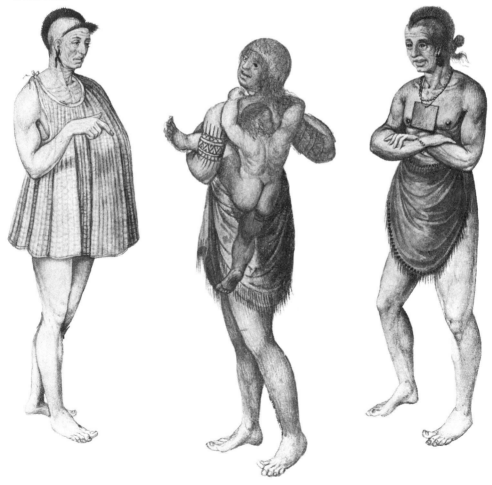

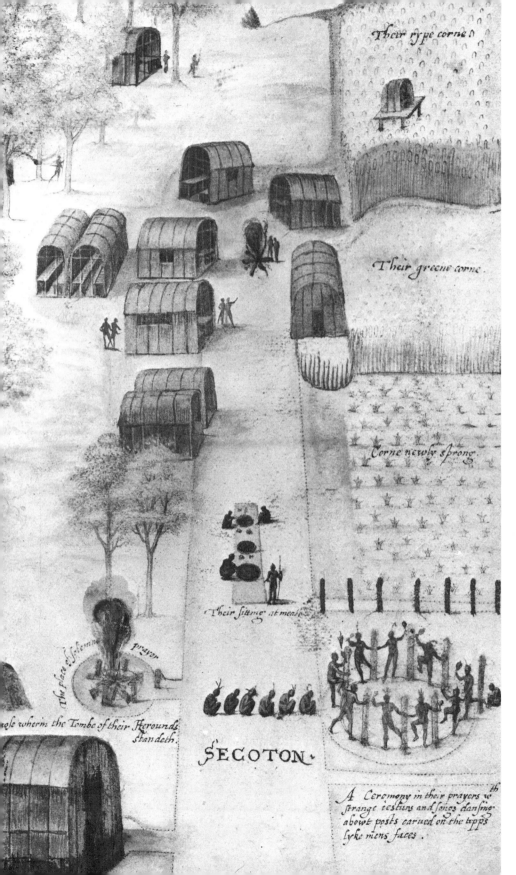

Their rype corne

Their greene corne

Corne newly sprong.

Their sitting at meate

The place of solemne prayer

those wherein the Tombe of their Herounds standeth

SECOTON

A Ceremony in their prayers wth strange iestures and songs dansing abowt posts carued on the topps lyke mens faces.

Indian daily life: (top left) two methods of broiling fish: on a grill over the flames and impaled by gills on sticks alongside fire; (top right) Indians fishing; (center left) couple eating; (bottom left) cooking corn in an earthenware pot; (bottom right) Indians dancing around a circle of posts with tops carved in the form of human heads

The manner of their fishing

ng of ts   *their meale . of earth .*

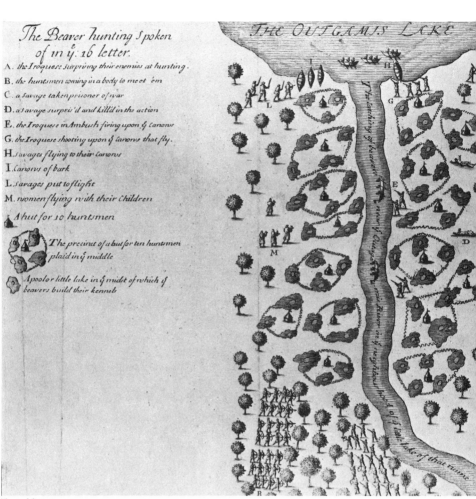

The Beaver hunting spoken
of in ÿ: 16 letter.

THE OUTGAMIS LAKE

A. the Iroquese surprising their enemies at hunting.
B. the huntsmen coming in a body to meet 'em
C. a savage taken prisoner of war
D. a savage surpris'd and kill'd in the action
E. the Iroquese in Ambush firing upon ÿ Canows
G. the Iroquese shooting upon ÿ Canows that fly.
H. savages flying to their Canows
I. Canows of bark
L. savages put to flight
M. women flying with their Children
N. a hut for 10 huntsmen

The precinct of a hut for ten huntsmen
plaid in ÿ middle

A pool or little lake in ÿ midst of which ÿ
beavers build their kennels

Iroquois Indians surprising some enemies who are hunting for beaver

(Left) Stages in the calumet (peace pipe) ceremony; (right) the calumet

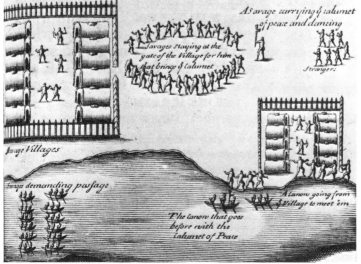

A savage carrying ÿ calumet
of peace and dancing

Savages staying at the
gate of the village for him
that brings ÿ calumet

Strangers

Savage Villages

Savages demanding passage

A canow going from
ÿ Village to meet 'em

The canow that goes
before with the
calumet of Peace

The calumet of peace being a great pipe &c:

Indians
of the
St. Lawrence

As a result of the fur trade, the French developed extensive relations with the northern Indians, particularly the Hurons, with whom they joined in an alliance against the Iroquois nations south of the St. Lawrence.

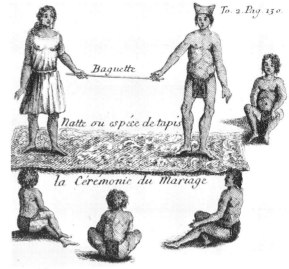

Library of Congress

Library of Congress

All illustrations, except below, from Lahoutan's "New Voyages to North America," 1703

Library of Congress

Method used by the Indians to hunt deer as depicted in Champlain's "Voyages," 1619

Library of Congress

1634

26.

The Oath of Freemen in Massachusetts

The Oath of a Freeman has dual historical significance. It was, in 1639, the first document printed on a press in America; and the second version of the oath, approved by the Massachusetts General Court May 14, 1634, contained a remarkably precise statement of the duties of a citizen toward his government. King Charles II objected to what he felt was an attitude of independence in the oath, which he attempted to subdue in 1665 by ordering that it be amended to include a pledge of "faith and true allegiance to our Sovereign Lord the King."

Source: Force, IV: "New-Englands Jonas Cast up at London, etc., etc.," p. 18.

I . . . BEING BY GOD'S PROVIDENCE an inhabitant and freeman within the jurisdiction of this commonwealth, do freely acknowledge myself to be subject to the government thereof; and therefore do swear by the great and dreadful name of the ever-living God that I will be true and faithful to the same, and will accordingly yield assistance and support thereunto with my person and estate, as in equity I am bound; and will also truly endeavor to maintain and preserve all the liberties and privileges thereof, submitting myself to the wholesome laws and orders made and established by the same. And further, that I will not plot or practise any evil against it, or consent to any that shall so do; but will timely discover and reveal the same to lawful authority now here established for the speedy preventing thereof.

Moreover, I do solemnly bind myself in the sight of God that, when I shall be called to give my voice touching any such matter of this state, in which freemen are to deal, I will give my vote and suffrage as I shall judge in my own conscience may best conduce and tend to the public weal of the body, without respect of persons or favor of any man. So help me God in the Lord Jesus Christ.

1636

27.

John Cotton: Democracy as Detrimental to Church and State

Political and religious pressures on the English Puritans became severe in the 1630s. As a result, certain Puritan members of Parliament, among them Lord Brooke and Lord Saye and Sele, who had helped to establish the Massachusetts Bay Company, conceived the idea of emigrating to America. They were anxious to maintain their hereditary privileges, however, including the right to a voice in governmental affairs, and when this demand was refused by the authorities in Massachusetts, the noble lords decided not to go. Formal rejection of their demands was undertaken by John Cotton. His reasons are set forth in the following selection, which includes a reply to "certain persons of quality" as a group and a private letter to Lord Saye. The antidemocratic sentiments of both letters were typical of the colony's leaders.

Source: Thomas Hutchinson, *The History of the Colony of Massachusett's Bay, etc., etc.,* 2nd edition, London, 1765, pp. 490-501.

I.

Proposals and Replies

Demand 1. That the Commonwealth should consist of two distinct ranks of men, whereof the one should be for them and their heirs, gentlemen of the country; the other for them and their heirs, freeholders.

Answer. Two distinct ranks we willingly acknowledge, from the light of nature and Scripture; the one of them called princes, or nobles, or elders (among whom gentlemen have their place); the other, the people. Hereditary dignity or honors we willingly allow to the former, unless, by the scandalous and base conversation of any of them, they become degenerate. Hereditary liberty, or estate of freemen, we willingly allow to the other, unless they also, by some unworthy and slavish carriage, do disfranchise themselves.

Dem. 2. That in these gentlemen and freeholders, assembled together, the chief power of the Commonwealth shall be placed, both for making and repealing laws.

Ans. So it is with us.

Dem. 3. That each of these two ranks

should, in all public assemblies, have a negative voice, so as, without a mutual consent, nothing should be established.

Ans. So it is agreed among us.

Dem. 4. That the first rank, consisting of gentlemen, should have power, for them and their heirs, to come to the parliaments or public assemblies and there to give their free votes personally; the second rank of freeholders should have the same power, for them and their heirs, of meeting and voting, but by their deputies.

Ans. Thus far this demand is practised among us. The freemen meet and vote by their deputies; the other rank give their votes personally, only with this difference: there be no more of the gentlemen that give their votes personally but such as are chosen to places of office, either governors, deputy governors, counselors, or assistants. All gentlemen in England have not that honor to meet and vote personally in Parliament, much less all their heirs. But of this more fully in an answer to the 9th and 10th demand[s].

Dem. 5. That for facilitating and dispatch of business, and other reasons, the gentlemen and freeholders should sit and hold their meetings in two distinct houses.

Ans. We willingly approve the motion, only as yet it is not so practised among us, but, in time, the variety and discrepancy of sundry occurrences will put them upon a necessity of sitting apart.

Dem. 6. That there shall be set times for these meetings, annually or half-yearly, or as shall be thought fit by common consent, which meetings should have a set time for their continuance, but should be adjourned or broken off at the discretion of both houses.

Ans. Public meetings, in General Courts, are by charter appointed to be quarterly, which, in this infancy of the colony, wherein many things frequently occur which need settling, have been of good use, but, when things are more fully settled in due order, it is likely that yearly or half-yearly meetings

will be sufficient. For the continuance or breaking up of these courts, nothing is done but with the joint consent of both branches.

Dem. 7. That it shall be in the power of this parliament, thus constituted and assembled, to call the governor and all public officers to account, to create new officers, and to determine them already set up; and, the better to stop the way to insolence and ambition, it may be ordered that all offices and fees of office shall, every parliament, determine, unless they be new confirmed the last day of every session.

Ans. This power to call governors and all officers to account, and to create new and determine the old, is settled already in the General Court or parliament, only it is not put forth but once in the year, viz., at the Great and General Court in May, when the governor is chosen.

Dem. 8. That the governor shall ever be chosen out of the rank of gentlemen.

Ans. We never practise otherwise, choosing the governor either out of the assistants, which is our ordinary course, or out of approved known gentlemen, as, this year, Mr. Vane.

Dem. 9. That, for the present, the Right Honorable the Lord Viscount Saye and Sele, the Lord Brooke, who have already been at great disbursements for the public works in New England, and such other gentlemen of approved sincerity and worth, as they, before their personal remove, shall take into their number, should be admitted for them and their heirs, gentlemen of the country. But, for the future, none shall be admitted into this rank but by the consent of both houses.

Ans. The great disbursements of these noble personages and worthy gentlemen we thankfully acknowledge, because the safety and presence of our brethren at Connecticut is no small blessing and comfort to us. But, though that charge had never been disbursed, the worth of the honorable persons named is so well known to all, and our need of such supports and guides is so sensible to ourselves, that we do not doubt the country would thankfully accept it as a singular favor from God and from them, if He should bow their hearts to come into this wilderness and help us. As for accepting them and their heirs into the number of gentlemen of the country, the custom of this country is, and readily would be, to receive and acknowledge, not only all such eminent persons as themselves and the gentlemen they speak of but others of meaner estate, so be it is of some eminency, to be for them and their heirs, gentlemen of the country. Only, thus standeth our case. Though we receive them with honor and allow them preeminence and accommodations according to their condition, yet we do not, ordinarily, call them forth to the power of election or administration of magistracy until they be received as members into some of our churches, a privilege, which we doubt not religious gentlemen will willingly desire (as David did in Ps. 27:4) and Christian churches will as readily impart to such desirable persons. Hereditary honors both nature and Scripture doth acknowledge (Eccles. 29:17), but hereditary authority and power standeth only by the civil laws of some commonwealths; and, yet, even among them, the authority and power of the father is nowhere communicated, together with his honors, unto all his posterity. Where God blesseth any branch of any noble or generous family with a spirit and gifts fit for government, it would be a taking of God's name in vain to put such a talent under a bushel, and a sin against the honor of magistracy to neglect such in our public elections. But if God should not delight to furnish some of their posterity with gifts fit for magistracy, we should expose them rather to reproach and prejudice, and the Commonwealth with them, than exalt them to honor, if we should call them forth, when God doth not, to public authority.

Dem. 10. That the rank of freeholders shall be made up of such as shall have so much personal estate there, as shall be thought fit for men of that condition, and have contributed some fit proportion to the public charge of the country, either by their disbursements or labors.

Ans. We must confess our ordinary practice to be otherwise; for, excepting the old planters, *i.e.,* Mr. Humfry, who himself was admitted an assistant at London, and all of them freemen before the churches here were established, none are admitted freemen of this Commonwealth but such as are first admitted members of some church or other in this country, and, of such, none are excluded from the liberty of freemen. And out of such only, I mean the more eminent sort of such it is that our magistrates are chosen. Both which points we should willingly persuade our people to change, if we could make it appear to them that such a change might be made according to God; for, to give you a true account of the grounds of our proceedings herein, it seemeth to them, and also to us, to be a Divine Ordinance (and moral) that none should be appointed and chosen by the people of God magistrates over them but men fearing God (Ex. 27:21), chosen out of their brethren (Deut. 17:15), saints (I Cor. 6:1). Yea, the apostle maketh it a shame to the Church, if it be not able to afford wise men from out of themselves which shall be able to judge all civil matters between their brethren (ver. 5). And Solomon maketh it the joy of a commonwealth when the righteous are in authority, and the calamity thereof when the wicked bear rule (Prov. 29:2).

Obj. If it be said, there may be many carnal men whom God hath invested with sundry eminent gifts of wisdom, courage, justice, fit for government.

Ans. Such may be fit to be consulted with and employed by governors, according to the quality and use of their gifts and parts, but yet are men not fit to be trusted with place of standing power or settled authority. Ahitophel's wisdom may be fit to be heard (as an oracle of God) but not fit to be trusted with power of settled magistracy, lest he at last call for 12,000 men to lead them forth against David (II Sam. 17:1-3). The best gifts and parts, under a covenant of works (under which all carnal men and hypocrites be), will at length turn aside by crooked ways to depart from God, and, finally, to fight against God, and are therefore, herein, opposed to good men and upright in heart (Ps. 125:4, 5).

Obj. If it be said again, that then the Church estate could not be compatible with any commonwealth under heaven.

Ans. It is one thing for the Church or members of the Church loyally to submit unto any form of government when it is above their calling to reform it; another thing to choose a form of government and governors discrepant from the rule. Now, if it be a divine truth that none are to be trusted with public permanent authority but godly men, who are fit materials for church fellowship, then from the same grounds it will appear that none are so fit to be trusted with the liberties of the Commonwealth as church members; for the liberties of the freemen of this Commonwealth are such as require men of faithful integrity to God and the state to preserve the same. Their liberties, among others, are chiefly these: (1) To choose all magistrates, and to call them to account at their General Courts. (2) To choose such burgesses, every General Court, as with the magistrates shall make or repeal all laws. Now, both these liberties are such as carry along much power with them, either to establish or subvert the Commonwealth, and therewith the Church, which power, if it be committed to men not according to their godliness, which makes them fit for church fellowship, but according to their wealth, which, as such, makes them no better than worldly men, then, in case worldly men should prove the major part, as soon they might do, they would as readily set over us magistrates like themselves, such as might hate us according to

the curse (Lev. 26:17), and turn the edge of all authority and laws against the Church and the members thereof, the maintenance of whose peace is the chief end which God aimed at in the institution of magistracy (I Tim. 2:1, 2).

II.

Letter to Lord Saye and Sele

IT IS VERY SUITABLE to God's all-sufficient wisdom and to the fullness and perfection of Holy Scriptures, not only to prescribe perfect rules for the right ordering of a private man's soul to everlasting blessedness with himself but also for the right ordering of a man's family, yea, of the Commonwealth too, so far as both of them are subordinate to spiritual ends, and yet avoid both the Church's usurpation upon civil jurisdictions, *in ordine ad spiritualia* [as ordained to the spiritual], and the Commonwealth's invasion upon ecclesiastical administrations, *in ordine* to civil peace and conformity to the civil state.

God's institutions (such as the government of Church and of Commonwealth be) may be close and compact, and coordinate one to another, and yet not confounded. God hath so framed the state of Church government and ordinances that they may be compatible to any commonwealth, though never so much disordered in His frame. But, yet, when a commonwealth hath liberty to mold His own frame . . . I conceive the Scripture hath given full direction for the right ordering of the same. . . .

Mr. Hooker doth often quote a saying out of Mr. Cartwright (though I have not read it in him) that no man fashioneth his house to his hangings, but his hangings to his house. It is better that the Commonwealth be fashioned to the setting forth of God's house, which is His church, than to accommodate the Church frame to the civil state. Democracy, I do not conceive, that ever God did ordain as a fit government either for Church or commonwealth. If the people be governors, who shall be governed? As for monarchy and aristocracy, they are both of them clearly approved and directed in Scripture, yet so as referreth the sovereignty to Himself, and setteth up theocracy in both as the best form of government in the commonwealth as well as in the Church.

The law, which Your Lordship instanceth in [that none shall be chosen to magistracy among us but a church member] was made and enacted before I came into the country; but I have hitherto wanted sufficient light to plead against it. . . . Nonmembership may be a just cause of nonadmission to the place of magistracy, but, yet, ejection out of his membership will not be a just cause of ejecting him out of his magistracy. . . .

Mr. Humfry was chosen for an assistant (as I hear) before the colony came over hither; and, though he be not as yet joined into church fellowship (by reason of the unsettledness of the congregation where he liveth), yet the Commonwealth do still continue his magistracy to him as knowing he waiteth for opportunity of enjoying church fellowship shortly.

When Your Lordship doubteth that this course will draw all things under the determination of the Church, *in ordine ad spiritualia* (seeing the Church is to determine who shall be members, and none but a member may have to do in the government of a commonwealth), be pleased (I pray you) to conceive that magistrates are neither chosen to office in the Church nor do govern by directions from the Church, but by civil laws, and those enacted in General Courts

and executed in courts of justice by the governors and assistants. In all which the Church (as the Church) hath nothing to do; only it prepareth fit instruments both to rule and to choose rulers, which is no ambition in the Church, nor dishonor to the Commonwealth. . . .

But Your Lordship doubteth that if such a rule were necessary then the Church estate and the best ordered commonwealth in the world were not compatible. But let not Your Lordship so conceive; for the Church submitteth itself to all the laws and ordinances of men, in what commonwealth soever they come to dwell. But it is one thing to submit unto what they have no calling to reform; another thing, voluntarily to ordain a form of government which, to the best discerning of many of us (for I speak not of myself), is expressly contrary to rule. Nor need Your Lordship fear (which yet I speak with submission to Your Lordship's better judgment) that this course will lay such a foundation as nothing but a mere democracy can be built upon it. . . .

Nor need we fear that this course will, in time, cast the Commonwealth into distractions and popular confusions. For (under correction) these three things do not undermine but do mutually and strongly maintain one another (even those three which we principally aim at) — authority in magistrates, liberty in people, purity in the Church. Purity, preserved in the Church, will preserve well-ordered liberty in the people, and both of them establish well-balanced authority in the magistrates. God is the Author of all these three, and neither is Himself the God of confusion, nor are His ways the ways of confusion but of peace.

1637

28.

John Winthrop: The Exclusion of Heretics

The Massachusetts General Court order defended in the following selection arose out of proceedings in March 1637 against the Reverend John Wheelwright, brother-in-law of Anne Hutchinson, in the course of which Wheelwright was convicted of sedition and contempt because his religious views departed from orthodox Puritanism. To stem the influx of other dissenters, the Court issued an order in May 1637 forbidding new settlers permanent residence in Massachusetts Bay Colony except by permission of the magistrates. The order was really directed against the Hutchinsonians led by former Bay Colony governor Sir Henry Vane; he deemed the order "tyranny" and protested so vigorously that John Winthrop issued the following defense of it. This in turn evoked a counterargument by Vane and an even longer Winthrop reply.

Source: *Winthrop Papers*, The Massachusetts Historical Society, 1943, Vol. III, pp. 422-426.

A Declaration of the Intent and Equity of the Order Made at the Last Court, to This Effect, That None Should Be Received to Inhabit Within This Jurisdiction but Such as Should Be Allowed by Some of the Magistrates

For clearing of such scruples as have arisen about this order, it is to be considered, first, what is the essential form of a commonweal or body politic such as this is, which I conceive to be this: The consent of a certain company of people, to cohabit together, under one government, for their mutual safety and welfare.

In this description all these things do concur to the well-being of such a body: (1) persons; (2) place; (3) consent; (4) government or order; (5) welfare.

It is clearly agreed, by all, that the care of safety and welfare was the original cause or occasion of commonweal and of many families subjecting themselves to rulers and laws; for no man has lawful power over another, but by birth or consent, so likewise, by the law of propriety, no man can have just interest in that which belongs to another, without his consent.

From the premises will arise these conclusions.

1. No commonweal can be founded but by free consent.

2. The persons so incorporating have a public and relative interest each in other, and in the place of their cohabitation and goods, and laws, etc., and in all the means of their welfare so as none other can claim privilege with them but by free consent.

3. The nature of such an incorporation ties every member thereof to seek out and entertain all means that may conduce to the welfare of the body, and to keep off whatsoever does appear to tend to their damage.

4. The welfare of the whole is to be put to apparent hazard for the advantage of any particular members.

From these conclusions I thus reason.

1. If we here be a corporation established by free consent, if the place of our cohabitation be our own, then no man has right to come into us, etc., without our consent.

2. If no man has right to our lands, our government privileges, etc., but by our consent, then it is reason we should take notice of before we confer any such upon them.

3. If we are bound to keep off whatsoever appears to tend to our ruin or damage, then we may lawfully refuse to receive such whose dispositions suit not with ours and whose society (we know) will be hurtful to us, and therefore it is lawful to take knowledge of all men before we receive them.

4. The churches take liberty (as lawfully they may) to receive or reject at their discretion; yea, particular towns make orders to the like effect; why then should the commonweal be denied the like liberty, and the whole more restrained than any part?

5. If it be sin in us to deny some men place, etc., among us, then it is because of some right they have to this place, etc., for to deny a man that which he has no right unto is neither sin nor injury.

6. If strangers have right to our houses or lands, etc., then it is either of justice or of mercy; if of justice, let them plead it, and we shall know what to answer; but if it be only in way of mercy, or by the rule of hospitality, etc., then I answer: (1) A man is not a fit object of mercy except he be in misery. (2) We are not bound to exercise mercy to others to the ruin of ourselves. (3) There are few that stand in need of mercy at their first coming hither. As for hospitality, that rule does not bind further than for some present occasion, not for continual residence.

7. A family is a little commonwealth, and a commonwealth is a great family. Now as a family is not bound to entertain all comers, no not every good man (otherwise than by way of hospitality) no more is a commonwealth.

8. It is a general received rule, *turpius ejicitur quam non admittitur hospes*, [*i.e.*] it is worse to receive a man whom we must cast out again than to deny him admittance.

9. The rule of the apostle (John 2:10) is that such as come and bring not the true doctrine with them should not be received to house, and by the same reason not into the commonweal.

10. Seeing it must be granted that there may come such persons (suppose Jesuits, etc.), which by consent of all ought to be rejected, it will follow that by this law (being only for notice to be taken of all that come to us, without which we cannot avoid such as indeed are to be kept out) is no other but just and needful, and if any should be rejected that ought to be received, that is not to be imputed to the law but to those who are betrusted with the execution of it. And herein is to be considered what the intent of the law is, and, by consequence, by what rule they are to walk who are betrusted with the keeping of it. The intent of the law is to preserve the welfare of the body; and for this end to have none received into any fellowship with it who are likely to disturb the same, and this intent (I am sure) is lawful and good. Now, then, if such to whom the keeping of this law is committed be persuaded in their judgments that such a man is likely to dis-

turb and hinder the public weal, but some others who are not in the same trust judge otherwise, yet they are to follow their own judgments rather than the judgments of others who are not alike interested; as in trial of an offender by jury, the twelve men are satisfied in their consciences, upon the evidence given, that the party deserves death; but there are twenty or forty standersby who conceive otherwise, yet is the jury bound to condemn him according to their own consciences, and not to acquit him upon the different opinion of other men, except their reasons can convince them of the error of their consciences, and this is according to the rule of the apostle (Rom. 14:5). Let every man be fully persuaded in his own mind.

If it be objected that some profane persons are received and others who are religious are rejected, I answer: (1) It is not known that any such thing has as yet fallen out. (2) Such a practice may be justifiable as the case may be, for younger persons (even profane ones) may be of less danger to the commonweal (and to the churches also) than some older persons, though professors of religion; for our Savior Christ, when he conversed with publicans, etc., says that such were nearer the Kingdom of Heaven than the religious Pharisees, and one that is of large parts and confirmed in some erroneous way is likely to do more harm to church and commonweal, and is of less hope to be reclaimed, than persons who have not yet become hardened, in the contempt of the means of grace.

Lastly, whereas it is objected that by this law we reject good Christians and, so consequently, Christ himself; I answer: (1) It is not known that any Christian man has been rejected. (2) A man that is a true Christian may be denied residence among us, in some cases, without rejecting Christ, as admit a true Christian should come over and should

maintain community of goods, or that magistrates ought not to punish the breakers of the first table, or the members of churches for criminal offenses; or that no man were bound to be subject to those laws or magistrates to which they should not give an explicit consent, etc. I hope no man will say that not to receive such an one were to reject Christ; for such opinions (though being maintained in simple ignorance, they might stand with a state of grace yet) they may be so dangerous to the public weal, in many respects, as it would be our sin and unfaithfulness to receive such among us, except it were for trial of their reformation. I would demand then in the case in question (for it is bootless curiosity to refrain openness in things public), whereas it is said that this law was made of purpose to keep away such as are of Mr. Wheelwright his judgment (admit it were so which yet I cannot confess), where is the evil of it? If we conceive and find by sad experience that his opinions are such, as by his own profession cannot stand with external peace, may we not provide for our peace by keeping of such as would strengthen him and infect others with such dangerous tenets? And if we find his opinions such as will cause divisions and make people look at their magistrates, ministers, and brethren as enemies to Christ and antichrists, etc., were it not sin and unfaithfulness in us to receive more of those opinions, which we already find the evil fruit of? Nay, why do not those who now complain join with us in keeping out of such, as well as formerly they did in expelling Mr. Williams for the like, though less dangerous? Where this change of their judgments should arise, I leave them to themselves to examine, and I earnestly entreat them so to do; and for this law let the equally minded judge what evil they find in it, or in the practice of those who are betrusted with the execution of it.

1639

29.

Fundamental Orders of Connecticut

The Connecticut settlement at Hartford was established in 1636 by settlers from the New Towne (now Cambridge), Massachusetts, congregation of the Reverend Thomas Hooker. This group had been preceded by others which had located at Windsor and Wethersfield. In January 1639, the freemen of these three townships assembled and drew up the so-called Fundamental Orders of Connecticut often hailed as the first written American constitution. Like similar agreements in Rhode Island at about the same time, it contained a preamble that is essentially a compact, the remainder being a body of laws. Hooker's move was prompted primarily by political considerations. He opposed the dominant figures at Boston, who looked down on democracy — believing it to be "no fit government either for church or commonwealth." However, despite popular elections, the Connecticut government remained for two centuries in the control of a small aristocratic faction.

Source: Poore, I, pp. 249-251.

FORASMUCH as it has pleased the Almighty God by the wise disposition of His Divine Providence so to order and dispose of things that we, the inhabitants and residents of Windsor, Hartford, and Wethersfield are now cohabiting and dwelling in and upon the river of Conectecotte [Connecticut] and the lands thereunto adjoining; and well knowing where a people are gathered together the Word of God requires that, to maintain the peace and union of such a people, there should be an orderly and decent government established according to God, to order and dispose of the affairs of the people at all seasons as occasion shall require; do therefore associate and conjoin ourselves to be as one public state or commonwealth, and do, for ourselves and our successors and such as shall be adjoined to us at any time hereafter, enter into combination and confederation together, to maintain and preserve the liberty and purity of the Gospel of our Lord Jesus which we now profess, as also the discipline of the churches, which, according to the truth of the said Gospel, is now practised among us.

As also in our civil affairs to be guided and governed according to such laws, rules, orders, and decrees as shall be made, ordered, and decreed, as follows:

1. It is ordered, sentenced, and decreed that there shall be yearly two general assemblies or courts; the one, the second Thursday in April, the other, the second Thursday in September following. The first shall be called the Court of Election, wherein shall be yearly chosen . . . so many magistrates and other public officers as shall be found requisite. Whereof one to be chosen governor for the year ensuing and until another be chosen, and no other magistrate to be chosen for more than one year; provided always there be six chosen besides the governor . . . which choice shall be made by all that are admitted freemen and have taken the oath of fidelity, and do cohabit within this jurisdiction (having been admitted inhabitants by the major part of the town wherein they live), or the major part of such as shall be then present. . . .

4. It is ordered . . . that no person be chosen governor above once in two years, and that the governor be always a member of some approved congregation, and formerly of the magistracy within this jurisdiction; and all the magistrates freemen of this Commonwealth. And that no magistrate or other public officer shall execute any part of his or their office before they are severally sworn, which shall be done in the face of the Court. . . .

5. It is ordered . . . that to the aforesaid Court of Election the several towns shall send their deputies, and, when the elections are ended, they may proceed in any public service as at other courts. Also, the other General Court in September shall be for making of laws, and any other public occasion which concerns the good of the Commonwealth. . . .

7. It is ordered . . . that after there are warrants given out for any of the said General Courts, the constable or constables of each town shall forthwith give notice distinctly to the inhabitants of the same in some public assembly or by going or sending from house to house that at a place and time by him or them limited and set, they meet and assemble themselves together to elect and choose certain deputies to be at the General Court then following to [manage] the affairs of the Commonwealth; which said deputies shall be chosen by all that are admitted inhabitants in the several towns and have taken the oath of fidelity; provided that none be chosen a deputy for any General Court which is not a freeman of this Commonwealth. . . .

8. It is ordered . . . that Windsor, Hartford, and Wethersfield shall have power, each town, to send four of their freemen as deputies to every General Court; and whatsoever other towns shall be hereafter added to this jurisdiction, they shall send so many deputies as the Court shall judge meet, a reasonable proportion to the number of freemen that are in the said towns . . . which deputies shall have the power of the whole town to give their votes and allowance to all such laws and orders as may be for the public good, and unto which the said towns are to be bound.

9. It is ordered . . . that the deputies thus chosen shall have power and liberty to appoint a time and a place of meeting together before any General Court to advise and consult of all such things as may concern the good of the public, as also to examine their own elections, whether according to the order, and, if they or the greatest part of them find any election to be illegal, they may seclude such for present from their meeting and return the same and their reasons to the Court; and, if it prove true, the Court may fine the party or parties so intruding and the town, if they see cause, and give out a warrant to go to a new election in a legal way. . . .

10. It is ordered . . . that every General Court . . . shall consist of the governor, or someone chosen to moderate the Court, and four other magistrates, at least, with the major part of the deputies of the several towns legally chosen; and in case the freemen or major part of them, through neglect or refusal of the governor and major part of the magistrates, shall call a Court, it shall consist of the major part of freemen that are present, or their deputies, with a moderator chosen by them. In which said General Courts shall consist the supreme power of the Commonwealth, and they only shall have power to make laws or repeal them, to grant levies, to admit of freemen, dispose of lands undisposed of to several towns or persons, and also shall have power to call either Court or magistrate or any other person whatsoever into question for any misdemeanor; and may for just causes displace or deal otherwise according to the nature of the offense; and also may deal in any other matter that concerns the good of this Commonwealth, except election of magistrates, which shall be done by the whole body of freemen.

In which Court, the governor or moderator shall have power to order the Court to give liberty of speech, and silence unseasonable and disorderly speakings, to put all things to vote, and, in case the vote be equal, to have the casting voice. But none of these courts shall be adjourned or dissolved without the consent of the major part of the Court.

11. It is ordered . . . that, when any General Court upon the occasions of the Commonwealth have agreed upon any sum or sums of money to be levied upon the several towns within this jurisdiction, that a committee be chosen to set out and appoint what shall be the proportion of every town to pay of the said levy, provided the committees be made up of an equal number out of each town.

———◆———

Connecticut, the little yellow spot [on the map] that makes the clock-peddler, the schoolmaster, and the senator. The first, gives you time; the second, tells you what to do with it; and the third makes your law and your civilization.

ALEXIS DE TOCQUEVILLE

1640

30.

Plan of Civil Government for Providence

Roger Williams, welcomed to Massachusetts in 1631 as a "godly minister," soon fell into disfavor for his criticisms of the civil governors in the Puritan colony. He claimed that they had no authority to enforce church law, and that the colonists' land claims violated Indian rights. On October 9, 1635, the Massachusetts General Court banished him from the colony for "propagating new and dangerous opinions." Williams and a small band of followers thus went, in 1636, to Narragansett Bay, where they founded the town of Providence. When they drew up the following plan of civil government in 1640, they determined the liberal character of the future Rhode Island colony in their pledge to "hold forth liberty of conscience" to all. This tolerant attitude caused other New England Puritans, who discouraged divergent religious beliefs within a single community, to look upon Providence as a veritable sink of iniquity.

Source: Hazard, I, pp. 464-466.

WE, Robert Coles, Chad Browne, William Harris, and John Warner, being freely chosen by the consent of our loving friends and neighbors, the inhabitants of this town of Providence, having many differences among us, they being freely willing and also bound themselves to stand to our arbitration in all differences among us, to rest contented in our determination being so betrusted, we have seriously and carefully endeavored to weigh and consider all those differences being desirous to bring to unity and peace, although our abilities are far short in the due examination of such weighty things;

yet, so far as we conceive in laying all things together, we have gone the fairest and the equalest way to produce our peace.

I. *Agreed.* We have with one consent agreed that in the parting those particular properties which some of our friends and neighbors have in Pawtuxet, from the general common of our town of Providence to run upon a straight line from a fresh spring being in the gulley, at the head of that cove running by that point of land called Saxafras unto the town of Mashipawog to an oak tree standing near unto the cornfield, being at this time the nearest cornfield unto Pawtuxet, the oak tree having four marks with an axe, till some other landmark be set for a certain bound. Also, we agree that if any meadow ground lying and joining to that meadow that borders upon the river of Pawtuxet come within the foresaid line, which will not come within a straight line from Long Cove to the marked tree, then for that meadow to belong to Pawtuxet, and so beyond the town of Mashipawog from the oak tree between the two fresh rivers Pawtuxet and Wanasquatucket of an even distance.

II. *Agreed.* We have with one consent agreed that for the disposing of those lands that shall be disposed belonging to this town of Providence to be in the whole inhabitants by the choice of five men for general disposal to be betrusted with disposal of lands and also of the town's stock, and all general things, and not to receive in any in six days as townsmen but first to give the inhabitants notice to consider if any have just cause to show against the receiving of him as you can apprehend, and to receive none but such as subscribe to this our determination. Also we agree that if any of our neighbors do apprehend himself wronged by these or any of these five disposers, that at the general town meeting he may have a trial.

Also we agree for the town to choose, besides the other five men, one or more to keep record of all things belonging to the town and lying in common.

We agree, as formerly has been the liberties of the town, so still, to hold forth liberty of conscience.

III. *Agreed.* That after many considerations and consultations of our own state and also of states abroad in way of government, we apprehend no way so suitable to our condition as government by way of arbitration. But if men agree themselves by arbitration, no state we know of disallows that, neither do we. But if men refuse that

which is but common humanity between man and man, then, to compel such unreasonable persons to a reasonable way, we agree that the five disposers shall have power to compel him either to choose two men himself, or if he refuse; for them to choose two men to arbitrate his cause; and if these four men chosen by every party do end the cause, then to see their determination performed and the faultive to pay the arbitrators for their time spent in it. But if those four men do not end it, then for the five disposers to choose three men to put an end to it; and for the certainty hereof we agree the major part of the five disposers to choose the three men, and the major part of the three men to end the cause having power from the five disposers by a note under their hand to perform it; and the faultive not agreeing in the first to pay the charge of the last, and for the arbitrators to follow no employment till the causes be ended without consent of the whole that have to do with the cause.

Instance. In the first arbitration, the offender may offer reasonable terms of peace, and the offended may exact upon him and refuse and trouble men beyond reasonable satisfaction, so for the last arbitrators to judge where the fault was, in not agreeing in the first, to pay the charge of the last.

IV. *Agreed.* That if any person damnify any man, either in goods or good name, and the person offended follow not the cause upon the offender, that if any person give notice to the five disposers, they shall call the party delinquent to answer by arbitration.

Instance. Thus, if any person abuse another in person or goods, maybe for peace sake a man will at present put it up, and it may so be resolved to revenge; therefore, for the peace of the state, the disposers are to look to it in the first place.

V. *Agreed,* for all the whole inhabitants to combine ourselves to assist any man in the pursuit of any party delinquent, with all our best endeavors to attack him; but if any man raise a hubbub, and there be no just cause, then for the party that raised the hubbub to satisfy men for their time lost in it.

VI. *Agreed.* That if any man have a difference with any of the five disposers which cannot be deferred till general meeting of the town, then he may have the clerk call the town together at his ———— for a trial.

Instance. It may be a man may be to depart the land, or to a far part of the land, or his estate may lie upon a speedy trial, or the like case may fall out.

VII. *Agreed.* That the town, by the five men, shall give every man a deed of all his lands lying within the bounds of the plantation, to hold it by for after ages.

VIII. *Agreed.* That the five disposers shall from the date hereof meet every month-day upon general things and at the quarter-day to yield a new choice and give up their old accounts.

IX. *Agreed.* That the clerk shall call the five disposers together at the month-day and the general town together every quarter, to meet upon general occasions from the date hereof.

X. *Agreed.* That the clerk is to receive for every cause that comes to the town for a trial 4*d*; for making each deed; 12*d*; and to give up the book to the town at the year's end, and yield to a new choice.

XI. *Agreed.* That all acts of disposal on both sides to stand since the difference.

XII. *Agreed.* That every man that has not paid in his purchase money for his plantation shall make up his 10*s*. to be 30*s*., equal with the first purchasers; and for all that are received, townsmen hereafter to pay the like sum of money to the town stock.

These being those things we have generally concluded on, for our peace, we desiring our loving friends to receive as our absolute determination, laying ourselves down as subjects to it.

1641

31.

Massachusetts Body of Liberties

As the only constitution of the Massachusetts Bay Colony was its corporate charter, there was no limit whatever to the authority of its all but self-appointed magistrates. In most cases, the administration of justice was equitable enough — no less so, at any rate, than what prevailed in England at the time. However, the grievances of the deputies in the General Court were serious enough to bring about a movement for a code of laws defining the liberties of the people. The first code of Massachusetts was based on a model drawn up by Nathaniel Ward and was adopted as law on December 10, 1641. The "Body of Liberties" was based for the most part on English common law and still retained a great deal of authority for the magistrates. While the effect of this document may not at first have been very great — owing to the opposition to it of Governor Winthrop, who opposed any premature codification of the peoples' liberties, and of the clergy, who insisted the "judges are Gods upon earth" — it at least circumscribed their authority as far as it went, and it led in 1648 to the adoption of The Book of the General Lawes and Libertyes, *a more popular code of laws that further increased the power of the people.*

Source: MHSC, 3rd series, VIII, pp. 216-237.

THE FREE FRUITION of such liberties, immunities, and privileges as humanity, civility, and Christianity call for as due to every man in his place and proportion without impeachment and infringement, has ever been and ever will be the tranquillity and stability of churches and commonwealths; and the denial or deprival thereof, the disturbance if not the ruin of both.

We hold it, therefore, our duty and safety, while we are about the further establishing of this government, to collect and express all such freedoms as for [the] present we foresee may concern us, and our posterity after us, and to ratify them with our solemn consent. We do, therefore, this day, religiously and unanimously decree and confirm these following rights, liberties, and privileges concerning our churches and civil state, to be respectively, impartially, and inviolably enjoyed and observed throughout our jurisdiction forever.

1. No man's life shall be taken away; no man's honor or good name shall be stained; no man's person shall be arrested, restrained, banished, dismembered, nor any ways punished; no man shall be deprived of his wife and children; no man's goods or

estate shall be taken away from him, nor any way endamaged under color of law or countenance of authority unless it be by virtue or equity of some express law of the country warranting the same, established by a General Court and sufficiently published, or in case of the defect of a law in any particular case, by the Word of God; and in capital cases, or in cases concerning dismembering or banishment, according to that Word to be judged by the General Court.

2. Every person within this jurisdiction, whether inhabitant or foreigner, shall enjoy the same justice and law that is general for the plantation, which we constitute and execute one toward another without partiality or delay.

3. No man shall be urged to take any oath or subscribe any articles, covenants, or remonstrance of a public and civil nature, but such as the General Court has considered, allowed, and required.

4. No man shall be punished for not appearing at or before any civil assembly, court, council, magistrate, or officer, nor for the omission of any office or service, if he shall be necessarily hindered by any apparent act or providence of God, which he could neither foresee nor avoid; provided that this law shall not prejudice any person of his just cost and damage in any civil action.

5. No man shall be compelled to any public work or service unless the impressment be grounded upon some act of the General Court, and have reasonable allowance therefor.

6. No man shall be impressed in person to any office, work, wars, or other public service that is necessarily and sufficiently exempted by any natural or personal impediment, as by want of years, greatness of age, defect of mind, failing of senses, or impotency of limbs.

7. No man shall be compelled to go out of the limits of this plantation upon any offensive wars which this Commonwealth or any of our friends or confederates shall voluntarily undertake; but only upon such vindictive and defensive wars in our own behalf or the behalf of our friends and confederates as shall be enterprised by the counsel and consent of a General Court, or by authority derived from the same.

8. No man's cattle or goods of what kind soever shall be impressed or taken for any public use or service, unless it be by warrant grounded upon some act of the General Court, nor without such reasonable prices and hire as the ordinary rates of the country do afford. And if his cattle and goods shall perish or suffer damage in such service, the owners shall be sufficiently recompensed.

9. No monopolies shall be granted or allowed among us, but of such new inventions that are profitable to the country, and that for a short time.

10. All our lands and heritages shall be free from all fines and license upon alienations, and from all heriots, wardships, liveries, primer-seisins, year day and waste, escheats, and forfeitures, upon the deaths of parents or ancestors, be they natural, casual, or judicial.

11. All persons which are of the age of twenty-one years, and of right understanding and memories, whether excommunicate or condemned, shall have full power and liberty to make their wills and testaments, and other lawful alienations of their lands and estates.

12. Every man, whether inhabitant or foreigner, free or not free, shall have liberty to come to any public court, council, or town meeting, and, either by speech or writing, to move any lawful, seasonable, and material question, or to present any necessary motion, complaint, petition, bill, or information, whereof that meeting has proper cognizance, so it be done in convenient time, due order, and respective manner.

13. No man shall be rated here for any es-

tate or revenue he has in England, or in any foreign parts till it be transported hither.

14. Any conveyance or alienation of land or other estate whatsoever made by any woman that is married, any child under age, idiot or distracted person shall be good if it be passed and ratified by the consent of a General Court.

15. All covenous [deceitful] or fraudulent alienations or conveyances of lands, tenements, or any hereditaments shall be of no validity to defeat any man due debts or legacies, or from any just title, claim, or possession, of that which is so fraudulently conveyed.

16. Every inhabitant that is a householder shall have free fishing and fowling in any great ponds and bays, coves and rivers, so far as the sea ebbs and flows within the precincts of the town where they dwell, unless the freemen of the same town or the General Court have otherwise appropriated them, provided that this shall not be extended to give leave to any man to come upon others' property without their leave.

17. Every man of or with this jurisdiction shall have free liberty, notwithstanding any civil power, to remove both himself and his family at their pleasure out of the same, provided there be no legal impediment to the contrary. . . .

26. Every man that finds himself unfit to plead his own cause in any court shall have liberty to employ any man against whom the court does not except to help him, provided he give him no fee or reward for his pains. This shall not exempt the party himself from answering such questions in person as the court shall think meet to demand of him. . . .

29. In all actions at law it shall be the liberty of the plaintiff and defendant by mutual consent to choose whether they will be tried by the bench or by a jury, unless it be where the law upon just reason has otherwise determined. The like liberty shall be granted to all persons in criminal cases.

30. It shall be in the liberty of plaintiff and defendant, and likewise every delinquent (to be judged by a jury), to challenge any of the jurors. And if his challenge be found just and reasonable by the bench, or the rest of the jury, as the challenger shall choose it shall be allowed him, and *tales de circumstantibus* [alternate jurors] impaneled in their room [stead]. . . .

36. It shall be in the liberty of every man cast, condemned, or sentenced in any cause in any inferior court to make their appeal to the Court of Assistants, provided they tender their appeal and put in security to prosecute it before the court be ended wherein they were condemned, and within six days next ensuing put in good security before some assistant to satisfy what his adversary shall recover against him; and if the cause be of a criminal nature, for his good behavior and appearance. And every man shall have liberty to complain to the General Court of any injustice done him in any Court of Assistants or other. . . .

42. No man shall be twice sentenced by civil justice for one and the same crime, offense, or trespass.

43. No man shall be beaten with above forty stripes, nor shall any true gentleman, nor any man equal to a gentleman, be punished with whipping, unless his crime be very shameful and his course of life vicious and profligate.

44. No man condemned to die shall be put to death within four days next after his condemnation, unless the court see special cause to the contrary, or in case of martial law; nor shall the body of any man so put to death be unburied twelve hours unless it be in case of anatomy [autopsy].

45. No man shall be forced by torture to confess any crime against himself nor any other unless it be in some capital case, where he is first fully convicted by clear and sufficient evidence to be guilty, after which, if the cause be of that nature that it is very apparent there be other conspirators or con-

federates with him, then he may be tortured, yet not with such tortures as be barbarous and inhumane.

46. For bodily punishments we allow among us none that are inhumane, barbarous, or cruel.

47. No man shall be put to death without the testimony of two or three witnesses, or that which is equivalent thereunto. . . .

LIBERTIES OF WOMEN

79. If any man at his death shall not leave his wife a competent portion of his estate, upon just complaint made to the General Court she shall be relieved.

80. Every married woman shall be free from bodily correction or stripes by her husband, unless it be in his own defense upon her assault. If there be any just cause of correction, complaint shall be made to authority assembled in some court, from which only she shall receive it.

LIBERTIES OF CHILDREN

81. When parents die intestate, the elder son shall have a double portion of his whole estate, real and personal, unless the General Court upon just cause alleged shall judge otherwise.

82. When parents die intestate having no heirs [males] of their bodies, their daughters shall inherit as copartners, unless the General Court upon just reason shall judge otherwise.

83. If any parents shall willfully and unreasonably deny any child timely or convenient marriage, or shall exercise any unnatural severity toward them, such children shall have free liberty to complain to authority for redress.

84. No orphan[s] during their minority which [were] not committed to tuition or service by the parents in their lifetime shall afterward be absolutely disposed of by any kindred, friend, executor, township, or

church, nor by themselves, without the consent of some court wherein two assistants at least shall be present.

LIBERTIES OF SERVANTS

85. If any servants shall flee from the tyranny and cruelty of their masters to the house of any freeman of the same town, they shall be there protected and sustained till due order be taken for their relief; provided due notice thereof be speedily given to their masters from whom they fled, and [to] the next assistant or constable where the party fleeing is harbored.

86. No servant[s] shall be put off for above a year to any other, neither in the lifetime of their master nor after their death by their executors or administrators, unless it be by consent of authority assembled in some court or two assistants.

87. If any man smite out the eye or tooth of his man-servant, or maid-servant, or otherwise maim or much disfigure him, unless it be by mere casualty, he shall let them go free from his service; and shall have such further recompense as the court shall allow him.

88. Servants that have served diligently and faithfully to the benefit of their masters seven years shall not be sent away empty. And if any have been unfaithful, negligent, or unprofitable in their service, notwithstanding the good usage of their masters, they shall not be dismissed till they have made satisfaction according to the judgment of authority.

LIBERTIES OF FOREIGNERS AND STRANGERS

89. If any people of other nations professing the true Christian religion shall flee to us from the tyranny or oppression of their persecutors, or from famine, wars, or the like necessary and compulsory cause, they shall be entertained and succored

among us, according to that power and prudence God shall give us.

90. If any ships or other vessels, be it friend or enemy, shall suffer shipwreck upon our coast, there shall be no violence or wrong offered to their persons or goods. But their persons shall be harbored and relieved, and their goods preserved in safety till authority may be certified thereof, and shall take further order therein.

91. There shall never be any bond slavery, villenage, or captivity among us unless it be lawful captives taken in just wars, and such strangers as willingly sell themselves or are sold to us. And these shall have all the liberties and Christian usages which the law of God, established in Israel concerning such persons, does morally require. This exempts none from servitude who shall be judged thereto by authority.

OF THE BRUTE CREATURE

92. No man shall exercise any tyranny or cruelty toward any brute creature[s] which are usually kept for man's use.

93. If any man shall have occasion to lead or drive cattle from place to place that is far off, so that they be weary, or hungry, or all sick, or lame, it shall be lawful to rest or refresh them, for competent time, in any open place that is not corn, meadow, or enclosed for some peculiar use.

94. *Capital Laws:*

I. If any man after legal conviction shall have or worship any other God but the Lord God, he shall be put to death (Deut. 13:6, 10; Deut. 17:2, 6; Ex. 22:20).

II. If any man or woman be a witch (that is, has or consults with a familiar spirit), they shall be put to death (Ex. 22:18; Lev. 20:27; Deut. 18:10).

III. If any person shall blaspheme the name of God, the Father, Son, or Holy Ghost, with direct, express, presumptuous, or high-handed blasphemy, or shall curse God in the like manner, he shall be put to death (Lev. 24:15, 16).

IV. If any person commit any willful murder, which is manslaughter, committed upon premeditated malice, hatred, or cruelty, not in a man's necessary and just defense, nor by mere casualty against his will, he shall be put to death (Ex. 21:12; Num. 35:13, 14, 30, 31).

V. If any person slay another suddenly in his anger or cruelty of passion, he shall be put to death (Num. 25:20, 21; Lev. 24:17).

VI. If any person shall slay another through guile, either by poisoning or other such devilish practice, he shall be put to death (Ex. 21:14).

VII. If any man or woman shall lie with any beast or brute creature by carnal copulation, they shall surely be put to death. And the beast shall be slain, and buried and not eaten (Lev. 20:15, 16).

VIII. If any man lies with mankind as he lies with a woman, both of them have committed abomination, they both shall surely be put to death (Lev. 20:13).

IX. If any person commits adultery with a married or espoused wife, the adulterer and adulteress shall surely be put to death (Lev. 20:19 and 18:20; Deut. 22:23, 24).

X. If any man steals a man or mankind, he shall surely be put to death (Ex. 21:16).

XI. If any man rise up by false witness, wittingly and of purpose to take away any man's life, he shall be put to death (Deut. 19:16, 18, 19).

XII. If any man shall conspire and attempt any invasion, insurrection, or public rebellion against our Commonwealth, or shall endeavor to surprise any town or towns, fort or forts therein, or shall treacherously and perfidiously attempt the alteration and subversion of our frame of polity or government fundamentally, he shall be put to death.

1642

32.

John Winthrop: A Negative View of Democracy

John Winthrop and other magistrates of the General Court of Massachusetts fell into disagreement with the town representatives, also members of the Court, as to whether the magistrates as officers of the Massachusetts Bay Company had the right to veto the representatives' actions. The dispute came to a head in a 1642 case in which the town representatives sided with the plaintiff and the magistrates upheld the defendant. Winthrop thereupon wrote a tract on the negative vote that included the following discussion of democracy. The magistrates and representatives settled their dispute in 1644 by dividing themselves into two bodies, each with the power to veto the other, thereby creating a bicameral legislature in Massachusetts.

Source: Robert C. Winthrop, *Life and Letters of John Winthrop, etc., etc.,*
2nd edition, Boston, 1869, Vol. II, pp. 427-438.

THAT WHICH MAKES a specific difference between one form of government and another is essential and fundamental. But the negative vote in the magistrates does so in our government; therefore, it is essential and fundamental.

The assumption is proved by this: That if the negative vote were taken away, our government would be a mere democracy, whereas now it is mixed. This I prove thus: Where the chief ordinary power and administration thereof is in the people, there is a democracy. This I prove thus: If it be in the deputies, it is in the people, but it will be in the deputies, governor, etc., for they are but the representative body of the people, and the matter lies not in the number of the people assembled, but in their power.

Again, the people are not bound to send their deputies, but they may come themselves, if they will. And though the magistrates be joined with them in the Court, as they were in Athens and other popular states in Greece, etc., yet they serve but as councilors, seeing they shall have but their single votes, as every one of the people has. Lastly, the answer: himself confesses that the deputies are the democratic part of our government.

Now if we should change from a mixed aristocracy to a mere democracy, first, we should have no warrant in Scripture for it; there was no such government in Israel. We should hereby voluntarily abase ourselves, and deprive ourselves of that dignity which the providence of God has put upon us, which is a manifest breach of the Fifth Commandment; for a democracy is, among most civil nations, accounted the meanest and worst of all forms of government; and therefore in writers it is branded with reproachful epithets as *bellua mutoru capitu*, a monster, etc., and histories do record that it has been always of least continuance and fullest of troubles. . . .

I say, we should incur scandal by undervaluing the gifts of God — as wisdom, learning, etc. — and the ordinance of magistracy, if the judgment and authority of any one of the common rank of the people should bear equal weight with that of the wisest and chiefest magistrate. . . . I acknowledge (and have always so done) that there are of the deputies men of wisdom and learning sufficient and, it may be, not inferior to some of the magistrates. But yet, if in common repute (especially in foreign parts) the magistrates be looked at as men [preeminent] in gifts and experience (for otherwise the people are misguided in their choice) then the scandal will remain, notwithstanding.

And, besides, I speak not positively but hypothetically, so as if there be at any time one or more deputies so weak as will hold no proportion with the most able of the magistrates, then my argument will hold good, without any scandal or offense given on my part. And whereas I style such a deputy "of the common rank of freemen," I hope it is no disparagement to any to be counted in that rank, which is allowed equal power with the governor and assistants in our highest Court, although a deputy in Court be of more value than any one freeman, seeing he represents many. Yet, before and after the Court, he is but as another freeman and so cannot be counted in the same rank with the magistrates.

And I should be willing to learn . . . how I might have spoken more modestly in this and suchlike passages and not have lost the force of my argument, which (the Lord knows) was the only thing I intended, and not to extol the gifts, etc., of the magistrates, nor to debase those of the deputies; for I acknowledge it my duty to honor the gifts of God wherever I find them; and, I hope, my ordinary practice has not been different.

1642 - 1646

33.

On Parental Duty and the Apprenticeship of Children

The Massachusetts Bay Colony School Law of May 1642 is one of the earliest laws on education in the American colonies. It reflected the concern of the New England settlers, even at that early date, with establishing a uniform code of education and confirmed an awareness that family responsibility for education had been, for the most part, a failure. In the Southern colonies, on the other hand, there was less concern with a public system of education; geographic, social, and economic conditions resulted in a system of apprenticeship and vocational training for the poor, while the children of wealthy families were educated by private tutors. Both the Massachusetts act and Virginia act of 1646 presented here did share, however, a common apprehension that lack of education might allow children to fall into corrupt ways.

Source: *The Charters and General Laws of the Colony and Province of Massachusetts Bay, etc., etc.*, Boston, 1814, pp. 73-76. Hening, I, pp. 336-337.

I.

Massachusetts Bay School Law

FORASMUCH AS THE GOOD EDUCATION of children is of singular behoof and benefit to any commonwealth, *and whereas* many parents and masters are too indulgent and negligent of their duty in that kind:

It is ordered that the selectmen of every town, in the several precincts and quarters where they dwell, shall have a vigilant eye over their brethren and neighbors to see, first, that none of them shall suffer so much barbarism in any of their families as not to endeavor to teach, by themselves or others, their children and apprentices so much learning as may enable them perfectly to read the English tongue, and knowledge of the capital laws; upon penalty of 20s. for each neglect therein.

Also that all masters of families do once a week (at the least) catechize their children and servants in the grounds and principles of religion; and if any be unable to do so much, that then at the least they procure such children and apprentices to learn some short orthodox catechism without book that they may be able to answer unto the questions that shall be propounded to them out of such catechism by their parents or masters, or any of the selectmen when they shall call them to a trial, of what they have learned in that kind.

And, further, that all parents and masters do breed and bring up their children and apprentices in some honest lawful calling, labor, or employment, either in husbandry or some other trade, profitable for themselves and the Commonwealth, if they will not or cannot train them up in learning, to fit them for higher employments.

And if any of the selectmen, after admonition by them given to such masters of families, shall find them still negligent of their duty in the particulars aforementioned, whereby children and servants become rude, stubborn, and unruly, the said selectmen, with the help of two magistrates, or the next county court for that shire, shall take such children or apprentices from them, and place them with some masters for years (boys till they come to twenty-one, and girls eighteen years of age complete), which will more strictly look unto and force them to submit unto government, according to the rules of this order, if by fair means and former instructions they will not be drawn unto it.

II.

Virginia Act for Training of Poor Children

Whereas sundry laws and statutes by act of Parliament established have with great wisdom ordained, for the better educating of youth in honest and profitable trades and manufactures, as also to avoid sloth and idleness wherewith such young children are easily corrupted, as also for relief of such parents whose poverty extends not to give them breeding, that the justices of the peace should, at their discretion, bind out children to tradesmen or husbandmen to be brought up in some good and lawful calling. *And whereas* God Almighty, among many His other blessings, has vouchsafed increase of children to this colony, who now are multiplied to a considerable number, who if instructed in good and lawful trades may much improve the honor and reputation of the country, and no less their own good and their parents' comfort; but forasmuch as for the most part the parents, either through fond indulgence or perverse obstinacy, are most averse and unwilling to part with their children, *Be it therefore enacted by authority of this Grand Assembly,* according to the aforesaid laudable custom in the Kingdom of England, that the commissioners of the several counties respectively do, at their discretion, make choice of two children in each county of the age of eight or seven years, at the least, either male or female, which are to be sent up to James City, between this and June next, to be employed in the public flax houses under such master and mistress as shall be there appointed, in carding, knitting, and spinning, etc. And that the said children be furnished from the said county with six barrels of corn, two coverlets, or one rug and one blanket, one bed, one wooden bowl or tray, two pewter spoons, a sow shoat of six months old, two laying hens, [and] with convenient apparel both linen and woolen, with hose and shoes. And for the better provision of housing for the said children, *It is enacted,* that there be two houses built by the first of April next of forty foot long apiece with good and substantial timber; the houses to be twenty foot broad apiece, eight foot high in the pitch, and a stack of brick chimnies standing in the middle of each house, and that they be lofted with sawn boards and made with convenient partitions. And it is further thought fit that the commissioners have caution not to take up any children but from such parents who by reason of their poverty are disabled to maintain and educate them, *Be it likewise agreed,* that the governor has agreed with the Assembly for the sum of 10,000 pounds of tobacco, to be paid him the next crop, to build and finish the said houses in manner and form before expressed.

1643

34.

The New England Confederation

The constant threat of attack by Indian tribes and the danger presented by the Dutch on the southwest and the French on the north brought the colonies of Massachusetts, Plymouth, Connecticut, and New Haven together in a common effort for protection in 1643. Representatives from each colony, meeting at Boston, drew up twelve articles of confederation that were ratified by the four colonies. Each member of this self-styled Confederation of the United Colonies of New England sent two representatives annually to determine the Indian policy, deal with foreign powers, and settle differences among themselves. The Confederation was the first attempt at federalism in America. But its affairs were dominated by Massachusetts, and, largely because of this, its activity virtually ceased after 1664 and by 1684 the union was terminated.

Source: Hazard, II, pp. 1-6.

ARTICLES OF CONFEDERATION between the plantations under the government of the Massachusetts, the plantations under the government of New Plymouth, the plantations under the government of Connecticut, and the government of New Haven with the plantations in combination therewith:

Whereas we all came into these parts of America with one and the same end and aim, namely, to advance the kingdom of our Lord Jesus Christ and to enjoy the liberties of the Gospel in purity with peace; *and whereas* in our settling (by a wise providence of God) we are further dispersed upon the seacoasts and rivers than was at first intended, so that we cannot according to our desire with convenience communicate in one government and jurisdiction; *and whereas* we live encompassed with people of several nations and strange languages which hereafter may prove injurious to us or our posterity; and forasmuch as the natives have formerly committed sundry insolences and outrages upon several plantations of the English and have of late combined themselves against us; and seeing by reason of those sad distractions in England which they have heard of, and by which they know we are hindered from that humble way of seeking advice, or reaping those comfortable fruits of protection, which at other times we might well expect, we, therefore, do conceive it our bounden duty, without delay, to enter into a present consociation among ourselves, for mutual help and strength in all our future concernments.

That, as in nation and religion so in other respects, we be and continue one according to the tenor and true meaning of the ensuing articles. Wherefore it is fully agreed and concluded by and between the parties of jurisdictions above named, and they jointly and severally do by these presents agree and conclude that they all be and henceforth be called by the name of the United Colonies of New England.

2. The said United Colonies, for themselves and their posterities, do jointly and severally hereby enter into a firm and perpetual league of friendship and amity for offense and defense, mutual advice and succor upon all just occasions, both for preserving and propagating the truth and liberties of the Gospel and for their own mutual safety and welfare.

3. It is further agreed that the plantations which at present are, or hereafter shall be, settled within the limits of the Massachusetts shall be forever under the Massachusetts, and shall have particular jurisdiction among themselves in all cases as an entire body; and that Plymouth, Connecticut, and New Haven shall each of them have like particular jurisdiction and government within their limits, and in reference to the plantations which already are settled, or shall hereafter be erected, or shall settle within their limits respectively; provided that no other jurisdiction shall hereafter be taken in as a distinct head or member of this confederation, nor shall any other plantation or jurisdiction in present being, and not already in combination or under the jurisdiction of any of these confederates, be received by any of them; nor shall any two of the confederates join in one jurisdiction without consent of the rest, which consent to be interpreted as is expressed in the 6th article ensuing.

4. It is by these confederates agreed that the charge of all just wars, whether offensive or defensive, upon what part or member of this confederation soever they fall, shall both in men and provisions and all other disbursements be borne by all the parts of this confederation in different proportions according to their different ability in manner following, namely, that the com-

missioners for each jurisdiction, from time to time as there shall be occasion, bring a true account and number of all the males in every plantation or any way belonging to or under their federal jurisdictions of what quality or condition soever they be from sixteen years old to threescore being inhabitants there. And that according to the different numbers which from time to time shall be found in each jurisdiction, upon a true and just account, the service of men and all charges of the war be borne by the poll; each jurisdiction or plantation being left to their own just course and custom of rating themselves and people according to their different estates with due respects to their qualities and exemptions among themselves though the confederation take no notice of any such privilege; and that according to their different charge of each jurisdiction and plantation, the whole advantage of the war (if it please God to bless their endeavors), whether it be in lands, goods, or persons, shall be proportionately divided among the said confederates.

5. It is further agreed that, if any of these jurisdictions or any plantation under or in combination with them be invaded by any enemy whomsoever, upon notice and request of any three magistrates of that jurisdiction so invaded, the rest of the confederates, without any further meeting or expostulation, shall forthwith send aid to the confederate in danger but in different proportions; namely, the Massachusetts, 100 men sufficiently armed and provided for such a service and journey, and each of the rest, 45 so armed and provided, or any less number, if less be required according to this proportion. . . . But in any such case of sending men for present aid, whether before or after such order or alteration, it is agreed that at the meeting of the commissioners for this confederation the cause of such war or invasion be duly considered; and if it appear that the fault lay in the parties so invaded that then that jurisdiction or plantation make just satisfaction, both to the invaders

whom they have injured, and bear all the charges of the war themselves, without requiring any allowance from the rest of the confederates toward the same. And, further, that if any jurisdiction see any danger of any invasion approaching, and there be time for a meeting, that in such case three magistrates of that jurisdiction may summon a meeting at such convenient place as themselves shall think meet, to consider and provide against the threatened danger; provided when they are met they may remove to what place they please. Only while any of these four confederates have but three magistrates in their jurisdiction, their request or summons from any two of them shall be accounted of equal force with the three mentioned in both the clauses of this article, till there be an increase of magistrates there.

6. It is also agreed that for the managing and concluding of all affairs proper and concerning the whole confederation, two commissioners shall be chosen by and out of each of these four jurisdictions; namely, two for the Massachusetts, two for Plymouth, two for Connecticut, and two for New Haven, being all in church fellowship with us, which shall bring full power from their several General Courts respectively to hear, examine, weigh, and determine all affairs of our war or peace leagues, aids, charges, and numbers of men for war, division of spoils and whatsoever is gotten by conquest, receiving of more confederates for plantations into combination with any of the confederates, and all things of like nature, which are the proper concomitants or consequents of such a confederation for amity, offense, and defense, not intermeddling with the government of any of the jurisdictions, which by the 3rd article is preserved entirely to themselves. . . . It is further agreed that these eight commissioners shall meet once every year, besides extraordinary meetings (according to the 5th article), to consider, treat, and conclude of all affairs belonging to this confederation. . . .

8. It is also agreed that the commissioners for this confederation hereafter at their meetings, whether ordinary or extraordinary, as they may have commission or opportunity, do endeavor to frame and establish agreements and orders in general cases of a civil nature, wherein all the plantations are interested, for preserving peace among themselves and preventing as much as may be all occasion of war or difference with others, as about the free and speedy passage of justice in every jurisdiction, to all the confederates equally as to their own, receiving those that remove from one plantation to another without due certificates; how all the jurisdictions may carry it toward the Indians, that they neither grow insolent nor be injured without due satisfaction, lest war break in upon the confederates through such miscarriage.

It is also agreed that if any servant run away from his master into any other of these confederated jurisdictions, that in such case, upon the certificate of one magistrate in the jurisdiction out of which the said servant fled, or upon other due proof, the said servant shall be delivered either to his master or any other that pursues and brings such certificate or proof. And that upon the escape of any prisoner whatsoever, or fugitive for any criminal cause, whether breaking prison, or getting from the officer, or otherwise escaping, upon the certificate of two magistrates of the jurisdiction out of which the escape is made, that he was a prisoner, or such an offender at the time of the escape, the magistrates, or some of them of that jurisdiction where for the present the said prisoner or fugitive abides, shall forthwith grant such a warrant as the case will bear for the apprehending of any such person, and the delivery of him into the hands of the officer or other person who pursues him. And if there be help required for the safe returning of any such offender, then it shall be granted to him that craves the same, he paying the charges thereof.

9. And for that the justest wars may be

of dangerous consequence, especially to the smaller plantations in these United Colonies, it is agreed that neither the Massachusetts, Plymouth, Connecticut, nor New Haven, nor any of the members of them, shall at any time hereafter begin, undertake, or engage themselves, or this confederation, or any part thereof in any war whatsoever (sudden exigents with the necessary consequents thereof excepted which are also to be moderated as much as the case will permit) without the consent and agreement of the forenamed eight commissioners, or at least six of them, as in the 6th article is provided; and that no charge be required of any of the confederates in case of a defensive war till the said commissioners have met and approved the justice of the war, and have agreed upon the sum of money to be levied, which sum is then to be paid by the several confederates in proportion according to the 4th article. . . .

11. It is further agreed that if any of the confederates shall hereafter break any of these present articles, or be any other ways injurious to any one of the other jurisdictions, such breach of agreement or injury shall be duly considered and ordered by the commissioners for the other jurisdictions, that both peace and this present confederation may be entirely preserved without violation.

35.

Anonymous: New England's First Fruits

The earliest educational efforts among the New England colonists were in the home, yet the efforts were earnest and reflected a strong desire for an educated citizenry. For reasons set forth in the following document, the leaders of the Massachusetts Bay Colony early determined to establish a school of higher education, to which end the General Court appropriated the very considerable sum of £400. The project was delayed for a time, but, in 1636, a Board of Overseers was appointed, a house was purchased in Cambridge, and a professor was engaged. In 1638, when a certain John Harvard died, leaving his library and half his estate to the enterprise, it was named Harvard College in his honor. The pamphlet reprinted here in part was published primarily as an appeal for funds. These were steadily forthcoming, despite the colony's lack of capital. From as distant a point as New Haven, farmers sent gifts of wheat, wampum, malt, corn, and apples in support of the college.

Source: MHSC, 1792, I, pp. 242-248.

After God had carried us safe to New England, and we had built our houses, provided necessaries for our livelihood, reared convenient places for God's worship, and settled the civil government, one of the next things we longed for and looked after was to advance learning and perpetuate it to posterity; dreading to leave an illiterate ministry to the churches, when our present ministers shall lie in the dust. And as we were thinking and consulting how to effect this great work, it pleased God to stir up the heart of one Mr. Harvard (a godly gentleman and a lover of learning, there living among us) to give the one-half of his estate (it being in all about £1,700) toward the erecting of a college, and all his library. After him, another gave £300; others after them cast in more; and the public hand of the state added the rest. The college was, by common consent, appointed to be at Cambridge (a place very pleasant and accommodate) and is called (according to the name of the first founder) Harvard College.

The edifice is very fair and comely within and without, having in it a spacious hall where they daily meet at commons, lectures, and exercises; and a large library with some books to it, the gifts of diverse of our friends, their chambers and studies also fitted for and possessed by the students, and all other rooms of office necessary and convenient with all needful offices thereto belonging. And by the side of the college, a fair grammar school for the training up of young scholars and fitting of them for academical learning, that still as they are judged ripe they may be received into the college of this school. Master Corlet is the master who has very well approved himself for his abilities, dexterity, and painfulness in teaching and education of the youths under him.

Over the college is Master Dunster placed as president, a learned, a conscionable, and industrious man, who has so trained up his pupils in the tongues and arts, and so seasoned them with the principles of divinity and Christianity, that we have to our great comfort (and in truth) beyond our hopes, beheld their progress in learning and godliness also. The former of these has appeared in their public declamations in Latin and Greek, and disputations logic and philosophy which they have been wonted (besides their ordinary exercises in the college hall) in the audience of the magistrates, ministers, and other scholars for the probation of their growth in learning, upon set days, constantly once every month to make and uphold. The latter has been manifested in sundry of them by the savory breathings of their spirits in their godly conversation; insomuch that we are confident, if these early blossoms may be cherished and warmed with the influence of the friends of learning and lovers of this pious work, they will, by the help of God, come to happy maturity in a short time.

Over the college are twelve overseers chosen by the General Court, six of them are of the magistrates, the other six of the ministers, who are to promote the best good of it and (having a power of influence into all persons in it) are to see that everyone be diligent and proficient in his proper place.

Rules and Precepts That Are Observed in the College.

1. When any scholar is able to understand Tully, or suchlike classical Latin author extempore, and make and speak true Latin in verse and prose, *suo ut aiunt Marte* [by his own effort, as they say]; and decline perfectly the paradigms of nouns and verbs in the Greek tongue, let him then and not before be capable of admission into the college.

2. Let every student be plainly instructed and earnestly pressed to consider well the main end of his life and studies is *to know God and Jesus Christ which is eternal life* (John 17:3), and therefore to lay Christ in the bottom as the only foundation of all sound knowledge and learning. And seeing the Lord only gives wisdom, let everyone seriously set himself by prayer in secret to seek it of Him (Prov. 2:3).

3. Everyone shall so exercise himself in reading the Scriptures twice a day that he shall be ready to give such an account of his proficiency therein, both in theoretical observations of the language and logic, and in practical and spiritual truths, as his tutor shall require, according to his ability; seeing *the entrance of the word giveth light, it giveth understanding to the simple* (Ps. 119:130).

4. That they eschewing all profanation of God's name, attributes, word, ordinances, and times of worship do study with good

conscience, carefully to retain God and the love of His truth in their minds, else let them know that (notwithstanding their learning) God may give them up to strong delusions, and, in the end, to a reprobate mind (II Thess. 2:11, 12; Rom. 1:28).

5. That they studiously redeem the time; observe the general hours appointed for all the students and the special hours for their own classes; and then diligently attend the lectures, without any disturbance by word or gesture. And if in anything they doubt, they shall inquire as of their fellows, so (in case of nonsatisfaction) modestly of their tutors.

6. None shall under any pretense whatsoever frequent the company and society of such men as lead an unfit and dissolute life. Nor shall any without his tutor's leave, or (in his absence) the call of parents or guardians, go abroad to other towns.

7. Every scholar shall be present in his tutor's chamber at the 7th hour in the morning, immediately after the sound of the bell, at his opening the Scripture and prayer, so also at the 5th hour at night, and then give account of his own private reading, as aforesaid in particular the 3rd, and constantly attend lectures in the hall at the hours appointed. But if any (without necessary impediment) shall absent himself from prayer or lectures, he shall be liable to admonition if he offend above once a week.

8. If any scholar shall be found to transgress any of the laws of God or the school, after twice admonition, he shall be liable, if not *adultus* [adult] to correction; if *adultus*, his name shall be given up to the overseers of the college that he may be admonished at the public monthly act.

The Times and Order Of Their Studies, Unless Experience Shall Show Cause To Alter. . . .

EVERY SCHOLAR that, on proof, is found able to read the originals of the Old and New Testament into the Latin tongue, and to resolve them logically, withal being of godly life and conversation, and at any public act has the approbation of the overseers and master of the college, is fit to be dignified with his first degree.

Every scholar that gives up in writing a system, or synopsis, or sum of logical, natural and moral philosophy, arithmetic, geometry, and astronomy, and is ready to defend his theses or positions, withal skilled in the originals as abovesaid, and of godly life and conversation, and so approved by the overseers and master of the college, at any public act, is fit to be dignified with his second degree.

The Manner Of The Late Commencement, Expressed In A Letter Sent Over From The Governor, And Diverse Of The Ministers, Their Own Words These.

THE STUDENTS of the first classes that have been these four years trained up in university learning (for their ripening in the knowledge of the tongues and arts) and are approved for their manners, as they have kept their public acts in former years, ourselves being present at them; so have they lately kept two solemn acts for their commencement, when the governor, magistrates, and the ministers from all parts, with all sorts of scholars and others in great numbers were present, and did hear their exercises; which were Latin and Greek orations and declamations, and Hebrew analysis, grammatical, logical, and rhetorical of the Psalms, and their answers and disputations in logical, ethical, physical, and metaphysical questions; and so were found worthy of the first degree (commonly called Bachelor) *pro more Academiarum in Anglia* [according to the custom of the academies in England]: being first presented by the president to the magistrates and ministers, and by him, upon their approbation, solemnly admitted unto the same degree, and a book of arts delivered into each of their hands, and power given them to read lectures in the hall upon any of the arts, when they shall be thereunto called, and a liberty of studying in the library.

All things in the college are at present like to proceed even as we can wish, may it but please the Lord to go on with His blessings in Christ, and stir up the hearts of His faithful and able servants in our own native country, and here (as He has graciously begun) to advance this honorable and most helpful work; the beginnings whereof and progress hitherto (generally) do fill our hearts with comfort, and raise them up to much more expectation of the Lord's goodness for us hereafter, for the good of posterity and the churches of Christ Jesus.

THUS FAR HAS THE GOOD HAND of God favored our beginning. See whether He has not engaged us to wait still upon His goodness for the future by such further remarkable passages of His providence to our plantation in such things as these:

I. In sweeping away great multitudes of the natives by the smallpox, a little before we went thither, that He might make room for us there.

II. In giving such marvelous safe passage from first to last, to so many thousands that went thither, the like has hardly been ever observed in any sea voyages.

III. In blessing us generally with health and strength, as much as ever (we might truly say) more than ever in our native land; many that were tender and sickly here are stronger and heartier there. That whereas diverse other plantations have been the graves of their inhabitants and their numbers much decreased, God has so prospered the climate to us that our bodies are hailer, and children there born stronger, whereby our numbers [are] exceedingly increased.

IV. In giving us such peace and freedom from enemies, when almost all the world is on a fire that (excepting that short trouble with the Pequots) we never heard of any sound of war to this day. And in that war which we made against them, God's hand from heaven was so manifested that a very few of our men, in a short time, pursued through the wilderness, slew and took prisoners about 1,400 of them, even all they could find, to the great terror and amazement of all the Indians to this day; so that the name of the Pequots (as of Amaleck) is blotted out from under heaven, there being not one that is or (at least) dare call himself a Pequot.

V. In subduing those erroneous opinions carried over from hence by some of the passengers, which for a time infested our church's peace, but (through the goodness of God) by conference preaching, a general assembly of learned men, magistrates' timely care, and, lastly, by God's own hand from heaven, in most remarkable strokes upon some of the chief fomenters of them, the matter came to such a happy conclusion that most of the seduced came humbly and confessed their errors in our public assemblies and abide to this day constant in the truth. The rest (that remained obstinate), finding no fit market there to vent their wares, departed from us to an island far off; some of whom also since that time have repented and returned to us and are received again into our bosoms. And from that time, not any unsound, unsavory, and giddy fancy have dared to lift up his head or abide the light among us.

VI. In settling and bringing civil matters to such a maturity in a short time among us, having planted fifty towns and villages, built thirty or forty churches, and more ministers' houses, a castle, a college, prisons, forts . . . and all these upon our own charges, no public hand reaching out any help; having comfortable houses, gardens, orchards, grounds fenced, cornfields, etc., and such a form and face of a commonwealth appearing in all the plantation, that strangers from other parts, seeing how much is done in so few years, have wondered at God's blessing on our endeavors.

VII. In giving such plenty of all manner of food in a wilderness, insomuch that all kinds of flesh, among the rest, store of venison in its season; fish both from sea and fresh water; fowl of all kinds, wild and tame; store of white meat, together with all sorts of English grain, as well as Indian, are plentiful among us; as also roots, herbs, and fruit, which being better digested by the sun, are far more fair, pleasant, and wholesome than here.

VIII. In prospering hemp and flax so well, that it is frequently sown, spun, and woven into linen cloth (and in a short time may serve for cordage); and so with cotton-wool (which we may have at very reasonable rates from the island); and our linen yarn, we can make dimities and fustians for our summer clothing. And having a matter of 1,000 sheep, which prosper well, to begin withal, in a competent time we hope to have woolen cloth there made. And great and small cattle, being now very frequently killed for food; their skins will afford us leather for boots and shoes and other uses. So that God is leading us by the hand into a way of clothing.

IX. In affording us many materials (which in part already are, and will in time further be, improved) for staple commodities, to supply all other defects, as:

1. Furs, beaver, otter, etc.

2. Clapboard, hoops, pipestaves, masts.

3. English wheat and other grain for Spain and West Indies; and all other provisions for victualing of ships.

4. Fish, as cod, haddock, herrings, mackerel, bass, sturgeon, seals, whales, seahorse.

5. Oil of sundry sorts, of whale, seahorse, etc.

6. Pitch and tar, rosin and turpentine, having pines, spruce, and pitch trees in our country to make these on.

7. Hemp and flax.

8. Minerals discovered and proved, as of iron in sundry places, black lead (many other in hopes) for the improving of which we are now about to carry over servants and instruments with us.

9. (Besides many boats, shallops, hoys, lighters, pinnaces) we are in a way of building ships, of 100, 200, 300, 400 tons, five of them are all ready at sea; many more in hand at this present, we being much encouraged herein, by reason of the plenty and excellency of our timber for that purpose, and seeing all the materials will be had there in short time.

10. In giving of such magistrates as are all of them godly men and members of our churches, who countenance those that be good and punish evildoers, that a vile person dares not lift up his head; nor need a godly man to hang it down, that (to God's praise be it spoken) one may live there from year to year and not see a drunkard, hear an oath, or meet a beggar. Now where sin is punished, and judgment executed, God is wont to bless that place and protect it. . . .

11. In storing that place with very many of His own people, and diverse of them eminent for godliness, now where His people are, there is His presence, and promise to be in the midst of them, a mighty God to save, and to joy over them with singing. . . .

12. Above all our other blessings, in planting His own name and precious ordinances among us (we speak it humbly and in His fear), our endeavor is to have all His own institutions, and no more than His own, and all those in their native simplicity, without having any humane dressings; having a liberty to enjoy all that God commands, and yet urged to nothing more than He commands. Now, wheresoever He records His name, thither He will come and bless. . . .

1646

36.

JOHN ELIOT: Puritan Missions to the Indians

*Attempts to Christianize the Indians in and around the Massachusetts colony were made
from the beginning, despite the difficulty of inculcating Puritan ethical values in a people
with so different a culture. The missionary spirit of one of the most zealous of the
Puritans, John Eliot, known as New England's "Apostle to the Indians," was undaunted by
frequent disappointments, and, in fact, he converted many Indians in the vicinity of
Massachusetts Bay. The following selection, taken from Eliot's* The Day-Breaking, if
not the Sun-Rising of the Gospell with the Indians in New-England, *reveals the strictness
with which the Puritans enforced their beliefs among the Indians. The pamphlet first
appeared in London under the pseudonym John Wilson.*

Source: MHSC, 3rd series, III, pp. 3-23.

METHINKS NOW that it is with the Indians as
it was with our New English ground when
we first came over — there was scarce any
man that could believe that English grain
would grow, or that the plow could do any
good in this woody and rocky soil. And
thus they continued in this supine unbelief
for some years, till experience taught them
otherwise; and now all see it to be scarce
inferior to Old English tillage, but bears
very good burdens. So we have thought of
our Indian people, and, therefore, have been
discouraged to put plow to such dry and
rocky ground, but God, having begun thus
with some few, it may be they are better
soil for the gospel than we can think.

I confess I think no great good will be
done till they be more civilized. But why
may not God begin with some few to
awaken others by degrees? Nor do I expect

any great good will be wrought by the English (leaving secrets to God, although the
English surely begin and lay the first stones
of Christ's kingdom and temple among
them), because God is wont ordinarily to
convert nations and peoples by some of
their own countrymen who are nearest to
them and can best speak, and, most of all,
pity their brethren and countrymen. But
yet, if the least beginnings be made by the
conversion of two or three, it is worth all
our time and travails, and cause of much
thankfulness for such seeds, although no
great harvests should immediately appear.

Surely this is evident, first, that they never heard heartbreaking prayer and preaching
before now in their own tongue, that we
know of. Second, that there were never
such hopes of a dawning of mercy toward
them as now. Certainly those abundant

tears which we saw shed from their eyes argue a mighty and blessed presence of the Spirit of Heaven in their hearts, which when once it comes into such kind of spirits will not easily out again.

The chief use that I can make of these hopeful beginnings, besides rejoicing for such shinings, is from Is. 2:5: "Oh, house of Israel, let us walk in the light of the Lord," considering that these blind natives begin to look toward God's mountain now.

The observations I have gathered by conversing with them are such as these:

1. That none of them . . . derided God's messenger: Woe unto those English that are grown bold to do that which Indians will not — heathens dare not.

2. That there is need of learning in ministers who preach to Indians, much more to Englishmen and gracious Christians, for these had sundry philosophical questions which some knowledge of the arts must help to give answer to; and without which these would not have been satisfied. Worse than Indian ignorance has blinded their eyes that renounce learning as an enemy to gospel ministries.

3. That there is no necessity of extraordinary gifts nor miraculous signs always to convert heathens . . . for we see the Spirit of God working mightily upon the hearts of these natives in an ordinary way, and I hope will, they being but a remnant, the Lord using to show mercy to the remnant. For there be but few that are left alive from the plague and pox, which God sent into those parts; and, if one or two can understand, they usually talk of it as we do of news — it flies suddenly far and near, and truth scattered will rise in time, for ought we know.

4. If Englishmen begin to despise the preaching of faith and repentance and humiliation for sin, yet the poor heathens will be glad of it and it shall do good to them; for so they are and so it begins to do. The Lord grant that the foundation of our English woe be not laid in the ruin and contempt of those fundamental doctrines of faith, repentance, humiliation for sin, etc., but rather relishing the novelties and dreams of such men as are surfeited with the ordinary food of the Gospel of Christ. Indians shall weep to hear faith and repentance preached, when Englishmen shall mourn, too late, that are weary of such truths.

5. That the deepest estrangements of man from God is no hindrance to His grace nor to the spirit of grace; for what nation or people ever so deeply degenerated since Adam's fall as these Indians, and yet the Spirit of God is working upon them?

6. That it is very likely if ever the Lord convert any of these natives that they will mourn for sin exceedingly and, consequently, love Christ dearly; for, if by a little measure of light such heartbreakings have appeared, what may we think will be when more is let in? They are some of them very wicked, some very ingenious. These latter are very apt and quick of understanding and naturally sad and melancholy (a good servant to repentance); and, therefore, there is the greater hope of great heartbreakings if ever God brings them effectually home, for which we should affectionately pray. . . .

We have cause to be very thankful to God who has moved the hearts of the General Court to purchase so much land for them to make their town in which the Indians are much taken with. And it is somewhat observable that, while the court were considering where to lay out their town, the Indians (not knowing of anything) were about that time consulting about laws for themselves, and their company who sit down with Waaubon. There were ten of them; two of them are forgotten.

Their laws were these:

1. That if any man be idle a week, at most a fortnight, he shall pay 5s.

2. If any unmarried man shall lie with a young woman unmarried, he shall pay 20s.

3. If any man shall beat his wife, his hands shall be tied behind him and [he shall

be] carried to the place of justice to be severely punished.

4. Every young man, if not another's servant and if unmarried, he shall be compelled to set up a wigwam and plant for himself, and not live shifting up and down to other wigwams.

5. If any woman shall not have her hair tied up but hang loose or be cut as men's hair, she shall pay 5s.

6. If any woman shall go with naked breasts, [she] shall pay 2s. 6d.

7. All those men that wear long locks shall pay 5s.

8. If any shall kill their lice between their teeth, they shall pay 5s. This law, though ridiculous to English ears, yet tends to preserve cleanliness among Indians.

It is wonderful in our eyes to understand by these two honest Indians what prayers Waaubon and the rest of them use to make, for he that preaches to them professes he never yet used any of their words in his prayers, from whom otherwise it might be thought that they had learned them by rote. One is this:

Amanaomen Jehovah tabassen metagh.

(Take away Lord my stony heart.)

Another:

Chechesom Jehovah kekowhogkew.

(Wash Lord my soul.)

Another:

(Lord lead me, when I die, to heaven.)

These are but a taste. They have many more, and these more enlarged than thus expressed, yet what are these but the sprinklings of the spirit and blood of Christ Jesus in their hearts?

And it is no small matter that such dry, barren, and long-accursed ground should yield such kind of increase in so small a time. I would not readily commend a fair day before night, nor promise much of such kind of beginnings, in all persons, nor yet in all of these, for we know the profession of very many is but a mere paint, and their best graces nothing but mere flashes and

pangs, which are suddenly kindled and as soon go out and are extinct again. Yet God does not usually send His plow and seedsman to a place but there is at least some little piece of good ground, although three to one be naught. And methinks the Lord Jesus would never have made so fit a key for their locks, unless He had intended to open some of their doors, and so to make way for His coming in. He that God has raised up and enabled to preach unto them is a man (you know) of a most sweet, humble, loving, gracious, and enlarged spirit, whom God hath blessed, and surely will still delight in and do good by.

I did think never to have opened my mouth to any to desire those in England to further any good work here, but now I see so many things inviting to speak in this business that it were well if you did lay before those that are prudent and able these considerations:

1. That it is pretty heavy and chargeable to educate and train up those children which are already offered us, in schooling, clothing, diet, and attendance, which they must have.

2. That in all probability, many Indians in other places, especially under our jurisdiction, will be provoked by this example in these, both to desire preaching and also to send their children to us, when they see that some of their fellows fare so well among the English, and the civil authority here so much favoring and countenancing of these; and if many more come in, it will be more heavy to such as only are fit to keep them, and yet have their hands and knees enfeebled so many ways besides.

3. That if any shall do anything to encourage this work, that it may be given to the college for such an end and use, that so from the college may arise the yearly revenue for their yearly maintenance. I would not have it placed in any particular man's hands for fear of cozenage or misplacing or careless keeping and improving; but at the

John Eliot, portrait by an anonymous painter, 1659

ed among us and instructed by us, complaining to us that they were not able to give anything to the English for their education. For this reason, there are, therefore, preparations made toward the schooling of them, and setting up a school among them or very near unto them. Sundry questions also were propounded by them to us, and of us to them; one of them being asked, "What is sin?" He answered, "A naughty heart." Another old man complained to us of his fears, viz., that he was fully purposed to keep the Sabbath, but still he was in fear whether he should go to hell or heaven; and thereupon the justification of a sinner by faith in Christ was opened unto him as the remedy against all fears of hell. Another complained of other Indians that did revile them and call them rogues and suchlike speeches for cutting off their locks, and for cutting their hair in a modest manner as the New English generally do; for since the Word has begun to work upon their hearts, they have discerned the vanity and pride which they placed in their hair, and have, therefore, of their own accord (none speaking to them that we know of), cut it modestly. They were therefore encouraged by some there present of chief place and account with us not to fear the reproaches of wicked Indians, nor their witchcraft and powwows and poisonings; but let them know that if they did not dissemble but would seek God unfeignedly, that they would stand by them, and that God also would be with them.

They told us also of diverse Indians who would come and stay with them three or four days and one Sabbath, and then they would go from them. But as for themselves, they told us they were fully purposed to keep the Sabbath, to which we encouraged them; and, night drawing on, [we] were forced to leave them for this time.

college it is under many hands and eyes, the chief and best of the country who have been and will be exactly careful of the right and comely disposing of such things. And, therefore, if anything be given, let it be put in such hands as may immediately direct it to the president of the college, who you know will soon acquaint the rest with it; and for this end if any in England have thus given anything for this end, I would have them speak to those who have received it to send it this way, which if it be withheld I think it is no less than sacrilege. But if God moves no hearts to such a work, I doubt not then but that [weaker] means shall have the honor of it in the Day of Christ.

THIS DAY BEING DECEMBER 9, the children being catechized, and that place of Ezekiel touching the dry bones being opened and applied to their condition, the Indians offered all their children to us to be educat-

1647

37.

Massachusetts School Law

In 1642, Massachusetts had passed the first American compulsory school law, which required the families of the colony to educate their youth. The law of 1647, reprinted here, took a substantial step forward in the development of elementary education by requiring every town of fifty families to provide a schoolmaster.

Source: *Records of the Governor and Company of the Massachusetts Bay in New England,* Nathaniel B. Shurtleff, ed., Boston, 1853, Vol. II, p. 203.

IT BEING ONE CHIEF PROJECT of that old deluder Satan to keep men from the knowledge of the Scriptures, as in former times by keeping them in an unknown tongue, so in these latter times by persuading from the use of tongues, that so at least the true sense and meaning of the original might be clouded by false glosses of saint-seeming deceivers, that learning may not be buried in the grave of our fathers in the church and commonwealth, the Lord assisting our endeavors:

It is therefore ordered that every township in this jurisdiction, after the Lord has increased them to the number of 50 householders, shall then forthwith appoint one within their town to teach all such children as shall resort to him to write and read, whose wages shall be paid either by the parents or masters of such children, or by the inhabitants in general, by way of supply, as the major part of those that order the prudentials of the town shall appoint; provided those that send their children be not oppressed by paying much more than they can have them taught for in other towns.

And it is further ordered that where any town shall increase to the number of 100 families or householders, they shall set up a grammar school, the master thereof being able to instruct youth so far as they may be fitted for the university, provided that if any town neglect the performance hereof above one year that every such town shall pay £5 to the next school till they shall perform this order.

38.

NATHANIEL WARD: The Simple Cobbler of Aggawam

After two generations of struggle, the Puritan cause in England reached a climax with the civil war of 1642-1646. During this chaotic period, the Puritans broke into sects or factions that threatened at first to exterminate one another; however, Oliver Cromwell prevailed upon them to tolerate each other's doctrinal differences. Such religious latitudinarianism profoundly shocked the Puritans of New England, and especially of Massachusetts, who were laboring to establish a society in the image of what they regarded as the one true church. In protest, Nathaniel Ward, the minister at Aggawam (Ipswich), completed a book in 1645 that affirmed the Massachusetts way of religious orthodoxy. The Simple Cobler of Aggawam . . . Willing to Help 'mend his Native Country, Lamentably Tattered, Both in the Upper-leather and Sole, with All the Honest Stitches He Can Take, *from which the following selection is extracted, was published for the first time in England in 1647 under the pseudonym Theodore de la Guard.*

Source: *The Simple Cobler of Aggawam in America,* David Pulsifer, ed., Boston, 1843, pp. 1-11.

EITHER I AM IN AN APOPLEXY, or that man is in a lethargy who does not now sensibly feel God shaking the heavens over his head, and the earth under his feet. The heavens so, as the sun begins to turn into darkness, the moon into blood, the stars to fall down to the ground; so that little light of comfort or counsel is left to the sons of men. The earth so, as the foundations are failing, the righteous scarce know where to find rest, the inhabitants stagger like drunken men; it is in a manner dissolved both in religions and relations. And no marvel, for they have defiled it by transgressing the laws, changing the ordinances, and breaking the everlasting Covenant. The truths of God are the pillars of the world, whereon states and churches may stand quiet if they will; if they will not, He can easily shake them off into delusions and distractions enough.

Satan is now in his passions; he feels his passion approaching; he loves to fish in roiled waters. Though that dragon cannot sting the vitals of the elect mortally, yet that Beelzebub can fly-blow their intellectuals miserably. The finer religion grows, the finer he spins his cobwebs; he will hold pace with Christ so long as his wits will serve him. He sees himself beaten out of gross idolatries, heresies, ceremonies, where the light breaks forth with power; he will, therefore, bestir him to prevaricate evangelical truths and ordinances, that if they will needs be walking, yet they shall *laborare varicibus* [work on legs with swollen veins], and not keep their path. He will put them out of time and place, assassinating for his engineers men of Paracelsian parts, well-complexioned for honesty; for such are fittest to mountebank his chemistry into sick churches and weak judgments.

Nor shall he need to stretch his strength overmuch in this work. Too many men having not laid their foundation sure, nor ballasted their spirits deep with humility and fear, are pressed enough of themselves to evaporate their own apprehensions. Those that are acquainted with story know it has ever been so in new editions of churches: such as are least able are most busy to putter in the rubbish, and to raise dust in the eyes of more steady repairers. Civil commotions make room for uncivil practices; religious mutations, for irreligious opinions; change of air discovers corrupt bodies; reformation of religion, unsound minds. He that has any well-faced fancy in his crown and does not vent it now, fears the pride of his own heart will dub him dunce forever. Such a one will trouble the whole Israel of God with his most untimely births, though he makes the bones of his vanity stick up, to the view and grief of all that are godly wise.

The devil desires no better sport than to see lightheads handle their heels, and fetch their careers in a time, when the roof of liberty stands open.

The next perplexed question, with pious and ponderous men, will be: What should be done for the healing of these comfortless exulcerations? I am the unablest adviser of a thousand, the unworthiest of ten thousand; yet I hope I may presume to assert what follows without just offense.

First, such as have given or taken any unfriendly reports of us New English should do well to recollect themselves. We have been reputed a colluvies [effluvium] of wild opinionists, swarmed into a remote wilderness to find elbowroom for our fanatic doctrines and practices. I trust our diligence past, and constant sedulity against such persons and courses, will plead better things for us. I dare take upon me, to be the herald of New England so far, as to proclaim to the world, in the name of our colony, that all Familists, Antinomians, Anabaptists, and other enthusiasts shall have free liberty to keep away from us, and such as will come to be gone as fast as they can, the sooner the better.

Second, I dare aver that God does no-

where in His Word tolerate Christian states, to give tolerations to such adversaries of His truth, if they have power in their hands to suppress them.

Here is lately brought us an extract of a Magna Carta, so called, compiled between the subplanters of a West Indian island; whereof the first article of constipulation firmly provides free stableroom and litter for all kind of consciences, be they never so dirty or jadish; making it actionable, yea, treasonable, to disturb any man in his religion, or to discommend it, whatever it be. We are very sorry to see such professed profaneness in English professors, as industriously to lay their religious foundations on the ruin of true religion; which strictly binds every conscience to contend earnestly for the truth; to preserve unity of spirit, faith, and ordinances, to be all like-minded, of one accord; every man to take his brother into his Christian care; to stand fast with one spirit, with one mind, striving together for the faith of the Gospel; and by no means to permit heresies or erroneous opinions. But God abhorring such loathsome beverages, has in His righteous judgment blasted that enterprise, which might otherwise have prospered well, for ought I know; I presume their case is generally known ere this.

If the devil might have his free option, I believe he would ask nothing else but liberty to enfranchise all false religions, and to embondage the true, nor should he need. It is much to be feared that lax tolerations upon state pretenses and planting necessities will be the next subtle stratagem he will spread, to distate the truth of God and supplant the peace of the churches. Tolerations in things tolerable, exquisitely drawn out by the lines of the Scripture, and pencil of the Spirit, are the sacred favors of truth, the due latitudes of love, the fair compartments of Christian fraternity; but irregular dispensations, dealt forth by the facilities of men, are the frontiers of error, the redoubts of schism, the perilous irritaments of carnal and spiritual enmity.

My heart has naturally detested four things: The standing of the Apocrypha in the Bible; foreigners dwelling in my country, to crowd our native subjects into the corners of the earth; alchemized coins; tolerations of diverse religions, or of one religion in segregant shapes. He that willingly assents to the last, if he examines his heart by daylight, his conscience will tell him he is either an atheist, or a heretic, or a hypocrite, or at best a captive to some lust. Poly-piety is the greatest impiety in the world. True religion is *ignis probationis*, which does *congregare homogenea segregare heterogenea* [ordeal by fire, which draws together the like and separates the unlike].

Not to tolerate things merely indifferent to weak consciences argues a conscience too strong; pressed uniformity in these, causes much disunity. To tolerate more than indifference, is not to deal indifferently with God; he that does it, takes His scepter out of His hand and bids Him stand by. Who has to do to institute religion but God. The power of all religion and ordinances lies in their purity; their purity in their simplicity; then are mixtures pernicious. I lived in a city where a Papist preached in one church, a Lutheran in another, a Calvinist in a third; a Lutheran one part of the day, a Calvinist the other, in the same pulpit; the religion of that place was but motley and meager, their affections leopardlike.

If the whole creature should conspire to do the Creator a mischief, or offer Him an insolency, it would be in nothing more than in erecting untruths against His truth, or by sophisticating His truths with humane medlies. The removing of some one iota in Scripture may draw out all the life and traverse all the truth of the whole Bible; but to authorize an untruth by a toleration of state is to build a sconce against the walls of heaven, to batter God out of His chair. To tell a practical lie is a great sin,

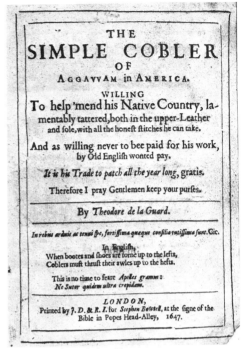

THE

SIMPLE COBLER

OF

AGGAWAM in AMERICA.

WILLING

To help 'mend his Native Country, lamentably tattered, both in the upper-Leather and sole, with all the honest stitches he can take.

And as willing never to bee paid for his work, by Old English wonted pay.

It is his Trade to patch all the year long, gratis.

Therefore I pray Gentlemen keep your purses.

By *Theodore de la Guard.*

In rebus arduis ac tenui spe, fortissima quaeque consilia tutissima sunt. Cic.

In English,

When bootes and shoes are torne up to the lefts, Coblers must thrust their awles up to the hefts.

This is no time to feare *Apelles gramm*: *Ne Sutor quidem ultra crepidam.*

LONDON,

Printed by *J. D. & R. I.* for *Stephen Bowtell*, at the signe of the Bible in Popes Head-Alley, 1647.

Title page from the first edition

but yet transient; but to set up a theoretical untruth is to warrant every lie that lies from its root to the top of every branch it has, which are not a few.

I would willingly hope that no member of the Parliament has skillfully ingratiated himself into the hearts of the House, that he might watch a time to midwife out some ungracious toleration for his own turn, and for the sake of that, some others. I would also hope that a word of general caution should not be particularly misapplied. I am the freer to suggest it, because I know not one man of that mind, my aim is general, and I desire may be so accepted. Yet good gentlemen, look well about you, and remember how Tiberius played the fox with the Senate of Rome, and how Fabius Maximus cropped his ears for his cunning.

That state is wise that will improve all pains and patience rather to compose than tolerate differences in religion. There is no

Divine truth but has much celestial fire in it from the Spirit of truth; nor no irreligious untruth, without its proportion of antifire from the spirit of error to contradict it. The zeal of the one, the virulency of the other, must necessarily kindle combustions. Fiery diseases seated in the spirit embroil the whole frame of the body; others, more external and cool, are less dangerous. They which divide in religion divide in God; they who divide in Him, divide beyond *genus generalissimum* [the most general species], where there is no reconciliation without atonement; that is, without uniting in Him, who is One, and in His truth, which is also one.

Wise are those men who will be persuaded rather to live within the pale of truth where they may be quiet, than in the purlieus, where they are sure to be hunted ever and anon, do authority what it can. Every singular opinion has a singular opinion of itself; and he that holds it a singular opinion of himself, and a simple opinion of all contrasentients; he that confutes them, must confute all three at once, or else he does nothing; which will not be done without more stir than the peace of the state or church can endure.

And prudent are those Christians that will rather give what may be given than hazard all by yielding nothing. To sell all peace of country, to buy some peace of conscience unseasonably, is more avarice than thrift, imprudence than patience. They deal not equally that set any truth of God at such a rate; but they deal wisely that will stay till the market is fallen.

My prognostics deceive me not a little, if once within three-seven years peace prove not such a pennyworth at most marts in Christendom, that he that would not lay down his money, his lust, his opinion, his will, I had almost said the best flower of his crown for it, while he might have had it, will tell his own heart he played the very ill husband.

Concerning tolerations I may further assert:

That persecution of true religion and toleration of false are the Jannes and Jambres to the Kingdom of Christ, whereof the last is far the worst. Augustine's tongue had not owed his mouth one penny rent though it had never spoken one word more in it, but this, *Nullum malum pejus libertate errandi* [There is no worse evil than mistaken liberty].

Frederick, duke of Saxon, spoke not one foot beyond the mark when he said he had rather the earth should swallow him up quick than he should give a toleration to any opinion against any truth of God.

He that is willing to tolerate any religion, or discrepant way of religion, besides his own, unless it be in matters merely indifferent, either doubts of his own or is not sincere in it.

He that is willing to tolerate any unsound opinion, that his own may also be tolerated, though never so sound, will for a need hang God's Bible at the devil's girdle.

Every toleration of false religions or opinions has as many errors and sins in it as all the false religions and opinions it tolerates, and one sound one more.

That state that will give liberty of conscience in matters of religion must give liberty of conscience and conversation in their moral laws, or else the fiddle will be out of tune and some of the strings crack.

He that will rather make an irreligious quarrel with other religions than try the truth of his own by valuable arguments and peaceable sufferings, either his religion or himself is irreligious.

Experience will teach churches and Christians that it is far better to live in a state united, though a little corrupt, than in a state whereof some part is incorrupt and all the rest divided. I am not altogether ignorant of the eight rules given by Orthodox divines about giving tolerations, yet with their favor I dare affirm.

That there is no rule given by God for any state to give an affirmative toleration to any false religion or opinion whatsoever; they must connive in some cases, but may not concede in any.

That the state of England (so far as my intelligence serves) might in time have prevented with ease, and may yet without any great difficulty, deny both toleration and irregular connivances, *salva republica* [a safe republic].

That if the state of England shall either willingly tolerate or weakly connive at such courses, the church of that kingdom will sooner become the devil's dancing school than God's temple; the civil state a bear garden than an exchange; the whole Realm a Pais base [Pays-Bas, Neth.], than an England. And what pity it is that that country which has been the staple of truth to all Christendom should now become the aviary of errors to the whole world, let every fearing heart judge.

I take liberty of conscience to be nothing but a freedom from sin and error. *Conscientia in tantum libera, in quantum ab errore liberata* [Conscience is free to the extent that it is freed from error]. And liberty of error nothing but a prison for conscience. Then small will be the kindness of a state to build such prisons for their subjects.

The Scripture says there is nothing makes free but truth, and Truth says there is no truth but one: If the states of the world would make it their sumoperous care to preserve this one truth in its purity and authority, it would ease them of all other political cares.

I am sure Satan makes it his grand if not only task to adulterate truth; falsehood is his sole scepter, whereby he first ruffled and ever since ruined the world.

If truth be but one, methinks all the opinionists in England should not be all in that one truth, some of them I doubt are out. He that can extract a unity out of such a disparity, or contract such a disparity into a unity, had need be a better artist than ever was Drebell.

If two centers (as we may suppose) be in one circle, and lines drawn from both to all the points of the compass, they will certainly cross one another, and probably cut through the centers themselves.

There is talk of a universal toleration, I would talk as loud as I could against it, did I know what more apt and reasonable sacrifice England could offer to God for His late performing all His heavenly truths than a universal toleration of all hellish errors, or how they shall make a universal reformation, but by making Christ's academy the devil's university, where any man may commence heretic *per saltum* [by a leap]; where he that is *filius diabolicus* [the devil's son], or *simpliciter pessimus* [outrightly most evil], may have his grace to go to hell *cum publico privilegio* [as a public right]; and carry as many after him as he can. . . .

If we will not be governed by God, we must be governed by tyrants.

WILLIAM PENN

1648

39.

The Cambridge Platform

In Massachusetts, the attempt to maintain religious orthodoxy only increased demands for toleration. The General Court was petitioned in 1646 to call a synod for the purpose of relaxing church discipline; the ruling clergy (which still included Winthrop) consented to the synod partly to forestall the intervention of more latitudinarian England in the colony's affairs. However, although the synod met promptly, both liberal and conservative forces delayed the enactment of a formal definition of authority for two years, by which time Cromwell's seizure of power in England had made interference from that quarter unlikely. As a result, the so-called Cambridge Platform of the synod, adopted in 1648, denied rather than affirmed the liberties that had been sought by the petitioners. The Platform, part of which appears below, is generally regarded as the high-water mark of clerical domination in Massachusetts.

Source: *The Creeds and Platforms of Congregationalism*, Williston Walker, ed., New York, 1893, pp. 194-237.

OF THE POWER OF THE CHURCH AND ITS PRESBYTERY

1. Supreme and lordly power over all the churches upon earth does only belong unto Jesus Christ, who is King of the church, and the Head thereof. He has the government upon His shoulders, and has all power given to Him, both in heaven and earth.

2. A company of professed believers ecclesiastically confederate as they are a church before they have officers, and without them; so even in that estate, subordinate church power, under Christ, delegated to them by Him, does belong to them in such a manner as is before expressed . . . and as flowing from the very nature and essence of a church; it being natural to all

bodies, and so unto a church body, to be furnished with sufficient power for its own preservation and subsistence.

3. This government of the church is a mixed government (and so has been acknowledged long before the term of independency was heard of), in respect of Christ, the Head and King of the church, and the sovereign power residing in Him, and exercised by Him, it is a monarchy; in respect of the body or brotherhood of the church and power from Christ granted unto them, it resembles a democracy; in respect of the presbytery and power committed unto them, it is an aristocracy. . . .

5. The power granted by Christ unto the body of the church and brotherhood is a prerogative or privilege which the church

does exercise: (1) in choosing their own officers, whether elders or deacons; (2) in admission of their own members and, therefore, there is great reason they should have power to remove any from their fellowship again. Hence, in case of offense, any one brother has power to convince and admonish an offending brother; and in case of not hearing him, to take one or two more to set on the admonition; and in case of not hearing them, to proceed to tell the church. And as his offense may require, the whole church has power to proceed to the public censure of him, whether by admonition or excommunication; and upon his repentance to restore him again unto his former communion. . . .

9. It belongs also unto the elders to examine any officers or members before they be received of the church; to receive the accusations brought to the church; and to prepare them for the church's hearing. In handling of offenses and other matters before the church, they have power to declare and publish the counsel and will of God touching the same, and to pronounce sentence with the consent of the church. Lastly, they have power, when they dismiss the people, to bless them in the name of the Lord.

10. This power of government in the elders does not anywise prejudice the power of privilege in the brotherhood as neither the power of privilege in the brethren does prejudice the power of government in the elders; but they may sweetly agree together. . . .

11. From the premises, namely, that the ordinary power of government belonging only to the elders, power of privilege remains with the brotherhood (as power of judgment in matters of censure, and power of liberty in matters of liberty). It follows that, in an organic church and right administration, all church acts proceed after the manner of a mixed administration, so as no church act can be consummated or perfected without the consent of both. . . .

OF THE ADMISSION OF MEMBERS INTO THE CHURCH

1. The doors of the churches of Christ upon earth do not by God's appointment stand so wide open that all sorts of people, good or bad, may freely enter therein at their pleasure; but such as are admitted thereto as members ought to be examined and tried first, whether they be fit and meet to be received into church society or not. . . .

5. A personal and public confession, and declaring of God's manner of working upon the soul, is both lawful, expedient, and useful, in sundry respects and upon sundry grounds. . . .

6. This profession of faith and repentance, as it must be made by such at their admission that were never in church society before, so nothing hinders but the same way also be performed by such as have formerly been members of some other church, and the church to which they now join themselves as members may lawfully require the same. . . .

7. The like trial is to be required from such members of the church as were born in the same, or received their membership and were baptized in their infancy, or minority, by virtue of the covenant of their parents, when, being grown up unto years of discretion, they shall desire to be made partakers of the Lord's Supper; unto which, because holy things must not be given unto the unworthy, therefore it is requisite that these as well as others should come to their trial and examination, and manifest their faith and repentance by an open profession thereof before they are received to the Lord's Supper, and otherwise not to be admitted thereunto.

Yet these church members that were so born, or received in their childhood, before they are capable of being made partakers of full communion, have many privileges which others (not church members) have not. They are in covenant with God; have the seal thereof upon them, viz., baptism; and so, if not regenerated, yet are in a more hopeful way of attaining regenerating grace and all the spiritual blessings both of the covenant and seal. They are also under church watch and, consequently, subject to the reprehensions, admonitions, and censures thereof for their healing and amendment, as need shall require.

OF CHURCH MEMBERS, THEIR REMOVAL FROM ONE CHURCH TO ANOTHER, AND OF LETTERS OF RECOMMENDATION AND DISMISSION

1. Church members may not remove or depart from the church, and so one from another, as they please, nor without just and weighty cause, but ought to live and dwell together, forasmuch as they are commanded not to forsake the assembling of themselves together. Such departure tends to the dissolution and ruin of the body, as the pulling of stones and pieces of timber from the building, and of members from the natural body, tend to the destruction of the whole.

2. It is therefore the duty of church members, in such times and places when counsel may be had, to consult with the church whereof they are members about their removal, that accordingly they have their approbation, may be encouraged, or otherwise desist. They who are joined with consent should not depart without consent, except forced thereunto. . . .

OF EXCOMMUNICATION AND OTHER CENSURES

1. The censures of the church are appointed by Christ for the preventing, removing, and healing of offenses in the church; for the reclaiming and gaining of offending brethren; for the deterring others from the like offenses; for purging out the leaven which may infect the whole lump; for vindicating the honor of Christ and of His church, and the holy profession of the Gospel; and for preventing the wrath of God that may justly fall upon the church if they should suffer His covenant and the seals thereof to be profaned by notorious and obstinate offenders.

2. If an offense be private (one brother offending another), the offender is to go and acknowledge his repentance for it unto his offended brother, who is then to forgive him; but if the offender neglect or refuse to do it, the brother offended is to go and convince and admonish him of it, between themselves privately. If, thereupon, the offender be brought to repent of his offense, the admonisher has won his brother; but if the offender hear not his brother, the brother offended is to take with him one or two more, that in the mouth of two or three witnesses, every word may be established (whether the word of admonition, if the offender receive it, or the word of complaint, if he refuse it); for if he refuse it, the offended brother is by the mouth of the elders to tell the church. And if he hear the church and declare the same by penitent confession, he is recovered and gained; and if the church discern him to be willing to hear yet not fully convinced of his offense, as in case of heresy, they are to dispense to him a public admonition; which declaring the offender to lie under the public offense of the church, does thereby withhold or suspend him from the holy fellowship of the Lord's Supper till his offense be removed by penitent confession. If he still continue obstinate, they are to cast him out by excommunication.

3. But if the offense be more public at first, and of a more heinous and criminal nature, to wit, such as are condemned by the light of nature, then the church, without such gradual proceeding, is to cast out the offender from their holy communion, for

the further mortifying of his sin and the healing of his soul, in the day of the Lord Jesus.

4. In dealing with an offender, great care is to be taken that we be neither overstrict or rigorous, nor too indulgent or remiss; our proceeding herein ought to be with a spirit of meekness, considering ourselves, lest we also be tempted; and that the best of us have need of much forgiveness from the Lord. Yet the winning and healing of the offender's soul, being the end of these endeavors, we must not daub with untempered mortar, nor heal the wounds of our brethren slightly. On some have compassion; others, save with fear.

5. While the offender remains excommunicate, the church is to refrain from all memberlike communion with him in spiritual things, and also from all familiar communion with him in civil things, further than the necessity of natural, or domestical, or civil relations do require; and are therefore to forbear to eat and drink with him, that he may be ashamed.

6. Excommunication being a spiritual punishment, it does not prejudice the excommunicate in, nor deprive him of, his civil rights, and therefore touches not princes or other magistrates in point of their civil dignity or authority. And the excommunicate, being but as a publican and a heathen, heathens being lawfully permitted to come to hear the word in church assemblies, we acknowledge therefore the like liberty of hearing the word may be permitted to persons excommunicate that is permitted unto heathen. And because we are not without hope of his recovery, we are not to account him as an enemy but to admonish him as a brother. . . .

OF THE COMMUNION OF CHURCHES ONE WITH ANOTHER

1. Although churches be distinct, and therefore may not be confounded one with another, and equal, and therefore have not dominion one over another, yet all the churches ought to preserve church communion one with another, because they are all united unto Christ, not only as a mystical but as a political head, whence is derived a communion suitable thereunto.

2. The communion of churches is exercised sundry ways: (1) by way of mutual care in taking thought for one another's welfare; (2) by way of consultation one with another, when we have occasion to require the judgment and counsel of other churches, touching any person or cause wherewith they may be better acquainted than ourselves. . . . (3) by way of admonition, to wit, in case any public offense be found in a church, which they either discern not or are slow in proceeding to use the means for the removing and healing of. . . . (4) by way of participation — the members of one church occasionally coming unto another, we willingly admit them to partake with us at the Lord's table, it being the seal of our communion not only with Christ, nor only with the members of our own church, but also with all the churches of the saints. In which regard, we refuse not to baptize their children presented to us, if either their own minister be absent or such a fruit of holy fellowship be desired with us. In like case, such churches as are furnished with more ministers ·than one do willingly afford one of their own ministers to supply the place of an absent or sick minister of another church for a needful season. . . .

OF THE CIVIL MAGISTRATES' POWER IN MATTERS ECCLESIASTICAL

1. It is lawful, profitable, and necessary for Christians to gather themselves into church estate, and therein to exercise all the ordinances of Christ, according unto the word, although the consent of the magis-

trate could not be had thereunto; because the apostles and Christians in their time did frequently thus practise when the magistrates, being all of them Jewish or pagan, and mostly persecuting enemies, would give no countenance or consent to such matters.

2. Church government stands in no opposition to civil government of commonwealths, nor any way entrenches upon the authority of civil magistrates in their jurisdiction; nor any whit weakens their hands in governing, but rather strengthens them and furthers the people in yielding more hearty and conscionable obedience unto them; whatsoever some ill-affected persons to the ways of Christ have suggested to alienate the affections of kings and princes from the ordinances of Christ; as if the Kingdom of Christ in His church could not rise and stand without the falling and weakening of their government, which is also of Christ. Whereas the contrary is most true, that they may both stand together and flourish, the one being helpful unto the other in their distinct and due administrations.

3. The power and authority of magistrates is not for the restraining of churches, or any other good works, but for helping in and furthering thereof; and therefore the consent and countenance of magistrates, when it may be had, is not to be slighted or lightly esteemed; but, on the contrary, it is part of that honor due to Christian magistrates to desire and crave their consent and approbation therein; which, being obtained, the churches may then proceed in their way with much more encouragement and comfort.

4. It is not in the power of magistrates to compel their subjects to become church members and to partake at the Lord's table; for the priests are reproved that brought unworthy ones into the sanctuary. Then, as it was unlawful for the priests, so it is as unlawful to be done by civil magistrates.

Those whom the church is to cast out if they were in, the magistrate ought not to thrust into the church nor to hold them therein.

5. As it is unlawful for church officers to meddle with the sword of the magistrate, so it is unlawful for the magistrate to meddle with the work proper to church officers. . . .

6. It is the duty of the magistrate to take care of matters of religion and to improve his civil authority for the observing of the duties commanded. . . .

7. The object of the power of the magistrate are not things merely inward, and so not subject to his cognizance and view, as unbelief, hardness of heart, erroneous opinions not vented; but only such things as are acted by the outward man. Neither is their power to be exercised in commanding such acts of the outward man, and punishing the neglect thereof, as are but mere inventions and devices of men, but about such acts as are commanded and forbidden in the word. Yea, such as the word does clearly determine, though not always clearly to the judgment of the magistrate or others, yet clearly in itself. In these, he of right ought to put forth his authority. . . .

8. Idolatry, blasphemy, heresy, venting corrupt and pernicious opinions that destroy the foundation, open contempt of the word preached, profanation of the Lord's Day, disturbing the peaceable administration and exercise of the worship and holy things of God, and the like are to be restrained and punished by civil authority.

9. If any church, one or more, shall grow schismatical, rending itself from the communion of other churches, or shall walk incorrigibly or obstinately in any corrupt way of their own, contrary to the rule of the word, in such a case the magistrate is to put forth his coercive power, as the matter shall require.

1650

40.

Charter of Harvard College

Harvard College was founded in 1636 to fill the need for a school to train a new generation of ministers for the Massachusetts Bay Colony. The school remained under the control of the ruling clergy until a formal charter was granted by the General Court of Massachusetts in 1650. The first president of Harvard, Henry Dunster, instigated the action that established the school as an independent corporation and is said to have written the first draft of the charter, which is still in effect today.

Source: Samuel A. Eliot, *A Sketch of the History of Harvard College and of its Present State*, Boston, 1848, pp. 130-133.

Whereas, through the good hand of God, many well-devoted persons have been, and daily are, moved and stirred up to give and bestow sundry gifts, legacies, lands, and revenues for the advancement of all good literature, arts, and sciences in Harvard College, in Cambridge in the county of Middlesex, and to the maintenance of the president and fellows, and for all accommodations of buildings and all other necessary provisions that may conduce to the education of the English and Indian youth of this country, in knowledge and godliness:

It is therefore ordered and enacted by this Court, and the authority thereof, that for the furthering of so good a work, and for the purposes aforesaid, from henceforth, that the said college, in Cambridge in Middlesex in New England, shall be a corpora-tion, consisting of seven persons; to wit, a president, five fellows, and a treasurer or bursar; and that Henry Dunster shall be the first president; Samuel Mather, Samuel Danforth, Masters of Art, [and] Jonathan Mitchell, Comfort Starr, and Samuel Eaton, Bachelors of Art, shall be the five fellows; and Thomas Danforth to be present trea-surer, all of them being inhabitants in the Bay, and shall be the first seven persons of which the said corporation shall consist. And that the said seven persons, or the greater number of them, procuring the pres-ence of the overseers of the college, and by their counsel and consent, shall have power and are hereby authorized, at any time or times, to elect a new president, fellows, or treasurer, so oft, and from time to time, as any of the said persons shall die or be removed; which said president and fellows, for the time being, shall forever hereafter, in name and fact, be one body politic and corporate in law, to all intents and purposes; and shall have perpetual succession; and shall be called by the name of president and fellows of Harvard College; and shall, from time to time, be eligible as aforesaid; and by that name they and their successors shall and may purchase and acquire to themselves, or take and receive upon free gift and donation, any lands, tenements, or hereditaments within this jurisdiction of the Massachusetts not exceeding £500 per annum, and any goods and sums of money whatsoever, to the use and behoof of the said president, fellows, and scholars of the said college; and also may sue and plead, or be sued and impleaded by the name aforesaid in all courts and places of judicature, within the jurisdiction aforesaid.

And that the said president, with any three of the fellows, shall have power and are hereby authorized, when they shall think fit, to make and appoint a common seal for the use of the said corporation. And the president and fellows, or major part of them, from time to time, may meet and choose such officers and servants for the college, and make such allowance to them and them also to remove; and after death or removal to choose such others, and to make, from time to time, such orders and bylaws for the better ordering and carrying on the work of the college as they shall think fit, provided the said orders be allowed by the overseers. And, also, that the president and fellows, or major part of them, with the treasurer, shall have power to make conclusive bargains for lands and tenements, to be purchased by the said corporation for valuable consideration.

And for the better ordering of the government of the said college and corporation, *be it enacted* by the authority aforesaid that the president and three more of the fellows shall and may from time to time, upon due

warning or notice given by the president to the rest, hold a meeting for the debating and concluding of affairs concerning the profits and revenues of any lands, and disposing of their goods (provided that all the said disposings be according to the will of the donors); and for direction in all emergent occasions; execution of all orders and bylaws; and for the procuring of a general meeting of all the overseers and society in great and difficult cases; and in case of nonagreement, in all which cases aforesaid, the conclusion shall be made by the major part, the said president having a casting voice, the overseers consenting thereunto. And that all the aforesaid transactions shall tend to and for the use and behoof of the president, fellows, scholars, and officers of the said college, and for all accommodations of buildings, books, and all other necessary provisions and furnitures, as may be for the advancement and education of youth, in all manner of good literature, arts, and sciences.

And further, *be it ordered* by this Court, and the authority thereof, that all the lands, tenements, and hereditaments, houses, or revenues, within this jurisdiction, to the aforesaid president or college appertaining, not exceeding the value of £500 per annum, shall, from henceforth, be freed from all civil impositions, taxes, and rates; all goods to the said corporation, or to any scholars thereof appertaining, shall be exempted from all manner of toll, customs, and excise whatsoever. And that the said president, fellows, and scholars, together with the servants and other necessary officers to the said president, or college appertaining, not exceeding ten, viz., three to the president and seven to the college belonging, shall be exempted from all personal civil offices, military exercises, or services, watchings, and wardings; and such of their estates, not exceeding £100 a man, shall be free from all country taxes or rates whatsoever, and no other.

41.

Anne Bradstreet: Two Poems

The earliest American poetess, Anne Bradstreet, arrived in Massachusetts with her husband Simon in 1630. For many years, she expressed her observations, her thoughts, and her emotions in poetry that was deeply influenced by a work highly favored by seventeenth-century readers, Du Bartas' "La Semaine." Mrs. Bradstreet's admiration for Du Bartas is reflected in the first poem reprinted below, "The Prologue" (1650). It was published along with others in London at the instigation of her brother-in-law and without her knowledge. The second poem, "To My Dear and Loving Husband," reveals her lifelong devotion to her husband. It was published posthumously in 1678.

Source: *The Works of Anne Bradstreet in Prose and Verse,* John Harvard Ellis, ed., Charleston, Mass., 1867, pp. 100-102, 394.

❦ THE PROLOGUE

To sing of wars, of captains, and of kings,
Of cities founded, commonwealths begun,
For my mean pen are too superior things:
Or how they all or each their dates have run,
Let poets and historians set these forth,
My obscure lines shall not so dim their worth.

But when my wondering eyes and envious heart
Great *Bartas'* sugared lines do but read o'er,
Fool I do grudge the Muses did not part
'Twixt him and me that overfluent store;
A *Bartas* can do what a *Bartas* will,
But simple I according to my skill.

From schoolboys' tongues no rhet'rick we expect,
Nor yet a sweet consort from broken strings,
Nor perfect beauty where's a main defect:
My foolish, broken, blemished Muse so sings
And this to mend, alas, no art is able,
'Cause nature made it so irreparable.

Nor can I, like that fluent sweet-tongued Greek
Who lisped at first, in future times speak plain;
By art he gladly found what he did seek —
A full requital of his striving pain.
Art can do much, but this maxim's most sure:
A weak or wounded brain admits no cure.

I am obnoxious to each carping tongue
Who says my hand a needle better fits,
A poet's pen all scorn I should thus wrong,
For such despite they cast on female wits:
If what I do prove well, it won't advance,
They'll say it's stolen, or else it was by chance.

But sure the antique Greeks were far more mild,
Else of our sex why feignéd they those nine,
And poesy made *Calliope's* own child?
So 'mongst the rest they placed the arts divine.
But this weak knot they will full soon untie —
The Greeks did nought but play the fools and lie.

Let Greeks be Greeks, and women what they are,
Men have precedency and still excel.
It is but vain unjustly to wage war,
Men can do best, and women know it well.
Preeminence in all and each is yours —
Yet grant some small acknowledgment of ours.

And oh ye high-flown quills that soar the skies,
And ever with your prey still catch your praise,
If e'er you deign these lowly lines your eyes,
Give thyme or parsley wreath, I ask no bays.
This mean and unrefinéd ore of mine
Will make your glistering gold but more to shine.

❧ TO MY DEAR AND LOVING HUSBAND

If ever two were one, then surely we.
If ever man were loved by wife, then thee;
If ever wife was happy in a man,
Compare with me ye women if you can.
I prize thy love more than whole mines of gold,
Or all the riches that the East doth hold.
My love is such that rivers cannot quench,
Nor ought but love from thee, give recompense.
Thy love is such I can no way repay,
The heavens reward thee manifold I pray.
Then while we live, in love let's so persevere,
That when we live no more, we may live ever.

42.

Connecticut Blue Laws

The kind of social legislation known as "blue laws" originated in the settlement at New Haven, but similar laws were enacted in many other colonies. Indeed, such laws, which restricted the manner of dress and prohibited certain types of "ungodly" activity, became widespread in New England even as Puritanism itself began to decline. They were often opposed, but the controversy about them died down during the Revolution, when other matters occupied men's minds. Legislation with a similar intent, such as Sunday closing laws, was revived in the following centuries, although in a different social context. Portions of the 1650 Code of the Connecticut General Court are reprinted below.

Source: *The Code of 1650, Being a Compilation of the Earliest Laws and Orders of the General Court of Connecticut, etc., etc.*, Hartford, 1822, pp. 20-94.

FORASMUCH AS THE FREE FRUITION of such liberties, immunities, privileges as humanity, civility and Christianity call for, as due to every man in his place and proportion, without impeachment and infringement, has ever been and ever will be the tranquillity and stability of churches and common-wealths; and the denial or deprival thereof, the disturbance, if not ruin of both: *It is thereof ordered by this Court, and authority thereof,* that no man's life shall be taken away; no man's honor or good name shall be stained; no man's person shall be arrested, restrained, banished, dismembered, nor any way punished; no man shall be deprived of his wife or children; no man's goods or estate shall be taken away from him nor anyways damaged, under color of law, or countenance of authority; unless it be by the virtue or equity of some express law of the country warranting the same, established by a General Court and sufficiently published, or in case of the defect of a law, in any particular case, by the Word of God.

ABILITY

It is ordered by this Court that all persons of the age of twenty-one years, and of right understanding and memory, whether ex-communicated, condemned, or otherways, have full power and liberty to make their wills, testaments, and other lawful aliena-tions of their goods and estates, and may be plaintiffs in a civil case. . . .

ARRESTS

It is ordered and decreed by this Court, and authority thereof, that no person shall be arrested or imprisoned for any debt or fine if the law can find any competent means of satisfaction otherwise from his estate, and if not, his person may be arrested and impris-oned, where he shall be kept at his own charge, not the plaintiff's, till satisfaction be made, unless the court that had cognizance of the cause, or some superior court, shall otherwise determine; provided, nevertheless, that no man's person shall be kept in prison for debt, but when there appears some estate which he will not produce, to which end, any court or commissioners authorized by the General Court, may administer an oath to the party, or any others suspected to be privy in concealing his estate, he shall satisfy by service, if the creditor require it; but shall not be sold to any but of the English nation. . . .

CAPITAL LAWS

1. If any man after legal conviction shall have or worship any other God but the Lord God, he shall be put to death. Deut. 13:6, 17:2; Ex. 22:20.

2. If any man or woman be a witch, that is, has or consults with a familiar spirit, they shall be put to death. Ex. 22:18; Lev. 20:27; Deut. 18:10, 11.

3. If any person shall blaspheme the name of God the Father, Son, or Holy Ghost with direct, express, presumptuous, or high-handed blasphemy, or shall curse in the like manner, he shall be put to death. Lev. 24:15, 16.

4. If any person shall commit any willful murder, which is manslaughter, committed upon malice, hatred, or cruelty, not in a man's necessary and just defense, nor by mere casualty against his will, he shall be put to death. Ex. 21:12-14; Num. 35:30,31.

5. If any person shall slay another through guile, either by poisonings or other such devilish practice, he shall be put to death. Ex. 21:14.

6. If any man or woman shall lie with any beast or brute creature, by carnal copulation, they shall surely be put to death, and the beast shall be slain and buried. Lev. 20:15, 16.

7. If any man lies with mankind as he lies with woman, both of them have committed abomination, they both shall surely be put to death. Lev. 20:13.

8. If any person commits adultery with a married or espoused wife, the adulterer and the adulteress shall surely be put to death. Lev. 20:10, 18:20; Deut. 22:23, 24.

9. If any man shall forcibly, and without consent, ravish any maid or woman that is lawfully married or contracted, he shall be put to death. Deut. 22:25.

10. If any man steals a man or mankind, he shall be put to death. Ex. 21:16.

11. If any man rise up by false witness, wittingly and of purpose to take away any man's life, he shall be put to death. Deut. 19:16, 18, 19.

12. If any man shall conspire or attempt any invasion, insurrection, or rebellion against the Commonwealth, he shall be put to death.

13. If any child or children above sixteen years old and of sufficient understanding shall curse or smite their natural father or mother, he or they shall be put to death; unless it can be sufficiently testified that the parents have been very unchristianly negligent in the education of such children, or so provoke them by extreme and cruel correction that they have been forced thereunto to preserve themselves from death, maiming. Ex. 21:15, 17; Lev. 20.

14. If any man have a stubborn and rebellious son of sufficient years and understanding, viz., sixteen years of age, which will not obey the voice of his father or the voice of his mother, and that when they have chastened him will not hearken unto them, then may his father and mother, being his natural parents, lay hold on him and bring him to the magistrates assembled in Court, and testify unto them that their son is stubborn and rebellious and will not obey their voice and chastisement, but lives in sundry notorious crimes, such a son shall be put to death. Deut. 21:20, 21. . . .

CHILDREN

FORASMUCH AS THE GOOD EDUCATION of children is of singular behoof and benefit to any commonwealth; and whereas many parents and masters are too indulgent and negligent of their duty in that kind: *It is therefore ordered by this Court, and authorized thereof,* that the selectmen of every town in the several precincts and quarters where they dwell shall have a vigilant eye over their brethren and neighbors, to see, first, that none of them shall suffer so much barbarism in any of their families, as not to endeavor to teach by themselves or others their children and apprentices so much learning as may enable them perfectly to read the English tongue, and knowledge of the capital laws, upon penalty of 20s. for each neglect therein. Also, that all masters of families do, once a week, at least, catechize their children and servants in the grounds and principles of religion, and if any be unable to do so much, that then, at the least, they procure such children or apprentices to learn some short orthodox catechism, without book, that they may be able to answer to the questions that shall be propounded to them out of such catechisms by their parents or masters, or any of the selectmen where they shall call them to a trial of what they have learned in this kind. And further, that all parents and masters do breed and bring up their children and apprentices in some honest, lawful calling, labor, or employment, either in husbandry or some other trade profitable for themselves and the Commonwealth, if they will not nor cannot train them up in learning, to fit them for higher employments. And if any of the selectmen, after admonition by them given to such masters of families, shall find them still negligent of their duty in the particulars aforementioned, whereby children and servants become rude, stubborn, and unruly, the said selectmen, with the help of two magistrates, shall take such children or apprentices from them and place them with some masters for years, boys till they come to twenty-one, and girls, eighteen years of age complete, which will more strictly look unto and force them to submit unto government, according to the rules of this order, if by fair means and former instructions they will not be drawn unto it. . . .

CRUELTY

It is ordered by this Court, and authority thereof, that no man shall exercise any tyranny or cruelty toward any brute creatures, which are usually kept for the use of man.

DAMAGES PRETENDED

It is ordered by this Court, that no man in any suit or action against another shall falsely pretend great damages or debts to vex his adversary; and if it shall appear any does so, the Court shall have power to set a reasonable fine on his head. . . .

ECCLESIASTICAL

FORASMUCH AS THE OPEN CONTEMPT of God's Word, and messengers thereof, is the desolating sin of civil states and churches, and that the preaching of the Word by those whom God does send is the chief ordinary means ordained by God for the converting, edifying, and saving the souls of the elect, through the presence and power of the Holy Ghost thereunto promised; and that the ministry of the Word is set up by God in His churches for those holy ends; and according to the respect or contempt of the same, and of those whom God has set apart for His own work and employment, the weal or woe of all Christian states, is much furthered and promoted: *It is therefore ordered and decreed,* that if any Christian, so called, within this jurisdiction, shall contemptuously bear himself toward the Word preached, or the messengers that are called to dispense the same in any congregation, when he does faithfully execute his service and office therein, according to the Will and Word of God, either by interrupting him in his preaching, or by charging him falsely with an error, which he has not taught, in the open face of the church, or like a son of Korah, cast upon his true doctrine, or himself, any reproach to the dishonor of the Lord Jesus, who has sent him, and to the disparagement of that His Holy Ordinance, and making God's ways contemptible and ridiculous, that every such person or persons, whatsoever censure the church may pass, shall, for the first scandal, be convented and reproved openly by the magistrates, at some lecture, and bound to their good behavior. And if a second time they break forth into the like contemptuous carriages, they shall either pay £5 to the public treasure, or stand two hours, openly, upon a block or stool four foot high, upon a lecture day, with a paper fixed on his breast written with capital letters, AN OPEN AND OBSTINATE CONTEMNER OF GOD'S HOLY ORDINANCES, that others may fear and be ashamed of breaking out into the like wickedness.

It is ordered and decreed by this Court, and authority thereof, that wheresoever the ministry of the Word is established, according to the order of the Gospel, throughout this jurisdiction, every person shall duly resort and attend thereunto respectively upon the Lord's Day, and upon such public fast days and days of thanksgiving as are to be generally kept by the appointment of authority. And if any person within this jurisdiction shall, without just and necessary cause, withdraw himself from hearing the public ministry of the Word, after due means of conviction used, he shall forfeit for his absence, from every such public meeting, 5s., all such offenses to be heard and determined by any one magistrate, or more, from time to time.

Forasmuch as the peace and prosperity of churches, and members thereof, as well as civil rights and liberties, are carefully to be maintained: *It is ordered by this Court and decreed,* that the civil authority here established has power and liberty to see the peace, ordinances, and rules of Christ be observed in every church, according to His Word; as also to deal with any church member in a way of civil justice, notwithstanding any church relation, office, or interest, so it be done in a civil and not in an

ecclesiastical way, nor shall any church censure degrade or depose any man from any civil dignity, office, or authority he shall have in the Commonwealth. . . .

GAMING

UPON COMPLAINT OF GREAT DISORDER, by the use of the game called shuffleboard, in houses of common entertainment, whereby much precious time is spent unfruitfully, and much waste of wine and beer occasioned: *It is therefore ordered and enacted by the authority of this Court,* that no person shall henceforth use the said game of shuffleboard in any such house, nor in any other house used as common for such purpose, upon pain for every keeper of such house to forfeit for every such offense 20s.; and for every person playing at the said game in any such house, to forfeit for every such offense 5s.; the like penalty shall be for playing in any place at any unlawful game. . . .

LYING

WHEREAS TRUTH IN WORDS as well as in actions is required of all men, especially of Christians, who are the professed servants of the Lord of Truth; and whereas all lying is contrary to truth, and some sorts of lies are not only sinful, as all lies are, but also pernicious to the public weal, and injurious to particular persons: *It is therefore ordered by this Court, and authority thereof,* that every person of the age of discretion, which is accounted fourteen years, who shall wittingly and willingly make or publish any lie which may be pernicious to the public weal, or tending to the damage or injury of any particular person, to deceive and abuse the people with false news or reports, and the same duly proved in any court, or before any one magistrate who has hereby power granted to hear and determine all offenses against this law, such persons shall be fined, for the first offense, 10s.; or if the party be unable to pay the same, then to be set in the stocks so long as the said Court or magistrate shall appoint, in some open place, not exceeding three hours. . . . And for all such as being under age of discretion, that shall offend in lying contrary to this order, their parents or masters shall give them due correction, and that in the presence of some officer, if any magistrate shall so appoint; provided, also, that no person shall be barred of his just action of slander, or otherwise, by any proceeding upon this order. . . .

MARRIAGE

FORASMUCH AS MANY PERSONS entangle themselves with rash and inconsiderate contracts for their future joining in marriage covenant, to the great trouble and grief of themselves and their friends, for the preventing thereof: *It is ordered by the authority of this Court,* that whosoever intends to join themselves in marriage covenant shall cause their purpose of contract to be published in some public place, and at some public meeting, in the several towns where such persons dwell, at the least eight days before they enter into such contract, whereby they engage themselves each to other; and that they shall forbear to join in marriage covenant at least eight days after the said contract.

And it is also ordered and declared, that no person whatsoever, male or female, not being at his or her own dispose, or that remains under the government of parents, masters, or guardians, or suchlike, shall either make or give entertainment to any motion or suit, in way of marriage, without the knowledge and consent of those they stand in such relation to, under the severe censure of the Court, in case of delinquency not attending this order; nor shall any third persons intermeddle in making any motion to any such without the knowledge and consent of those under whose government they are under the same penalty. . . .

SCHOOLS

IT BEING ONE CHIEF PROJECT of that old deluder, Satan, to keep men from the knowledge of the Scriptures, as in former times, keeping them in an unknown tongue, so in these latter times, by persuading them from the use of tongues, so that at least the true sense and meaning of the original might be clouded with false glosses of saint-seeming deceivers; and that learning may not be buried in the grave of our forefathers in church and Commonwealth. . . . *It is therefore ordered by this Court . . .* that every township within this jurisdiction, after the Lord has increased them to the number of fifty householders, shall then forthwith appoint one within their town to teach all such children, as shall resort to him, to write and read, whose wages shall be paid either by the parents or masters of such children or by the inhabitants in general, by way of supply, as the major part of those who order the prudentials of the town shall appoint; provided that those who send their children be not oppressed by paying much more than they can have them taught for in other towns.

And it is further ordered, that where any town shall increase to the number of one hundred families or householders, they shall set up a grammar school, the masters thereof being able to instruct youths so far as they may be fitted for the university. And if any town neglect the performance hereof, above one year, then every such town shall pay £5 per annum to the next such school till they shall perform this order.

The propositions concerning the maintenance of scholars at Cambridge, made by the commissioners, is confirmed.

And it is ordered, that two men shall be appointed in every town within this jurisdiction who shall demand what every family will give, and the same to be gathered and brought into some room, in March; and this to continue yearly, as it shall be considered by the commissioners.

43.

ADRIAEN VAN DER DONCK *et al.*: Criticisms of New Netherland

The Dutch settlements along the Delaware, Hudson, and Connecticut rivers, collectively called New Netherland, were beset by a variety of problems in the ten years preceding 1650. Among the more serious were Indian raids, encroachments by English colonists, and declining trade. The diverse nature of the population made unity of purpose impossible, and the policies of the governors, Willem Kieft and Peter Stuyvesant, seemed only to aggravate the situation. In 1650 a group of settlers led by Adriaen van der Donck drew up a paper entitled The Representation of New Netherland, *in which they aired their complaints to the West India Company, in Holland, which was charged with overseeing the colony's affairs. A selection from the report, which was especially critical of the two governors, is reprinted below. Fifteen years later, as a result of the second Anglo-Dutch War, New Netherland became an English colony.*

Source: *Collections of the New York Historical Society*, 2nd series, Vol. II, New York, 1849, pp. 288-321.

As WE SHALL SPEAK of the reasons and causes which have brought New Netherland into the ruinous condition in which it is now found to be, we deem it necessary to state the very first difficulties and, for this purpose, regard it as we see and find it in our daily experience. As far as our understanding goes, to describe it in one word (and none better presents itself), it is *bad government*, with its attendants and consequences, that is the true and only *foundation stone* of the decay and ruin of New Netherland. This government from which so much abuse proceeds is twofold; that is, in the fatherland by the managers and in this country. We shall first, briefly and in some order, point out the mistakes in fatherland and afterward proceed to show how abuses have grown up and obtained strength here.

The managers of the Company adopted a wrong course at first, and, as we think, had more regard for their own interest than for the welfare of the country, trusting rather to evil than just counsels. This is proven by the unnecessary expenses incurred from time to time, the heavy accounts of New Netherland, the registering of manors — in which business most of the managers themselves engaged and in reference to which they have regulated the trade — and finally the not peopling the country. It seems as if, from the first, the Company has sought to stock this land with their own employees, which was a great mistake, for when their time was out they returned home, taking nothing with them, except a little in their purses and a bad name for the country, in regard to its means of sustenance and in other respects. In the meantime, there was no profit, but, on the contrary, heavy monthly expenditures, as the accounts of New Netherland will show. . . .

Trade, without which, when it is legitimate, no country is prosperous, is by their acts so decayed that the like is nowhere else. It is more suited for slaves than freemen, in consequence of the restrictions upon it and the annoyances which accompany the exercise of the right of inspection. We approve of inspection, however, so far as relates to contraband. This contraband trade has ruined the country, though it is now excluded from every part of it by orders given by the managers to their officers. These orders should be executed without partiality, which is not always the case. The recognition [export duty] runs high, and of inspection and confiscation there is no lack; hence true trade is entirely diverted, except a little, which exists *pro forma* as a cloak to carry on smuggling.

In the meantime, the Christians are treated almost like Indians in the purchase of the necessaries with which they cannot dispense. This causes great complaint, distress, and poverty; as, for example, the merchants sell those goods which are liable to little depreciation at 100 percent and more profit, when there is no particular demand or scarcity of them. And the traders who come with small cargoes, and others engaged in the business, buy them up from the merchants and sell them again to the common man, who cannot do without them, oftentimes at 100 percent advance, and higher or lower according as it suits them. Upon liquors, which are liable to much leakage, they take more; and those who buy from them retail them in the same manner as we have described in regard to dry wares, and generally at as much profit; so that the goods are in first, second, and sometimes in third hands, at 100 and 200 percent and more advance.

We are not able to think of all the practices which are contrived for advancing individual gain. Little attention is given to populating the land. The people, moreover, have been driven away by harsh and unreasonable proceedings, for which Their Honors gave the orders; for the managers wrote to Director Kieft to prosecute when there was no offense and to consider a partial offense (*faute*) an entire one and so forth. . . .

The directors here, though far from their masters, were close by their profit. They have always known how to manage their own matters with little loss and under pretext of the public business. They have also conducted themselves just as if they were the sovereigns of the country. As they desired to have it, so always has it been; and as they willed, so was it done. "The managers," they say, "are masters in fatherland, but we are masters in this land." As they understand it, so it is; there is no appeal. And it has not been difficult for them hitherto to maintain this doctrine in practice; for the people were few and for the most part very simple and uninformed, and, besides, had transactions with the directors every day. As there were some intelligent men among them *who could go upon their own feet,* them it was sought to oblige.

They could not understand at first the arts of the directors, which were always subtle and dark, inasmuch as they were very frequently successful and for a long time quite advantageous. Director Kieft said himself, and let it be said also by others, that he was sovereign in this country, the same as the Prince in Netherland. This was told him several times here, and he never made any particular objection to it. The refusing to allow appeals, and other similar acts, prove clearly that in regard to us it is just as they say and not otherwise. The present director does the same; and, in the denial of appeal, he is at home. He asserts the maxim, "the Prince is above the law," and applies it so boldly to his own person that he is even ashamed of it himself.

These directors, having then the power in their own hands, can do and have done what they chose according to their goodwill and pleasure; and whatever was, was right, because it was agreeable to them. It is well known that those who accept power and use it to command what they will frequent-

ly command and will more than they
ought, whether it appear well or not. So
too there are always some persons who applaud such conduct, some out of a desire to
make mischief, others from fear; and yet
still complain with Jan Vergas *de clementia
ducis*, of the clemency of the duke.

But in order that we give nobody cause
to suspect that we *blow any too hard*, it will
be proper to illustrate by examples the government of Mr. Director Kieft at its close,
and the administration of Mr. Director
Stuyvesant just prior to the time of our departure thence. We frankly admit, however,
that we will not be able to speak of them
fully because they were conducted so secretly and with such duplicity and craft. We
will nevertheless expose some of their proceedings according to our ability, and thus
let the lion be judged of from his paw.

Casting our eyes upon the government of
Director Kieft, the church first meets us,
and we will therefore speak of the public
property, ecclesiastical and civil. . . .

Before the time that Director Kieft
brought the unnecessary war upon the
country, his principal aim and endeavors
were to provide well for himself and to
leave a great name after him, but without
any expense to himself or the Company. He
never did anything remarkable for the country by which it was improved. Thus he
considered the erection of a church a very
necessary public work, the more so as it
was contemplation to build one at that time
at Renselaers-Wyck. With this view, he
communicated with the church wardens —
of which body he himself was one — and
they willingly agreed to and seconded the
project. The place where it should stand
was then debated. The director contended
that it should be placed in the fort, and
there it was erected in spite of the others
and, indeed, as suitably as a fifth wheel to a
wagon; for, besides that the fort is small
and lies upon a point of land which must
be very valuable in case of an increase of

population, the church ought to be owned
by the congregation at whose cost it was
built. . . .

We must now speak of the property belonging to the church, and, to do the truth
no violence, we do not know that there has
ever been any, or that the church has any
income except what is given to it. There
has never been any exertion made either by
the Company or by the director to obtain
or provide any.

The bowl has been going round a long
time for the purpose of erecting a common
school and it has been built with words, but
as yet the first stone is not laid. Some materials only are provided. The money, nevertheless, given for the purpose has all
found its way out and is mostly spent; so
that it falls short and no permanent benefit
has as yet been derived from it.

For the poor, who are, however, otherwise well provided for, nothing is done except the alms collected among the people,
and some fines and donations of the inhabitants. A considerable portion of this money
is in the possession of the Company, who
have been spending it from time to time,
and have promised, for a year and upward,
to pay interest. Little attention, however, is
given to this promise, so that neither principal nor interest can be obtained from them.
Flying reports about asylums for orphans,
for the sick and aged, and the like have occasionally been heard but as yet no attempt,
order, or direction has been made in relation to them.

From all these facts, then, it sufficiently
appears that scarcely any proper care or diligence has been used by the Company or its
officers for any ecclesiastical property whatever — at least, nothing as far as is known
— from the beginning to this time; but, on
the contrary, great industry and exertion
have been used to attach and bind closely
to them their minions. . . .

And now let us proceed to the consideration of what public measures of a civil char-

acter had been adopted up to the time of our departure, in order to make manifest the diligence and care of the directors in this particular.

There was not, at first, under the government of Director Kieft, so much opportunity as there has since been; because the recognition of the peltries was then paid in the fatherland, and the freemen gave nothing for excise; but, after that public calamity, the rash war was brought upon us, the recognition of the peltries began to be collected in this country, and a beer excise was sought to be established, about which a conference was had. . . .

After the war was, as the director himself said, finished — though in our opinion it will never be finished until the country is populated — everyone hoped that this impost would be removed, but Director Kieft put off the removal until the arrival of a new director, who was delayed for some time thereafter. When finally he did appear, it was like the crowning of Rehoboam, for, instead of abolishing the beer excise, his first business was to impose a wine excise and other intolerable burdens; so that some of the commonalty, as they had no remedy, were constrained to remonstrate against the same. Instead, however, of obtaining the relief which they expected, they received abuse from the director. Subsequently a written answer was given them that a director like him usually had such large and ample powers that poor common people as are here made mistakes in relation to them and should submit to them without relief. Further attempts have accordingly been made from time to time to introduce new taxes and duties.

In fine, it was so managed in Director Kieft's time that a large yearly sum was received from the recognition and other sources, calculated to amount annually to 16,000 guilders, besides the recognition which was paid in the fatherland and which was paid in effect here by the poor com-

monalty; for the goods were thereby run up exorbitantly high and sold to them. In Director Stuyvesant's administration, the revenue has reached a much higher sum, and it is estimated that about 30,000 guilders are now derived yearly from the people by recognitions, confiscations, excise and other taxes.

Though it is not right that the more one has the more he should have, yet this was submitted to in order to give as much as possible, when it was designed for the public weal. And whereas in all the proclamations it was promised and declared that the money should be employed for laudable and necessary public works, let us now look for a moment and see what laudable public works there are in this country, and what fruits all the donations and contributions have hitherto borne. . . .

According to the proclamations during the administration of Director Kieft, if we rightly consider and examine them all, we cannot learn or discover that anything — we say *anything*, large or small — worth relating was done, built, or made which concerned or belonged to the commonalty, the church excepted, whereof we have heretofore spoken. Yea, it has gone on so badly and negligently that nothing has ever been designed, understood, or done that gave appearance of content to the people, even externally, but on the contrary, what came from the commonalty has even been mixed up with the effects of the Company, and even the Company's property and means have been everywhere neglected in order to make friends, to secure witnesses, and to avoid accusers about the management of the war.

The Negroes, also, who came from Tamandare, were sold for pork and peas, from the proceeds of which something wonderful was to be performed, but they just dripped through the fingers. There are, also, various other Negroes in this country, some of whom have been made free for their long service, but their children have remained slaves, though it is contrary to the laws of every people that anyone born of a Christian mother should be a slave and be compelled to remain in servitude.

It is impossible to relate everything that has happened. Whoever did not give his assent and approval was watched and, when it was convenient, was summoned. We submit to all intelligent persons to consider what fruit this has borne, and what a way this was to obtain good testimony. Men are by nature covetous, especially those who are needy. . . .

But to proceed now to the administration of Director Stuyvesant, and to see how affairs have been conducted up to the time of our departure. Mr. Stuyvesant has most all the time from his first arrival up to our leaving been busy building, laying masonry, making, breaking, repairing, and the like, but generally in matters of the Company and with little profit to it; for upon some things more was spent than they were worth. And though, at the first, he put in order the church, which came into his hands very much out of repair, and shortly afterward made a wooden wharf, both of which are very serviceable and convenient, yet after this time we do not know that anything has been done or made that is entitled to the name of a public work, though there has been income enough as is to be seen in the statement of the yearly revenue. Nothing more was afterward attempted, as is the case with dropsical people.

Thus, in a short time, very great discontent has sprung up on all sides, not only among the burghers, who had little to say, but also among the Company's officers themselves; so that various protests were made by them on account of the expense and waste consequent upon unnecessary councilors, officers, servants, and the like, who are not known by the mayors, and also on account of the monies and means which were given in common, being privately appropriated and used. But it was all

in vain — there was very little or no amendment; and the greater the endeavors to help, restore, and raise up everything, the worse has it been; for pride has ruled when justice dictated otherwise, just as if it were disgraceful to follow advice, and as if everything should come from one head. . . .

Great distrust has also been created among the inhabitants on account of Heer Stuyvesant being so ready to confiscate. There scarcely comes a ship in or near here which, if it does not belong to friends, is not regarded as a prize by him. There will be great pretenses (though little comes of them) made concerning these matters, about which we will not dispute; but confiscating has reached such a pitch in New Netherland that nobody who has any visible property considers it to be at all safe.

Besides this, the country of the Company is so taxed, and is burdened and kept down in such a manner, that the inhabitants are not able to appear beside their neighbors of Virginia or New England or to undertake any enterprise. It seems — and thus much is known by us — that all the inhabitants of New Netherland admit that the managers have scarce any care or regard for New Netherland, except when there is something to receive, for which reason, however, they receive less.

The great extremity of war into which we have been thrown clearly demonstrates that the managers care not whether New Netherland sink or swim; for, when, in that emergency, aid and assistance were sought from them — which they indeed were bound by honor and by promises half unsolicited, to grant, pursuant to the exemptions — they made no attempt to furnish them at their own expense. We let the expense go; they have never established any good order or regulation concerning it, although the plenitude of Their High Mightinesses had decreed and commanded it. Neither have they ever allowed the true causes and reasons of the war to be investigated, nor have they attempted to punish those who had rashly begun it. . . .

If the inhabitants, or we ourselves, go to the director or other officers of the Company and speak of the flourishing condition of our neighbors, and complain of our own desolate and ruinous state, we get for answer from them that they see and observe it, but cannot remedy it, as they follow the Company's orders, which they are compelled to do; and that if we have anything to say, we must petition their masters, the managers, or Their High Mightinesses, which, in truth, we have judged to be necessary. It is now more than a year since the commonalty deemed it expedient, and proposed to send a deputation to Their High Mightinesses. The director commended the project and not only assented to it but urged it strongly. It was put well in the mill, so that we had already spoken of a person to go, when it fell through, for these reasons: When it was proposed, the director desired that it should be communicated according to his wishes; which some who perceived the object would not consent to, and the matter therefore fell asleep. . . .

In our opinion this country will never flourish under the government of the Honorable Company but will pass away and come to an end of itself, unless the Honorable Company be reformed; and therefore it would be more profitable for them, and better for the country, that they should be rid thereof and their effects transported hence.

To speak specifically: Care ought to be taken of the public property, as well ecclesiastical as civil, which, in beginnings, can be illy dispensed with. It is doubtful whether divine worship will not have to cease altogether in consequence of the departure of the minister and the inability of the Company. There should be a public school, provided with at least two good masters, so that first of all, in so wild a country, where there are many loose people, the youth be well taught and brought up, not only in reading and writing but also in the knowl-

edge and fear of the Lord. As it is now, the school is kept very irregularly, one and another keeping it according to his pleasure and as long as he thinks proper. There ought also to be an almshouse and an orphan asylum and other similar institutions. The minister, who now goes home, can give a much fuller explanation thereof.

The country must also be provided with godly, honorable, and intelligent rulers who are not very indigent or, indeed, are not too covetous. A covetous governor makes poor subjects. The manner the country is now governed falls severely upon it and is intolerable, for nobody is unmolested or secure in his property longer than the director pleases, who is generally strongly inclined to confiscating; and if everything be well done, and the property given to the Heer, one must still study always to please him if he would have quiet. A good population would be the consequence of a good government, as we have shown according to our ability in our petition; and although to give free passage and equip ships, if it be necessary, would be expensive at first, yet, if the result be considered, it would ultimately be a wise measure, if by that means farmers and laborers together with other poor people were brought into the country with the little property which they have; of whom the fatherland has enough to spare.

We believe it would then prosper, especially as good privileges and exemptions, which we regard as the mother of population, would encourage the inhabitants to carry on commerce and lawful trade. Everyone would be allured hither by the pleasantness, situation, salubrity, and fruitfulness of the country, if protection were secured within the already established boundaries. It would all, with God's assistance, then, according to human judgment, go well, and New Netherland would in a few years be a brave place and be able to do service to the Netherland nation, to repay richly the cost, and to thank its benefactors.

1651

44.

Sumptuary Regulations in New England

Puritan regulations regarding wearing apparel were normally conceived as a defense against "irreligious" and "immoral" ostentation, but sensitivity to social standing and rank was sometimes equally apparent as a motive. Some of the wealthier colonists, seeking to emulate the English aristocracy in the manner of their dress, were greatly offended when their poorer neighbors copied the same fashions. In order that the social classes might be more clearly distinguished, a law — supported mainly by the rich — was passed in the Massachusetts Bay Colony in 1651 that specifically forbade the poor to adopt "excessive dress."

Source: *The Colonial Laws of Massachusetts,* Boston, 1887, p. 5.

ALTHOUGH SEVERAL DECLARATIONS and orders have been made by this Court against excess in apparel, both of men and women, which have not taken that effect as were to be desired, but on the contrary, we cannot but to our grief take notice that intolerable excess and bravery have crept in upon us, and especially among people of mean condition, to the dishonor of God, the scandal of our profession, the consumption of estates, and altogether unsuitable to our poverty. And, although we acknowledge it to be a matter of much difficulty, in regard of the blindness of men's minds and the stubbornness of their wills, to set down exact rules to confine all sorts of persons, yet we cannot but account it our duty to commend unto all sorts of persons the sober and moderate use of those blessings which, beyond expectation, the Lord has been pleased to afford unto us in this wilderness. And

also to declare our utter detestation and dislike that men and women of mean condition should take upon them the garb of gentlemen by wearing gold or silver lace, or buttons, or points at their knees, or to walk in great boots; or women of the same rank to wear silk or tiffany hoods, or scarves, which, though allowable to persons of greater estates or more liberal education, yet we cannot but judge it intolerable. . . .

It is therefore ordered by this Court, and the authority thereof, that no person within this jurisdiction, nor any of their relations depending upon them, whose visible estates, real and personal, shall not exceed the true and indifferent value of £200, shall wear any gold or silver lace, or gold and silver buttons, or any bone lace above 2s. per yard, or silk hoods, or scarves, upon the penalty of 10s. for every such offense and every such delinquent to be presented by the grand jury. And forasmuch as distinct and particular rules in this case suitable to the estate or quality of each person cannot easily be given: *It is further ordered by the authority aforesaid,* that the selectmen of every town, or the major part of them, are hereby enabled and required, from time to time, to have regard and take notice of apparel of any of the inhabitants of their several towns respectively; and whosoever they shall judge to exceed their ranks and abilities in the costliness or fashion of their apparel in any respect, especially in the wearing of ribbons or great boots (leather being so scarce a commodity in this country), lace, points, etc., silk hoods, or scarves, the selectmen aforesaid shall have power to assess such persons, so offending in any of the particulars above mentioned, in the country rates, at £200 estates, according to that proportion that such men use to pay to whom such apparel is suitable and allowed; provided this law shall not extend to the restraint of any magistrate or public officer of this jurisdiction, their wives and children, who are left to their discretion in wearing of apparel, or any settled military officer or soldier in the time of military service, or any other whose education and employment have been above the ordinary degree, or whose estate have been considerable, though now decayed.

45.

Peter Bulkeley: A City Set Upon a Hill

According to the so-called doctrine of the Gospel covenant, which combined political and religious ideas, the New England colonists enjoyed a special covenant with God and were therefore called upon to form a political and religious community wholly dedicated to Him. Those Puritans who embraced Arminianism tended to interpret the doctrine as an attempt to reconcile the Calvinist principle of salvation by God's grace alone with the principle that a man's right actions could influence God's attitude toward him. The Reverend Peter Bulkeley, preacher at and one of the founders of Concord, Massachusetts, maintained the Calvinist principle of predestination but qualified it by a strong emphasis on right living which he implied, if he did not explicitly assert, might win God's favor. This departure from strict Calvinism paved the way for the more liberal religious ideas of the eighteenth and nineteenth centuries. The portion of Bulkeley's famous sermon, The Gospel-Covenant, *that appears below is taken from the 1651 revised edition of the work.*

Source: *The Gospel-Covenant; or The Covenant of Grace Opened,* 2nd edition, London, 1651, pp. 431-432.

CONSIDER A TIME of separation must come wherein the Lord Jesus will divide and separate the holy from the unholy, as a shepherd separates the sheep from the goats. It will be good to be found among the saints at that day, and to stand in the assembly of the righteous. Woe, then, unto all those that are secluded from them, to all those that must stand without and be among dogs and devils, having no fellowship with

Christ nor with his saints. It is good, therefore, to be holy. It will be found so then; woe unto the profane and ungodly at that day.

And for ourselves here, the people of New England, we should in a special manner labor to shine forth in holiness above other people. We have that plenty and abundance of ordinances and means of grace, as few people enjoy the like; we are as a city set upon a hill, in the open view of all the earth, the eyes of the world are upon us, because we profess ourselves to be a people in covenant with God, and therefore not only the Lord our God, with whom we have made covenant, but heaven and earth, angels and men, that are witnesses of our profession, will cry shame upon us if we walk contrary to the covenant which we have professed and promised to walk in. If we open the mouths of men against our profession, by reason of the scandalousness of our lives, we (of all men) shall have the greater sin. . . .

Let us study so to walk that this may be our excellency and dignity among the nations of the world among which we live; that they may be constrained to say of us, only this people is wise, a holy and blessed people; that all that see us may see and know that the name of the Lord is called upon us; and that we are the seed which the Lord hath blessed (Deut. 28:10; Isa. 61:9).

There is no people but will strive to excel in something. What can we excel in, if not in holiness? If we look to number, we are the fewest; if to strength, we are the weakest; if to wealth and riches, we are the poorest of all the people of God through the whole world. We cannot excel (nor so much as equal) other people in these things; and if we come short in grace and holiness, too, we are the most despicable people under heaven; our worldly dignity is gone. If we lose the glory of grace, too, then is the glory wholly departed from our Israel, and we are become vile. Strive we, therefore, herein to excel, and suffer not this crown to be taken away from us. Be we a holy people, so shall we be honorable before God and precious in the eyes of His saints.

———◆———

God hath sifted a whole nation, that he might send choice grain into this wilderness.

WILLIAM STOUGHTON

1652

46.

Roger Williams: The Hireling Ministry — None of Christ's

Throughout his stormy career as a Puritan minister, converted Baptist, and "Seeker" of the "pure truth," Roger Williams continued to maintain the Calvinist principle that a ministry sent from God was necessary to the existence of the true church. During a visit to England in 1651 he became embroiled in a controversy raging there over forced tithes for the support of established church ministers. In The Hireling Ministry, Williams denounced compulsory support for the clergy, arguing that ministers who bargained for salary were not those truly ordained by Christ.

Source: *The Hireling Ministry None of Christs, etc., etc.*, London, 1652, pp. 3-30.

THE CIVIL STATE of the nations, being merely and essentially civil, cannot (Christianly) be called "Christian states," after the pattern of that holy and typical land of Canaan, which I have proved at large in the *Bloudy Tenent* to be a nonesuch and an unparalleled figure of the spiritual state of the church of Christ Jesus, dispersed yet gathered to Him in all nations.

The civil sword (therefore) cannot (rightfully) act either in restraining the souls of the people from worship, etc., or in constraining them to worship, considering that there is not a tittle in the New Testament of Christ Jesus that commits the forming or reforming of His spouse and church to the civil and worldly powers. . . .

If it shall please our most noble governors to search into the institution and con-

stitution (as they have done of the diocesan so also) of the national and parish churches. . . .

If they please to take off the yokes, the soul yokes of binding all persons to such parochial or parish forms, permitting them to enjoy their own belief, whether within or without such parish worships, parish maintenance, parish marryings, parish buryings, by which the souls and consciences of so many have been inbondaged in life and death, and (their bodies, in respect of buryings) after death.

If they shall please so far (if not to countenance yet) to permit impartially all consciences, and especially the consciences, the meetings and assemblings of faithful and conscionable people (the volunteers in preaching Christ Jesus), so as that what people and persons please, may peaceably frequent and repair to such spiritual meetings and assemblies as they do the parish churches, I am humbly confident that, as to the point of converting souls to God (so far as the present state of Christianity can be so promoted), the souls of thousands will bless God more than if millions of hirelings were sent abroad from all the universities, both of popish and Protestant countries.

[And] upon the grounds first laid, I observe the great and wonderful mistake, both our own and our fathers, as to the civil powers of this world, acting in spiritual matters. I have read . . . the last will and testament of the Lord Jesus over many times, and yet I cannot find by one tittle of that testament that if He had been pleased to have accepted of a temporal crown and government that ever He would have put forth the least finger of temporal or civil power in the matters of His spiritual affairs and Kingdom.

Hence must it lamentably be against the testimony of Christ Jesus for the civil state to impose upon the souls of the people a religion, a worship, a ministry, oaths (in religious and civil affairs), tithes, times, days, marryings, and buryings in holy ground, yet in force, as I have (I hope), by the help of God, fully debated that great question with Master Cotton, and washed off all his late washings of that bloody tenent of persecution, etc.

What is then the express duty of the civil magistrate as to Christ Jesus, His Gospel and Kingdom?

I answer: I know how woefully that Scripture, "Kings shall be thy nursing fathers," etc., has been abused. . . . I humbly conceive that the great duty of the magistrate, as to spirituals, will turn upon these two hinges:

First, in removing the civil bars, obstructions, hindrances in taking off those yokes that pinch the very souls and consciences of men, such as yet are the payments of tithes and the maintenance of ministers they have no faith in; such are the enforced oaths and some ceremonies therein, in all the courts of justice; such are the holy marryings, holy buryings, etc.

Second, in a free and absolute permission of the consciences of all men in what is merely spiritual. . . .

But how will this propagate the Gospel of Christ Jesus?

I answer thus: The first grand design of Christ Jesus is to destroy and consume His mortal enemy antichrist. This must be done by the breath of His mouth in His prophets and witnesses. Now, the nations of the world have impiously stopped this heavenly breath and stifled the Lord Jesus in His servants. Now, it shall please the civil state to remove the state bars set up to resist the holy spirit of God in His servants (whom yet finally to resist is not in all the powers of the world), I humbly conceive that the civil state has made a fair progress in promoting the Gospel of Jesus Christ.

This mercy and freedom is due to the (merely) religious consciences of all men in the world. Is there no more due from the magistrate to Christ Jesus, His saints and Kingdom?

I answer: While I plead the conscience of all men to be at liberty, doubtless I must plead the liberty of the magistrate's conscience also; and, therefore, were his bounties and donations to his bishops and ministers as large as those of Constantine — who but the Holy Spirit of God in the mouths of His prophets can restrain him? . . .

But under the pretense of propagating the Gospel of Christ Jesus (it may be said), what horrible opinions and spirits will be vented, as woeful experience has manifested.

I answer: Opinions offensive are of two sorts: some savoring of impiety, and some of incivility.

Against the first, Christ Jesus never called for the sword of steel to help the sword of the spirit, that two-edged sword that comes out of the mouth of the Lord Jesus. . . .

The second sort, to wit, opinions of incivility, doubtless the opinions as well as practices are the proper object of the civil sword. . . .

But ought not the civil magistrates to repeal their ordinance for tithes, and also to appoint some course for the maintenance of the ministry?

I answer: Upon that ground of removing soul yokes, and not restraining nor constraining conscience, I humbly conceive that the civil state cannot by any rule from Christ Jesus either forbid the payment of tithes to such whose conscience is to pay them, or enjoin them where the conscience is not so persuaded. For the further clearing of which assertion, I distinguish of the people of this nation into two sorts:

First, such as have a freedom in their mind to frequent the public parish assemblies of the nation; and they are also of two sorts: (1) such as conscientiously frequent such places, either out of a conscientious zeal of worshiping of God, or out of a superstitious and traditional awe; (2) such as can go or not go, and care not what religion themselves and the state be of.

There is a second sort of people in this nation which, out of conscience, dare not frequent such places, and they are such: (1) such as indeed fear God and are in their consciences persuaded of an indelible character of holiness upon such temples as temples dedicated to a parish worship; (2) such as, out of an utter dislike of all Protestant worship and a high esteem of their own Catholic faith, are as far from love to such places as the former sort.

Now, all these consciences (yea, the very conscience of the Papists, Jews, etc., as I have proved at large in my answer to Master Cotton's washings) ought freely and impartially to be permitted their several respective worships, their ministers of worships, and what way of maintaining them they freely choose.

But if the civil state enjoin not the maintenance of the ministry, if they quite let loose the golden reins of discipline (as the Parliament expressed and the Scots objected), what will become of the ministry of the Gospel and the souls of men? For if each man's conscience be at liberty to come to church or not, to pay to the minister or not, the profane and loose will neither pay nor pray, but turn atheistic and irreligious. The ministers of worship will be discouraged and destitute, and parents will have little mind to expend their monies to make their children scholars, when the hope of their preferment is cut off.

I answer, first, that the Supreme Court in their declaration never declared to bar up all the doors and windows of that honorable House, so that no further light from Heaven should break into their . . . councils from the most glorious sun of all righteousness, the Lord Jesus.

Although the loose will be more loose (yet) possibly being at more liberty they may be put upon consideration and choice of ways of life and peace, yet, however, it is infinitely better that the profane and loose be unmasked than to be muffled up under the veil and hood of traditional hypocrisy, which turns and dulls the very edge of all conscience either toward God or man.

Third, it is not to be doubted but that each conscience, the Papists and the Protestants, both Presbyterians and Independents, will . . . strive for (their not only conscience but) credit sake to excel and win the garland in the fruits of bounty, etc. Thus a Jesuit once in Newgate boasted of the Papists' charity to a Protestant . . . for, pulling out his hand full of gold, look here (said he) are the fruits of our religion.

Fourth, such parents or children as aim at the gain and preferment of religion do often mistake gain and gold for godliness, godbelly for the true God, and some false for the true Lord Jesus. I add, such priests or ministers as can force a maintenance of tithes or otherwise, by the sword, or else cease preaching for want of such or such a maintenance, or can remove from bishoprics or benefices . . . for fatter and ranker pastures, or, wanting spiritual work and maintenance, are too fine to work with their hands as the first patterns, Christ's first ministers, did — how can they say, as Peter to Christ Jesus, "Lord, Thou knowest all things, Thou knowest I love Thee," etc.?

[Therefore] lastly, the Father of Spirits graciously be pleased to preserve the spirits of our higher powers from laying on the hay and stubble, though upon the golden foundation Christ Jesus, for all such work in matters spiritual which our forefathers, either popish or Protestant, in their several changes in this nation have made, they have been consumed and burned (like hay and stubble) and come to nothing.

The *summa totalis* of all the former particulars is this:

First, since the people of this nation have been forced into a national way of worship, both popish and Protestant (as the wheels of time's revolutions, by God's mighty Providence and permission, have turned about), the civil state is bound before God to take off that bond and yoke of soul op-

pression, and to proclaim free and impartial liberty to all the people of the three nations to choose and maintain what worship and ministry their souls and consciences are persuaded of; which act, as it will prove an act of mercy and righteousness to the enslaved nations, so is it of a binding force to engage the whole and every interest and conscience to preserve the common freedom and peace; however, an act most suiting with the piety and Christianity of the Holy Testament of Christ Jesus.

Second, the civil state is humbly to be implored to provide in their high wisdom for the security of all the respective consciences, in their respective meetings, assemblings, worshipings, preachings, disputings, etc., and that civil peace and the beauty of civility and humanity be maintained among the chief opposers and dissenters.

Third, it is the duty of all that are in authority, and of all that are able, to countenance, encourage, and supply such true volunteers as give and devote themselves to the service and ministry of Christ Jesus in any kind, although it be also the duty, and will be the practice, of all such whom the spirit of God sends upon any work of Christ's . . . than the work and service of their Lord and Master should be neglected.

1654

47.

EDWARD JOHNSON: Sions Saviour in New England

Representing the rank and file of the Massachusetts Bay Colony rather than its leaders (though he was no less devout), Edward Johnson wrote a history of the colony entitled Wonder-Working Providence of Sions Saviour in New England, a portion of which appears here. Johnson lacked a university education; as a result, he never learned the celebrated "plain style" of the New England clergy but wrote in a manner which by comparison was long-winded and ornate. He also included in his history a number of clumsy though pious verses. Yet the work, "written," as Samuel Eliot Morison has said, "with the avowed purpose to overwhelm the enemies of Massachusetts by evidence of divinely ordained success, and to hearten friends by stories of marvelous providences," was thoroughly and wholeheartedly Puritan in its conception. Begun in 1650, it was first published in London in 1654.

Source: *Wonder-Working Providence of Sions Saviour in New England*, Andover, 1867, pp. 8-13, 106-112, 133, 164-165, 205-206.

OF THE CIVIL GOVERNMENT IN NEW ENGLAND AND THEIR NURTURE OF THE PEOPLE UPON THEIR TENDER KNEES

THE VERNAL OF THE YEAR 1637, being now in its prime, and as the season of the year grew hotter, so the minds of many were hot in the eager pursuit of their self-conceited opinions, and verily had not authority stepped in, it was much to be doubted they would not have proceeded from words to blows. Great hold and keep there was about choice of magistrates this year, the choice being retarded by a paper called a petition, but indeed a mere device to hinder the election until the erroneous party were strengthened, their number increasing daily. But the Lord Christ, graciously providing for the peace of His people, toward the end of the day the honored John Winthrop, Esq., was chosen governor and the number of freemen added this year was about 125.

Here according to promise the reader shall have an account of the civil government of this little commonwealth. As their whole aim in their removal from their native country was to enjoy the liberties of the Gospel of Christ, so in serving up civil government, they daily direct their choice to make use of such men as mostly endeavor to keep the truths of Christ pure and unspotted, and assuredly they can digest any wrongs or injuries done them in their estates or trade better than the wresting of their right in the freedom of the Gospel out of their hands. This the erronists knowing right well (to save their heads whole), they persuade men it is not for civil government to meddle with matters of religion; and also to help out with their damnable doctrines, they report it in all places where they come that New England government does persecute the people and churches of Christ. Which to speak truth they have hitherto been so far from, that they have endeavored to expel all such beasts of prey (who will not be reclaimed), that here might be none left to hurt or destroy in all God's holy mountain, and therefore are ready to put the churches of Christ in mind of their duty herein. Yea, and sometimes going before them in their civil censures that they may not only profess the truth, but also hate every false way, not that they would compel men to believe by the power of the sword, but to endeavor all may answer their profession, whether in church covenant or otherwise, by knowing they do not bare the sword in vain. Neither do they exercise civil power to bring all under their obedience to a uniformity in every point of religion, but to keep them in the unity of the spirit, and the bond of peace; nor yet have they ever mixed their civil powers with the authority peculiarly given by Christ to His churches and officers of them, but from time to time have labored to uphold their privileges, and only commune one with another.

The chief court or supreme power of this little commonwealth consists of a mixed company, part aristocracy and part democracy of magistrates, that are yearly chosen by the majority vote of the whole body of the freemen throughout the country; and deputies chosen by the several towns. They have hitherto had about twelve or thirteen magistrates in the colony of Massachusetts;

the other colonies have not above five or six. They have hitherto been volunteers, governing without pay from the people, only the governor of Massachusetts has some years £100 allowed him, and sometimes less. . . .

And now seeing it is the opinion of many in these days of reformation, that all sorts of sectaries (that acknowledge a Christ) should be tolerated by civil government, except Papist, and this government has hitherto and is for future time resolved to practice otherwise (the Lord assisting), having met already with more blasphemous sectaries, than are Papists; wherefore it will not be amiss if our countrymen be acquainted with the one and twenty years experience of this wilderness work in point of government.

First, it is their judgment, and that from Scripture taught them, that those who are chosen to a place in government, must be men truly fearing God, wise and learned in the truths of Christ, (if so) as hitherto it has been New England's practice; then surely such will be utterly unfit to tolerate all sorts of sectaries, because they have taken up Joshua's resolution to serve the Lord, and a man cannot serve two masters, much less many masters. Then surely such as would have all sorts of sinful opinions upheld by the civil government must be sure to make choice of the most atheistical persons they can find to govern, such as are right Gallios; for New England has found by experience that every man will most favor his own way of profession, and labor tooth and nail to maintain it, and if any have complied with other, that have been of a contrary sinful opinion to their own, it has been because they would have their own escape scot free. But assuredly the Lord Christ will allow of no such ways for favoring the professors of his truths, nor may any magistrate do evil that good may come of it, in favoring dangerous and deceivable doctrines, that others may favor the true servants of Christ. Neither is there any such need, for it is their honors (if the will of God be so) to suffer, nor can the people of New England (I mean the better part) be persuaded to set up any other to govern, but those who are zealous for the maintenance of the truths of Christ.

Yet of late there is a buzzing noise, as if it were injury to the churches for civil power to meddle in matters of religion; but to be sure there are many that strive for a toleration: yet the people of Christ, who are the natural mothers of this government, resolve never to see their living child so divided, looking at such a government to be no better to them than a living child divided in twain. They therefore desire their loving countrymen to bear with them in this point, and if any notwithstanding shall force it to be so, we shall show our natural affection, and leave all to them, choosing rather to dwell on the backside of this desert (a place as yet inaccessible), knowing assuredly our God will appear for our deliverance.

Yet let them also know the soldiers of Christ in New England are not of such a pusillanimous spirit, but resolve as that valiant Jephthah did to keep in possession the towns his God had given them, so we are resolved (the Lord willing) to keep the government our God has given us, and for witness He has so done, let this history manifest. For we chose not the place for the land, but for the government, that our Lord Christ might reign over us, both in churches and commonwealth. And although the Lord has been pleased by an extraordinary blessing upon his people's industry to make the place fruitful (as at this day indeed it is), yet all may know the land in itself is very sterile.

The upholding of the truths of Christ is the chief cause why many have hitherto come; and further, if the servants of Christ be not much mistaken, the downfall of Antichrist is at hand, and then the kingdoms of the earth shall become the Kingdom of our Lord Christ in a more peculiar manner,

than now they are. And surely godly civil government shall have a great share in that work, for they are exhorted to fill her double of the cup she has given to them. And also know our magistrates, being conscious of ruling for Christ, dare not admit of any bastardly brood to be nursed up upon their tender knees; neither will any Christian of a sound judgment vote for any, but those who earnestly contend for the faith, although the increase of trade and traffic may be a great inducement to some. . . .

[In 1638] although the estates of these pilgrim people were much wasted, yet seeing the benefit that would accrue to the churches of Christ and civil government, by the Lord's blessing upon learning, they began to erect a college. The Lord by His provident hand giving His approbation to the work, in sending over a faithful and godly servant of His, the Reverend Mr. John Harvard, who, joining with the people of Christ at Charlestown, suddenly after [he] departed this life, and gave near a thousand pound[s] toward this work; wherefore the government thought it meet to call it Harvard College in remembrance of him. . . .

For place they fix their eye upon New-Town, which to tell their posterity whence they came is now called Cambridge; and withal to make the whole world understand that spiritual learning was the thing they chiefly desired . . . they chose this place, being then under the orthodox and soul-flourishing ministry of Mr. Thomas Shepheard. . . . The situation of this college is very pleasant, at the end of a spacious plain, more like a bowling green than a wilderness, near a fair navigable river, environed with many neighboring towns of note, being so near that their houses join with her suburbs. . . . It has the conveniences of a fair hall, comfortable studies and a good library, given by the liberal hand of some magistrates and ministers, with others. . . . The government has endeavored to grant them all the privileges fit for a college, and accordingly the governor and magistrates, together with the president of the college . . . have a continual care of ordering all matters for the good of the whole. This college has brought forth and nursed up very hopeful plants to the supplying of some churches here.

OF THE GREAT PAINS AND CARE TAKEN BY THOSE IN AUTHORITY, FOR THE COMPILING OF LAWS FOR THIS LITTLE COMMONWEALTH

THIS YEAR THE GENERAL COURT appointed a committee of diverse persons to draw up a body of laws for the well-ordering of this little commonwealth; and to the end that they might be most agreeable with the rule of Scripture, in every county there were appointed two magistrates, two ministers, and two able persons from among the people, who, having provided such a competent number as was meet, together with the former that were enacted newly amended, they presented them to the General Court, where they were again perused and amended. Then another committee was chosen to bring them into form, and present them to the Court again, who the year following passed an act of confirmation upon them and so committed them to the press.

In the year 1648 they were printed, and now are to be seen by all men, to the end that none may plead ignorance, and that all who intend to transport themselves hither, may know this is no place of licentious liberty, nor will this people suffer any to trample down this vineyard of the Lord, but with diligent execution will cut off from the City of the Lord the wicked doers, and if any man can show wherein any of them derogate from the Word of God, very willingly will they accept thereof, and amend their imperfections (the Lord assisting). But let not any ill-affected persons find fault with them, because they suit not with their own humor, or because they meddle with matters of religion. For it is no wrong to any man, that a people who have spent their estates, many of them, and ventured their lives to keep faith and a pure conscience, should use all means that the Word of God allows for maintenance and continuance of the same (especially since they have taken up a desolate wilderness to be their habitation), and not deluded any by keeping their profession in huggermug, but print and proclaim to all the way and course they intend, God willing, to walk in.

If any will yet notwithstanding seek to jostle them out of their own right, let them not wonder if they meet with all the opposition a people put to their greatest straits can make. As in all their undertaking, their chiefest aim has been to promote the ordinances of Christ, so also in contriving their laws, liberties, and privileges, they have not been wanting, which has caused many to malign their civil government, and more especially for punishing any by a law, that walk contrary to the rule of the Gospel which they profess. But to them it seems unreasonable and savors too much of hypocrisy, that any people should pray unto the Lord for the speedy accomplishment of His Word in the overthrow of Antichrist, and in the meantime become a patron to sinful opinions and damnable errors that oppose the truths of Christ, admit it be but in the bare permission of them.

─────◆─────

Any government is free to the people under it where the laws rule and the people are a party to the laws.

WILLIAM PENN, *Frame of Government* 1682

1655

48.

Exclusion of Jews from Military Service in New Amsterdam

When, in 1655, Peter Stuyvesant was preparing a military expedition and needed to augment his 200 man force, certain Jewish citizens of New Amsterdam petitioned the Burgher Council for admission to the guard. The petition was rejected because of the "disinclination and unwillingness" of other militiamen to serve with them and the lack of any such precedent in Holland. The Council resolution of August 28, 1655, reprinted here, announced the decision and in addition imposed a special tax on the Jews because of their exemption from service. Only a few days later the city was raided by a party of Indians, and a number of citizens were killed before the undermanned guard could repulse the attack.

Source: *Ecclesiastical Records, State of New York*, Albany, 1901, Vol. I, p. 340.

THE CAPTAINS AND OFFICERS of the train-bands of this city, having asked the director general and Council whether the Jewish people who reside in this city should also train and mount guard with the citizens' bands, this was taken in consideration and deliberated upon. First, the disgust and un-willingness of these trainbands to be fellow soldiers with the aforesaid nation and to be on guard with them in the same guard-house, and, on the other side, that the said nation was not admitted or counted among the citizens, as regards trainbands or com-mon citizens' guards, neither in the illustri-ous city of Amsterdam nor (to our knowl-edge) in any city in Netherland. But in or-der that the said nation may honestly be taxed for their freedom in that respect, it is directed by the director general and Coun-cil, to prevent further discontent, that the aforesaid nation shall, according to the us-ages of the renowned city of Amsterdam, remain exempt from the general training and guard duty, on condition that each male person over sixteen and under sixty years contribute for the aforesaid freedom toward the relief of the general municipal taxes sixty-five stivers [one stiver equals two cents] every month. And the military coun-cil of the citizens is hereby authorized and charged to carry this into effect until our further orders, and to collect, pursuant to the above, the aforesaid contribution once in every month, and, in case of refusal, to collect it by legal process. Thus done in Council at Fort Amsterdam.

49.

ANDREW MARVELL: "Bermudas"

Andrew Marvell, one of the greatest of the so-called metaphysical poets of the English seventeenth century, never visited America and probably knew next to nothing about it. Nevertheless, his "Bermudas" expresses the feeling of many Englishmen who did come as well as any poem of the time. Long an admirer of Oliver Cromwell, Marvell may have conceived "Bermudas" while serving as tutor to Cromwell's ward, William Dutton, in the house of John Oxenbridge, who had made a voyage to Bermuda. In fact, however, several of Marvell's other poems throw more light on "Bermudas" than investigations into his biography would probably do. He was fascinated by the idea of the earthly paradise, and it is to be supposed that he could believe that New England, or Bermuda — doubtless it was all one to him — was in some sense a new Garden of Eden beyond the sea. In any event, a number of actual colonists, among them such men as John Cotton and Peter Bulkeley, entertained similar views.

Source: *Poems*, G. A. Aitken, ed., London, n.d.

❧ BERMUDAS

Where the remote Bermudas ride
In the ocean's bosom unespied,
From a small boat that rowed along,
The listening winds received this song:

"What should we do but sing His praise,
That led us through the watery maze,
Unto an isle so long unknown,
And yet far kinder than our own?
Where He the huge sea monsters wracks,
That lift the deep upon their backs,
He lands us on a grassy stage,
Safe from the storms, and prelate's rage.
He gave us this eternal spring,
Which here enamels everything,
And sends the fowls to us in care,
On daily visits through the air;
He hangs in shades the orange bright,
Like golden lamps in a green night,
And does in the pomegranates close
Jewels more rich than Ormus shows;

He makes the figs our mouths to meet,
And throws the melons at our feet;
But apples plants of such a price,
No tree could ever bear them twice;
With cedars chosen by His hand,
From Lebanon, He stores the land,
And makes the hollow seas, that roar,
Proclaim the ambergris on shore.
He cast (of which we rather boast)
The gospel's pearl upon our coast,
And in these rocks for us did frame
A temple where to sound His name.
Oh! let our voice His praise exalt,
Till it arrive at heaven's vault,
Which, thence perhaps rebounding, may
Echo beyond the Mexique Bay."

Thus sung they, in the English boat,
An holy and a cheerful note;
And all the way, to guide their chime,
With falling oars they kept the time.

1657

50.

Toleration for Quakers

Quaker missionaries were active in New Netherland for a brief period in 1656-1657 before the leaders of New Amsterdam issued proclamations enjoining the missionaries from practising their faith. Severe punishments were meted out to those who defied these injunctions. Such harsh treatment aroused the sympathies of twenty-six citizens of Flushing, Long Island, who addressed the following letter of December 27, 1657, to Peter Stuyvesant and the colonial authorities, asking them to show tolerance to the Quakers. The Flushing "Remonstrance," like Roger Williams' Bloudy Tenent of Persecution, was an early and articulate plea for the establishment of religious freedom.

Source: *Ecclesiastical Records, State of New York*, Albany, 1901, Vol. I, pp. 412-414.

YOU HAVE BEEN PLEASED to send up unto us a certain prohibition or command that we should not receive or entertain any of those people called Quakers, because they are supposed to be, by some, seducers of the people. For our part we cannot condemn them in this case, neither can we stretch out our hands against them to punish, banish, or persecute them, for out of Christ, God is a consuming fire, and it is a fearful thing to fall into the hands of the living God. We desire, therefore, in this case, not to judge lest we be judged, neither to condemn lest we be condemned, but rather let every man stand and fall to his own. . . .

We are bound by the law to do good unto all men, especially to those of the household of faith; and, though, for the present, we seem to be unsensible of the law and the lawgiver, yet when death and the law assault us, if we have (not) our advocate to seek, who shall plead for us in this case of conscience between God and our own souls?

The powers of this world can neither attack us neither excuse us, for if God justify who can condemn, and if God condemn, there is none can justify; and for those jealousies and suspicions which some have of them — that they are destructive unto magistracy and ministry — that cannot be; for the magistrate has the sword in his hand and the minister has the sword in his hand, as witness those two great examples which all magistrates and ministers are to follow — Moses and Christ, whom God raised up, maintained, and defended against all the enemies both of flesh and spirit. And, therefore, that which is of God will stand, and that which is of man will (come) to nothing. And as the Lord has taught Moses, or the civil power, to give an outward liberty in the state by the law written in His heart designed (for) the good of all and can truly judge who is good and who is evil, who is true and who is false, and can pass definitive sentence of life or (death) against that man which rises up against the fundamental law of the States General, so (He) has made His ministers a savor of life unto (life) and a savor of death unto death.

The law of love, peace, and liberty in the states extending to Jews, Turks, and Egyptians, as they are considered the sons of Adam, which is the glory of the outward state of Holland; so love, peace, and liberty, extending to all in Christ Jesus condemns hatred, war, and bondage; and because our Savior says it is impossible but that offense will come, but woe be unto him by whom they come, our desire is not to offend one of His little ones in whatsoever form, name, or title he appears in, whether Presbyterian, Independent, Baptist, or Quaker; but shall be glad to see anything of God in any of them, desiring to do unto all men as we desire all men should do unto us, which is the true law both of church and state; for our Savior says this is the law and the prophets. Therefore, if any of these said persons come in love unto us, we cannot in conscience lay violent hands upon them, but give them free egress into our town and houses as God shall persuade our consciences. And in this we are true subjects both of the church and state; for we are bound by the law of God and man to do good unto all men and evil to no man; and this is according to the patent and charter of our town given unto us in the name of the States General, which we are not willing to infringe and violate but shall hold to our patent and shall remain your humble subjects, the inhabitants of Flushing.

When your people come to me, they are permitted to use their own fashions, and I expect the same liberty when I come to you.
        MIANTUNNUMOH, a sachem of the Narragansetts; said to Governor Dudley in 1640

1660 - 1669

51.

Virginia Slave Laws

Throughout the seventeenth century, indentured servants, who agreed to work for a stated number of years in return for their passage to the New World, were a convenient source of labor for the American colonies. Both Negroes and whites served under the system. White servants, after working out their period of indenture, often rose to respected positions in the community. However, Negroes, who numbered about 2,000 in Virginia in 1670, were seldom accorded the same treatment. By the middle of the century they were generally considered servants for life. In the late 1650s, laws referring to slaves began to appear in the Virginia statutes; the following sampling of Virginia Laws, passed between 1660 and 1669, clearly marks the distinction between white servants and Negro slaves.

Source: Hening, II, pp. 26, 170, 260, 266, 270.

I.

ON RUNNING AWAY WITH
NEGROES (MARCH 1660)

Be it enacted that in case any English servant shall run away in company with any Negroes who are incapable of making satisfaction by addition of time . . . the English so running away in company with them shall serve for the time of the said Negroes' absence as they are to do for their own by a former act.

II.

ON THE NATIVITY CONDITIONS
OF SLAVERY (DECEMBER 1662)

Whereas some doubts have arisen whether children got by any Englishman upon a Negro woman should be slave or free, *be it therefore enacted and declared by this present Grand Assembly,* that all children born in this country shall be held bond or free only according to the condition of the mother; and that if any Christian shall commit fornication with a Negro man or woman, he or she so offending shall pay double the fines imposed by the former act.

III.

ON BAPTISM AND BONDAGE
(SEPTEMBER 1667)

Whereas some doubts have risen whether children that are slaves by birth, and by the charity and piety of their owners made partakers of the blessed sacrament of baptism, should by virtue of their baptism be made free, *it is enacted and declared by this Grand Assembly, and the authority thereof,* that the conferring of baptism does not alter the condition of the person as to his bondage or freedom; that diverse masters, freed from this doubt may more carefully endeavor the propagation of Christianity by permitting children, though slaves, or those of greater growth if capable, to be admitted to that sacrament.

IV.

ON CORPORAL PUNISHMENT
(SEPTEMBER 1668)

Whereas it has been questioned whether servants running away may be punished with corporal punishment by their master or magistrate, since the act already made gives the master satisfaction by prolonging their time by service, *it is declared and enacted by this Assembly* that moderate corporal punishment inflicted by master or magistrate upon a runaway servant shall not deprive the master of the satisfaction allowed by the law, the one being as necessary to reclaim them from persisting in that idle course as the other is just to repair the damages sustained by the master.

V.

ON THE KILLING OF SLAVES (OCTOBER 1669)

Whereas the only law in force for the punishment of refractory servants resisting their master, mistress, or overseer cannot be inflicted upon Negroes, nor the obstinacy of many of them be suppressed by other than violent means, *be it enacted and declared by this Grand Assembly* if any slave resists his master (or other by his master's order correcting him) and by the extremity of the correction should chance to die, that his death shall not be accounted a felony, but the master (or that other person appointed by the master to punish him) be acquitted from molestation, since it cannot be presumed that premeditated malice (which alone makes murder a felony) should induce any man to destroy his own estate.

Pray! what thing in the world can be worse toward us than if men should rob or steal us away and sell us for slaves to strange countries, separating husband from wife and children?

Resolutions of Germantown Mennonites, 1688

1661

52.

Anonymous: Incentives for Building Towns in Virginia

Between 1620 and 1660 the development of self-sustaining farms in the Chesapeake Bay area dispersed the population widely. Induced by land grants and the lessening of the Indian menace, settlers moved out from fortified posts, returning only periodically for supplies and occasionally for church. The resultant lack of communal spirit or interest in education and religious life was the special concern of the following report, presented to Lord Guilbert, bishop of London, by the petitioner "R.G." on September 2, 1661. The report, titled Virginia's Cure: or An Advisive Narrative Concerning Virginia, *sought to strengthen the church by building additional towns where the people could congregate. The tract was subsequently published in London in 1662.*

Source: Force, III, 15.

THAT PART OF VIRGINIA which has at present craved Your Lordship's assistance to preserve the Christian religion and to promote the building God's church among them, by supplying them with sufficient ministers of the gospel . . . is divided into several counties. And those counties contain in all about fifty parishes, the families whereof are dispersedly and scatteringly seated upon the sides of rivers, some of which, running very far into the country, bear the English plantations above a hundred miles, and, being very broad, cause the inhabitants of either side to be listed in several parishes. . . .

The families of such parishes being seated after this manner, at such distances from each other, many of them are very remote from the house of God, though placed in the midst of them. Many parishes as yet want both churches and glebes; and I think not above a fifth part of them are supplied with ministers. Where there are ministers the people meet together weekly, but once upon the Lord's Day, and sometimes not at all, being hindered by extremities of wind and weather. And diverse of the more remote families being discouraged by the length or tediousness of the way, through extremities of heat in summer, frost and snow in winter, and tempestuous weather in both, do very seldom repair thither.

By which brief description of their manner of seating themselves in that wilderness, Your Lordship may easily apprehend that their very manner of planting themselves has caused hitherto to rob God in a great measure of that public worship and service, which, as a homage due to His great name,

He requires to be constantly paid to Him at the times appointed for it in the public congregations of His people in His house of prayer.

This sacrilege I judge to be the prime cause of their long-languishing, improsperous condition. . . . But, though this be the saddest consequence of their dispersed manner of planting themselves (for what misery can be greater than to live under the curse of God?), yet this has a very sad train of attendants which are likewise consequences of their scattered planting. For, hence is the great want of Christian neighborhood, or brotherly admonition, of holy examples of religious persons, of the comfort of theirs and their ministers' administrations in sickness, and distresses, of the benefit of Christian and civil conference and commerce. . . .

Their almost general want of schools, for the education of their children, is another consequence of their scattered planting, of most sad consideration, most of all bewailed of parents there, and therefore the arguments drawn from thence most likely to prevail with them cheerfully to embrace the remedy. This want of schools, as it renders a very numerous generation of Christians' children born in Virginia (who naturally are of beautiful and comely persons, and generally of more ingenious spirits then these in England) unserviceable for any great employments either in church or state, so likewise it obstructs the hopefulest way they have for the conversion of the heathen, which is, by winning the heathen to bring in their children to be taught and instructed in our schools, together with the children of the Christians. . . .

The cause of their dispersed seating was at first a privilege indulged by the royal grant of having a right to fifty acres of land for every person they should transport at their own charges; by which means some men transporting many servants thither, and others purchasing the rights of those that did, took possession of great tracts of land at their pleasure; by degrees scattered their plantations through the country after the manner before described, although, therefore, from the premises, it is easy to conclude that the only way of remedy for Virginia's disease (without which all other help will only palliate, not cure) must be by procuring towns to be built and inhabited in their several counties. Yet, lest any man be hereby injured in his just right, even this remedy ought to be procured after such a manner as the present manner of planting themselves, their poverty, and mean condition will permit. According to which, whether the building towns in each county of Virginia will be best promoted by reviving a former act of that country for markets in stated places of each county . . . or whether they may best be promoted by some other way (it being out of my sphere), I dare not presume to determine. . . .

What way soever they determine to be best, I shall humbly, in obedience to Your Lordship's command, endeavor to contribute toward the compassing this remedy by propounding:

1. That Your Lordship would be pleased to acquaint the King with the necessity of promoting the building towns in each county of Virginia, upon the consideration of the forementioned sad consequences of their present manner of living there.

2. That Your Lordship, upon the foregoing consideration, be pleased to move the pitiful and charitable heart of His Gracious Majesty (considering the poverty and needs of Virginia) for a collection to be made in all the churches of his three kingdoms (there being considerable numbers of each kingdom) for the promoting a work of so great charity to the souls of many thousands of his loyal subjects, their children, and the generations after them, and of numberless poor heathen. And that the ministers of each congregation be enjoined with more than ordinary care and pains to stir up the people to a free and liberal contribution

toward it; or, if this way be not thought sufficient, that some other way be taken to do it.

3. That the way of dispensing such collections for sending workmen over for the building towns and schools, and the assistance the persons that shall inhabit them shall contribute toward them, may be determined here by the advice of Virginia's present or late honorable governors, if in London; and whom they shall make choice of for their assistants (who have formerly lived in Virginia). And that the King (if he shall approve what is so determined) may be humbly petitioned to authorize it by his special command, lest what is duly ordered here be perverted there.

4. That those planters who have such a considerable number of servants, as may be judged may enable them for it, if they be not willing (for I have heard some express their willingness, and some their averseness) may, by His Majesty's authority, be enjoined to contribute the assistance that shall be thought meet for them, to build themselves houses in the towns nearest to them and to inhabit them; for, they having horses enough in that country, may be convenienced, as their occasions require, to visit their plantations. And the masters who shall inhabit the towns, having families of servants upon remote plantations, may be ordered to take care that upon Saturday afternoons (when, by the custom of Virginia, servants are freed from their ordinary labor), their servants (except one or two, left by turns to secure their plantations) may repair to their houses in the towns, and there remain with their masters until the public worship and service of the Lord's Day be ended.

5. That for a continual supply of able ministers for their churches, after a set term of years, Your Lordship would please to endeavor the procuring an act of Parliament whereby a certain number of fellowships, as they happen to be next proportionably vacant in both the universities, may bear the name of Virginia fellowships, so long as the needs of that church shall require it. And none be admitted to them but such as shall engage by promise to hold them seven years and no longer; and, at the expiration of those seven years, transport themselves to Virginia and serve that church in the office of the ministry seven years more (the church there providing for them), which being expired, they shall be left to their own liberty to return or not. And if they perform not the conditions of their admittance, then to be incapable of any preferment.

These things being procured, I think Virginia will be in the most probable way (that her present condition can admit) of being cured of the forementioned evils of her scattered planting. . . .

Men may wonder why the attempts made by the . . . honorable governors to reduce Virginia's planters into towns did never succeed, and perhaps it may be hard for any that never lived among them rightly to conjecture. But the truth in plain English is this:

Whatsoever is of public concernment in Virginia is determined by their Grand Assemblies, which are usually held once a year, and consist of governor and Council, which make the Upper House, and the burgesses, which represent the people, and make the Lower House, and are chosen out of every county by the people after the manner that burgesses are chosen for parliaments in England, and are more or fewer according as the people agree, who are to defray their charges.

Whatsoever passes into an act of Assembly must be agreed upon by the major part of burgesses, and these are usually such as went over servants thither; and, though, by time and industry, they may have attained competent estates, yet, by reason of their poor and mean education, they are unskillful in judging of a good estate, either of church or commonwealth, or of the means of procuring it. No marvel, therefore, if the best proposals which have been made to such persons for reducing them into towns, offending in the least against their present private, worldly interest (though never so promising for the future), have been from time to time bandied against by such major parts of their burgesses, and the fewer wise heads overvoted by them. . . .

To contemplate the poor church (whose plants now grow wild in that wilderness) become like a garden enclosed, like a vineyard fenced, and watched like a flock of sheep with their lambs safely folded by night and fed by day; all which are the promised fruits of well-ordered towns, under religious pastors and magistrates, with what joy and delight may you likewise think upon their comely and most ingenious children, like hopeful plants growing up in nurseries of learning and piety; and, when their time of fruit is come, transplanted into the enclosed gardens of God, and becoming fruitful and useful trees of righteousness; which is the promised happiness and benefit of well-ordered schools, in well-governed towns. . . .

For encouragement, therefore, of ministers to adventure thither to help them, I humbly propound:

First, that Your Lordship be pleased to procure that the next Grand Assembly in Virginia may enact that what tobacco any parish agrees to pay their minister shall be paid of the best tobacco of every man's own crop, and with cask, otherwise experience has shown that a minister's livelihood there will be very uncertain.

Second, that, at the same Assembly, it be enacted that every parish choose a vestry (in case they have not one already chosen), and the vestry of each parish be enjoined to subscribe what quantity of corn and tobacco of the best of their own crops, with cask, they will allow a sufficient minister yearly.

Third, that, in the next and every Assembly, the act for paying 15 lb. of tobacco per annum for every tithable person in every parish destitute of a minister (which act was made at an Assembly, March 27, 1656) be

carefully executed and strict inquiry made whether the tobacco due by that act be duly collected and employed to the ends expressed in that act; viz., building churches, purchasing glebes and stocks of cattle to belong to them. . . .

Fourth, that the act made in the same Assembly concerning disposing intestate estates to public uses, in case no administrator of kin to the deceased proprietor appears, may serve in the first place the needs of the church for furnishing each parish with glebes, and the glebes with stocks of cattle before any part of such estates be employed to any other use.

Fifth, that there being diverse persons already in the colony fit to serve the church in the office of deacon, a bishop be sent over so soon as there shall be a city for his see. As for other needs of that church, so also, that, after due probation and examination, such persons may be ordained deacons, and their duty and service be appointed by the bishop.

Sixth, that the ministers that go thither be not hired by the year, as is now usual, but firmly instituted and induced into livings of stated value. . . .

Seventh, that all ministers desirous to go to Virginia, and not able to transport themselves, be acquainted with an act of Assembly of that country, whereby it is provided that whatsoever sufficient minister shall not be able to pay for his transportation, any merchant that shall defray the charge of it (if such minister agree not with him upon other conditions) shall receive £20 sterling for his passage from the parish that entertains him, or 2,000 lb. of tobacco, who shall also repay any sums of money disbursed for his accommodation, and the minister to be free to choose his parish. . . .

This is all I can think meet to propound at present, only for a conclusion I shall add, for the encouragement both of bishop and ministers that shall adventure thither out of pity and compassion to the souls of so many of their poor brethren, that, as their reward will be great in Heaven, so also they shall (in a very pleasant and fruitful land) meet with a people which generally bear a great love and respect to their ministers. And (if they behave themselves as becomes their high calling) they shall find there ready help and assistance in their needs; and (which should be much more encouraging) they will find a people which generally bear a great love to the stated constitutions of the Church of England, in her government and public worship; which gave us (who went thither under the late persecutions of it) the advantage of liberty to use it constantly among them, after the naval force had reduced that colony under the power (but never to the obedience) of the usurpers; which liberty we could not have enjoyed had not the people generally expressed a great love to it.

And I hope even this will be a consideration (not of least regard) to move Your Lordship to use all possible care and endeavor to supply Virginia's needs with sufficient orthodox ministers, in the first place, and before any other of our foreign plantations which crave your help, because, in the late times of our Church's persecution, her people alone cheerfully and joyfully embraced, encouraged, and maintained the orthodox ministers that went over to them, in their public conformity to the Church of England, in her doctrine and stated manner of public worship.

53.

Constitutionalism in Massachusetts

The charter of 1629 creating the Massachusetts Bay Company omitted any specific reference to Parliamentary authority over the Company's affairs. Thus, when the Company removed to America and was known as a colony, it was possible to claim that Parliament had no power in Massachusetts, which was bound only by such laws as the Company officers (who were also the colony's governors) chose to make. This at any rate was what both Governor Winthrop and John Cotton seem to have understood, and such a view of the matter was later implied in the colony's Body of Liberties *(1641). The selection reprinted here is still another attempt to distinguish the liberties of freemen in the colony from their allegiance to the King. It was approved by the General Court on June 10, 1661. It was in response to these and other assertions of autonomy that the Crown at last, in 1684, revoked the colony's charter.*

Source: *Records of the Governor and Company of the Massachusetts Bay in New England,* Nathaniel B. Shurtleff, ed., Boston, 1854, Vol. IV, Pt. 2, pp. 25-26.

CONCERNING OUR LIBERTIES

1. We conceive the patent (under God) to be the first and main foundation of our civil polity here, by a Governor and Company, according as is therein expressed.

2. The Governor and Company are, by the patent, a body politic, in fact and name.

3. This body politic is vested with power to make freemen.

4. These freemen have power to choose annually a governor, deputy governor, assistants, and their select representatives or deputies.

5. This government has also to set up all sorts of officers, as well superior as inferior, and point out their power and places.

6. The governor, deputy governor, assistants, and select representatives or deputies have full power and authority, both legislative and executive, for the government of all the people here, whether inhabitants or strangers, both concerning ecclesiastics and in civils, without appeal, excepting law or laws repugnant to the laws of England.

7. The government is privileged by all fitting means (yea, if need be, by force of arms) to defend themselves, both by land and sea, against all such person or persons as shall at any time attempt or enterprise the destruction, invasion, detriment, or annoyance of this plantation, or the inhabitants therein, besides other privileges mentioned in the patent, not here expressed.

8. We conceive any imposition prejudicial to the country contrary to any just law of ours, not repugnant to the laws of England, to be an infringement of our right.

CONCERNING OUR DUTIES OF ALLEGIANCE TO OUR SOVEREIGN LORD, THE KING

1. We ought to uphold and, to our power, maintain this place, as of right belonging to Our Sovereign Lord, The King, as holden of His Majesty's manor of East Greenwich, and not to subject the same to any foreign prince or potentate whatsoever.

2. We ought to endeavor the preservation of His Majesty's royal person, realms, and dominions, and so far as lies in us, to discover and prevent all plots and conspiracies against the same.

3. We ought to seek the peace and prosperity of Our King and nation by a faithful discharge in the governing of this people committed to our care:

First, by punishing all such crimes (being breaches of the First or Second Table) as are committed against the peace of Our Sovereign Lord, The King, his Royal Crown, and dignity.

Second, in propagating the Gospel, defending and upholding the true Christian or Protestant religion according to the faith given by our Lord Christ in His word; our dread sovereign being styled "defender of the faith."

The premises considered, it may well stand with the loyalty and obedience of such subjects as are thus privileged by their rightful sovereign (for Himself, His Heirs, and Successors forever) as cause shall require, to plead with their prince against all such as shall at any time endeavor the violation of their privileges. . . . And, also, that the General Court may do safely to declare that in case (for the future) any legally obnoxious, and flying from the civil justice of the state of England, shall come over to these parts, they may not here expect shelter.

Somerset House conference which brought peace between England and Spain in 1604; painting after Gheeraerts

CHALLENGE TO THE SPANISH

After the defeat of her armada in 1588 and the end of war with England in 1604, Spain's ability to police the sea weakened while the strength of her rivals grew. Attracted at first by the old dreams of gold or a route to the Indies, the English, Dutch, and French planted or renewed colonies in North America. Development of the real wealth of the New World — tobacco, lumber, fur, and fish — led to new rivalry for mercantile control of the continent.

Compared to the Spanish and French colonies, the English offered more self-government and, overall, more religious toleration. Fertile land and encouragement of settlers in the English colonies caused a population growth that proved decisive in the coming struggle between the colonial powers.

Fanciful views from Capt. John Smith's "Generall Historie of Virginia," 1624, describing the early years of the Jamestown colony with himself as the central figure (below) lottery ticket sold in London to raise money for the Virginia Company

Jamestown

Sent by the London Company in 1607 to seek gold and a passage to India, planted in a malarial swamp, populated by misfits and "gentlemen" who would not work, and poorly governed, Jamestown barely survived its first two years. It began to thrive only after the development of tobacco.

A Declaration for the certaine time of dravving the great standing Lottery.

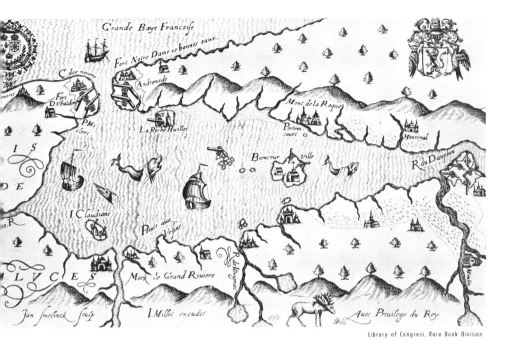

New France

The French made extensive explorations of the interior of North America, but fur traders, rocky soil, religious restrictions in New France, religious wars in old France, and the Thirty Years War in Europe acted together to retard French permanent settlement in Canada.

(Above) French settlement at Port Royal, Nova Scotia, from map by Lescarbot, 1609; (left) Samuel de Champlain, portrait by Ducornet; (below) upper St. Lawrence River on a 1609 map in "Histoire de la Nouvelle France" by Lescarbot

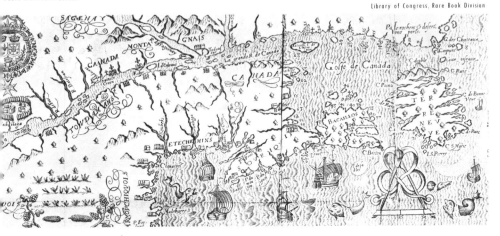

Courtesy, Metropolitan Museum of Art

Pilgrim Society, Plymouth

Library of Congress, Rare Book Division

(Top) "A Quay at Leyden" by Jan van der Heyden. Many of the Separatists congregated at Leyden during the repressive reign of James I in England; (bottom left) this portrait of Gov. Edward Winslow, painted in 1651, is the only known likeness of a Mayflower passenger; (bottom right) detail of a 17th-century map of New England. Plymouth appears opposite the tip of Cape Cod

Plymouth and Massachusetts Bay

James I asserted the authority of the Church of England and repressed the Separatists, many of whom took refuge temporarily in the Netherlands. Most of these Pilgrims, as they called themselves, could afford the passage to America only by contracting their labor for seven years to the Plymouth Company. Ten years after the Separatists settled Plymouth, a group of Puritans bought a charter for themselves as the Massachusetts Bay Company and founded Boston. Massachusetts Bay overshadowed the smaller and less prosperous Pilgrim settlement, and finally annexed Plymouth in 1691.

John Endecott (top) and John Winthrop (center), leaders of the Massachusetts Bay colonists; (bottom) sketch map of Massachusetts Bay about 1633 with a key by John Winthrop. Boston is located on the peninsula, center, and at the right is the road to Plymouth

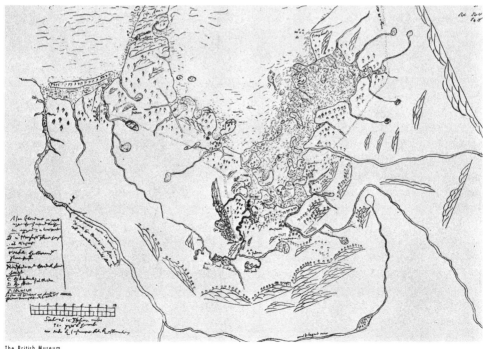

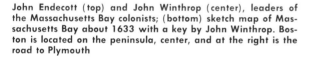

t' Fort nieuw Amsterdam op de Manhatans

The earliest known view of Manhattan

The Dutch East India Company shipyards in Holland

Gov. Peter Stuyvesant (1610-1672)

New Amsterdam

In the 1620s the Dutch colonized the Hudson Valley, where the Pilgrims had meant to land. Mainly interested in the East Indies, the Dutch gave poor governors to New Amsterdam, which the British took without a struggle in 1664.

Redraft of the Castello Plan of New Amsterdam in the Medici Library, 1660

Maryland

George Calvert, a convert to Catholicism, nevertheless remained friends with Charles I. In 1632 Charles favored Calvert, later Lord Baltimore, with a proprietary grant in America. Under the astute management of the Calverts, Maryland colony prospered. Intended in part as a haven for Catholics, but with toleration for all Christians, Maryland soon had a Protestant majority.

(Below) George Calvert, 1st Lord Baltimore (d. 1632); (above right) Cecil Calvert (1605-1675), 2nd Lord Baltimore, sent settlers to Maryland under the leadership of his brother, Leonard (right); (below right) a portion of Cecil Calvert's instructions to the colonists, 1633

1666

54.

Anonymous: Opportunities for Settlers in Carolina

South Carolina was originally a proprietary colony — i.e., the rights of government were included in its grant — that was established on land given by Charles II in 1663 to eight of his friends. Some seven years passed before these proprietors could arrange for actual settlement, which began at Charles Town (Charleston) in 1670. In the interval, among other preparations, they arranged for and possibly wrote at least one pamphlet, of which a portion follows, setting forth the privileges they were prepared to grant to any settlers. A Brief Description of the Province of Carolina, on the Coasts of Floreda *was published in London in 1666.*

Source: *Historical Collections of South Carolina, etc., etc.,* B. R. Carroll, ed., New York, 1836, Vol. II, pp. 10-18.

CAROLINA is a fair and spacious province on the continent of America. . . . The land is of diverse sorts as in all countries of the world. That which lies near the sea is sandy and barren, but bears many tall trees, which make good timber for several uses; and this sandy ground is by experienced men thought to be one cause of the healthfulness of the place. But up the river about twenty or thirty mile[s], where they have made a town, called Charles Town, there is plenty of as rich ground as any in the world. . . . The woods are stored with deer and wild turkeys, of a great magnitude, weighing many times above 50 lb. a piece, and of a more pleasant taste than in England, being in their proper climate; other sorts of beasts in the woods that are good for food, and also fowls, whose names are not known to them.

This is what they found naturally upon the place; but they have brought with them most sorts of seeds and roots of the Barbadoes which thrive [in] the most temperate clime . . . and they have potatoes, and the other roots and herbs of Barbadoes growing and thriving with them; as also from Virginia, Bermuda, and New England, what they could afford. They have indigo, tobacco, very good, and cotton wool; lime trees, orange, lemon, and other fruit trees they brought, thrive exceedingly. They have two crops of Indian corn in one year, and great increase every crop. Apples, pears, and other

English fruit grow there out of the planted kernels.

The marshes and meadows are very large, from 1,500 to 3,000 acres and upwards, and are excellent food for cattle, and will bear any grain being prepared. Some cattle, both great and small, will live well all the winter, and keep their fat without fodder; hogs find so much mast and other food in the woods that they want no other care than a swineherd to keep them from running wild. The meadows are very proper for rice, rapeseed, linseed, etc., and may many of them be made to overflow at pleasure with a small charge.

Here are as brave rivers as any in the world, stored with great abundance of sturgeon, salmon, bass, plaice, trout, and Spanish mackerel, with many other most pleasant sorts of fish, both flat and round, for which the English tongue has no name. Also, in the little winter they have, abundance of wild geese, ducks, teals, widgeons, and many other pleasant fowl. And (as it is said before) the rivers are very deep and navigable above 100 miles up; also there are wholesome springs and rivulets.

Last of all, the air comes to be considered, which is not the least considerable to the well being of a plantation, for without a wholesome air all other considerations avail nothing. And this is it which makes this place so desirable, being seated in the glorious light of heaven brings many advantages, and His convenient distance secures them from the inconvenience of His scorching beams. . . .

If, therefore, any industrious and ingenious persons shall be willing to partake of the felicities of this country, let them embrace the first opportunity, that they may obtain the greater advantages.

The chief of the privileges are as follows:

First, there is full and free liberty of conscience granted to all, so that no man is to be molested or called in question for matters of religious concern; but everyone to be obedient to the civil government, worshiping God after their own way.

Second, there is freedom from custom for all wine, silk, raisins, currants, oil, olives, and almonds that shall be raised in the province for seven years, after four ton of any of those commodities shall be imported in one bottom.

Third, every freeman and freewoman that transport themselves and servants by the 25th of March next, being 1667, shall have for himself, wife, children, and menservants, for each 100 acres of land for him and his heirs forever, and for every womanservant and slave, 50 acres, paying at most ½d. per acre, per annum, in lieu of all demands, to the Lords Proprietors; provided always that every man be armed with a good musket full bore, 10 lb. powder, and 20 lb. of bullet, and six-months provision for all, to serve them while they raise provision in that country.

Fourth, every manservant, at the expiration of their time, is to have of the country 100 acres of land to him and his heirs forever, paying only ½d. per acre, per annum, and the women, 50 acres of land on the same conditions; their masters also are to allow them two suits of apparel and tools such as he is best able to work with, according to the custom of the country.

Fifth, they are to have a governor and council appointed from among themselves to see the laws of the Assembly put in due execution; but the governor is to rule but three years, and then learn to obey; also he has no power to lay any tax or make or abrogate any law without the consent of the colony in their Assembly.

Sixth, they are to choose annually from among themselves a certain number of men, according to their divisions, which constitute the General Assembly with the governor and his council, and have the sole power of making laws and laying taxes for the common good when need shall require.

These are the chief and fundamental privileges, but the Right Honorable Lords Proprietors have promised (and it is their interest so to do) to be ready to grant what other privileges may be found advantageous for the good of the colony.

Is there, therefore, any younger brother who is born of gentile blood, and whose spirit is elevated above the common sort, and yet the hard usage of our country has not allowed suitable fortune; he will not surely be afraid to leave his native soil to advance his fortunes equal to his blood and spirit, and so he will avoid these unlawful ways too many of our young gentlemen take to maintain themselves according to their high education, having but small estates. Here, with a few servants and a small stock, a great estate may be raised, although his birth have not entitled him to any of the land of his ancestors, yet his industry may supply him so, as to make him the head of as famous a family.

Such as are here tormented with much care how to get worth to gain a livelihood, or that with their labor can hardly get a comfortable subsistence, shall do well to go to this place, where any man whatever that is but willing to take moderate pains may be assured of a most comfortable subsistence, and be in a way to raise his fortunes far beyond what he could ever hope for in England. Let no man be troubled at the thoughts of being a servant for four or five years, for I can assure you that many men give money with their children to serve seven years, to take more pains and fare

nothing so well as the servants in this plantation will do. Then, it is to be considered that so soon as he is out of his time, he has land and tools, and clothes given him, and is in a way of advancement.

Therefore, all artificers, as carpenters, wheelwrights, joiners, coopers, bricklayers, smiths, or diligent husbandmen and laborers that are willing to advance their fortunes and live in a most pleasant healthful and fruitful country, where artificers are of high esteem and used with all civility and courtesy imaginable, may take notice that there is an opportunity offered now by the Virginia Fleet, from whence Cape Fear is but three or four days' sail, and then a small stock carried to Virginia will purchase provisions at a far easier rate than to carry them from hence; also the freight of the said provisions will be saved, and be more fresh, and there wants not conveyance from Virginia thither.

If any maid or single woman have a desire to go over, they will think themselves in the Golden Age, when men paid a dowry for their wives; for if they be but civil, and under fifty years of age, some honest man or other will purchase them for their wives.

Those that desire further advice, or servants that would be entertained, let them repair to Mr. Matthew Wilkinson, ironmonger, at the sign of the Three Feathers in Bishopsgate Street, where they may be informed when the ships will be ready, and what they must carry with them.

1674 - 1677

55.

Plymouth Colony School Laws

Massachusetts Bay was the first colony to enact laws establishing standards of education (1642) and requiring towns of a certain size to supply educational facilities (1647). Most of the other New England colonies followed suit. The Plymouth laws of 1674 and 1677, reprinted here, provided that public schools be established in towns large enough to support them and that the profits of the Cape Cod fisheries be appropriated for building and maintaining schools.

Source: *The Compact with the Charter and Laws of the Colony of New Plymouth, etc., etc.,* Boston, 1836, Pt. 3, pp. 172, 185.

I.

Fishery Profits for Schools

THIS COURT has received from the deputies of the several towns the decision of the major part of the freemen of this colony that all the profits of the fishing at Cape Cod, granted by the Court for the erecting and maintaining of a school, shall continue to be given for that end if a sufficient number of scholars appear to be devoted thereunto, which this Court judges not to be less than eight or ten. We do, therefore, hereby confirm the grant of the aforesaid profits of the fishing at Cape Cod to the maintenance of the school; and that there be no further de-

mands, besides the said profits of the Cape, asked of the country for the maintenance of the said school.

II.

A School for Each Fifty Families

FORASMUCH as the maintenance of good literature tends to the advancement of the welfare and flourishing estate of societies and republics, this Court therefore orders that in every township whatever in this government consisting of fifty families or more, any meet man should be obtained to teach a grammar school. Such township shall allow at least £12 in current merchantable pay to be raised by rate on all the inhabitants of such a town, and those that have the more immediate benefit thereof by their children's good and the general good shall make up the residue necessary to maintain the same. The profits arising from the Cape fishing, heretofore ordered to maintain a grammar school in this colony, shall be distributed to such towns as have grammar schools. This is not to exceed £5 per annum to any such town unless the Court treasurer or other appointed person sees good cause to add to that sum for any . . . town.

And further, this Court orders that every town consisting of more than seventy families and which has no grammar school shall allow and pay to the next town which has a grammar school the sum of £5 per annum in current merchantable pay, to be levied on the inhabitants of such defective towns by rate and gathered and delivered by the constables of such towns as a warrant from any magistrate in this jurisdiction shall require.

1675

56.

Benjamin Tompson: New England's Crisis

Benjamin Tompson's epic poem New-England's Crisis *laments the loss of religious fervor in an age that saw New England settlers pursuing economic and social success with a zeal once reserved for the church. The Prologue, reprinted here, is at once nostalgic for the simple, disciplined faith of old New England and scornful of the "softness" and "decadence" of the new. In a community just fifty-five years old, Tompson mourned the loss of all the earlier graces, from conscience and manners to housewifery and cooking. The poem was written in 1675, and was published the following year.*

Source: *New-England's Crisis*, Boston, 1894.

The time wherein Old Pompion was a saint,
When men fared hardly, yet without complaint,
On vilest cates; the dainty Indian maize
Was eat with clamshells out of wooden trays,
Under thatched huts, without the cry of rent,
And the best sauce to every dish, content.
When flesh was food and hairy skins made coats,
And men as well as birds had chirping notes.
When simnels were accounted noble blood
Among the tribes of common herbage food.
Of Ceres' bounty formed was many a knack,
Enough to fill *Poor Robin's Almanack.*
These golden times (too fortunate to hold)
Were quickly sinned away for love of gold.
'Twas then among the bushes not the street,
If one in place did an inferior meet,
"Good morrow, brother! is there aught you want?
Take freely of me, what I have you ha'n't."
Plain Tom and Dick would pass as current now,
As ever since "Your Servant, Sir!" and bow.
Deep-skirted doublets, puritanic capes,
Which now would render men like upright apes,

Was comelier wear, our wiser fathers thought,
Than the cast fashions from all Europe brought.
'Twas in those days an honest grace would hold
Till a hot pudding grew at heart a cold,
And men had better stomachs to religion,
Than I to capon, turkey-cock, or pigeon;
When honest sisters met to pray, not prate,
About their own and not their neighbor's state.
During Plain Dealing's reign, that worthy stud
Of th' ancient planters' race before the flood,
These times were good, merchants cared not a rush
For other fare than jonakin and mush.
Although men fared and lodgéd very hard,
Yet innocence was better than a guard.
'Twas long before spiders and worms had drawn
Their dingy webs, or hid with cheating lawn
New England's beauties, which still seemed to me
Illustrious in their own simplicity.
'Twas ere Virginia's neighboring land had broke
The hogsheads of her worse than hellish smoke.
'Twas ere the islands sent their presents in,
Which but to use counted next to sin.
'Twas ere a barge had made so rich a freight
As chocolate, dust-gold, and bits of eight.
Ere wines from France and Moscovadoe, too,
Without the which the drink will scarcely do;
From western isles ere fruits and delicacies
Did rot maids' teeth and spoil their handsome faces.
Or ere these times did chance, the noise of war
Was from our towns and hearts removéd far.
No bugbear comets in the crystal air
To drive our Christian planters to despair.
No sooner pagan malice peepéd forth
But valor snibbed it; then were men of worth,
Who by their prayers slew thousands, angel-like;
Their weapons are unseen with which they strike.
Then had the churches rest; as yet the coals
Were covered up in most contentious souls.
Freeness in judgment, union in affection,
Dear love, sound truth, they were our grand protection:
These were the twins which in our councils sat,
These gave prognostics of our future fate.
If these be longer lived our hopes increase,
These wars will usher in a longer peace.
But if New England's love die in its youth,
The grave will open next for blessed truth. . . .
This is the *Prologue* to thy future woe;
The *Epilogue* no mortal yet can know.

1676

57.

Regulation of Wages and Prices in Connecticut

The founding fathers of the New England colonies found it difficult to adjust their religious ideas to the increasing commercial interests of their communities. The competitive spirit of the growing number of merchants, whose business transactions often ignored the welfare of the community as a whole, prompted John Winthrop to remark that "the care of the public must over-sway all private respect." The Calvinist ethic forbade taking "excess" profits in response to short supplies, rising demands, or losses in other areas. The following Connecticut law of May 1676 is typical of legal restraints employed throughout New England to curb profits and wages.

Source: *The Public Records of the Colony of Connecticut, from October, 1706, to October, 1716, etc., etc.,* Charles J. Hoadly, ed., Hartford, 1870, Vol. V, pp. iv-v.

WHEREAS A GREAT CRY of oppression is heard among us, and that principally pointed at workmen and traders, which is hard to regulate without a standard prepared both for advance and for pay duly set as money, it is therefore ordered that the price of provision be duly set at each of our General Courts annually, according to true intelligence from Boston, for money sold, and then for such pay within six months paid, no merchant or trader shall advance above 2*d.* upon the shilling for profit, charge, and venture from Boston, or other market of like distance, for goods well bought with ready money; trustings and trifles under a shilling being left to each man's agreement, discretion, and moderation, according to a good conscience, to deal.

All goods as are subject to waste, the waste to be allowed as part of the first price or cost of the goods. And all breaches of this order to be punished proportionable to the value of the oppression, treble to the oppression; one-third to be restored to the party oppressed, and the residue half of it to the complainer that shall prove the fact, and half to the county treasury where the offense is committed.

And as for those tradesmen whose commodities are partly their own labor and partly materials they work upon, as tanners, shoemakers, smiths, and suchlike, as also such whose day's labor cannot ordinarily be known how much they daily effect, as weavers, tailors, and suchlike, and day laborers, there being great difficulty to regulate the prices of their ware and work, this Court, purposing in season to state orders respecting those things which at present is not attainable, do in the interim recommend it to all such tradesmen and laborers to consider the religious end of their callings, which is that receiving such moderate profit as may enable them to serve God and their neighbors with their arts and trades comfortably, they do not enrich themselves suddenly and inordinately (by oppressing prices and wages to the impoverishing their neighbors and rendering them in great measure incapable of convenient subsistence) live in the practice of that crying sin of oppression, but avoid it.

58.

WILLIAM HUBBARD: The Happiness of a People

A rising tide of democratic sentiment and the desire of the people to have a voice in their civil and religious government became manifest in America during the second half of the seventeenth century. In Puritan New England, change was facilitated by geography — dissatisfied colonists could leave the established societies to found new communities in the wilderness. Furthermore, doubts were being raised about the Calvinist principle of the chosen few. As political power began to slip from the hands of the "saints," clergymen such as William Hubbard warned their parishioners of the dangers of popular rule. On May 3, 1676, Hubbard gave an election day sermon, The Happiness of a People in the Wisdom of their Rulers Directing and in Obedience of their Brethren Attending Unto What Israel Ought To Do, *a portion of which follows. In good Calvinist fashion, he summoned biblical analogies to prove that the few chosen men of wisdom were best equipped to rule.*

Source: *The Happiness of a People in the Wisdom of their Rulers, etc., etc.,* Boston, 1676.

I WILL NOT HERE ENGAGE in any dispute as to whether it is necessary or convenient for a free people to use their liberty in often changing their magistrates or chief rulers. Concerning inferior officers, such as are fiscals and treasurers, whose places (by reason of the profit they are usually attended with) are more liable to temptation and corruption, there is no matter of danger in their change. . . .

But the supreme rulers, being as the heart and vitals of the commonwealth, it is not expedient to run a hazard in often changing them. Another speaks to the same purpose, that unless a country is very full of skillful and expert men, by often changing their rulers, the government will fall into the hands of rude and ignorant mechanics.

But where the wisdom of any country has by long experience seen cause to continue the same rulers, they had need be well-advised who would promote any innovation, especially at any difficult juncture of affairs. It cannot but be dangerous to put the helm into the hands of an unexperienced pilot in a tempestuous or stormy season. . . .

Let wisdom and knowledge be found in our electors, as well as in our elected rulers, and that will be the stability of our times and the strength of salvation. Our election is the foundation of our government. A small and inconsiderable error in the foundation may put the whole building much out of order. As in the body natural, a defect in the first connection is seldom helped by the second; so will it be found in the body politic. And in all ages, as the rulers are, so will be the people both in church and state. Therefore, how much it concerns those who have an opportunity in their hands, not only to keep it but to improve it and manage it aright, for the upholding and maintaining of good order and discipline, both in church and state. For if I mistake not, any man may make both a true prognostication and diagnosis of the state of your people through the whole order of your government, both ecclesiastical and civil, by your elections, and the quality of the persons you choose into places of trust, be they superiors or inferiors, in things sacred as well as civil. . . .

If any should expect that a character should here be given as to how to judge such men as may be accounted meet to be heads or leaders of Israel, the text is a full description; those who have understanding of the times know what Israel ought to do, and they who are such do discover themselves, or may be distinguished from others by these qualifications:

1. The fear of the Lord and the love of righteousness. The fear of the Lord is the beginning or chief part of wisdom, as the text tells us. He that is not wise for himself or for his own soul will never be wise for the commonwealth. They that are not of Israel will not much care to know what Israel ought to do. . . . So, to know or do that which is right, unless it is out of integrity of their hearts and conformity to the mind of God, does not in God's account demonstrate a man wise, or one that knows what Israel ought to do. God may make use of the common gifts of the spirit or natural endowments of men unsanctified for the good of His people (and often does when

the government is unavoidably devolved upon them), but it may be questioned whether a people can expect a blessing under rulers of their own voluntary choice whose piety may upon certain and good grounds be suspected, or denied, whatever their other qualifications may be.

2. Human learning in conjunction with the former. Those who, by the benefit of natural parts, experience, education, and study, have advantage above others to be acquainted with the world abroad, as well as with the laws and customs of their own people at home; for seeing that persons of that alloy have generally the chief managing of affairs in other nations, as much of that kind as may be had, cannot but be necessary for the better ordering of the affairs of Israel. . . .

The chief leaders of Israel, before the kings, were called judges . . . though the chief part of their work was generally to be captains of their wars, yet they received their title from their power of judging, which certainly required skill and knowledge of the laws by which they were to judge; how well it could be attained without the help of human learning I cannot understand. It was well replied by an officer of state to a nobleman who made small account of learning in the education of his son (aiming at no higher learning than to be able to ride a horse, or fly a hawk) that if it were so, then noblemen's sons must be content that mean men's children should govern the kingdom.

3. Constancy or steadiness is another property of a wise man, at least of one fit to be a leader of others. Not but that a wise man may sometimes change his mind, and his wisdom may lead him to so do. Sometimes we say second thoughts are best, but to be of a fickle, unconstant mind is the character of one, as Jacob said to Reuben, that will never excel; he is unstable as water which is neither easy to keep in any bounds nor observant of one constant motion, but apt to change direction upon

every occasion. . . . A wise man always sails by the same compass, though not always by the same wind. Particular actions may be changed upon occasion, though the same mark may still be aimed at.

4. Moderation is another property of wisdom, for if peace and truth be the best end, then all ought to aim at moderation and pacific ways, and principles that run not in extremes are certainly the directed ways that lead thereunto. Therefore, it is observed that men of moderate and peaceable tempers are both the wisest and most useful men in all societies. Extremes are always dangerous; for as the philosopher says of virtue, that it lies in the middle between two vices; as the extremes are on the either hand, so may truth generally be found in the middle between two errors. Some may think they can never run far enough from that which they hate, whereas wise men can see as dangerous a precipice of error before them as that which they left behind them. This is too evident in most of the controversies which have been bandied for and against in our times, in most of which he that has taken the least view of the managing of such controversies will find that men of rigid and severe spirits have missed both peace and truth, the design of all good and wise men. . . .

5. Peaceableness is another property of wisdom which ought to be esteemed by the tendency it has toward the obtaining of the great end that all ought to aim at for the honor of God and the good of societies, which is much more promoted by peace than by the proceeding of force. . . . There is nothing more easy than to begin a war, and nothing more difficult than to manage it aright, or bring it to a good issue; therefore is peace in a wise man's eyes a rich booty. "Contention," said Solomon, "is like the breaking forth of water"; therefore, his advice is to leave off before it be meddled with (Prov. 17:14). . . . War is welcome to none but those who never made trial of

it, as I fear New England may find by woeful experience, which will leave a reflection of the deeper guilt, if any have had any needless hand in the inviting of such an unwelcome guest into the country. But I judge charitably of the present auditors, and dare not censure others. . . .

For all necessary and fundamental truths, we cannot be too resolved in contention for them; but for opinions of less certainty and moment, where wise and good men have always needed a latitude wherein to differ and turn aside one for the other, it can be no part of wisdom to be too eager or rigorous about them. Some of the disciples in Luke 9:54, 55 are ready to think he deserves no less than to be destroyed by fire from heaven, that follows not with them, whom yet our Savior justly reproves for giving too much way to their own spirits.

6. Condescension may in the next place be added as another property of wisdom. Humility, the ground of condescension, is nearly allied to wisdom; both are the procreant causes of great blessings to the sons of men (Prov. 22:4). The wisdom that is from above is gentle, easy to be entreated. No man ever thought Abraham was the less wise because he was willing to yield in the controversy between him and Lot. Those parts of the natural body that are the most yielding are the strongest and the most useful. Were all the other parts of our body as hard and as stiff as the bones, how uncomfortable would our actions and motions be. If any find it better to break than bow, they may thereby gain some reputation for their willfulness, but not for their wisdom.

This must always be understood of things lawful and expedient to be yielded to, else Moses, the meekest man on earth, will not move an inch, nor Paul, the most humble of Christians, will not yield or give place for an hour; both of whom in other places could deny themselves and yield very far.

7. Deliberation is the last property of wisdom which I need mention. It can hard-

ly be thought consistent with wisdom to do anything rashly in matters of moment. Temerity of counsel argues height of folly and pride rather than depth of wisdom; for in so doing, we should lay aside reason, our most faithful and best counselor, and commit ourselves to be transported with passion. What is to be appointed forever after had need be a long time deliberated upon. For although our statutes are not unalterable, like those of the Medes and Persians, yet that which is maturely agreed upon at first will stand in the less need of alteration or abrogation; the frequency of either of which abates much of the rigor of the laws and honor of the lawmakers. Many things in human affairs admit not of second thoughts, notwithstanding they are generally known to be the best. "Therefore," says Solomon, "with good advice make war, and manage likewise with the same care, lest there be no room to play an after game." And wise men account it the best way, to put as little as possible to peradventure. . . . Much deliberation in public affairs, especially if the case is about matters of moment, is rarely found a disadvantage. . . . Deliberation is of use in the enacting as well as in the executing of all civil constitutions and decrees; therefore, wise lawyers have been always wont to account that laws of difficult terms and doubtful event had need be deliberately thought upon before they be enacted or put in execution. . . .

THE CONCERNS belonging unto you in reference to Israel are either ecclesiastical or political; the latter are civil and military, so that, as you see, they are threefold — sacred, civil, and military. I shall briefly, as the matter will allow, touch upon all three in their order.

First, the sacred or religious concerns of Israel are under your care and conduct; *imperative*, as they say, though not *elicitive*. I need not take up time (it were not to spend but to misspend it) in proving that civil rulers have to do with matters of religion. That text alone, Matt. 22:37, is enough to prove it: "Thou shalt love the Lord thy God with all thy heart, with all thy soul, and with all thy might." Love is ready to summon in all the powers and faculties within its reach, to attend the will of Him whom it loves, as its last end. It was said by the prophet, "the merchandise of Tyre shall be holiness to the Lord"; may it not as well be said that the magistracy of Rome, as the merchandise of Tyre, was to be holiness to the Lord? . . .

Nor is this doctrine any new upstart invention, but a truth owned by the doctors and fathers of the church, as they were called in Constantine's time. But to prevent any mistake here, by speaking more particularly about the civil magistrate's power and duty concerning matters of religion, it may be reduced to these three heads: (1) the establishing of the true religion where it never was; (2) the maintaining and upholding of it where it is; (3) the reforming of it where it is grown corrupt.

1. Concerning the first of these, it is made, by learned and judicious writers, one of the undoubted rights of sovereignty to determine what religion shall be publicly professed and exercised within their dominions, *i.e.*, what in their consciences is most agreeable to the Word of God and the Divine Law. What reason can be rendered why the popish religion is professed only in Spain, the Lutheran in some kingdoms and provinces of Europe, the Calvinist in others, and indulgence granted in some kingdoms to differing professions, but that the chief rulers, kings or princes of state, are this or that way affected? Why else do we in New England, who possess the doctrine of Calvin, yet practise the discipline of them called Independent or Congregational churches, but because the authority of the country believes that to be most agreeable to the mind of God? . . .

2. In the second place, therefore, the same power is necessarily required to uphold and maintain the true religion, which was at first to establish it, that is to maintain the public profession thereof. Creation and Providence are the issues of the same Being and Power. If the true religion had not been publicly professed without the countenance of the civil power, it is not likely to be professed longer than the same power will give allowance or command or encouragement. Now this is or ought to be done, first, by taking care that public ministers be sent forth to preach the word of truth, administer the sacraments, and celebrate all other rites and ordinances that concern the true religion. . . .

3. By setting up and encouraging the schools of learning, for he that wills the end is supposed also to will the means. It is not meet that the Israelites should always go down to the Philistines to sharpen their weapons, which they are to use in fighting against the enemies of God's church, or for whetting the tools they must use in tilling God's field. Christian emperors of old were wont to adorn Christian temples with the spoils of the Gentiles; Julian complained that the Christians beat the heathen philosophers with their own weapons; therefore did he fully contrive to deprive the Christians of the benefit of schools and other means of humane learning, thinking that to be the likeliest means whereby to overthrow the Christian religion. . . .

4. By the calling of synods or councils, as need may require, to discuss points of religion in controversy, and to hear matters of differences and determine them, and be of use whenever there is want of truth or peace in the churches. . . .

5. By preventing the spreading and growth of corrupt doctrine and heretical opinions. . . . Heresy, schism, or corrupt doctrine is not without due ground, so to be judged and condemned. I shall not here entertain you with any sharp invective or declaiming against a boundless toleration of all religions lest it should be an insinuation that some here present are inclined that way, which I believe there was never any occasion given to suspect. . . .

FOR THE CIVIL CONCERNS of the leaders in Israel there are exigents in reference to this, as well as the former, that require much prudence and skill to know what Israel ought to do in and about the same.

There are two things principally to be attended here: (1) the moderation of the civil power to a due temperament; (2) the faithful improvement of it for the public good. For the first, it is very true, what a learned person observed, that power is very apt to overflow in whatever vessel it is put, unless it be tempered with a due proportion of wisdom and goodness, and is apt though never so necessary in itself, to prove pernicious and destructive to them that are concerned in it. . . .

As they are heads, so they ought to go before the members of the civil body by their pious and grave examples, as well as by their prudent counsels, and their just and wholesome laws; for 'tis true, examples of rulers are always observed to take more place with their people than their precepts. Posterity will as much honor the piety of him that left a good pattern of honesty or bounty as they will the wisdom of him that left a good body of just and useful laws. And some princes have inherited the title and surname of good and liberal, as well as for other perfections of wisdom or justice. . . .

They are as pillars that uphold the foundation of the state, which in a sense may be said to be built thereon. . . .

They are the watchmen set upon the gate of Jerusalem, to descry danger afar off; which has its truth in reference to civil magistrates as well as spiritual watchmen, by the consent of the best interpreters.

It is not safe to give false alarms, because it may occasion true ones to be the less regarded; nor yet to give an uncertain sound, for who then can be prepared for the battle? Yet in such cases, a godly jealousy should not be complained of: if a watchman shall cry an enemy, when a friend comes he ought more to be commended for his care than blamed for his error, as some have said.

They are nursing fathers to Israel, and physicians to Gilead; it is the office of the head, not only to prevent the evil that may befall the other members of the body but also to heal it; and therefore they must be endued with much patience to bear with the forwardness of those to whom they stand so related. . . .

They are lawgivers, to prescribe wholesome laws and rules of living; the fountains of justice, whence flow the streams that refresh and make fruitful the heritage of Israel. Yea, a ruler is a living law. "The law," says one, "is a heart without affection, a mind without passion, a treasurer to keep what we have, and a steward to distribute what we ought to have." But it had needs be considered that the life and virtue of laws lie in their execution; therefore, the making of more laws than need or can be executed may weaken the authority of those that are in force and necessary to be attended. Yea, it is found by experience that leniency in the executing of laws is more hurtful than severity. The best way to keep an instrument in good tune is to leave the strings upon a sharp, they being naturally apt to fail of themselves. And mankind is continually bent to declining. Politicians use to account violation of laws not so hurtful as nonexecution. In this sense, he that is slothful in his work is brother to him that is a great waster (Prov. 18:9).

They are lords as well as lawgivers. Nothing more truly denotes lordship than a power to give laws. No debt is more justly due than homage and tribute to the lords of a people, which, if it were freely paid, need not be exacted; where we are required to render to God the things that are God's, in the same clause it is added likewise, to Caesar the things that are Caesar's. Yet the less of the dead fly of covetousness that is found in the ointment, the more precious will the savor thereof be found. . . .

In fine, they are God's, whose wisdom and goodness they ought to imitate as well as His power; He by His wise Providence maintains a sweet harmony in the whole world, though it is made up of contrary elements, all of which notwithstanding, peace and concord is maintained in the universe by a wise and equal temperament of those several qualities. . . .

Thus much of the civil affairs relating to the heads of Israel.

THE MILITARY CONCERNMENTS of Israel call for no little prudence and skill; sometimes as much stress and difficulty is found here as in the former. Intricacies may be so interwoven that it may prove very difficult to know what Israel ought to do. The church is sometimes compared to a lily among thorns; there will be need of gloves of iron to handle such thorns and pricking briars. These may want as well courage to know *how*, as wisdom to know *what* to do. Yea, sometimes God may be provoked to vex a people with all adversity. He may raise such a tempest in a nation that both head and members may be at their wit's end, not knowing what to do.

Hence it has been found in former times that no manner of persons ever gained more interest in the hearts of people than those that have manfully undertaken and successfully accomplished their wars. . . .

1. It is never safe to take a dog by the ears: so Solomon tells us (Prov. 26:15); that is, to meddle with an unnecessary strife

or begin a war without just ground. This is one part of the power of the sword, which as the magistrate bears not in vain, so neither must he take it in vain. "For he that so taketh the sword," as our Savior speaks in Matt. 26:52, "may expect to perish by the sword." There is nothing more necessary than self-preservation, and our friends, as our country, are part of ourselves. Nor is actual confederation always necessary for taking up arms in the behalf of our friends, as appears by the instance of Abraham and Lot, yet there had need be great care that an unnecessary war be not undertaken, for the war is on one side a heinous evil or murder, and on both it is a judgment.

2. War ought not to be made without good advice (Prov. 20:18 and 24:6), which is to be understood as well of the managing as of the first engaging in a war. Josiah, by overhasty resolves, engaged himself and his people in a fatal war, which proved the ruin of both. 'Tis true, when a nation or people are ripe for a judgment, God judiciously brings it upon them, yet according to the mediate causality, it may be the imprudences, indiscretion, and want of faith in God's promises, not asking counsel at God's oracle, that may be the immediate cause. . . .

3. Offer violence to no man (Luke 3:14). A necessary rule for all men of war to walk by, for then we must not do wrong to the innocent, be they Indians or English. . . .

4. Let not him that puts on his harness boast of himself as he that puts it off (I Kings 20:10, 11). It is not the wisest way to divide the bear's skin, before the bear is killed. They that overcome before they begin to fight never may have cause to boast of their victory. . . .

5. Let them that undertake a war first sit down and count whether they can with 10,000 men deal with them that come against them with 20,000 men (Luke 14:31). . . .

6. Wisdom is better than weapons or war, for wisdom delivered the city when the strength of the inhabitants failed. And wisdom will direct when the iron is blunt. Joab deserved to be captain more for his conduct than his courage, though he was not defective in the latter. And may it not be said of many of our young men that have so sadly fallen by the edge of the sword of late that it was for want of something else, more than for lack of courage? . . .

7. Looking up to God, who is the Lord of Hosts, He turns the scale of victory to which side He pleases. He taught David's hands to war and his fingers to fight; he was a man of war from his youth, experienced in all feats of arms, difficulties of wars, hazard of battle, and danger of secret ambushments, yet was he always fearful of encounters until he saw God marching before him in the head of his army (I Chron. 14:15). He was designed by God to cut down the trees of the wilderness that overshadowed the vine brought out of Egypt, which never thrived nor became very fruitful till David had the pruning of it, or the dressing of the ground where it was planted.

59.

Anonymous: On Bacon's Rebellion in Virginia

The first popular revolt in the English colonies arose from the refusal of Governor William Berkeley and the Virginia House of Burgesses to protect small landowners from brutal Indian attacks. When Berkeley disbanded a volunteer army of 300 colonists, whom he branded as rebels, 60 of the group followed Nathaniel Bacon in retaliatory raids on the Indians. A new assembly at Jamestown then granted Bacon an official commission as an Indian fighter. Berkeley launched several military expeditions against Bacon's group, but Bacon managed to seize control of the government and called a reform assembly to repeal low tobacco price scales and high taxes. "Bacon's Rebellion" collapsed shortly thereafter when Bacon died of fever late in 1676. The following account of the Rebellion was written in 1705, at the request of a British investigating commission, by a colonist known only as "T.M."

Source: Force, I: "The Beginning, Progress, and Conclusion of Bacon's Rebellion in Virginia, In the Years 1675 and 1676."

My dwelling was in Northumberland, the lowest county on [the] Potomac River, Stafford being the upmost, where having also a plantation, servants, cattle, etc., my overseer there had agreed with one Robt. Hen to come thither and be my herdsman, who then lived ten miles above it. But on a Sabbath day morning in the summer [of] 1675, people [on] their way to church saw this Hen lying athwart his threshold, and an Indian without the door, both chopped on their heads, arms and other parts, as if done with Indian hatchets, the Indian was dead, but Hen when asked who did that? answered Doegs Doegs, and soon died. Then a boy came out from under a bed, where he had hid himself, and told them Indians had come at break of day and, done those murders.

From this Englishman's blood did (by degrees) arise Bacon's Rebellion, with the following mischiefs which overspread all Virginia and twice endangered Maryland, as by the ensuing account is evident. . . .

In these frightful times the most exposed small families withdrew into our houses of better numbers, which we fortified with palisades and redoubts. Neighbors in bodies joined their labors from each plantation to others alternately, taking their arms into the fields and setting sentinels. No man stirred out-of-doors unarmed. Indians were (ever and anon) espied, three, four, five, or six in a party lurking throughout the whole land, yet (what was remarkable) I rarely heard of any houses burned, though abundance was forsaken, nor ever of any corn or tobacco cut up, or other injury done, besides murders, except the killing a very few cattle and swine. Frequent complaints of bloodshed were sent to Sir Wm. Berkeley (then Governor) from the heads of the rivers, which were as often answered with promises of assistance.

These at the heads of James and York rivers (having now most people destroyed by the Indians flight thither from Potomac) grew impatient at the many slaughters of

their neighbors and rose for their own defense, who choosing Mr. Bacon for their
leader, sent oftentimes to the Governor,
humbly beseeching a commission to go
against those Indians at their own charge;
which His Honor as often promised, but
did not send. The mysteries of these delays
were wondered at, and which I never heard
any could penetrate into, other than the effects of his passion and a new (not to be
mentioned) occasion of avarice, to both
which he was (by the common vogue)
more than a little addicted; whatever were
the popular surmises and murmurings, viz.,
"that no bullets would pierce beaver skins";
"rebels' forfeitures would be loyal inheritances," etc.

During these protractions and people often slain, most or all the officers, civil and
military, with as many dwellers next the
heads of the rivers as made up 300 men,
taking Mr. Bacon for their commander, met
and concerted together, the danger of going
without a commission on the one part and
the continual murders of their neighbors on
the other part (not knowing whose or how
many of their own turns might be next),
and came to this resolution, viz., to prepare
themselves with necessaries for a march, but
interim to send again for a commission,
which if could or could not be obtained by
a certain day, they would proceed, commission or no commission.

This day lapsing and no commission
come, they marched into the wilderness in
quest of these Indians, after whom the
Governor sent his proclamation, denouncing
all rebels who should not return within a
limited day; whereupon those of estates
obeyed. But Mr. Bacon, with fifty-seven
men, proceeded until their provisions were
near spent, without finding enemies when
coming nigh a fort of friend[ly] Indians, on
the other side a branch of James River, they
desired relief, offering payment; which these
Indians kindly promised to help them with
on the morrow, but put them off with
promises until the third day, so as having

then eaten their last morsels they could not
return, but must have starved in the way
homeward. And now 'twas suspected these
Indians had received private messages from
the Governor, and those to be the causes of
these delusive procrastinations; whereupon
the English waded shoulder deep through
that branch to the fort's palisades, still entreating and tendering pay for victuals. But
that evening a shot from the place they left
on the other side of that branch killed one
of Mr. Bacon's men, which made them believe those in the fort had sent for other
Indians to come behind and cut them off.

Hereupon, they fired the palisades,
stormed and burned the fort and cabins,
and (with the loss of three English) slew
150 Indians.

The circumstances of this expedition Mr.
Bacon entertained me with, at his own
chamber, on a visit I made him, the occasion whereof is hereafter mentioned.

From hence they returned home, where
writs were come up to elect members for
an assembly, when Mr. Bacon was unanimously chosen for one, who coming down
the river was commanded by a ship with
guns to come on board, where waited Major Hone, the high sheriff of Jamestown,
ready to seize him, by whom he was carried
down to the Governor and by him received
with a surprising civility in the following
words, "Mr. Bacon, have you forgot to be
a gentleman." "No, may it please Your
Honor," answered Mr. Bacon. "Then," replied the Governor, "I'll take your parole,"
and gave him his liberty.

In March 1675-6 writs came up to Stafford to choose their two members for an
assembly to meet in May, when Colonel
Mason, Captain Brent, and other gentlemen
of that county invited me to stand a candi-
date — a matter I little dreamed of, having
never had inclinations to tamper in the precarious intrigues of government and my
hands being full of my own business. They
presented several cogent arguments, and I,
having considerable debts in that county,

besides my plantation concerns, where (in one and the other) I had much more severely suffered than any of themselves by the Indian disturbances in the summer and winter foregoing, I held it not (then) discreet to disoblige the rulers of it. So Colonel Mason with myself were elected without objection. He, at time convenient, went on horseback; I took my sloop, and, the morning I arrived to Jamestown after a week's voyage, was welcomed with the strange acclamations of, "All's over; Bacon is taken," having not heard at home of the southern commotions, other than rumors like idle tales of one Bacon risen up in rebellion, nobody knew for what, concerning the Indians.

The next forenoon, the Assembly being met in a chamber over the General Court and our speaker chosen, the Governor sent for us down, where His Honor with a pathetic emphasis, made a short, abrupt speech wherein were these words: "If they had killed my grandfather and grandmother, my father and mother and all my friends, yet if they had come to treat of peace, they ought to have gone in peace and sat down."

The two chief commanders at the forementioned siege, who slew the four Indian great men, [were] present and part of our Assembly.

The Governor stood up again and said, "If there be joy in the presence of the angels over one sinner that repents, there is joy now, for we have a penitent sinner come before us. Call Mr. Bacon." Then did Mr. Bacon, upon one knee at the bar, deliver a sheet of paper confessing his crimes, and begging pardon of God, the King, and the Governor. Whereto (after a short pause) he answered, "God forgive you, I forgive you," thrice repeating the same words, when Colonel Cole (one of the Council) said, "And all that were with him." Yea, said the Governor and all that were with him, twenty or more persons being then in irons who were taken coming down in the same and other vessels with Mr. Bacon.

About a minute after this, the Governor starting up from his chair a third time, said, "Mr. Bacon! if you will live civilly but till next Quarter Court (doubling the words) but till next Quarter Court, I will promise to restore you again to your place there," pointing with his hand to Mr. Bacon's seat, he having been of the Council, before these troubles, though he had been a very short time in Virginia, but was deposed by the foresaid proclamation. And in the afternoon, passing by the court door in my way to our chamber, I saw Mr. Bacon on his quondam [former] seat with the Governor and Council, which seemed a marvelous indulgence to one whom he had so lately proscribed as a rebel.

The Governor had directed us to consider of means for security from the Indian insults and to defray the charge, etc., advising us to beware of two rogues among us, naming Lawrence and Drumond, both dwelling at Jamestown and who were not at the Pascataway siege. . . .

While some days passed in settling the quotas of men, arms and ammunition, provisions, etc., each county was to furnish, one morning early a bruit ran about the town: "Bacon is fled, Bacon is fled." . . .

But Bacon was escaped into the country, having intimation that the Governor's generosity in pardoning him and his followers, and restoring him to his seat in Council, were no other than previous wheedles to amuse him and his adherents and to circumvent them by stratagem; forasmuch as the taking Mr. Bacon again into the Council was, first, to keep him out of the Assembly, and, in the next place, the Governor knew the country people were hastening down with dreadful threatenings to double revenge all wrongs should be done to Mr. Bacon or his men, or whoever should have had the least hand in them. . . .

In three or four days after this escape, upon news that Mr. Bacon was thirty miles up the river, at the head of 400 men, the

(Above) Courtesy, Maurice du Pont Lee, photo from Winterthur Libraries; (right) British Museum

(Above) Sir William Berkeley, portrait by an unknown artist; (right) protest sent to the King by Bacon's group in an attempt to remove Berkeley from office

Governor sent to the parts adjacent, on both sides [of the] James River, for the militia and all the men could be gotten to come and defend the town. Expresses came almost hourly of the army's approaches, who in less than four days after the first account of them at two o'clock, entered the town, without being withstood, and formed a body upon a green, not a flight shot from the end of the statehouse, of horse and foot, as well regular as veteran troops, who forthwith possessed themselves of all the avenues, disarming all in town, and coming thither in boats or by land.

In half an hour after this, the drum beat for the House to meet, and in less than an hour more, Mr. Bacon came with a file of fusiliers on either hand, near the corner of the statehouse, where the Governor and Council went forth to him. We saw from the window the Governor open [expose] his breast, and Bacon strutting between his two files of men with his left arm akimbo, flinging his right arm every way, both like men distracted; and if, in this moment of fury, that enraged multitude had fallen upon the Governor and Council, we of the Assembly expected the same immediate fate. I stepped down, and among the crowd of spectators found the seamen of my sloop, who prayed me not to stir from them, when in two minutes, the Governor walked toward his private apartment, a quoit's cast distant at the other end of the statehouse, the gentlemen of the Council following him. And after them walked Mr. Bacon, with outrageous postures of his head, arms, body, and legs, often tossing his hand from his sword to his hat; and after him came a detachment of fusiliers (muskets not being there in use), who, with their cocks bent, presented their fusils at a window of the Assembly chamber filled with faces, repeating with menacing voices, "We will have it, we will have it," [for] half a minute; when, as one of our House, a person known to many of them, shook his handkerchief out at the window, saying, "You shall have it, you shall have it" three or four times.

At these words, they set down their fusils, unbent their cocks, and stood still, until Bacon, coming back, followed him to their main body. In this hubbub, a servant of mine got so nigh as to hear the Governor's words, and also followed Mr. Bacon, and heard what he said, who came and told me that when the Governor opened his breast, he said "Here! shoot me. Before God, fair, mark, shoot," often rehearsing [repeating] the same, without any other words. Whereto, Mr. Bacon answered, "No, may it please Your Honor we will not hurt a hair of your head, nor of any other man's. We are come for a commission to save our lives from the Indians, which you have so often promised, and now we will have it before we go."

But when Mr. Bacon followed the Governor and Council with the aforementioned impetuous (like delirious) actions, while that party presented their fusils at the window full of faces, he said "Damn my blood, I'll kill Governor, Council, Assembly, and all, and then I'll sheathe my sword in my own heart's blood." And afterward 'twas said Bacon had given a signal to his men, who presented their fusils at those gazing out at the window, that if he should draw his sword, they were on sight of it to fire and slay us, so near was the massacre of us all that very minute, had Bacon in that paroxysm of frantic fury but drawn his sword before the pacific handkerchief was shaken out at window.

In an hour or more after these violent concussions, Mr. Bacon came up to our chamber and desired a commission from us to go against the Indians. Our speaker sat silent, when one Mr. Blayton, a neighbor to

Mr. Bacon and elected with him a member of Assembly for the same county (who therefore dared speak to him), made answer, "It was not in our province, or power, nor of any other, save the King's vicegerent, our Governor." He pressed hard nigh half an hour's harangue on the preserving our lives from the Indians, inspecting the public revenues, the exorbitant taxes, and redressing the grievances and calamities of that deplorable country, whereto having no other answer, he went away dissatisfied. . . .

I never had been conversant in military matters, and also having lived tenderly, my service could be of no benefit because the hardships and fatigues of a wilderness campaign would put a speedy period to my days. Little expecting to hear of more intestine broils, I went home to Potomac, where reports were afterward various: we had account that General Bacon was marched with 1,000 men into the forest to seek the enemy Indians; and, in a few days after, our next news was that the Governor had summoned together the militia of Gloucester and Middlesex counties, to the number of 1,200 men, and proposed to them to follow and suppress that rebel Bacon; whereupon arose a murmuring before his face "Bacon, Bacon, Bacon," and all walked out of the field, muttering as they went "Bacon, Bacon, Bacon," leaving the Governor and those that came with him to themselves, who being thus abandoned, wafted over Chesapeake Bay thirty miles to Accomac, where are two counties of Virginia.

Mr. Bacon, hearing of this, came back part of the way, and sent out parties of horse patrols through every county, carrying away prisoners, all whom he distrusted might any more molest his Indian prosecution, yet giving liberty to such as pledged him their oaths to return home and live quiet; the copies or contents of which oaths I never saw but heard were very strict, though little observed.

About this time was a spy detected pretending himself a deserter, who had twice or thrice come and gone from party to party, and was by council of war sentenced to death, after which Bacon declared openly to him that if any one man in the army would speak a word to save him, he should not suffer, which no man appearing to do, he was executed. Upon this manifestation of clemency, Bacon was applauded for a merciful man, not willing to spill Christian blood; nor indeed was it said that he put any other man to death in cold blood, or plunder any house.

Nigh the same time came Major Langston, with his troop of horses, and quartered two nights at my house, who (after high compliments from the general) told me I was desired to accept the lieutenancy for preserving the peace in the northern counties between Potomac and Rappahannock rivers. I humbly thanked His Honor, excusing myself, as I had done before on that invitation of the like nature at Jamestown, but did hear he was mightily offended at my evasions and threatened to remember me.

The Governor made a second attempt, coming over from Accomac, with what men he could procure, in sloops and boats forty miles up the river to Jamestown, which Bacon hearing of came, again down from his forest pursuit, and finding a bank not a flight shot long, cast up thwart the neck of the peninsula there in Jamestown. He stormed it and took the town, in which attack were twelve men slain and wounded, but the Governor, with most of his followers, fled back down the river in their vessels.

Here, resting a few days, they concerted [agreed to] the burning of the town, wherein Mr. Lawrence and Mr. Drumond, owning the two best houses save one, set fire each to his own house, which example the soldiers following laid the whole town (with church and statehouse) in ashes, saying the rogues should harbor no more there.

On these reiterated molestations, Bacon called a convention at Middle Plantation, fifteen miles from Jamestown, in the month of August 1676, where an oath with one or more proclamations were formed, and writs by him issued for an assembly. The oaths or writs I never saw, but one proclamation commanded all men in the land, on pain of death, to join him and retire into the wilderness upon arrival of the forces expected from England, and oppose them until they should propose or accept to treat of an accommodation, which we who lived comfortably could not have undergone, so as the whole land must have become an Aceldama if God's exceeding mercy had not timely removed him. . . .

Mr. Bacon now returned from his last expedition sick of a flux; without finding any enemy Indians, having not gone far by reason of the vexations behind him. Nor had he one dry day in all his marches to and fro in the forest while the plantations (not fifty miles distant) had a summer so dry as stinted the Indian corn and tobacco, etc., which the people ascribed to the *pawawings, i.e.,* the sorceries, of the Indians. In a while Bacon died and was succeeded by his lieutenant general, Ingram . . . whereupon hastened over the Governor to York River, and with him they articled for themselves and whom else they could. And so all submitted and were pardoned; exempting those nominated and otherwise proscribed, in a proclamation of indemnity, the principal of whom were Lawrence and Drumond. . . .

This Mr. Drumond was a sober Scotch gentleman of good repute with whom I had not a particular acquaintance, nor do I know the cause of that rancor His Honor had against him, other than his pretensions in common for the public. But meeting him by accident the morning I left the town, I advised him to be very wary, for he saw the Governor had put a brand upon him. He (gravely expressing my name) answered, "I am in over shoes, I will be over boots," which I was sorry to hear and left him.

The last account of Mr. Lawrence was from an uppermost plantation, whence he and four others . . . with horses, pistols, etc., marched away in a snow ankle deep, who were thought to have cast themselves into a branch of some river rather than to be treated like Drumond.

Bacon's body was so made away as his bones were never found to be exposed on a gibbet as was purposed, stones being laid in his coffin, supposed to be done by Lawrence.

Near this time arrived a small fleet with a regiment from England — Sir John Berry, admiral; Col. Herbert Jefferies [Jeffries], commander of the land forces; and Colonel Morrison, who had one year been a former governor. There, all three joined in commission with or to Sir William Barclay, soon after when a General Court and also an Assembly were held, where some of our former Assembly (with so many others) were put to death, diverse whereof were persons of honest reputations and handsome estates, as that the Assembly petitioned the Governor to spill no more blood. And Mr. Pres-ley, at his coming home, told me he believed the Governor would have hanged half the country, if they had let him alone.

The first was Mr. Bland, whose friends in England had procured his pardon to be sent over with the fleet, which he pleaded at his trial was in the Governor's pocket (though whether 'twas so or how it came there I know not, yet did not hear 'twas openly contradicted); but he was answered by Colonel Morrison that he pleaded his pardon at sword's point, which was looked upon an odd sort of reply, and he was executed (as was talked) by private instructions from England, the Duke of York having sworn, "By God, Bacon and Bland should die."

The Governor went in the fleet to London (whether by command from His Majesty or spontaneous I did not hear), leaving Colonel Jefferies in his place. And by next shipping came back a person who waited on His Honor in his voyage and until his death, from whom a report was whispered about that the King did say, "that old fool has hanged more men in that naked country than he had done for the murder of his father."

Whereof, the Governor hearing, died soon after without having seen His Majesty; which shuts up this tragedy.

1677

60.

Charter of West New Jersey

West New Jersey came under the proprietorship of the Quakers by an indirect route. King Charles II granted the territory that later became New York and New Jersey to his brother James (later King James II), who conveyed New Jersey to Lord John Berkeley and Sir George Carteret. In 1674, Berkeley sold western New Jersey to the Quakers John Fenwicke and Edward Byllynge. The Concessions and Agreements of March 13, 1677, probably drafted by William Penn, guaranteed many of the Quaker principles of civil government, including freedom of religion and trial by jury. The chapters printed below comprise the entire charter of the colony.

Source: Thorpe, V, pp. 2548-2551.

That these following concessions are the common law, or fundamental rights, of the Province of West New Jersey.

That the common law or fundamental rights and privileges of West New Jersey are individually agreed upon by the proprietors and freeholders thereof to be the foundation of the government, which is not to be altered by the legislative authority or free Assembly hereafter mentioned and constituted, but that the said legislative authority is constituted according to these fundamentals, to make such laws as agree with and maintain the said fundamentals, and to make no laws that in the least contradict, differ, or vary from the said fundamentals, under what pretense or allegation soever.

But if it so happen that any person or persons of the said General Assembly shall therein designedly, willfully, and maliciously move or excite any to move any matter or thing whatsoever that contradicts or any ways subverts any fundamentals of the said laws in the constitution of the government of this Province, it being proved by seven honest and reputable persons, he or they shall be proceeded against as traitors to the said government.

That these concessions, law, or great charter of fundamentals be recorded in a fair table, in the Assembly House, and that they be read at the beginning and dissolving of every general free Assembly. And it is further agreed and ordained that the said concessions, common law, or great charter of fundamentals be written in fair tables, in every common hall of justice within this Province, and that they be read in solemn manner four times every year, in the presence of the people, by the chief magistrates of those places.

That no men nor number of men upon earth have power or authority to rule over men's consciences in religious matters, therefore, it is consented, agreed, and ordained that no person or persons whatsoever within the said Province, at any time or times hereafter, shall be any ways upon any pretense whatsoever called in question, or in the least punished or hurt, either in person, estate, or privilege, for the sake of his opinion, judgment, faith, or worship toward God in matters of religion. But that all and every such person and persons may, from time to time, and at all times, freely and fully have and enjoy his and their judgments, and the exercises of their consciences in matters of religious worship throughout all the said Province.

That no proprietor, freeholder, or inhabitant of the said Province of West New Jersey shall be deprived or condemned of life, limb, liberty, estate, property, or any ways hurt in his or their privileges, freedoms, or franchises, upon any account whatsoever, without a due trial, and judgment passed by twelve good and lawful men of his neighborhood first had. And that in all causes to be tried, and in all trials, the person or persons arraigned may except against any of the said neighborhood without any reason rendered (not exceeding thirty-five), and in case of any valid reason alleged, against every person nominated for that service.

And that no proprietor, freeholder, free denizen, or inhabitant in the said Province shall be attached, arrested, or imprisoned for or by reason of any debt, duty, or thing whatsoever (cases felonious, criminal, and treasonable excepted) before he or she have personal summon or summons, left at his or her last dwelling place, if in the said Province, by some legal authorized officer constituted and appointed for that purpose, to appear in some court of judicature for the said Province, with a full and plain account of the cause or thing in demand, as also the name or names of the person or persons at whose suit, and the court where he is to appear, and that he has at least fourteen days' time to appear and answer the said suit, if he or she live or inhabit within forty English miles of the said court: and if at a further distance, to have for every twenty miles, two days' time more for his and their appearance, and so proportionably for a larger distance of place.

That upon the recording of the summons and nonappearance of such person and persons, a writ or attachment shall or may be issued out to arrest or attach the person or persons of such defaulters, to cause his or their appearance in such court, returnable at a day certain, to answer the penalty or penalties in such suit or suits. And if he or they shall be condemned by legal trial and judgment, the penalty or penalties shall be paid and satisfied out of his or their real or personal estate so condemned, or cause the person or persons so condemned to lie in execution [detention] till satisfaction of the debt and damages be made.

Provided always, if such person or persons so condemned shall pay and deliver such estate, goods, and chattels which he or any other person has for his or their use, and shall solemnly declare and aver that he or they have not any further estate, goods, or chattels wheresoever to satisfy the person or persons (at whose suit he or they are condemned) their respective judgments, and shall also bring and produce three other persons as compurgators, who are well known and of honest reputation and approved of by the commissioners of that division where they dwell or inhabit, which shall in such open court likewise solemnly declare and aver that they believe in their consciences such person and persons so condemned have not wherewith further to pay the said condemnation or condemnations, he or they shall be thence forthwith discharged from their said imprisonment, any law or custom to the contrary thereof, heretofore in the said Province, notwithstanding. . . .

That there shall be in every court three justices or commissioners, who shall sit with the twelve men of the neighborhood, with them to hear all causes, and to assist the said twelve men of the neighborhood in case of law; and that they, the said justices, shall pronounce such judgment as they shall receive from, and be directed by the said twelve men, in whom only the judgment resides, and not otherwise.

And in case of their neglect and refusal, that then one of the twelve, by consent of the rest, pronounce their own judgment as the justices should have done.

And if any judgment shall be passed, in any case, civil or criminal, by any other person or persons, or any other way than according to this agreement and appointment, it shall be held null and void, and such person or persons so presuming to give judgment shall be severely fined, and, upon complaint made to the General Assembly, by them be declared incapable of any office or trust within this Province.

That in all matters and causes, civil and criminal, proof is to be made by the solemn and plain averment, of at least two honest and reputable persons; and in case that any person or persons shall bear false witness, and bring in his or their evidence contrary to the truth of the matter as shall be made plainly to appear, that then every such person or persons shall in civil causes suffer the penalty which would be due to the person or persons he or they bear witness against. And in case any witness or witnesses, on the behalf of any person or persons indicted in a criminal cause, shall be found to have borne false witness for fear, gain, malice or favor, and thereby hinder the due execution of the law and deprive the suffering person or persons of their due satisfaction, that then and in all other cases of false evidence such person or persons shall be first severely fined, and next that he or they shall forever

be disabled from being admitted in evidence, or into any public office, employment, or service within this Province.

That all and every person and persons whatsoever who shall prosecute or prefer any indictment or information against others for any personal injuries or matter criminal, or shall prosecute for any other criminal cause (treason, murder, and felony, only excepted), shall and may be master of his own process and have full power to forgive and remit the person or persons offending against him or herself only, as well before as after judgment and condemnation, and pardon and remit the sentence, fine, and punishment of the person or persons offending, be it personal or other whatsoever.

That the trials of all causes, civil and criminal, shall be heard and decided by the verdict or judgment of twelve honest men of the neighborhood, only to be summoned and presented by the sheriff of that division or propriety where the fact or trespass is committed; and that no person or persons shall be compelled to fee [pay] any attorney or counselor to plead his cause, but that all persons have free liberty to plead his own cause, if he please. And that no person nor persons imprisoned upon any account whatsoever within this Province shall be obliged to pay any fees to the officer or officers of the said prison, either when committed or discharged.

That in all public courts of justice for trials of causes, civil or criminal, any person or persons, inhabitants of the said Province, may freely come into and attend the said courts, and hear and be present at all or any such trials as shall be there had or passed, that justice may not be done in a corner nor in any covert manner, being intended and resolved, by the help of the Lord and by these our concessions and fundamentals, that all and every person and persons inhabiting the said Province shall, as far as in us lies, be free from oppression and slavery.

1682

61.

William Penn: First Frame of Government of Pennsylvania

The province of Pennsylvania was chartered in 1681, and in the following year its "Frame of Government" was drawn up by William Penn. The "Frame" presupposed the existence of the royal charter granting to Penn and his heirs the right to lay taxes, appoint officers, administer justice, incorporate towns, and dispose of land in the province. Though Penn had the advice of John Locke, Algernon Sidney, and others in preparing the "Frame," it proved unworkable as a governmental structure, notwithstanding a penal code attached to it that was advanced for its time. A Quaker by faith and an enemy of all oppression, Penn nevertheless believed in government for the people by enlightened gentlemen like himself and thought those he ruled would be content with his genuine liberality; he found instead that they insisted upon defining their own rights.

Source: Thorpe, V, pp. 3052-3059.

THE PREFACE

When the great and wise God had made the world of all His creatures, it pleased him to choose man His deputy to rule it; and to fit him for so great a charge and trust, He did not only qualify him with skill and power but with integrity to use them justly. This native goodness was equally his honor and his happiness; and while he stood here, all went well. There was no need of coercive or compulsive means; the precept of divine love and truth, in his bosom, was the guide and keeper of his innocency. But lust prevailing against duty made a lamentable breach upon it; and the law, that before had no power over him, took place upon him, and his disobedient posterity, that such as would not live conformable to the holy law within should fall under the reproof and correction of the just law without in a judicial administration.

This the apostle teaches in diverse of his epistles: "The law (says he) was added because of transgression." In another place, "Knowing that the law was not made for the righteous man but for the disobedient and ungodly, for sinners, for unholy and profane, for murderers, for whoremongers, for them that defile themselves with mankind, and for man-stealers, for liars, for perjured persons," etc., But this is not all; he opens and carries the matter of government a little further: "Let every soul be subject to the higher powers; for there is no power but of God. The powers that be are ordained of God; whosoever therefore resisteth the power, resisteth the ordinance of God. For rulers are not a terror to good works but to evil; wilt thou then not be afraid of the power? Do that which is good, and thou shalt have praise of the same." "He is the minister of God to thee for good." "Wherefore ye must needs be subject, not only for wrath but for conscience sake."

This settles the divine right of government beyond exception, and that for two ends: first, to terrify evildoers; second, to cherish those that do well, which gives government a life beyond corruption and makes it as durable in the world, as good men shall be; so that government seems to me a part of religion itself, a thing sacred in its institution and end. For, if it does not directly remove the cause, it crushes the effects of evil, and is as such (though a lower, yet) an emanation of the same Divine Power that is both author and object of pure religion; the difference lying here, that the one is more free and mental, the other more corporal and compulsive in its operations. But that is only to evildoers; government itself being otherwise as capable of kindness, goodness, and charity as a more private society.

They weakly err that think there is no other use of government than correction, which is the coarsest part of it. Daily experience tells us that the care and regulation of many other affairs, more soft and daily necessary, make up much of the greatest part of government; and which must have followed the peopling of the world, had

Adam never fell, and will continue among men on earth under the highest attainments they may arrive at, by the coming of the blessed Second Adam, the Lord from heaven. Thus much of government in general, as to its rise and end.

For particular frames and models, it will become me to say little; and comparatively I will say nothing. My reasons are:

First, that the age is too nice and difficult for it, there being nothing the wits of men are more busy and divided upon. It is true, they seem to agree to the end, to wit, happiness; but, in the means, they differ as to divine, so to this human felicity; and the cause is much the same, not always want of light and knowledge, but want of using them rightly. Men side with their passions against their reason, and their sinister interests have so strong a bias upon their minds that they lean to them against the good of the things they know.

Second, I do not find a model in the world that time, place, and some singular emergencies have not necessarily altered; nor is it easy to frame a civil government, that shall serve all places alike.

Third, I know what is said by the several admirers of monarchy, aristocracy, and democracy, which are the rule of one, a few, and many, and are the three common ideas of government, when men discourse on the subject. But I choose to solve the controversy with this small distinction, and it belongs to all three: Any government is free to the people under it (whatever be the frame) where the laws rule, and the people are at party to those laws, and more than this is tyranny, oligarchy, or confusion.

But, lastly, when all is said, there is hardly one frame of government in the world so ill designed by its first founders that, in good hands, would not do well enough; and story tells us the best, in ill ones, can do nothing that is great or good — witness the Jewish and Roman states. Governments, like clocks, go from the motion men give them; and as governments are made and moved by men, so by them they are ruined too. Wherefore, governments rather depend upon men than men upon governments. Let men be good, and the government cannot be bad; if it be ill, they will cure it. But, if men be bad, let the government be never so good, they will endeavor to warp and spoil it to their turn.

I know some say let us have good laws, and no matter for the men that execute them; but let them consider that though good laws do well, good men do better; for good laws may want good men, and be abolished or evaded by ill men; but good men will never want good laws, nor suffer ill ones. It is true, good laws have some awe upon ill ministers, but that is where they have not power to escape or abolish them, and the people are generally wise and good; but a loose and depraved people (which is the question) love laws and an administration like themselves. That, therefore, which makes a good constitution must keep it, viz.: men of wisdom and virtue, qualities, that because they descend not with worldly inheritances must be carefully propagated by a virtuous education of youth; for which after ages will owe more to the care and prudence of founders, and the successive magistracy, than to their parents, for their private patrimonies.

These considerations of the weight of government, and the nice and various opinions about it, made it uneasy to me to think of publishing the ensuing frame and conditional laws, foreseeing both the censures they will meet with, from men of differing humors and engagements, and the occasion they may give of discourse beyond my design.

But, next to the power of necessity (which is a solicitor that will take no denial) this induced me to a compliance that we have (with reverence to God, and good conscience to men) to the best of our skill, contrived and composed the frame and laws of this government, to the great end of all government, viz.: To support power in reverence with the people, and to secure the people from the abuse of power; that they may be free by their just obedience, and the magistrates honorable, for their just administration; for liberty without obedience is confusion, and obedience without liberty is slavery. To carry this evenness is partly owing to the constitution, and partly to the magistracy; where either of these fail, government will be subject to convulsions; but where both are wanting, it must be totally subverted; then where both meet, the government is like to endure. Which I humbly pray and hope God will please to make the lot of this of Pennsylvania. Amen.

THE FRAME

To all persons to whom these presents may come.

Whereas, King Charles II, by his letters patents, under the great seal of England, bearing date the 4th day of March in the thirty-and-third year of the King, for diverse considerations therein mentioned, hath been graciously pleased to give and grant unto me, William Penn, by the name of William Penn, Esquire, son and heir of Sir William Penn, deceased, and to my heirs and assigns forever, all that tract of land, or province, called Pennsylvania, in America, with diverse great powers, preeminences, royalties, jurisdictions, and authorities necessary for the well-being and government thereof: Now know ye, that for the well-being and government of the said province, and for the encouragement of all the freemen and planters that may be therein concerned, in pursuance of the powers aforementioned, I, the said William Penn, have declared, granted, and confirmed, and by these presents, for me, my heirs, and assigns, do declare, grant, and confirm unto all the freemen, planters, and adventurers of, in, and to the said province, these liberties, franchises, and properties, to be held, enjoyed and kept by the freemen, planters, and inhabitants . . . forever.

Imprimis, that the government of this province shall, according to the powers of the patent, consist of the governor and freemen of the said province, in form of a provincial Council and General Assembly, by whom all laws shall be made, officers chosen, and public affairs transacted, as is hereafter respectively declared, that is to say —

II. That the freemen of the said province shall, on the 20th day of the twelfth month, which shall be in this present year 1682, meet and assemble in some fit place, of which timely notice shall be beforehand given by the governor or his deputy; and then and there shall choose out of themselves seventy-two persons of most note for their wisdom, virtue, and ability, who shall meet, on the 10th day of the first month next ensuing, and always be called, and act as, the provincial Council of the said province.

III. That, as the first choice of such provincial Council, one-third part of the said provincial Council shall be chosen to serve for three years, then next ensuing; one-third part, for two years then next ensuing; and one-third part, for one year then next ensuing such election, and no longer; and that the said third part shall go out accordingly. And on the 20th day of the twelfth month, as aforesaid, yearly forever afterward, the freemen of the said province shall, in like manner, meet and assemble together, and then choose twenty-four persons, being one-third of the said number, to serve in provincial Council for three years; it being intended that one-third part of the whole provincial Council (always consisting, and to consist, of seventy-two persons, as aforesaid) falling off yearly, it shall be yearly supplied by such new yearly elections, as aforesaid; and that no one person shall continue therein longer than three years. And, in case any member shall decease before the last election during his time, that then at the next election ensuing his decease, anoth-

er shall be chosen to supply his place for the remaining time he was to have served, and no longer.

IV. That after the first seven years, every one of the said third parts, that goeth yearly off, shall be incapable of being chosen again for one whole year following; that so all may be fitted for government, and have experience of the care and burden of it.

V. That the provincial Council, in all cases and matters of moment, as their arguing upon bills to be passed into laws, erecting courts of justice, giving judgment upon criminals impeached, and choice of officers, in such manner as is hereinafter mentioned, not less than two-thirds of the whole provincial Council shall make a quorum, and that the consent and approbation of two-thirds of such quorum shall be had in all such cases and matters of moment. And moreover that, in all cases and matters of lesser moment, twenty-four members of the said provincial Council shall make a quorum, the majority of which twenty-four shall, and may, always determine in such cases and causes of lesser moment.

VI. That in this provincial Council, the governor or his deputy shall or may always preside, and have a treble voice; and the said provincial Council shall always continue and sit upon its own adjournments and committees.

VII. That the governor and provincial Council shall prepare and propose to the General Assembly, hereafter mentioned, all bills which they shall, at any time, think fit to be passed into laws, within the said province; which bills shall be published and affixed to the most noted places, in the inhabited parts thereof, thirty days before the meeting of the General Assembly, in order to the passing them into laws or rejecting of them, as the General Assembly shall see meet.

VIII. That the governor and provincial Council shall take care that all laws, statutes, and ordinances, which shall at any time be made within the said province, be duly and diligently executed.

IX. That the governor and provincial Council shall, at all times, have the care of the peace and safety of the province, and that nothing be by any person attempted to the subversion of this frame of government.

X. That the governor and provincial Council shall, at all times, settle and order the situation of all cities, ports, and market towns in every county, modeling therein all public buildings, streets, and market places, and shall appoint all necessary roads and highways in the province.

XI. That the governor and provincial Council shall, at all times, have power to inspect the management of the public treasury, and punish those who shall convert any part thereof to any other use than what hath been agreed upon by the governor, provincial Council, and General Assembly.

XII. That the governor and provincial Council shall erect and order all public schools, and encourage and reward the authors of useful sciences and laudable inventions in the said province.

XIII. That, for the better management of the powers and trust aforesaid, the provincial Council shall, from time to time, divide itself into four distinct and proper committees for the more easy administration of the affairs of the province, which divides the seventy-two into four eighteens, every one of which eighteens shall consist of six out of each of the three orders, or yearly elections, each of which shall have a distinct portion of business, as followeth: First, a committee of plantations, to situate and settle cities, ports, and market towns, and highways, and to hear and decide all suits and controversies relating to plantations. Second, a committee of justice and safety, to secure the peace of the province, and punish the maladministration of those who subvert justice to the prejudice of the public, or private, interest. Third, a committee of trade and treasury, who shall regulate all trade and

commerce according to law, encourage manufacture and country growth, and defray the public charge of the province. And, fourth, a committee of manners, education, and arts, that all wicked and scandalous living may be prevented, and that youth may be successively trained up in virtue and useful knowledge and arts. The quorum of each of which committees being six, that is, two out of each of the three orders, or yearly elections, as aforesaid, make a constant and standing Council of twenty-four, which will have the power of the provincial Council, being the quorum of it, in all cases not excepted in the 5th Article; and in the said committees, and standing Council of the province, the governor, or his deputy, shall or may preside, as aforesaid; and in the absence of the governor, or his deputy, if no one is by either of them appointed, the said committees or Council shall appoint a president for that time, and not otherwise; and what shall be resolved at such committees shall be reported to the said Council of the province, and shall be by them resolved and confirmed before the same shall be put in execution; and that these respective committees shall not sit at one and the same time, except in cases of necessity.

XIV. And to the end that all laws prepared by the governor and provincial Council aforesaid may yet have the more full concurrence of the freemen of the province, it is declared, granted, and confirmed that, at the time and place or places for the choice of a provincial Council, as aforesaid, the said freemen shall yearly choose members to serve in a General Assembly, as their representatives, not exceeding 200 persons, who shall yearly meet on the 20th day of the second month, which shall be in the year 1683 following, in the capital town or city of the said province, where, during eight days, the several members may freely confer with one another; and, if any of them see meet, with a committee of the provincial Council (consisting of three out of each of the four committees aforesaid, being twelve in all) which shall be, at that time, purposely appointed to receive from any of them proposals for the alterations or amendment of any of the said proposed and promulgated bills. And on the ninth day from their so meeting, the said General Assembly, after reading over the proposed bills by the clerk of the provincial Council, and the occasions and motives for them being opened by the governor or his deputy, shall give their affirmative or negative, which to them seemeth best, in such manner as hereinafter is expressed. But not less than two-thirds shall make a quorum in the passing of laws, and choice of such officers as are by them to be chosen.

XV. That the laws so prepared and proposed, as aforesaid, that are assented to by the General Assembly, shall be enrolled as laws of the province, with this style: By the governor, with the assent and approbation of the freemen in provincial Council and General Assembly.

XVI. That, for the establishment of the government and laws of this province, and to the end there may be a universal satisfaction in the laying of the fundamentals thereof: the General Assembly shall, or may, for the first year, consist of all the freemen of and in the said province; and ever after it shall be yearly chosen, as aforesaid; which number of 200 shall be enlarged as the country shall increase in people, so as it do not exceed 500 at any time. The appointment and proportioning of which, as also the laying and methodizing of the choice of the provincial Council and General Assembly, in future times, most equally to the divisions of the hundreds and counties, which the country shall hereafter be divided into, shall be in the power of the provincial Council to propose, and the General Assembly to resolve.

XVII. That the governor and the provincial Council shall erect, from time to time, standing courts of justice, in such places and number as they shall judge convenient for the good government of the said province. And that the provincial Council shall, on the 13th day of the first month, yearly, elect and present to the governor, or his deputy, a double number of persons, to serve for judges, treasurers, masters of rolls within the said province for the next year ensuing. And the freemen of the said province, in the county courts, when they shall be erected, and till then in the General Assembly, shall, on the 23rd of the second month, yearly, elect and present to the governor, or his deputy, a double number of persons to serve for sheriffs, justices of the peace, and coroners, for the year next ensuing; out of which respective elections and presentments, the governor or his deputy shall nominate and commissionate the proper number for each office, the third day after the said presentments, or else the first named in such presentment for each office shall stand and serve for that office the year ensuing.

XVIII. But forasmuch as the present condition of the province requires some immediate settlement, and admits not of so quick a revolution of officers; and to the end the said province may, with all convenient speed, be well ordered and settled, I, William Penn, do therefore think fit to nominate and appoint such persons for judges, treasurers, masters of the rolls, sheriffs, justices of the peace, and coroners as are most fitly qualified for those employments; to whom I shall make and grant commissions for the said offices, respectively, to hold to them, to whom the same shall be granted, for so long time as every such person shall well behave himself in the office, or place, to him respectively granted, and no longer. And upon the decease or displacing of any of the said officers, the succeeding officer, or officers, shall be chosen, as aforesaid.

XIX. That the General Assembly shall continue so long as may be needful to impeach criminals, fit to be there impeached, to pass bills into laws that they shall think fit to pass into laws, and till such time as the governor and provincial Council shall declare that they have nothing further to propose unto them for their assent and approbation; and that declaration shall be a dismiss to the General Assembly for that time; which General Assembly shall be, notwithstanding, capable of assembling together upon the summons of the provincial Council at any time during that year, if the said provincial Council shall see occasion for their so assembling.

XX. That all the elections of members, or representatives of the people, to serve in provincial Council and General Assembly, and all questions to be determined by both, or either of them, that relate to passing of bills into laws, to the choice of officers, to impeachments by the General Assembly, and judgment of criminals upon such impeachments by the provincial Council, and to all other cases by them respectively judged of importance, shall be resolved and determined by the ballot; and unless on sudden and indispensable occasions, no business in provincial Council, or its respective committees, shall be finally determined the same day that it is moved.

XXI. That at all times when, and so often as it shall happen that the governor shall or may be an infant, under the age of one-and-twenty years, and no guardians or commissioners are appointed in writing by the father of the said infant, or that such guardians or commissioners shall be deceased; that during such minority, the provincial Council shall, from time to time, as they shall see meet, constitute and appoint guardians or commissioners, not exceeding three; one of

which three shall preside as deputy and chief guardian during such minority, and shall have and execute, with the consent of the other two, all the power of a governor, in all the public affairs and concerns of the said province.

XXII. That, as often as any day of the month, mentioned in any article of this charter, shall fall upon the first day of the week, commonly called the Lord's Day, the business appointed for that day shall be deferred till the next day, unless in case of emergency.

XXIII. That no act, law, or ordinance whatsoever shall, at any time hereafter, be made or done by the governor of this province, his heirs, or assigns, or by the freemen in the provincial Council, or the General Assembly to alter, change, or diminish the form, or effect, of this charter, or any part or clause thereof, without the consent of the governor, his heirs, or assigns, and six parts of seven of the said freemen in provincial Council and General Assembly.

XXIV. And lastly, that I, the said William Penn, for myself, my heirs, and assigns, have solemnly declared, granted and confirmed, and do hereby solemnly declare, grant, and confirm, that neither I, my heirs, nor assigns shall procure or do anything or things, whereby the liberties in this charter contained and expressed shall be infringed or broken; and if anything be procured by any person or persons contrary to these premises, it shall be held of no force or effect.

In witness whereof, I, the said William Penn, have unto this present charter of liberties set my hand and broad seal, this 25th day of the second month, vulgarly called April, in the year of Our Lord 1682.

1684

62.

INCREASE MATHER: An Arrow Against Profane and Promiscuous Dancing

The social life of New England was strictly limited by a Puritan leadership that was anxious to avoid the sinful frivolities — as they were supposed to be — of life back in England. However, within the narrow limits prescribed by rigorous codes in almost every colony, there was still room for disagreement on the nature and value of expressions of merriment. Thus, although as early as 1625 John Cotton could express the moderate view that "dancing (yea though mixt) I would not simply condemn," almost sixty years later Increase Mather could condemn it not only simply but absolutely in his Arrow Against Profane and Promiscuous Dancing. *This strange work, which proclaimed all mixed dancing to be intolerable, was prompted by a discussion with fellow ministers on the subject. The* Arrow *filled thirty pages; the sharpest paragraphs are reprinted below.*

Source: *An Arrow Against Profane and Promiscuous Dancing Drawn out of the Quiver of the Scriptures*, Boston, 1684.

CONCERNING THE CONTROVERSY about dancing, the question is not whether all dancing be in itself sinful. It is granted that pyrrhical or polemical saltation, *i.e.*, when men vault in their armor to show their strength and activity, may be of use. Nor is the question whether a sober and grave dancing of men with men or of women with women be not allowable; we make no doubt of that, where it may be done without offense, in due season and with moderation. The Prince of Philosophers has observed truly that dancing or leaping is a natural expression of joy; so that there is no more sin in it than in laughter or any outward expression of inward rejoicing.

But our question is concerning gynecandrical dancing, or that which is commonly called mixed or promiscuous dancing, viz., of men and women (be they elder or younger persons) together. Now this we affirm to be utterly unlawful and that it cannot be tolerated in such a place as New England without great sin.

And that it may appear that we are not transported by affection without judgment, let the following arguments be weighed in the balance of the sanctuary.

That which the Scripture condemns is sinful. None but atheists will deny this proposition; but the Scripture condemns promiscuous dancing. This assumption is proved from the Seventh Commandment. It is an eternal truth to be observed in expounding the Commandments that whenever any sin is forbidden, not only the highest acts of that sin but all degrees thereof and all occasions leading thereto are prohibited. Now we cannot find one orthodox and judicious divine that writes on the Commandments but mentions promiscuous dancing as a breach of the Seventh Commandment, as being an occasion and an incentive to that which is evil in the sight of God.

Yea, this is so manifest as that the assembly in the larger catechism do expressly take notice of dancings as a violation of the Commandments. . . .

The unchaste touches and gesticulations used by dancers have a palpable tendency to that which is evil. Whereas some object that they are not sensible of any ill motions occasioned in them, by being spectators or actors in such saltations, we are not bound to believe all which some pretend concerning their own mortification. . . .

Now then, shall the gentiles, who had only the dark light of nature to show them what things are good and what evil, condemn petulant dancings? And shall Christians, who have the Scriptures and the glorious light of the Gospel to illuminate them, practise or plead for such works of darkness? And shall that abomination be set up in New England (the place where the light of the Gospel has shined so gloriously), which moral heathen have detested? The Lord lay not this great sin to the charge of any who have at all been guilty of it. . . .

A Christian should do nothing wherein he cannot exercise grace or put a respect of obedience to God on what he does. This in lawful recreations may be done. . . . But who can seriously pray to the Holy God to be with him when he is going to a promiscuous dance? It is that which hinders religious exercises, especially for persons to go immediately from hearing a sermon to a gynecandrical dance. It is a high degree of profaneness, an impudent contempt put upon the Gospel. The devil thereby catches away the good seed of the Word, and the former religious exercise is rendered ineffectual. . . .

Now, they that frequent promiscuous dancings, or that send their children thereunto, walk disorderly and contrary to the apostles' doctrine. It has been proved that such a practice is a scandalous immorality and therefore to be removed out of churches by discipline, which is the broom of Christ, whereby He keeps His churches clean. . . .

But will you that are professors of religion have your children to be thus taught? The Lord expects that you should give the children who are baptized into His name another kind of education, that you should bring them up in the nurture and admonition of the Lord. And do you not hear the Lord expostulating the case with you and saying, you have taken my children, the children that were given unto me; the children that were solemnly engaged to renounce the pomps of Satan; but is this a light matter that you have taken these my children and initiated them in the pomps and vanities of the wicked one, contrary to your covenant? What will you say in the day of the Lord's pleading with you?

We have that charity for you as to believe that you have erred through ignorance and not wickedly; and we have, therefore, accounted it our duty to inform you in the truth. If you resolve not on reformation, you will be left inexcusable. However it shall be, we have now given our testimony and delivered our own souls. Consider what we say, and the Lord give you understanding in all things.

1688

63.

Against the Traffic of Mens-body

The first Negro slaves brought to the English colonies in America by Dutch traders arrived in Virginia in 1619, though slavery as an institution was not formally recognized by the colony until 1661. While the number of slaves remained small throughout the seventeenth century, their status inspired protests from various quarters, notably the Quakers and the kindred Mennonite Germans of Pennsylvania. The Mennonites, a radical Protestant sect whose members settled at Germantown near Philadelphia in 1683, were especially critical of the institution, for reasons set forth in the following resolutions of their monthly meeting of February 1688. It is the earliest known protest of its kind in the American colonies.

Source: *The Pennsylvania Magazine of History and Biography*, Philadelphia, 1880, Vol. IV, pp. 28-30.

This is to the Monthly Meeting held at Rigert Worrell's.

These are the reasons why we are against the traffic of mens-body as follows: Is there any that would be done or handled at this manner, viz., to be sold or made a slave for all the time of his life? How fearful and fainthearted are many on sea when they see a strange vessel, being afraid it should be a Turk, and they should be taken and sold for slaves in Turkey. Now what is this better done as Turks do? Yea, rather is it worse for them which say they are Christians, for we hear that the most part of such Negroes are brought hither against their will and consent, and that many of them are stolen. Now, though they are black, we cannot conceive there is more liberty to have them slaves as it is to have other white ones. There is a saying that we shall do to all men like as we will be done ourselves, making no difference of what generation, descent, or color they are. And those who steal or rob men, and those who buy or purchase them, are they not all alike? Here is liberty of conscience, which is right and reasonable. Here ought to be likewise liberty of the body, except of evildoers, which is another case. But to bring men hither, or to rob and sell them against their will, we stand against.

In Europe there are many oppressed for conscience sake; and here there are those oppressed which are of a black color. And we, who know that men must not commit adultery, some do commit adultery in others, separating wives from their husbands and giving them to others, and some sell the children of those poor creatures to other men. Oh! do consider well this thing, you who do it, if you would be done at this manner, and if it is done according [to] Christianity? You surpass Holland and Germany in this thing. This makes an ill report in all those countries of Europe, where they hear of that the Quakers do here handle men like they handle there the cattle. And for that reason some have no mind or inclination to come hither.

And who shall maintain this your cause or plead for it? Truly we cannot do so except you shall inform us better hereof, viz., that Christians have liberty to practise these things. Pray! What thing in the world can be done worse toward us than if men should rob or steal us away and sell us for slaves to strange countries, separating husbands from their wives and children.

Being now this is not done at that manner we will be done at, therefore, we contradict and are against this traffic of mensbodies. And we who profess that it is not lawful to steal must likewise avoid to purchase such things as are stolen, but rather help to stop this robbing and stealing if possible and such men ought to be delivered out of the hands of the robbers and set free as well as in Europe. Then is Pennsylvania to have a good report; instead it has now a bad one for this sake in other countries. Especially whereas the Europeans are desirous to know in what manner the Quakers do rule in their province, and most of them do look upon us with an envious eye. But if this is done well, what shall we say is done evil?

If once these slaves (which they say are so wicked and stubborn men) should join themselves, fight for their freedom and handle their masters and mistresses as they did handle them before, will these masters and mistresses take the sword at hand and war against these poor slaves, like we are able to believe some will not refuse to do? Or have these Negroes not as much right to fight for their freedom as you have to keep them slaves?

Now consider well this thing, if it is good or bad. And in case you find it to be good to handle these blacks at that manner, we desire and require you hereby lovingly that you may inform us herein, which at this time never was done, viz., that Christians have liberty to do so, to the end we shall be satisfied in this point, and satisfy likewise our good friends and acquaintances in our native country, to whom it is a terror or fearful thing that men should be handled so in Pennsylvania.

64.

New England ABC

For more than a century the New England Primer, *first published, perhaps as early as 1688, by Benjamin Harris, was the leading textbook for elementary education in early America. "The Little Bible," as it came to be known, combined religious instruction with lessons in grammar. The eighty-page booklet taught the alphabet with the help of crude woodcuts, moral texts, and couplets as in the selection below. The child's prayer, "Now I Lay Me Down to Sleep," also first appeared in the* Primer, *probably in 1748.*

Source: *New England Primer.*

In *A*dam's fall
We sinned all.

Thy life to mend
This *B*ook attend.

The *C*at doth play
And after slay.

A *D*og will bite
A thief at night.

An *E*agle's flight
Is out of sight.

The idle *F*ool
Is whipt at school.

As runs the *G*lass
Man's life doth pass.

My book and *H*eart
Shall never part.

*J*ob feels the rod,
Yet blesses God.

*K*ings should be good;
Not men of blood.

The *L*ion bold
The *L*amb doth hold.

The *M*oon gives light
In time of night.

*N*ightingales sing
In time of Spring.

Young *O*badias,
David, Josias,
All were pious.

*P*eter denies
His Lord, and cries.

*Q*ueen Esther sues,
And saves the Jews.

*R*achel doth mourn
For her first-born.

*S*amuel anoints
Whom God appoints.

*T*ime cuts down all
Both great and small.

*U*riah's beauteous wife
Made David seek his life.

*W*hales in the sea
God's voice obey.

*X*erxes the great did die
And so must you and I.

*Y*outh forward slips;
Death soonest nips.

*Z*accheus he
Did climb the tree
His Lord to see.

1689

65.

ANONYMOUS: On the Rebellion Against Governor Andros

The crisis of 1688-1689 in the American colonies, paralleling developments in England as William of Orange and his wife Mary succeeded James II on the throne, was largely precipitated by James's colonial policies. To facilitate closer political and economic control over the colonies, Charles II had, in 1684, annulled the 1629 charter of Massachusetts. James, who succeeded Charles in 1685, went even further by the formation of a union of English colonies ultimately reaching from Maine to the Delaware River, appointing Sir Edmund Andros governor-general. In Massachusetts, where economic success had blunted original Puritan zeal, Andros' policies reinforced the position of a group of religious moderates, and were interpreted by the remaining Puritans as divine retribution for their loss of faith. Andros was finally overthrown in April 1689 — for political and economic, as well as religious, reasons. The following account of the rebellion was set down three weeks later by "A.B.," an anonymous reporter hurrying to issue his version before any "false reports" might reach England.

Source: Force, IV, 10, pp. 6-12.

I. We have seen more than a decade of years rolled away, since the English world had the discovery of a horrid popish plot; wherein the bloody devotees of Rome had in their design and prospect no less than the extinction of the Protestant religion; which mighty work they called "the utter subduing of a pestilent heresy"; wherein (they said) there never were such hopes of success since the death of Queen Mary, as now in our days. And we were of all men the most insensible if we should apprehend a country so remarkable for the true profession and pure exercise of the Protestant religion as New England is, wholly unconcerned in the infamous plot. To crush and break a country so entirely and signally made up of Reformed Churches, and at length to involve it in the miseries of an utter extirpation, must needs carry even a supererogation of merit with it among such as were intoxicated with a bigotry inspired into them by the great Scarlet Whore.

II. To get us within the reach of the des-

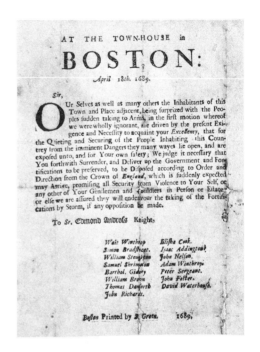

(Above) Courtesy, the Rhode Island State Archives, (right) Massachusetts Historical Society

(Above) Sir Edmund Andros, portrait by F. S. Batcheler; (right) broadside warning Gov. Andros to surrender, 1689

olation desired for us, it was no improper thing that we should first have our Charter vacated, and the hedge which kept us from the wild beasts of the field effectually broken down. The accomplishment of this was hastened by the unwearied solicitations and slanderous accusations of a man, for his malice and falsehood, well known unto us all. Our Charter was with a most injurious pretense (and scarce that) of law, condemned before it was possible for us to appear at Westminster in the legal defense of it; and without a fair leave to answer for ourselves concerning the crimes falsely laid to our charge, we were put under a president and Council, without any liberty for an Assembly, which the other American plantations have, by a commission from His Majesty.

III. The commission was as illegal for the form of it as the way of obtaining it was malicious and unreasonable; yet we made no resistance thereunto as we could easily have done; but chose to give all mankind a

demonstration of our being a people sufficiently dutiful and loyal to our King; and this with yet more satisfaction, because we took pains to make ourselves believe as much as ever we could of the wheedle then offered unto us — that His Majesty's desire was no other than the happy increase and advance of these provinces by their more immediate dependence on the Crown of England.

And we were convinced of it by the courses immediately taken to damp and spoil our trade; whereof decays and complaints presently filled all the country; while in the meantime neither the honor nor the treasure of the King was at all advanced by this new model of our affairs, but a considerable charge added unto the Crown.

IV. In little more than half a year we saw this commission superseded by another, yet more absolute and arbitrary, with which Sir Edmund Andros arrived as our governor; who besides his power, with the advice and consent of his Council, to make laws and raise taxes as he pleased, had also authority by himself to muster and employ all persons residing in the territory as occasion shall serve; and to transfer such forces to any English plantation in America, as occasion shall require. And several companies of soldiers were now brought from Europe to support what was to be imposed upon us, not without repeated menaces that some hundreds more were intended for us.

V. The government was no sooner in these hands but care was taken to load preferments principally upon such men as were strangers to and haters of the people. And everyone's observation has noted what qualifications recommended a man to public offices and employments, only here and there a good man was used, where others could not easily be had. The Governor himself, with assertions now and then falling from him, made us jealous that it would be thought for His Majesty's interest, if this people were removed and another succeeded in their room; and his far-fetched instruments that were growing rich among us would gravely inform us that it was not for His Majesty's interest that we should thrive.

But of all our oppressors we were chiefly squeezed by a crew of abject persons, fetched from New York, to be the tools of the adversary, standing at our right hand. By these were extraordinary and intolerable fees extorted from everyone upon all occasions, without any rules but those of their own insatiable avarice and beggary; and even the probate of a will must now cost as many pounds perhaps as it did shillings heretofore; nor could a small volume contain the other illegalities done by these horse leeches in the two or three years that they have been sucking of us; and what laws they made it was as impossible for us to know as dangerous for us to break. But we shall leave the men of Ipswich and of Plymouth (among others) to tell the story of the kindness which has been shown them upon this account. Doubtless a land so

ruled as once New England was has not without many fears and sighs beheld the wicked walking on every side, and the vilest men exalted.

VI. It was now plainly affirmed, both by some in open Council, and by the same in private converse, that the people in New England were all slaves, and the only difference between them and slaves is their not being bought and sold; and it was a maxim delivered in open court unto us by one of the Council that we must not think the privileges of Englishmen would follow us to the end of the world. Accordingly, we have been treated with multiplied contradictions to Magna Carta, the rights of which we laid claim unto. Persons who did but peaceably object against the raising of taxes without an Assembly have been for it fined, some £20, some £30, and others £50. Packed and picked juries have been very common things among us, when, under a pretended form of law, the trouble of some honest and worthy men has been aimed at; but when some of this gang have been brought upon the stage for the most detestable enormities that ever the sun beheld, all men have with admiration seen what methods have been taken that they might not be treated according to their crimes. Without a verdict, yea, without a jury sometimes, have people been fined most unrighteously; and some not of the meanest quality have been kept in long and close imprisonment without any the least information appearing against them, or a habeas corpus allowed unto them. In short, when our oppressors have been a little out of money, it was but pretending some offense to be inquired into, and the most innocent of men were continually put into no small expense to answer the demands of the officers, who must have money of them, or a prison for them, though none could accuse them of any misdemeanor.

VII. To plunge the poor people everywhere into deeper incapacities, there was one very comprehensive abuse given to us. Multitudes of pious and sober men through the land scrupled the mode of swearing on the Book, desiring that they might swear with an uplifted hand, agreeable to the ancient custom of the colony. And though we think we can prove that the common law among us (as well as in some other places under the English Crown) not only indulges but even commands and enjoins the rite of lifting the hand in swearing, yet they that had this doubt were still put by from serving upon any juries; and many of them were most unaccountably fined and imprisoned. Thus, one grievance is a Trojan horse, in the belly of which it is not easy to recount how many insufferable vexations have been contained.

VIII. Because these things could not make us miserable fast enough, there was a notable discovery made of we know not what flaw in all our titles to our lands; and, though besides our purchase of them from the natives, and besides our actual peaceable unquestioned possession of them for near threescore years, and besides the promise of King Charles II, in his proclamation sent over to us in the year 1683, that no man here shall receive any prejudice in his freehold or estate. We had the grant of our lands, under the seal of the Council of Plymouth; which grant was renewed and confirmed unto us by King Charles I under the Great Seal of England; and the General Court, which consisted of the patentees and their associates, had made particular grants hereof to the several towns (though it was now denied by the Governor, that there was any such thing as a town) among us; to all which grants the General Court annexed for the further securing of them "A General Act," published under the seal of the colony, in the year 1684.

Yet were we every day told that no man was owner of a foot of land in all the colony. Accordingly, writs of intrusion began everywhere to be served on people, that

after all their sweat and their cost upon their formerly purchased lands, thought themselves freeholders of what they had. And the Governor caused the lands pertaining to these and those particular men to be measured out for his creatures to take possession of; and the right owners, for pulling up the stakes, have passed through molestations enough to tire all the patience in the world. They are more than a few that were by terrors driven to take patents for their lands at excessive rates, to save them from the next that might petition for them. And we fear that the forcing of the people at the eastward hereunto gave too much rise to the late unhappy invasion made by the Indians on them. Blank patents were got ready for the rest of us, to be sold at a price, that all the money and moveables in the territory could scarce have paid. And several towns in the country had their commons begged by persons (even by some of the Council themselves) who have been privately encouraged thereunto, by those that sought for occasions to impoverish a land already peeled, meted out, and trodden down.

IX. All the Council were not engaged in these ill actions, but those of them which were true lovers of their country were seldom admitted to, and seldomer consulted at, the debates which produced these unrighteous things. Care was taken to keep them under disadvantages; and the Governor, with five or six more, did what they would. We bore all these, and many more such things, without making any attempt for any relief. Only Mr. Mather, purely out of respect unto the good of his afflicted country, undertook a voyage into England; which, when these men suspected him to be preparing for, they used all manner of craft and rage, not only to interrupt his voyage but to ruin his person too. God having through many difficulties given him to arrive at Whitehall, the King, more than once or twice, promised him a certain Magna

Carta for a speedy redress of many things which we were groaning under; and in the meantime said that our Governor should be written unto, to forbear the measures that he was upon. However, after this, we were injured in those very things which were complained of; and besides what wrong has been done in our civil concerns, we suppose the ministers and the churches everywhere have seen our sacred concerns apace going after them. How they have been discountenanced has had a room in the reflections of every man that is not a stranger in our Israel.

X. And yet that our calamity might not be terminated here, we are again briared in the perplexities of another Indian war; how, or why, is a mystery too deep for us to unfold. And though it is judged that our Indian enemies are not above 100 in number, yet an army of 1,000 English has been raised for the conquering of them; which army of our poor friends and brethren now under popish commanders (for in the army, as well as in the Council, papists are in commission) has been under such a conduct, that not one Indian has been killed, but more English are supposed to have died through sickness and hardship than we have adversaries there alive. And the whole war has been so managed that we cannot but suspect in it a branch of the plot to bring us low; which we leave to be further inquired into in due time.

XI. We did nothing against these proceedings but only cry to our God; they have caused the cry of the poor to come unto Him, and He hears the cry of the afflicted. We have been quiet hitherto, and so still we should have been had not the Great God at this time laid us under a double engagement to do something for our security; besides, what we have in the strangely unanimous inclination, which our countrymen by extremest necessities are driven unto. For, first, we are informed that the rest of the English America is alarmed with just and great fears, that they may be attacked by the French, who have lately (it is said) already treated many of the English with worse than Turkish cruelties. And while we are in equal danger of being surprised by them, it is high time we should be better guarded than we are like to be while the government remains in the hands by which it has been held of late. Moreover, we have understood (though the Governor has taken all imaginable care to keep us all ignorant thereof) that the Almighty God has been pleased to prosper the noble undertaking of the Prince of Orange, to preserve the three kingdoms from the horrible brinks of popery and slavery, and to bring to a condign punishment those worst of men, by whom English liberties have been destroyed; in compliance with which glorious action, we ought surely to follow the patterns which the nobility, gentry, and commonalty in several parts of those kingdoms have set before us, though they therein chiefly proposed to prevent what we already endure.

XII. We do therefore seize upon the persons of those few ill men which have been (next to our sins) the grand authors of our miseries; resolving to secure them for what justice, orders from His Highness, with the English Parliament shall direct, lest, ere we are aware, we find (what we may fear, being on all sides in danger) ourselves to be by them given away to a foreign power, before such orders can reach unto us; for which orders we now humbly wait. In the meantime, firmly believing that we have endeavored nothing but what mere duty to God and our country calls for at our hands; we commit our enterprise unto the blessing of Him who hears the cry of the oppressed, and advise all our neighbors, for whom we have thus ventured ourselves, to join with us in prayers and all just actions for the defense of the land.

1691

66.

Right to the Land by Occupancy

The Revolution in New-England Justified, probably written by Edward Rawson and published in Boston in 1691, was one of many tracts composed in defense of the overthrow of the Dominion of New England and Governor Edmund Andros in Massachusetts. Since the Dominion had been established and Andros installed by King James II, the New England Puritans seized on James's forced abdication in favor of William and Mary as a rationale for their revolt; they had, they said, returned a Protestant Crown colony to a rightful Protestant monarch. The portion of Rawson's work reprinted here includes a report of a discussion that took place between Governor Andros and John Higginson, minister at Salem. Higginson's argument was designed to show that the English King had never had any rights to land in America. Although it was specifically devised to justify the Puritans' actions during the "Glorious Revolution" in America, it does represent a view commonly held by the Puritans.

Source: Force, IV, 9: "The Revolution in New-England Justified, etc., etc."

THAT IN THE TIME of his [Andros'] government, he, without form or color of legal authority, made laws destructive of the liberty of the people, imposed and levied taxes, threatened and imprisoned them that would not be assisting to the illegal levies, denied that they had any property in their lands without patents from him, and, during the time of actual war with the Indians, he did supply them with ammunition, and several Indians declared that they were encouraged by him to make war upon the English, and he discountenanced making defense against the Indians. . . .

That Sir Edmund Andros, etc., did make laws destructive to the liberty of the subjects is notoriously known, for they made what laws they pleased without any consent of the people, either by themselves or representatives, which is indeed to destroy the fundamentals of the English and to erect a French government. . . . And whereas, by constant usage, any person might remove out of the country at his pleasure, a law was made that no man should do so without the governor's leave. And all fishing boats, coasters, etc., were to enter into £1,000 bond, whereby fees were raised for himself and creatures. This law could not pass at Boston, because many of Sir Edmund's council there opposed it; but then a junto of them, meeting at New York, passed it. And after that law was made, how should any dissatisfied persons ever obtain liberty to go for England to complain of their being oppressed by arbitrary governors?

But besides all this, they made laws for the levying monies without the consent of the people either by themselves or by an assembly; for, in order to the supporting their own government, they did, by an act bearing date March 3, 1686, raise considerable sums of money on the King's subjects in that part of his dominions, viz., a penny in the pound on all estates, personal or real, 20d. per head as poll money, a penny in the pound for goods imported, besides an excise on wine, rum, and other liquors. . . .

They did not only act according to these illegal taxes but they did inflict severe punishment on those true Englishmen who did oppose their arbitrary proceedings. . . .

That those who were in confederacy with Sir Edmund Andros for the enriching themselves on the ruins of New England, did invade the property as well as liberty of the subject, is in the next place to be cleared, and we trust will be made out beyond dispute. When they little imagined that there should ever be such a revolution in England as that which by means of His present Majesty this nation is blessed with, they feared not to declare their sentiments, to the inexpressible exasperation of the people whom they were then domineering over. They gave out that now their charter was gone, all their lands were the King's; that [they] themselves did represent the King; and that, therefore, men that would have any legal title to their lands must take patents of them, on such terms as they should see meet to impose. What people that had the spirits of Englishmen could endure this? That when they had, at vast charges of their own, conquered a wilderness and been in possession of their estates forty, nay, sixty years, that now a parcel of strangers, some of them indigent enough, must come and inherit all that the people now in New England, and their fathers before them, had labored for! Let the whole nation judge whether these men were not driving on a French design and had not fairly erected a French government. And that our adversaries may not insult and say these are words without proof, we shall here subjoin the testimonies of the Rev. Mr. Higginson, and several other worthy persons, given in upon oath concerning this matter:

Being called by those in present authority to give my testimony to the discourse between Sir Edmund Andros and myself, when he came from the Indian war, as he passed through Salem going for Boston in March 1688-9, I cannot refuse it and therefore declare as follows what was the substance of that discourse. Sir Edmund Andros, then governor, being accompanied with the Attorney General Graham, Secretary West, Judge Palmer, the room being also full of other people, most of them his attendants, he was pleased to tell me he would have my judgment about this question — Whether all the lands in New England were not the King's? I told him I was surprised with such a question and was not willing to speak to it; that being a minister, if it was a question about a matter of religion, I should not be averse, but, this being a state matter, I did not look upon it as proper for me to declare my mind in it; therefore entreated again and again that I might be excused.

Sir Edmund Andros replied and urged me with much importunity, saying, "Because you are a minister, therefore we desire to know your judgment in it." Then I told him, if I must speak to it, I would only speak as a minister from Scripture and reason, not meddling with the law. He said the King's attorney was present there to inform what was law. I then said I did not understand that the lands of New England were the King's, but the King's subjects, who had for more than sixty years had the possession and use of them by a twofold right, warranted by the word of God: (1) By a right of just occupation from the grand charter in Genesis, first and ninth chapters, whereby God gave the earth to the sons of Adam and Noah, to be subdued and replenished; (2) By a right of purchase from the Indians, who were native inhabitants and had possession of the land before the English came hither; and, that having lived here sixty years, I did certainly know that from the beginning of these plantations our fathers entered upon the land, partly as a wilderness and *vacuum domicilium* and partly by the consent of the Indians, and therefore care was taken to treat with them and to gain their consent, giving them such a valuable consideration as was to their satisfaction. And this I told them I had the more certain knowledge of because, having learned the Indian language in my younger time, I was at several times made use of by the government and by divers particular plantations as an interpreter in treating with the Indians about their lands, which being done and agreed on, the several townships and proportions of lands of particular men were ordered and settled by the government of the country; and therefore I did believe that the lands of New England were the subjects' properties and not the King's lands.

Sir Edmund Andros and the rest replied that the lands were the King's, and that he gave the lands within such limits to his subjects by a charter upon such conditions as were not performed, and therefore all the lands of New England have returned to the King, and that the attorney general then present could tell what was law. [He] spoke divers things to the same purpose as Sir Edmund Andros had done, slighting what I had said, and vilifying the Indian title, saying they were brutes, etc., and if we had possessed and used the land, they said we were the King's subjects, and what land the

King's subjects have, they are the King's. And one of them used such an expression, "Wherever an Englishman sets his foot, all that he has is the King's," and more to the same purpose. I told them that so far as I understood, we received only the right and power of government from the King's charter within such limits and bounds, but the right of the land and soil we had received from God according to his grand charter to the sons of Adam and Noah, and with the consent of the native inhabitants, as I had expressed before.

They still insisted on the King's right to the land as before, whereupon I told them I had heard it was a standing principle in law and reason, *nil dat qui non habet* [he gives nought that owns not]; and from thence I propounded this argument — He that has no right can give no right to another, but the King had no right to the lands of America before the English came hither, therefore he could give no right to them. I told them I knew not of any that could be pleaded but from a popish principle that Christians have a right to the lands of heathen, upon which the pope, as the head of the Christians, had given the West Indies to the king of Spain, but this was disowned by all Protestants. Therefore I left it to them to affirm and prove the King's title. They replied and insisted much upon that, that the King had a right by his subjects coming and taking possession of this land.

And, at last, Sir Edmund Andros said with indignation, "Either you are subjects or you are rebels," intimating, as I understood him, according to the whole scope and tendency of his speeches and actions, that if we would not yield all the lands of New England to be the King's, so as to take patents for lands and to pay rent for the same, then we should not be accounted subjects but rebels and treated accordingly.

There were many other various replies and answers on both sides, but this is the sum and substance of that discourse.

1692

67.

Thomas Brattle: Condemnation of Witchcraft Trials

Witchcraft hysteria seized Salem Village (now Danvers), Massachusetts, in the spring of 1692, when a group of young women began experiencing hysterical pains and delusions. The local physician could find no physical cause, so the Reverend Samuel Parris and a conference of ministers attributed the malady to witchcraft, a notion the Puritans brought with them from England. When the afflicted girls began accusing certain villagers of acting as "agents of the devil," a special court was formed to try the cases. Of the several hundred persons accused, many were imprisoned, nineteen were hanged, and one, Giles Corey, was pressed to death for refusing to answer charges; contrary to popular legend, no one was burned at the stake. Thomas Brattle, later treasurer of Harvard College, rendered a vivid account of the episode in the following letter of October 8, 1692, to an unknown English clergyman.

Source: MHSC, 1798, V, pp. 61-79.

I SHOULD BE VERY LOATH to bring myself into any snare by my freedom with you, and therefore hope that you will put the best construction on what I write, and secure me from such as would interpret my lines otherwise than they are designed. Obedience to lawful authority I evermore accounted a great duty; and willingly I would not practise anything that might thwart and contradict such a principle. Too many are ready to despise dominions, and speak evil of dignities; and I am sure the mischiefs which arise from a factious and rebellious spirit are very sad and notorious; insomuch that I would sooner bite my fin- gers' ends than willingly cast dirt on au- thority, or any way offer reproach to it. Far, therefore, be it from me to have any- thing to do with those men your letter mentions, whom you acknowledge to be men of a factious spirit, and never more in their element than when they are declaim- ing against men in public place, and con- triving methods that tend to the disturbance of the common peace. I never accounted it a credit to my cause to have the good liking of such men. "My son! (says Solomon) fear thou the Lord and the king, and meddle not with them that are given to change" (Prov. 24:21).

However, sir, I never thought judges infallible, but reckoned that they, as well as private men, might err; and that when they were guilty of erring, standers-by, who possibly had not half their judgment, might, notwithstanding, be able to detect and behold their errors. And, furthermore, when errors of that nature are thus detected and observed, I never thought it an interfering with dutifulness and subjection for one man to communicate his thoughts to another thereabout, and with modesty and due reverence to debate the premised failings; at least, when errors are fundamental and palpably pervert the great end of authority and government; for as to circumstantial errors, I must confess my principle is that it is the duty of a good subject to cover with his silence a multitude of them.

But I shall no longer detain you with my preface, but pass to some things you look for, and whether you expect such freedom from me, yea or no, yet shall you find that I am very open to communicate my thoughts unto you, and in plain terms to tell you what my opinion is of the Salem proceedings.

First, as to the method which the Salem justices do take in their examinations, it is truly this: A warrant being issued out to apprehend the persons that are charged and complained of by the afflicted children, as they are called; said persons are brought before the justices, the afflicted being present. The justices ask the apprehended why they afflict those poor children; to which the apprehended answer, they do not afflict them. The justices order the apprehended to look upon the said children, which accordingly they do; and at the time of that look (I dare not say *by* that look, as the Salem gentlemen do), the afflicted are cast into a fit. The apprehended are then blinded, and ordered to touch the afflicted; and at that touch, though not *by* the touch (as above), the afflicted ordinarily do come out of their fits. The afflicted persons then declare and affirm that the apprehended have afflicted them; upon which the apprehended persons, though of never so good repute, are forthwith committed to prison on suspicion for witchcraft.

One of the Salem justices was pleased to tell Mr. Alden (when upon his examination) that truly he had been acquainted with him these many years, and had always accounted him a good man; but, indeed, now he should be obliged to change his opinion. This there are more than one or two did hear, and are ready to swear to, if not in so many words, yet as to its natural and plain meaning. He saw reason to change his opinion of Mr. Alden because that, at the time he touched the poor child, the poor child came out of her fit. I suppose His Honor never made the experiment whether there was not as much virtue in his own hand as there was in Mr. Alden's, to cure by a touch. I know a man that will venture two to one with any Salemite whatever that, let the matter be duly managed, and the afflicted person shall come out of her fit upon the touch of the most religious hand in Salem. It is worthily noted by some that at some times the afflicted will not presently come out of their fits upon the touch of the suspected; and, then, forsooth, they are ordered by the justices to grasp hard, harder yet, etc., insomuch that at length the afflicted come out of their fits; and the reason is very good, because that a touch of any hand, and process of time, will work the cure; infallibly they will do it, as experience teaches.

I cannot but condemn this method of the justices, of making this touch of the hand a rule to discover witchcraft; because I am fully persuaded that it is sorcery, and a superstitious method, and that which we have no rule for, either from reason or religion. . . .

I would fain know of these Salem gentlemen, but as yet could never know how it comes about, that if these apprehended persons are witches, and, by a look of the eye, do cast the afflicted into their fits by poisoning them, how it comes about, I say, that, by a look of their eye, they do not cast others into fits, and poison others by their looks; and in particular, tender, fearful women who often are beheld by them, and as likely as any in the whole world to receive an ill impression from them. This Salem philosophy some men may call the new philosophy; but I think it rather deserves the name of Salem superstition and sorcery, and it is not fit to be named in a land of such light as New England is. I think the matter might be better solved another way; but I shall not make any attempt that way further than to say that these afflicted children, as they are called, do hold correspondence with the devil, even in the esteem and account of the Salem gentlemen; for when the black man, *i.e.*, say these gentlemen, the devil, does appear to them, they ask him many questions, and accordingly give information to the inquirer; and if this is not holding correspondence with the devil, and something worse, I know not what is.

But, furthermore, I would fain know of these Salem justices what need there is of further proof and evidence to convict and condemn these apprehended persons than this look and touch, if so be they are so certain that this falling down and arising up, when there is a look and a touch, are natural effects of the said look and touch, and so a perfect demonstration and proof of witchcraft in those persons. What can the jury or judges desire more to convict any man of witchcraft than a plain demonstration that the said man is a witch? Now if this look and touch, circumstanced as before, be a plain demonstration, as their philosophy teaches, what need they seek for further evidences, when, after all, it can be but a demonstration? But let this pass with the Salem gentlemen for never so plain and natural a demonstration; yet certain is it

that the reasonable part of the world, when acquainted herewith, will laugh at the demonstration, and conclude that the said Salem gentlemen are actually possessed, at least, with ignorance and folly. . . .

Second, with respect to the confessors, as they are improperly called, or such as confess themselves to be witches (the second thing you inquire into in your letter), there are now about fifty of them in prison, many of which I have again and again seen and heard; and I cannot but tell you that my faith is strong concerning them, that they are deluded, imposed upon, and under the influence of some evil spirit, and therefore unfit to be evidences, either against themselves or anyone else. I now speak of one sort of them, and of others afterward.

These confessors, as they are called, do very often contradict themselves, as inconsistently as is usual for any crazed, distempered person to do. This the Salem gentlemen do see and take notice of; and even the judges themselves have, at some times, taken these confessors in flat lies, or contradictions, even in the courts; by reason of which one would have thought that the judges would have frowned upon the said confessors, discarded them, and not minded one tittle of anything that they said. But instead thereof, as sure as we are men, the judges vindicate these confessors and salve their contradictions by proclaiming that the devil takes away their memory and imposes upon their brain. If this reflects anywhere, I am very sorry for it. I can but assure you that, upon the word of an honest man, it is truth, and that I can bring you many credible persons to witness it, who have been eye and ear witnesses to these things.

These confessors, then, at least some of them, even in the judges' own account, are under the influence of the devil; and the brain of these confessors is imposed upon by the devil, even in the judges' account. But now, if, in the judges' account, these confessors are under the influence of the

(Left) William Stoughton, chief justice at the witchcraft trials, portrait by an unknown 18th century artist; (right) Samuel Sewall, jurist at the trials, portrait by John Smibert

devil, and their brains are affected and imposed upon by the devil so that they are not their own men, why then should these judges, or any other men, make such account of, and set so much by, the words of these confessors, as they do? In short, I argue thus:

If the devil does actually take away the memory of them at some times, certainly the devil, at other times, may very reasonably be thought to affect their fancies, and to represent false ideas to their imagination. But, now, if it be thus granted that the devil is able to represent false ideas (to speak vulgarly) to the imaginations of the confessors, what man of sense will regard the confessions, or any of the words, of these confessors?

The great cry of many of our neighbors now is — What, will you not believe the confessors? Will you not believe men and women who confess that they have signed to the devil's book? that they were baptized by the devil; and that they were at the mock sacrament once and again? What! will you not believe that this is witchcraft, and that such and such men are witches,

although the confessors do own and assert it?

Thus, I say, many of our good neighbors do argue; but methinks they might soon be convinced that there is nothing at all in all these their arguings, if they would but duly consider of the premises.

In the meantime, I think we must rest satisfied in it, and be thankful to God for it, that all men are not thus bereft of their senses; but that we have here and there considerate and thinking men who will not thus be imposed upon, and abused, by the subtle endeavors of the crafty one.

In the next place, I proceed to the form of their indictments and the trials thereupon.

The indictment runs for sorcery and witchcraft, acted upon the body of such a one (say M. Warren), at such a particular time . . . and at diverse other times before and after, whereby the said M. W. is wasted and consumed, pined, etc.

Now for the proof of the said sorcery and witchcraft, the prisoner at the bar pleading not guilty.

(Above) Increase Mather, portrait by John Van-
derspriet, 1688; (right) death warrant of Bridget
Bishop, June 10, 1692

1. The afflicted persons are brought into court, and, after much patience and pains taken with them, do take their oaths that the prisoner at the bar did afflict them. And here I think it very observable that often, when the afflicted do mean and intend only the appearance and shape of such a one (say G. Proctor), yet they positively swear that G. Proctor did afflict them; and they have been allowed so to do, as though there was no real difference between G. Proctor and the shape of G. Proctor. This, methinks, may readily prove a stumbling block to the jury, lead them into a very fundamental error, and occasion innocent blood, yea, the innocentest blood imaginable, to be in great danger. Whom it belongs unto, to be eyes unto the blind and to remove such stumbling blocks, I know full well; and yet you, and everyone else, do know as well as I who do not.

2. The confessors do declare what they know of the said prisoner; and some of the confessors are allowed to give their oaths, a thing which I believe was never heard of in this world, that such as confess themselves to be witches, to have renounced God and

Christ and all that is sacred, should yet be allowed and ordered to swear by the name of the great God! This indeed seems to me to be a gross taking of God's name in vain. I know the Salem gentlemen do say that there is hope that the said confessors have repented; I shall only say that, if they have repented, it is well for themselves, but if they have not, it is very ill for you know who. But then,

3. Whoever can be an evidence against the prisoner at the bar is ordered to come into court; and here it scarce ever fails but that evidences, of one nature and another, are brought in; though, I think, all of them altogether alien to the matter of indictment, for they none of them do respect witchcraft upon the bodies of the afflicted, which is the alone matter of charge in the indictment.

4. They are searched by a jury; and as to some of them, the jury brought in, that on such or such a place there was a preternatural excrescence. And I wonder what person there is, whether man or woman, of whom it cannot be said but that, in some part of their body or other, there is a preternatural

excrescence. The term is a very general and inclusive term.

Some of the Salem gentlemen are very forward to censure and condemn the poor prisoner at the bar because he sheds no tears; but such betray great ignorance in the nature of passion, and as great heedlessness as to common passages of a man's life. Some there are who never shed tears; others there are that ordinarily shed tears upon light occasions, and yet for their lives cannot shed a tear when the deepest sorrow is upon their hearts. And who is there that knows not these things? Who knows not that an ecstasy of joy will sometimes fetch tears, when as the quite contrary passion will shut them close up? Why then should any be so silly and foolish as to take an argument from this appearance? But this is by the by. In short, the prisoner at the bar is indicted for sorcery and witchcraft acted upon the bodies of the afflicted. Now, for the proof of this, I reckon that the only pertinent evidences brought in are the evidences of the said afflicted.

It is true that over and above the evidences of the afflicted persons there are many evidences brought in against the prisoner at the bar; either that he was at a witch meeting; or that he performed things which could not be done by an ordinary natural power; or that she sold butter to a sailor, which, proving bad at sea, and the seamen exclaiming against her, she appeared, and soon after there was a storm, or the like. But what if there were ten thousand evidences of this nature; how do they prove the matter of indictment? And if they do not reach the matter of indictment, then I think it is clear that the prisoner at the bar is brought in guilty and condemned, merely from the evidences of the afflicted persons. . . .

As to the late executions, I shall only tell you that in the opinion of many unprejudiced, considerate, and considerable spectators, some of the condemned went out of the world not only with as great protesta-tions but also with as good shows of innocence as men could do.

They protested their innocence as in the presence of the great God, whom forthwith they were to appear before. They wished, and declared their wish, that their blood might be the last innocent blood shed upon that account. With great affection they entreated Mr. Cotton Mather to pray with them; they prayed that God would discover what witchcrafts were among us; they forgave their accusers, they spoke without reflection on jury and judges for bringing them in guilty and condemning them; they prayed earnestly for pardon for all *other* sins, and for an interest in the precious blood of our dear Redeemer. . . .

Deacon Fry's wife, Captain Osgood's wife, and some others, remarkably pious and good people in repute, are apprehended and imprisoned; and that which is more admirable, the forementioned women are become a kind of confessors, being first brought thereto by the urgings and arguings of their good husbands, who, having taken up that corrupt and highly pernicious opinion, that whoever were accused by the afflicted were guilty, did break charity with their dear wives, upon their being accused, and urge them to confess their guilt; which so far prevailed with them as to make them say they were afraid of their being in the snare of the devil. And which, through the *rude and barbarous methods*[1] that were afterward used at Salem, issued in somewhat plainer degrees of confession, and was attended with imprisonment. The good deacon and captain are now sensible of the error they were in; do grieve and mourn bitterly that they should break their charity with their wives, and urge them to confess themselves witches. They now see and ac-

---

1. You may possibly think that my terms are too severe; but should I tell you what a kind of blade was employed in bringing these women to their confession; what methods from damnation were taken; with what violence urged; how unseasonably they were kept up; what buzzings and chuckings of the hand were used, and the like. I am sure that you would call them, as I do, rude and barbarous methods.

knowledge their rashness and uncharitableness, and are very fit objects for the pity and prayers of every good Christian. . . .

I cannot but admire that the justices, whom I think to be well-meaning men, should so far give ear to the devil, as merely upon his authority to issue out their warrants and apprehend people. Liberty was evermore accounted the great privilege of an Englishman; but certainly, if the devil will be heard against us and his testimony taken, to the seizing and apprehending of us, our liberty vanishes, and we are fools if we boast of our liberty. Now, that the justices have thus far given ear to the devil, I think may be mathematically demonstrated to any man of common sense. And for the demonstration and proof hereof, I desire, only, that these two things may be duly considered, viz.:

1. That several persons have been apprehended purely upon the complaints of these afflicted, to whom the afflicted were perfect strangers, and had not the least knowledge of [them] imaginable, before they were apprehended.

2. That the afflicted do own and assert, and the justices do grant, that the devil does inform and tell the afflicted the names of those persons that are thus unknown unto them. Now these two things being duly considered, I think it will appear evident to anyone that the devil's information is the fundamental testimony that is gone upon in the apprehending of the aforesaid people.

If I believe such or such an assertion as comes immediately from the minister of God in the pulpit, because it is the Word of the everliving God, I build my faith on God's testimony; and if I practise upon it, this my practice is properly built on the Word of God; even so in the case before us.

If I believe the afflicted persons as informed by the devil, and act thereupon, this my act may properly be said to be grounded upon the testimony or information of the devil. And now, if things are thus, I think it ought to be for a lamentation to

you and me, and all such as would be accounted good Christians.

If any should see the force of this argument, and upon it say (as I heard a wise and good judge once propose) that they know not but that God Almighty, or a good spirit, does give this information to these afflicted persons, I make answer thereto and say that it is most certain that it is neither Almighty God, nor yet any good spirit, that gives this information; and my reason is good, because God is a God of truth, and the good spirits will not lie; whereas these informations have several times proved false, when the accused were brought before the afflicted. . . .

These things I cannot but admire and wonder at. Now, if so be it is the effect of my dullness that I thus admire, I hope you will pity, not censure me; but if, on the contrary, these things are just matter of admiration, I know that you will join with me in expressing your admiration hereat.

The chief judge is very zealous in these proceedings, and says he is very clear as to all that has as yet been acted by this court, and, as far as ever I could perceive, is very impatient in hearing anything that looks another way. I very highly honor and reverence the wisdom and integrity of the said judge, and hope that this matter shall not diminish my veneration for His Honor. However, I cannot but say my great fear is that wisdom and counsel are withheld from His Honor as to this matter, which yet I look upon not so much as a judgment to His Honor as to this poor land.

But although the chief judge, and some of the other judges, be very zealous in these proceedings, yet this you may take for a truth, that there are several about the Bay, men for understanding, judgment, and piety inferior to few, if any, in New England that do utterly condemn the said proceedings, and do freely deliver their judgment in the case to be this, viz., that these methods will utterly ruin and undo poor New England. . . .

Finally, the principal gentlemen in Boston, and thereabout, are generally agreed that irregular and dangerous methods have been taken as to these matters.

Sir, I would not willingly lead you into any error and therefore would desire you to note:

1. That when I call these afflicted "*the afflicted children*," I would not be understood as though I meant that all that are afflicted are *children.* There are several young men and women that are afflicted, as well as children; but this term has most prevailed among us, because of the younger sort that were first afflicted, and therefore I make use of it.

2. That when I speak of the Salem gentlemen, I would not be understood as though I meant every individual gentleman in Salem; nor yet as though I meant that there were no men but in Salem that run upon these notions. Some term they must have, and this seems not improper, because in Salem this sort of gentlemen does most abound.

3. That other justices in the country, besides the Salem justices, have issued out their warrants and imprisoned, on the accusations of the afflicted as aforesaid; and, therefore, when I speak of the Salem justices, I do not mean them exclusively.

4. That as to the above-mentioned judges, that are commissioned for this court at Salem, five of them do belong to Suffolk County; four of which five do belong to Boston; and therefore I see no reason why Boston should talk of Salem as though their own judges had had no hand in these proceedings at Salem.

Nineteen persons have now been executed, and one pressed to death for a mute; seven more are condemned, two of which are reprieved because they pretend their being with child; one . . . from the intercession of some friends; and two or three more because they are confessors.

The court is adjourned to the first Tuesday in November, then to be kept at Salem; between this and then will be the Great Assembly, and this matter will be a peculiar matter of their agitation. I think it is matter of earnest supplication and prayer to Almighty God that He would afford His gracious presence to the said Assembly, and direct them aright in this weighty matter. Our hopes are here; and if, at this juncture, God does not graciously appear for us, I think we may conclude that New England is undone and undone.

I am very sensible that it is irksome and disagreeable to go back, when a man's doing so is an implication that he has been walking in a wrong path; however, nothing is more honorable than, upon due conviction, to retract and undo, so far as may be, what has been amiss and irregular.

I would hope that, in the conclusion, both the judges and justices will see and acknowledge that such were their best friends and advisers as dissuaded from the methods which they have taken, though hitherto they have been angry with them, and apt to speak very hardly of them.

I cannot but highly applaud, and think it our duty to be very thankful, for the endeavors of several elders, whose lips, I think, should preserve knowledge, and whose counsel should, I think, have been more regarded, in a case of this nature, than as yet it has been. . . .

Thus, sir, I have given you as full a narrative of these matters as readily occurs to my mind, and I think every word of it is matter of fact. . . . What will be the issue of these troubles, God only knows. I am afraid that ages will not wear off that reproach and those stains which these things will leave behind them upon our land. I pray God pity us, humble us, forgive us, and appear mercifully for us in this our mount of distress.

1693

68.

INCREASE MATHER: Insufficiency of Evidence Against Witches

Like most of his less learned and sophisticated fellow Puritans, Increase Mather believed firmly in the reality of witches. Indeed, the fact that Mather, a scholar and church leader, entertained what now seems to us an intellectual aberration is the best possible evidence for the prevalence of such beliefs in New England in the later seventeenth century. To believe is one thing, however, to act another, and the Mather family's reputation has long suffered from the part Increase and his son Cotton took in the Salem trials. Actually, Increase's role in the trials, which was less prominent than that of his son, was largely that of a restraining influence. In his work of 1693, Cases of Conscience Concerning Evil Spirits Personating Men *(part of which is reprinted here), he asserted the relatively humane doctrine that justice required more "scientific" proof than the accusations of "bewitched" accusers who, he implied, may have been doing no more than acting out their fantasies.*

Source: *A Library of American Literature, etc., etc.,* Edmund C. Stedman and Helen M. Hutchinson, eds., New York, 1889, Vol. II, pp. 99-106.

IF THE THINGS which have been mentioned are not infallible proofs of guilt in the accused party, it is then queried: Whether there are any discoveries of this crime which jurors and judges may with a safe conscience proceed upon to the conviction and condemnation of the persons under suspicion?

Let me here premise two things:

1. The evidence in this crime ought to be as clear as in any other crimes of a capital nature. The Word of God does nowhere intimate that a less clear evidence, or that fewer or other witnesses may be taken as sufficient to convict a man of sorcery, which would not be enough to convict him were he charged with another evil worthy of death. If we may not take the oath of a distracted person, or of a possessed person in a case of murder, theft, felony of any sort, then neither may we do it in the case of witchcraft.

2. Let me premise this also, that there have been ways of trying witches long used

in many nations, especially in the dark times of paganism and popery, which the righteous God never approved of, but which (as judicious Mr. Perkins expresseth it in plain English) were invented by the devil, that so innocent persons might be condemned and some notorious witches escape. Yea, many superstitious and magical experiments have been used to try witches by. Of this sort is that of scratching the witch . . . yea, and that way of discovering witches by tying their hands and feet, and casting them on the water to try whether they will sink or swim. I did publicly bear my testimony against this superstition in a book printed at Boston eight years past.

I hear that of late some in a neighbor colony have been playing with this diabolical invention. It is to be lamented that, in such a land of uprightness as New England once was, a practice which Protestant writers generally condemn as sinful, and which the more sober and learned men among papists themselves have not only judged unlawful but (to express it in their own terms) to be no less than a mortal sin, should ever be heard of. Were it not that the coming of Christ to judge the earth draweth near, I should think that such practices are an unhappy omen that the devil and pagans will get these dark territories into their possession again. But that I may not be thought to have no reason for my calling the impleaded experiment into question, I have these things further to allege against it. .

1. It has been rejected long agone by Christian nations as a thing superstitious and diabolical. In Italy and Spain it is wholly disused, and in the Low Countries and in France, where the judges are men of learning. In some parts of Germany old paganism customs are observed more than in other countries; nevertheless, all the academies throughout Germany have disapproved of this way of purgation.

2. The devil is in it, all superstition is from him; and when secret things or latent crimes are discovered by superstitious practices, some compact and communion with the devil is the cause of it, as Austin has truly intimated. And so it is here; for if a witch cannot be drowned, this must proceed either from some natural cause, which it doth not, for it is against nature for human bodies, when hands and feet are tied, not to sink under the water. Besides, they that plead for this superstition say that if witches happen to be condemned for some other crime and not for witchcraft, they will not swim like a cork above water, which cause showeth that the cause of this natation is not physical. And if not, then either it must proceed from a divine miracle to save a witch from drowning; or, lastly, it must be a diabolical wonder.

This superstitious experiment is commonly known by the name of "The Vulgar Probation," because it was never appointed by any lawful authority, but from the suggestion of the devil taken up by the rude rabble. And some learned men are of opinion that the first explorator (being a white witch) did explicitly covenant with the devil that he should discover latent crimes in this way. And that it is by virtue of that first contract that the devil goeth to work to keep his servants from sinking when this ceremony of his ordaining is used. Moreover, we know that *Diabolus est Dei simia,* the devil seeks to imitate divine miracles. We read in ecclesiastical story that some of the martyrs, when they were by persecutors ordered to be drowned, proved to be immersible. This miracle would the devil imitate in causing witches, who are his martyrs, not to sink when they are cast into the waters.

3. This way of purgation is of the same nature with the old ordeals of the pagans. If men were accused with any crime, to clear their innocency, they were to take a hot iron into their hands, or to suffer scalding water to be poured down their throats; and, if they received no hurt, thereby they were acquitted. This was the devil's invention,

and many times (as the devil would have it) they that submitted to these trials suffered no inconvenience. Nevertheless, it is astonishing to think what innocent blood has been shed in the world by means of this satanical device. Witches have often (as Sprenger observes) desired that they might stand or fall by this trial by hot iron, and sometimes come off well.

Indeed, this ordeal was used in other cases, and not in cases of witchcraft only. And so was "The Vulgar Probation" by casting into the water practised upon persons accused with other crimes as well as that of witchcraft. How it came to be restrained to that of witchcraft I cannot tell; it is as supernatural for a body whose hands and feet are tied to swim above the water as it is for their hands not to feel a red hot iron. If the one of these ordeals is lawful to be used, then so is the other too. But as for the fiery ordeal it is rejected and exploded out of the world; for the same reason then the trial by water should be so.

4. It is a tempting of God when men put the innocency of their fellow creatures upon such trials; to desire the Almighty to show a miracle to clear the innocent or to convict the guilty is a most presumptuous tempting of Him. Was it not a miracle when Peter was kept from sinking under the water by the omnipotency of Christ? As for Satan, we know that his ambition is to make his servants believe that his power is equal to God's, and that therefore he can preserve whom he pleaseth. I have read of certain magicians who were seen walking on the water. If then guilty persons shall float on the waters, either it is the devil that causes them to do so (as no doubt it is), and what have men to do to set the devil on work; or else it is a divine miracle, like that of Peter's not sinking, or that of the iron that swam at the word of Elisha. And shall men try whether God will work a miracle to make a discovery? If a crime cannot be found out but by miracle, it is not for any judge on earth to usurp that judgment

which is reserved for the Divine Throne.

5. This pretended gift of immersibility attending witches is a most fallible deceitful thing; for many a witch has sunk under water. . . . Besides, it has sometimes been known that persons who have floated on the water when the hangman has made the experiment on them, have sunk down like a stone, when others have made the trial.

6. The reasons commonly alleged for this superstition are of no moment. It is said they hate the water; whereas they have many times desired that they might be cast on the water in order to their purgation. It is alleged that water is used in baptism, therefore witches swim. A weak fancy; all the water in the world is not consecrated water. Cannot witches eat bread or drink wine, notwithstanding those elements are made use of in the Blessed Sacrament? But (say some) the devils by sucking of them make them so light that the water bears them; whereas some witches are twice as heavy as many an innocent person. Well, but then they are possessed with the devil. Suppose so; is the devil afraid if they should sink that he should be drowned with them? But why then were the Gadaren's hogs drowned when the devil was in them?

These things being premised, I answer the question affirmatively: There are proofs for the conviction of witches which jurors may with a safe conscience proceed upon so as to bring them in guilty. The Scripture which saith, "Thou shalt not suffer a witch to live," clearly implies that some in the world may be known and proved to be witches. For until they be so, they may and must be suffered to live. Moreover, we find in Scripture that some have been convicted and executed for witches. "For Saul cut off those that had familiar spirits, and the wizards out of the land" (I Sam. 28:9). . . .

But then the inquiry is: What is sufficient proof?

This case has been with great judgment answered by several divines of our own, particularly by Mr. Perkins and Mr. Bernard. Also Mr. John Gaul, a worthy minister at Staughton, in the county of Huntington, has published a very judicious discourse called, "Select Cases of Conscience touching Witches and Witchcrafts," printed at London A.D. 1646, wherein he does with great prudence and evidence of Scripture lightly handle this and other cases. Such jurors as can obtain those books, I would advise them to read, and seriously as in the fear of God to consider them, and so far as they keep to the law and to the testimony, and speak according to that word, receive the light which is in them. But the books being now rare to be had, let me express my concurrence with them in these two particulars.

1. That a free and voluntary confession of the crime made by the person suspected and accused after examination is a sufficient ground of conviction.

Indeed, if persons are distracted or under the power of frenetic melancholy, that alters the case; but the jurors that examine them, and their neighbors that know them, may easily determine that case; or if confession be extorted, the evidence is not so clear and convictive; but if any persons out of remorse of conscience, or from a touch of God in their spirits, confess and show their deeds, as the converted magicians in Ephesus did, nothing can be more clear. Suppose a man to be suspected for murder, or for committing a rape, or the like nefarious wickedness, if he does freely confess the accusation, that's ground enough to condemn him. The Scripture approveth of judging the wicked servant out of his own mouth. It is by some objected that persons in discontent may falsely accuse themselves. I say, if they do so, and it cannot be proved that they are false accusers of themselves, they ought to die for their wickedness, and their blood will be upon their own heads; the jury, the judges, and the land is clear. . . .

2. If two credible persons shall affirm upon oath that they have seen the party accused speaking such words, or doing things which none but such as have familiarity with the devil ever did or can do, that's a sufficient ground for conviction.

Some are ready to say that wizards are not so unwise as to do such things in the sight or hearing of others, but it is certain that they have very often been known to do so. How often have they been seen by others using enchantments? Conjuring to raise storms? And have been heard calling upon their familiar spirits? And have been known to use spells and charms? And to show in a glass or in a show stone persons absent? And to reveal secrets which could not be discovered but by the devil? And have not men been seen to do things which are above human strength, that no man living could do without diabolical assistances? . . .

The devil never assists men to do supernatural things undesired. When, therefore, such like things shall be testified against the accused party, not by specters, which are devils in the shape of persons either living or dead, but by real men or women who may be credited, it is proof enough that such a one has that conversation and correspondence with the devil as that he or she, whoever they be, ought to be exterminated from among men. This notwithstanding I will add: It were better that ten suspected witches should escape than that one innocent person should be condemned.

———◆———

Whoever is right, the persecutor must be wrong.
WILLIAM PENN, *Some Fruits of Solitude*, 1693

69.

COTTON MATHER: Wonders of the Invisible World

Cotton Mather played a prominent role in the Salem witchcraft trials by virtue of his position as head of the Puritan church in Boston. Although his 1689 essay, Memorable Providences Relating to Witchcraft and Possessions, *had fostered much of the hysteria surrounding the trials, Mather, like his father Increase, did attempt to exclude "spectral evidence" from the trials and to induce the courts to hand down lenient punishments. In the following selection from* The Wonders of the Invisible World *(1693), Mather described the "witchcraft delusion" and attempted to justify the procedures and outcome of the trials at Salem.*

Source: *The Wonders of the Invisible World,* London, 1862, pp. 9-17.

THE NEW ENGLANDERS are a people of God settled in those, which were once the devil's territories. And it may easily be supposed that the devil was exceedingly disturbed when he perceived such a people here accomplishing the promise of old made unto our Blessed Jesus — that He should have the utmost parts of the earth for His possession. There was not a greater uproar among the Ephesians when the Gospel was first brought among them than there was among the powers of the air (after whom those Ephesians walked), when first the silver trumpets of the Gospel here made the joyful sound. The devil, thus irritated, immediately tried all sorts of methods to overturn this poor plantation; and so much of the church, as was fled into this wilderness, immediately found the serpent cast out of his mouth a flood for the carrying of it away.

I believe that never were more satanical devices used for the unsettling of any people under the sun than what have been employed for the extirpation of the vine which God has here planted, casting out the heathen, and preparing a room before it, and causing it to take deep root and fill the land; so that it sent its boughs unto the Atlantic Sea, eastward, and its branches unto the Connecticut River, westward; and the hills were covered with the shadow thereof. But, all those attempts of hell have hitherto been abortive, many an Ebenezer has been erected unto the praise of God, by His poor people here. And, having obtained help from God, we continue to this day.

Wherefore, the devil is now making one attempt more upon us; an attempt more difficult, more surprising, more snarled with unintelligible circumstances than any that we have hitherto encountered; an attempt so critical, that if we get well through, we shall soon enjoy halcyon days, with all the vultures of hell trodden under our feet. He has wanted his incarnate legions to persecute us, as the people of God have in the other hemisphere been persecuted; he has, therefore, drawn forth his more spiritual ones to make an attack upon us. We have been advised by some credible Christians yet alive that a malefactor, accused of witchcraft as well as murder, and executed in this place more than forty years ago, did then give notice of a horrible *plot* against the country by *witchcraft,* and a foundation of *witchcraft* then laid, which if it were not seasonably discovered would probably blow up and pull down all the churches in the country.

And we have now with horror seen the discovery of such a *witchcraft!* An army of devils is horribly broke in upon the place which is the center, and after a sort, the firstborn of our English settlements. And the houses of the good people there are filled with the doleful shrieks of their children and servants, tormented by invisible hands, with tortures altogether preternatural. After the mischiefs there endeavored, and since in part conquered, the terrible plague of evil angels has made its progress into some other places, where other persons have been in like manner diabolically handled.

These our poor afflicted neighbors, quickly, after they become infected and infested with these demons, arrive to a capacity of discerning those which they conceive the shapes of their troublers; and notwithstanding the great and just suspicion that the demons might impose the shapes of innocent persons in their spectral exhibitions upon the sufferers (which may perhaps prove no small part of the witch plot in the issue), yet many of the persons thus represented, being examined, several of them have been convicted of a very damnable witchcraft. Yea, more than twenty-one have confessed that they have signed unto a book, which the devil showed them, and engaged in his hellish design of bewitching and ruining our land.

We know not, at least I know not, how far the delusions of Satan may be interwoven into some circumstances of the confessions; but one would think all the rules of understanding human affairs are at an end, if after so many most voluntary, harmonious confessions, made by intelligent persons of all ages, in sundry towns, at several times, we must not believe the main strokes wherein those confessions all agree; especially when we have a thousand preternatural things every day before our eyes, wherein the confessors do acknowledge their concernment, and give demonstration of their being so concerned. If the devils now can strike the minds of men with any poisons of so fine a composition and operation that scores of innocent people shall unite in confessions of a crime which we see actually committed, it is a thing prodigious, beyond the wonders of the former ages, and it threatens no less than a sort of a dissolution upon the world.

Now, by these confessions it is agreed that the devil has made a dreadful knot of witches in the country, and by the help of witches has dreadfully increased that knot; that these witches have driven a trade of commissioning their confederate spirits to do all sorts of mischiefs to the neighbors; whereupon there have ensued such mischievous consequences upon the bodies and estates of the neighborhood as could not otherwise be accounted for; yea, that at prodigious witch meetings the wretches have proceeded so far as to concert and consult the methods of rooting out the Christian religion from this country, and setting up instead of it perhaps a more gross diabolism than ever the world saw before. And yet it will be a thing little short of miracle if, in so spread a business as this, the devil should not get in some of his juggles to confound the discovery of all the rest.

1696

70.

WILLIAM PENN: The People Called Quakers

Primitive Christianity Revived was William Penn's attempt to show that the beliefs and practices of the Society of Friends were the same as those of the early Christian church, and were, in fact, the correct way to godliness. Penn emphasized the Quaker doctrine of the light of Christ in man, a "divine principle" that, even though it was not inherent in man's nature, was bestowed by God on all men. Accordingly, Quakers held in high regard humanitarian and equalitarian principles, since each individual carried within him a spark of Divine Spirit. The doctrine, which ascribed the Inner Light to all men, regardless of race or creed, marked the rise of a new religious liberalism and a spirit of toleration, especially in Pennsylvania.

Source: *The Select Works of William Penn*, 4th edition, London, 1825, Vol. III, pp. 473-512.

THAT WHICH THE PEOPLE called Quakers lay down as a main fundamental in religion is this, "That God, through Christ, has placed a principle in every man to inform him of his duty, and to enable him to do it; and that those that live up to this principle are the people of God; and those that live in disobedience to it are not God's people, whatever name they may bear or profession they may make of religion." This is their ancient, first, and standing testimony; with this they began, and this they bore, and do bear, to the world.

By this principle they understand something that is divine; and though in man, yet not of man, but of God; and that it came from Him, and leads to Him all those that will be led by it.

There are diverse ways of speaking they have been led to use, by which they declare and express what this principle is, about which I think fit to precaution the reader; viz., they call it "the light of Christ within man," or, "light within," which is their ancient, and most general and familiar phrase, also the manifestation or appearance of Christ; the witness of God, the seed of God; the seed of the kingdom; wisdom, the word in the heart; the grace that appears to all men; the spirit given to every man to profit with; the truth in the inward parts; the spiritual leaven that leavens the whole lump of man — which are many of them figurative expressions, but all of them such as the Holy Ghost had used, and which will be used in this treatise, as they are most frequently in the writings and ministry of this people. But that this variety and manner of expression may not occasion any misapprehension or confusion in the understanding of the reader, I would have him know that they always mean by these terms, or denominations, not another but the same principle, before mentioned; which, as I said, though it be in man, is not of man but of God, and therefore divine; and-one in itself, though diversely expressed by the holy men, according to the various manifestations and operations thereof.

It is to this principle of light, life, and grace that this people refer all; for they say it is the great agent in religion; that, without which, there is no conviction, so no conversion, or regeneration, and consequently no entering into the kingdom of God. That is to say, there can be no true sight of sin, nor sorrow for it, and therefore no forsaking or overcoming of it, or remission or justification from it. A necessary and powerful principle, indeed, when neither sanctification nor justification can be had without it. In short, there is no becoming virtuous, holy, and good without this principle; no acceptance with God, nor peace of soul, but through it. But, on the contrary, that the reason of so much irreligion among Christians, so much superstition instead of devotion, and so much profession without enjoyment, and so little heart reformation, is because people, in religion, overlook this principle and leave it behind them.

They will be religious without it and Christians without it, though this be the only means of making them so indeed. So natural is it to man, in his degenerate state, to prefer sacrifice before obedience, and to make prayers go for practice, and so flatter himself to hope by ceremonial and bodily service, to excuse himself with God from the stricter discipline of this principle in the soul, which leads man to take up the cross, deny himself, and do that which God requires of him. And that is every man's true religion, and every such man is truly religious; that is, he is holy, humble, patient, meek, merciful, just, kind, and charitable; which, they say, no man can make himself, but that this principle will make them all so that will embrace the convictions and teachings of it, being the root of all true religion in man, and the good seed from whence all good fruits proceed. To sum up what they say upon the nature and virtue of it, as contents of that which follows, they declare that this principle is, first, divine; second, universal; third, efficacious, in that it gives man:

First, the knowledge of God, and of himself; and therein a sight of his duty and disobedience to it.

Second, it begets a true sense and sorrow for sin in those that seriously regard the convictions of it.

Third, it enables them to forsake sin, and sanctifies from it.

Fourth, it applies God's mercies, in Christ, for the forgiveness of sins that are past, unto justification, upon such sincere repentance and obedience.

Fifth, it gives, to the faithful, perseverance unto a perfect man, and the assurance of blessedness, world without end.

To the truth of all which, they call in a threefold evidence: First, the Scriptures, which give an ample witness, especially those of the New and better Testament. Second, the reasonableness of it in itself. And, last, a general experience, in great measure, but particularly their own, made credible by the good fruits they have brought forth, and the answer God has given to their ministry; which, to impartial observers, have commended the principle.

EXPANDING COLONIAL INTERESTS

In the 17th century the British and French colonies became securely established in North America. Along the eastern seaboard, new settlements arose as Europeans immigrated to new proprietary colonies such as Pennsylvania and southern Carolina to find better religious, economic, or political conditions. For similar reasons, other colonies were established as earlier American settlers re-migrated to Rhode Island, Connecticut, and northern Carolina. The mi-

nor colonies of Sweden and the Netherlands in Pennsylvania and New York had neither the population nor the power to resist the growing British strength in these areas.

New France was not thickly settled during the 17th century, but her fur trade was prosperous, her explorers audacious. By 1671 the Mississippi had been explored, and all of North America west of it claimed for the King of France.

Defeat of the Indians in the Pequot War, 1637, opened the Connecticut Valley to large scale settlement

Library of Congress, Rare Book Division

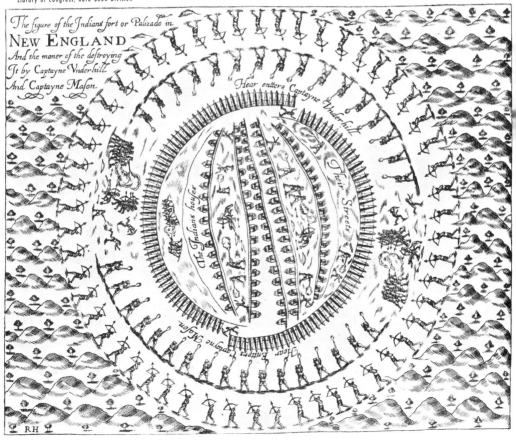

Map of New England by John Foster, 1677

Connecticut

Connecticut was founded by Puritans from Massachusetts, who settled the Hartford area, and from London, who settled New Haven. The Hartford Puritans drew up the Fundamental Orders of Connecticut in 1639, which established representative government and the Congregational Church. New Haven, though separate, had a similar arrangement. In 1662 the area of modern Connecticut was defined when Hartford and New Haven were united by royal charter.

(Top) Rev. John Davenport, co-founder of the New Haven colony in 1638, portrait by John Foster; (middle) William Pynchon, a fur trader from Massachusetts, settled at Springfield, Mass., in 1636

(Below) The Charter of Connecticut granted by Charles II; it united Connecticut under Gov. John Winthrop (right)

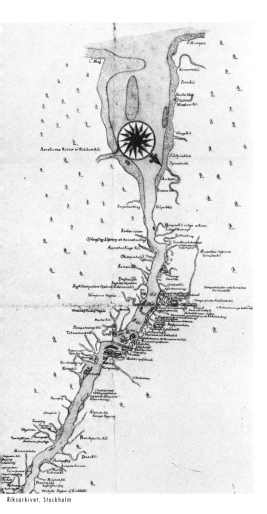

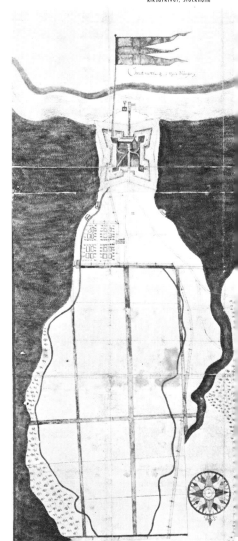

(Above) Map of New Sweden on the Delaware River; (above right) Johan Printz, governor of New Sweden, 1643-53, is said to have weighed 300 pounds; (right) plan of Ft. Christina and the projected settlement there drawn by Per Lindstrom

New Sweden

The brief colonial endeavor of the Swedes began at the invitation of the founder of the Dutch West India Company. Gustavus Adolphus planned to recoup in New Sweden some of the cost of the Thirty Years' War, then in progress, and in which he was to lose his life. After the establishment of Fort Christina on the Delaware River, the Swedes bought out the Dutch interests in the venture. But Dutch colonists in America regarded the Swedes as rivals, and in 1655 captured Fort Christina, ending Sweden's power in America.

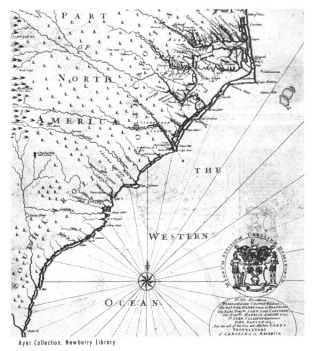

Carolina

Anthony Ashley Cooper's vast Carolina proprietorship, granted by Charles II in 1663, did not begin to prosper until wealthy French Huguenots, refugees from persecution in France after 1685, developed slave-grown rice as a cash crop in southern Carolina. Regional differences grew as northern Carolina was settled by poor white refugees from Virginia, where slave-grown tobacco dominated the economy.

(Above right) Anthony Ashley Cooper, 1st Earl Shaftesbury; (left) plan of Charleston and nearby plantations

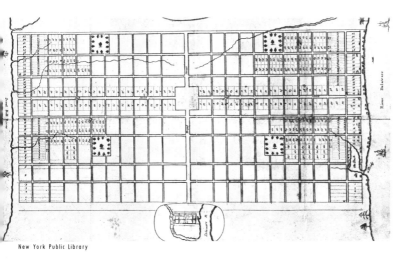

Surveyor's plan for Philadelphia by Thomas Holme, prepared for Penn and his backers in 1683

New York Public Library

Pennsylvania

Although a Quaker, William Penn was in good standing with Charles II, owing to services rendered the King by his father, an admiral. His proprietary colony, intended as a refuge for Quakers, was founded on the principle of religious toleration. This combined with fair treatment of Indians and considerable local autonomy, helped make Pennsylvania a prosperous colony that remained in the Penn family until the Revolution.

(Left) "Indian deed for lands to Wm. Penn 1683" for which the three Delaware chiefs accepted "150 fathom of wampum" and a quantity of goods, including guns, lead and powder, pots and pans, shoes and "three papers of beads"

Lots in Philadelphia for Penn and his daughter, 1698

Library of Congress, Map Division

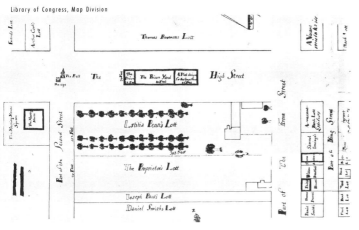

Historical Society of Pennsylvania

William Penn, pastel portrait considered most authentic likeness extant

(Above) The disasters of La Salle's second trip to America were chronicled by Father Hennepin in "Nouveau Voyage d'un Pays Plus Grand que l'Europe," 1698; (below) Robert Cavelier, sieur de la Salle (1643-1687)

New France

Canada remained basically a trading outpost, with a population numbered only in the hundreds in the mid-17th century. Nevertheless, exploration was extensive. Most ambitious of all was Sieur de la Salle, who traveled the Mississippi to its mouth in 1682. Dreaming of a trade monopoly of the entire Mississippi Valley, La Salle sailed into the Gulf of Mexico in 1684, could not find the mouth of the Mississippi, and was eventually assassinated by mutineers.

Detail from a 1688 map showing a series of forts established by the French in the interior

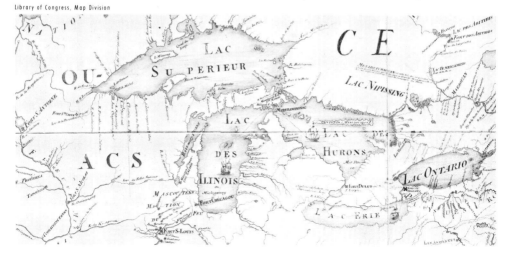

(Above) The main French interest in America, as shown in these prints, was fishing and the fur trade; (left) Louis Jolliet's "Smaller Map," 1673, details his discoveries in the Great Lakes, particularly the water routes between the St. Lawrence and the Mississippi (Riviere Colbert); (below) Quebec, shown in 1688, was the center for Jesuit missionary work and the only real city in New France

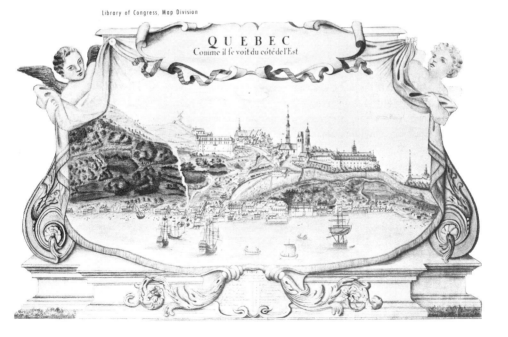

QUEBEC
Comme il se voit du côté de l'Est

1697

71.

WILLIAM PENN: Plan of Union for the English Colonies in America

Rivalries between the French and English colonies in America for land, fur, and Indian allegiance erupted into war in 1689. For nearly eight years the New England borderlands suffered continuous attacks from both the French and their Indian allies; the few united efforts of the English colonies to launch defensive attacks against French posts ended in failure and, in addition to the "Bloodless Revolution" of 1688 in England, precipitated colonial rebellions and disputes among different sections of New England. Although a treaty was finally signed in 1697, ending the so-called King William's War, the colonies continued to have difficulties. During this period (1684-1699), William Penn, the proprietor of Pennsylvania, was in England. However, his continued concern for the welfare of the English possessions prompted him to devise the following Plan of Union that he presented to the London Board of Trade in 1697. It was one of the earliest schemes to promote military and economic unity among the colonies.

Source: *Documents Relative to the Colonial History of the State of New-York*, E. B. O'Callaghan, ed., Vol. IV, Albany, 1854, pp. 296-297.

A BRIEF AND PLAIN SCHEME how the English colonies in the north parts of America, viz., Boston, Connecticut, Rhode Island, New York, New Jerseys, Pennsylvania, Maryland, Virginia, and Carolina, may be made more useful to the Crown and one another's peace and safety, with a universal concurrence.

1. That the several colonies before mentioned do meet once a year, and oftener if need be during the war, and at least once in two years in times of peace, by their stated and appointed deputies, to debate and resolve of such measures as are most advisable for their better understanding and the public tranquillity and safety.

2. That in order to it, two persons, well qualified for sense, sobriety, and substance, be appointed by each province as their representatives or deputies, which in the whole make the congress to consist of twenty persons.

3. That the King's commissioner, for that purpose specially appointed, shall have the chair and preside in the said congress.

4. That they shall meet as near as conveniently may be to the most central colony for ease of the deputies.

5. Since that may, in all probability, be New York, both because it is near the center of the colonies, and for that it is a frontier and in the King's nomination, the governor of that colony may therefore also be the King's high commissioner during the session, after the manner of Scotland.

6. That their business shall be to hear and adjust all matters of complaint or difference between province and province. As, (1) where persons quit their own province and go to another that they may avoid their just debts, though they be able to pay them; (2) where offenders fly justice or justice cannot well be had upon such offenders in the provinces that entertain them; (3) to prevent or cure injuries in point of commerce;

(4) to consider the ways and means to support the union and safety of these provinces against the public enemies. In which congress the quotas of men and charges will be much easier and more equally set than it is possible for any establishment made here to do; for the provinces, knowing their own condition and one another's, can debate that matter with more freedom and satisfaction, and better adjust and balance their affairs in all respects for their common safety.

7. That, in times of war, the King's high commissioner shall be general or chief commander of the several quotas upon service against the common enemy, as he shall be advised, for the good and benefit of the whole.

1700

72.

Francis D. Pastorius: German Settlers in Pennsylvania

The founding of Germantown, Pennsylvania, by German Mennonites in 1683, was undertaken by the Frankfort Land Company, whose agent in the New World was Francis D. Pastorius. Because of a similarity of beliefs, Pastorius and his followers soon united with the Pennsylvania Society of Friends. As the settlement grew and prospered, it attracted other Germans coming to the colonies. The success of the settlement was largely owing to the personal influence of Pastorius. He was to the Pennsylvania Quakers what Bradford and Winthrop were to the Puritans in Massachusetts. Pastorius is probably the author of the memorial against slaveholding (the first such protest against Negro slavery) adopted by the Germantown Friends in 1688. The following selection, written in 1700, is taken from his Description of . . . Pennsylvania. *It is likely that it was sent to Germany as an inducement for new settlers.*

Source: OSL 95: "A Particular Geographical Description of the Lately Discovered
   Province of Pennsylvania, Situated on the Frontiers of this Western World, America."

THE GERMAN SOCIETY commissioned myself, Francis Daniel Pastorius, as their licensed agent, to go to Pennsylvania and to superintend the purchase and survey of their lands.

I set out from Frankfurt am Main, went to London, (where I made the purchase), and then embarked for America.

Under the protection of the Almighty, I arrived safely at Philadelphia; and I was enabled to send my report home to Germany on the 7th of March, 1684.

The lands I purchased were to be as follows: 15,000 acres in one tract on some navigable stream; 300 acres in the City Liberties, which is the strip of land lying between the Rivers Delaware and Schuylkill, above Philadelphia; three lots in the city proper for the purpose of building thereon.

Upon my arrival I applied to the governor, William Penn, for warrants, so as to survey and take possession of the aforesaid lands. His first answer, concerning the 300 acres in the Liberties and the three lots in the city, was this; that these could by right not be claimed by the German Company, because they had been purchased after he had left London, the books closed, and all the lots previously disposed of. He, however, had three lots in the city surveyed for me, out of his youngest son's portion, instead of those above mentioned. . . .

The governor, William Penn, laid out the city of Philadelphia between the two rivers Delaware and Schuylkill, naming it with the pious wish and desire that its inhabitants might dwell together in brotherly love and unity. The Delaware is deep enough so that the largest vessels can come up close to the bank, which is but about a stone's cast from the city.

Another English company [has] laid out the new town of Frankfort, five miles above Philadelphia, at which, now so flourishing and pleasant place, they have already established several good mills, a glasshouse, pottery, and some stores and trading houses.

New Castle lies forty miles from the ocean on the Delaware, and has a very good harbor. The town of Uplandt is twenty miles above New Castle on the river, and is a fine, large place, inhabited mostly by Swedes.

On the 24th day of October, 1685, I, Francis Daniel Pastorius, with the wish and concurrence of our governor, laid out and planned a new town, which we called Germantown, or Germanopolis, in a very fine and fertile district, with plenty of springs of fresh water, being well supplied with oak, walnut, and chestnut trees, and having besides excellent and abundant pasturage for the cattle. At the commencement there were but twelve families of forty-one individuals, consisting mostly of German mechanics and weavers. The principal street of this, our town, I made sixty feet in width, and the cross street, forty feet. The space or lot for each house and garden I made three acres in size; for my own dwelling, however, six acres.

Before my laying out of this town, I had already erected a small house in Philadelphia, thirty feet by fifteen in size. The windows, for the want of glass, were made of oiled paper. Over the door I had placed the following inscription: *Parva domus, sed amica bonis, procul este prophani* [A small house, but friendly to the good; let the evil take themselves hence], at which our governor, when he paid me a visit, laughed heartily, at the same time encouraging me to build more.

I have also obtained 15,000 acres of land for our company, in one tract, with this condition; that within one year at least thirty families should settle on it; and thus we may, by God's blessing, have a separate German province where we can all live together in one.

Inasmuch as this region lies in the same degree of latitude as Montepelier and Naples, but has a much richer soil, and that better watered by its many springs and rivulets, it is but reasonable to suppose that such a country must be well calculated to produce all kinds of fruit. The air is pure and serene, the summer is longer and warmer than it is in Germany, and we are cultivating many kinds of fruits and vegetables, and our labors meet with rich reward.

Of cattle we have a great abundance, but for want of proper accommodation they roam at large for the present. . . .

Although this far-distant land was a dense wilderness — and it is only quite recently that it has come under the cultivation of the Christians — there is much cause of wonder and admiration how rapidly it has already, under the blessing of God, advanced, and is still advancing, day by day. The first part of the time we were obliged to obtain our provisions from the Jerseys for money, and at a high price; but now we not only have enough for ourselves but a considerable surplus to dispose of among our neighboring colonies. Of the most needful mechanics we have enough now; but day laborers are very scarce, and of them we stand in great need. Of mills, brick kilns, and tile ovens, we have the necessary number.

Our surplus of grain and cattle we trade to Barbados for rum, syrup, sugar, and salt. The furs, however, we export to England for other manufactured goods.

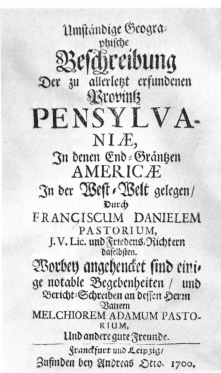

Umſtändige Geogra-
phiſche
Beſchreibung
Der zu allerletzt erfundenen
Provintz
PENSYLVA-
NIÆ,
In denen End-Gräntzen
AMERICÆ
In der Weſt-Welt gelegen/
Durch
FRANCISCUM DANIELEM
PASTORIUM,
J. V. Lic. und Friedens-Richtern
daſelbſten.

Worbey angehencket ſind eini-
ge notable Begebenheiten / und
Bericht-Schreiben an deſſen Herrn
Vattern
MELCHIOREM ADAMUM PASTO-
RIUM,
Und andere gute Freunde.

Francfurt und Leipzig/
Zufinden bey Andreas Otto. 1700.

Courtesy, the Library of Congress, Rare Book Division

Title page from "An accurate description of the recently founded province of Pennsylvania" by Pastorius, who established the first German settlement
in the colonies, 1700

We are also endeavoring to introduce the cultivation of the vine, and also the manufacture of woolen cloths and linens, so as to keep our money as much as possible in the country. For this reason we have already established fairs to be held at stated times, so as to bring the people of different parts together for the purposes of barter and trade, and thereby encourage our own industry and prevent our little money from going abroad.

The inhabitants may be divided into three classes: (1) the aborigines, or, as they are called, the savages; (2) those Christians who have been in the country for years and are called old settlers; (3) the newly arrived colonists of the different companies.

1. The savages, or Indians, are in general strong, nimble, and well-shaped people, of a dark, tawny complexion, and wore no clothing whatever when the first Europeans came to this country. Now, however, they hang a blanket about their shoulders, or some of them also have shirts.

They have straight black hair which they cut off close to the head, save one tuft, which they leave stand on the right side. Their children they anoint with the fat of the bears and other animals, so as to make their skin dark, for by nature they would be white enough. They cultivate among themselves the most scrupulous honesty, are unwavering in keeping promises, defraud and insult no one, are very hospitable to strangers, obliging to their guests, and faithful even to death toward their friends.

Their huts, or wigwams, they make by bending down several young trees and covering them with bark.

They use neither tables nor chairs nor furniture of any kind, except, perhaps, a single pot or kettle to cook their food.

I once saw four of them dining together in great enjoyment of their feast. It consisted in nothing more than a pumpkin, simply boiled in water, without salt, butter, or spice of any kind. Their seat and table was the bare ground, their spoons were seashells, wherewith they supped the warm water, and their plates were the leaves of the nearest tree, which, after they were done their meal, they had no occasion of washing or any need of carefully preserving for future use. I thought to myself on witnessing this scene how these poor savages, who have never heard of the Savior's doctrines and maxims of contentment and temperance, how far superior they are to ourselves, so-called Christians, at least so far as these virtues are concerned.

They are otherwise very grave and reserved, speak but little, and in few words, and are greatly surprised when they hear much needless and even foolish talking and tale bearing among us Christians.

They are true and faithful in their matrimonial relations, abhorring licentiousness in the extreme. Above all do they despise deception and falsehood. They have no idols, but adore one great, good spirit, who keeps the devil in subjection. They believe in the immortality of the soul, and, according as they have lived in this world, do they expect a reward or punishment in the future.

Their peculiar mode ·of worship consists principally in singing and dancing, during which they make use of the most singular contortions and positions of the body; and, when the remembrance of the death of parents or dear friends is brought to their mind, they break forth into the most piteous cries and lamentations.

They are fond of hearing us speak about the Creator of heaven and the earth, and of His wisdom and divine power, and particularly do they listen with emotion to the narrative of the Savior's life and sufferings; but it is greatly to be regretted that we are not yet sufficiently acquainted with their language so as to explain the great plan of salvation to them fully. They behave with the greatest respect and decorum whenever they attend public worship in our churches; and it is my firm belief that many of these poor American savages will in the great day rise up in judgment with those of Tyre and Sidon against our own wicked and perverse generation.

As regards their domestic arrangements, the men attend to the chase, hunting, and fishing; the women bring up their children, instructing them in virtue and honor. They raise some few vegetables, such as corn and beans; but, as to any extensive farming and cultivation, they concern themselves nothing about it, but are rather surprised that we, as Christians, should have so many cares and anxieties as to our support and nourishment, just as if we did not believe that God will and can sustain and provide for us.

They speak a most beautiful and grave language, which sounds very much like the Italian, although it has entirely different words.

They are in the habit of painting their faces with various colors, and the women as well as the men are very fond of tobacco.

2. The earlier Europeans or old settlers. These never had the proper motives in settling here; for, instead of instructing the poor Indians in the Christian virtues, their only desire was gain, without ever scrupling about the means employed in obtaining it.

By these means they have taught those natives who had dealings with them nothing but deception and many other evil habits, so that there is very little virtue or honesty remaining on either side.

These wicked people make it a custom to pay the savages in rum and other liquors for the furs they bring to them, so that these poor, deluded Indians have become very intemperate, and sometimes drink to such excess that they can neither walk nor stand. On such occasions they often commit thefts and other vices.

3. The newly arrived colonists of our and other companies. We who have come over to this land with good and honest intentions have purchased considerable tracts of land where we will settle and endeavor to live in happiness and contentment; and we are living in the hope and expectation that we can in time do something for the eternal welfare and salvation of the aborigines. May our God prosper and bless our undertakings!

The aborigines of this country had their own chiefs and kings. We Christians acknowledge as our governor and chief magistrate the oft-named and excellent, the Hon. William Penn, to whom this region was granted and given as his own by His Majesty of England, Charles II, with the express command that all the previous and future colonists should be subject to Penn's laws and jurisdiction.

This wise and truly pious ruler and governor did not, however, take possession of the province thus granted without having first conciliated, and at various councils and treaties duly purchased from, the natives of this country the various regions of Pennsylvania. He, having by these means obtained good titles to the province, under the sanction and signature of the native chiefs, I therefore have purchased from him some 30,000 acres for my German colony.

Now, although the oft-mentioned William Penn is one of the sect of Friends, or Quakers, still he will compel no man to belong to his particular society; but he has granted to everyone free and untrammeled exercise of their opinions and the largest and most complete liberty of conscience.

The native Indians have no written religious belief or creed; and their own peculiar ideas, which are by no means so rude or so barbarous as those of many other heathens, have to be transmitted from the parents to their children only *per traditionem* [through tradition].

The English and the Dutch adhere to the Calvinistic persuasion. The colonists of William Penn are nearly all Quakers. The Swedes and Germans are Evangelical Lutherans, under the jurisdiction of the Bishop of Uppsala. The Swedes have their own churches. The name of their clergyman is Fabricius, of whom I must say with deep regret that he is an intemperate man, and, as regards spiritual things, very dark and ignorant.

We in Germantown built a little chapel for ourselves in 1686, but did not so much care for a splendid stone edifice as for having a humble but true temple devoted to the living God, in which true believers might be edified to the salvation of their souls. The ministers here might have an excellent opportunity to obey and practise the command of the Savior, "Go ye into all the world and preach the gospel"; but, unfortu-

nately, they seek more their own comfort and ease than they do the glory of the Redeemer. . . .

Our German Society have in this place now established a lucrative trade in woolen and linen goods, together with a large assortment of other useful and necessary articles, and have entrusted this extensive business to my own direction. Besides this they have now purchased and hold over 30,000 acres of land, for the sake of establishing an entirely German colony. In my newly laid out Germantown there are already sixty-four families in a very prosperous condition. Such persons, therefore, and all those who still arrive, have to fall to work and swing the axe most vigorously; for wherever you turn the cry is, *Itur in antiquam sylvam* [Let us go through the primeval forest], nothing but endless forests. So that I have been often wishing for a number of stalwart Tyroleans to throw down these gigantic oak and other forest trees, but which we will be obliged to cut down ourselves by degrees and with almost incredible labor and exertion, during which we can have a very forcible illustration of the sentence pronounced upon our poor old father Adam, that *in the sweat of his brow he should eat his bread.*

To our successors, and others coming after us, we would say that they must not only bring over money but a firm determination to labor and make themselves useful to our infant colony. Upon the whole, we may consider that man blessed whom the devil does not find idling. In the meantime we are employing the wild inhabitants as day laborers, for which they are, however, not much inclined; and we ourselves are gradually learning their language, so to instruct them in the religion of Christ, inviting them to attend our church services, and therefore have the pleasing hope that the spirit of God may be the means of enlightening many of these poor heathens unto their souls' salvation. To Him be honor, praise, thanks, and glory, forevermore. Amen.

73.

Samuel Sewall: On Accommodating the Indians

Samuel Sewall, eminent jurist and Puritan leader, exhibited a rare but characteristic humanitarianism in his efforts to secure just treatment for the Indians. In the following letter of May 3, 1700, Sewall expressed to Sir William Ashurst his concern with such practical problems as fixing fair boundaries for Indian lands, as well as a plan for recruiting missionaries from Indians converted to Christianity.

Source: MHSC, 6th series, I, pp. 231-233.

Last fall, I had notice of my being entrusted with a share in managing the Indian affairs, and presently upon it, the Commissioners were pleased to appoint me their secretary. As I account it an honor to be thus employed, so according to my mean ability, I shall endeavor faithfully to serve the Corporation and Commissioners, as I shall receive instructions from them.

I have met with an observation of some grave divines, that ordinarily when God intends good to a nation, He is pleased to make use of some of themselves to be instrumental in conveying of that good unto them. Now God has furnished several of the Indians with considerable abilities for the work of the ministry, and teaching school. And therefore I am apt to believe that if the Indians so qualified were more taken notice of in suitable rewards, it would conduce very much to the propagation of the Gospel among them. Besides the content they might have in a provision of necessary food and raiment, the respect and honor of it would quicken their industry and allure others to take pains in fitting themselves for a fruitful discharge of those offices.

One thing more I would crave leave to suggest. We have had a very long and grievous war with the Eastern Indians, and

it is of great concernment to His Majesty's interests here that a peace be concluded with them upon firm and sure foundations; which in my poor opinion cannot well be while our articles of accord with them remain so very general as they do. I should think it requisite that convenient tracts of land should be set out to them; and that by plain and natural boundaries, as much as may be — as lakes, rivers, mountains, rocks — upon which for any Englishman to encroach should be accounted a crime. Except this be done, I fear their own jealousies, and the French friars, will persuade them that the English, as they increase and think they want more room, will never leave till they have crowded them quite out of all their lands. And it will be a vain attempt for us to offer Heaven to them if they take up prejudices against us, as if we did grudge them a living upon their own earth.

The Savoy Confession of Faith, English on one side and Indian on the other, has been lately printed here; as also several sermons of the president's [of Harvard, Increase Mather] have been transcribed into Indian and printed; which I hope in God's time will have a very good effect. To see it and be employed in giving Your Honor an account of it would be a very desirable piece of service to [me].

74.

Samuel Sewall: The Selling of Joseph

Samuel Sewall is remembered chiefly for his diary. In it for fifty-seven years, he set down the events of his own and other lives in Boston — revealing in the process all of his many crotchets and vanities, but showing, too, the courage that led him, on January 14, 1697, to have his pastor read from the pulpit of his church his repentance for having concurred in the sentences that had lately condemned nineteen persons to death as witches. Sewall was among other things a judge, with a concern for the unfortunate that was not always belated. His protest against slavery in the province of Massachusetts, called The Selling of Joseph, *was first printed in 1700.*

Source: *The Selling of Joseph: A Memorial*, Boston, 1700.

Forasmuch as liberty is in real value next unto life, none ought to part with it themselves, or deprive others of it, but upon most mature consideration.

The numerousness of slaves at this day in the province, and the uneasiness of them under their slavery, has put many upon thinking whether the foundation of it be firmly and well laid, so as to sustain the vast weight that is built upon it. It is most certain that all men, as they are the sons of Adam, are coheirs, and have equal right unto liberty, and all other outward comforts of life. "God hath given the earth (with all its commodities) unto the sons of Adam" (Ps. 115:16). "And hath made of one blood, all nations of men, for to dwell on all the face of the earth, and hath determined the times before appointed, and the bounds of their habitation, that they should seek the Lord. Forasmuch then as we are the offspring of God," etc. (Acts 17:26, 27, 29).

Now, although the title given by the last Adam does infinitely better men's estates respecting God and themselves, and grants them a most beneficial and inviolable lease under the broad seal of heaven, who were before only tenants at will; yet, through the indulgence of God to our first parents after the Fall, the outward estate of all and every of their children remains the same as to one another; so that, originally and naturally, there is no such thing as slavery. Joseph was rightfully no more a slave to his brethren than they were to him; and they had no more authority to sell him than they had to slay him. And if they had nothing to do to sell him, the Ishmaelites bargaining with them and paying down twenty pieces of silver, could not make a title. Neither could Potiphar have any better interest in him than the Ishmaelites had (Gen. 37:20, 27, 28); for he that shall in this case plead alteration of property seems to have forfeited a great part of his own claim to humanity. There is no proportion between twenty pieces of silver and *liberty*. The commodity itself is the claimer. If Arabian gold be imported in any quantities, most are afraid to meddle with it, though they might have it at easy rates, lest if it should have been wrongfully taken from the owners, it should kindle a fire to the consumption of their whole estate.

'Tis pity there should be more caution used in buying a horse or a little lifeless dust than there is in purchasing men and women. Whenas they are the offspring of God, and their liberty is *Auro pretiosior omni* [more precious than all gold].

And seeing God has said, "He that stealeth a man and selleth him, or if he be found in his hand, he shall surely be put to death" (Ex. 21:16). This law being of everlasting equity, wherein manstealing is ranked among the most atrocious of capital crimes, what louder cry can there be made of that celebrated warning, *Caveat emptor!* [Let the buyer beware.]

And all things considered, it would conduce more to the welfare of the province to have white servants for a term of years than to have slaves for life. Few can endure to hear of a Negro's being made free, and indeed they can seldom use their freedom well; yet their continual aspiring after their forbidden liberty renders them unwilling servants. And there is such a disparity in their conditions, color, and hair that they can never embody with us and grow up into orderly families, to the peopling of the land, but still remain in our body politic as a kind of extravasat[ed] blood. As many Negro men as there are among us, so many empty places there are in our train bands, and the places taken up of men that might make husbands for our daughters. And the sons and daughters of New England would become more like Jacob and Rachel, if this slavery were thrust quite out-of-doors. Moreover, it is too well known what temptations masters are under to connive at the fornication of their slaves, lest they should be obliged to find them wives, or pay their fines. It seems to be practically pleaded that they might be lawless; 'tis thought much of, that the law should have satisfaction for

their thefts and other immoralities; by which means, holiness to the Lord is more rarely engraven upon this sort of servitude.

It is likewise most lamentable to think, how in taking Negroes out of Africa and selling of them here, that which God has joined together men do boldly rend asunder — men from their country, husbands from their wives, parents from their children. How horrible is the uncleanness, mortality, if not murder, that the ships are guilty of that bring great crowds of these miserable men and women. Methinks, when we are bemoaning the barbarous usage of our friends and kinfolk in Africa, it might not be unseasonable to inquire whether we are not culpable in forcing the Africans to become slaves among ourselves. And it may be a question whether all the benefit received by Negro slaves will balance the account of cash laid out upon them, and for the redemption of our own enslaved friends out of Africa, besides all the persons and estates that have perished there.

Objection 1. These blackamoors are of the posterity of Ham, and therefore are under the curse of slavery (Gen. 9:25-27).

Answer. Of all offices, one would not beg this; viz., uncalled for, to be an executioner of the vindictive wrath of God, the extent and duration of which is to us uncertain. If this ever was a commission, how do we know but that it is long since out of date? Many have found it to their cost that a prophetical denunciation of judgment against a person or people would not warrant them to inflict that evil. If it would, Hazael might justify himself in all he did against his Master and the Israelites, from II Kings 8:10, 12.

But it is possible that by cursory reading this text may have been mistaken. For Canaan is the person cursed three times over, without the mentioning of Ham. Good expositors suppose the curse entailed on him, and that this prophesy was accomplished in the extirpation of the Canaanites and in the servitude of the Gibeonites. *Vide pareum* [see Pareus]. Whereas the blackamoors are not descended of Canaan but of Cush (Ps. 68:31). Princes shall come out of Egypt (Mizraim), Ethiopia (Cush) shall soon stretch out her hands unto God; under which names all Africa may be comprehended, and their promised conversion ought to be prayed for (Jer. 13:23). Can the Ethiopian change his skin? This shows that black men are the posterity of Cush, who time out of mind have been distinguished by their color. And for want of the true, Ovid assigns a fabulous cause of it.

Sanguine tum credunt in corpora summa vocato Aethiopum populus nigrum traxisse, colorem [It was then, as men think, that the peoples of Ethiopia became black-skinned, since the blood was drawn to the surface of their bodies by the heat]. [*Metamorphoses*, II.]

Objection 2. The Negroes are brought out of a pagan country into places where the Gospel is preached.

Answer. Evil must not be done that good may come of it. The extraordinary and comprehensive benefit accruing to the Church of God, and to Joseph personally, did not rectify his brethren's sale of him.

Objection 3. The Africans have wars one with another. Our ships bring lawful captives taken in those wars.

Answer. For ought is known, their wars are much such as were between Jacob's sons and their brother Joseph. If they be between town and town, provincial or national, every war is upon one side unjust. An unlawful war can't make lawful captives. And by receiving, we are in danger to promote and partake in their barbarous cruelties. I am sure, if some gentlemen should go down to the Brewster's to take the air, and fish, and a stronger party from Hull

should surprise them and sell them for slaves to a ship outward bound, they would think themselves unjustly dealt with — both by sellers and buyers. And yet 'tis to be feared, we have no other kind of title to our Negroes. "Therefore, all things whatsoever ye would that men should do to you, do ye even so to them; for this is the Law and the Prophets" (Matt. 7:12).

Objection 4. Abraham had servants bought with his money and born in his house.

Answer. Until the circumstances of Abraham's purchase be recorded, no argument can be drawn from it. In the meantime, charity obliges us to conclude that he knew it was lawful and good.

It is observable that the Israelites were strictly forbidden the buying or selling one another for slaves (Lev. 25:39, 46; Jer. 34:8-22). And God gaged [pledged] His blessing in lieu of any loss they might conceive they suffered thereby (Deut. 15:18). And since the partition wall is broken down, inordinate self-love should likewise be demolished. God expects that Christians should be of a more ingenuous and benign frame of spirit. Christians should carry it to all the world, as the Israelites were to carry it one toward another. And for men obstinately to persist in holding their neighbors and brethren under the rigor of perpetual bondage seems to be no proper way of gaining assurance that God has given them spiritual freedom.

Our Blessed Savior has altered the measures of the ancient love song and set it to a most excellent new tune, which all ought to be ambitious of learning (Matt. 5:43, 44; John 13:34). These Ethiopians, as black as they are, seeing they are the sons and daughters of the first Adam, the brethren and sisters of the last Adam, and the offspring of God, they ought to be treated with a respect agreeable.

1701

75.

Cotton Mather: A Christian at His Calling

The Puritan creed was as much an exhortation to work as to worship. In the true Puritan community, each member was obeying the call of God in his everyday life, even if the task that God had summoned him to perform was business. In the following tract, Cotton Mather outlined the moral code that Christian business should follow. A Christian at His Calling was first printed in Boston in 1701. With only slight changes in emphasis, the sermon's main point has been repeated thousands of times in churches of every denomination in America.

Source: *A Christian at His Calling; Two Brief Discourses, One Directing a Christian in his General Calling; Another Directing Him in his Personal,* Boston, 1701, pp. 36ff. Original on deposit in Yale University Library.

Genesis: 47:3
What is your Occupation?

THERE ARE TWO CALLINGS to be minded by all Christians. Every Christian hath a general calling, which is to serve the Lord Jesus Christ, and save his own soul, in the services of religion, that are incumbent on all the children of men. God hath called us to believe on His Son, and repent of our sin, and observe the sacred means of our communion with Himself, and bear our testimony to His truths and ways in the world. And every man in the world should herein conform to the calls of that God, who hath called us with this holy calling.

But, then, every Christian hath also a personal calling, or a certain particular employment, by which his usefulness in his neighborhood is distinguished. God hath made man a sociable creature. We expect benefits from human society. It is but equal that human society should receive benefits from us. We are beneficial to human society by the works of that special occupation in which we are to be employed, according to the order of God.

A Christian, at his two callings, is a man in a boat, rowing for heaven, the house which our Heavenly Father hath intended for us. If he mind but one of his callings, be it which it will, he pulls the oar, but on one side of the boat, and will make but a poor dispatch to the shore of eternal blessedness. It is not only necessary that a Christian should follow his general calling; it is of necessity that he follow his personal calling, too.

The case, therefore, now before us, is — *What is that good account that a Christian should be able to give of his occupation?* Or, *How should a Christian be occupied in the business of his personal calling, that he may give a good account of it?* We will thus proceed in our discourse upon it.

1. A Christian should be able to give this account, *that he hath an occupation.* Every Christian ordinarily should have a calling. That is to say, there should be some special business and some settled business wherein a Christian should for the most part spend the most of his time; and this, that so he may glorify God by doing of good for others and getting of good for himself. . . . 'Tis not honest nor Christian that a Christian should have no business to do. There is a variety of callings in the world, even as there are various objects about which the callings of men are conversant, and various designs unto which the callings of men are intended. Some callings are more immediately to serve the souls of our neighbors; and some their safety; and some their defense; and some their bodies; and some their estates; and some their delights. But it is not lawful for a Christian ordinarily to live without some calling or another, until infirmities have unhappily disabled him. . . .

2. But upon that inquiry — what is your occupation? — a Christian should be able to give this further account, that he hath an allowable occupation, yea, an agreeable occupation; and that he entered into it with a suitable disposition. . . . If our calling be that whereby God will be offended, it cannot be a calling wherein we shall be ourselves befriended. What can any man be the better for a calling that will bring him under the wrath of God? But the wrath of God will cleave to all the gain gotten by a calling that shall be forbidden by the Word of God. The man and his posterity will gain but little by a calling whereto God hath not called him. For our course of life, then, we must consult the Word of God if

we would not fall into a course of sin when we go to choose our occupation. . . .

Let this be taken for granted; except a calling have a tendency to the happiness of mankind, and except the spiritual, or the temporal, good of other men be helped forward by a calling, a man may not meddle with it; the calling is naught, the good God calls you to let it alone. . . .

Every calling whereby God will be dishonored; every calling whereby none but the lusts of men are nourished; every calling whereby men are damnified in any of their true interests; every such calling is to be rejected. . . . I say then, a Christian may not get his living by a calling, the intention whereof is against sobriety, or equity, or piety. No instrument of sin can be allowable.

But this is not enough. A Christian should have it contrived that his calling be agreeable as well as allowable. It is a wonderful inconvenience for a man to have a calling that won't agree with him. See to it, O parents, that when you choose callings for your children, you wisely consult their capacities and their inclinations, lest you ruin them. And, Oh! cry mightily to God, by prayer, yea, with fasting and prayer, for His direction when you are to resolve upon a matter of such considerable consequence. But, O children, you also should be thoughtful and prayerful when you are going to fix upon your callings; and, above all, propose deliberately right ends unto yourselves in what you do. . . .

3. A Christian should be able to give a good account, not only what is his occupation but also, what he is in his occupation. It is not enough that a Christian have an occupation, but he must mind his occupation, as it becomes a Christian. Well then that a Christian may be able to give a good account of his occupation, there are certain virtues of Christianity with which he is to follow it; particularly,

1. A Christian should follow his occupation with *industry.* . . . It seems a man

slothful in business is not a man serving the Lord. By slothfulness men bring upon themselves, what, but poverty, but misery, but all sorts of confusion. . . . On the other side, a man by diligence in his business, what may he not come to? A diligent man is very rarely an indigent man. Would a man rise by his business? I say, then, let him rise to his business. . . . I tell you, with diligence a man may do marvelous things. Young man, work hard while you are young; you'll reap the effects of it when you are old. Yea, how can you ordinarily enjoy any rest at night if you have not been well at work in the day? Let your business engross the most of your time. . . .

Come, come, for shame, away to your business. Lay out your strength in it; put forth your skill for it; avoid all impertinent avocations. Laudable recreations may be used now and then; but, I beseech you, let those recreations be used for sauce, but not for meat. If recreations go to encroach too far upon your business, give to them that put off. . . . It may be there are some that neglect their occupation and squander away one hour, and perhaps one day, after another, drinking, and gaming, and smoking, and fooling at those drinking houses that are so sinful as to entertain them. Unto you, O Miserables, I must address a language like that of our Savior: Thou wicked and slothful person, reform thy ways or thou art not far from outer darkness. Is it nothing to thee that by much slothfulness thy money and credit and all is decaying, and by the idleness of thy hands thy house is coming to nothing? Is it nothing to thee that thou art contracting the character of a vagabond and a prodigal? . . . If the Lord Jesus Christ might find thee in thy storehouse, in thy shop, or in thy ship, or in thy field, or where thy business lies, who knows what blessings He might bestow upon thee? . . .

2. A Christian should follow his occupation with *discretion*. . . . It is a dishonor to the profession of religion if there be no dis-

cretion expressed in the affairs of its professors. Every man should with a praiseworthy emulation strive to get the praise once given to Joseph: There is none so discreet as thou art.

More particularly, one memorandum for you is this: Let every man have the discretion to be well instructed in, and well acquainted with, all the mysteries of his occupation. Be a master of your trade; count it a disgrace to be no workman. And as discretion would bid you to have an insight in your business, thus it also bids you have a foresight in it. . . . Let every man, therefore, in his business, observe the most proper time for everything; for there is a time to every purpose. The wise man says, "There is a time to buy, and a time to sell." And a wise man will do what he can to discern the time.

The same discretion must show a man how to proportion his business unto his ability. 'Tis an indiscreet thing for a man to overcharge himself in his business; for a man to distract his mind, to confound his health, to launch out beyond his estate in his business, is a culpable indiscretion. Be therewithal well advised by the rules of discretion with another caveat: and that is to suit your expenses unto your revenues. Take this advice, O Christians: 'Tis a sin, I say, 'tis ordinarily a sin, and it will at length be a shame, for a man to spend more than he gets, or make his layings out more than his comings in.

A frequent inspection into the state of your business is, therefore, not among the least rules of discretion. It was among the maxims of wisdom given of old, *Be thou diligent for to know the state of thy flocks;* that is to say, often examine the condition of thy business to see whether thou go forward or backward, and learn how to order thy concerns accordingly. . . .

3. A Christian should follow his occupation with *honesty*. . . . Truly, justice, justice must be exactly followed in that calling by

which we go to get our living. A Christian in all his business ought so altogether justly to do everything that he should be able to say with Him: (Acts 23:1) "Men and brethren, I have lived in all good conscience." A Christian should imitate his Lord, of whom 'tis said, *He is righteous in all His ways.* In your business you have dealings with other persons; but a certain vein of honesty, unspotted and resolved honesty, should run through all your dealings. You aim at the getting of silver and gold by your occupation; but you should always act by the Golden Rule. . . . Shall I be more particular? I say then: Let a principle of honesty in your occupation cause you to speak the truth, and nothing but the truth, on all occasions. . . .

Well, then, don't conceal from any customer that which you ought in equity or charity to acquaint him withal; and, more especially, if your customer do rely upon your sincerity. Don't exceed the truth, either in commendations or disparagements of commodities. Don't assert anything that is contrary to truth about the kind or the use or the price of them. . . . In every bargain that you make in your business, let a principle of honesty keep you from every fraudulent or oppressive action. . . . Wherefore, take no advantage, either from the necessity or from the unskillfulness, of those with whom you are concerned. It is uncharitable, it is disingenuous, it is inhumane for one man to prey upon the weakness of another.

And, therefore, also, never, never make any bargain with such as you suspect have no just propriety in what you go to purchase from them. If you fear that stolen goods are offered you, never touch those burning coals, nor incur that brand, when thou saw a thief then thou contended with him. Are there also any manufactures that you are to work up for others? Let them all be well wrought. Give every manufacture its due perfection. Cheat no man with any-

thing that shall be unserviceable to him. Do nothing slightly, do nothing basely, do nothing deceitfully.

But I have yet another thing to say. Let a principle of honesty cause you carefully to pay the debts which in your business must fall upon you. Run into debt as little as you may. . . . But being in debt, be as ready to get out of it as ever you were to get into it. Sirs, I must go to law with you; I'll bring you to the law; all I mean is only to show you the law! . . . Don't carelessly run into debt, and then as carelessly live in it. Indeed, business cannot ordinarily be carried on (especially as the world now goes) without something of debtor and creditor. Well, but let it be uneasy unto you, at any time to think, I have so much of another man's estate in my hands, and I to his damage detain it from him. Some, 'tis said, when they are fallen far into debt, will use I know not what counterfeits to cheat their creditors. But unto those, I cannot use easier terms than these: Thou thief, the great God knows all thy counterfeit and underhand practices; and thou shalt not prosper in them. And, in fine, I have yet one thing more to say: Let a principle of honesty cause you to keep your word, in all your business. You sometimes give your word; let that word then be as good as your bond.

4. A Christian should follow his occupation with *contentment.* . . . A Christian should not be too ready to fall out with his calling. It is the singular favor of God unto a man that he can attend his occupation with contentment and satisfaction. That one man has a spirit formed and fitted for one occupation, and another man for another, this is from the operation of that God who forms the spirit of man within him. . . . Yea, but when a man comes to dislike his occupation, and everything disturbs him and vexes him in it, I am very much afraid that man is nigh unto mischief! Wherefore, the thing to be first pressed upon you is this: Count not your business to be your burden

or your blemish. Let not a proud heart make you ashamed of that business wherein you may be a blessing. For my part, I can't see an honest man hard at work in the way of his occupation, be it never so mean (and though, perhaps, driving of a wheelbarrow) but I find my heart sensibly touched with respect for such a man.

'Tis possible, you may see others in some greater and richer business; and you may think that you might be, yourselves, greater and richer if you were in some other business. Yea, but hath not the God of heaven cast you into that business which now takes you up? . . . Is your business here clogged with any difficulties and inconveniences? Contentment under those difficulties is no little part of your homage to that God who hath placed you where you are. Fall not into any fretful discontent; but with patience make the conclusion of the prophet: Truly, this is a grief and I must bear it! I must bear it! . . .

And, hence, another thing to be pressed upon you is this: Let all persons take heed of too suddenly leaving that business wherein God has fixed them. When a man is become unfit for his business, or his business becomes unfit for him, unquestionably he may leave it; and a man may be otherwise invited, sometimes justly, to change his business. I make no question of it. But many a man, merely from covetousness and from discontent, throws up his business; and how many, do you think, repent of their doing so? . . . I refer it unto your own particular observations.

For my own part, I have a special value for the neighbors who go down to the sea in ships, and do business on the great waters. They are a sort of men that lay the public under as great obligation as almost the men of any occupation whatsoever. And the genius of many young men leading them to the sea, it must not be discouraged. But yet, say, O my young men, very many of you were in good business ashore, and

might have made a good subsistence on your business. But the hope of getting more at sea has too far enchanted some of them. To sea they have betaken themselves. Query: Whether ten to one have not been undone by doing so! All I will say is this: Holy Mr. Tindal said, "I take God to witness to my conscience; I desire of God for myself no more of this world than that without which I cannot keep His laws." If some could have said so, it had been well for them!

5. A Christian should with *piety* follow his occupation. . . . Oh, let every Christian walk with God when he works at his calling; and act in his occupation with an eye to God, act as under the eye of God. Sirs, 'tis a wondrous thing that I am going to say! A poor man, that minds the business of his calling and weaves a thread of holiness into all his business, may arrive to some of the highest glories in heaven at the last. . . .

But now, these things call for your attention.

First, let not the business of your personal calling swallow up the business of your general calling. Man, be jealous lest the fate of Korah's company be thy fate; even to be swallowed up of the earth. . . . Forget not, O mortal man, that thou hast an immortal soul to be provided for. Let not that care, What shall I eat or drink and wherewithal shall I be clothed? make you forgetful of that care, What shall I do to be saved? It may be said to many a man who is drowned in the encumbrances of his occupation, as Luke 10:41, 42: "Thou art careful and troubled about many things; but one thing is needful." Thus, thou art careful to do the business that must be done for the relief of thy bodily wants. It is well; do it, do it. But, thy soul, thy soul, the salvation of thy soul, an acquaintance with Christ, and a union with Christ, the only Savior of thy soul — this is the *one thing* that is needful. Be not so foolish and unwise as to neglect that, whatever thou doest! Oh, try and see if you don't upon trial find, besides the vast blessings of eternity, the fulfillment of that word: (Matt. 6:33) "Seek first the kingdom of God, and all these things shall be added unto you."

Wherefore, be your business never so much, yet use prayer with meditation on the Word of God, every day, both by yourselves and with your families, and this both morning and evening. Rob not the Almighty God of this daily sacrifice, whatever pressure of business may lie upon you. And be assured, all your business will go on the better, all the day, for your being thus faithful to God.

But much more, let your business give way to the Lord's Day. On the Lord's Day, lay aside all business but that of conversing with God in the exercises of devotion. . . . This I would urge; let there be no buying and selling on the Lord's Day. Don't profane the Lord's Day with so much as any thoughts about your secular business. Let all but the exercises of devotion be shut out of your souls; let them lodge without until our Sabbath be over. Sirs, I am verily persuaded that if you would make the experiment, you would ordinarily find that you prosper all the week in your occupation according to your strictness in keeping the first day of the week.

Second, let *obedience* to God be the spring and the strain of all your business. . . .

Third, when you follow your business, have your dependence on God for the succeeding of it.

Fourth, intermix with all your business devotionary thoughts and ejaculatory prayers innumerable. How many thousands of heavenly thoughts may you have in the midst of all your business? You may spiritualize the most earthly business in the world by a chemistry that shall fetch heavenly thoughts out of it. These thoughts you may turn into prayers, even while you are at your business. And you may dart up your prayers to the heavens, notwithstanding what you are doing on earth. Here, here would be a walk in the spirit indeed! What life and peace would it bring to be so spiritually minded!

Why do you find so many occupations mentioned in the Scriptures? 'Tis partly that so you may think on the Scriptures in the midst of your occupations. The Bible directs the merchant unto this desire — May I be a wise merchant and find the pearl of great price! The husbandman is directed unto this desire — May the fallow ground of my heart be ploughed up! The mariner unto this — May I have the anchor of my hope cast within the vail! The carpenter unto this — May I be built up in my most holy faith! The goldsmith to this — May I be enriched with the true gold tried in the fire. The tailor to this — May my soul be furnished with the garments of salvation! And who are they that should come to desire — May my feet be shod with the preparation of the gospel of peace! . . .

May you all follow your good occupations, and may goodness and mercy follow you all in your occupations.

[The poor] have a more comfortable life here, and far less danger as to the next life. . . . A rich man has a miserable life; for he is always full of fear and care. . . . Whereas a man that has but food and raiment with honest labour is free from these fears and cares. . . . We need to pity and love rich men.

JOSEPH MORGAN, *The Nature of Riches*, 1732

1705

76.

ROBERT BEVERLEY: Low Character of Immigrants to Virginia

Robert Beverley, considered one of the best early historians of Virginia, was asked by an English book dealer, in 1703, to appraise John Oldmixon's British Empire in America. *So faulty did Beverley find the book that he set out to write his own interpretation of the Virginia he knew.* The History and Present State of Virginia, *published in 1705, is a sometimes humorous and often perceptive description of those "persons of low circumstances" who became the tobacco planters of early Virginia and who failed, in Beverley's opinion, to display a proper enterprising spirit. An excerpt from the work appears below.*

Source: *The History and Present State of Virginia, In Four Parts*, London, 1705, Pt. 3, Chs. 15, 16.

I CAN EASILY IMAGINE with Sir Josiah Child, that this, as well as all the rest of the plantations, was for the most part at first peopled by persons of low circumstances, and by such as were willing to seek their fortunes in a foreign country. Nor was it hardly possible it should be otherwise; for 'tis not likely that any man of a plentiful estate should voluntarily abandon a happy certainty to roam after imaginary advantages in a New World. Besides which uncertainty, he must have proposed to himself to encounter the infinite difficulties and dangers that attend a new settlement. These discouragements were sufficient to terrify any man that could live easy in England from going to provoke his fortune in a strange land.

Those that went over to that country first were chiefly single men, who had not the encumbrance of wives and children in England; and if they had, they did not expose them to the fatigue and hazard of so long a voyage, until they saw how it should fare with themselves. From hence it came to pass that, when they were settled there in a comfortable way of subsisting a family, they grew sensible of the misfortune of wanting wives, and such as had left wives in England sent for them; but the single men were put to their shifts. They excepted against the Indian women, on account of their being pagans, and for fear they should conspire with those of their own nation to destroy their husbands.

Under this difficulty they had no hopes but that the plenty in which they lived might invite modest women of small fortunes to go over thither from England. However, they would not receive any but such as could carry sufficient certificate of their modesty and good behavior. Those, if they were but moderately qualified in all other respects, might depend upon marrying very well in those days, without any fortune. Nay, the first planters were so far from expecting money with a woman that 'twas a common thing for them to buy a deserving wife at the price of £100 and make themselves believe they had a hopeful bargain.

But this way of peopling the colony was only at first; for after the advantages of the climate and the fruitfulness of the soil were well known, and all the dangers incident to infant settlements were over, people of better condition retired thither with their families, either to increase the estates they had before, or else to avoid being persecuted for their principles of religion or government.

Thus in the time of the Rebellion in England, several good Cavalier families went thither with their effects to escape the tyranny of the usurper. And so again, upon the Restoration, many people of the opposite party took refuge there, to shelter themselves from the King's resentment. But they had not many of these last, because that country was famous for holding out the longest for the royal family of any of the English dominions; for which reason, the Roundheads went for the most part to New England, as did most of those that in the reign of King Charles II were molested on the account of their religion, though some of these fell likewise to the share of Virginia. As for malefactors condemned to transportation, they have always received very few, and for many years last past, their laws have been severe against them.

1710

77.

Cotton Mather: Proposal for Discussion Groups

"Talking things out" is an American tradition, particularly in New England. Cotton Mather, an indefatigable writer in the cause of righteousness, was a firm believer in the value of public discussion of improvements of all kinds — personal, civil, and religious. The passages below are taken from a book published by him in 1710, called Bonifacius, *or* Essays To Do Good. *The procedures outlined by Mather were later followed by Benjamin Franklin in his adult discussion groups — the Junto — in Philadelphia.*

Source: *Essays To Do Good, etc., etc.,* Boston, 1808, pp. 67-69.

WE CANNOT DISMISS this part of the subject without offering a proposal to animate and regulate private meetings of religious persons for the exercises of religion. It is very certain that when such private meetings have been maintained and well conducted, the Christians who have composed them have, like so many "coals of the altar," kept one another alive, and been the means of maintaining a lively Christianity in the neighborhood. Such societies have been strong and approved instruments, to uphold the power of godliness. The disuse of such societies has been accompanied with a visible decay of religion, in proportion as they have been discontinued or disregarded in any place, the less has godliness flourished.

The rules observed by some associated families may be offered with advantage, on this occasion. They will show us what good may be done in a neighborhood by the establishment of such societies.

1. It is proposed that a select number of families, perhaps about twelve, agree to meet (the men and their wives) at each other's houses alternately, once in a fortnight or a month, or otherwise, as shall be thought most proper, and spend a suitable time together in religious exercises.

2. The exercises of religion proper for such a meeting are: for the brethren in rotation to commence and conclude with prayer; for psalms to be sung; and for sermons to be repeated.

3. It were desirable for the ministers, now and then, to be present at the meeting, and pray with them, instruct and exhort them, as they may see occasion.

4. Candidates for the ministry may do well to perform their first offices here, and thereby prepare themselves for further services.

5. One special design of the meeting should be with united prayers to ask the

blessing of Heaven on the family where they are assembled, as well as on the rest; that with the wondrous force of united prayers "two or three may agree on earth to ask such things" as are to be done for the families, by "our Father which is in heaven."

6. The members of such a society should consider themselves as bound up in one "bundle of love," and count themselves obliged, by very close and strong bonds, to be serviceable to one another. If anyone in the society should fall into affliction, all the rest should presently study to relieve and support the afflicted person in every possible way. If anyone should fall into temptation, the rest should watch over him, and with the "spirit of meekness," with "meekness of wisdom," endeavor to recover him. It should be like a law of the Medes and Persians to the whole society — that they will, upon all just occasions, affectionately give and receive mutual admonitions of anything that they may see amiss in each other.

7. It is not easy to calculate the good offices which such a society may do to many other persons, besides its own members. The prayers of such well-disposed societies may fetch down marvelous favors from Heaven on their pastors; their lives may be prolonged, their gifts augmented, their graces brightened, and their labors prospered, in answer to the supplications of such associated families. The interests of religion may be also greatly promoted in the whole flock by their fervent supplications; and the Spirit of Grace mightily poured out upon the rising generation; yea, the country at large may be the better for them.

8. The society may, on peculiar occasions, set apart whole days for fasting and prayer. The success of such days has been sometimes very remarkable, and the savor which they have left on the minds of those who have engaged in them, has been such as

greatly to prepare them to "show forth the death of the Lord," at His holy table; yea, to meet their own death when God has been pleased to appoint it.

9. It is very certain that the devotions and conferences carried on in such a society will not only have a wonderful tendency to produce the "comfort of love" in the hearts of good men toward one another but that their ability to serve many valuable interests will also thereby be much increased.

10. Unexpected opportunities to do good will arise to such a society; and especially if such a plan as the following were adopted: That the men who compose the society would now and then spend half an hour by themselves in considering that question — What good is there to be done? More particularly,

Who are to be called upon to do their duty in coming to special ordinances?

Who are in any peculiar adversity, and what may be done to comfort them?

What contention or variance may there be among any of our neighbors, and what may be done for healing it?

What open transgressions do any live in, and who shall be desired to carry faithful admonitions to them?

Finally: What is there to be done for the advantage and advancement of our holy religion?

In the primitive times of Christianity, much use was made of a saying which was ascribed to Matthias the apostle: "If the neighbor of an elect or godly man sin, the godly man himself has also sinned." The intention of that saying was to point out the obligation of neighbors watchfully to admonish one another. O, how much may Christians, associated in religious societies, effect by watchful and faithful admonitions to prevent their being "partakers in other men's sins"! The man, who shall produce and promote such societies will do an incalculable service to the neighborhood.

1711

78.

John Urmstone: Self-Reliance on the Frontier

The history of America's frontier settlements is a story of the determination, as well as the independence and self-reliance of men and women willing to forego the comforts of an established community. For the earliest pioneers in North Carolina, land was ample and productive, but labor was scarce. Frontier families had to work until they were almost exhausted to produce the bare necessities of life. One such North Carolina family was headed by the Reverend John Urmstone, who on July 7, 1711, addressed the following letter to the secretary of the Society for Propagating the Gospel. It is an illuminating account of man's ability to provide for himself.

Source: Francis L. Hawks, *History of North Carolina*, Fayetteville, N.C., 1858, Vol. II, p. 215.

WORKMEN ARE DEAR AND SCARCE. I have about a dozen acres of clear ground, and the rest woods; in all, 300 acres. Had I servants and money, I might live very comfortably upon it, raise good corn of all sorts, and cattle, without any great labor or charges, could it once be stocked; but for want thereof shall not make any advantage of my land. I have bought a horse some time ago; since that, three cows and calves, five sheep, and some fowls of all sorts, but most of them unpaid for, together with fourteen bushels of wheat, for all which I must give English goods.

At this rate I might have had anything that either this government or any of the neighboring colonies afford; but had I stock, I need not fear wanting either butter, cheese, beef, or mutton, of my own raising, or good grain of all sorts. I am forced to work hard with axe, hoe, and spade. I have not a stick to burn for any use but what I cut down with my own hands. I am forced to dig a garden, raise beans, peas, etc., with the assistance of a sorry wench my wife brought with her from England. Men are generally of all trades, and women the like within their spheres, except some who are the posterity of old planters and have great numbers of slaves, who understand most handicraft. Men are generally carpenters, joiners, wheelwrights, coopers, butchers, tanners, shoemakers, tallow-chandlers, watermen, and what not; women, soap-makers, starch-makers, dyers, etc. He or she that cannot do all these things, or has not slaves that can, over and above all the common occupations of both sexes, will have but a bad time of it; for help is not to be had at any rate, everyone having business enough of his own. This makes tradesmen turn planters, and these become tradesmen.

1717

79.

JOHN WISE: On Democracy in Church Government

During the first decade of the eighteenth century, the Mathers and others among the Puritan clergy led a movement to form an association that would assume control over certain areas of church government that up to this time had been handled by the members (including lay) of the individual churches. A Congregational minister in Ipswich, John Wise, was outspoken in his opposition to such action and advocated instead democracy and autonomy in church government. His publication of 1717, A Vindication of the Government of New-England Churches, *excerpts from which appear below, is a brilliantly contrived and closely thought out defense of democracy in church as well as in civil government.*

Source: *A Vindication of the Government of New England Churches,* Boston, 1772, pp. 28-66.

THE FIRST HUMAN SUBJECT and origin of civil power is the people; for as they have a power every man over himself in a natural state, so upon a combination they can and do bequeath this power unto others and settle it according as their united discretion shall determine; for that this is very plain, that when the subject of sovereign power is quite extinct, that power returns to the people again. And, when they are free, they may set up what species of government they please; or, if they rather incline to it, they may subside into a state of natural being if it be plainly for the best. . . .

The formal reason of government is the will of a community, yielded up and surrendered to some other subject, either of one particular person, or more, conveyed in the following manner:

Let us conceive in our mind a multitude of men, all naturally free and equal, going about voluntarily to erect themselves into a new commonwealth. Now their condition being such, to bring themselves into a political body, they must needs enter into diverse covenants.

(1) They must interchangeably each man covenant to join in one lasting society, that they may be capable to concert the measures of their safety by a public vote.

(2) A vote or decree must then nextly pass to set up some particular species of government over them. And if they are joined in their first compact upon absolute terms to stand to the decision of the first vote concerning the species of government, then all are bound by the majority to acquiesce in that particular form thereby settled,

though their own private opinion incline them to some other model.

(3) After a decree has specified the particular form of government, then there will be need of a new covenant, whereby those on whom sovereignty is conferred engage to take care of the common peace and welfare; and the subjects, on the other hand, to yield them faithful obedience. In which covenant is included that submission and union of wills by which a state may be conceived to be but one person. So that the most proper definition of a civil state is this, viz.: A civil state is a compound moral person whose will (united by those covenants before passed) is the will of all; to the end it may use and apply the strength and riches of private persons toward maintaining the common peace, security, and well-being of all, which may be conceived as though the whole state was now become but one man, in which the aforesaid covenants may be supposed, under God's Providence, to be the Divine Fiat, pronounced by God: Let us make man. And, by way of resemblance, the aforesaid being may be thus anatomized.

i. The sovereign power is the soul infused, giving life and motion to the whole body.

ii. Subordinate officers are the joints by which the body moves.

iii. Wealth and riches are the strength.

iv. Equity and laws are the reason.

v. Counselors the memory.

vi. *Salus populi,* or the happiness of the people, is the end of its being, or main business to be attended and done.

vii. Concord among the members and all estates is the health.

viii. Sedition is sickness, and civil war death. . . .

The forms of a regular state are three only, which forms arise from the proper and particular subject in which the supreme power resides. As,

1. A democracy, which is when the sovereign power is lodged in a council consisting of all the members and where every member has the privilege of a vote. This form of government appears in the greatest part of the world to have been the most ancient. For that reason seems to show it to be most probable, that when men (being originally in a condition of natural freedom and equality) had thoughts of joining in a civil body, would without question be inclined to administer their common affairs by their common judgments and so must necessarily, to gratify that inclination, establish a democracy. . . .

A democracy is then erected when a number of free persons do assemble together in order to enter into a covenant for uniting themselves in a body; and such a preparative assembly has some appearance already of a democracy. It is a democracy in embryo, properly in this respect, that every man has the privilege freely to deliver his opinion concerning the common affairs. Yet he who dissents from the vote of the majority is not in the least obliged by what they determine, till by a second covenant a popular form be actually established, for not before then can we call it a democratic government, viz., till the right of determining all matters relating to the public safety is actually placed in a general assembly of the whole people, or by their own compact and mutual agreement determine themselves the proper subjects for the exercise of sovereign power. And to complete this state and render it capable to exert its power to answer the end of a civil state, these conditions are necessary:

(1) That a certain time and place be assigned for assembling.

(2) That when the assembly be orderly met, as to time and place, that then the vote of the majority must pass for the vote of the whole body.

(3) That magistrates be appointed to exercise the authority of the whole for the better dispatch of business, of everyday's oc-

currence, who also may, with more mature diligence, search into more important affairs; and, if in case anything happens of greater consequence, may report it to the assembly, and be peculiarly serviceable in putting all public decrees into execution, because a large body of people is almost useless in respect of the last service, and of many others, as to the more particular application and exercise of power. Therefore, it is most agreeable with the law of nature that they institute their officers to act in their name and stead.

2. The second species of regular government is an aristocracy, and this is said then to be constituted when the people or assembly, united by a first covenant and having thereby cast themselves into the first rudiments of a state, do then, by common decree, devolve the sovereign power on a council consisting of some select members; and these, having accepted of the designation, are then properly invested with sovereign command, and then an aristocracy is formed.

3. The third species of a regular government is a monarchy, which is settled when the sovereign power is conferred on some one worthy person. It differs from the former, because a monarch, who is but one person in natural as well as in moral account, and so is furnished with an immediate power of exercising sovereign command in all instances of government; but the forenamed must needs have particular time and place assigned; but the power and authority is equal in each.

Mixed governments, which are various and of diverse kinds . . . yet possibly the fairest in the world is that which has a regular monarchy settled upon a noble democracy as its basis. . . .

In general, concerning rebellion against government, for particular subjects to break in upon regular communities, duly established, is from the premises to violate the law of nature, and is a high usurpation upon the first grand immunities of mankind. Such rebels in states and usurpers in churches affront the world with a presumption that the best of the brotherhood are a company of fools, and that themselves have fairly monopolized all the reason of human nature. Yea, they take upon them the boldness to assume a prerogative of trampling underfoot the natural original equality and liberty of their fellows; for to push the proprietors of settlements out of possession of their old, and impose new, schemes upon them is virtually to declare them in a state of vassalage, or that they were born so; and, therefore, will the usurper be so gracious as to insure them they shall not be sold at the next market. They must esteem it a favor, for by this time all the original prerogatives of man's nature are intentionally a victim, smoking to satiate the usurper's ambition. . . .

Where the constitution of a nation is such that the laws of the land are the measures both of the sovereign's commands and the obedience of the subjects, whereby it is provided that as the one are not to invade what by concessions and stipulations is granted to the ruler, so the other is not to deprive them of their lawful and determined rights and liberties, then the prince who strives to subvert the fundamental laws of the society is the traitor and the rebel and not the people, who endeavor to preserve and defend their own. It is very applicable to particular men in their rebellions or usurpations in church or state. . . .

It is certainly a great truth that man's original liberty, after it is resigned (yet under due restrictions), ought to be cherished in all wise governments, or otherwise, a man in making himself a subject, he alters himself from a freeman into a slave, which to do is repugnant to the law of nature. Also, the natural equality of men among men must be duly favored, in that government was never established by God or nature to give one man a prerogative to insult over another. Therefore, in a civil as well as in a natural state of being, a just equality is to be indulged so far as that every man is bound to honor every man, which is agreeable both with nature and religion (I Peter 2:17): *Honor all men.*

The end of all good government is to cultivate humanity, and promote the happiness of all and the good of every man in all his rights, his life, liberty, estate, honor, etc., without injury or abuse done to any. Then certainly it cannot easily be thought that a company of men that shall enter into a voluntary compact to hold all power in their own hands, thereby to use and improve their united force, wisdom, riches, and strength for the common and particular good of every member, as is the nature of a democracy; I say it cannot be that this sort of constitution will so readily furnish those in government with an appetite or disposition to prey upon each other or embezzle the common stock, as some particular persons may be apt to do when set off and entrusted with the same power.

And, moreover, this appears very natural that, when the aforesaid government or power, settled in all, when they have elected certain capable persons to minister in their affairs, and the said ministers remain accountable to the assembly, these officers must needs be under the influence of many wise cautions from their own thoughts (as well as under confinement by their commission) in their whole administration. And from thence it must needs follow that they will be more apt and inclined to steer right for the main point, viz., the peculiar good and benefit of the whole and every particular member fairly and sincerely.

And why may not these stand for very rational pleas in church order? For certainly, if Christ has settled any form of power in His church, He has done it for His church's safety and for the benefit of every member. Then He must needs be presumed to have made choice of that government as

should least expose His people to hazard, either from the fraud or arbitrary measures of particular men. And it is as plain as daylight, there is no species of government like a democracy to attain this end. . . .

If the government of the gospel churches be a democracy, these consequences must necessarily follow:

1. That the right of convoking councils ecclesiastical is in the churches.

2. That such a council has only consultative not a juridical power in it. A juridical power committed to such a representative body is both needless and also dangerous to the distinct and perfect states they derive from. Complete states settled upon a body of immutable and imperial laws as its basis may want council; but to create a new subject of juridical power is some way to endanger the being of the creators.

3. That all the members of an ecclesiastical council deriving from a democracy are subjects of equal power. Whatever the power is, the several delegates must, from the nature of the government they derive from, be equal sharers in it. Democratic states, in their representative body, can make but one house, because they have but one subject of supreme power in their nature, and, therefore, their delegates, let them be who or what they may be, are under equal trust; so that none can justly claim superiority over their fellows or pretend to a higher power in their suffrage.

Indeed, in such kingdoms where the sovereign power is distributed and settled in diverse subjects that the balance of power may be more even, for the safety of the whole and of all parts under all acts of sovereign power, from such a settlement of power there arises several distinct states in the same government, which, when convened as one subject of sovereign power, they make different houses in their grand sessions. And so one house or state can negative another.

But in every distinct house of these states, the members are equal in their vote — the most ayes make the affirmative vote, and the most noes, the negative. They don't weigh the intellectual furniture, or other distinguishing qualifications of the several voters, in the scales of the golden rule of fellowship; they only add up the ayes and the noes, and so determine the suffrage of the house. . . .

In the last century, God has been very admirable in the works of Providence, and has therein highly dignified our constitution. And we want no other evidence . . . than the recognition of what God has done for these famous English colonies in North America, who have all along distinguished themselves from all the world by their singular regard, both to the faith and practice of the true religion. Now, let any other constitution on earth but parallel ours in the eminent shines of Providence and in religious effects and we will resign the whole cause. But [until] then, we will go on and rejoice in the Grace of God that we, in these countries, are by His good Providence over us the subjects of the most ancient, rational, and noble constitution in church order that ever was, will be, or can be, while the laws of nature and grace remain unrepealed. For that it is a constitution which infinite wisdom has authorized and founded in the law of nature, and His omnificent Providence has eminently honored and dignified, both by the smiles and frowns of His countenance, through all the ages of the Christian world, to this very morning.

And though some of the reverend churches within this grand consociation (who settled upon the same platform with us) have with too great a precipitation made a defection from the constitution, yet this is our comfort — that their alteration is not so firm as the laws of the Medes and Persians; for that those who turned them off may by the same power bring them on to their old basis again. And let Christ pity and help them; for certainly their present state is portentous, from what may be observed from the proceedings of Providence through the whole Christian Era, unto this day.

1718

80.

Indenture of Apprentices in New York

In New York, as in the other colonies, the practice of binding apprentices to their masters by a contract, or indenture, was common. However, all of the advantages in such a contract did not lie with the master. Apprenticeship was a means of acquiring training in a useful vocation, and although the apprentice was bound to serve his master for a stated number of years, the master was bound to teach his trade to his apprentice in return. The daily school session stipulated in this typical New York contract of October 2, 1718, resulted from the New York school law of 1665.

Source: *Collections of the New-York Historical Society for the Year 1909,* New York, 1910, pp. 113-114.

THIS INDENTURE WITNESSES that I, William Mathews, son of Marrat of the city of New York, a widow . . . does voluntarily and of his own free will and accord and by the consent of his said mother put himself as an apprentice cordwainer to Thomas Windover of the city aforesaid.

He will live and (after the manner of an apprentice) serve from August 15, 1718, until the full term of seven years be completed and ended. During all of this term, the said apprentice shall faithfully serve his said master, shall faithfully keep his secrets, and gladly obey his lawful commands everywhere. He shall do no damage to his said master, nor see any done by others without giving notice to his said master. He shall not waste his said master's goods nor lend them unlawfully to any. He shall not commit fornication nor contract matrimony within the said term.

At cards, dice, or any other unlawful game, he shall not play (whereby his said master may have damage) with his own goods or the goods of others. Without a license from his master he shall neither buy nor sell during the said term. He shall not absent himself day or night from his master's service without his leave, nor haunt alehouses, but in all things he shall behave himself as a faithful apprentice toward his master all during his said term.

The said master, during the said term, shall, by the best means or methods, teach or cause the said apprentice to be taught the art or mystery of a cordwainer. He shall find and provide unto the said apprentice sufficient meat, drink, apparel, lodging, and washing fit for an apprentice. During the said term, every night in winter he shall give the apprentice one quarter of schooling. At the expiration of the said term he shall provide him with a sufficient new suit of apparel, four shirts, and two necklets.

1721

81.

JEREMIAH DUMMER: A Defense of the New England Charters

Jeremiah Dummer grew up in Boston, but around 1705 he left for England, never to return. However, his interest in his native land never dwindled, and he worked on its behalf for the rest of his life, serving as colonial agent for both Massachusetts and Connecticut. The occasion of his Defence of the New-England Charters was a Parliamentary attack on them in 1715. Dummer strongly defended the colonies, and insisted that they had done nothing to merit the revocation of their charters, which, because they had been granted for "services to be performed," should be considered even more inviolable than the charters of other English corporations. The Defence, a portion of which is reprinted here, was first printed in 1721.

Source: *A Defence of the New-England Charters*, Boston, 1745.

THE GENERAL NAME OF NEW ENGLAND includes in its common acceptation the province of the Massachusetts Bay, the colony of Connecticut, the government of Rhode Island, with Providence plantations, and the province of New Hampshire. The three former are charter governments; the last, viz.: New Hampshire never had any peculiar privileges, but is under the immediate and absolute direction of the Crown. The Massachusetts, as it is the first of all the colonies in extent of territory and number of inhabitants, was the first incorporated, having obtained their charter from King Charles I, in the fourth year of his reign. The colony of Connecticut received theirs from King Charles II in 1662, and the fourteenth year of his reign.

These charters agreed in all the main points, confirming to the patentees their title to the soil, and giving them ample privileges for the well-ordering and governing the respective plantations. They had power to make a common seal; to plead and be impleaded; to call general assemblies; to make laws, so as they were not repugnant to the laws of England; to assess the freemen; to constitute all civil officers; to array the inhabitants in warlike posture, and use the martial law when occasion required. And it was provided further that in case any doubts should arise, the charters should have the most favorable construction for the benefit of the several corporations. . . .

I. I shall endeavor to show that the charter governments have a good and undoubted right to their respective charters.

II. That they have not forfeited them by

any misgovernment or maladministration.

III. That if they had, it would not be the interest of the Crown to accept the forfeitures. And,

IV. I shall make some observations upon the extraordinary method of proceeding against the charters by a bill in Parliament.

As to the first point, there can be no difficulty. The charters were granted by the Crown, and the king is acknowledged to be the head and fountain of all corporations and franchises; for though My Lord Coke takes notice that a body politic may be established by prescription, yet such prescription is only valid upon a presumption that there was an ancient grant of the Crown, which by the injury of time was afterward lost. I need not insist upon what nobody controverts; but it is material to observe that the American charters are of a higher nature and stand on a better foot than the corporations in England. For these latter were granted upon improvements already made, and therefore were acts of mere grace and favor in the Crown; whereas the former were given as premiums for services to be performed, and therefore are to be considered as grants upon a valuable consideration; which adds weight and strength to the title.

To increase the nation's commerce and enlarge her dominions, must be allowed a work of no little merit, if we consider the hardships to which the Adventurers were exposed; or the expense in making their settlements; or lastly, the great advantages thence accruing to the Crown and nation. . . .

As great, however, as this expense was, I believe it will appear that the settlement of New England was not more chargeable to the Adventurers than it has been in its consequence profitable to Great Britain. There is no sort of British manufacture but what the subjects there demand in a greater or less proportion, as they have ability to pay for it; everything for the use, convenience, ornament, and (I say it with regret) for the luxury and pride of life. Some of the oldest and most experienced traders to those parts have by computation made these exports arise to the value of £300,000 per annum. The imports from thence are equally beneficial to the Kingdom. . . .

What I have said amounts to this: That New England received her charters on this express condition, of settling colonies for the benefit of the Crown:

That she was at a vast expense, and through incredible difficulties, accomplished the work, even beyond what was ever hoped or expected.

And then the conclusion that I would draw from these premises is this: That to strip the country of their charters after the service has been so successfully performed is abhorrent from all reason, equity, and justice. . . .

I believe it will be generally allowed that my argument is thus far right, if I can make good my second proposition, viz.: That these governments have by no misbehavior forfeited back their charters to the Crown. . . .

The first charge in the bill against the charter governments is that they have neglected the defense of the inhabitants. This I must own, if true, and such neglect was voluntary, while they had the means and power of defense in their hands, was a high and treasonable breach of their trust, and would be the strongest argument that could be brought for a resumption of the charters. But, now, if I should prove that these governments, especially the Massachusetts and Connecticut, have in all past times defended the inhabitants, both by sea and land, as well against the French as Indian enemy; if I shall prove that they have all the late war protected one of the king's provinces lying on their confines, which would otherwise inevitably have been lost; and that another of those provinces took no part in the war, but maintained a shameful neutrality with the enemy, whereby the whole weight of the war fell on the Massachusetts; if I shall prove that they have frequently carried offensive arms into the French territories, and made one important conquest, since annexed to the British Crown; and that all this was done at their own vast expense; then, I hope, New England will stand fairly acquitted of this supposed crime of neglecting to defend the inhabitants, and be allowed not only irreprehensible in this respect, but to have highly merited of the Crown and nation. . . .

The other charge in the bill is that they have exercised arbitrary power. If this be aimed at the proprietary governments, which however I don't accuse, I have nothing to say, but am sure that the charter governments stand clear of it. The thing speaks loudly for itself; for in the governments where there are charters, and those charters entire, all officers, civil and military, are elected by the people, and that annually; than which constitution nothing under heaven can be a stronger barrier against arbitrary rule; for should it be allowed that the people, corrupted or deceived, might instead of wise magistrates choose tyrants and oppressors to lord over them one year, yet it can't be imagined that, after they have felt the smart of it, they will do so the next. Nor can there be a greater obligation on the rulers themselves to administer justice than that their election depends on it the next year. Hence, the frequent choice of magistrates has been ever a main pillar upon which all who have aimed at freedom in their schemes of government have depended.

As the reason is incontestable so the fact is apparent, that these governments, far from retrenching the liberty of the subject, have improved it in some important articles, which the circumstances of things in Great Britain perhaps don't require, or won't easily admit.

To instance in a few: There has been from the beginning an office erected by law in every country where all conveyances of land are entered at large, after the grantors have first acknowledged them before a justice of peace; by which means much fraud is prevented, no person being able to sell his estate twice, or take up more money upon it than it's worth. Provision has likewise been made for the security of the life and property of the subject in the matter of juries, who are not returned by the sheriff of the county, but are chosen by the inhabitants of the town a convenient time before the sitting of the courts. And this election is under the most exact regulation, in order to prevent corruption, so far as human prudence can do it. It must be noted that sheriffs in the plantations are comparatively but little officers, and therefore not to be trusted as here, where they are men of ample fortunes. And yet even here such flagrant corruptions have been found in returning juries by sheriffs that the House of Commons thought it necessary, in their last session, to amend the law in this point, and passed a bill for choosing them by ballot.

Redress in their courts of law is easy, quick, and cheap. All processes are in English, and no special pleadings or demurrers are admitted, but the general issue is always given, and special matters brought in evidence; which saves time and expense; and in this case a man is not liable to lose his estate for a defect in form, nor is the merit of the cause made to depend on the niceties of clerkship. By a law of the country, no writ may be abated for a circumstantial error, such as a slight misnomer or any informality. And by another law, it is enacted that every attorney taking out a writ from the clerk's office shall endorse his surname upon it, and be liable to pay to the adverse party his costs and charges in case of nonprosecution or discontinuance, or that the plaintiff be nonsuit, or judgment pass against him. And it is provided in the same act that if the plaintiff shall suffer a nonsuit by the attorney's mislaying the action, he shall be obliged to draw a new writ without a fee, in case the party shall see fit to revive the suit.

I can't but think that everybody, except gentlemen of the long robe and the attornies, will think this a wholesome law, and well calculated for the benefit of the subject. For the quicker dispatch of causes, declarations are made parts of the writ, in which the case is fully and particularly set forth. If it be matter of account, the account is annexed to the writ, and copies of both left with the defendant; which being done fourteen days before the sitting of the court, he is obliged to plead directly, and the issue is then tried; whereas, by the practice of the Court of King's Bench, three or four months time is often lost after the writ is served before the cause can be brought to issue. . . .

This being the case of the charter governments, let us turn the tables and see how it fared with them when in an evil reign they lost their charters. Then, the governor of New England, with four or five strangers of his council, men of desperate fortunes, and bad, if any, principles, made what laws and levied what taxes they pleased on the people. They, without an assembly, raised a penny in the pound on all the estates in the country, and another penny on all imported goods, besides 20*d.* per head as poll money, and an immoderate excise on wine, rum, and other liquors. Several worthy persons, having in a humble address represented this proceeding as a grievance, were committed to the common jail for a high misdemeanor; denied the benefit of the habeas corpus act; tried out their own county; fined exorbitantly; and obliged to pay £160 for fees, when the prosecution would hardly have cost them so many shillings in Great Britain. And to complete the oppression, when they upon their trial claimed the privileges of Englishmen, they were scoffingly told those things would not follow them to the ends of the earth.

Unnatural insult; must the brave adventurer, who with the hazard of his life and fortune seeks out new climates to enrich his mother country, be denied those common

Courtesy, the Yale University Art Gallery

Jeremiah Dummer, portrait by an unidentified English artist, early 18th century

rights which his countrymen enjoy at home in safe and indolence? Is he to be made miserable and a slave by his own acquisitions? Is the laborer alone unworthy of his hire, and shall they only reap who have neither sown nor planted? Monstrous absurdity! Horrid inverted order!

These proceedings, however arbitrary and oppressive, were but the prelude: The catastrophe was, if possible, yet more dismal. Having invaded their liberties, by an easy transition, the next attack was directly on their properties. Their titles to their lands [were] absolutely denied by the governor and his creatures upon two pretenses: One, that their conveyances were not according to the law of England; the other, that if they might be thought to have had something like a title formerly, yet it now ceased by the revocation of their charters; so that they who had fairly purchased their lands, and held them in quiet possession for above fifty years, were now obliged to accept new deeds from the governor, and pay for them a third part of their value, in order to ascertain their titles, or otherwise they would be seized for the Crown. . . .

I should not have thus far entered into the detail of things so long past but to show from experience, as well as from the reason and nature of the thing, that charters are not the causes of arbitrary government but, indeed, strong works raised against it, which, once thrown down, oppression rushes in like a tide and bears down everything before it. . . .

What I have heard most insisted on is that the Acts of Trade and Navigation, made on purpose to render the plantations beneficial to Great Britain, are disregarded in the charter governments; and that this evil cannot be effectually cured but by a resumption of the charters. To which I answer very particularly and distinctly:

First, the complaints on this head are for the most part of an old date, and when the bill against the charters was pending in the House of Commons, were produced from the files of the Plantation Board, whither they had been transmitted in former reigns, when customhouse officers in the plantations were such great rarities that one collector served four entire provinces. And can it be thought strange that merchants, whose business is gain, should have sometimes, for lucre, transgressed the Acts of Trade, when there were no officers to see them duly observed? The case is vastly different now. Officers of the Revenue are multiplied, and are extremely rigorous, so that instead of their complaints of unfair traders, the merchants, on the other hand, greatly complain of the oppression of the officers. . . .

Second, if there be some late complaints, perhaps upon examination, they will appear to be ill-grounded. I can speak this knowingly, with respect to a complaint transmitted not long since by the surveyor general of North America, and the collector of New London against His Majesty's colony of Connecticut. These gentlemen, one or both of them, drew up a charge against that innocent and loyal colony, in very severe terms, as setting the laws of trade and navigation at the utmost defiance; whereas, in truth and in fact, the instances they produced of such defiance were clear proofs of that colony's inclination to support the laws of trade and their own traffic; and on the contrary, what the customhouse officers insisted on was manifestly subversive of both, and could serve no end in the world but enhancing the collector's fees. . . .

Third, if it were true that some persons did now and then concern themselves in an illegal trade, can it be thought just or reasonable that the whole community should suffer for their private fault? . . .

Another thing alleged against the American charters is that their governments have made laws repugnant to the laws of Great Britain, contrary to the powers given them, and thereby have incurred a forfeiture of the charters.

If the Massachusetts charter were singly in question, this allegation would have no place, because no act passed by that Assembly has the force of a law till the king's governor has assented to it, and then it comes home for His Majesty's approbation, who, if he pleases, annuls it. There is, therefore, no danger of their making laws repugnant to the laws of Great Britain; or if they should, there being a remedy always at hand, if it be not made use of, the fault will lie somewhere else, and can't affect the province.

But let us examine a little whether any of the other governments acting under charters may deserve this censure; in order to which, we must consider what this phrase [repugnant to the laws of England] imports. I believe it will be easily allowed that a law may be various from the laws of England and yet not repugnant to them; or otherwise these governments must make no laws at all, which nobody will say who knows that a right of legislature is the most essential part of their charters, and what indeed the reason and nature of the thing make absolutely necessary. Every country has circumstances peculiar to itself in respect of its soil, situation, inhabitants, and commerce, to all which convenient laws must, with the nicest care and judgment, be adapted; whereas the laws of England are calculated for their own meridian, and are many of them no ways suitable to the plantations, and others not possible to be executed there. . . .

Having premised this distinction, I answer the question in direct terms: That then a law in the plantations may be said to be repugnant to a law made in Great Britain, when it flatly contradicts it, so far as the law made here mentions and relates to the plantation. . . .

It is the 7th and 8th of King William, which . . . enacts that all laws, bylaws, usages, or customs at this time, or which hereafter shall be in practice, or endeavored or pretended to be in force or practice in any of the plantations, which are in anywise repugnant to the before-mentioned laws or any of them, *so far as they do relate to the said plantations, or any of them,* or which are any ways repugnant to this present act, or any other law hereafter to be made in this Kingdom, *so far as such law shall relate to and mention the said plantations,* are illegal, null, and void, to all intents and purposes whatsoever. . . .

If the words will receive any other construction than what the act of Parliament has put upon them, I think it must be supposed to be this: That the patentees should not under color of their particular charters presume to make any laws inconsistent with the Great Charter and other laws of England, by which the lives, liberties, and properties of Englishmen are secured. It seems reasonable enough to think that the Crown might intend by this injunction to provide for all its subjects, that they might not be oppressed by arbitrary power; but in whatever distant part of the world they were settled, being still subjects, they should have the usage of Englishmen, be protected by the same mild laws, and enjoy the same happy government as if they continued within the realm.

Consider the expression in this light, and the colonies (which I am defending) are still safe, having in no respect impaired, but many ways improved the liberty of the subject, as I have before shown under another head. If hereafter so unaccountable a thing should happen, that those privileges which were designed as fences against oppression and despotic power prove the means to introduce both, and the body of the people should petition to be relieved from the yoke of their charters, for my part, I'll be no longer an advocate for them. Only in the meantime, I heartily wish they may not be disturbed, but rest in peace till then.

There is one thing more I have heard often urged against the charter colonies, and indeed 'tis what one meets with from people of all conditions and qualities, though, with due respect to their better judgments, I can see neither reason nor color for it. 'Tis said that their increasing numbers and wealth, joined to their great distance from Britain, will give them an opportunity in the course of some years to throw off their dependence on the nation and declare themselves a free state, if not curbed in time, by being made entirely subject to the Crown; whereas, in truth, there's nobody, though but little acquainted with these or any of the northern plantations, who does not know and confess that their poverty and the declining state of their trade is so great at present that there's far more danger of their sinking, without some extraordinary support from the Crown, than of their ever revolting from it. So that I may say, without being ludicrous, that it would not be more absurd to place two of His Majesty's Beefeaters to watch an infant in the cradle, that it don't rise and cut its father's throat, than to guard these weak infant colonies, to prevent their shaking off the British yoke. Besides, they are so distinct from one another in their forms of government, in their religious rites, in their emulation of trade, and, consequently, in their affections that they can never be supposed to unite in so dangerous an enterprise.

It is for this reason I have often wondered to hear some great men profess their belief of the feasibleness of it, and the probability of its sometime or other actually coming to pass, who yet with the same breath advise that all the governments on the Continent be formed into one, by being brought under one viceroy, and into one assembly. For surely, if we in earnest believed that there was or would be hereafter a disposition in the provinces to rebel, and declare themselves independent, it would be good policy to keep them disunited; because if it were possible they could contrive so wild and rash an undertaking, yet they would not be hardy enough to put it in execution, unless they could first strengthen themselves by a confederacy of all the parts. . . .

Another proposition I advanced was that if these governments should be adjudged to have forfeited their charters back to the Crown, yet it is not the true interest of the Crown to resume them.

It is a generally received opinion that the people in the plantations have an interest distinct from that of the Crown; when it is supposed at the same time that the interest of the governors, they being the king's representatives, is one with the Crown; and from these premises it is concluded that there can't be too much power given to the governors, or too little to the people. Whereas, with humble submission, I conceive this to be a very wrong judgment, and that the reverse of it is true. The only interest of the people is to thrive and flourish in their trade, which is the true interest of the Crown and nation, because they reap the profit of it. When, on the other hand, the view that governors generally have is private gain, which being too often acquired by discouraging and oppressing trade, it is not only an interest distinct from that of the Crown but extremely prejudicial to it.

The trade of a young plantation is like a tender plant, and should be cherished with the fondest care; but if instead of that it meets with the rough hand of oppression, it will soon die. The proper nursery for this plant is a free government, where the laws are sacred, property secure, and justice not only impartially but expeditiously distributed. For to what purpose shall the merchant expose his estate to the dangers of the sea, the enemy, and many more accidents, if after all he can't save it at home from rapine and violence? . . .

To enlarge then the power of governors is to give them greater power to oppress; and to vacate the charter is to enlarge their power, the government in that case, of course, devolving upon them, as we see in those plantations which never had any charters, but are immediately dependent on the Crown. There they have, in a manner, the entire legislative and executive powers, or at least so great an influence on the constituent parts of the former, as leaves them little more than nominal sharers, serving rather as screens to the governor than a defense to the people. The militia is absolutely vested in the governors, which influences all elections of representatives. They appoint judges, justices, sheriffs, and other civil officers, with the consent, it's said indeed, of the Council. But that such consent, voluntary or involuntary, will ever be refused, seems too much to be expected, if we consider, that though the governors do not indeed appoint the Council, yet they recommend proper persons to the king; and it may be supposed, that a gentleman who is entrusted with the chief command of a province, and is actually on the spot, will be thought the best judge who are fit to serve, and therefore his recommendations will almost always prevail. . . .

The sum of my argument is that the benefit which Great Britain receives from the plantations arises from their commerce; that oppression is the most opposite thing in the world to commerce and the most destructive enemy it can have; that governors have, in all times and in all countries, been too much inclined to oppress; and, consequently, it cannot be the interest of the nation to increase their power and lessen the liberties of the people. I am so sanguine in this opinion that I really think it would be for the service of the Crown and nation to incorporate those governments which have no charters, rather than disfranchise those that have.

The last thing I proposed to consider was how far it may be consistent with justice to deprive the colonies of their charters without giving them a fair trial or any previous notice.

It is certain that bills of attainder, such as this would be, have been seldom used in England, and then only upon the most extraordinary occasions. . . . Now this is the case of the charter governments. How great the purchase-consideration was has been before laid; but how valuable the charters themselves are can never be said, liberty being estimable. And for the time they have enjoyed them, were they not on record, it would be what the civilians call "immemorial," one of them being above fourscore years standing.

It seems, therefore, a severity without a precedent that a people who have the misfortune of being a thousand leagues distant from their sovereign, a misfortune great enough in itself should, *unsummoned, unheard, in one day*, be deprived of all their valuable privileges, which they and their fathers have enjoyed for near a hundred years. It's true, the legislative power is absolute and unaccountable, and king, lords and commons may do what they please; but the question here is not about power, but right — and shall not the supreme judicature of all the nation do right? One may say, that what the Parliament can't do justly, they can't do at all. *In maximis minima est licentia*: the higher the power is, the greater caution is to be used in the execution of it,

because the sufferer is helpless and without resort. . . .

I know of but one thing more that can be said to palliate a proceeding against the charters in this way, which is: That the provinces always have their respective agents at court, who may be heard by petition before the bill passes into an act. To which I answer: First, that sometimes they have agents here, and at other times they have not. Next, that a bill may pass into an act without the knowledge of the agents, they having no citation. This had once like to have been the case when a bill of this nature was formerly brought into the House of Commons; and certainly had proved so if the agent for New England had at that nice juncture been indisposed in his health, or but a day's journey out of town, or if he had not been more than ordinarily active and diligent when he was in town. And lastly, I must observe that agents are only instructed in things that fall within the ordinary course of business and when anything of a new and extraordinary nature is brought on the carpet, they have a general instruction to pray for time in order to notify their principals, and receive their special commands. . . .

To conclude, what these governments desire of their superiors at home is: That they may not be judged and condemned unheard. And I cannot but flatter myself they will obtain it, whether I consider the reasonableness of the demand itself, or the celebrated justice and lenity of His Majesty's government, or the importance of the thing in question to the provinces concerned. I mention this last particular, being sure they would reckon the loss of their privileges a greater calamity than if their houses were all in flames at once. Nor can they be justly blamed — the one being a repairable evil, but the other irreparable. Burned houses may rise again out of their ashes, and even more beautiful than before, but 'tis to be feared that liberty, once lost, is lost forever.

82.

Theodorus Frelinghuysen: A Revivalist Sermon

What is often called the first wave of the Great Awakening that swept New England between 1730 and 1745 began among the Dutch colonists in New Jersey, under the influence of Theodorus Frelinghuysen. On January 17, 1720, shortly after his arrival from Holland, Frelinghuysen delivered a sermon in New York that touched off a controversy which continued throughout his ministry. Conservatives objected to his use of English rather than Dutch, and to his disregard of many traditional practices as unnecessary formalism. But his evangelical preaching converted many souls despite what appear, at first blush, to be demands on one's piety that very few could meet. The following selection, taken from a sermon delivered around 1721, is a good example of the fervor that prompted many lethargics to avow conversion.

Source: *Sermons by Theodorus Jacobus Frelinghuysen*, translated by William Demarest, New York, 1856, pp. 51-70: "The Acceptable Communicant."

THE PIOUS OF FORMER TIMES were characterized by exceeding great care and circumspection in admitting to the Holy Supper. . . . Who will take it ill of a minister of the Gospel that he endeavors to preserve this sacred ordinance from profanation? None but the formal, blind, nominal Christian who desires to be dealt with, not according to the Word of God but his own distorted conceptions. When it is considered how awful is the sin of partaking unworthily (for thus Jesus is greatly dishonored, as if He were the head of ungodly and unholy men; the covenant of God is profaned; the wrath of God is kindled against the whole congregation; the unworthy partaker rendered liable to a severe doom), what minister, if he fear God and love his neighbor, would not carefully watch as well that God's sanctuary should not be profaned, as that none of his hearers should approach unworthily and eat death and destruction? Yourselves, I pray you, decide: should not one who is zealous for the honor of Christ and the welfare of his neighbor, rather, after the example of Chrysostom, that pious doc-tor of the ancient Christian church, prefer losing his life to making himself chargeable with so great a sin?

But alas! how far have we departed from the purity of the primitive churches. Oh! how far do we yet daily depart! For not only was this the sentiment of the early reformers but it is still the confession of our whole Church, that when but one is admitted to the Lord's Supper, who by doctrine and life shows himself to be unbelieving and ungodly, the covenant of God is violated, and His wrath kindled against the whole congregation; and therefore rulers are under obligation to debar the disorderly by Christian discipline. But where is now the faithfulness that is required in a steward of the mysteries of God (1 Cor. 4:2)? Truly, it is manifest that the Lord's Supper is now frequently thus desecrated; for not only does one unworthily approach, but how many of those who receive the sacred elements are either ignorant or ungodly — as drunkards, slanderers, backbiters, profaners of God's name and day, vain and worldly minded, or merely moral persons who do not possess but hate true godliness!

It is an undoubted truth (declared by the Rev. D'Outrein . . . [pastor at Amsterdam in the Netherlands]):

> When we attentively consider the mode of procedure in our churches, we are compelled to acknowledge that this weighty business is by many not correctly viewed, much less, properly attended to. Members are admitted who do not possess a definite knowledge of the truth which is according to godliness; nay, who have not a correct idea of the design of the Lord's Supper, of the duty to be there performed, and the things signified and sealed by the outward circumstances. And where things are conducted in the best manner, the members who present themselves for admittance are indeed examined somewhat respecting their knowledge of fundamental truths and their external deportment; but by many scarcely an inquiry is made in regard to true repentance, faith, and holiness of life, not to mention the fact that none but those in whom these things are at least hopefully found should be admitted to a participation in this holy meat and drink, which, to employ the language of the form, Christ hath ordained only for the faithful.

It is the doctrine of the Reformed Church that no unconverted persons may approach, but that the ungodly must be repelled. How happens it, then, that this sacrament is so lightly extended to all who but ask it and bear the name of members, though often as ignorant as heathen, openly living in gross sins and not marked by the least morality, not to speak of true godliness? With what reason may we exclaim, with the holy Polycarp: "O good God! To what evil times hast Thou preserved me!" For it has now come to this, that many may be found who bear the name of the Reformed and yet are ignorant of the Reformed doctrines, and oppose, calumniate, and practically deny them.

I have three times (it is now the fourth time) administered the Lord's Supper and urged this point, that the unconverted may not approach, and that the wicked must, according to our doctrine, be debarred. But what murmuring has this excited? How many tongues, set on fire of hell, have uttered their slanders? Yea, such as it least became! I would ask you, who have been and, perhaps, still are so greatly displeased on this account? Is not this the doctrine of the Reformed Church? I imagine that no one will deny it (for whosoever has not willfully closed his ears must have sufficiently heard it). Why, then, disobey the truth? Why make yourselves guilty of such slanders and backbitings? Say you that I speak too hard and sharply? Must I not speak in accordance with the Word of God? Does not the spirit of God say by the mouth of Paul (1 Cor. 11:29), "He that eateth and drinketh unworthily, eateth and drinketh judgment to himself?" Can a more awful denunciation be conceived of? Does not our catechism declare that if we grant access to the ungodly, the covenant of God is profaned, and His wrath kindled against the whole congregation? Could anything harder than this be said? Truly, you cannot do otherwise than condemn yourselves; and were not your consciences insensible, did you but see and know what you have done, you would tremble in view of God's wrath!

But upon this I may no longer dwell. As far as I myself am concerned, I little care what is said behind my back by ignorant, carnal men who desire to substitute their own perverted ideas for God's truth. They are greatly deceived if they imagine that they will thus put me to silence; for I would sooner die a thousand deaths than not preach the truth.

Much-loved hearers, who have so often been at the Lord's table, do you know that the unconverted may not approach? Have you then, with the utmost care, examined whether you be born again? Were you aware what is required in order to an acceptable observance when you so composedly approached? Or did you go blindly forward, not only without a wedding garment but even without concern respecting it, not examining whether you were of the number of those who are invited?

Say you, I was not aware that so much is required? You should have known it; you should at least have been acquainted with your catechism. Is it so dangerous a thing unworthily to partake of the Sacred Supper, since, by so doing, guilt so great is contracted and a fearful judgment incurred? How, then, is it possible that Satan should so blind men as to cause them so lightly to esteem it, so little to fear God's judgments, and so thoughtlessly to lay hold upon that food which, instead of eternal life, may seal to them eternal death? How is it possible that in a matter of so great importance men should act in so inconsiderate and trifling a manner?

Remain, I beseech you, my hearers, no longer ignorant respecting this truth, but at length lay it to heart; for, if there be aught concerning which we should be circumspect, it is this. Let us then here be careful, if we would anywhere be so! He who loves danger deserves to fall into it; nowhere is danger so great as here! Here, by a morsel and swallow, can the covenant of God be desecrated, His wrath brought upon the whole congregation; and ourselves made liable to temporal and eternal punishment.

Reflect, therefore, upon and bear in mind this truth; and remember that, though moral and outwardly religious, if still you be unregenerate and destitute of spiritual life, you have no warrant for an approach to the table of grace. Ye ignorant, worldly minded, and ungodly persons who live in your sins, know that we dare not grant you access but are under obligation to debar you; not to your destruction but for your good, that you may thus amend your lives and turn to

the Lord; and if you give evidence of real amendment, with good conscience and the utmost cheerfulness, will we admit you.

Remember, also, that each member is bound to subject himself to the examination of the minister of Christ, and thus give a reason of the faith and hope which are in him, but with meekness and fear. This is God's command (1 Pet. 3:15; Heb. 13:17). Who dares resist the command of God? Although the knowledge and persuasion of one's conversion is not the ground upon which he is to be admitted (as the Labadists erroneously maintain), it is yet the duty of a minister to examine members, according to Prov. 27; Ex. 44:23; for the ministers of Jesus are the spiritual fishermen described in the parable (Matt. 13:48), who, sitting down upon the shore, gather out of the fish drawn up by the net of the Gospel the good into vessels but cast the bad away; which act is declared by the Lord to be significant of the severing of the evil and the just. They are (figuratively speaking) the angels in the gates of the new Jerusalem, who determine who may enter into the city (Rev. 21:27).

Very fitly is the duty under consideration described by the distinguished Mr. D'Outrein. . . . Ministers (he observes), to whom especially is entrusted the duty of receiving members, must not only with the utmost care previously instruct those whom they receive in the principles of the doctrine of Christ or, if they have been instructed by others, test their ability to make confession of the truth, but they must also examine whether they be marked by true repentance, sincere saving faith, and heart-renewing conversion. The necessity for these things they must earnestly impress upon their minds, and examine whether they be in possession of them, with cautions against self-deception; for if without carefully examining them and faithfully warning them they admit any, and thus afford them occasion to eat and drink judgment to themselves, is it possible that the guilt should not, to some extent, rest upon them (Ezek. 33:7, 8)?

Shall, then, an overseer with good conscience receive or admit one, he must see to it that he make a good confession of the truth, of his sins, of his faith in Christ, his purpose of leading a holy life; and that his walk be not at variance with his confession. Such is the requirement of the Constitution, Article 61:

> No one shall be admitted to the Supper of the Lord except he have made confession of the Reformed religion, according to the custom of the churches with which he connects himself; having at the same time the testimony of a godly walk, without which also those who come from other churches shall not be received.

But this is not sufficient for the communicant himself, who must be a true believer, sorrowful on account of his sins, seek salvation and forgiveness in Christ, and aim to lead a holy life, in order properly and profitably to observe the ordinance.

Therefore, examine whether you have a right to the Lord's Supper; whether these things be found in you. Prove yourselves, says Paul (2 Cor. 13:5); for it is an undoubted truth, which has been in the clearest manner shown, that none other may approach; but he who is really possessed of these properties of the divine life not only *may* but *must* approach. He should, therefore, remember that he engages in an important undertaking who proposes to repair to the Lord's table, and should accordingly make personal and particular preparation; upon which, however, we shall not now enlarge but conclude with the words of the psalmist: "Whoso is wise, let him observe these things; and so shall he understand the loving kindness of the Lord" (Ps. 107:43).

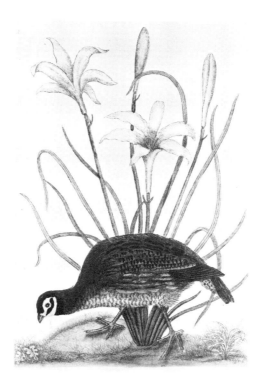

1722

83.

WILLIAM DOUGLASS: Against Inoculation for Smallpox

During the summer of 1721 Boston suffered a serious smallpox epidemic. Cotton Mather urged Zabdiel Boylston (the physician who first introduced smallpox vaccinations to America) to inoculate the people of the city. William Douglass, another physician, strongly protested, holding that the disease might be spread by this method. In an attempt to persuade others of his views, he wrote four pamphlets, three anonymously, attacking the practice. The following letter of May 1, 1722, describing the epidemic and the results of inoculation, was addressed to Dr. Cadwallader Colden of New York. Thirty years later Douglass had reversed his position: "The novel practice of procuring the small-pox by inoculation," he stated in 1751, "is a very considerable and most beneficial improvement in that article of medical practice."

Source: MHSC, 4th series, II, pp. 167-170.

YOURS OF THE 12TH OF MARCH last I received, and the enclosed to Captain Kennedy I forwarded by a ship which sailed in a few hours after the receipt thereof. Your letter concerning the Indians I lent to a news writer that he might extract something for the public, but not with a design of inserting it at length, there being some words in it which ought to have been omitted; however, in time coming, write me freely. It shall be safe unless you give me some innuendo that it may be public.

Your reasons against inoculation of the smallpox are strong, and I return you thanks for the communication. Having the opportunity of my good friend Mr. Relf, I could not neglect writing, and your present entertainment shall be the general history of our smallpox in 1720 in Boston, and the inoculation thereof, without descending to particulars. I have by me some practical observations relating to the history and method of cure in this distemper, which, if desired, shall candidly communicate, providing you give a large allowance for the imperfections of a young practitioner. About eighty have died with purple spots and profuse hemorrhage, which cases I have particularly noted. The cases of the inoculated, as far as I have been able to learn and of which I am assured for fact, being either eye witness or from good information, shall also in due time communicate.

After nineteen years intermission we received, via Saltertudas from Barbados, the smallpox, middle of April 1721, and by the January following it was nearly over, having affected only Boston and two or three adjacent towns, which demonstrates that no condition of air, etc., can produce the smallpox without some real communication of infection from a smallpox illness. At first it makes but small progress, the month of May proving a cold, wet month and the infected houses being shut up and guards set over them. About the change of the moon, middle of June, it spread so much that the watches being of no use were removed; of this first parcel very few died. Beginning of July another and large parcel taken down whereof several die; thus in the beginning they were taken all in distinct parcels at about sixteen or eighteen days distance from seizure to seizure; but when the infection became universal this could not be so distinctly observed.

Hence I made this remark, that the more decumbents, the infection was the more intense (abstracting from the influence of the weather and season, *i.e.,* in October, though a fine autumn month, was the time of the greatest decumbiture and mortality) and more died than in proportion to the number of the sick. My second remark is, I have frequently observed all along our sick time that, if one of a family by some accidental infection was taken down, it proved generally sixteen or eighteen days thereafter before the rest of the family were ill (if the infection was received at home). I shall not pretend to account for this, only I observe first that about the eighth, ninth, or tenth day of decumbiture, the smallpox pustules begin to crack, run and smell, the infection then perspiring and making its way abroad; second, that the inoculated generally begin to sicken the seventh or eighth day from

their inoculation; and of those who were taken ill of the smallpox at sea, having received the infection ashore, none, so far as I can learn, exceeded nine or ten days being from home.

Our smallpox burials were as follows: May, 1; June, 8; July, 20; August, 26; September, 101; October, 402; November, 249; December, 31; January, 6; in all 844 persons in Boston. Last February an exact scrutiny was made; it was found that Boston consisted of 10,565 souls, whereof 6,000 have now had the smallpox and of those 899 died; about 700 who never had it escaped and a few who remained in the country are free of it.

Having, sometime before the smallpox arrived, lent to a credulous vain preacher, Mather, Jr., the *Philosophical Transactions, No. 339 and 377,* which contain Timonius' and Pylermus' accounts of inoculation from the Levant, that he might have something to send home to the Royal Society, who had long neglected his communications as he complained, he sets inoculation to work in month of June. By 18th of November, 100 were inoculated, and by January, in all, some few more than 250 in town and country. Whereof some have been inoculated oftener than once before it took effect; with some it never wrought. They all complained much of head disorders, even with those who had but very few, and these imperfect, pustules; their incisions grew up in a few days, as in common superficial wounds of the skin. But about the seventh or eighth day generally they begin to complain (some few sooner or later), are feverish, their incisions inflame, open, and discharge profusely with a peculiar noisome fetor [stench], and continue running some weeks after their smallpox pimples are dried up; and they abroad about their affairs, infect wherever they go (this spreading the infection and consequently rendering it more intense is a great objection against inoculation practised at random in a place whose greatest part of the people are liable to the distemper).

We all knew of nine or ten inoculation deaths, besides abortions that could not be concealed. We suspect more who died in the height of the smallpox, it being only known to their nearest relations whether they died of inoculation or in the natural way. Some had the confluent kind, many were very full of a distinct kind; some had a large red burrow round every pustule, in some they appeared like red face pimples, but not of a determined round as in the natural distinct sort, some like the chicken pox, others so free and without pus that they can scarce be said to have had the smallpox. In some the running of their incision sores has been troublesome many months and endangered the loss of limbs; with some there still remains a crusty scab which falls and returns on the place of incision. Many have had a good genuine distinct kind.

What the consequences may be and if some of them may not be liable to the smallpox in the natural way, time only can determine. But to speak candidly for the present it seems to be somewhat more favorably received by inoculation than received in the natural way. I oppose this novel and dubious practice, not being sufficiently assured of its safety and consequences. In short, I reckon it a sin against society to propagate infection by this means and bring on my neighbor a distemper which might prove fatal and which perhaps he might escape (as many have done) in the ordinary way, and which he might certainly secure himself against by removal in this country, where it prevails seldom. However, many of our clergy had got into it and they scorn to retract; I had them to appease, which occasioned great heats (you may perhaps admire how they reconcile this with their doctrine of predestination). The enclosed pamphlets, which unwillingly I was obliged to publish, may inform you more at large of the controversy. They were calculated for New York, and I am afraid will scarce bear reading anywhere else. Our people at present are generally averse to it.

Favor me with the nature and cure of that distemper you call "pain in the side" in New York, as also of your dry bellyache.

NEW ENGLAND

Two great influences on New England were the sea and the Bible. New England, like old England, came to rely on seafaring for her prosperity, and ships from Boston sailed the Atlantic and Caribbean buying and selling what the market demanded, including molasses, pepper, and slaves. Farms were small and no cash crop dominated the economy as did tobacco in the South.

Many New Englanders were also con-cerned with salvation, although the number seemed to be waning before the Great Awakening. The Puritan prescription that every individual read the Bible had two notable results: first, an emphasis on education that made New England foremost among the colonies in the number of schools and colleges; second, numerous disputes concerning interpretation of the Bible, and a flow of dissenters and new sects.

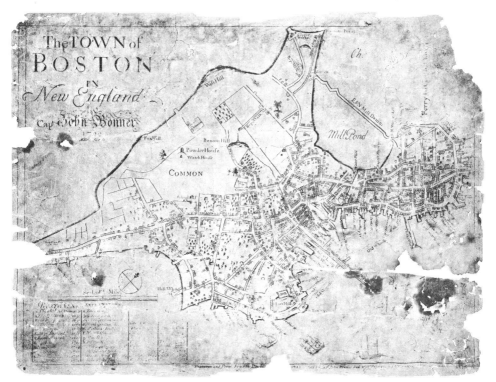

John Bonner map of Boston, 1722

Self-portrait by Thomas Smith, 17th-century New England sea captain

Boston

Boston owed its prominence in New England not only to its being the major source of New England Puritanism, but, increasingly, to its importance as a leading American seaport.

Peter Faneuil, wealthy Boston merchant, portrait by John Smibert

Woodcut showing pillory being used for public punishment of man accused of passing counterfeit money

View of Boston in the 1760s

Faneuil Hall, given to the city of Boston as a market house by Faneuil; the structure was designed by John Smibert and completed in 1742

Captain John Larrabee, portrait
by Joseph Badger

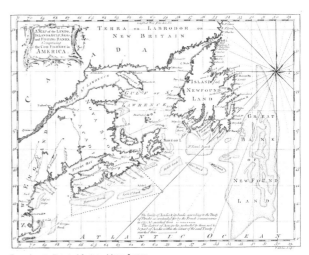

Map of North Atlantic fisheries in the 18th century

Print dated 1720 showing the steps in cod-
fishing in Newfoundland

Fishing and Commerce

Codfish from the waters off New England
and Newfoundland were exchanged in Europe for wine or other goods that in turn
were traded for British products. New England captains also regularly stopped in Africa and the West Indies.

"Sea Captains Carousing in Surinam," painting by John Greenwood, mid-18th century

Woodcut from "Plain Truth" by Franklin

Benjamin Church, who led colonial forces against King Philip, 1675-76

New England Frontier

Improved farming and decreasing fur trade in favor of fishing and trade changed the New Englander's attitude toward the Indian. Instead of being useful, Indians became an obstacle to new settlement, and battles over territory became frequent.

Woodcut from "A New Guide to the English Tongue," a child's primer by Thomas Dilworth

King Philip, chief of the Wampanoags, led Indians against frontier towns

Examples of plows in use in the 18th century

New England Likenesses

Worcester Art Museum

Museum of Fine Arts, Boston

(Above) Margaret Gibbs, and (below) Elizabeth and Mary Freake, John Freake, all painted in Boston, 1670-75, by an unknown "limner"; (above right) Judge Edmund Quincy, and (right) Nathaniel Byfield, both by John Smibert, who painted in Boston, 1730-48, and was the best portraitist before Copley

Worcester Art Museum

Metropolitan Museum of Art

Worcester Art Museum

The stern expressions and stiff poses in most early colonial portraits may not give true characterizations, but they convey something of the spiritual rigors associated with Puritan New England, even while revealing a taste for not altogether austere finery. However, only the wealthy or respected were painted and the diversity, vitality, irreverence, even crudity of the population at large are absent.

(Above) Mrs. John Edwards, by Joseph Badger, who was active in Boston, 1748-60; his primitive technique was aided by bold characterizations; (left) Gov. William Shirley, mezzotint engraving by Peter Pelham (c. 1695-1751), from a Smibert portrait; Pelham was the stepfather and tutor of John Singleton Copley; (below) James Bowdoin II, 1748, and (below left) self-portrait 1750, both by Robert Feke

(Left) Rev. Timothy Cutler, Congregationalist minister who converted to the Church of England, 1722, portrait by Peter Pelham, 1750; (center) Benjamin Colman, leader of the liberal Presbyterian group in Massachusetts, portrait by John Smibert; (right) Increase Mather, leading Puritan minister, portrait attributed to Pelham

Religion in New England

The authoritarian nature of the Massachusetts Bay theocracy conflicted with the individualism inherent in Puritanism and produced rebels whose confidence in their own insight into the Scriptures, or lack of confidence in that of others, led them to settle new areas where they could worship according to their own lights. Although such theological disputes fired the intellectual controversies of the time, Puritanism was becoming less strict as the colonies prospered.

Rev. John Rogers, a Baptist in Rhode Island, opposed an established clergy and founded the Rogerenes

Gov. Gurdon Saltonstall was influential in founding Yale and locating it at New Haven

Harvard College, 1739

Continued emphasis on an educated clergy led to the establishment of new colleges primarily for the training of ministers, but increasingly attended by gentlemen with a commercial future.

The belief that the colonies were in spiritual decline led some clergymen to support revivalist preaching in the 1730s and 1740s. Owing to the enthusiasm generated by such exciting revivalists as George Whitefield, combined with the intellectual stimulus of Jonathan Edwards, the period became known as the Great Awakening. Conservative in doctrine but histrionic in style, the preachers of the Awakening had a strong impact on colonial religion.

A *Isaac Doy...*

TREATISE
Concerning

Religious Affections,

In Three PARTS;

PART I. Concerning the Nature of the *Affections*, and their Importance in *Religion*.
PART II. Shewing what are *no certain Signs* that *religious Affections* are gracious, or that they are *not*.
PART III. Shewing what are *distinguishing Signs* of truly gracious and *holy Affections*.

By *Jonathan Edwards*, A.M.
And Pastor of the *first* Church in *Northampton*.

Levit. ix. ult. and x. 1, 2. *And there came a Fire out from before the Lord,----upon the Altar; -----which when all the People saw, they shouted and fell on their Faces. And Nadab and Abihu ----- offered strange Fire before the Lord, which he commanded them not: And there went out a Fire from the Lord, and devoured them, and they died before the Lord.*
Cant. ii. 12, 13. *The Flowers appear on the Earth, the Time of the Singing of Birds is come, and the Voice of the Turtle is heard in our Land; the Fig-tree putteth forth her green Figs, and the Vines with the tender Grape, give a good Smell.* Ver. 15. *Take us the Foxes, the little Foxes, which spoil the Vines; for our Vines have tender Grapes.*

B O S T O N:
Printed for S. KNEELAND and T. GREEN in *Queen-street*, over against the Prison. 1 7 4 6.

Title page of Edwards' defense of revivals

Rev. Jonathan Edwards, author of "Faithful Narrative of the Surprising Work of God," which gave impetus to the revival; portrait by Joseph Badger

George Whitefield, painted by John Wollaston

Charles Chauncy, spokesman for liberals in the Congregational Church, was Edwards' opponent on the issue of revivalism

John Wesley, founder of Methodism, incorporated revivalist techniques into his evangelical work in England. His followers later brought religion to America

1723

84.

SAMUEL SHUTE: Self-Government in Massachusetts

In most colonies royal governors served at the pleasure of the Crown and received their salaries directly from the King. The case of Massachusetts was significantly different, however, for its Assembly had the right to determine, and to pay, the salary of its governor. As a result, the Massachusetts Assembly indulged from time to time in a kind of legislative blackmail, withholding the governor's salary on one pretext or another until he had approved all of the Assembly's actions. The following memorial, written by Governor Samuel Shute to the Privy Council in August 1723, pointed out to the King the impracticality of the arrangement.

Source: *Calendar of State Papers, Colonial Series, America and West Indies, 1722-1723,*
Cecil Headlam, ed., Vol. XXVIII, London, 1934, pp. 324-330.

I SOON CALLED the General Assembly together upon arrival in the Massachusetts Bay in October 1716. I found the House of Representatives, who are chosen annually, possessed of all the same powers of the House of Commons, and of much greater; they having the power of nominating once a year the persons that constitute Your Majesty's Council etc., and giving the salary of the governor and lieutenant governor, but from six months to six months; and likewise giving such only as is no way suitable to the rank of Your Majesty's governor and lieutenant governor, or to the known abilities of the province, and this notwithstanding Your Majesty's instructions directing them to settle a salary suitable to their stations, and for such time as they shall continue in [them].

The said House likewise appoint the salary of the treasurer every year, whereby they have in effect the sole authority over that important office, which they often use in order to intimidate the treasurer from obeying the proper orders for issuing money, if such orders are not agreeable to their views and inclinations. By all which means the House of Representatives are in a manner the whole legislative, and in a good measure the executive, power of the province.

This House consists of about one hundred, who by an act of Assembly must be persons residing in the respective towns, which they represent; whereby it happens that the greatest part of them are of small fortunes and mean education — men of the best sense and circumstances generally residing in or near Boston — so that by the artifice of a few designing members, together with the insinuations of some people in the town of Boston, the country representatives are easily made to believe that the House is barely supporting the privileges of the people, while they are invading the undoubted prerogatives of the Crown. Were it not for this act, the Assembly would certainly consist of men of much better sense, temper, and fortune than they do at present.

The Assembly usually sits at Boston, the capital of this province, a large and populous town, supposed to contain about 18,000 inhabitants, under no magistracy, by the want of which, many of the inhabitants become too much disposed to a leveling spirit, too apt to be mutinous and disorderly, and to support the House of Representatives in any steps they take toward encroaching on the prerogative of the Crown. That this is too much the prevailing temper, in the majority of the inhabitants of this town, is plain from hence, that if I have at any time, according to the known power vested in Your Majesty's governor of that province, with the strongest reasons, given my negative to any person nominated to be of Your Majesty's Council there, the said town have hardly ever failed to choose him their representative.

Three negatived councilors are the present representatives of the town of Boston. This practice is so notoriously known and justified that it is a common maxim that a negatived councilor makes a good representative. The House of Representatives, thus constituted and abetted, notwithstanding the many uncommon privileges they enjoy by virtue of their charter, far from being contented therewith, have for some years last past been making attempts upon the few prerogatives that have been reserved to the Crown; which for that reason, as well as from the obligation of my oath, and the trust reposed in me by Your Majesty, I have endeavored, to my utmost, to maintain against all invasions whatsoever.

I would humbly beg leave to lay before Your Majesty some instances in which they have endeavored to wrest those prerogatives out of your royal hands.

1. The House of Representatives have denied Your Majesty's right to the woods in the province of Maine, contrary to the reservations in their charter, to an act of Parliament of Great Britain, and the instructions I received from Your Majesty, etc. The said House, having received an account of a great quantity of trees that were felled, and cut into logs in the county of York, many of them fit for masting the Royal Navy, voted that a committee of that House should be joined with a committee of the Council to make inquiry into that affair, and to dispose of those logs for the use of the province; to which the Council, at my instance, made the following amendment, viz.: "saving to His Majesty his right." But the House of Representatives refused to agree to that amendment. After which, without either my consent or the Council's, they sent a committee of their own with orders to dispose of the said logs for the use of the province.

2. The House of Representatives would have refused me the power of a negative on the choice of their speaker; which I thought it necessary to make use of against Mr. Cooke, when he was chosen to that office, he having publicly opposed Your Majesty's known rights to those woods. And the said House, insisting on their choice notwithstanding the negative I had given it, I dissolved that Assembly, and then made a representation of the whole matter to the Right Honorable the Lords of Trade, etc., who sent me the opinion of Your Majesty's attorney general, that the power was vested in Your Majesty's governor for the time being. And when they acquainted me, at the next meeting of the House of Representatives, by a message, that they had chosen Mr. Clarke for their speaker, and I had returned them for answer that I approved their said choice, the House of Representa-

tives sent me this message, viz.: "that they did not send up the foregoing message for my approbation but for my information only," and since that time, whenever the speaker has been absent by sickness or otherwise, they have never failed to choose the said Mr. Cooke speaker pro tempore.

3. The House of Representatives voted a public fast throughout Your Majesty's said province — a thing never attempted by any of their predecessors, it being very well known that that power was always vested in and exercised by Your Majesty's governor in that and all other colonies in America.

4. Though the Royal Charter has vested in the governor only the power of proroguing the General Assembly, yet the House of Representatives sent up a vote to the Council adjourning the General Assembly to the town of Cambridge; to which I refused to give my assent. And yet after this, they adjourned themselves for several days without my consent or privity; and did not meet me on the day to which I had adjourned the General Assembly.

5. I had hoped that the House of Representatives, upon making due reflection on the several attempts they had unwarrantably made against these Your Majesty's undoubted prerogatives, and the constant opposition they had met with from me therein, would have desisted from any further attempts of this kind. But to my great surprise they have endeavored to wrest the sword out of your royal hands, as will appear by the following instances.

Though the charter, as well as Your Majesty's commission, gives the command of all the forts in the said province to Your Majesty's governor, and the sole power of building and demolishing such forts, yet the House of Representatives voted that a committee of their House should go down to Your Majesty's Castle William to take an account of all the stores there; and to take receipts from the officers for the same, without any application made to me, for

my leave. And in the same manner, without asking my consent, ordered the treasurer that he should pay no more subsistence money to the officers and soldiers of Fort Mary, at Winter Harbor; and directed him to take speedy care that the provisions of ordnance, arms, and ammunition, and all other stores of war at that Fort should be transported to Boston and lodged with him. Upon which, I must beg leave to observe to Your Majesty, that the last of these is the only fort and harbor that can secure the fishing vessels of Your Majesty's subjects in the eastern parts. The inhabitants have been so sensible of the danger of dismantling this fort that 132 persons at Marblehead, etc., have petitioned the House of Representatives, since my departure, that the said Fort may not be dismantled; whereupon the House has desisted from any further attempts that way, and ordered it to be supported.

This instance may serve at the same time to show the disposition of the House, to wrest the sword out of your royal hands, and that by their assuming this undue power to themselves, the people are taught to address them in cases, where they should only apply to him that has the honor of commanding in chief over your forces there.

6. The House of Representatives voted that Mr. Moody, a major in Your Majesty's forces there, should be suspended, and that even unheard; which vote they sent up [for] concurrence. But the Council nonconcurring, the said House of Representatives ordered Moody should be no longer paid. And upon my expostulating with the House on their proceeding against a major in Your Majesty's service, so manifestly contrary to all rules of justice, they sent me a message justifying their proceedings against him, in terms that have not been usually given to one that has the honor of being Your Majesty's governor in that province. And . . . they have of late addressed the Chair in terms much less respectful than any of their predecessors.

7. The House of Representatives ordered a committee to command the officers at the eastern and western parts of the province to draw out their forces and muster them; only under color of an order signed by their speaker. And the said House has been so far from returning to a just sense of their duty, and from acknowledging this unprecedented violation of the most important and undoubted right of Your Crown, that they have since my departure from the said province, by Your Majesty's leave, repeated this unprecedented attempt by pretending to the power of drawing off the forces from the place where they were; which bold pretense of theirs has not gone without a proper animadversion and reprimand from Your Majesty's lieutenant governor. These charges may be made good by their own votes.

I would with humble submission further lay before Your Majesty that, upon my arrival, I had good reason given me to expect that they would allow me for my salary £1,500 per annum of the money current there; but they gave me no more the first year than £1,200 of that money; at which time £160 there was equal in value to £100 sterling. And they did likewise continue the same allowance for two years after; and though provisions have been much dearer since, they have given me no more than £1,000 per annum of that money, which is now so much reduced in its value that £260 is but equal to £100 sterling, and, therefore, is now above a third less in value than when I first arrived there, so that £385 sterling per annum is all which they in reality now allow me. They vote me that sum by moiety's at each session of their Assembly, which is once in six months; but even that they don't give me till I have passed the bills in the respective sessions, thereby to constrain me as far as they can to consent to any bills they lay before me. In the last sessions of the Assembly, they have voted me no salary at all;

so that I have been, and must be, without any support from them for some time.

And because I did all in my power to prevent their encroachments on Your Majesty's just prerogative, they have endeavored to make me uneasy by other ways, as well as by reducing the salary or allowance which they formerly gave me; as appears by comparing the salary of the three first years with the salary or allowance of the three last; and as might be made appear to Your Majesty by other instances, if that was necessary. They voted the lieutenant governor for his service of three years no more than £35 of that country money; which he thought below the honor of his commission to accept; for which unjust treatment I know no other reason than that he is firmly attached to the just prerogatives of the Crown.

It is but justice to the province, after making these observations on the House of Representatives, and on too great a part of the town of Boston, humbly to acquaint Your Majesty that the whole clergy of the province, as well as the generality of the people, are zealously affected to Your Majesty's person and government, and the succession of the Crown in your royal family. And that the unjustifiable proceedings of the House of Representatives are disapproved by those in the province who are most distinguished for their wealth, understanding, and probity; though by reason of the constitution of that government, which in effect excludes many of the richest of representatives, they are not able to prevent or redress.

I am also humbly of opinion that this province may deserve Your Majesty's attention, the rather because it is of great extent, well peopled, capable of being made a strong frontier, to several of Your Majesty's other colonies; furnishes pitch, tar, masts, and planks for Your Royal Navy; and other valuable commodities which they exchange for British manufactures.

1725

85.

Pennsylvania Flour Inspection Law

The attempt to secure and maintain foreign markets led many colonial governments to pass legislation regulating the quality of produce intended for export. The Pennsylvania Flour Inspection Law that appears below was passed on March 20, 1725, and was largely responsible for Philadelphia's preeminent position as an exporter of wheat. The law successfully maintained the quality of the world famous "Philadelphia superfine" flour and at the same time inspired other colonies to establish similar standards.

Source: *The Statutes at Large of Pennsylvania from 1682 to 1801,* James T. Mitchell and Henry Flanders, eds., Harrisburg, 1897, Vol. IV, pp. 3-8.

Whereas by the laws of this Province lately made and provided for preventing the exportation of flour not merchantable, the credit of the trade of this Province in one of its most considerable branches has in some good measure been retrieved. But forasmuch as those laws continue in force no longer than three years from the publication thereof:

Therefore, to the end that the said credit of our trade and the benefits thence arising may be continued and improved:

Section 1. Be it enacted, by Sir William Keith, Baronet, Governor of the Province of Pennsylvania, etc., by and with the advice and consent of the freemen of the Province aforesaid in General Assembly met, and by the authority of the same, that

every bolter [sifter] of flour and baker of bread residing or (at any time hereafter during the continuance of this present act) to reside within this Province shall each one for himself provide and have a distinguishable brand mark; and shall therewith brand each and every cask of flour or biscuit of his own bolting or baking before the same shall be removed from the place where the same was so as aforesaid bolted or baked.

But before any such bolter or baker shall bolt any flour or bake any bread for exportation out of this Province, every such bolter and baker shall cause such his brand mark, together with his name and place of abode, to be entered with the clerk of the Court of Quarter Sessions for the county where he does reside (if not already entered), and so from time to time as often as any such bolter or baker shall move the place of his residence from one county of this Province into another, he shall there cause his mark, name, and place of residence to be entered with the clerk of the respective county, for recording whereof the said clerk shall have and receive 1s. each and no more: and every bolter and baker offending in all or any of the premises on due proof thereof made shall forfeit and pay the sum of 5s. for every such offense.

Section 2. And be it enacted, by the authority aforesaid, that all wheat flour bolted and packed for exportation from and after the 13th day of May next ensuing the publication of this act shall by the bolter thereof be and be made merchantable and of due fineness, without any mixture of coarser or other flour, and honestly and well-packed in well-seasoned cask with the tare thereof thereupon marked, the cask being first weighed by weights tried by or made according to the standard of weights in this Province, wherewith the flour and bread packed shall be also weighed. And if any bolter shall offend therein he shall forfeit and pay for every such offense the sum of 1s. per cask. . . .

Section 4. And be it enacted, by the authority aforesaid, that no merchant or person whatsoever shall lade or ship any flour for exportation out of this Province before he shall first submit the same to the view and examination of the officer appointed by or by the direction of this act, who shall search and try the same in order to judge of its goodness; and if the said officer shall judge the same to be merchantable, according to the direction of this present act, he shall brand every such cask of flour on the quarter with the provincial brand mark, which the said officer shall provide and have for that end and purpose, sufficient and capable to impress in a fair and distinguishable manner the arms of the Province of Pennsylvania with the letter *P* on each

side, for which trouble of the said officer he shall have and receive of the shipper, 1d. per cask and no more.

Provided always, nevertheless, that if any dispute shall happen to arise between the said officer and possessor of such flour concerning the fineness or goodness thereof, application being made to one of the magistrates of the city or county where the said dispute arises, who shall issue his warrant to two indifferent, judicious persons of skill and integrity to view and search the said flour and make report forthwith according as they find the same, and the said magistrate is hereby empowered and required to give judgment accordingly. And in case the said flour is judged not fit to be exported, the said magistrate shall order it not to be exported under the penalty of forfeiture of all such flour, and shall also award and order the owner or possessor of the said flour to pay the said officer 1s. per cask for all such flour as shall be adjudged not fit for exportation as aforesaid with reasonable charges, who shall recover the said costs and charges from the bolter and maker thereof.

But in case the said flour upon trial shall be found to be good and merchantable according to the directions of this act, the charges of prosecution shall be paid by the said officer. And in case any flour shall upon trial be found not merchantable or fit to be exported, the officer shall take the bolter's brand and the marks and numbers of such casks of flour; and if the same flour be afterwards shipped in order for exportation, the proof that it is not the said flour shall lie wholly on the owner or shipper thereof and shall not be incumbent on the said officer.

Section 5. And be it enacted, by the authority aforesaid, that the said officer (or his deputies) shall have full power and authority by virtue of this act and without any further or other warrant to enter on board any ship, sloop, or vessel whatsoever lying or being in any port or place of this Province, and into any house, store, or place whatsoever within the Province aforesaid, to search for and make discovery of any flour shipped or intended to be shipped for exportation; and if the owner or possessor thereof or their servants or others shall deny him or them entrance, or if the said officer or his deputies shall be anyways molested in making such discovery as aforesaid, or if such merchant or owner shall refuse to permit the said officer or his deputies to view and examine any flour or not permit him or them to brand the same if merchantable, according to the directions of this act, every such person so offending shall forfeit and pay the sum of £10; or shall ship off any cask or casks of flour not branded with the provincial brand mark aforesaid, every such person so offending shall forfeit and pay the sum of 5s. for every cask of flour so shipped. . . .

Section 9. And be it enacted, by the authority aforesaid, that no owner, possessor, or occupier of any grist mill in this Province shall by himself, servant, or others presume to grind or suffer to be ground into meal for bolting for exportation out of this Province any unsound, ill-dressed, or unmerchantable wheat; and whatsoever owner, possessor or occupier of any such mill as aforesaid shall so grind or suffer to be ground any such unsound, ill-dressed, or unmerchantable wheat, to be bolted for exportation out of this Province contrary to the true intent and meaning of this act, he, she, or they so offending in the premises shall forfeit and pay for every such offense the sum of 35s. on due proof thereof by one or more credible witnesses before any one justice of the peace in this Province.

Section 10. And be it enacted, by the authority aforesaid, that if any person or persons shall counterfeit the said provincial brand mark or impress or brand the same on any cask of flour, he, she, or they being thereof legally convicted shall, for the first offense, forfeit and pay the sum of £5; for the second offense, the sum of £10; and for the third and every other such offense the offender shall be committed to gaol [jail], and sentenced to the pillory, there to stand the space of two hours on market day in any city, borough, or town of the respective counties of this Province where the fact was committed.

Section 11. And be it enacted, by the authority aforesaid, that all and singular the fines, forfeitures, and charges mentioned in this act, where the same respectively exceed not 40s., the same shall be recovered in the same manner as other debts under 40s. by the laws of this Province; and where the same shall exceed 40s., they may be sued for and shall be recovered in any court of record in this Province by bill, plaint, or information, wherein no essoin, protection, or wager of law nor any more than one imparlance shall be allowed. All which said forfeitures not hereinbefore directed how to be applied shall be paid to the prosecutor, one-half thereof for the use of the poor, which he is hereby strictly required immediately on receipt thereof to pay to the overseers of the poor of the place where the forfeiture shall happen, and the other half for the said prosecutor, which he may detain to his own use as prosecutor, any law, usage, or custom to the contrary in anywise notwithstanding.

86.

"The Little Mohee"

This touching ditty has been traced back to the early years of the eighteenth century (the year 1725, of course, is hardly more than a guess). The song has been sung in many versions, usually to the tune of "Down in the Valley"; this one was taught to one of the editors by his grandmother, who had learned it from her grandmother, before the Civil War. The story is sentimental and almost surely has no historical foundation; rather, it reflects what may be a perennial longing — that the simple people of the New World should turn out to be somehow truer and more loyal than those of the Old.

THE LITTLE MOHEE

As I was a-walking for pleasure one day,
In sweet recreation I careless did stray.

As I went a-walking all by the seashore,
The wind it did whistle, the water did roar.

As I sat amusing myself on the grass,
Oh who should I spy but a young Indian lass.

She came, sat down beside me, took hold of my hand,
And said "You're a stranger, and in a strange land.

But if you will follow you're welcome to come
And dwell in the cottage where I call it my home."

Together we wander, together we roam,
Till we come to the cottage where she calls it her home.

She asked me to marry and offered her hand,
Said "My father's the chieftain all over this land.

My father's a chieftain and ruler is he,
I'm his only daughter, my name is Mohee."

"Oh no, my dear maiden, that never can be,
For I have a sweetheart in my own country.

I will not forsake her, for I know she loves me;
Her heart is as true as any Mohee."

It was early one morning, one morning in May,
I broke her poor heart by the words I did say.

"I'm going to leave you, so fare you well, dear;
My ship's sails are spreading, over home I must steer."

The last time I saw her, she knelt on the strand,
And as my ship passed by her she waved me her hand,

Crying "When you get over to the girl that you love,
Remember the Mohee in the coconut grove."

My friends and companions around me I see;
But none can compare with the little Mohee.

The girl I had trusted proved untrue to me;
I turned my course backward far over the sea.

I turned my course backward, and backward did flee
To spend my last days with the little Mohee.

1727

87.

Statutes of the College of William and Mary

On February 8, 1693, the College of William and Mary was established under a charter granted to the Reverend James Blair by the English King and Queen, after whom the school was named. The second institution of higher education in the colonies, Harvard being the first (Yale was the third), William and Mary comprised a grammar, an Indian, a philosophy, and a divinity school. The latter two were not active until around 1729. Most of the early records of the school were lost by fire, and the statutes of 1727, reprinted here, are among the oldest of the school's documents to survive.

Source: *The Charter, Transfer and Statutes of the College of William and Mary in Virginia*, Williamsburg, 1758, pp. 109-161.

NOWHERE WAS THERE any greater danger on account of ignorance and want of instruction than in the English colonies of America; in which the first planters had much to do, in a country overrun with woods and briers and for many years infested with the incursions of the barbarous Indians, to earn a mean livelihood with hard labor.

There were no schools to be found in those days, nor any opportunity for good education. Some few, and very few indeed, of the richer sort, sent their children to England to be educated. And there, after many dangers from the seas and enemies and unusual distempers occasioned by the change of country and climate, they were often taken off by the smallpox and other diseases. It was no wonder if this occasioned a great defect of understanding and all sort of literature, and that it was followed with a new generation of men, far short of their forefa-thers, which, if they had the good fortune, though at a very indifferent rate, to read and write had no further commerce with the muses or learned sciences, but spent their life ignobly at the hoe and spade and other employments of an uncultivated and unpolished country. There remained, still notwithstanding, a small remnant of men of better spirit, who had either had the benefit of better education themselves in their mother country, or at least had heard of it from others.

These men's private conferences among themselves being communicated to greater numbers in the like circumstances, produced at last a scheme of a free school and college, which was by them exhibited to the president and council, in the year 1690, a little before the arrival of Lieutenant Governor Nicholson, which was afterward recommended by them with applause to the next ensuing General Assembly. This work so luckily begun made a very considerable progress under his government. For, although being tied up by injunctions from My Lord Effingham, chief governor, who was then in England, he was not allowed to call an assembly so soon as he would, yet that designed good work did not sleep in the meantime; for in that interval of assemblies he and the council sent out briefs, by which, and their own good example, they invited and encouraged the subscriptions of the inhabitants. These briefs were recommended to the care and management of Mr. Commissary Blair, a minister, who had been one of the first projectors of this good work and was a little before this made commissary to the bishop of London; with the help of his surrogates, some of the most creditable ministers of the country, and brought in subscriptions to the value of £2,000 sterling.

Upon this followed that famous General Assembly of the year 1691. This assembly not only approved that scheme of a college, as well fitted to this country, but resolved upon a humble petition to King William and Queen Mary for a charter to empower certain trustees that they named to found such a college, and that Their Majesties would likewise assist in the funds necessary for building the edifices and maintaining the president and masters. To deliver this petition and to negotiate this whole affair, they made Mr. Blair their agent to solicit it at the Court of England. Though both the King and Queen were exceeding well inclined, and the good bishops, especially Dr. Tillotson, archbishop of Canterbury, and Dr. Compton, bishop of London, gave all assistance, and Mr. Blair followed it with diligence and dexterity, it was a long time before all the difficulties, which were objected, were got over.

But at last, after two years spent in that service, an ample charter was obtained, with several gifts, both for building and endowment for paying the president's and masters'

salaries; and Mr. Blair, by advice of the General Assembly in Virginia and the bishops in England, being made president of the college, returned to see all put in execution. . . . For many years afterward he was involved in a great number of difficulties, some of which threatened the total subversion of the design, especially when, in the year 1705, the buildings and library were destroyed by fire, and there was no money to repair the loss. Yet at length, by patience and good husbandry of the revenues and the bounty of Queen Anne, the work was finished a second time to everyone's admiration.

But to go on to another necessary branch of this design, which we are now about, other obstructions being in good measure removed, there seems to be nothing more necessary than that, according to the advice of our Most Reverend Chancellor Dr. Wake, archbishop of Canterbury, some rules and statutes should be made for the good government of the college, and of the president and masters and scholars and all others that either live in it or are employed in the management of its affairs abroad, after mature deliberation with the said Lord Archbishop, our chancellor. But because in progress of time many things will be found to be more expedient, when from small beginnings the college shall have come to greater perfection, and some things too will want to be corrected and altered, as future cases and circumstances may require, all these things we are very willing to leave to the visitors and governors, for the time being, to be added, diminished, and changed according to the different circumstances of the college, for promoting the study of the learned languages and liberal arts, according to the powers granted them by the college charter.

Only that nothing may be enacted rashly, in the heat of disputation, no old statute suddenly changed, or new one made, we recommend it for a rule in these matters that no new statute be enacted or prescribed until it has been duly proposed, read, and considered at two several meetings of the governors of the college. . . .

CONCERNING THE PRESIDENT, AND MASTERS, AND SCHOOLS

THERE ARE THREE THINGS which the founders of this college proposed to themselves, to which all its statutes should be directed.

The first is that the youth of Virginia should be well educated to learning and good morals.

The second is that the churches of America, especially Virginia, should be supplied with good ministers after the doctrine and government of the Church of England, and that the college should be a constant seminary for this purpose.

The third is that the Indians of America should be instructed in the Christian religion, and that some of the Indian youth that are well behaved and well inclined, being first well prepared in the Divinity School, may be sent out to preach the gospel to their countrymen in their own tongue, after they have duly been put in orders of deacons and priests.

For carrying on these noble designs, let there be four schools assigned within the college precincts, of which, together with the masters or professors belonging to them, some directions must be given.

THE GRAMMAR SCHOOL

IN THIS GRAMMAR SCHOOL let the Latin and Greek tongues be well taught. As for rudiments and grammars and classic authors of each tongue, let them teach the same books which by law or custom are used in the schools of England. Nevertheless, we allow the schoolmaster the liberty, if he has any observations on the Latin or Greek grammars or any of the authors that are taught in his school, that with the approbation of the president he may dictate them to the scholars. Let the master take special care

that, if the author is never so well approved on other accounts, he teach no such part of him to his scholars as insinuates anything against religion and good morals.

Special care likewise must be taken of their morals, that none of the scholars presume to tell a lie, or curse or swear, or talk or do anything obscene, or quarrel and fight, play at cards or dice, or set in to drinking, or do anything else that is contrary to good manners. And that all such faults may be so much the more easily detected, the master shall choose some of the most trusty scholars for public observators, to give him an account of all such transgressions, and, according to the degrees of heinousness of the crime, let the discipline be used without respect of persons. . . .

THE PHILOSOPHY SCHOOL

FORASMUCH AS WE SEE NOW daily a further progress in philosophy than could be made by Aristotle's *Logic* and *Physics,* which reigned so long alone in the schools and shut out all other, therefore, we leave it to the president and masters, by the advice of the chancellor, to teach what systems of logic, physics, ethics, and mathematics they think fit in their schools. Further, we judge it requisite that, besides disputations, the studious youth be exercised in declamations and themes on various subjects but not any taken out of the Bible. Those we leave to the Divinity School. In the Philosophy School we appoint two masters or professors, who for their yearly salary shall each of them receive £80 sterling and 20s. sterling a year from each scholar, except such poor ones as are entertained at the college charge upon the foundations; for they are to be taught gratis.

One of these masters shall teach rhetoric, logic, and ethics; the other physics, metaphysics, and mathematics.

And that the youth of the college may the more cheerfully apply themselves to these studies and endeavor to rise to the academic degrees, we do, according to the form and institution of the two famous universities in England, allot four years before they attain to the degree of Bachelor, and seven years before they attain the degree of Master of Arts.

THE DIVINITY SCHOOL

IN THIS SCHOOL let there be two professors, with a salary of £ 150 sterling to each; they are to have nothing from the students or candidates of theology.

Let one of these professors teach the Hebrew tongue and critically expound the literal sense of the Holy Scripture both of the Old and New Testament. Let the other explain the common places of divinity and the controversies with heretics; and let them have prelections and disputations on those subjects.

And let the students of divinity divide their time between those two professors.

THE INDIAN SCHOOL

THERE IS BUT ONE MASTER in this school who is to teach the Indian boys to read, and write, and vulgar arithmetic. And especially he is to teach them thoroughly the catechism and the principles of the Christian religion. For a yearly salary, let him have £ 40 or £ 50 sterling, according to the ability of that school, appointed by the Honorable Robert Boyle, or to be further appointed by other benefactors. And in the same school the master may be permitted to teach other scholars from the town, for which he is to take the usual wages of 20s. a year. . . .

OF THE SCHOLARS

THERE ARE TWO SORTS OF SCHOLARS; one is of them who are maintained at their own charge and pay school wages in the schools where the masters are allowed to take wages as above; the other sort is of those who are maintained at the college's charge.

As to the first sort of scholars, we leave their parents and guardians at liberty whether they shall lodge and eat within the college or elsewhere in the town, or any country village near the town. For it being our intention that the youth, with as little charge as they can, should learn the learned languages and the other liberal arts and sciences, if any have their houses so near the college that from thence the college bells can be heard and the public hours of study be duly observed, we would not, by these our statutes, hinder them from boarding their own children or their friends or from lodging them at their own houses. Nevertheless we hope that all things relating to the table or lodging will be so well supplied within the college that they can be nowhere cheaper or better accommodated.

Let the spare chambers of the college, over and above what are necessary for the president and masters and other officers of the college, be let out at moderate rents to the better sort of the big boys; and let the money they yield be laid out in the reparation of the edifices of the college.

Out of the scholars let there be chosen to be put upon the foundation as many as the college can maintain out of the funds allotted for that purpose. And let them be thereafter diligently instructed and maintained, till they are put in orders and preferred to some place and office in the church. The election of this sort of scholars let it be in the visitors; and in that election let them chiefly regard, besides their poverty, their ingeniousness, learning, piety, and good behavior as to their morals. And the more any one of the candidates excels in these things, he has so much the better title to be preferred; and let him be preferred accordingly.

1728

88.

BENJAMIN FRANKLIN: Credo

The life of Benjamin Franklin was many lives, and hardly any other American, of his age or after it, ever manifested so great a variety of talents. Printer, almanac-maker, maxim-monger, essayist, inventor, philanthropist, diplomat, statesman, and wit, he was "everything but a poet," as Herman Melville later said. Perhaps it was because he was everything but a poet — because, at any rate, he held both mystery and metaphysics in contempt — that Franklin had no inclination toward the transcendent and inscrutable God of the Puritans, but subscribed instead to the faith set forth in his Articles of Belief and Acts of Religion *(1728). Formulated when he was only twenty-two, this creed or private religious ceremony served him all his life. In substance it embodied the principles of Deism, the religion or philosophy of life that was publicly professed by a small but influential number of eighteenth-century Americans, including Washington and Jefferson.*

Source: Sparks, II, pp. 1-3.

I BELIEVE there is one supreme, most perfect Being, Author and Father of the gods themselves.

For I believe that man is not the most perfect being but one, but rather that there are many degrees of beings superior to him.

Also, when I stretch my imagination through and beyond our system of planets, beyond the visible fixed stars themselves, into that space that is every way infinite, and conceive it filled with suns like ours, each with a chorus of worlds forever moving round him; then this little ball on which we move seems, even in my narrow imagination, to be almost nothing, and myself less than nothing, and of no sort of consequence.

When I think thus, I imagine it great vanity in me to suppose, that the Supremely Perfect does in the least regard such an inconsiderable nothing as man; more especially, since it is impossible for me to have any clear idea of that which is infinite and incomprehensible, I cannot conceive otherwise, than that He, the Infinite Father, expects or requires no worship or praise from us, but that He is even infinitely above it.

But, since there is in all men something like a natural principle which inclines them to *devotion*, or the worship of some unseen power;

And since men are endowed with reason superior to all other animals that we are in our world acquainted with;

Therefore, I think it seems required of me, and my duty as a man, to pay divine regards to *something*.

I conceive, then, that the *infinite* has created many beings or gods, vastly superior to man, who can better conceive his perfections than we, and return him a more rational and glorious praise; as, among men, the praise of the ignorant or of children is not regarded by the ingenious painter or architect, who is rather honored and pleased with the approbation of wise men and artists.

It may be these created gods are immortal; or it may be that, after many ages, they are changed and others supply their places.

Howbeit, I conceive that each of these is exceeding wise and good, and very powerful; and that each has made for himself one glorious sun, attended with a beautiful and admirable system of planets.

It is that particular wise and good God, who is the Author and Owner of our system, that I propose for the object of my praise and adoration; for I conceive that He has in Himself some of those passions He has planted in us; and that, since He has given us reason whereby we are capable of observing His wisdom in the creation, He is not above caring for us, being pleased with our praise, and offended when we slight Him, or neglect His glory.

I conceive, for many reasons, that He is a *good being*; and, as I should be happy to have so wise, good, and powerful a being my friend, let me consider in what manner I shall make myself most acceptable to Him.

Next to the praise resulting from and due to His wisdom, I believe He is pleased and delights in the happiness of those He has created; and, since without virtue a man can have no happiness in this world, I firmly believe He delights to see me virtuous, because He is pleased when He sees me happy.

And since He has created many things, which seem purely designed for the delight of man, I believe He is not offended when He sees His children solace themselves in any manner of pleasant exercises and innocent delights; and I think no pleasure innocent that is to man hurtful.

I *love* Him, therefore, for His goodness, and I *adore* Him for His wisdom.

Let me not fail, then, to praise my God continually, for it is His due, and it is all I can return for His many favors and great goodness to me; and let me resolve to be virtuous, that I may be happy, that I may please Him, who is delighted to see me happy. Amen!

The body of Benjamin Franklin, printer, (like the cover of an old book, its contents torn out and stript of its lettering and gilding), lies here, food for worms; but the work shall not be lost, for it will (as he believed) appear once more in a new and more elegant edition, revised and corrected by the Author.

BENJAMIN FRANKLIN, epitaph written for himself sixty-two years before his death

89.

WILLIAM BYRD: Surveying the Frontier

In his History of the Dividing Line, *William Byrd recorded the daily activities of a Virginia commission assigned to survey and relocate the boundary between Virginia and North Carolina. The 1728-1729 survey was frequently hampered by quarrels with a North Carolina surveying·party. Byrd placed the blame for these on the Carolinians, dubbing them "Knights of the Rum-Cask." The colorful background material in Byrd's* History *includes a sketch of the Virginia countryside and some caustic comments on the character of North Carolinians. Parts of the work, which remained unpublished until 1841, are reprinted here.*

Source: *William Byrd's Histories of the Dividing Line Betwixt Virginia and North Carolina*, William K. Boyd, ed., Raleigh, 1929, pp. 52-86.

March 9. The surveyors entered early upon their business this morning and ran the line through Mr. Eyland's plantation, as far as the banks of North River. They passed over it in the pirogue and landed in Gibbs's marsh, which was a mile in breadth and tolerably firm. They trudged through this marsh without much difficulty as far as the highland, which promised more fertility than any they had seen in these parts. But this firm land lasted not long before they came upon the dreadful pocoson [swamp] they had been threatened with. Nor did they find it one jot better than it had been painted to them. The beavers and otters had rendered it quite impassable for any creature but themselves.

Our poor fellows had much ado to drag their legs after them in this quagmire, but, disdaining to be balked, they could hardly be persuaded from pressing forward by the surveyors, who found it absolutely necessary to make a traverse in the deepest place to prevent their sticking fast in the mire and becoming a certain prey to the turkey buzzards.

This horrible day's work ended two miles to the northward of Mr. Merchant's plantation, divided from Northwest River by a narrow swamp, which is causewayed over. We took up our quarters in the open field not far from the house, correcting, by a fire as large as a Roman funeral pile, the aguish exhalations arising from the sunken grounds that surrounded us.

The neck of land included between North River and Northwest River, with the adjacent marsh, belonged formerly to Governor Gibbs but, since his decease, to Colonel Bladen, in right of his first lady, who was Mr. Gibbs's daughter. It would be a valuable tract of land in any country but North Carolina, where, for want of navigation and commerce, the best estate affords little more than a coarse subsistence.

10. The Sabbath happened very opportunely to give some ease to our jaded people, who rested religiously from every work but that of cooking the kettle. We observed very few cornfields in our walks, and those very small, which seemed the stranger to us because we could see no other tokens of husbandry or improvement. But upon further inquiry, we were given to understand people only made corn for themselves and not for their stocks, which know very well how to get their own living. . . .

The only business here is raising of hogs, which is managed with the least trouble and affords the diet they are most fond of. The truth of it is, the inhabitants of North Carolina devour so much swine's flesh that it fills them full of gross humors. For want, too, of a constant supply of salt, they are commonly obliged to eat it fresh, and that begets the highest taint of scurvy. Thus, whenever a severe cold happens to constitutions thus vitiated, 'tis apt to improve into the yaws, called there very justly the country distemper. This has all the symptoms of the pox, with this aggravation, that no preparation of mercury will touch it. First it seizes the throat, next the palate, and lastly shows its spite to the poor nose, of which 'tis apt in a small time treacherously to undermine the foundation.

11. We ordered the surveyors early to their business, who were blessed with pretty dry grounds for three miles together. But they paid dear for it in the next two, consisting of one continued frightful pocoson, which no creatures but those of the amphibious kind ever had ventured into before. This filthy quagmire did in earnest put the men's courage to a trial, and though I can't say it made them lose their patience, yet they lost their humor for joking. They kept their gravity like so many Spaniards, so that a man might then have taken his opportunity to plunge up to the chin without danger of being laughed at. However, this unusual composure of countenance could not fairly be called complaining.

Their day's work ended at the mouth of Northern's Creek, which empties itself into Northwest River; though we chose to quarter a little higher up the river, near Mossy Point. This we did for the convenience of an old house to shelter our persons and baggage from the rain, which threatened us

hard. We judged the thing right, for there fell a heavy shower in the night that drove the most hardy of us into the house. Though indeed our case was not much mended by retreating thither, because that tenement having not long before been used as a pork store, the moisture of the air dissolved the salt that lay scattered on the floor, and made it as wet within doors as without. However, the swamps and marshes we were lately accustomed to had made such beavers and otters of us that nobody caught the least cold.

We had encamped so early that we found time in the evening to walk near half a mile into the woods. There we came upon a family of mulattoes that called themselves free, though by the shyness of the master of the house, who took care to keep least in sight, their freedom seemed a little doubtful. It is certain many slaves shelter themselves in this obscure part of the world, nor will any of their righteous neighbors discover them. On the contrary, they find their account in settling such fugitives on some out-of-the-way corner of their land to raise stocks for a mean and inconsiderable share, well knowing their condition makes it necessary for them to submit to any terms.

Nor were these worthy borderers content to shelter runaway slaves, but debtors and criminals have often met with the like indulgence. But if the government of North Carolina has encouraged this unneighborly policy in order to increase their people, it is no more than what ancient Rome did before them, which was made a city of refuge for all debtors and fugitives, and from that wretched beginning grew up in time to be mistress of a great part of the world. And considering how fortune delights in bringing great things out of small, who knows but Carolina may, one time or other, come to be the seat of some other great empire? . . .

16. The line was this day carried one mile and a half and sixteen poles. The soil continued soft and miry, but fuller of trees, especially white cedars. Many of these, too, were thrown down and piled in heaps, high enough for a good Muscovite fortification. The worst of it was the poor fellows began now to be troubled with fluxes, occasioned by bad water and moist lodging, but chewing of rhubarb kept that malady within bounds. . . .

We passed by no less than two Quaker meeting houses, one of which had an awkward ornament on the west end of it, that seemed to ape a steeple. I must own I expected no such piece of foppery from a sect of so much outside simplicity. That persuasion prevails much in the lower end of Nansemond County, for want of ministers to pilot the people a decenter way to heaven. The ill reputation of tobacco planted in those lower parishes makes the clergy unwilling to accept of them, unless it be such whose abilities are as mean as their pay. Thus, whether the churches be quite void or but indifferently filled, the Quakers will have an opportunity of gaining proselytes. 'Tis a wonder no popish missionaries are sent from Maryland to labor in this neglected vineyard, who we know have zeal enough to traverse sea and land on the meritorious errand of making converts.

Nor is it less strange that some wolf in sheep's clothing arrives not from New England to lead astray a flock that has no shepherd. People uninstructed in any religion are ready to embrace the first that offers. It is natural for helpless man to adore his Maker in some form or other, and were there any exception to this rule, I should suspect it to be among the Hottentots of the Cape of Good Hope and of North Carolina. . . .

17. They were, however, forced to keep the Sabbath in spite of their teeth, contrary to the dispensation our good chaplain had given them. Indeed, their short allowance of provision would have justified their making the best of their way, without distinction of

William Byrd II, portrait by an unknown artist, *c.* 1720

days. 'Twas certainly a work both of necessity and self-preservation to save themselves from starving. Nevertheless, the hard rain had made everything so thoroughly wet that it was quite impossible to do any business. They therefore made a virtue of what they could not help and contentedly rested in their dry situation.

Since the surveyors had entered the Dismal, they had laid eyes on no living creature: neither bird nor beast, insect nor reptile came in view. Doubtless the eternal shade that broods over this mighty bog and hinders the sunbeams from blessing the ground makes it an uncomfortable habitation for anything that has life. Not so much as a Zealand frog could endure so aguish a situation. It had one beauty, however, that delighted the eye, though at the expense of all the other senses: the moisture of the soil preserves a continual verdure and makes every plant an evergreen, but at the same time the foul damps ascend without ceasing, corrupt the air, and render it unfit for respiration. Not even a turkey buzzard will venture to fly over it, no more that the Italian vultures will over the filthy Lake Avernus, or the birds in the Holy Land over the Salt Sea where Sodom and Gomorrah formerly stood.

In these sad circumstances, the kindest thing we could do for our suffering friends was to give them a place in the litany. Our chaplain, for his part, did his office and rubbed us up with a seasonable sermon. This was quite a new thing to our brethren of North Carolina, who live in a climate where no clergyman can breathe any more than spiders in Ireland.

For want of men in holy orders, both the members of the council and justices of the peace are empowered by the laws of that country to marry all those who will not take one another's word; but for the ceremony of christening their children, they trust that to chance. If a parson come in their way, they will crave a cast of his office, as they call it, else they are content their offspring should remain as errant pagans as themselves. They account it among their greatest advantages that they are not priest-ridden, not remembering that the clergy is rarely guilty of bestriding such as have the misfortune to be poor.

One thing may be said for the inhabitants of that province, that they are not troubled with any religious fumes and have the least superstition of any people living. They do not know Sunday from any other day, any more than Robinson Crusoe did, which would give them a great advantage were they given to be industrious. But they keep so many Sabbaths every week that their disregard of the seventh day has no manner of cruelty in it, either to servants or cattle. . . .

21. The surveyors and their attendants began . . . to be alarmed with apprehensions of famine. . . . Their provisions were now near exhausted. They had this morning made the last distribution, that so each might husband his small pittance as he pleased. Now it was that the fresh colored young man began to tremble, every joint of him, having dreamed the night before that the Indians were about to barbecue him over live coals. The prospect of famine determined the people at last, with one consent, to abandon the line for the present, which advanced but slowly, and make the best of their way to firm land.

Accordingly, they set off very early, and, by the help of the compass which they carried along with them, steered a direct westwardly course. They marched from morning till night and computed their journey to amount to about four miles, which was a great way considering the difficulties of the ground. It was all along a cedar swamp, so dirty and perplexed that, if they had not traveled for their lives they could not have reached so far. On their way they espied a turkey buzzard that flew prodigiously high to get above the noisome exhalations that ascend from that filthy place. This they were willing to understand as a good omen, according to the superstitions of the ancients, who had great faith in the flight of vultures. However, after all this tedious journey, they could yet discover no end of their toil, which made them very pensive, especially after they had eaten the last morsel of their provisions. But, to their unspeakable comfort, when all was hushed in the evening, they heard the cattle low and the dogs bark very distinctly, which, to men in that distress, was more delightful music than Faustina or Farinelli could have made. In the meantime the commissioners could get no news of them from any of their visitors, who assembled from every point of the compass. . . .

22. Our patrol happened not to go far enough to the northward this morning; if they had, the people in the Dismal might have heard the report of their guns. For this reason they returned without any tidings, which threw us into a great though unnecessary perplexity. This was now the ninth day since they entered into that inhospitable swamp, and consequently we had reason to believe their provisions were quite spent. We knew they worked hard and therefore would eat heartily so long as they had wherewithal to recruit their spirits, not imagining the swamp so wide as they found it. Had we been able to guess where the line would come out, we would have sent men to meet them with a fresh supply; but as we could know nothing of that, and as we had neither compass nor surveyor to guide a messenger on such an errand, we were unwilling to expose him to no purpose; therefore, all we were able to do for them, in so great an extremity, was to recommend them to a merciful Providence.

However long we might think the time, yet we were cautious of showing our uneasiness, for fear of mortifying our landlord. He had done his best for us, and therefore we were unwilling he should think us dissatisfied with our entertainment. In the midst of our concern, we were most agreeably surprised, just after dinner, with the news that the Dismalites were all safe. . . .

24. This being Sunday, we had a numerous congregation, which flocked to our quarters from all the adjacent country. The news that our surveyors were come out of the Dismal increased the number very much, because it would give them an opportunity of guessing, at least, whereabouts the line could cut, whereby they might form some judgment whether they belonged to Virginia or Carolina. Those who had taken up land within the disputed bounds were in great pain lest it should be found to lie in Virginia; because this being done contrary to an express order of that government, the patentees had great reason to fear they should in that case have lost their land. But their apprehensions were now at an end when they understood that all the territory which had been controverted was like to be left in Carolina. . . .

27. Between this and Edenton there are many thuckleberry slashes, which afford a convenient harbor for wolves and foxes. The first of these wild beasts is not so large and fierce as they are in other countries more northerly. He will not attack a man in the keenest of his hunger but run away from him as from an animal more mischievous than himself. The foxes are much bolder and will sometimes not only make a stand but likewise assault anyone that would balk them of their prey. The inhabitants hereabouts take the trouble to dig abundance of wolfpits, so deep and perpendicular that when a wolf is once tempted into them he can no more scramble out again than a husband who has taken the leap can scramble out of matrimony.

Most of the houses in this part of the country are loghouses, covered with pine or cypress shingles, three feet long and one broad. They are hung upon laths with pegs, and their doors, too, turn upon wooden hinges and have wooden locks to secure them, so that the building is finished without nails or other ironwork. They also set up their pales without any nails at all, and indeed more securely than those that are nailed. There are three rails mortised into the posts, the lowest of which serves as a sill, with a groove in the middle big enough to receive the end of the pales; the middle part of the pale rests against the inside of the next rail, and the top of it is brought forward to the outside of the uppermost. Such wreathing of the pales in and out makes them stand firm, and much harder to unfix than when nailed in the ordinary way.

Within three or four miles of Edenton the soil appears to be a little more fertile, though it is much cut with slashes, which seem all to have a tendency toward the Dismal. This town is situated on the north side of Albemarle Sound, which is there about five miles over. A dirty slash runs all along the back of it, which in the summer is a foul annoyance and furnishes abundance of that Carolina plague, mosquitoes. There may be forty or fifty houses, most of them

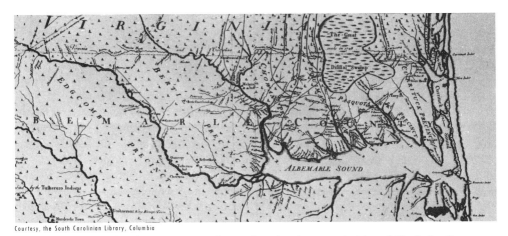

Detail from map by Edward Moseley, 1733, showing boundary between Virginia and North Carolina as surveyed by William Byrd

small and built without expense. A citizen here is counted extravagant if he has ambition enough to aspire to a brick chimney. Justice herself is but indifferently lodged, the courthouse having much the air of a common tobacco house.

I believe this is the only metropolis in the Christian or Mohammedan world where there is neither church, chapel, mosque, synagogue, or any other place of public worship of any sect or religion whatsoever. What little devotion there may happen to be is much more private than their vices. The people seem easy without a minister as long as they are exempted from paying him. Sometimes the Society for Propagating the Gospel has had the charity to send over missionaries to this country; but unfortunately the priest has been too lewd for the people, or, which oftener happens, they too lewd for the priest. For these reasons these reverend gentlemen have always left their flocks as errant heathen as they found them. Thus much, however, may be said for the inhabitants of Edenton, that not a soul has the least taint of hypocrisy or superstition, acting very frankly and aboveboard in all their excesses. . . .

They are rarely guilty of flattering or making any court to their governors, but treat them with all the excesses of freedom and familiarity. They are of opinion their rulers would be apt to grow insolent if they grew rich, and for that reason take care to keep them poorer and more dependent, if possible, than the saints in New England used to do their governors. They have very little coin, so they are forced to carry on their home traffic with paper money. This is the only cash that will tarry in the country, and for that reason the discount goes on increasing between that and real money. . . .

April 1. The surveyors, getting now upon better ground quite disengaged from underwoods, pushed on the line almost twelve miles. They left Somerton Chapel near two miles to the northward, so that there was now no place of public worship left in the whole province of North Carolina. . . .

If the governor's hands have been weak in that province, under the authority of the lord proprietors, much weaker than were the hands of the magistrate, who, though he might have had virtue enough to endeavor to punish offenders, which very rarely happened, yet that virtue had been quite impotent for want of ability to put it in execution. Besides, there might have been some danger, perhaps, in venturing to be so rigorous, for fear of undergoing the fate of an honest justice in Currituck precinct. This bold magistrate, it seems, taking upon him to order a fellow to the stocks for being disorderly in his drink, was for his intemperate zeal carried thither himself, and narrowly escaped being whipped by the rabble into the bargain.

This easy day's work carried the line to the banks of Somerton Creek, that runs out of Chowan River a little below the mouth of Nottoway. . . .

7. The next day being Sunday, we ordered notice to be sent to all the neighborhood that there would be a sermon at this place, and an opportunity of christening their children. But the likelihood of rain got the better of their devotion, and, what perhaps might still be a stronger motive, of their curiosity. In the morning we dispatched a runner to the Nottoway town to let the Indians know we intended them a visit that evening, and our honest landlord was so kind as to be our pilot thither, being about four miles from his house.

Accordingly in the afternoon we marched in good order to the town, where the female scouts, stationed on an eminence for that purpose, had no sooner spied us but they gave notice of our approach to their fellow citizens by continual whoops and cries, which could not possibly have been more dismal at the sight of their most implacable enemies. This signal assembled all their great men, who received us in a body and conducted us into the fort.

This fort was a square piece of ground enclosed with substantial puncheons, or strong palisades, about ten feet high, and leaning a little outward to make a scalade more difficult. Each side of the square might be about a hundred yards long, with loopholes at proper distances through which they may fire upon the enemy. Within this enclosure we found bark cabins sufficient to lodge all their people in case they should be obliged to retire thither. These cabins are no other but close arbors made of saplings, arched at the top, and covered so well with bark as to be proof against all weather. The fire is made in the middle, according to the Hibernian fashion, the smoke whereof finds no other vent but at the door, and so keeps the whole family warm, at the expense both of their eyes and complexion.

The Indians have no standing furniture in their cabins but hurdles to repose their persons upon which they cover with mats or deerskins. We were conducted to the best apartments in the fort, which just before had been made ready for our reception, and adorned with new mats that were sweet and clean. The young men had painted themselves in a hideous manner, not so much for ornament as terror. In that frightful equipage they entertained us with sundry war dances wherein they endeavored to look as formidable as possible. The instrument they danced to was an Indian drum, that is, a large gourd with a skin braced taut over the mouth of it. The dancers all sang to this music, keeping exact time with their feet, while their heads and arms were screwed into a thousand menacing postures.

Upon this occasion the ladies had arrayed themselves in all their finery. They were wrapped in their red and blue match coats, thrown so negligently about them that their mahogany skins appeared in several parts, like the Lacedaemonian damsels of old. Their hair was braided with white and blue peak and hung gracefully in a large roll upon their shoulders. This peak consists of small cylinders cut out of a conch shell, drilled through and strung like beads. It serves them both for money and jewels, the blue being of much greater value than the white, for the same reason that Ethiopian mistresses in France are dearer than French, because they are more scarce. The women wear necklaces and bracelets of these precious materials when they have a mind to appear lovely. Though their complexions be a little sad colored, yet their shapes are very straight and well proportioned. Their faces are seldom handsome, yet they have an air of innocence and bashfulness, that with a little less dirt would not fail to make them desirable.

Such charms might have had their full effect upon men who had been so long deprived of female conversation, but that the whole winter's soil was so crusted on the skins of those dark angels that it required a very strong appetite to approach them. The bear's oil, with which they anoint their persons all over, makes their skins soft, and at the same time protects them from every species of vermin that use to be troublesome to other uncleanly people. We were unluckily so many that they could not well make us the compliment of bedfellows, according to the Indian rules of hospitality, though a grave matron whispered one of the commissioners very civilly in the ear that, if her daughter had been but one year older, she should have been at his devotion.

It is by no means a loss of reputation among the Indians for damsels that are single to have intrigues with the men; on the contrary, they count it an argument of superior merit to be liked by a great number of gallants. However, like the ladies that game, they are a little mercenary in their amours and seldom bestow their favors out of stark love and kindness. But after these women have once appropriated their charms by marriage, they are from thenceforth faithful to their vows and will hardly ever be tempted by an agreeable gallant or be provoked by a brutal or even by a fumbling husband to go astray. The little work that is done among the Indians is done by the poor women, while the men are quite idle or at most employed only in the gentlemanly diversions of hunting and fishing.

In this, as well as in their wars, they use nothing but firearms, which they purchase of the English for skins. Bows and arrows are grown into disuse, except only among their boys. Nor is it ill policy, but on the contrary very prudent, thus to furnish the Indians with firearms, because it makes them depend entirely upon the English, not only for their trade but even for their subsistence. Besides, they were really able to do more mischief while they made use of arrows, of which they would let silently fly several in a minute with wonderful dexterity, whereas now they hardly ever discharge their firelocks more than once, which they insidiously do from behind a tree, and then retire as nimbly as the Dutch horse used to do now and then formerly in Flanders.

We put the Indians to no expense but only of a little corn for our horses, for which in gratitude we cheered their hearts with what rum we had left, which they love better than they do their wives and children. Though these Indians dwell among the English and see in what plenty a little industry enables them to live, yet they choose to continue in their stupid idleness and to suffer all the inconveniences of dirt, cold, and want, rather than to disturb their heads with care or defile their hands with labor.

The whole number of people belonging to the Nottoway town, if you include women and children, amount to about 200. These are the only Indians of any consequence now remaining within the limits of Virginia. The rest are either removed or dwindled to a very inconsiderable number, either by destroying one another or else by the smallpox and other diseases — though nothing has been so fatal to them as their ungovernable passion for rum, with which, I am sorry to say it, they have been but too liberally supplied by the English that live near them.

And here I must lament the bad success Mr. Boyle's charity has hitherto had toward converting any of these poor heathens to Christianity. Many children of our neighboring Indians have been brought up in the College of William and Mary. They have been taught to read and write, and have been carefully instructed in the principles of the Christian religion, till they came to be men. Yet, after they returned home, instead of civilizing and converting the rest, they have immediately relapsed into infidelity and barbarism themselves.

And some of them, too, have made the worst use of the knowledge they acquired among the English by employing it against their benefactors. Besides, as they unhappily forget all the good they learn and remember the ill, they are apt to be more vicious and disorderly than the rest of their countrymen. . . .

I'm sorry I can't give a better account of the state of the poor Indians with respect to Christianity, although a great deal of pains has been and still continues to be taken with them. For my part, I must be of opinion, as I hinted before, that there is but one way of converting these poor infidels and reclaiming them from barbarity, and that is, charitably to intermarry with them, according to the modern policy of the most Christian king in Canada and Louisiana. Had the English done this at the first settlement of the colony, the infidelity of the Indians had been worn out at this day, with their dark complexions, and the country had swarmed with people more than it does with insects.

It was certainly an unreasonable nicety that prevented their entering into so good-natured an alliance. All nations of men have the same natural dignity, and we all know that very bright talents may be lodged under a very dark skin. The principal difference between one people and another proceeds only from the different opportunities of improvement. The Indians by no means want understanding, and are in their figure tall and well proportioned. Even their copper-colored complexion would admit of blanching if not in the first, at the farthest in the second generation. I may safely venture to say, the Indian women would have made altogether as honest wives for the first planters as the damsels they used to purchase from aboard the ships. It is strange, therefore, that any good Christian should have refused a wholesome, straight bedfellow, when he might have had so fair a portion with her as the merit of saving her soul. . . .

November 16. We gave orders that the horses should pass Roanoke River at Monisep Ford, while most of the baggage was transported in a canoe. We landed at the plantation of Cornelius Keith, where I beheld the wretchedest scene of poverty I had ever met with in this happy part of the world. The man, his wife, and six small children lived in a pen, like so many cattle, without any roof over their heads but that of heaven. And this was their airy residence in the daytime, but then there was a fodder stack not far from this enclosure in which the whole family sheltered themselves anights and in bad weather.

However, 'twas almost worthwhile to be as poor as this man was, to be as perfectly contented. All his wants proceeded from indolence and not from misfortune. He had good land, as well as good health and good limbs to work it, and, besides, had a trade very useful to all the inhabitants round about. He could make and set up quern [handmill] stones very well and had proper materials for that purpose just at hand, if he could have taken the pains to fetch them. There is no other kind of mills in these remote parts, and, therefore, if the man would have worked at his trade, he might have lived very comfortably. The poor woman had a little more industry and spun cotton enough to make a thin covering for her own and her children's nakedness.

I am sorry to say it, but idleness is the general character of the men in the southern part of this colony as well as in North Carolina. The air is so mild, and the soil so fruitful, that very little labor is required to fill their bellies, especially where the woods afford such plenty of game. These advantages discharge the men from the necessity of killing themselves with work, and, then, for the other article of raiment, a very little of that will suffice in so temperate a climate. But so much as is absolutely necessary falls to the good women's share to provide. They all spin, weave, and knit, whereby they make a good shift to clothe the whole family; and to their credit be it recorded many of them do it very completely and thereby reproach their husbands' laziness in the most inoffensive way — that is to say, by discovering a better spirit of industry in themselves.

From hence we moved forward to Colonel Mumford's other plantation, under the care of Miles Riley, where, by that gentleman's directions, we were again supplied with many good things. Here it was we discharged our worthy friend and fellow traveler, Mr. Bearskin, who had so plentifully supplied us with provisions during our long expedition. We rewarded him to his heart's content, so that he returned to his town laden both with riches and the reputation of having been a great discoverer.

17. This being Sunday, we were seasonably put in mind how much we were obliged to be thankful for our happy return to the inhabitants. Indeed, we had great reason to reflect with gratitude on the signal mercies we had received. First, that we had, day by day, been fed by the bountiful hand of Providence in the desolate wilderness, insomuch that if any of our people wanted one single meal during the whole expedition, it was entirely owing to their own imprudent management. Second, that not one man of our whole company had any violent distemper or bad accident befall him, from one end of the line to the other. The very worst that happened was that one of them gave himself a smart cut on the pan of his knee with a tomahawk, which we had the good fortune to cure in a short time, without the help of a surgeon.

As for the misadventures of sticking in the mire and falling into rivers and creeks, they were rather subjects of mirth than complaint, and served only to diversify our travels with a little farcical variety. And, lastly, that many uncommon incidents have concurred to prosper our undertaking. . . .

22. A little before noon we all took leave and dispersed to our several habitations, where we were so happy as to find all our families well. This crowned all our other blessings and made our journey as prosperous as it had been painful. Thus ended our second expedition, in which we extended the line within the shadow of the Cherokee Mountains, where we were obliged to set up our pillars, like Hercules, and return home.

We had now, upon the whole, been out sixteen weeks, including going and returning, and had traveled at least 600 miles, and no small part of that distance on foot. Below, toward the seaside, our course lay through marshes, swamps, and great waters; and above, over steep hills, craggy rocks, and thickets, hardly penetrable. Notwithstanding this variety of hardships, we may say, without vanity, that we faithfully obeyed the King's orders, and performed the business effectually in which we had the honor to be employed.

Nor can we by any means reproach ourselves of having put the Crown to any exorbitant expense in this difficult affair, the whole charge, from beginning to end, amounting to no more than £1,000. But let no one concerned in this painful expedition complain of the scantiness of his pay, so long as His Majesty has been graciously pleased to add to our reward the honor of his royal approbation, and to declare, notwithstanding the desertion of the Carolina commissioners, that the line by us run shall hereafter stand as the true boundary between the governments of Virginia and North Carolina.

1729

90.

WILLIAM DOUGLASS: Plan for a Map of North America

William Douglass and Cadwallader Colden, two prominent colonial physicians, dabbled in a number of other fields of scientific investigation besides medicine. Cartography was one of Colden's special interests, and he devoted many efforts to a project for creating an accurate map of the country. Colden, a New Yorker, asked his friends for help, and Douglass, a Bostonian, wrote him in September 1729, giving geographical information about New England.

Source: MHSC, 4th series, II, pp. 185-188.

IT IS WITH PLEASURE I understand that you incline to oblige the world with a correct map of North America. I am sorry that it is not in my power to contribute toward it by sending you a good map of the provinces of New England; there is not one extant but what is intolerably and grossly erroneous. I have at times (with a design of learning the country) traveled the greatest part of our four colonies of Massachusetts Bay, Connecticut, Rhode Island, and New Hampshire, but cannot pretend to reduce them to an exact plan. I may, however, send you some hints which may enable you to make the maps far more exact than any hitherto published. When you have favored me (which I earnestly desire, as also the true boundaries of New York government in writing) with a copy of your map of New York and the adjacent Indian countries, I shall by that pattern be more capable of reducing my loose hints to some short, intelligible method.

In general, that you may not fall into the same mistake with former publishers, you are to observe that the lines or boundaries of our provinces here at present are not exactly the same as laid down in the charters and grants but have been enlarged by consent; as for instance the Massachusetts heads Rhode Island and Connecticut governments by a due east and northwest line according to the charters; this line, by consent of Rhode Island, is an east and west line without any variation allowed, and consequently to the prejudice of Rhode Island property, with Connecticut to some towns no variation allowed, to others 9° variation allowed, so that it makes a sort of indented line.

I presume the most natural, easy and exact method of beginning a draft or map is by first laying down some certain fixed points accurately determined as to latitude and longitude, and the other principal parts laid down according to their exact distances and bearings from these invariable points will prevent any gross mistake. I know not what fixed points you may have collected for the Carolinas, Virginia, and Maryland. Sir William Keith, I find by the *Philosophical Transactions,* has been at some pains to ascertain the latitude and longitude of Philadelphia; New York is in your own observation. Boston is accurately fixed by the observations of Mr. Robie (a Fellow and sufficiently practised in observing) at Cambridge College, which is about three and a half miles west southerly from Boston. Cambridge is in 42°29′ north latitude; its longitude he has endeavored to determine by sundry observations with a twenty-four-foot telescope.

I shall only trouble you with the most exact which was of an eclipse of the moon on the 15th of March, 1707, which eclipse happened also to be observed at Paris by Cassini and De la Hire. By those observations collated, Cambridge is 4ʰ 55′ 50″ west of Paris (subducting 9′ 40″ London's westing from Paris) and consequently 4ʰ 46′ 10″ from London; so that with sufficient exactness Boston may be fixed at 42° 25′ north latitude, and 4ʰ 45′ 57″ west from the meridian of London, that is in west longitude 71°29′ *circiter.* Thus Boston is 12′ 43″ east from New York, or 3°10′ difference of longitude, that is to say Boston is *circiter* 142 geographical miles east, and 105 of the same north of New York; and the nearest distance about 180 geographical miles, or 207 English; the common post road by its turnings, via Providence, New London, and New Haven to New York, is 265 miles (as I computed in my progress), but the nearest, though less used road, is via Mendon, Woodstock, Hartford and New Haven, to New York; 254 measured English miles.

As to other helps, we have a very exact draft of our most considerable River Merrimac as it was surveyed three years ago by

order of our government. I may send you a copy of it from the records; by it you will have a very exact map of New Hampshire government (for by this survey we are in hopes to swallow up that petty government according to the letter of our charter) and of about one-quarter part of the Massachusetts. Rhode Island and Connecticut governments are small. When you have their outlines (which I can send you with great exactness) as settled some years ago by consent of the several assemblies, there will be no great difficulty in placing the rivers and towns. I could procure from the secretary's office plans of our several towns as they were when first granted, but the subsequent assemblies have made such considerable alterations in dividing, dismembering, uniting, etc., that they will not answer your design. I can, however, from my own travels give you in general their situation with respect to one another and the considerable rivers, which may be sufficient for a general map.

Our station ships, Captain Durel, a very ingenious draftsman, in his several cruises has made a very exact sealine (with the makings and bearings of the land which are not in your way) of our coast from Boston Bay to Canso near Cape Breton; but as he designs to make a present of it at home, it is not proper for me to desire a copy of it here. Judge Dudley has for some years been hammering out a map of this country, but I fancy it will not make its appearance yet awhile. He pretends to be a sort of virtuoso; therefore communicates nothing freely to a friend, lest he should be prevented in the reputation of being the author.

To conclude for this time, I wish I could with you sing *Deus nobis haec otia fecit* [God made this leisure (time) for us]; our labors in practice of physic here are many and gains not much above a competency, and therefore cannot fall into sundry amusements which I could desire.

1732

91.

JONATHAN BELCHER: Power of the Purse — Legislative Revolt in Massachusetts

Throughout his term as governor of Massachusetts, Jonathan Belcher, who had been born in the colony, tried unsuccessfully to fulfill the demands both of the Crown that had appointed him and of his fellow colonists. The Massachusetts Assembly, which had traditionally been allowed to levy its own taxes and to control public expenditures, was unwilling to provide sufficient funds to support the King's armies and officials. The Assembly was, in effect, using its prerogative to maintain its independence of both the King and the royal governor. As Belcher pointed out in a letter of December 23, 1732, to the Board of Trade, the Crown's officers were becoming useless figureheads, for without the power of the purse, their decisions lacked authority.

Source: MHSC, 6th series, VI, pp. 226-228.

I HAD THE HONOR of writing to Your Lordships the 21st of the last month, of which a duplicate is also gone. The General Assembly of this province being still sitting, I cannot by this conveyance write Your Lordships so fully on the state of the public affairs as I hope to do when the General Court rises, and which will be in a few days.

The speech I made at the opening of this session will show Your Lordships what a miserable condition the province is in for want of the Assembly's making the proper and seasonable supplies of money to the public treasury, where there has not been a shilling for nineteen months past, although there is now upward of £40,000 due to the officers and soldiers of the king's forts and garrisons, the judges, the secretary of the province, and other people. Nor am I yet able to judge whether the Assembly will raise any money before they rise; but as they have, My Lords, taken a very extraordinary step upon His Majesty's royal instructions to me (the 16th and 30th) by addressing His Majesty a third time to withdraw them, and in case His Majesty will not hear them, then their agent is instructed to apply to the House of Commons.

This, My Lords, is what I take to be very extraordinary, to complain to His Majesty's dutiful and faithful Commons of the severity of His Majesty's proceedings with his people here. I believe, I say, this is without precedent. Nor have I ever heard that any of the king's plantations have presumed upon anything of this nature. Nor is there that I can see any occasion for treating His Majesty so indecently and disrespectfully.

The justice and strength of his royal orders will undoubtedly appear plain to all men of sense and understanding by comparing them with the charter of this province, and if the construction of any paragraph thereof falls into dispute, or seems dubious, why cannot the judges of England determine such points? I know no reason unless that the Assembly here love to be clamorous and troublesome. His Majesty's instructions, of the 16th and 30th, to me in my humble opinion are excellently calculated for supporting the honor of his government, and for the peace, welfare, and happiness of his people. I therefore hope in justice, mercy, and favor to his good subjects he will not recede from any part of them.

As to the instruction of the 16th, which limits or restrains the striking of credit bills, I believe every man of thought and substance is highly thankful that the Assembly are kept from ruining all the estates of the province by issuing out floods of those pernicious bills. At an emission of £50,000 or £60,000, every man that has outstanding debts sinks at least a fifth part of his capital, the bills growing in three or four months' time of so much less value than before such an emission.

And whereas £125 of the lawful money of the province would purchase £100 sterling, yet £350 of the vile bills that have been issued by the government will not at this day purchase that sum; so that to allow any further liberty of making these bills than for the annual expense of the province, or to extend the calling them in beyond the year in which they are issued, would have a direct tendency to ruin the king's government and people, and would prove a fraud and cheat upon all the merchants of England, who have always large effects in this country.

As to the instruction of the 30th, My Lords, I think nothing can be plainer than that it exactly quadrates with the charter; and for His Majesty to give it up or condescend to the House of Representatives examining the public accounts of charge of the government, I should think it would be as well to suffer them to appoint their own governor. For really, My Lords, all the struggle in that matter is for power. If every account of the province must be subjected to a House of Representatives, the king's governor will be of very little signification. They that have the control of the money will certainly have the power; and I take the single question on this head to be, whether the king shall appoint his own governor, or whether the House of Representatives shall be governor of the province?

I have, My Lords, with the best assistance and information I could get, drawn up the state of the case respecting the instruction of the 30th in the enclosed sheets, which is humbly submitted to your correction, and to be used as Your Lordships shall judge proper. When the sitting of the Assembly is over, I shall do myself the honor of writing Your Lordships the further needful for His Majesty's service in the government under my care.

There are three faithful friends: an old wife, an old dog, and ready money.
BENJAMIN FRANKLIN, *Poor Richard's Almanac*

THE SOUTHERN COLONIES

The coastal and tidewater regions of the southern colonies were the first to be settled, and became the site of large plantations of tobacco or rice grown by slaves and sold in world markets. Later settlers in the back country regions were subsistence farmers who found the governments of the colonies from Maryland to Georgia controlled by the tidewater planters. Indeed, the back country settlers of both North and South had more in common with each other than either did with the older coastal residents of their colonies, and until the early 19th century the most important sectional difference in the country was that between East and West.

The large plantations made agriculture the dominant economic activity, and in this the South differed from the more commercial North. As slaves increased in numbers the social structure became increasingly rigid in the southern colonies. The Anglican Church was established, though Presbyterians were common in the back country. Public schools were lacking, and education was conducted at home or in private schools, for those who could afford it — a situation that prevailed until the Civil War.

Virginia

(Above) Yorktown's deep-water harbor made it a busy tobacco port. This sketch was made on a British warship in the late 18th century; (right) Alexander Spotswood, outstanding governor of colonial Virginia from 1710-22, helped open the Shenandoah Valley to settlement; (below left) a 1750 engraving from the British "Universal Magazine" showing several stages in tobacco manufacture; (below right) evidence of English influence on Virginian tastes in portraiture is revealed in this painting of a lady of the Howard family

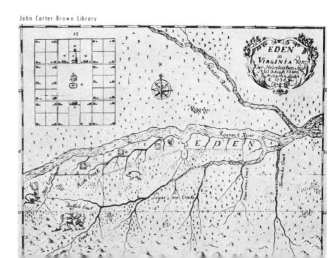

(Top left) Rev. James Blair, founder of the College of William and Mary; (top right) "Bodleian Plate" depicting William and Mary, second oldest college in America; (center left) portrait of Anne Byrd; (center right) the manners and wealth of tidewater aristocrats are shown in this anonymous painting of a man and a child drinking tea; (right) William Byrd hoped to induce people to settle on his property with advertisements for "Eden in Virginia"

Baltimore, pictured here in 1752, had grown little since its founding in 1729, because most planters shipped tobacco from their own wharves and did not need a central port

Cultural activity in Annapolis is represented by this drawing of the Grand Rehearsal of the Anniversary Ode of the Tuesday Club, 1746

Maryland

(Above) Benedict Leonard Calvert, governor, 1727-31; (below left) Charles Calvert, 3rd Lord Baltimore; (below) the second Charles Calvert, 5th Lord Baltimore

Maryland was generally well-governed under its proprietors, the Calvert family, but the colony was withheld from them by the crown from 1692 to 1715 until Benedict Calvert renounced Catholicism

Two paintings by Henrietta Johnston, a lady artist active in Charleston about 1711-29; (left) William Rhett, foe of pirates who preyed on Charleston's shipping; (right) Anne Broughton, a fashionable young lady

Carolina

(Above left) Gov. Sir Nathaniel Johnson (c. 1645-1713) attempted to introduce silk culture in South Carolina; (above right) interior of a water-powered mill for cleaning rice, an important South Carolina crop; (below) Charleston, South Carolina, was a busy port in 1739 involved in trade with the West Indies, with Indians to the west, and in exporting rice and indigo

1733

92.

Molasses Act

Theoretically, at least, the Crown had chartered the colonies in America for its economic benefit, but the Crown was sometimes inconsistent in carrying out this policy. The Molasses Act of 1733 was an example. Rum distilling was one of the leading New England industries; the molasses for the rum was imported from both the British and the French West Indies. The act was passed to protect the interests of English planters in the British sugar islands; but it had the effect of raising the price of molasses in New England, and thus of depressing the distilling business there. The practice of bribing customs officials to allow the import of cheaper French rum became common as a result, and the act thereby became ineffective. Had it been systematically enforced, New England's economy would have been crippled, and the system of trade that had evolved over the years would have been destroyed.

Source: Pickering, XVI, pp. 374-379.

An act for the better securing and encouraging the trade of His Majesty's sugar colonies in America.

Whereas the welfare and prosperity of Your Majesty's sugar colonies in America are of the greatest consequence and importance to the trade, navigation, and strength of this Kingdom: *And whereas* the planters of the said sugar colonies have of late years fallen under such great discouragements that they are unable to improve or carry on the sugar trade upon an equal footing with the foreign sugar colonies without some advantage and relief be given to them from Great Britain; for remedy whereof, and for the good and welfare of Your Majesty's subjects, we, Your Majesty's most dutiful and loyal subjects, the Commons of Great Britain, do most humbly beseech Your Majesty that it may be enacted . . . that from and after December 25, 1733, there shall be raised, levied, collected, and paid unto and for the use of His Majesty, His Heirs, and Successors upon all rum or spirits of the produce or manufacture of any of the colonies or plantations in America, not in the possession or under the dominion of His

Majesty . . . which at any time or times within or during the continuance of this act shall be imported or brought into any of the colonies or plantations in America . . . the sum of 9*d.*, money of Great Britain, to be paid according to the proportion and value of 5*s.* 6*d.* the ounce in silver for every gallon thereof, and after that rate for any greater or lesser quantity; and upon all molasses or syrups of such foreign produce or manufacture as aforesaid, which shall be imported or brought into any of the said colonies or plantations of or belonging to His Majesty, the sum of 6*d.* of like money for every gallon thereof . . . and upon all sugars and panelas [brown sugar] of such foreign growth, produce, or manufacture as aforesaid, which shall be imported into any of the said colonies or plantations of or belonging to His Majesty, a duty after the rate of 5*s.* of like money for every hundredweight avoirdupois. . . .

II. *It is hereby further enacted* . . . that all and every the said duties hereby imposed . . . shall be paid down in ready money by the importers thereof before the landing of the same, respectively.

III. *And be it further enacted* that, in case any of the said commodities shall be landed or put on shore in any of His Majesty's said colonies or plantations in America, out of any ship or vessel, before due entry be made thereof at the port or place where the same shall be imported, and before the duties . . . shall be duly paid, or without a warrant for the landing and delivering the same, first signed by the collector or impost officer . . . all such goods . . . shall be forfeited and . . . may be seized by the governor or commander in chief, for the time being, of the colonies or plantations where the same shall be so landed. . . . And all and every such offense and forfeitures shall and may be prosecuted for and recovered in any Court of Admiralty in His Majesty's colonies or plantations in America . . . or in any court of record in the said colonies or

plantations where such offense is committed. . . .

V. *And it is hereby further enacted* . . . that if any person or persons shall be aiding and assisting in bringing on shore or landing any such sugar, panelas, syrups, or molasses, rum, or spirits into . . . any of His Majesty's colonies or plantations in America, contrary to the true intent and meaning of this act, or shall receive into his, her, or their house or custody any of the commodities aforementioned, knowing the same to be imported or landed . . . contrary to this act, every such person so offending shall forfeit treble the value of such goods, to be estimated and computed according to the best price that each respective commodity bears at the place where any such seizures shall be made. . . .

VII. *And it is hereby further enacted* . . . that if any of His Majesty's subjects who is or shall be master, or have the charge of any ship or vessel, shall . . . permit . . . syrups or molasses, rum or spirits . . . brought on shore and landed in any of His Majesty's plantations in America . . . every such master or other person so offending shall forfeit and pay the sum of £100. . . .

IX. *And it is hereby further enacted* . . . that in case any sugar or panelas of the growth, produce, or manufacture of any of the colonies or plantations belonging to or in the possession of His Majesty . . . which shall have been imported into Great Britain after June 24, 1733, shall at any time within one year after the importation thereof be again exported out of Great Britain and that due proof be first made by certificate from the proper officers of the due entry and payment of the subsidies or duties charged or payable upon the importation thereof, together with the oath of the merchant, or his agent, importing and exporting the same, or in case such merchant or agent shall be one of the people called Quakers by his solemn affirmation to the truth thereof, and that all other requisites shall be performed that are by law to be performed in cases where any of the said subsidies or duties are to be paid by any former statute, all the residue and remainder of the subsidy or duty, by any former act or acts of Parliament granted and charged on such sugar or panelas as aforesaid, shall without any delay or reward be repaid to such merchant or merchants, who do export the same, within one month after demand thereof.

X. *And it is hereby further enacted . . .* that from and after June 24, 1733, for every hundredweight of sugar refined in Great Britain . . . which shall be exported out of this Kingdom, there shall be, by virtue of this act, repaid at the customhouse to the exporter, within one month after the demand thereof, over and above the several sums of 3s. and 1s. per hundred, payable by two former acts of Parliament . . . the fur-

ther sum of 2s., oath or solemn affirmation as aforesaid being first made by the refiner that the said sugar so exported was produced from brown and muscovado sugar, and that, as he verily believes, the same was imported from some of the colonies or plantations in America belonging to and in the possession of the Crown of Great Britain, and that, as he verily believes, the duty of the said . . . sugar was duly paid at the time of the importation thereof, and that the same was duly exported. . . .

XIV. *And it is hereby declared and enacted* that this present act shall be taken to be a public act, of which all judges and justices shall take notice. . . . And the same shall continue and be in force for the space of five years, to be computed from June 24, 1733, and to the end of the then next session of Parliament.

1735

93.

JAMES ALEXANDER: The Trial of John Peter Zenger

John Peter Zenger, printer and publisher of the New York Weekly Journal, *was arrested in 1734 for printing articles critical of the New York colonial governor, and charged with seditious libel. His trial, which became a* cause célèbre, *turned on the issue of whether the liberties of the colonists were in accord with those of citizens in England. James Alexander served as Zenger's counsel before being declared in contempt of court and struck from the roster of attorneys. Alexander's successor, Andrew Hamilton, argued the famous legal doctrine that "the truth is a defense against libel" — that is, a statement, even if defamatory, is not libelous if it is proved to be true — and thereby not only won Zenger's acquittal but helped establish an important precedent in common law. The case is a landmark in the history of freedom of speech and of the press in America, and it gave impetus to the voicing of grievances against the Crown in subsequent years; it was cited, for example, by those who protested in 1765 against the Stamp Act, which, it was charged, restricted the freedom of the press by requiring that government stamps be placed on all newspapers. Alexander wrote an account of the trial, from which the following selection, focusing on Hamilton's arguments for the defense, is taken.*

Source: *A Brief Narrative of the Case and Trial of John Peter Zenger, Printer of the New York Weekly Journal,* Stanley N. Katz, ed., Cambridge, 1963, pp. 58-101.

MR. ATTORNEY GENERAL opened the information, which was as follows:

Mr. Attorney. May it please Your Honors, and you, gentlemen of the jury; the information now before the Court, and to which the Defendant Zenger has pleaded *not guilty,* is an information for printing and publishing *a false, scandalous, and seditious libel,* in which His Excellency the Governor of this Province, who is the King's immediate representative here, is greatly and unjustly scandalized as a person that has no regard to law nor justice; with much more, as will appear upon reading the information. This of libeling is what has always been discouraged as a thing that tends to create differences among men, ill blood among the people, and oftentimes great bloodshed between the party libeling and the party libeled. There can be no doubt but you gentlemen of the jury will have the same ill opinion of such practices as the judges have always shown upon such occasions. But I shall say no more at this time until you hear the information, which is as follows:

New York, Supreme Court.

Of the term of January, in the eighth year of the reign of Our Sovereign Lord, King George II., etc.
New York, Ss. Be it remembered that Richard Bradley, Esq., Attorney General of Our Sovereign Lord the King, for the Province of New York, who for Our said Lord the King in this part prosecutes, in his own proper person comes here into the Court of Our said Lord the King, and for Our said Lord the King gives the Court here to understand and be informed that John Peter Zenger, late of the City of New York, printer (being a seditious person and a frequent printer and publisher of false news and seditious libels, and wickedly and maliciously devising the government of Our said Lord the King of this His Majesty's Province of New York under the administration of His Excellency William Cosby, Esq.; Captain General and Governor-in-Chief of the said Province, to traduce, scandalize and vilify, and His Excellency the said Governor and the ministers and officers of Our said Lord the King, of and for the said Province to bring into suspicion and the ill opinion of the subjects of Our said Lord the King residing within the said Province) the 28th day of January, in the seventh year of the reign of Our Sovereign Lord, George II, by the grace of God, of Great Britain, France and Ireland, King, Defender of the Faith, etc., at the City of New York, *did falsely, seditiously, and scandalously* print and publish, and cause to be printed and published, a certain *false, malicious, seditious, scandalous libel,* entitled *The New York Weekly Journal, containing the Freshest Advices, Foreign and Domestic;* in which libel (of and concerning His Excellency the said Governor, and the ministers

and officers of Our said Lord the King, **of** and for the said Province) among other things therein contained are these words:

Your appearance in print at last gives a pleasure to many, though most wish you had come fairly into the open field, and not appeared behind retrenchments made of the supposed laws against libeling and of what other men have said and done before; these retrenchments, gentlemen, may soon be shown to you and all men to be weak, and to have neither law nor reason for their foundation, so cannot long stand you in stead. Therefore, you had much better as yet leave them, and come to what the people of this City and Province (the City and Province of New York meaning) think are the points in question (to wit): They (the people of the City and Province of New York meaning) think as matters now stand that their *liberties* and *properties* are precarious, and that *slavery* is like to be entailed on them and their posterity if some past things be not amended, and this they collect from many past proceedings. (Meaning many of the past proceedings of His Excellency the said Governor, and of the ministers and officers of Our said Lord the King, of and for the said Province.)

And the said Attorney General of Our said Lord the King, for Our said Lord the King, likewise gives the Court here to understand and be informed that the said John Peter Zenger afterwards (to wit) the 8th day of April, in the seventh year of the reign of Our said Lord the King, at the City of New York aforesaid, did *falsely, seditiously, and scandalously* print and publish, and cause to be printed and published, another *false, malicious, seditious, and scandalous* libel entitled *The New York Weekly Journal, containing the Freshest Advices, Foreign and Domestic.* In which libel (of and concerning the government of the said Province of New York, and of and concerning His Excellency the said Governor and the ministers and officers of Our said Lord the King, of and for the said Province) among other things therein contained as these words:

One of our neighbors (one of the inhabitants of New Jersey meaning) being in company, observing the strangers (some of the inhabitants of New York meaning) full of complaints, endeavored to persuade them to remove into Jersey; to which it was replied, that would be leaping out of the frying pan into the fire, for, says he, we both are under the same governor (His Excellency the said Governor meaning) and your Assembly have shown with a witness what is to be expected from them; one that was then moving to Pennsylvania (meaning one that was then removing from New York with intent to reside at Pennsylvania), to which place it is reported several considerable men are removing (from New York meaning) expressed, in terms very moving, much concern for the circumstances of New York (the bad circumstances of the Province and people of New York meaning) seemed to think them very much owing to the influence that some men (whom he called tools) had in the administration (meaning the administration of government of the said Province of New York) said he was now going from them, and was not to be hurt by any measures they should take, but could not help having some concern for the welfare of his countrymen, and should be glad to hear that the Assembly (meaning the General Assembly of the Province of New York) would exert themselves as became them by showing that they have the interest of their country more at heart than the gratification of any private view of any of their members, or being at all affected by the smiles or frowns of a governor (His Excellency the said Governor meaning), both which ought equally to be despised when the interest of their country is at stake. You, says he, complain of the lawyers, but I think the law itself is at an end; WE (the people of the Province of New York meaning) SEE MEN'S DEEDS DESTROYED, JUDGES ARBITRARILY DISPLACED, NEW COURTS ERECTED WITHOUT CONSENT OF THE LEGISLATURE (Within the Province of New York meaning) BY WHICH, IT SEEMS TO ME, TRIALS BY JURIES ARE TAKEN AWAY WHEN A GOVERNOR PLEASES (His Excellency the said Governor meaning), MEN OF KNOWN ESTATES DENIED THEIR VOTES CONTRARY TO THE RECEIVED PRACTICE, THE BEST EXPOSITOR OF ANY LAW. Who is then in that Province

(meaning the Province of New York) that call (can call meaning) anything his own, or enjoy any libery (liberty meaning) longer than those in the administration (meaning the administration of government of the said Province of New York) will condescend to let them do it, for which reason I have left it (the Province of New York meaning), as I believe more will.

To the great disturbance of the peace of the said Province of New York, to the great scandal of Our said Lord the King, of His Excellency the said Governor, and of all others concerned in the administration of the government of the said Province, and against the peace of Our Sovereign Lord the King, his crown, and dignity, etc. Whereupon the said Attorney General of Our said Lord the King, for Our said Lord the King, prays the advisement of the Court here, in the premises, and the due process of the law, against him, the said John Peter Zenger, in this part to be done, to answer to Our said Lord the King of and in the premises, etc.

R. Bradley, Attorney General.

To this information the Defendant has pleaded *not guilty,* and we are ready to prove it.

[Mr. Chambers has not been pleased to favor me with his notes, so I cannot, for fear of doing him injustice, pretend to set down his arguments; but here Mr. Chambers set forth very clearly the nature of a libel, the great allowances that ought to be made for what men speak or write, that in all libels there must be some particular persons so clearly pointed out that no doubt must remain about who is meant; that he was in hopes Mr. Attorney would fail in his proof as to this point; and therefore he desired that he would go on to examine his witnesses.]

Then Mr. Hamilton, who at the request of some of my friends was so kind as to come from Philadelphia to assist me on the trial, spoke.

Mr. Hamilton. May it please Your Honor; I am concerned in this cause on the part of Mr. Zenger, the Defendant. The information against my client was sent me a few days before I left home, with some instructions to let me know how far I might rely upon the truth of those parts of the papers set forth in the information and which are said to be libelous. And though I am perfectly of the opinion with the gentleman who has just now spoken on the same side with me as to the common course of proceedings, I mean in putting Mr. Attorney upon proving that my client printed and published those papers mentioned in the information. Yet I cannot think it proper for me (without doing violence to my own principles) to deny the publication of a complaint which I think is the right of every freeborn subject to make when the matters so published can be supported with truth; and therefore I'll save Mr. Attorney the trouble of examining his witnesses to that point; and I do (for my client) confess that he both printed and published the two newspapers set forth in the information, and I hope in so doing *he* has committed no crime.

Mr. Attorney. Then if Your Honor pleases, since Mr. Hamilton has confessed the fact, I think our witnesses may be discharged; we have no further occasion for them.

Mr. Hamilton. If you brought them here only to prove the printing and publishing of these newspapers, we have acknowledged that, and shall abide by it.

[Here my journeyman and two sons (with several others subpoenaed by Mr. Attorney to give evidence against me) were discharged, and there was silence in the Court for some time.]

Mr. Chief Justice. Well Mr. Attorney, will you proceed?

Mr. Attorney. Indeed sir, as Mr. Hamilton has confessed the printing and publishing these libels, I think the jury must find a verdict for the King; for supposing they were true, the law says that they are not the less libelous for that; nay, indeed the law says their being true is an aggravation of the crime.

Mr. Hamilton. Not so neither, Mr. Attorney, there are two words to that bargain. I hope it is not our bare printing and publishing a paper that will make it a libel. You will have something more to do before you make my client a libeler; for the words themselves must be libelous, that is, *false, scandalous, and seditious,* or else we are not guilty.

[As Mr. Attorney has not been pleased to favor us with his argument, which he read, or with the notes of it, we cannot take upon us to set down his words, but only to show the book cases he cited and the general scope of his argument which he drew from those authorities. He observed upon the excellency as well as the use of government, and the great regard and reverence which had been constantly paid to it, both under the law and the Gospel. That by government we were protected in our lives, religion, and properties; and that for these reasons great care had always been taken to prevent everything that might tend to scandalize magistrates and others concerned in the administration of the government, especially the supreme magistrate. And that there were many instances of very severe judgments, and of punishments inflicted upon such as had attempted to bring the government into contempt by publishing false and scurrilous libels against it, or by speaking evil and scandalous words of men in authority; to the great disturbance of the public peace.

And to support this, he cited 5 Coke 121 (suppose it should be 125), Wood's Instit. 430, 2 Lilly 168, 1 Hawkins 73.11.6. From these books he insisted that a libel was a malicious defamation of any person, expressed either in printing or writing, signs or pictures, to asperse the reputation of one that is alive or the memory of one that is dead; if he is a private man, the libeler deserves a severe punishment, but if it is against a magistrate or other public person, it is a greater offense; for this concerns not only the breach of the peace but the scandal of the government; for what greater scandal of government can there be than to have corrupt or wicked magistrates to be appointed by the King to govern his subjects under him? And a greater imputation to the state cannot be than to suffer such corrupt men to sit in the sacred seat of justice, or to have any meddling in or concerning the administration of justice.

And from the same books Mr. Attorney insisted that whether the person defamed is a private man or a magistrate, whether living or dead, whether the libel is true or false, or if the party against whom it is made is of good or evil fame, it is nevertheless a libel: For in a settled state of government the party aggrieved ought to complain for every injury done him in the ordinary course of the law. And as to its publication, the law had taken so great care of men's reputations that if one maliciously repeats it, or sings it in the presence of another, or delivers the libel or a copy of it over to scandalize the party, he is to be punished as a publisher of a libel. He said it was likewise evident that libeling was an offense against the law of God (Acts 23:5): "Then said Paul, I wist not brethren, that he was the High Priest: For it is written, thou shalt not speak evil of the ruler of the People"; (II Pet. 2:10): "Despise government, presumptuous are they, self-willed, they are not afraid to speak evil of dignitaries," etc.

He then insisted that it was clear, both by the law of God and man, that it was a very great offense to speak evil of or to revile those in authority over us; and that Mr. Zenger had offended in a most notorious and gross manner in scandalizing His Excellency our Governor, who is the King's immediate representative and the supreme magistrate of this province; for can there be anything more scandalous said of a governor than what is published in those papers? Nay, not only the Governor, but both the Council and Assembly are scandalized; for there it is plainly said that as matters now stand, their liberties and properties are precarious, and that slavery is like to be entailed on them and their posterity.

And then again Mr. Zenger says the Assembly ought to despise the smiles or frowns of a governor; that he thinks the law is at an end; that we see men's deeds destroyed, judges arbitrarily displaced, new courts erected without consent of the legislature; and that it seems trials by juries are

taken away when a governor pleases; that none can call anything their own longer than those in the administration will condescend to let them do it. And Mr. Attorney added that he did not know what could be said in defense of a man that had so notoriously scandalized the Governor and principal magistrates and officers of the government by charging them with depriving the people of their rights and liberties, and taking away trials by juries, and, in short, putting an end to the law itself.

If this was not a libel, he said, he did not know what was one. Such persons as will take those liberties with governors and magistrates he thought ought to suffer for stirring up sedition and discontent among the people. And concluded by saying that the government had been very much traduced and exposed by Mr. Zenger before he was taken notice of; that at last it was the opinion of the Governor and Council that he ought not to be suffered to go on to disturb the peace of the government by publishing such libels against the Governor and the chief persons in the government; and therefore they had directed this prosecution to put a stop to this scandalous and wicked practice of libeling and defaming His Majesty's government and disturbing His Majesty's peace.

Mr. Chambers then summed up to the jury, observing with great strength of reason on Mr. Attorney's defect of proof that the papers in the information were *false, malicious, or seditious,* which was incumbent on him to prove to the jury, and without which they could not on their oaths say that they were so, as charged.]

Mr. Hamilton. May it please Your Honor; I agree with Mr. Attorney that government is a sacred thing, but I differ very widely from him when he would insinuate that the just complaints of a number of men who suffer under a bad administration is libeling that administration. Had I believed that to be the law, I should not have given the Court the trouble of hearing anything that I should say in this cause. I own when I read the information I had not the art to find out (without the help of Mr. Attorney's innuendoes) that the Governor was the person meant in every period of that newspaper; and I was inclined to believe that they were written by some who from an extraordinary zeal for liberty had misconstrued the conduct of some persons in authority into crimes; and that Mr. Attorney out of his too great zeal for power had exhibited this information to correct the indiscretion of my client; and at the same time to show his superiors the great concern he had lest they should be treated with any undue freedom. But from what Mr. Attorney has just now said, to wit, that this prosecution was directed by the Governor and Council, and from the extraordinary appearance of people of all conditions which I observe in Court upon this occasion, I have reason to think that those in the administration have by this prosecution something more in view, and that the people believe they have a good deal more at stake, than I apprehended. And, therefore, as it is become my duty to be both plain and particular in this cause, I beg leave to bespeak the patience of the Court.

I was in hopes, as that terrible Court, where those dreadful judgments were given and that law established which Mr. Attorney has produced for authorities to support this cause, was long ago laid aside as the most dangerous court to the liberties of the people of England that ever was known in that kingdom; that Mr. Attorney knowing this would not have attempted to set up a Star Chamber here, nor to make their judgments a precedent to us; for it is well known that what would have been judged treason in those days for a man to speak, I think, has since not only been practised as lawful but the contrary doctrine has been held to be law.

In Brewster's case for printing that the subjects might defend their rights and liberties by arms, in case the King should go about to destroy them, he was told by the Chief Justice that it was a great mercy he was not proceeded against for his life; for that to say the King could be resisted by arms in any case whatsoever was express treason. And yet we see since that time Dr. Sacheverell was sentenced in the highest court in Great Britain for saying that such a resistance was not lawful. Besides, as times have made very great changes in the laws of England, so in my opinion there is good reason that places should do so too.

Is it not surprising to see a subject, upon his receiving a commission from the King to be a governor of a colony in America, immediately imagining himself to be vested with all the prerogatives belonging to the sacred person of his Prince? And which is yet more astonishing, to see that a people can be so wild as to allow of and acknowledge those prerogatives and exemptions, even to their own destruction? Is it so hard a matter to distinguish between the majesty of our Sovereign and the power of a governor of the plantations? Is not this making very free with our Prince, to apply that regard, obedience, and allegiance to a subject which is due only to our Sovereign? And yet in all the cases which Mr. Attorney has cited to show the duty and obedience we owe to the supreme magistrate, it is the King that is there meant and understood, though Mr. Attorney is pleased to urge them as authorities to prove the heinousness of Mr. Zenger's offense against the Governor of New York. The several plantations are compared to so many large corporations, and perhaps not improperly; and can anyone give an instance that the mayor or head of a corporation ever put in a claim to the sacred rights of majesty? Let us not (while we are pretending to pay a great regard to our Prince and his peace) make bold to transfer that allegiance to a subject which we owe to our King only.

What strange doctrine is it to press everything for law here which is so in England? I believe we should not think it a favor, at present at least, to establish this practice. In England so great a regard and reverence is had to the judges that if any man strikes another in Westminster Hall while the judges are sitting, he shall lose his right hand and forfeit his land and goods for so doing. And though the judges here claim all the powers and authorities within this government that a Court of King's Bench has in England, yet I believe Mr. Attorney will scarcely say that such a punishment could be legally inflicted on a man for committing such an offense in the presence of the judges sitting in any court within the Province of New York. The reason is obvious; a quarrel or riot in New York cannot possibly be attended with those dangerous consequences that it might in Westminster Hall; nor (I hope) will it be alleged that any misbehavior to a governor in the plantations will, or ought to be, judged of or punished as a like undutifulness would be to our Sovereign.

From all which, I hope Mr. Attorney will not think it proper to apply his law cases (to support the cause of his Governor) which have only been judged where the King's safety or honor was concerned. It will not be denied but that a freeholder in the Province of New York has as good a right to the sole and separate use of his lands as a freeholder in England, who has a right to bring an action of trespass against his neighbor for suffering his horse or cow to come and feed upon his land, or eat his corn, whether enclosed or not enclosed; and yet I believe it would be looked upon as a strange attempt for one man here to bring an action against another, whose cattle and horses feed upon his grounds not enclosed, or indeed for eating and treading down his corn, if that were not enclosed. Numberless are the instances of this kind that might be given to show that what is good law at one time and in one place is not so at another time and in another place; so that I think the law seems to expect that in these parts of the world men should take care, by a good fence, to preserve their property from the injury of unruly beasts. And perhaps there may be as good reason why men should take the same care to make an honest and upright conduct a fence and security against the injury of unruly tongues.

Mr. Attorney. I don't know what the gentleman means by comparing cases of freeholders in England with freeholders here. What has this case to do with actions of trespass, or men's fencing their ground? The case before the Court is whether Mr. Zenger is guilty of libeling His Excellency the Governor of New York, and indeed the whole administration of the government. Mr. Hamilton has confessed the printing and publishing, and I think nothing is plainer than that the words in the information are *scandalous, and tend to sedition, and to disquiet the minds of the people of this Province.* And if such papers are not libels, I think it may be said there can be no such things as a libel.

Mr. Hamilton. May it please Your Honor; I cannot agree with Mr. Attorney; for though I freely acknowledge that there are such things as libels, yet I must insist at the same time that what my client is charged with is not a libel. And I observed just now that Mr. Attorney in defining a libel made use of the words "scandalous, seditious, and tend to disquiet the people"; but (whether with design or not I will not say) he omitted the word "false."

Mr. Attorney. I think I did not omit the word "false"; but it has been said already that it may be a libel notwithstanding it may be true.

Mr. Hamilton. In this I must still differ with Mr. Attorney; for I depend upon it, we are to be tried upon this information now before the Court and jury, and to which we have pleaded not guilty, and by it we are charged with printing and publishing a certain false, malicious, seditious and scandalous libel. This word "false" must have some meaning, or else how came it there? I hope Mr. Attorney will not say he put it there by chance, and I am of opinion his information would not be good without it. But to show that it is the principal thing which, in my opinion, makes a libel, I put the case, if the information had been for printing and publishing a certain *true* libel, would that be the same thing? Or could Mr. Attorney support such an information by any precedent in the English law? No, the falsehood makes the scandal, and both make the libel. And to show the Court that I am in good earnest and to save the Court's time and Mr. Attorney's trouble, I will agree that if he can prove the facts charged upon us to be *false*, I'll own them to be *scandalous, seditious* and *a libel*. So the work seems now to be pretty much shortened, and Mr. Attorney has now only to prove the words *false* in order to make us guilty.

Mr. Attorney. We have nothing to prove; you have confessed the printing and publishing; but if it was necessary (as I insist it is not) how can we prove a negative? But I hope some regard will be had to the authorities that have been produced, and that supposing all the words to be true, yet that will not help them, that Chief Justice Holt in his charge to the jury in the case of Tutchin made no distinction whether Tutchin's papers were true or false; and as Chief Justice Holt has made no distinction in that case, so none ought to be made here; nor can it be shown in all that case there was any question made about their being false or true.

Mr. Hamilton. I did expect to hear that a negative cannot be proved, but everybody knows there are many exceptions to that general rule; for if a man is charged with killing another, or stealing his neighbor's horse, if he is innocent in the one case, he may prove the man said to be killed to be really alive, and the horse said to be stolen, never to have been out of his master's stable, etc.; and this I think is proving a negative. But we will save Mr. Attorney the trouble of proving a negative, and take the

onus probandi [the burden of proof] upon ourselves and prove those very papers that are called libels to be *true.*

Mr. Chief Justice. You cannot be admitted, Mr. Hamilton, to give the truth of a libel in evidence. A libel is not to be justified; for it is nevertheless a libel that it is true.

Mr. Hamilton. I am sorry the Court has so soon resolved upon that piece of law; I expected first to have been heard to that point. I have not in all my reading met with an authority that says we cannot be admitted to give the truth in evidence upon an information for a libel.

Mr. Chief Justice. The law is clear, that you cannot justify a libel.

Mr. Hamilton. I own that, may it please Your Honor, to be so; but, with submission, I understand the word "justify" there to be a justification by plea, as it is in the case upon an indictment for murder, or an assault and battery; there the prisoner cannot justify, but plead not guilty. Yet it will not be denied but he may, and always is admitted, to give the truth of the fact or any other matter in evidence, which goes to his acquittal; as in murder, he may prove it was in defense of his life, his house, etc., and in assault and battery, he may give in evidence that the other party struck first, and in both cases he will be acquitted. And in this sense I understand the word "justify," when applied to the case before the Court.

Mr. Chief Justice. I pray show that you can give the truth of a libel in evidence.

Mr. Hamilton. I am ready, both from what I understand to be the authorities in the case and from the reason of the thing, to show that we may lawfully do so. But here I beg leave to observe that informations for libels is a child, if not born, yet nursed up and brought to full maturity in the Court of Star Chamber.

Mr. Chief Justice. Mr. Hamilton you'll find yourself mistaken; for in *Coke's Insti-*

tutes you'll find informations for libels long before the Court of Star Chamber.

Mr. Hamilton. I thank Your Honor; that is an authority I did propose to speak to by and by; but as you have mentioned it, I'll read that authority now. I think it is in 3 Coke under title "Libel"; it is the case of John de Northampton for a letter written to Robert de Ferrers, one of the King's Privy Council, concerning Sir William Scot, Chief Justice, and his fellows; but it does not appear to have been upon information; and I have good grounds to say it was upon indictment, as was the case of Adam de Ravensworth, just mentioned before by Lord Coke under the same title; and I think there cannot be a greater, at least a plainer, authority for us than the judgment in the case of John de Northampton, which My Lord has set down at large. *Et quia praedictus Johannes cognovit dictam litteram per se scriptam Roberto de Ferrers, qui est de Concilio Regis, qua littera continet in se nullam veritatem,* etc. [and since the aforementioned John admits writing the said letter to Robert de Ferrers of the King's Council, which letter contains no truth whatever].

Now, sir, by this judgment it appears the libelous words were utterly false, and there the falsehood was the crime and is the ground of that judgment. And is not that what we contend for? Do not we insist that the falsehood makes the scandal, and both make the libel? And how shall it be known whether the words are libelous, that is, true or false, but by admitting us to prove them true, since Mr. Attorney will not undertake to prove them false? Besides, is it not against common sense that a man should be punished in the same degree for a true libel (if any such thing could be) as for a false one? I know it is said that truth makes a libel the more provoking, and therefore the offense is the greater, and consequently the judgment should be the heavier. Well, suppose it were so, and let us agree for once that truth is a greater sin than falsehood;

yet as the offenses are not equal, and as the punishment is arbitrary, that is, according as the judges in their discretion shall direct to be inflicted, is it not absolutely necessary that they should know whether the libel is true or false, that they may by that means be able to proportion the punishment? For would it not be a sad case if the judges, for want of a due information, should chance to give as severe a judgment against a man for writing or publishing a lie as for writing or publishing a truth? And yet this (with submission), as monstrous and ridiculous as it may seem to be, is the natural consequence of Mr. Attorney's doctrine that truth makes a worse libel than falsehood, and must follow from his not proving our papers to be false, or not suffering us to prove them to be true.

But this is only reasoning upon the case, and I will now proceed to show what in my opinion will be sufficient to induce the Court to allow us to prove the truth of the words which in the information are called libelous. And first, I think there cannot be a greater authority for us than the judgment I just now mentioned in the case of John de Northampton, and that was in early times, and before the Star Chamber came to its fullness of power and wickedness. In that judgment, as I observed, the falsehood of the letter which was written is assigned as the very ground of the sentence. And agreeable to this it was urged by Sir Robert Sawyer, in the trial of the seven bishops, *that the falsity, the malice, and sedition of the writing were all facts to be proved.* But here it may be said Sir Robert was one of the bishops' counsel, and his árgument is not to be allowed for law; but I offer it only to show that we are not the first who have insisted that to make a writing a libel it must be false. And if the argument of a counsel must have no weight, I hope there will be more regard shown to the opinion of a judge, and therefore I mention the words of Justice Powell in the same trial, where he says (of the petition of the bishops, which was called a libel, and upon which they were prosecuted by information) that to make it a libel, it must be false and malicious and tend to sedition; and declared, as he saw no falsehood or malice in it, he was of opinion that it was no libel.

Now I should think this opinion alone, in the case of the King, and in a case which that King had so much at heart and which to this day has never been contradicted, might be a sufficient authority to entitle us to the liberty of proving the truth of the papers which in the information are called false, malicious, seditious, and scandalous. If it be objected that the opinions of the other three judges were against him, I answer that the censures the judgments of these men have undergone, and the approbation Justice Powell's opinion, his judgment and conduct upon that trial has met with, and the honor he gained to himself for daring to speak truth at such a time, upon such an occasion, and in the reign of such a King, is more than sufficient in my humble opinion to warrant our insisting on his judgment as a full authority to our purpose; and it will lie upon Mr. Attorney to show that this opinion has since that time been denied to be law, or that Justice Powell, who delivered it, has ever been condemned or blamed for it in any lawbook extant at this day, and this I will venture to say Mr. Attorney cannot do.

But to make this point yet more clear, if anything can be clearer, I will on our part proceed and show that in the case of Sir Samuel Barnardiston, his counsel, notwithstanding he stood before one of the greatest monsters that ever presided in an English court (Judge Jeffreys), insisted on the want of proof to the malice and seditious intent of the author of what was called a libel. And in the case of Tutchin, which seems to be Mr. Attorney's chief authority, that case is against him; for he was upon his trial put upon showing the truth of his papers, but did not; at least the prisoner was asked by the King's counsel whether he would say they were true? And as he never pretended that they were true, the Chief Justice was not to say so.

But the point will still be clearer on our side from Fuller's case, for falsely and wickedly causing to be printed a false and scandalous libel, in which (among other things) were contained these words, "Mr. Jones has also made oath that he paid £5,000 more by the late king's order to several persons in places of trust that they might complete my ruin and invalidate me forever. Nor is this all; for the same Mr. Jones will prove by undeniable witness and demonstration that he has distributed more than £180,000 in eight years last past by the French king's order to persons in public trust in this kingdom."

Here you see is a scandalous and infamous charge against the late king; here is a charge no less than high treason against the men in public trust for receiving money of the French king, then in actual war with the Crown of Great Britain; and yet the Court were far from bearing him down with that Star Chamber doctrine, to wit, that it was no matter whether what he said was true or false. No, on the contrary, Lord Chief Justice Holt asks Fuller, "Can you make it appear they are true? Have you any witnesses? You might have had subpoenas for your witnesses against this day. If you take upon you to write such things as you are charged with, it lies upon you to prove them true, at your peril. If you have any witnesses, I will hear them. How came you to write those books which are not true? If you have any witnesses, produce them. If you can offer any matter to prove what you have written, let us hear it." Thus said and thus did that great man, Lord Chief Justice Holt, upon a trial of the like kind with ours, and the rule laid down by him in this case, is that he who will take upon him to write things, it lies upon him to prove them at his peril. Now, sir, we have acknowledged the printing and publishing of those papers set forth in the information, and (with the leave of the Court) agreeable to the rule laid down by Chief Justice Holt, we are ready to prove them to be true, at our peril.

Mr. Chief Justice. Let me see the book.

[Here the Court had the case under consideration a considerable time, and everyone was silent.]

Mr. Chief Justice. Mr. Attorney, you have heard what Mr. Hamilton has said, and the cases he has cited, for having his witnesses examined to prove the truth of the several facts contained in the papers set forth in the information. What do you say to it?

Mr. Attorney. The law in my opinion is very clear; they cannot be admitted to justify a libel; for, by the authorities I have already read to the Court, it is not the less a libel because it is true. I think I need not trouble the Court with reading the cases over again; the thing seems to be very plain, and I submit it to the Court.

Mr. Chief Justice. Mr. Hamilton, the Court is of opinion you ought not to be permitted to prove the facts in the papers. These are the words of the book, "It is far from being a justification of a libel that the contents thereof are true, or that the person upon whom it is made had a bad reputation, since the greater appearance there is of truth in any malicious invective, so much the more provoking it is."

Mr. Hamilton. These are Star Chamber cases, and I was in hopes that practice had been dead with the Court.

Mr. Chief Justice. Mr. Hamilton, the Court have delivered their opinion, and we expect you will use us with good manners; you are not to be permitted to argue against the opinion of the Court.

Mr. Hamilton. With submission, I have seen the practice in very great courts, and never heard it deemed unmannerly to —

Mr. Chief Justice. After the Court have declared their opinion, it is not good man-

ners to insist upon a point in which you are overruled.

Mr. Hamilton. I will say no more at this time; the Court I see is against us in this point; and that I hope I may be allowed to say.

Mr. Chief Justice. Use the Court with good manners, and you shall be allowed all the liberty you can reasonably desire.

Mr. Hamilton. I thank Your Honor. Then, gentlemen of the jury, it is to you we must now appeal for witnesses to the truth of the facts we have offered and are denied the liberty to prove; and let it not seem strange that I apply myself to you in this manner — I am warranted so to do both by law and reason. The law supposes you to be summoned out of the neighborhood where the fact is alleged to be committed; and the reason of your being taken out of the neighborhood is because you are supposed to have the best knowledge of the fact that is to be tried. And were you to find a verdict against my client, you must take upon you to say the papers referred to in the information, and which we acknowledge we printed and published, are false, scandalous, and seditious; but of this I can have no apprehension. You are citizens of New York; you are really what the law supposes you to be, honest and lawful men; and, according to my brief, the facts which we offer to prove were not committed in a corner; they are notoriously known to be true; and therefore in your justice lies our safety.

And as we are denied the liberty of giving evidence to prove the truth of what we have published, I will beg leave to lay it down as a standing rule in such cases, that the suppressing of evidence ought always to be taken for the strongest evidence; and I hope it will have that weight with you. But since we are not admitted to examine our witnesses I will endeavor to shorten the dispute with Mr. Attorney, and to that end I desire he would favor us with some standard definition of a libel, by which it may

Numb. XLVII.

THE

New - York Weekly JOURNAL.

Containing the freſheſt Advices, Foreign, and Domeſtick.

MUNDAY September 23d, 1734.

ond Continuation of the Letter from
ddletown.

Ray (ſays the Councellor very
gravely) if a Nullity of Laws is
to be inferred from the Governours voting in Council,
what will become of the Sup-
Government? Our Governours
) have always done ſo, and believe
ſo in the Neighbouring Govern-
of *York* and *Penſilvania,* &c. and I
heard that the Councils (whoſe Buſi-
it was) either there or here, ever op-
d the Governour's Sitting and Acting
Council: And, Sir, do you conſider
e dangerous Conſequence of a Nullity of

ments of his Oppreſſion; upon which he
was recalled. Look a little farther, and
under the Adminiſtration of General *Hunter* (who was a Man as tenacious of Power
and knew as well how to uſe it as moſt Men)
you will find the Aſſembly ſending their
Bills up to the Council, and in particular
to the Preſident of the Council; all this he
admitted, and never once attempted to dif-
poſſeſs the Meſſengers that brought them,
on the Pretence that they ought to have
been delivered to him: If he had; That
Aſſembly conſiſting of Members who had
no private left Handed Views, were not ſo
weak and low Spirited as to ſuffer ſuch an
Attempt to paſs without Remarking, in a
Manner ſuitable to the Violence of ſuch

(Above) Library of Congress; (left) Historical Society of Pennsylvania

(Above) Page from the newspaper printed by Zenger;
(left) Andrew Hamilton, counsel for Zenger, portrait
copied from an original by an unknown artist

be certainly known whether a writing be a libel, yea or not.

Mr. Attorney. The books, I think, have given a very full definition of a libel; they say it is in a strict sense taken for a malicious defamation, expressed either in printing or writing, and tending either to blacken the memory of one who is dead, or the reputation of one who is alive, and to expose him to public hatred, contempt, or ridicule.

2. But it is said that in a larger sense the notion of a libel may be applied to any defamation whatsoever, expressed either by signs or pictures, as by fixing up a gallows against a man's door, or by painting him in a shameful and ignominious manner.

3. And since the chief cause for which the law so severely punishes all offenses of this nature is the direct tendency of them to a breach of public peace by provoking the parties injured, their friends and families, to acts of revenge, which it would be impossible to restrain by the severest laws, were there no redress from public justice for injuries of this kind, which of all others are most sensibly felt; and since the plain meaning of such scandal as is expressed by signs or pictures is as obvious to common sense, and as easily understood by every common capacity, and altogether as provoking, as that which is expressed by writing or printing, why should it not be equally criminal?

4. And from the same ground it seems also clearly to follow that such scandal as is expressed in a scoffing and ironical manner makes a writing as properly a libel as that which is expressed in direct terms; as where a writing, in a taunting manner reckoning up several acts of public charity done by one, says you will not play the Jew, nor the hypocrite, and so goes on in a strain of ridicule to insinuate that what he did was owing to his vainglory; or where a writing, pretending to recommend to one the characters of several great men for his imitation, instead of taking notice of what they are generally esteemed famous for, pitched on such qualities only which their enemies charge them with the want of, as by proposing such a one to be imitated for his courage who is known to be a great statesman but no soldier, and another to be imi-

tated for his learning who is known to be a great general but no scholar, etc., which kind of writing is as well understood to mean only to upbraid the parties with the want of these qualities as if it had directly and expressly done so.

Mr. Hamilton. Ay, Mr. Attorney; but what certain standard rule have the books laid down by which we can certainly know whether the words or the signs are malicious? Whether they are defamatory? Whether they tend to the breach of the peace, and are a sufficient ground to provoke a man, his family, or friends to acts of revenge, especially those of the ironical sort of words? And what rule have you to know when I write ironically? I think it would be hard, when I say such a man is a very worthy honest gentleman, and of fine understanding, that therefore I meant he was a knave or a fool.

Mr. Attorney. I think the books are very full; it is said in 1 Hawkins p. 193, just now read, that such scandal as is expressed in a scoffing and ironical manner makes a writing as properly a libel as that which is expressed in direct terms; as where a writing, in a taunting manner says, reckoning up several acts of charity done by one, says, you will not play the Jew or the hypocrite, and so goes on to insinuate that what he did was owing to his vainglory, etc. Which kind of writing is as well understood to mean only to upbraid the parties with the want of these qualities, as if it had directly and expressly done so. I think nothing can be plainer or more full than these words.

Mr. Hamilton. I agree the words are very plain, and I shall not scruple to allow (when we are agreed that the words are false and scandalous, and were spoken in an ironical and scoffing manner, etc.) that they are really libelous; but here still occurs the uncertainty which makes the difficulty to know what words are scandalous and what not; for you say they may be scandalous, true or false. Besides, how shall we know

whether the words were spoken in a scoffing and ironical manner, or seriously? Or how can you know whether the man did not think as he wrote? For by your rule, if he did, it is no irony, and consequently no libel. But under favor, Mr. Attorney, I think the same book and the same section will show us the only rule by which all these things are to be known. The words are these: which kind of writing is as well *understood* to mean only to upbraid the parties with the want of these qualities, as if they had directly and expressly done so. Here it is plain the words are scandalous, scoffing, and ironical only as they are *understood*. I know no rule laid down in the books but this, I mean, as the words are *understood*.

Mr. Chief Justice. Mr. Hamilton, do you think it so hard to know when words are ironical, or spoke in a scoffing manner?

Mr. Hamilton. I own it may be known; but I insist the only rule to know is, as I do or can *understand* them; I have no other rule to go by, but as I *understand* them.

Mr. Chief Justice. That is certain. All words are libelous or not, as they are understood. Those who are to judge of the words must judge whether they are scandalous or ironical, tend to the breach of the peace, or are seditious; there can be no doubt of it.

Mr. Hamilton. I thank Your Honor; I am glad to find the Court of this opinion. Then it follows that those twelve men must understand the words in the information to be scandalous, that is to say false; for I think it is not pretended they are of the ironical sort; and when they understand the words to be so, they will say we are guilty of publishing a false libel, and not otherwise.

Mr. Chief Justice. No, Mr. Hamilton; the jury may find that Zenger printed and published those papers, and leave it to the Court to judge whether they are libelous. You know this is very common; it is in the nature of a special verdict, where the jury leave the matter of law to the Court.

Mr. Hamilton. I know, may it please Your Honor, the jury may do so; but I do likewise know they may do otherwise. I know they have the right beyond all dispute to determine both the law and the fact, and where they do not doubt of the law, they ought to do so. This of leaving it to the judgment of the Court, whether the words are libelous or not, in effect renders juries useless (to say no worse) in many cases; but this I shall have occasion to speak to by and by. And I will with the Court's leave proceed to examine the inconveniencies that must inevitably arise from the doctrines Mr. Attorney has laid down; and I observe, in support of this prosecution, he has frequently repeated the words taken from the case of *Libely Famosis* in 5 Coke.

This is indeed the leading case, and to which almost all the other cases upon the subject of libels do refer; and I must insist upon saying that according as this case seems to be understood by the Court and Mr. Attorney, it is not law at this day; for though I own it to be base and unworthy to scandalize any man, yet I think it is even villainous to scandalize a person of public character, and I will go so far into Mr. Attorney's doctrine as to agree that if the faults, mistakes, nay, even the vices, of such a person be private and personal, and don't affect the peace of the public or the liberty or property of our neighbor, it is unmanly and unmannerly to expose them either by word or writing. But when a ruler of a people brings his personal failings, but much more his vices, into his administration, and the people find themselves affected by them, either in their liberties or properties, that will alter the case mightily, and all the high things that are said in favor of rulers, and of dignities, and upon the side of power, will not be able to stop people's mouths when they feel themselves oppressed — I mean in a free government.

It is true in time past it was a crime to speak truth, and in that terrible Court of Star Chamber many worthy and brave men suffered for so doing; and yet even in that Court and in those bad times, a great and good man dared say what I hope will not be taken amiss of me to say in this place, to wit; "The practice of informations for libels is a sword in the hands of a wicked king and an arrant coward to cut down and destroy the innocent; the one cannot because of his high station, and the other dares not because of his want of courage, revenge himself in another manner."

Mr. Attorney. Pray, Mr. Hamilton, have a care what you say; don't go too far neither; I don't like those liberties.

Mr. Hamilton. Sure, Mr. Attorney, you won't make any applications; all men agree that we are governed by the best of kings, and I cannot see the meaning of Mr. Attorney's caution. My well-known principles, and the sense I have of the blessings we enjoy under His present Majesty, makes it impossible for me to err, and I hope, even to be suspected, in that point of duty to my King. May it please Your Honor, I was saying, notwithstanding all the duty and reverence claimed by Mr. Attorney to men in authority, they are not exempt from observing the rules of common justice, either in their private or public capacities; the laws of our mother country know no exemption.

It is true, men in power are harder to be come at for wrongs they do either to a private person or to the public; especially a governor in the plantations, where they insist upon an exemption from answering complaints of any kind in their own government. We are indeed told and it is true they are obliged to answer a suit in the King's Courts at Westminster for a wrong done to any person here. But do we not know how impracticable this is to most men among us, to leave their families (who depend upon their labor and care for their livelihood) and carry evidences to Britain, and at a great, nay, a far greater expense than almost any of us are able to bear, only to prosecute a governor for an injury done here? But, when the oppression is general, there is no remedy even that way.

No, our constitution has (blessed be God) given us an opportunity, if not to have such wrongs redressed, yet by our prudence and resolution we may in a great measure prevent the committing of such wrongs by making a governor sensible that it is his interest to be just to those under his care; for such is the sense that men in general (I mean freemen) have of common justice that when they come to know that a chief magistrate abuses the power with which he is trusted for the good of the people, and is attempting to turn that very power against the innocent, whether of high or low degree, I say mankind in general seldom fail to interpose, and as far as they can, prevent the destruction of their fellow subjects. And has it not often been seen (and I hope it will always be seen) that when the representatives of a free people are by just representations or remonstrances made sensible of the sufferings of their fellow subjects by the abuse of power in the hands of a governor, they have declared (and loudly too) that they were not obliged by any law to support a governor who goes about to destroy a province or colony, or their privileges, which by His Majesty he was appointed, and by the law he is bound to protect and encourage?

But I pray it may be considered of what use is this mighty privilege if every man that suffers must be silent? And if a man must be taken up as a libeler for telling his sufferings to his neighbor? I know it may be answered, Have you not a legislature? Have you not a House of Representatives to whom you may complain? And to this I answer, we have. But what then? Is an Assembly to be troubled with every injury done by a governor? Or are they to hear of nothing but what those in the administra-

tion will please to tell them? Or what sort of a trial must a man have? And how is he to be remedied; especially if the case were, as I have known it to happen in America in my time, that a governor who has places (I will not say pensions, for I believe they seldom give that to another which they can take to themselves) to bestow, and can or will keep the same Assembly (after he has modeled them so as to get a majority of the House in his interest) for near twice seven years together? I pray, what redress is to be expected for an honest man who makes his complaint against a governor to an Assembly who may properly enough be said to be made by the same governor against whom the complaint is made? The thing answers itself.

No, it is natural, it is a privilege, I will go farther, it is a right which all freemen claim, and are entitled to complain when they are hurt; they have a right publicly to remonstrate the abuses of power in the strongest terms, to put their neighbors upon their guard against the craft or open violence of men in authority, and to assert with courage the sense they have of the blessings of liberty, the value they put upon it, and their resolution at all hazards to preserve it as one of the greatest blessings heaven can bestow. And when a House of Assembly composed of honest freemen sees the general bent of the people's inclinations, that is it which must and will (I'm sure it ought to) weigh with a legislature, in spite of all the craft, caressing, and cajoling made use of by a governor to divert them from hearkening to the voice of their country. As we all very well understand the true reason why gentlemen take so much pains and make such great interest to be appointed governors, so is the design of their appointment not less manifest.

We know His Majesty's gracious intentions to his subjects. He desires no more than that his people in the plantations should be kept up to their duty and allegiance to the Crown of Great Britain; that peace may be preserved among them, and justice impartially administered; that we may be governed so as to render us useful to our mother country, by encouraging us to make and raise such commodities as may be useful to Great Britain. But will anyone say that all or any of these good ends are to be effected by a governor's setting his people together by the ears, and by the assistance of one part of the people to plague and plunder the other? The commission which governors bear while they execute the powers given them according to the intent of the Royal Grantor expressed in their commissions, requires and deserves very great reverence and submission; but when a governor departs from the duty enjoined him by his Sovereign, and acts as if he was less accountable than the Royal Hand that gave him all that power and honor which he is possessed of, this sets people upon examining and inquiring into the power, authority, and duty of such a magistrate, and to compare those with his conduct; and just as far as they find he exceeds the bounds of his authority, or falls short in doing impartial justice to the people under his administration, so far they very often, in return, come short in their duty to such a governor.

For power alone will not make a man beloved, and I have heard it observed that the man who was neither good nor wise before his being made a governor, never mended upon his preferment, but has been generally observed to be worse. For men who are not endowed with wisdom and virtue can only be kept in bounds by the law; and by how much the further they think themselves out of the reach of the law, by so much the more wicked and cruel men are. I wish there were no instances of the kind at this day. And wherever this happens to be the case of a governor, unhappy are the people under his administration, and in the end he will find himself so

too; for the people will neither love him nor support him.

I make no doubt but there are those here who are zealously concerned for the success of this prosecution, and yet I hope they are not many, and even some of those I am persuaded (when they consider what lengths such prosecutions may be carried, and how deeply the liberties of the people may be affected by such means) will not all abide by their present sentiments. I say *not all*; for the man who from an intimacy and acquaintance with a governor has conceived a personal regard for him, the man who has felt none of the strokes of his power, the man who believes that a governor has a regard for him and confides in him, it is natural for such men to wish well to the affairs of such a governor; and as they may be men of honor and generosity, may, and no doubt will, wish him success, so far as the rights and privileges of their fellow citizens are not affected. But as men of honor I can apprehend nothing from them; they will never exceed that point. There are others that are under stronger obligations, and those are such as are in some sort engaged in support of a governor's cause by their own or their relations' dependence on his favor for some post or preferment; such men have what is commonly called duty and gratitude to influence their inclinations, and oblige them to go his lengths.

I know men's interests are very near to them, and they will do much rather than forgo the favor of a governor and a livelihood at the same time; but I can with very just grounds hope, even from those men, whom I will suppose to be men of honor and conscience too, that when they see the liberty of their country is in danger, either by their concurrence, or even by their silence, they will, like Englishmen, and like themselves, freely make a sacrifice of any preferment of favor rather than be accessory to destroying the liberties of their country and entailing slavery upon their posterity.

There are indeed another set of men of whom I have no hopes; I mean such who lay aside all other considerations, and are ready to join with power in any shapes and with any man or sort of men by whose means or interest they may be assisted to gratify their malice and envy against those whom they have been pleased to hate; and that for no other reason but because they are men of abilities and integrity, or at least are possessed of some valuable qualities far superior to their own. But as envy is the sin of the devil, and therefore very hard, if at all, to be repented of, I will believe there are but few of this detestable and worthless sort of men, nor will their opinions or inclinations have any influence upon this trial.

But to proceed. I beg leave to insist that the right of complaining or remonstrating is natural; and the restraint upon this natural right is the law only, and those restraints can only extend to what is false; for as it is truth alone which can excuse or justify any man for complaining of a bad administration, I as frankly agree that nothing ought to excuse a man who raises a false charge or accusation, even against a private person, and that no manner of allowance ought to be made to him who does so against a public magistrate. *Truth* ought to govern the whole affair of libels, and yet the party accused runs risk enough even then; for if he fails of proving every tittle of what he has written, and to the satisfaction of the Court and jury too, he may find to his cost that when the prosecution is set on foot by men in power, it seldom wants friends to favor it. And from thence (it is said) has arisen the great diversity of opinions among judges about what words were or were not scandalous or libelous.

I believe it will be granted that there is not greater uncertainty in any part of the law than about words of scandal; it would be misspending of the Court's time to mention the cases; they may be said to be numberless; and therefore the utmost care ought to be taken in following precedents; and the times when the judgments were given which are quoted for authorities in the case of libels are much to be regarded. I think it will be agreed that ever since the time of the Star Chamber, where the most arbitrary and destructive judgments and opinions were given that ever an Englishmen heard of, at least in his own country— I say prosecutions for libels since the time of that arbitrary Court, and until the Glorious Revolution, have generally been set on foot at the instance of the Crown or its ministers. And it is no small reproach to the law that these prosecutions were too often and too much countenanced by the judges, who held their places at pleasure (a disagreeable tenure to any officer, but a dangerous one in the case of a judge). To say more to this point may not be proper. And yet I cannot think it unwarrantable to show the unhappy influence that a sovereign has sometimes had, not only upon judges but even upon Parliaments themselves. It has already been shown how the judges differed in their opinions about the nature of a libel in the case of the seven bishops. . . .

If then, upon the whole, there is so great an uncertainty among judges (learned and great men) in matters of this kind; if power has had so great an influence on judges, how cautious ought we to be in determining by their judgments, especially in the plantations and in the case of libels? There is heresy in law as well as in religion, and both have changed very much. And we well know that it is not two centuries ago that a man would have been burned as a heretic for owning such opinions in matters of religion as are publicly written and printed at this day. They were fallible men, it seems, and we take the liberty not only to differ from them in religious opinions but to condemn them and their opinions too. And I must presume that in taking these freedoms in thinking and speaking about matters of faith or religion, we are in the right; for, though it is said there are very great liberties of this kind taken in New York, yet I have heard of no information preferred by Mr. Attorney for any offenses of this sort. From which I think it is pretty clear that in New York a man may make very free with his God, but he must take special care what he says of his governor.

It is agreed upon by all men that this is a reign of liberty, and while men keep within the bounds of truth, I hope they may with safety both speak and write their sentiments of the conduct of men in power. I mean of that part of their conduct only which affects the liberty or property of the people under their administration. Were this to be denied, then the next step may make them slaves; for what notions can be entertained of slavery beyond that of suffering the greatest injuries and oppressions without the liberty of complaining; or if they do, to be destroyed, body and estate, for so doing?

It is said and insisted on by Mr. Attorney that government is a sacred thing; that it is to be supported and reverenced; it is government that protects our persons and estates; that prevents treasons, murders, robberies, riots, and all the train of evils that overturns kingdoms and states and ruins particular persons; and if those in the administration, especially the supreme magistrate, must have all their conduct censured by private men, government cannot subsist. This is called a licentiousness not to be tolerated. It is said that it brings the rulers of the people into contempt, and their authority not to be regarded, and so in the end, the laws cannot be put in execution. These I say, and such as these, are the general topics insisted upon by men in power and their advocates. But I wish it might be considered at the same time how often it has happened that the abuse of power has been the primary cause of these evils, and that it was the injustice and oppression of these great men which has commonly brought them into contempt with the people. The

craft and art of such men is great, and who that is the least acquainted with history or law can be ignorant of the specious pretenses which have often been made use of by men in power to introduce arbitrary rule and destroy the liberties of a free people. . . .

If a libel is understood in the large and unlimited sense urged by Mr. Attorney, there is scarce a writing I know that may not be called a libel, or scarce any person safe from being called to an account as a libeler; for Moses, meek as he was, libeled Cain; and who is it that has not libeled the devil? For according to Mr. Attorney, it is no justification to say one has a bad name. Echard has libeled our good King William; Burnet has libeled among many others King Charles and King James; and Rapin has libeled them all. How must a man speak or write, or what must he hear, read, or sing? Or when must he laugh, so as to be secure from being taken up as a libeler?

I sincerely believe that were some persons to go through the streets of New York nowadays and read a part of the Bible, if it was not known to be such, Mr. Attorney, with the help of his innuendoes, would easily turn it into a libel. As for instance, Isa. 9:16; "The leaders of the people cause them to err, and they that are led by them are destroyed." But should Mr. Attorney go about to make this a libel, he would read it thus; "The leaders of the people" [innuendo, the Governor and Council of New York] "cause them" [innuendo, the people of this Province] "to err, and they" [the people of this Province meaning] "that are led by them" [the Governor and Council meaning] "are destroyed" [innuendo, are deceived into the loss of their liberty], which is the worst kind of destruction. Or if some persons should publicly repeat, in a manner not pleasing to his betters, the 10th and 11th verses of Chapter 56 of the same book, there Mr. Attorney would have a large field to display his skill in the artful application of his innuendoes. The words are; "His watchmen are all blind, they are ignorant, etc. Yea, they are greedy dogs, that can never have enough." But to make them a libel, there is, according to Mr. Attorney's doctrine, no more wanting but the aid of his skill in the right adapting his innuendoes. As for instance; "His watchmen" [innuendo, the Governor's Council and Assembly] "are all blind, they are ignorant" [innuendo, will not see the dangerous designs of His Excellency]. "Yea, they" [the Governor and Council meaning] "are greedy dogs, which can never have enough" [innuendo, enough of riches and power].

Such an instance as this is seems only fit to be laughed at; but I may appeal to Mr. Attorney himself whether these are not at least equally proper to be applied to His Excellency and his ministers as some of the inferences and innuendoes in his information against my client. Then if Mr. Attorney is at liberty to come into court, and file an information in the King's name without leave, who is secure whom he is pleased to prosecute as a libeler? And as the Crown law is contended for in bad times, there is no remedy for the greatest oppression of this sort, even though the party prosecuted is acquitted with honor. And give me leave to say as great men as any in Britain have boldly asserted that the mode of prosecuting by information (when a Grand Jury will not find *billa vera* [a true bill]) is a national grievance, and greatly inconsistent with that freedom which the subjects of England enjoy in most other cases. But if we are so unhappy as not to be able to ward off this stroke of power directly, yet let us take care not to be cheated out of our liberties by forms and appearances; let us always be sure that the charge in the information is made out clearly even beyond a doubt; for though matters in the information may be called form upon trial, yet they may be and often have been found to be matters of substance upon giving judgment.

Gentlemen, the danger is great in proportion to the mischief that may happen through our too great credulity. A proper confidence in a court is commendable; but as the verdict (whatever it is) will be yours, you ought to refer no part of your duty to the discretion of other persons. If you should be of opinion that there is no falsehood in Mr. Zenger's papers, you will, nay (pardon me for the expression), you ought to say so; because you don't know whether others (I mean the Court) may be of that opinion. It is your right to do so, and there is much depending upon your resolution as well as upon your integrity.

The loss of liberty to a generous mind is worse than death; and yet we know there have been those in all ages who for the sake of preferment or some imaginary honor have freely lent a helping hand to oppress, nay, to destroy their country. . . .

Power may justly be compared to a great river, while kept within its due bounds, is both beautiful and useful; but when it overflows its banks, it is then too impetuous to be stemmed, it bears down all before it and brings destruction and desolation wherever it comes. If then this is the nature of power, let us at least do our duty, and, like wise men (who value freedom), use our utmost care to support liberty, the only bulwark against lawless power, which in all ages has sacrificed to its wild lust and boundless ambition the blood of the best men that ever lived.

I hope to be pardoned, sir, for my zeal upon this occasion; it is an old and wise caution that when our neighbor's house is on fire, we ought to take care of our own. For though blessed be God, I live in a government where liberty is well understood and freely enjoyed; yet experience has shown us all (I'm sure it has to me) that a bad precedent in one government is soon set up for an authority in another; and therefore I cannot but think it mine and every honest man's duty that, while we pay all due obedience to men in authority, we ought at the same time to be upon our guard against power wherever we apprehend that it may affect ourselves or our fellow subjects.

I am truly very unequal to such an undertaking on many accounts. And you see I labor under the weight of many years, and am borne down with great infirmities of body; yet old and weak as I am, I should think it my duty, if required, to go to the utmost part of the land where my service could be of any use in assisting to quench the flame of prosecutions upon informations set on foot by the government to deprive a people of the right of remonstrating (and complaining too) of the arbitrary attempts of men in power — men who injure and oppress the people under their administration, provoke them to cry out and complain; and then make that very complaint the foundation for new oppressions and prosecutions. I wish I could say there were no instances of this kind.

But to conclude. The question before the Court and you gentlemen of the jury is not of small or private concern; it is not the cause of a poor printer, nor of New York alone, which you are now trying. No! It may in its consequence affect every freeman that lives under a British government on the main of America. It is the best cause. It is the cause of liberty; and I make no doubt but your upright conduct this day will not only entitle you to the love and esteem of your fellow citizens, but every man who prefers freedom to a life of slavery will bless and honor you as men who have baffled the attempt of tyranny; and by an impartial and uncorrupt verdict, have laid a noble foundation for securing to ourselves, our posterity, and our neighbors that to which nature and the laws of our country have given us a right — the liberty — both of exposing and opposing arbitrary power (in these parts of the world, at least) by speaking and writing truth.

[Here Mr. Attorney observed that Mr. Hamilton had gone very much out of the way. . . . All that the jury had to consider of was Mr. Zenger's printing and publishing two scandalous libels, which very highly reflected on His Excellency and the principal men concerned in the administration of this government, which is confessed — that is, the printing and publishing of the *Journals* set forth in the information is confessed. And concluded that as Mr. Hamilton had confessed the printing and there could be no doubt but they were scandalous papers, highly reflecting upon His Excellency and the principal magistrates in the Province; and therefore he made no doubt but the jury would find the Defendant guilty, and would refer to the Court for their direction.]

Mr. Chief Justice. Gentlemen of the jury, the great pains Mr. Hamilton has taken to show how little regard juries are to pay to the opinion of the judges, and his insisting so much upon the conduct of some judges in trials of this kind, is done no doubt with a design that you should take but very little notice of what I might say upon this occasion. I shall therefore only observe to you that as the facts or words in the information are confessed, the only thing that can come in question before you is whether the words as set forth in the information make a libel. And that is a matter of law, no doubt, and which you may leave to the Court. But I shall trouble you no further with anything more of my own, but read to you the words of a learned and upright judge in a case of the like nature.

To say that corrupt officers are appointed to administer affairs is certainly a reflection on the government. If people should not be called to account for possessing the people with an ill opinion of the government, no government can subsist, for it is very necessary for all governments that the people should have a good opinion of it. And nothing can be worse to any government than to endeavor to procure animosities; as to the management of it, this has been always looked upon as a crime, and no government can be safe without it be punished.

Now you are to consider whether these words I have read to you do not tend to beget an ill opinion of the administration of the government? To tell us that those that are employed know nothing of the matter, and those that do know are not employed? Men are not adapted to offices, but offices to men, out of a particular regard to their interest, and not to their fitness for the places; this is the purport of these papers.

Mr. Hamilton. I humbly beg Your Honor's pardon. I am very much misapprehended if you suppose what I said was so designed. Sir, you know, I made an apology for the freedom I found myself under a necessity of using upon this occasion. I said there was nothing personal designed; it arose from the nature of our defense.

The jury withdrew and in a small time returned. And being asked by the clerk whether they were agreed of their verdict, and whether John Peter Zenger was guilty of printing and publishing the libels in the information mentioned, they answered by Thomas Hunt, their foreman, NOT GUILTY; upon which there were three huzzas in the hall, which was crowded with people and the next day I was discharged from my imprisonment.

1740

94.

Civil Rights for Religious Minorities

Participation in the development of domestic industries and foreign trade had gained for the Jews of England sufficient power to obtain from King George II the following Act of 1740, conferring citizenship on Jews in the American colonies. The status of "natural-born subject" granted under the terms of the act entitled Protestants, Quakers, and Jews (but not Catholics) full rights of citizenship in the colonies, in order further to promote England's economic growth. The last provision of the act carefully limited such citizenship to Jews living in America, excluding them from similar privileges in Great Britain or Ireland.

Source: *Publications of the American Jewish Historical Society*, No. 1, 2nd edition, 1905, pp. 94-98.

An Act for naturalizing such foreign Protestants, and others therein mentioned, as are settled or shall settle in any of His Majesty's colonies in America.

Whereas the increase of people is a means of advancing the wealth and strength of any nation or country; *And whereas* many foreigners and strangers from the lenity of our government, the purity of our religion, the benefit of our laws, the advantages of our trade, and the security of our property might be induced to come and settle in some of His Majesty's colonies in America, if they were made partakers of the advantages and privileges which the natural-born subjects of this realm do enjoy; *Be it therefore enacted,* by the King's Most Excellent Majesty, by and with the advice and con-

sent of the Lords spiritual and temporal, and Commons, in this present Parliament assembled, and by the authority of the same, that from and after the 1st day of June in the year of Our Lord 1740, all persons born out of the legiance of His Majesty, His Heirs, or Successors, who have inhabited and resided, or shall inhabit or reside for the space of seven years or more in any of His Majesty's colonies in America, and shall not have been absent out of some of the said colonies for a longer space than two months at any one time during the said seven years, and shall take and subscribe the oaths, and make, repeat, and subscribe the declaration appointed by an act made in the first year of the reign of His late Majesty King George I, entitled "An Act for the further Security of His Majesty's Person and Government, and the Succession of the Crown in the Heirs of the late Princess Sophia, being Protestants"; and for extinguishing the hopes of the pretended Prince of Wales, his open and secret abettors; or, being of the people called Quakers, shall make and subscribe the declaration of fidelity, and take and affirm the effect of the abjuration oath, appointed and prescribed by an act made in the eighth year of the reign of His said late Majesty, entitled "An Act for granting the People called Quakers such Forms of Affirmation or Declaration, as may remove the Difficulties which many of them lie under"; and also make and subscribe the profession of his Christian belief, appointed and subscribed by an act made in the first year of the reign of Their late Majesties, King William and Queen Mary, entitled "An Act for exempting Their Majesties' Protestant Subjects, from the Penalties of certain Laws"; before the chief judge, or other judge of the colony wherein such persons respectively have so inhabited and resided, or shall so inhabit and reside, shall be deemed, adjudged, and taken to be His Majesty's natural-born subjects of this Kingdom, to all intents, constructions, and purposes, as if they and every of them had been or were born within this Kingdom.

Which said oath or affirmation and subscription of the said declarations respectively, the chief judge or other judge of every of the said colonies is hereby enabled and empowered to administer and take; and the taking and subscribing of every such oath or affirmation, and the making, repeating, and subscribing of every such declaration shall be before such chief judge or other judge, in open court, between the hours of nine and twelve in the forenoon; and shall be entered in the same court, and also in the secretary's office of the colony wherein such person shall so inhabit and reside; and every chief judge or other judges of every respective colony before whom such oaths or affirmation shall be taken and every such declaration shall be made, repeated, and subscribed as aforesaid, is hereby required to make a due and proper entry thereof in a book to be kept for that purpose in the said court; for the doing whereof 2s. and no more shall be paid at each respective place, under the penalty and forfeiture of £10 of lawful money of Great Britain. . . .

And in like manner every secretary of the colony wherein any person shall so take the said oaths or affirmation, and make, repeat, and subscribe the said declarations respectively, as aforesaid, is hereby required to make a due and proper entry thereof in a book to be kept for that purpose in his office, upon notification thereof to him by the chief judge or other judges of the same colony, under the like penalty and forfeiture for every such neglect or omission.

II. *Provided always and be it enacted,* by the authority aforesaid, that no person, of what quality, condition, or place soever, other than and except such of the people called Quakers as shall qualify themselves and be naturalized by the ways and means hereinbefore mentioned, or such who profess the Jewish religion, shall be naturalized by virtue of this act, unless such persons shall have received the sacrament of the Lord's Supper in some Protestant and Reformed congregation within this Kingdom of Great Britain, or within some of the said colonies in America, within three months next before his taking and subscribing the said oaths, and making, repeating, and subscribing the said declaration; and shall, at the time of his taking and subscribing said oaths, and making, repeating, and subscribing the said declaration, produce a certificate signed by the person administering the said sacrament, and attested by two credible witnesses, whereof an entry shall be made in the secretary's office of the colony, wherein such person shall so inhabit and reside, as also in the court where the said oaths shall be so taken as aforesaid, without any fee or reward.

III. *And whereas* the following words are contained in the latter part of the oath of abjuration, *videlicet* (upon the true faith of a Christian); *And whereas* the people professing the Jewish religion may thereby be prevented from receiving the benefit of this act, *Be it further enacted,* by the authority aforesaid, that whenever any person professing the Jewish religion shall present himself to take the said oath of abjuration in pursuance of this act, the said words (upon the true faith of a Christian) shall be omitted out of the said oath in administering the same to such person, and the taking and subscribing the said oath by such person professing the Jewish religion, without the words aforesaid, and the other oaths appointed by the said act in like manner as Jews were permitted to take the oath of abjuration by an act made in the tenth year of the reign of His late Majesty King George I, entitled "An Act for explaining and amending an Act of the last Session of Parliament, entitled 'An Act to oblige all Persons, being Papists, in that part of Great Britain called Scotland, and all persons in Great Britain, refusing or neglecting to take the Oaths appointed for the Security of His Majesty's Person and Government,' by several Acts herein mentioned, to register their Names and real Estates"; and for enlarging the time for taking the said oaths, and making such registers, and for allowing further time for the enrollment of deeds or wills made by Papists, which have been omitted to be enrolled pursuant to an act of the third year of His Majesty's reign; and also for giving relief to Protestant lessees, shall be deemed a sufficient taking of the said oaths, in order to entitle such person to the benefit of being naturalized by virtue of this act.

IV. *And be it further enacted,* by the authority aforesaid, that a testimonial or certificate under the seal of any of the said colonies, of any persons having resided and inhabited for the space of seven years or more as aforesaid within the said colonies or some of them, to be specified in such certificate, together with the particular time of residence in each of such respective colonies (whereof the colony under the seal of which such certificate shall be given to be one) and of his having taken and subscribed the said oaths, and of his having made, repeated, and subscribed the said declaration, and in case of a Quaker of his having made and subscribed the declaration of fidelity, and of his having taken and affirmed the effect of the abjuration oath as aforesaid, and in the case of a person professing the Jewish religion, of his having taken the oath of abjuration as aforesaid, within the same colony, under the seal whereof such certificate shall be given as aforesaid, shall be deemed and taken to be a sufficient testimony and proof thereof, and of his being a natural-born subject of Great Britain, to all intents and purposes whatsoever, and as such shall be allowed in every court within the Kingdoms of Great Britain and Ireland, and also in the said colonies in America.

V. *And be it further enacted,* by the authority aforesaid that every secretary of the said respective colonies for the time being shall and is hereby directed and required at the end of every year, to be computed from the said 1st day of June in the year of Our Lord 1740, to transmit and send over to the office of the Commissioners for Trade and Plantations kept in the City of London or Westminster, a true and perfect list of the names of all and every person and persons who have in that year entitled themselves to the benefit of this act, under the penalty and forfeiture of £50 of lawful money of Great Britain for every neglect or omission; all which said lists so transmitted and sent over shall, from year to year, be duly and regularly entered by the said Commissioners, in a book or books to be had and kept for that purpose in the said office, for public view and inspection as occasion shall require.

VI. *Provided always, and it is hereby further enacted*, that no person who shall become a natural-born subject of this Kingdom by virtue of this act, shall be of the Privy Council, or a member of either House of Parliament, or capable of taking, having, or enjoying any office or place of trust within the Kingdoms of Great Britain or Ireland, either civil or military, or of having, accepting, or taking any grant from the Crown to himself, or to any other in trust for him, of any lands, tenements, or hereditaments within the Kingdoms of Great Britain or Ireland; anything hereinbefore contained to the contrary thereof in anywise notwithstanding.

95.

Royal Currency Order

The practice of issuing paper money and bills of credit to pay current expenses was initiated by Massachusetts in the 1690s. The practice spread to other colonies, and British merchants and creditors suffered losses as a result of the depreciation of colonial currency. Their complaints were met by royal proclamations forbidding or restricting such issues. However, the royal governors, who were charged with implementing the policies of the Crown, found that in this as in other cases they were unable to control the colonial legislatures over which they had nominal authority. On August 5, 1740, the Crown issued an ultimatum to the governors: Enforce the royal demands or be removed from office. Despite the harshness of the penalty, the order proved ineffectual.

Source: *Documents Relating to the Colonial History of the State of New Jersey*, William A. Whitehead, ed., Newark, 1882, Vol. VI, pp. 95-98.

Whereas an Act of Parliament was passed in the sixth year of Her late Majesty Queen Anne entitled *An Act for Ascertaining the Rates of Foreign Coins in Her Majesty's Plantations in America*, which Act the respective governors of all the plantations in America have from time to time been instructed to observe and carry into due execution; *and whereas* notwithstanding the same, complaints have been made that the said Act has not been observed as it ought to have been in many of His Majesty's colonies and plantations in America, by means whereof many indirect practices have grown up and various and illegal currencies have been introduced in several of the said colonies and plantations, contrary to the true intent and meaning of the said Act and to the prejudice of the trade of His Majesty's subjects.

In consequence of which complaints, a humble address was presented the last sessions by the House of Commons to His Majesty that he would be graciously pleased to require and command the respective governors of his colonies and plantations in America effectually to observe His Majesty's royal instruction, directing them that the Act of the sixth year of the reign of Her Majesty Queen Anne entitled *An Act for Ascertaining the Rate of Foreign Coins in Her*

Majesty's Plantations in America be punctually and bona fide observed and put in execution according to the true intent and meaning of the said Act. It is therefore His Majesty's royal will and pleasure, and you are hereby strictly required and commanded, under pain of His Majesty's highest displeasure and of being removed from your government, to take the most effectual care for the future that the said Act be punctually and bona fide observed and put in execution according to the true intent and meaning thereof.

And to the end that His Majesty's commands herein may be fully made known to all his subjects within your government, and that none of them may pretend ignorance thereof, you are hereby further required and commanded to publish this instruction in such manner as may best answer His Majesty's gracious intentions herein signified.

And whereas, for preventing the many and great inconveniences that had arisen in some of His Majesty's colonies and plantations in America by passing laws for striking bills of credit and issuing out the same in lieu of money, the respective governors and commanders in chief of His Majesty's colonies and plantations for the time being have been particularly instructed not to give their assent to or pass any such laws for the future without a clause be inserted in such act declaring that the same shall not take effect until the said act shall have been approved and confirmed by His Majesty, His Heirs, or Successors.

And whereas notwithstanding such His Majesty's commands to the said governors in that behalf, paper bills of credit have been created and issued in His Majesty's said colonies and plantations by virtue of acts of assembly there, making it obligatory on all persons to take such bills of credit in payment for debts, dues, and demands, whereby the good intention of the aforementioned Act of the sixth of Her late Majesty Queen Anne for ascertaining the rates of foreign coins in Her Majesty's plantations in America has been frustrated, and a great discouragement has been brought on the commerce of this kingdom by occasioning a confusion in dealings and a lessening of credit in those parts.

And whereas a humble address was presented the last session by the House of Commons to His Majesty that he would be graciously pleased to require and command the respective governors of his colonies and plantations in America, punctually and effectually to observe His Majesty's royal instructions not to give assent to or to pass any act whereby bills of credit may be issued in lieu of money without a clause be inserted in such act declaring that the same shall be approved by His Majesty.

It is therefore His Majesty's will and pleasure, and you are hereby also further required and commanded under pain of His Majesty's highest displeasure and of being removed from your government, punctually and effectually to observe His Majesty's royal instruction not to give assent to or pass any act whereby bills of credit may be issued in lieu of money without a clause be inserted in such act declaring that the same shall not take effect until the said act shall be approved by His Majesty, His Heirs, or Successors.

1741

96.

Jonathan Edwards: Sinners in the Hands of an Angry God

This, the most famous of Jonathan Edwards' sermons, was delivered at Enfield, Connecticut, on July 8, 1741. It is often cited as an instance of the Puritan delight in visions of hellfire, and while no conception could misrepresent Edwards more profoundly, his eloquence here was designed to terrify. *So, in the words of his biographer, Perry Miller, the sermon "slowly, with implacable slowness, coils a monstrous accusation against mankind, until the bow of God's wrath is bent and the arrow justifiably aimed at the entrails of the race." Only the arrow is not shot. There were moanings and cryings among the congregation at the time, and Edwards had to pause until they spent themselves. Yet the ultimate result seemed not to be destructive, but on the contrary, witnesses were struck by the cheerfulness and pleasantness on the faces of people afterwards. It appeared that the minister, desiring that his audience should feel at last the force of God's inexplicable mercy, had brought about the purgation he sought.*

Source: *The Works of President Edwards, etc., etc.*, New York, 1844, Vol. IV, pp. 313-321.

Deuteronomy 32:35 — *Their foot shall slide in due time.*

In this verse is threatened the vengeance of God on the wicked, unbelieving Israelites that were God's visible people, and lived under means of grace; and that notwithstanding all God's wonderful works that He had wrought toward that people, yet remained, as is expressed verse 28, void of counsel, having no understanding in them; and that, under all the cultivations of heaven, brought forth bitter and poisonous fruit,

as in the two verses next preceding the text.

The expression that I have chosen for my text, *Their foot shall slide in due time*, seems to imply the following things relating to the punishment and destruction that these wicked Israelites were exposed to.

1. That they were always exposed to destruction, as one that stands or walks in slippery places is always exposed to fall. This is implied in the manner of their destruction's coming upon them, being represented by their foot's sliding. The same is expressed (Ps. 73:18): "Surely thou didst

set them in slippery places; thou castedst them down into destruction."

2. It implies that they were always exposed to sudden, unexpected destruction, as he that walks in slippery places is every moment liable to fall, he cannot foresee one moment whether he shall stand or fall the next; and when he does fall, he falls at once, without warning, which is also expressed in that Ps. 73:18, 19: "Surely thou didst set them in slippery places; thou castedst them down into destruction: how are they brought into desolation as in a moment."

3. Another thing implied is that they are liable to fall of themselves, without being thrown down by the hand of another, as he that stands or walks on slippery ground needs nothing but his own weight to throw him down.

4. That the reason why they are not fallen already, and do not fall now, is only that God's appointed time is not come; for it is said that when that due time, or appointed time, comes, *their feet shall slide.* Then they shall be left to fall, as they are inclined by their own weight. God will not hold them up in these slippery places any longer, but will let them go; and then, at that very instant, they shall fall into destruction, as he that stands in such slippery declining ground on the edge of a pit that he cannot stand alone; when he is let go he immediately falls and is lost.

The observation from the words that I would now insist upon is this: There is nothing that keeps wicked men at any one moment out of hell but the mere pleasure of God.

By the mere pleasure of God, I mean His sovereign pleasure, His arbitrary will, restrained by no obligation, hindered by no manner of difficulty, anymore than if nothing else but God's mere will had in the least degree or in any respect whatsoever, any hand in the preservation of wicked men one moment.

The truth of this observation may appear by the following considerations:

1. There is no want of power in God to cast wicked men into hell at any moment. Men's hands cannot be strong when God rises up: the strongest have no power to resist Him, nor can any deliver out of His hands. He is not only able to cast wicked men into hell, but He can most easily do it.

Sometimes an earthly prince meets with a great deal of difficulty to subdue a rebel that has found means to fortify himself, and has made himself strong by the number of his followers. But it is not so with God. There is no fortress that is any defense against the power of God. Though hand join in hand, and vast multitudes of God's enemies combine and associate themselves, they are easily broken in pieces; they are as great heaps of light chaff before the whirlwind, or large quantities of dry stubble before devouring flames. We find it easy to tread on and crush a worm that we see crawling on the earth; so it is easy for us to cut or singe a slender thread that anything hangs by; thus easy it is for God, when He pleases, to cast His enemies down to hell. What are we that we should think to stand before Him, at whose rebuke the earth trembles, and before whom the rocks are thrown down!

2. They deserve to be cast into hell; so that divine justice never stands in the way, it makes no objection against God's using His power at any moment to destroy them. Yea, on the contrary, justice calls aloud for an infinite punishment of their sins. Divine justice says of the tree that brings forth such grapes of Sodom: "Cut it down, why cumbereth it the ground?" (Luke 13:7). The sword of divine justice is every moment brandished over their heads, and it is nothing but the hand of arbitrary mercy and God's mere will that holds it back.

3. They are already under a sentence of condemnation to hell. They do not only justly deserve to be cast down thither, but

the sentence of the law of God, that eternal and immutable rule of righteousness that God has fixed between Him and mankind, is gone out against them; and stands against them; so that they are bound over already to hell (John 3:18): "He that believeth not is condemned already." So that every unconverted man properly belongs to hell; that is his place; from thence he is (John 8:23): "Ye are from beneath": and thither he is bound; it is the place that justice, and God's word, and the sentence of His unchangeable law assign to him.

4. They are now the objects of that very same anger and wrath of God that is expressed in the torments of hell; and the reason why they do not go down to hell at each moment is not because God, in whose power they are, is not then very angry with them; as angry as He is with many of those miserable creatures that He is now tormenting in hell, and do there feel and bear the fierceness of His wrath. Yea, God is a great deal more angry with great numbers that are now on earth; yea, doubtless, with many that are now in this congregation — that, it may be, are at ease and quiet — than He is with many of those that are now in the flames of hell.

So that it is not because God is unmindful of their wickedness and does not resent it that He does not let loose His hand and cut them off. God is not altogether such a one as themselves, though they may imagine Him to be so. The wrath of God burns against them; their damnation does not slumber; the pit is prepared; the fire is made ready; the furnace is now hot; ready to receive them; the flames do now rage and glow. The glittering sword is whet and held over them, and the pit hath opened her mouth under them.

5. The devil stands ready to fall upon them and seize them as his own, at what moment God shall permit him. They belong to Him; He has their soul in his possession and under His dominion. The Scripture represents them as His goods (Luke 11:21). The devils watch them; they are ever by them, at their right hand; they stand waiting for them like greedy hungry lions that see their prey and expect to have it, but are for the present kept back. If God should withdraw His hand by which they are restrained, they would in one moment fly upon their poor souls. The old serpent is gaping for them; hell opens its mouth wide to receive them; and if God should permit it, they would be hastily swallowed up and lost.

6. There are in the souls of wicked men those hellish principles reigning that would presently kindle and flame out into hellfire, if it were not for God's restraints. There is laid in the very nature of carnal men a foundation for the torments of hell; there are those corrupt principles, in reigning power in them and in full possession of them, that are the beginnings of hellfire. These principles are active and powerful, exceeding violent in their nature; and if it were not for the restraining hand of God upon them, they would soon break out, they would flame out after the same manner as the same corruptions, the same enmity does in the hearts of damned souls, and would beget the same torments in them as they do in them.

The souls of the wicked are in Scripture compared to the troubled sea (Isa. 57:20). For the present, God restrains their wickedness by His mighty power, as He does the raging waves of the troubled sea, saying, "Hitherto shalt thou come, and no further"; but if God should withdraw that restraining power, it would soon carry all before it. Sin is the ruin and misery of the soul; it is destructive in its nature; and if God should leave it without restraint, there would need nothing else to make the soul perfectly miserable. The corruption of the heart of man is a thing that is immoderate and boundless in its fury; and while wicked men live here, it is like fire pent up by

God's restraints, whereas if it were let loose, it would set on fire the course of nature; and as the heart is now a sink of sin, so, if sin was not restrained, it would immediately turn the soul into a fiery oven, or a furnace of fire and brimstone.

7. It is no security to wicked men, for one moment, that there are no visible means of death at hand. It is no security to a natural man that he is now in health, and that he does not see which way he should now immediately go out of the world by any accident, and that there is no visible danger in any respect in his circumstances. The manifold and continual experience of the world in all ages shows that this is no evidence that a man is not on the very brink of eternity, and that the next step will not be into another world. The unseen, unthought of ways and means of persons going suddenly out of the world are innumerable and inconceivable. Unconverted men walk over the pit of hell on rotten covering, and there are innumerable places in this covering so weak that they will not bear their weight, and these places are not seen.

The arrows of death fly unseen at noonday; the sharpest sight cannot discern them. God has so many different, unsearchable ways of taking wicked men out of the world and sending them to hell that there is nothing to make it appear that God had need to be at the expense of a miracle, or go out of the ordinary course of His providence to destroy any wicked man, at any moment. All the means that there are of sinners going out of the world are so in God's hands, and so absolutely subject to His power and determination, that it does not depend at all less on the mere will of God, whether sinners shall at any moment go to hell, than if means were never made use of, or at all concerned in the case.

8. Natural men's prudence and care to preserve their own lives, or the care of others to preserve them, do not secure them a moment. This, Divine Providence and universal experience do also bear testimony to. There is this clear evidence that men's own wisdom is no security to them from death; that if it were otherwise we should see some difference between the wise and politic men of the world, and others, with regard to their liableness to early and unexpected death; but how is it in fact? "How dieth the wise man? As the fool" (Eccles. 2:16).

9. All wicked men's pains and contrivance they use to escape hell, while they continue to reject Christ, and so remain wicked men, do not secure them from hell one moment. Almost every natural man that hears of hell flatters himself that he shall escape it; he depends upon himself for his own security; he flatters himself in what he has done, in what he is now doing, or what he intends to do. Everyone lays out matters in his own mind how he shall avoid damnation, and flatters himself that he contrives well for himself, and that his schemes will not fail. They hear indeed that there are but few saved, and that the bigger part of men that have died heretofore are gone to hell; but each one imagines that he lays out matters better for his own escape than others have done. He does not intend to come to that place of torment; he says within himself that he intends to take care that shall be effectual, and to order matters so for himself as not to fail.

But the foolish children of men do miserably delude themselves in their own schemes; and in their confidence in their own strength and wisdom, they trust to nothing but a shadow. The bigger part of those that heretofore have lived under the same means of grace, and are now dead, are undoubtedly gone to hell; and it was not because they were not as wise as those that are now alive; it was not because they did not lay out matters as well for themselves to secure their own escape. If it were so that we could come to speak with them, and could inquire of them, one by one, whether they expected, when alive, and when they used to hear about hell, ever to be subjects of that misery, we, doubtless, should hear one and another reply, "No, I never intended to come here. I had laid out matters otherwise in my mind. I thought I should contrive well for myself. I thought my scheme good. I intended to take effectual care; but it came upon me unexpectedly. I did not look for it at that time, and in that manner. It came as a thief; death outwitted me; God's wrath was too quick for me. O my cursed foolishness! I was flattering myself and pleasing myself with vain dreams of what I would do hereafter; and when I was saying peace and safety, then sudden destruction came upon me."

10. God has laid Himself under no obligation, by any promise, to keep any natural man out of hell one moment. God certainly has made no promises either of eternal life or of any deliverance or preservation from eternal death, but what are contained in the Covenant of Grace, the promises that are given in Christ, in whom all the promises are yea and amen. But surely they have no interest in the promises of the Covenant of Grace that are not the children of the Covenant, and that do not believe in any of the promises of the Covenant, and have no interest in the Mediator of the Covenant.

So that, whatever some have imagined and pretended about promises made to natural men's earnest seeking and knocking, it is plain and manifest that whatever pains a natural man takes in religion, whatever prayers he makes, till he believes in Christ, God is under no manner of obligation to keep him a moment from eternal destruction.

So that thus it is that natural men are held in the hand of God over the pit of hell; they have deserved the fiery pit and are already sentenced to it; and God is dreadfully provoked — His anger is as great toward them as to those that are actually suffering the executions of the fierceness

of His wrath in hell, and they have done nothing in the least to appease or abate that anger; neither is God in the least bound by any promise to hold them up one moment. The devil is waiting for them; hell is gaping for them; the flames gather and flash about them, and would fain lay hand on them and swallow them up; the fire pent up in their own hearts is struggling to break out; and they have no interest in any Mediator — there are no means within reach that can be any security to them. In short, they have no refuge, nothing to take hold of; all that preserves them every moment is the mere arbitrary will and uncovenanted, unobliged forbearance of an incensed God.

APPLICATION

The use may be of awakening to unconverted persons in this congregation. This that you have heard is the case of every one of you that are out of Christ. That world of misery, that lake of burning brimstone, is extended abroad under you. There is the dreadful pit of the glowing flames of the wrath of God; there is hell's wide, gaping mouth open; and you have nothing to stand upon, nor anything to take hold of. There is nothing between you and hell but the air; it is only the power and mere pleasure of God that holds you up.

You probably are not sensible of this; you find you are kept out of hell, but do not see the hand of God in it; but look at other things, as the good state of your bodily constitution, your care of your own life, and the means you use for your own preservation. But indeed these things are nothing; if God should withdraw His hand, they would avail no more to keep you from falling than the thin air to hold up a person that is suspended in it.

Your wickedness makes you as it were heavy as lead, and to tend downward with great weight and pressure toward hell; and if God should let you go, you would immediately sink and swiftly descend and plunge into the bottomless gulf, and your healthy constitution, and your own care and prudence, and best contrivance, and all your righteousness would have no more influence to uphold you and keep you out of hell than a spider's web would have to stop a falling rock. Were it not that so is the sovereign pleasure of God, the earth would not bear you one moment; for you are a burden to it; the creation groans with you; the creature is made subject to the bondage of your corruption, not willingly; the sun does not willingly shine upon you to give you light to serve sin and Satan; the earth does not willingly yield her increase to satisfy your lusts; nor is it willingly a stage for your wickedness to be acted upon; the air does not willingly serve you for breath to maintain the flame of life in your vitals, while you spend your life in the service of God's enemies.

God's creatures are good, and were made for men to serve God with, and do not willingly subserve to any other purpose, and groan when they are abused to purposes so directly contrary to their nature and end. And the world would spew you out were it not for the sovereign hand of Him who hath subjected it in hope. There are the black clouds of God's wrath now hanging directly over your heads, full of the dreadful storm, and big with thunder; and were it not for the restraining hand of God, it would immediately burst forth upon you. The sovereign pleasure of God, for the present, stays His rough wind; otherwise it would come with fury, and your destruction would come like a whirlwind, and you would be like the chaff of the summer threshing floor.

The wrath of God is like great waters that are dammed for the present; they increase more and more, and rise higher and higher, till an outlet is given; and the longer the stream is stopped, the more rapid and mighty is its course, when once it is let loose. It is true that judgment against your evil work has not been executed hitherto. The floods of God's vengeance have been withheld; but your guilt in the meantime is constantly increasing, and you are every day treasuring up more wrath; the waters are continually rising, and waxing more and more mighty; and there is nothing but the mere pleasure of God that holds the waters back, that are unwilling to be stopped and press hard to go forward. If God should only withdraw His hand from the floodgate, it would immediately fly open, and the fiery floods of the fierceness and wrath of God would rush forth with inconceivable fury, and would come upon you with omnipotent power; and if your strength were ten thousand times greater than it is — yea, ten thousand times greater than the strength of the stoutest, sturdiest devil in hell — it would be nothing to withstand or endure it.

The bow of God's wrath is bent, and the arrow made ready on the string, and justice bends the arrow at your heart, and strains the bow, and it is nothing but the mere pleasure of God, and that of an angry God, without any promise or obligation at all, that keeps the arrow one moment from being made drunk with your blood.

Thus are all you that never passed under a great change of heart, by the mighty power of the Spirit of God upon your souls; all that were never born again, and made new creatures, and raised from being dead in sin to a state of new, and before altogether unexperienced, light and life (however you may have reformed your life in many things, and may have had religious affections, and may keep up a form of religion in your families and closets and in the houses of God, and may be strict in it), you are thus in the hands of an angry God; it is nothing but His mere pleasure that keeps you from being this moment swallowed up in everlasting destruction.

However unconvinced you may now be of the truth of what you hear, by and by you will be fully convinced of it. Those that are gone from being in the like circumstances with you see that it was so with them; for destruction came suddenly upon most of them, when they expected nothing of it, and while they were saying, peace and safety. Now they see that those things that they depended on for peace and safety were nothing but thin air and empty shadows.

The God that holds you over the pit of hell, much as one holds a spider or some loathsome insect over the fire, abhors you, and is dreadfully provoked. His wrath toward you burns like fire; He looks upon you as worthy of nothing else but to be cast into the fire; He is of purer eyes than to bear to have you in His sight; you are ten thousand times so abominable in His eyes as the most hateful and venomous serpent is in ours. You have offended Him infinitely more than ever a stubborn rebel did his prince; and yet it is nothing but His hand that holds you from falling into the fire every moment. It is ascribed to nothing else that you did not go to hell the last night; that you were suffered to awake again in this world after you closed your eyes to sleep; and there is no other reason to be given why you have not dropped into hell since you arose in the morning, but that God's hand has held you up. There is no other reason to be given why you have not gone to hell, since you have sat here in the house of God, provoking His pure eyes by your sinful, wicked manner of attending His solemn worship; yea, there is nothing else that is to be given as a reason why you do not this very moment drop down into hell.

O sinner! consider the fearful danger you are in: it is a great furnace of wrath, a wide and bottomless pit, full of the fire of wrath, that you are held over in the hand of that God, whose wrath is provoked and incensed as much against you as many of the damned in hell. You hang by a slender thread, with the flames of divine wrath flashing about it, and ready every moment to singe it and burn it asunder; and you have no interest in any Mediator, and nothing to lay hold of to save yourself, nothing to keep off the flames of wrath, nothing of your own, nothing that you ever have done, nothing that you can do to induce God to spare you one moment.

And consider here more particularly several things concerning that wrath that you are in such danger of:

1. Whose wrath it is. It is the wrath of the infinite God. If it were only the wrath of man, though it were of the most potent prince, it would be comparatively little to be regarded. The wrath of kings is very much dreaded, especially of absolute monarchs that have the possessions and lives of their subjects wholly in their power, to be disposed of at their mere will (Prov. 20:2): "The fear of a king is as the roaring of a lion: whoso provoketh him to anger, sinneth against his own soul." The subject that very much enrages an arbitrary prince is liable to suffer the most extreme torments that human art can invent, or human power can inflict. But the greatest earthly potentates, in their greatest majesty and strength, and when clothed in their greatest terrors, are but feeble, despicable worms of the dust in comparison of the great and almighty Creator and King of heaven and earth; it is but little that they can do when most enraged, and when they have exerted the utmost of their fury. All the kings of the earth before God are as grasshoppers; they are nothing, and less than nothing; both their love and their hatred is to be despised. The wrath of the great King of kings is as much more terrible than theirs, as His majesty is greater (Luke 12:4, 5): "And I say unto you, my friends, be not afraid of them that kill the body, and after that have no more that they can do. But I will forewarn you whom you shall fear: fear Him, which after He hath

killed, hath power to cast into hell; yea, I say unto you, fear Him."

2. It is the fierceness of His wrath that you are exposed to. We often read of the fury of God, as in Isa. 59:18: "According to their deeds, accordingly He will repay fury to his adversaries." So Isa. 66:15: "For behold, the Lord will come with fire and with His chariots like a whirlwind, to render His anger with fury, and His rebuke with flames of fire." And so in many other places. So we read of God's fierceness, Rev. 19:15. There we read of "the wine press of the fierceness and wrath of Almighty God." The words are exceedingly terrible; if it had only been said, "the wrath of God," the words would have implied that which is infinitely dreadful; but it is not only said so, but "the fierceness and wrath of God": the fury of God! the fierceness of Jehovah! Oh how dreadful must that be! Who can utter or conceive what such expressions carry in them! But it is not only said so, but "the fierceness and wrath of Almighty God." As though there would be a very great manifestation of His almighty power in what the fierceness of His wrath should inflict, as though omnipotence should be as it were enraged, and exerted, as men are wont to exert their strength in the fierceness of their wrath. Oh! then, what will be the consequence! What will become of the poor worm that shall suffer it! Whose hands can be strong! And whose heart endure! To what a dreadful, inexpressible, inconceivable depth of misery must the poor creature be sunk who shall be the subject of this!

Consider this, you that are here present, that yet remain in an unregenerate state. That God will execute the fierceness of His anger implies that He will inflict wrath without any pity. When God beholds the ineffable extremity of your case, and sees your torment so vastly disproportioned to your strength, and sees how your poor soul is crushed, and sinks down, as it were, into an infinite gloom, He will have no compassion upon you, He will not forbear the executions of His wrath, or in the least lighten His hand. There shall be no moderation or mercy, nor will God then at all stay His rough wind; He will have no regard to your welfare, nor be at all careful lest you should suffer too much in any other sense, than only that you should not suffer beyond what strict justice requires. Nothing shall be withheld, because it is so hard for you to bear (Ezek. 8:18): "Therefore will I also deal in fury; mine eye shall not spare, neither will I have pity; and though they cry in mine ears with a loud voice, yet will I not hear them."

Now God stands ready to pity you; this is a day of mercy; you may cry now with some encouragement of obtaining mercy; but when once the day of mercy is past, your most lamentable and dolorous cries and shrieks will be in vain; you will be wholly lost and thrown away of God, as to any regard to your welfare; God will have no other use to put you to, but only to suffer misery; you shall be continued in being to no other end, for you will be a vessel of wrath fitted to destruction; and there will be no other use of this vessel, but only to be filled full of wrath. God will be so far from pitying you when you cry to Him that it is said He will only "laugh and mock" (Prov. 1:25, 26, etc.).

How awful are those words (Isa. 63:3) which are the words of the great God: "I will tread them in mine anger, and trample them in my fury, and their blood shall be sprinkled upon my garments, and I will stain all my raiment." It is perhaps impossible to conceive of words that carry in them greater manifestations of these three things, viz., contempt and hatred and fierceness of indignation. If you cry to God to pity you, He will be so far from pitying you in your doleful case, or showing you the least regard or favor, that instead of that He will only tread you underfoot; and though He will know that you cannot bear the weight of omnipotence treading upon you, yet He will not regard that, but He will crush you under His feet without mercy; He will crush out your blood and make it fly, and it shall be sprinkled on His garments so as to stain all His raiment. He will not only hate you but He will have you in the utmost contempt; no place shall be thought fit for you but under His feet, to be trodden down as the mire in the streets.

3. The misery you are exposed to is that which God will inflict to that end, that He might show what that wrath of Jehovah is. God hath had it on His heart to show to angels and men, both how excellent His love is and also how terrible His wrath is. Sometimes earthly kings have a mind to show how terrible their wrath is by the extreme punishments they would execute on those that provoke them. Nebuchadnezzar, that mighty and haughty monarch of the Chaldean Empire, was willing to show his wrath when enraged with Shadrach, Meshech, and Abednego; and accordingly gave order that the burning fiery furnace should be heated seven times hotter than it was before; doubtless it was raised to the utmost degree of fierceness that human art could raise it. But the great God is also willing to show His wrath, and magnify His awful majesty and mighty power in the extreme sufferings of His enemies (Rom. 9:22): "What if God, willing to show His wrath and to make His power known, endured with much long-suffering the vessels of wrath fitted to destruction?"

And seeing this is His design and what He has determined, to show how terrible the unmixed, unrestrained wrath, the fury, and fierceness of Jehovah is, He will do it to effect. There will be something accomplished and brought to pass that will be dreaded with a witness. When the great and angry God hath risen up and executed His awful vengeance on the poor sinner, and the wretch is actually suffering the infinite weight and power of His indignation, then will God call upon the whole universe to behold that awful majesty and mighty power that is to be seen in it (Isa. 33:12-14): "And the people shall be as the burnings of lime, as thorns cut up shall they be burnt in the fire. Hear ye, that are afar off, what I have done; and ye that are near, acknowledge my might. The sinners in Zion are afraid; fearfulness hath surprised the hypocrites," etc.

Thus it will be with you that are in an unconverted state if you continue in it; the infinite might, and majesty, and terribleness of the Omnipotent God shall be magnified upon you in the ineffable strength of your torments; you shall be tormented in the presence of the holy angels, and in the presence of the Lamb; and when you shall be in this state of suffering, the glorious inhabitants of heaven shall go forth and look on the awful spectacle, that they may see what the wrath and fierceness of the Almighty is; and when they have seen it, they will fall down and adore that great power and majesty (Isa. 66:23, 24): "And it shall come to pass that, from one moon to another, and from one Sabbath to another, shall all flesh come to worship before me, said the Lord. And they shall go forth and look upon the carcasses of the men that have transgressed against me; for their worm shall not die, neither shall their fire be quenched, and they shall be abhorring unto all flesh."

4. It is everlasting wrath. It would be dreadful to suffer this fierceness and wrath of Almighty God one moment; but you must suffer it to all eternity. There will be no end to this exquisite, horrible misery; when you look forward, you shall see a long forever, a boundless duration before you, which will swallow up your thoughts and amaze your soul; and you will absolutely despair of ever having any deliverance, any end, any mitigation, any rest at all. You will know certainly that you must wear out long ages, millions of millions of

ages, in wrestling and conflicting with this almighty, merciless vengeance; and then when you have so done, when so many ages have actually been spent by you in this manner, you will know that all is but a point to what remains. So that your punishment will indeed be infinite. Oh, who can express what the state of a soul in such circumstances is! All that we can possibly say about it gives but a very feeble, faint representation of it; it is inexpressible and inconceivable, for "who knows the power of God's anger?"

How dreadful is the state of those that are daily and hourly in danger of this great wrath and infinite misery! But this is the dismal case of every soul in this congregation that has not been born again, however moral and strict, sober and religious they may otherwise be. Oh, that you would consider it, whether you be young or old! There is reason to think that there are many in this congregation now hearing this discourse that will actually be the subjects of this very misery to all eternity. We know not who they are, or in what seats they sit, or what thoughts they now have. It may be they are now at ease, and hear all these things without much disturbance, and are now flattering themselves that they are not the persons — promising themselves that they shall escape. If we knew that there was one person, and but one, in the whole congregation, that was to be the subject of this misery, what an awful thing it would be to think of! If we knew who it was, what an awful sight would it be to see such a person! How might all the rest of the congregation lift up a lamentable and bitter cry over him! But alas! Instead of one, how many is it likely will remember this discourse in hell! And it would be a wonder if some that are now present should not be in hell in a very short time, before this year is out. And it would be no wonder if some persons that now sit here in some seats of this meetinghouse in health, and quiet and

secure, should be there before tomorrow morning.

Those of you that finally continue in a natural condition, that shall keep out of hell longest, will be there in a little time! Your damnation does not slumber; it will come swiftly and, in all probability, very suddenly upon many of you. You have reason to wonder that you are not already in hell. It is doubtless the case of some whom you have seen and known, that never deserved hell more than you, and that heretofore appeared as likely to have been now alive as you. Their case is past all hope; they are crying in extreme misery and perfect despair; but here you are in the land of the living and in the house of God, and have an opportunity to obtain salvation. What would not those poor, damned, hopeless souls give for one day's such opportunity as you now enjoy!

And now you have an extraordinary opportunity, a day wherein Christ has thrown the door of mercy wide open, and stands in the door calling and crying with a loud voice to poor sinners; a day wherein many are flocking to Him, and pressing into the kingdom of God. Many are daily coming from the east, west, north, and south; many that were very lately in the same miserable condition that you are in, are now in a happy state, with their hearts filled with love to Him who has loved them, and washed them from their sins in his own blood, and rejoicing in hope of the glory of God.

How awful is it to be left behind at such a day! To see so many others feasting, while you are pining and perishing! To see so many rejoicing and singing for joy of heart, while you have cause to mourn for sorrow of heart, and howl for vexation of spirit! How can you rest one moment in such a condition? Are not your souls as precious as the souls of the people at Suffield, where they are flocking from day to day to Christ?

Are there not many here that have lived long in the world and are not to this day born again? and so are aliens from the commonwealth of Israel, and have done nothing ever since they have lived but treasure up wrath against the day of wrath? Oh, sirs, your case, in an especial manner, is extremely dangerous. Your guilt and hardness of heart is extremely great. Do you not see how generally persons of your years are passed over and left in the present remarkable and wonderful dispensation of God's mercy? You had need to consider yourselves, and wake thoroughly out of sleep. You cannot bear the fierceness and wrath of the infinite God.

And you, young men and young women, will you neglect this precious season which you now enjoy, when so many others of your age are renouncing all youthful vanities and flocking to Christ? You especially have now an extraordinary opportunity; but if you neglect it, it will soon be with you as it is with those persons who spent all the precious days of youth in sin, and are now come to such a dreadful pass in blindness and hardness. And you, children, who are unconverted, do not you know that you are going down to hell, to bear the dreadful wrath of that God who is now angry with you every day and every night? Will you be content to be the children of the devil, when so many other children in the land are converted, and are become the holy and happy children of the King of kings?

And let everyone that is yet out of Christ, and hanging over the pit of hell, whether they be old men and women, or middle-aged, or young people, or little children, now hearken to the loud calls of God's word and providence. This acceptable year of the Lord, a day of such great favors to some, will doubtless be a day of as remarkable vengeance to others. Men's hearts harden, and their guilt increases apace at such a day as this if they neglect their souls; and never was there so great danger of such persons being given up to hardness of heart and blindness of mind.

God seems now to be hastily gathering in His elect in all parts of the land; and probably the greater part of adult persons that ever shall be saved will be brought in now in a little time; and that it will be as it was on that great outpouring of the Spirit upon the Jews in the apostles' days — the election will obtain, and the rest will be blinded. If this should be the case with you, you will eternally curse this day, and will curse the day that ever you were born, to see such a season of the pouring out of God's Spirit, and will wish that you had died and gone to hell before you had seen it. Now undoubtedly it is, as it was in the days of John the Baptist, the axe is in an extraordinary manner laid at the root of the trees, that every tree that brings not forth good fruit may be hewn down and cast into the fire. Therefore, let everyone that is out of Christ now awake and fly from the wrath to come. The wrath of Almighty God is now undoubtedly hanging over great part of this congregation. Let everyone fly out of Sodom: "Haste and escape for your lives, look not behind you, escape to the mountain, lest you be consumed."

———◆———

Resolved, *That I will act so, in every respect, as I think I shall wish I had done, if I should at last be damned.*

Jonathan Edwards, July 8, 1723

1742

97.

CHARLES CHAUNCY: Revivalism and True Religion

The Great Awakening, with its ecstasies, groans, foot stampings, and shrieks, was regarded with distrust by most of the established clergy in New England. Their ablest voice was Charles Chauncy, a minister of the First Church of Boston and an exponent of liberal or rationalistic theology in his day. In the following letter, addressed to a Scottish minister on August 4, 1742, and later published as a pamphlet, Chauncy described disapprovingly the preaching of George Whitefield, the English evangelist who had lately toured the colonies, Gilbert Tennent, who had led the revival in New Jersey, and James Davenport of Long Island, who was considered a ranter even by those who defended the religious fervor of the times.

Source: *The Clarendon Historical Society's Reprints*, 1st series, Edinburgh, 1883, pp. 5-15: "A Letter from a Gentleman in Boston to Mr. George Wishart, etc., etc."

Reverend Sir,

I perceive by a printed letter from a friend in Edinburgh, containing excerpts of letters concerning the success of the Gospel in these parts, that marvelous accounts have been sent abroad of a most glorious work of grace going on in America, as begun by Mr. Whitefield, and helped forward by those in his way of preaching and acting. I should be glad there had been more truth in those accounts. Some of the things related are known falsehoods, others strangely enlarged upon; and the representations, in general, such as exhibit a wrong idea of the religious state of affairs among us. I had thoughts of sending you the needful corrections of that pamphlet; but my circumstances being such, at present, as not to allow of this, must content myself with giving you the following summary narration of things as they have appeared among us.

The minds of people in this part of the world had been greatly prepossessed in favor of Mr. Whitefield, from the accounts transmitted of him, from time to time, as a wonder of piety, a man of God, so as no one was like him. Accordingly, when he came to town, about two years since, he was received as though he had been an angel of God; yea, a god come down in the likeness of man. He was strangely flocked after by all sorts of persons, and much admired by the vulgar, both great and small. The ministers had him in veneration, at least in appearance, as much as the people; encouraged his preaching, attended it themselves every day in the week, and mostly twice a day. The grand subject of conversation was Mr. Whitefield, and the whole business of the town to run from place to place to hear him preach. And as he preached under such uncommon advantages, being high in the opinion of the people and having the body of the ministers hanging on his lips, he soon insinuated himself still further into the affections of multitudes, insomuch that it became dangerous to mention his name without saying something in commendation of him.

His reception as he passed through this and the neighboring governments of Connecticut and New York, till he came to Philadelphia, was after much the same manner, save only that he met with no admirers among the clergy, unless here and there one, anywhere but in Boston; and whether the ministers here in general really thought better of him than they did elsewhere, I will not be too positive to affirm. 'Tis possible they might act as though they had a great veneration for him, and so as to lead people into such an apprehension, from cowardice, affectation of popularity, or a rigid attachment to some sentiments in divinity, they might imagine there was now an advantage to establish and propagate; and I would not undertake to prove that they might none of them be under an undue influence from some or other of these motives.

Much began to be now said of a glorious work of God going on in the land. Evening lectures were set up in one place and another; no less than six in this town, four weekly, and two monthly ones, though the town does not consist of above 5,000 families at the largest computation. At some of these lectures, it was common to mention Mr. Whitefield by name, both in the prayers and sermons; giving God thanks for sending such an extraordinary man among us, and making him the instrument of such extraordinary good to so many souls. He was indeed spoken of as the angel flying through heaven with the everlasting Gospel, and such honors sacrificed to him as were due to no mere man. Nay, to such a height did this spirit rise that all who did not express a very high thought of Mr. Whitefield were looked upon with an evil eye; and as to those who declared their dislike of what they judged amiss of the times, they were stigmatized as enemies of God and true religion. Yea, they were openly represented, both from the pulpit and the press, as in danger of committing the sin against the Holy Ghost, if not actually guilty even of this unpardonable sin.

And here you will doubtless be disposed to inquire what was the great good this gentleman was the instrument of. In answer whereto, I freely acknowledge, wherever he went he generally moved the passions, especially of the younger people, and the females among them; the effect whereof was a great talk about religion, together with a disposition to be perpetually hearing sermons to neglect of all other business; especially as preached by those who were sticklers for the *new way,* as it was called. And in these things chiefly consisted the goodness so much spoken of.

I deny not but there might be here and there a person stopped from going on in a course of sin; and some might be made really better. But so far as I could judge upon the nicest observation, the town, in general, was not much mended in those things wherein a reformation was greatly needed. I could not discern myself, nor many others whom I have talked with and challenged on this head, but that there was the same pride and vanity, the same luxury and intemperance, the same lying and tricking and cheating as before this gentleman came among us.

There was certainly no remarkable difference as to these things, and 'tis vain in any to pretend there was. This I am sure of, there was raised such a spirit of bitter, censorious, uncharitable judging as was not known before; and is, wherever it reigns, a scandal to all who call themselves Christians. Nor was it ever evident to me but that the greatest friends to Mr. Whitefield were as much puffed up with conceit and pride as any of their neighbors; and as to some of them, and the more eminent too, I verily believe they possess a worse spirit than before they heard of his name, and it had been as well for them if they had never seen his face.

But I have only entered as yet upon that scene of things which has made so much noise in the country. A number of ministers in one place and another were by this time formed into Mr. Whitefield's temper, and began to appear and go about preaching with a zeal more flaming, if possible, than his. One of the most famous among these was Mr. Gilbert Tennent, a man of no great parts or learning. His preaching was in the extemporaneous way, with much noise and little connection. If he had taken suitable care to prepare his sermons and followed nature in the delivery of them, he might have acquitted himself as a middling preacher; but, as he preached, he was an awkward imitator of Mr. Whitefield, and too often turned off his hearers with mere stuff, which he uttered with a spirit more bitter and uncharitable than you can easily imagine. All were Pharisees, hypocrites, carnal, unregenerate wretches, both ministers and people, who did not think just as he did, particularly as to the doctrines of Calvinism; and those who opposed him, and the work of God he was sure he was carrying on, would have opposed Christ Jesus himself and his apostles, had they lived in their day.

This gentleman came from New Brunswick in the Jersies to Boston, in the middle of winter (a journey of more than 300 miles), to water the good seed sown by Mr. Whitefield in this place. It was indeed at Mr. Whitefield's desire, and in consequence of a day of fasting and prayer kept on purpose to know the mind of God as to this matter, that he came among us; the ministers in the town, though fourteen in number, being thought insufficient to carry on the good work he had begun here in the hearts of people. And though the design this gentleman professedly came upon was a barefaced affront to the body of the ministers, yet not only the people (which is not to be wondered at) but some of the ministers themselves admired and followed him as much as they had done Mr. Whitefield before him. And here he was, by their encouragement, a great part of the winter, preaching every day in the week, to the taking people off from their callings and the introducing a neglect of all business but that of hearing him preach. He went from Boston to the eastward to visit the places where Mr. Whitefield had been; and on his return home passed through the country, preaching everywhere as he went along, in the same manner and with the same spirit he did here in Boston.

And now it was that Mr. Whitefield's doctrine of inward feelings began to discover itself in multitudes, whose sensible perceptions arose to such a height as that they cried out, fell down, swooned away, and, to all appearance, were like persons in fits; and this, when the preaching (if it may be so called) had in it as little well-digested and connected good sense as you can well suppose. Scores in a congregation would be in such circumstances at a time; nay, some hundreds in some places, to the filling the houses of worship with confusion not to be expressed in words, nor indeed conceived of by the most lively imagination, unless where persons have been eye and ear witnesses to these things. Though I may add here that to a person in possession of himself and capable of observation this surprising scene of things may be accounted for.

The speaker delivers himself with the greatest vehemence both of voice and gesture, and in the most frightful language his genius will allow of. If this has its intended effect upon one or two weak women, the shrieks catch from one to another, till a great part of the congregation is affected; and some are in the thought that it may be too common for those zealous in the new way to cry out themselves on purpose to move others and bring forward a general scream. Visions now became common, and trances also, the subjects of which were in their own conceit transported from earth to heaven, where they saw and heard most glorious things; conversed with Christ and holy angels; had opened to them the Book of Life and were permitted to read the names of persons there; and the like. And what is a singular instance (so far as I remember) of the working of enthusiasm, laughing — loud hearty laughing — was one of the ways in which our new converts, almost everywhere, were wont to join together in expressing their joy at the conversion of others.

'Tis scarce imaginable what excesses and extravagancies people were running into, and even encouraged in, being told such things were arguments of the extraordinary presence of the Holy Ghost with them. The same houses of worship were scarce emptied night nor day for a week together, and unheard of instances of supposed religion were carried on in them. Some would be praying, some exhorting, some singing, some clapping their hands, some laughing, some crying, some shrieking and roaring out; and so invincibly set were they in these ways, especially when encouraged by any ministers (as was too often the case), that it was a vain thing to argue with them to show them the indecency of such behavior;

and whoever indeed made an attempt this way might be sure aforehand of being called an opposer of the spirit and a child of the devil.

At these times there were among the people what we call here *exhorters;* these are such as are esteemed to be converts in the new way. Sometimes they are children, boys and girls, sometimes women; but most commonly raw, illiterate, weak, and conceited young men or lads. They pray with the people, call upon them to come to Christ, tell them they are dropping into hell, and take upon them what they imagine is the business of preaching. They are generally much better thought of than any ministers, except those in the new way, I mean by the friends to the extraordinaries prevalent in the land; and they are the greatest promoters of them. 'Tis indeed at the exhortations of these poor ignorant creatures that there is ordinarily the most noise and confusion; and, what may be worth a particular remark, 'tis seldom there are any great effects wrought till the gloominess of the night comes on. It is in the evening, or more late in the night, with only a few candles in a meetinghouse, that there is the screaming and shrieking to the greatest degree; and the persons thus affected are generally children, young people, and women. Other instances there may have been, but they are more rare; these bear the chief part.

I shall here insert a paragraph of a letter sent me by a friend living at New Haven, the seat of one of our colleges, a gentleman of known integrity and veracity, giving an account of the managements of one of the preachers of Mr. Whitefield's making, with the appearance following thereupon. Says he:

After the conclusion of the exercises usual in our religious assemblies, he came down from the pulpit into the deacon's seat. His exercises were: (1) short prayers, wherein he used very uncommon expressions, and such as had no tendency, at least in my mind, to excite devotion; which he delivered with a boisterous voice and in a manner to me very disagreeable; (2) singing psalms and hymns, which he himself repeated with an awful tone and frightful gestures; (3) exhorting, as they called it, to which many laymen were admitted as assistants.

In performing these exercises they observed no stated method, but proceeded as their present thought or fancy led them. And by this means the meetinghouse would be filled with what I could not but judge great confusion and disorder; for the whole house would many times seem to be in a perfect hubbub, and people filled with consternation. These meetings they would continue till ten, eleven, twelve o'clock at night; in the midst of them, sometimes ten, twenty, thirty, and sometimes many more would scream and cry out, or send forth the most lamentable groans, while others made great manifestations of joy by clapping their hands, uttering ecstatic expressions, singing psalms, and inviting and exhorting others. Some would swoon away under the influence of distressing fears and others swallowed up with insupportable joy. While some were fainting, others labored under convulsive twitches of body, which they said were involuntary. But in vain shall I pretend to describe all the proceedings at those meetings. But what appeared to me most dangerous and hurtful was that very much stress was laid on these extraordinaries, as though they were sure marks, or at least sufficient evidences of a just conviction of sin, on the one hand; or, on the other, of that joy which there is in believing, and so of an interest in the favor of God.

You may be ready, perhaps, to think I have here given you a romantic representation of things; but it is the real truth of the case without a figure. Yea, this has been the appearance in all parts of the land more or less, and so known to have been so that there is no room for debate upon the matter. Nay, those who are friends to the new way were once so far from being ashamed of these things that they boasted of them,

and entertained an ill opinion of all who did not speak of them as evidences of the wonderful power of the spirit of God. I say they at first boasted of these things, and some of them do so still; though the generality have begun, for some time, to speak publicly of the subtility of Satan, to tell people he may appear as an angel of light, and to warn them against being carried away by his devices.

Nay, Mr. Tennent himself, one of the main instruments of all our disorders, has, in a couple of letters to some of his friends, published in the prints, expressed his fears lest the churches should be undone with a spirit of enthusiasm and these exhorters which have risen up everywhere in the land. He seems indeed to have quite turned about, the reason whereof may be this: The Moravians who came to Philadelphia with Count Zinzendorf have been among his people, and managed with them as he did elsewhere, and brought the like confusion among them. And now he cries out of danger, and expresses himself much as those did, whom before he had sent to the devil by wholesale.

Various are the sentiments of persons about this unusual appearance among us. Some think it to be a most wonderful work of God's grace; others, a most wonderful spirit of enthusiasm. Some think there is a great deal of religion, with some small mixture of extravagance; others, a great deal of extravagance, with some small mixture of that which may be called good. Some think the country was never in such a happy state on a religious account; others, that it was never in a worse.

For myself, I am among those who are clearly in the opinion that there never was such a spirit of superstition and enthusiasm reigning in the land before; never such gross disorders and barefaced affronts to common decency; never such scandalous reproaches on the Blessed Spirit, making Him the author of the greatest irregularities and confusions. Yet, I am of opinion also that the appearances among us (so much out of the ordinary way, and so unaccountable to persons not acquainted with the history of the world) have been the means of awakening the attention of many; and a good number, I hope, have settled into a truly Christian temper. Though I must add, at the same time, that I am far from thinking that the appearance, in general, is any other than the effect of enthusiastic heat.

The goodness that has been so much talked of, 'tis plain to me, is nothing more, in general, than a commotion in the passions. I can't see that men have been made better, if hereby be meant their being formed to a nearer resemblance to the Divine Being in moral holiness. 'Tis not evident to me that persons, generally, have a better understanding of religion, a better government of their passions, a more Christian love to their neighbor, or that they are more decent and regular in their devotions toward God. I am clearly of the mind they are worse in all these regards. They place their religion so much in the heat and fervor of their passions that they too much neglect their reason and judgment; and instead of being more kind and gentle, more full of mercy and good fruits, they are more bitter, fierce, and implacable.

And what is a grand discriminating mark of this work, wherever it takes place, is that it makes men spiritually proud and conceited beyond measure; infinitely censorious and uncharitable to neighbors, to relations, even the nearest and dearest, to ministers in a special manner; yea, to all mankind who are not as they are, and don't think and act as they do. And there are few places where this work has been in any remarkable manner but they have been filled with faction and contention; yea, in some they have divided into parties, and openly and scandalously separated from one another.

Truly, the accounts sent abroad were sent too soon; too soon, I am satisfied, to reflect honor upon the persons who wrote them. They betray such a want of judgment as I was really sorry to see them falling into. There are few persons now, perhaps none, but such as are evidently overheated, but begin to see that things have been carried too far, and that the hazard is great, unless God mercifully interpose, lest we should be overrun with enthusiasm. And to speak the plain truth, my fear is lest the end of these things should be Quakerism and infidelity. These we have now chiefly to guard against.

A particular account of one Mr. James Davenport, with his strange conduct in town and elsewhere, I doubt not would have been agreeable; but I have exceeded already. He is the wildest enthusiast I ever saw, and acts in the wildest manner; and, yet, he is vindicated by some in all his extravagancies.

I now beg pardon, sir, for thus trespassing upon your patience. As Mr. Whitefield has been in Scotland, and human nature is the same everywhere, this narration of the effects he has been the instrument of producing here may excite your zeal to guard the people in time against any such extravagancies, if there should be danger of them where you may be concerned.

Young man, my advice to you is that you cultivate an acquaintance with, and a firm belief in, the Holy Scriptures. This is your certain interest.

BENJAMIN FRANKLIN

98.

Henry Melchior Mühlenberg: On the Right to Appoint Clergy

During the early decades of the eighteenth century, the Lutherans of America were relatively few and, under the nominal leadership of the overbearing Pietist, Count Zinzendorf, divided into disputing factions. The Lutheran churches of Pennsylvania, far from content with the situation, called on the church in Germany for assistance. In response to this call, Henry Melchior Mühlenberg arrived in Philadelphia on November 25, 1742. But his position in Pennsylvania was not at first secure. He was distrusted by the skeptical Philadelphia Germans, and he found Zinzendorf opposed to his attempt to unify the Lutheran parishes. Mühlenberg was finally able to do this, but the turning point in his career was a confrontation with Zinzendorf that occurred in late December of 1742. Mühlenberg wrote the following account of their meeting in his Journal.

Source: *The Journals of Henry Melchior Mühlenberg,* translated by Theodore G. Tappert and John W. Doberstein, Philadelphia, 1942, Vol. I, pp. 76-78.

THE COUNT HAD, from the beginning, set himself up as a Lutheran pastor, and won the confidence of the people to such an extent that they had given him a written call. However, the call was not subscribed by anyone. On one occasion, when he had preached to the Lutherans in a house which they rented jointly with the Reformed, a few buttons of the sheep's clothing flew open and the other side of his face was revealed, which made the sheep suspicious and scattered them. Whatever each could snatch on the run he took with him. One had taken the church record book, another the alms bag, a third the alms chest, a fourth the chalice, a fifth the key, and so on. Afterward, a Lutheran deacon, Thomas Mayor, had put a lock on the church house.

On the Sunday reserved for the Lutherans, the Count sent to the church his adjunct, Mr. Pirlaeus, and the people he had enticed away from the Lutherans. When they found the lock there, they broke it off with a piece of iron, went in, began to sing, and Mr. Pirlaeus was about to preach. The Lutherans and the Reformed also gathered outside the door and saw that the lock had been broken off. A Lutheran elder thereupon went in and exhorted Mr. Pirlaeus to leave. When he repeatedly refused and accused the elder of not being a Lutheran and told him that he was going astray, the Reformed people rushed in and dragged the adjunct out. During all this rough work on a Sunday, they trampled, pushed, and knocked each other about, and the women began to scream; in short, there was a tumult. The Zinzendorfers brought suit in the affair, and the Reformed and Lutherans contested it; and the upshot is that it is in the hands of the court and has developed into a long, drawn-out lawsuit.

Now the question was: Who had rented the house? The house belonged to a leading, respectable merchant in the city. The Count got next to the owner and tried to make him believe that his people were the real Lutherans who, together with the Reformed, had rented the house. A few others called themselves Lutherans, and this minority had illegally put on the lock. Several Lutheran deacons, however, had taken a vote among their people who far outnumbered the Moravians, and submitted it to the owner. Since the Count had won over to his side two of the Lutheran deacons who had possession of the key to the alms chest, the chalice, and the church book, he thought he could accomplish something in this way. The above-described disturbance occurred on July 18, 1742, old style. About two weeks afterward, when the Lutherans had gathered to edify themselves with singing and reading in their jointly rented house, the Count himself came in again with his people and wanted to preach. The Lutheran deacons warned him earnestly, however, that he should leave and not disturb them. He withdrew and went away.

For some time they tried to reach an amicable agreement and settle the affair peaceably, and to this end some of the elders of the Lutheran congregation, along with one deacon from Providence, even had a meeting with them. The Count, on his part, had commissioned Peter Böhler to speak for him and through him presented a number of written articles to which they were to subscribe. The articles, however, were so curious that they were unable in good conscience to sign them; so the affair remained in process. Our people confronted Mr. Peter Böhler with the misdemeanor of having torn the lock off the door, and he replied that they should not attach much importance to that affair, for when swine come to their sty and find the door locked, they put their snout under the door and lift it off the hinges. Our people had no objection to make to this pretty remark and so the meeting broke up without success. . . .

I sent two of our deacons to the above-mentioned brewer to demand that he send back our church book and the copper chalice since they belonged to our congregation. He sent back the reply that he had turned them both over to Count Zinzendorf. Then the two deacons wanted to send over to the Count's, but, before they reached there, the Count sent Mr. Peter Böhler to me to say that he thought it very strange that when I was in Philadelphia I did not come to visit him. Mr. Böhler entered into a dispute with me concerning their affairs in the presence of our deacons. Finally, he said that I should speak with Mr. von Thürnstein himself. After dinner the Count sent word to me, politely requesting that I should visit him. I went, expecting to speak to the Count alone. When I arrived, however, there was in the room a large gathering of his generals and corporals, the Count presiding at a small table. This was the first time I ever saw the Count face to face, and I expected to hear something great from the *Reformator Ecclesiae*. The Count asked me first about a number of circumstances with regard to Grosshennersdorf in Upper Lusatia. What I knew I answered. Then the following ensued:

Count. On what conditions are you here?
Reply. I have been called and sent through the Rev. Court Preacher Zigenhagen, who had a commission from the congregation.
Count. What sort of commission did Mr. Zigenhagen have?
Reply. The three Lutheran congregations in New Hanover, Providence, and Philadelphia had been urgently requesting a pastor for several years past. The copies are deposited in Providence and the letters in London, which can be published at any time, if necessary.
Count. When did the congregation last petition for a pastor?
Reply. I do not know; I must look it up in the copies.
Count. You must say at once when they

wrote the last letter to Mr. Zigenhagen.
(The brewer and several others of his
people chimed in and said that the last letter may have reached there about 1739. I
did not know, because nothing had been
said to me about it.)

[*Reply.*] I really cannot say just now, and
besides, it is of no importance, for I have
been called, sent, and accepted. The deacons
and elders of the three congregations have
signed an acceptance.

Count. Here in Philadelphia no deacons
of the Lutheran congregation gave their sig-
natures, for the deacons of the Lutheran
congregation are sitting here, and there is
no other Lutheran congregation and church
here other than the one we have. Haven't
you seen the church yet, which was just recently built?

Reply. I know nothing about it, because I
am convinced that I preached to Lutheran
people and was accepted by them.

Count. They are not Lutherans but rebels,
brawlers; and you have become the head of
such people and preached to them in the
house from which they expelled my adjunct
Pirlaeus. The rebels must first come to us
and apologize.

Reply. My dear Count, your people must
first come and apologize to our Lutherans
because they broke the lock off our church
and started the tumult.

Count. That is not true!

Reply. It is true to the extent that they
are still involved in a lawsuit over it.

Count. I know of no lawsuit.

Reply. Well, everybody knows what happened last summer, July 18.

Count. Let us stick to the subject. The
last time I asked Mr. Zigenhagen how
things stood as far as Pennsylvania was concerned, he replied that he could send no
preacher there because the congregations
were not willing to stipulate the salary.
Now, since Mr. Zigenhagen knew that I
had come in here, why did he send you afterward?

Reply. I was sent to investigate conditions
here and to see whether order cannot be
established.

Count. Mr. Zigenhagen is an archliar and
hypocrite! When I am in his presence, he is
meek and humble and submissive; when I
am away from him, he inveighs and slanders. This is another spiteful trick which he
and Mr. Franke are playing off on me! I
shall tell him of it to his face when I get to
London.

Reply. My dear Count, it is a shame to
speak that way. I have often heard in Germany that you, yourself, were a liar. Am I
not forced to believe it?

Count. I have heard that you have read
all my writings. Did you not read that I
have established a Lutheran consistory here
in Philadelphia?

Reply. I read in Charlestown the printed
reports of seven conferences, and through
them learned that a certain Mr. von
Thürnstein had caused disturbances in various places, but I did not know that the
Count had established a Lutheran consistory.

Count. These are Jesuitical tricks.

Reply. I once heard in Germany that you
were appointed a Moravian bishop by a
Reformed preacher. How does that jibe
with your being able to establish a Lutheran consistory?

Count. I am inspector of all Lutheran
churches in Pennsylvania and Lutheran pastor in Philadelphia. I have held synods in
the country and here, also installed pastors
in several places, and even deposed a pastor
named Stöver.

Reply. Can a Reformed preacher give such
authority to you?

Count. Don't you understand canonical
law? Don't you know that in Wittenberg
the foremost Lutheran theologian, was ordained by a Catholic?

Reply. But how is it that sometimes you
can be a Moravian bishop and sometimes
an inspector and a Lutheran pastor?

Count. I publicly resigned my episcopal office in Holland in the presence of lords and princes.

Reply. You change frequently.

Count. I have been called as pastor in writing by the Lutheran congregation here in Philadelphia, . . .

Reply. Is your call signed by anybody? *Count.* It doesn't need it.

Reply. My call has been signed and I shall trouble myself no further, but just follow the instructions of my superiors in Europe. If this does not please you, you can settle it with them.

99.

CADWALLADER COLDEN: Encroachment on Indian Lands

The following selection, taken from a famous book by Cadwallader Colden, is an account of informal negotiations that took place between Indian leaders and Pennsylvania officials on July 7, 1742. As usual, the talk centered on land rights and boundary violations by the white settlers on the frontier. But other and more serious problems underlay the exchange of amenities. The English colonists were anxious to open up the Ohio Valley for trade, and at the same time feared French interference, which would be intensified by a French alliance with the Indians. The principal speakers were the Iroquois chief Canassateego and the lieutenant governor of Pennsylvania, George Thomas.

Source: *The History of the Five Indian Nations of Canada, etc., etc.,* 3rd edition, London, 1755, Vol. II, pp. 18-24.

"BRETHREN, the Governor and Council, and all present,

"According to our promise we now propose to return you an answer to the several things mentioned to us yesterday, and shall beg leave to speak to public affairs first, though they were what you spoke to last. On this head you yesterday put us in mind, first, of William Penn's early and constant care to cultivate friendship with all the Indians; of the treaty we held with one of his sons, about ten years ago; and of the necessity there is at this time of keeping the roads between us clear and free from all obstructions.

"We are all very sensible of the kind regard that good man William Penn had for all the Indians, and cannot but be pleased to find that his children have the same. We well remember the treaty you mention held with his son on his arrival here, by which we confirmed our league of friendship, that is to last as long as the sun and moon endure. In consequence of this, we, on our part, shall preserve the road free from all encumbrances; in confirmation whereof we lay down this string of wampum.

"You, in the next place, said you would enlarge the fire and make it burn brighter, which we are pleased to hear you mention; and assure you we shall do the same by adding to it more fuel, that it may still flame out more strongly than ever.

"In the last place, you were pleased to say that we are bound by the strictest leagues to watch for each others preservation; that we should hear with our ears for you, and you hear with your ears for us. This is equally agreeable to us; and we shall not fail to give you early intelligence, whenever anything of consequence comes to our knowledge. And to encourage you to do the same, and to nourish in your hearts what you have spoke to us with your tongues about the renewal of our amity and the brightening of the chain of friendship, we confirm what we have said with another belt of wampum.

"Brethren, we received from the Proprietors yesterday some goods in consideration of our release of the lands on the west side of Susquehanna. It is true, we have the full quantity according to agreement; but if the Proprietor had been here himself, we think, in regard of our numbers and poverty, he would have made an addition to them. If the goods were only to be divided among the Indians present, a single person would

have but a small portion; but if you consider what numbers are left behind, equally entitled with us to a share, there will be extremely little. We therefore desire, if you have the keys of the Proprietor's chest, you will open it and take out a little more for us.

"We know our lands are now become more valuable. The white people think we do not know their value; but we are sensible that the land is everlasting, and the few goods we receive for it are soon worn out and gone. For the future, we will sell no lands but when Brother Onas is in the country; and we will know beforehand the quantity of the goods we are to receive. Besides, we are not well used with respect to the lands still unsold by us. Your people daily settle on these lands, and spoil our hunting. We must insist on your removing them, as you know they have no right to settle to the northward of Kittochtinny Hills. In particular, we renew our com-

Map of the five Iroquois nations from "History of the Five Indian Nations" by Colden, 1755

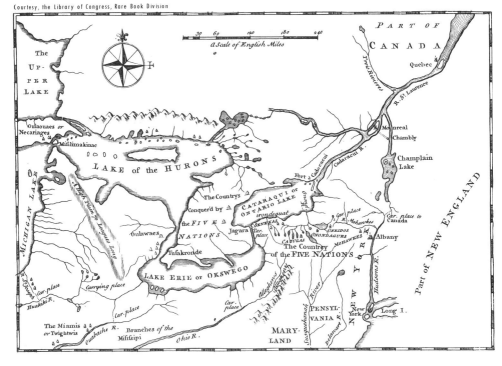

plaints against some people who are settled at Juniata, a branch of Susquehanna, and all along the banks of that river, as far as Mahaniay; and desire they may be forthwith made to go off the land, for they do great damage to our cousins the Delawares.

"We have further to observe, with respect to the lands lying on the west side of Susquehanna that though Brother Onas (meaning the Proprietor) has paid us for what his people possess, yet some parts of that country have been taken up by persons whose place of residence is to the south of this province, from whom we have never received any consideration. This affair was recommended to you by our chiefs at our last treaty; and you then, at our earnest desire, promised to write a letter to that person who has the authority over those people, and to procure us his answer.

"As we have never heard from you on this head, we want to know what you have done in it. If you have not done anything, we now renew our request, and desire you will inform the person whose people are seated on our lands that that country belongs to us, in right of conquest; we having bought it with our blood, and taken it from our enemies in fair war; and we expect, as owners of that land, to receive such a consideration for it as the land is worth. We desire you will press him to send a positive answer. Let him say Yes or No; if he says Yes, we will treat with him; if No, we are able to do ourselves justice, and we will do it by going to take payment ourselves.

"It is customary with us to make a present of skins whenever we renew our treaties. We are ashamed to offer our brethren so few, but your horses and cows have eaten the grass our deer used to feed on. This has made them scarce, and will, we hope, plead in excuse for our not bringing a larger quantity. If we could have spared more, we would have given more; but we are really poor; and desire you'll not consider the quantity, but, few as they are, accept them

Courtesy, the Metropolitan Museum of Art, bequest of Grace Wilkes, 1922
Cadwallader Colden, portrait by John Wollaston

in testimony of our regard." Here they gave the Governor a bundle of skins. The Governor immediately replied.

"Brethren, we thank you for the many declarations of respect you have given us, in this solemn renewal of our treaties. We receive and shall keep your string and belts of wampum as pledges of your sincerity, and desire those we gave you may be carefully preserved, as testimonies of ours.

"In answer to what you say about the Proprietaries — they are all absent, and have taken the keys of their chest with them; so that we cannot, on their behalf, enlarge the quantity of goods. Were they here, they might, perhaps, be more generous; but we cannot be liberal for them. The government will, however, take your request into consideration; and in regard to your poverty, may, perhaps, make you a present. I but just mention this now, intending to refer this part of your speech to be answered at our next meeting.

"The number of guns, as well as everything else, answers exactly with the particulars specified in your deed of conveyance, which is more than was agreed to be given you. It was your own sentiments that the lands on the west side of Susquehanna were not so valuable as those on the east; and an abatement was to be made proportionable to the difference in value. But the Proprietor overlooked this, and ordered the full quantity to be delivered, which you will look on as a favor.

"It is very true that lands are of late becoming more valuable; but what raises their value? Is it not entirely owing to the industry and labor used by the white people in their cultivation and improvement? Had not they come among you, these lands would have been of no use to you, any further than to maintain you. And is there not, now you have sold so much, enough left for all the purposes of living? What you say of the goods, that they are soon worn out, is applicable to everything; but you know very well that they cost a great deal of money; and the value of land is no more than it is worth in money.

"On your former complaints against people's settling the lands on Juniata, and from thence all along on the River Susquehanna as far as Mahaniahy, some magistrates were sent expressly to remove them, and we thought no persons would presume to stay after that."

Here they interrupted the Governor. . . . "These persons who were sent did not do their duty. So far from removing the people, they made surveys for themselves, and they are in league with the trespassers. We desire more effectual methods may be used, and honester persons employed."

Which the Governor promised, and then proceeded:

"I shall conclude what I have to say at this time with acknowledgements for your present, which is very agreeable to us, from the expressions of regard used by you in presenting it — gifts of this nature receiving their value from the affection of the giver, and not from the quantity or price of the thing given."

"Brethren, according to the promise made at our last treaty with you, Mr. Logan, who was at that time president, did write to the governor of Maryland, that he might make you satisfaction for such of your lands as his people had taken up, but did not receive one word from him upon that head. I will write to him again, and endeavor to procure you a satisfactory answer. We do not doubt but he will do you justice. But we exhort you to be careful not to exercise any acts of violence toward his people, as they likewise are our brethren, and subjects of the same great King; and therefore violence toward them must be productive of very evil consequences."

———◆———

The Father of Waters.
The Mississippi. The name of the river is derived from the Algonquin *misi,* meaning great, and *sipi,* meaning river. Le Page du Pratz, *Histoire de la Louisiane,* 1758, translated the word erroneously as *le vieux père des rivières.*

RIVAL COLONIAL EMPIRES

The struggle for control of the continent intensified in the 18th century. Already excluded from most of North America, the Spanish strengthened their fortifications in Florida in anticipation of increased French and English colonial expansion. The Spanish also pressed forward with numerous missionary settlements in the Southwest, under the characteristic dual administration of church and military.

But the main contestants in North America were the English and the French. The European wars of these powers were paralleled by four major colonial conflicts, in which the army regulars and colonial militias on both sides were joined by Indian allies.

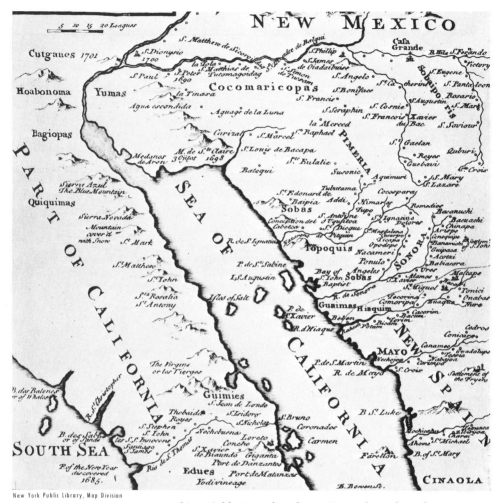

Map of Baja California and northwest Mexico drawn by Father Kino, 1701

The Spanish Missions

The countless missions established by the Spanish in Mexico account for the prevalence of Catholicism in that country today. Farther north, in the present southwestern United States, the influence of the missions did not outlast the 19th century as the Indian populations they served were moved or wiped out by advancing Protestant settlers from the East.

1691 sketch of hive-shaped huts of the Caddo Indians in Texas

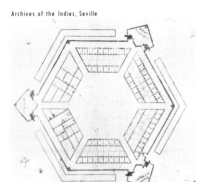

Plan of the Presidio at Adaes, Texas,
1721

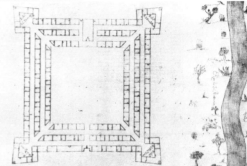

Presidio of San Antonio, 1722

Map showing
the Presidio
of San Anto-
nio and the
missions of
Texas, 1764

Spanish settlement at Pensacola, Florida, 1743

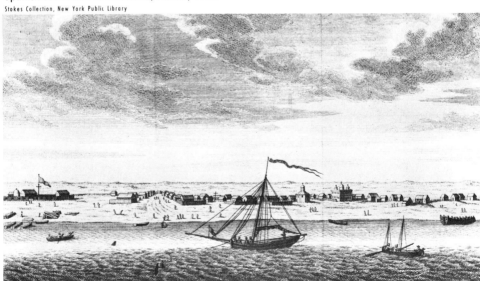

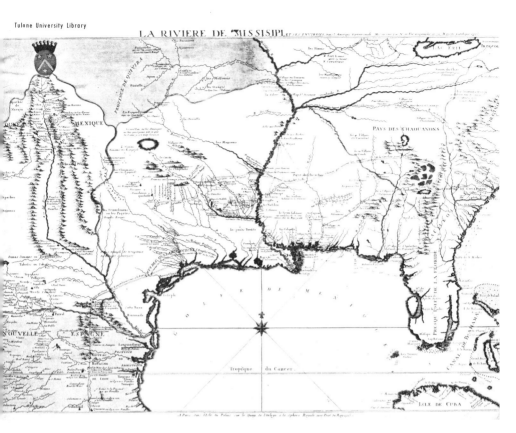

New French Settlements

The St. Lawrence Valley remained the principal area of French settlement in the 18th century. However, prompted by the fur trade, French exploration into the interior continued. Forts were built in the Mississippi Valley and alliances with the Indians were sought as a matter of policy. French control over the Mississippi, extending along the Gulf Coast, encircled the English colonies and threatened the Spanish claim to the Southwest.

(Above) Map of the Mississippi River drawn by Nicolas de Fer, 1715; (left) plan of Mobile, showing the French fort built in 1702

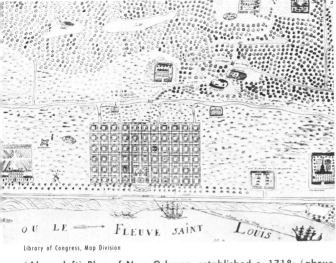

(Above left) Plan of New Orleans, established c. 1718; (above right) Pierre le Moyne, founder of Louisiana, 1698; (center) birch bark map showing route between Lake Superior and Lake of the Woods drawn by the Indian guide of Pierre de la Verendrye, 1728; (bottom) French settlement of Cascaskies (Kaskaskia, Ill.), established in the early 17th century

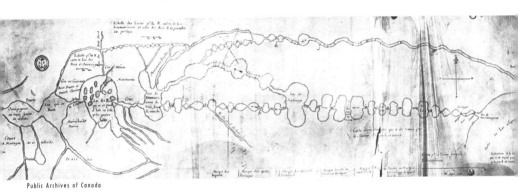

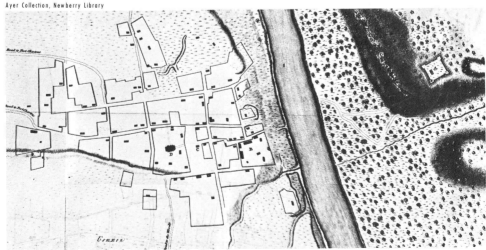

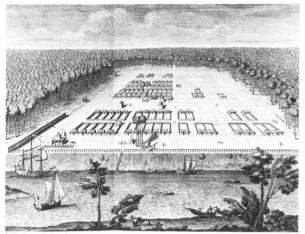

Savannah, Georgia, 1734

James Oglethorpe

**Lutherans from Salzburg
leaving for Georgia, 1732**

Oglethorpe's fleet attacking St. Augustine, 1740

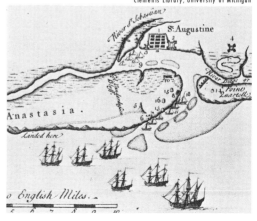

Georgia

The last colony to be founded
was Georgia, in 1733. James
Oglethorpe expected the colony to
be settled by British debtors, although many early settlers were
Protestants from western Europe.
Oglethorpe also intended the colony as a buffer against the Spanish
in Florida, and Georgia was soon
involved in the "War of Jenkins'
Ear," in 1739.

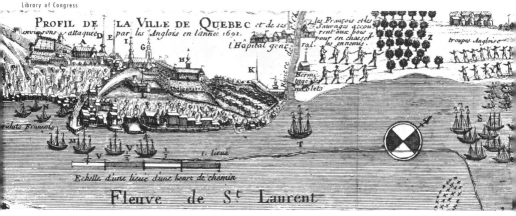

PROFIL DE LA VILLE DE QUEBEC et de ses environs attaquée par les Anglois en lannée 1691.

Fleuve de St Laurent

(Above) Quebec under attack by the English, 1691; (right) Sir William Phips, leader of the attack

Colonial Wars

Two strong fortresses enabled the French to control Canada and harass New England fishing and commerce during a hundred years of colonial rivalry. Quebec resisted repeated British attacks until 1759. Louisbourg fell in 1745, but was traded back to France by treaty in 1748.

(Below left) English expedition against Louisbourg, 1745; (below right) Sir William Pepperrell, commander of the English forces

1743

100.

WILLIAM BOLLAN: Smuggling in the Colonies

By 1743, Britain's New England colonies had become important manufacturing as well as trading centers, often in more or less direct competition with the mother country. Despite repeated attempts to control this competition, British laws like the Molasses Act of 1733 were for the most part unenforceable. New England was usually able either to ignore or to evade regulation — which she had to do, indeed, in order to remain prosperous. One result was that smuggling was widespread. The Board of Trade in London sent frequent inquiries to the royal governors concerning the extent of illegal trade and commerce. The following reply to one such inquiry was written by William Bollan, the advocate general of Massachusetts, on February 26, 1743.

Source: *Publications of the Colonial Society of Massachusetts*, Vol. VI, Boston, 1904, pp. 299-304.

My Lords:

Mr. Shirley, the governor and vice-admiral of this province, soon after his being made such, was pleased to appoint me the King's advocate; and, according to the practice, here it is the duty of the person filling that place to prosecute all offenders against the Acts of Trade, the discharge of which trust has been lately attended with such discoveries, and is at present accompanied with so many difficulties, that after communicating them to His Excellency, he gave me orders to make them particularly known to Your Lordships. And, indeed, I conceive them to be of such nature and consequence that, had I not received his commands to that end, I should have thought myself obliged in faithfulness to the

Crown to lay them before Your Lordships.

After mentioning which I shall make no further apology for giving Your Lordships this trouble but proceed to inform you that there has lately been carried on here a large illicit trade (destructive to the interest of Great Britain in her trade to her own plantations and contrary to the main intent of all her laws made to regulate that trade) by importing into this province large quantities of European goods of almost all sorts from diverse parts of Europe, some of which are by the laws wholly prohibited to be imported into the plantations, and the rest are prohibited to be imported there unless brought directly from Great Britain.

To show forth to Your Lordships the rise, progress, and extent of this pernicious practice would, I fear, far exceed the proper compass of a letter from me to Your Lordships, and therefore I shall content myself with saying, first, that a considerable number of ships have . . . lately come into this country directly from Holland, laden, some wholly, some in part, with reels of yarn or spun hemp, paper, gunpowder, iron, and goods of various sorts used for men and women's clothing. Second, that some vessels have also come directly from other foreign parts of Europe with like cargoes. Third, that some of those vessels were laden chiefly and others in part with the goods of the produce and manufacture of old Spain prohibited under large penalties to be imported into Great Britain during the present war. Fourth, that to carry on this sort of trade, diverse vessels have been fitted out here laden with provisions, and though they appear wholly English in the plantations, yet, by means of their being commanded and navigated by French refugees naturalized, or such persons as may easily pass for Frenchmen and by the help of French papers and passes procured by French merchants concerned in the matter, they have carried the English provisions to their open enemies and landed them out of those vessels in the ports of Spain.

Fifth, that a considerable part of the illicit trade from Holland is carried on by factors here for the sake of their commissions, Dutch merchants having the property in the goods imported. Sixth, that one of these illicit traders, lately departed hence for Holland, proposed to one of the greatest sellers of broadcloths here (and to how many others I can't say) to supply him with black cloths from thence, saying that this country might be better and cheaper supplied with broadcloths of that color from Holland than from England; but to prevent, or rather increase, Your Lordships' surprise on this head, I need only to acquaint you that I write this, clad in a superfine French cloth which I bought on purpose that I might

wear about the evidence of these illegal traders having already begun to destroy the vital parts of the British commerce; and to use a memento to myself and the customhouse officers to do everything in our power toward cutting off this trade so very pernicious to the British nation.

Seventh, that the persons concerned in this trade are many, some of them of the greatest fortunes in this country, and who have made great gains by it; and, having all felt the sweets of it, they begin to espouse and justify it, some openly, some covertly; and having persuaded themselves that their trade ought not to be bound by the laws of Great Britain, they labor, and not without success, to poison the minds of all the inhabitants of the province, and matters are brought to such a pass that it is sufficient to recommend any trade to their general approbation and favor that it is unlawful. And as examples of this kind soon spread their influence on the other plantations around, 'tis too plain almost to need mentioning that if care be not soon taken to cure this growing mischief, the British trade to these plantations and their proper dependence on their mother country will in a great measure, ere long, be lost.

I shall now recount to Your Lordships the difficulties which attend the suppression of this mischief. The first and one of the principal whereof is that the breaches of the statute . . . entitled "An Act for the Encouragement of Trade," and made purposely to keep the plantations in a firm dependence upon England; and to render them advantageous to it in the vent [sale] of English woolen and other commodities; and which provides that all European goods and manufactures imported into the plantations shall be shipped in England, are not cognizable in the Court of Admiralty, and a prosecution in the common law courts here will be unavoidably attended with great delay and too many difficulties and discouragements to be generally overcome.

For, in the first place, by the course of judicial proceedings established in this province, there will be a necessity for the prosecutor to pass through various trials (and frequently in distant counties) in courts disinclined to the prosecution, and with scarce any hopes of success; for, in the next place, the prosecutor cannot there have process to compel an appearance of unwilling witnesses (and all witnesses for the Crown in cases of this nature are generally such); and, finally, a trial by jury here is only trying one illicit trader by his fellows, or at least his well-wishers. How it happened that the offenses against this statute, which is the main ligament whereby the plantation trade is fastened and secured to Great Britain, should not be cognizable in the Court of Admiralty, when the cognizance of other Acts of Trade of much less consequence to the nation are given to that court from the common consideration of the interest or desire that the juries have here to defeat all seizures and prosecutions for the Crown, I cannot say; but the inconveniences that at present proceed from the Court of Admiralty's want of jurisdiction over offenses against that statute are certainly very great.

Another difficulty that attends the suppressing this illegal trade arises from the nature and situation of the country which abounds with outports, where vessels employed in this trade unlade their cargoes into small vessels, wherein they afterward carry their prohibited goods with ease into some proper places of safety. And a further difficulty grows out of the corruption of those who are employed to carry on this trade, which is become so great that we have had some late instances of oaths taken at the customhouse by masters of vessels in direct contradiction to their certain knowledge of the truth, and to this crime these illicit traders have lately added this contrivance; viz., to conceal or spirit away the seamen who might otherwise be witnesses and by their testimony possibly cause a condemnation of some of the vessels employed this way; and thus, when vast quantities of goods are illegally imported here, after they are unladen and secured, the master appears boldly and is ready to swear anything for the good of the voyage, and the sailors are dispersed and gone, and there is nothing to be found but an empty vessel, against which no proof can be obtained.

Having thus laid before Your Lordships the principal difficulties that attend the carrying the Acts of Trade into execution here, it may perhaps be expected that I should propose some remedies which appear to us who are upon the spot, and there observe the working of these things to be most likely to effect the cure of these mischiefs; wherefore, I shall now proceed to mention them for the consideration of Your Lordships.

The first thing that seems necessary to be done, and that by Parliament, is to grant to the Court of Admiralty cognizance of all past and future offenses against the abovementioned statute . . . or (which would be much better) to provide by act of Parliament that all offenses whatever, past and future, against the Acts of Trade committed in the plantations, and the penalties and forfeitures arising therefrom, may be prosecuted for and recovered in any Court of Admiralty in the plantations. There is really a greater want of a certain and general jurisdiction in the Courts of Admiralty in the plantations over breaches of the Acts of Trade there than at first may be imagined.

For among other things the statute . . . for preventing frauds and regulating abuses in the plantation trade is so obscurely penned in the point of the Admiralty's jurisdiction that it has received different constructions, and that court has been frequently prohibited in this province to take cognizance of some of the main offenses against that statute. And of late I hear that like prohibitions have been granted in the province of New York, though the intent of the

Parliament that made that statute (as I think) doubtless was to give that Admiralty jurisdiction of all offenses against it. The granting to the Admiralty a general jurisdiction over all breaches of the Laws of Trade will, without question, be of advantage to the Crown and Kingdom and save much trouble to the officers prosecuting illicit traders. And, indeed, no reason can be assigned for giving the Admiralty cognizance of offenses against some of the Acts of Trade, but what holds equally good for giving the like jurisdiction over the rest. But let what will be done with respect to granting the Admiralty courts in the plantations such general jurisdiction, I think it is very plain that to suffer the offenses against [that statute], to remain only punishable in the courts of common law, is to leave it in the power of illicit traders (notwithstanding that statute) to import into these plantations any European goods directly from any foreign countries to their great profit and with little peril.

Another thing I would propose to Your Lordships as a cure of this mischievous trade is that actions of detinue be brought against some of the principal offenders importing here goods from foreign parts in order to recover the goods imported, or their value, against the importer of them. Such actions will be warranted by the judgment given in Westminster Hall by the Court of King's Bench . . . in the case of Roberts against Wetheral. . . . The effect of a few such actions properly pursued and recoveries thereupon had, will, I think, unquestionably have the greatest possible tendency to break up this trade; for the security of the persons concerned in it according to their understanding of the matter rests in this: that if they can but prevent the officers

seizing the goods illegally imported (and therein they generally meet with no great difficulty, as has been already observed), then they are, according to their present judgments, safe in all respects. But when once the importers come to find that they are chargeable with actions for the goods illegally imported, or their value, after they have imported them safely and disposed of them, I think they cannot but be deterred from making such unlawful importations; for then they will see a new danger, great and of long duration, such as upon the whole they will have but little (if any) hopes to secure themselves from. . . .

And though I have said so much to Your Lordships touching this matter, yet I cannot avoid adding that this illicit trade is carried on to so great a degree and in so many various shapes that I make no doubt but if proper preventive measures be not soon taken, a great part of the bounty money given by Great Britain to the importers of naval stores from the plantations will in a short time be laid out in Holland or other parts of Europe in the purchase of goods there to be illegally imported here, if that has not been already practised.

I cannot conclude without observing to Your Lordships that, unless effectual measures are speedily taken to stop this growing evil, the illicit traders will by their numbers, wealth, and wiles have got such power in these parts that laws and orders may come too late from Great Britain to have their proper effect against it.

Your Lordships' commands to me (if you have any touching these matters) signified to His Excellency the Governor, or in whatever manner you please, shall be obeyed with the utmost care and dispatch.

101.

Jonathan Edwards: On the Great Religious Revival

Between 1730 and 1745 there swept over the American colonies from Maine to Georgia a religious revival known as the Great Awakening. Particularly in the back country, where hundreds of isolated communities had neither church nor minister, and where the social instinct was all but wholly frustrated, a passion developed for religious conversion. Meetings were held and sects were formed, while itinerant preachers gave fervent sermons on the certainty of sin and the hope of salvation. For the revival movement, unlike the earlier doctrine of the Puritans, promised the grace of God to all who could experience a desire for it. Details of the second wave of the Great Awakening in Northampton, Massachusetts, are given in the following letter of December 12, 1743, addressed by Jonathan Edwards to the Reverend Thomas Prince in Boston. The Mr. Whitefield to whom Edwards refers was the Reverend George Whitefield, the English evangelist who toured the American colonies in 1740 preaching to huge revival meetings. It was said of him that he could make his voice audible to as many as 25,000 persons. Edwards' letter, which was printed by Prince in the Boston Christian History *of January 14, 21, and 28, 1744, gives some indication of the reasons why in the following year Edwards started to cast doubt on the conversions within his own congregation — an act that virtually destroyed his public career.*

Source: *Christian History, Containing Accounts of the Revival*, Boston, January 14, 21, 28, 1743/4.

EVER SINCE THE GREAT WORK OF GOD THAT was wrought here about nine years ago, there has been a great abiding alteration in this town in many respects. There has been vastly more religion kept up in the town, among all sorts of persons, in religious exercises and in common conversation than used to be before. There has remained a more general seriousness and decency in attending the public worship. There has been a very great alteration among the youth of the town with respect to reveling, frolicking, profane and unclean conversation, and lewd songs. Instances of fornication have been very rare. There has also been a great alter-ation among both old and young with respect to tavern haunting. I suppose the town has been in no measure so free of vice in these respects for any long time together for this sixty years as it has been this nine years past.

There has also been an evident alteration with respect to a charitable spirit to the poor (though I think with regard to this we in this town, as the land in general, come far short of Gospel rules). And though after that great work nine years ago there has been a very lamentable decay of religious affections and the engagedness of people's spirit in religion, yet many societies for prayer and social religion were all along kept up; and there were some few instances of awakening and deep concern about the things of another world, even in the most dead time.

In the year 1740, in the spring, before Mr. Whitefield came to this town, there was a visible alteration. There was more seriousness and religious conversation, especially among young people; those things that were of ill tendency among them were more forborne. And it was a more frequent thing for persons to visit their minister upon soul accounts; and in some particular persons there appeared a great alteration about that time. And thus it continued till Mr. Whitefield came to town, which was about the middle of October following. He preached here four sermons in the meeting-house (besides a private lecture at my house) — one on Friday, another on Saturday, and two upon the Sabbath. The congregation was extraordinarily melted by every sermon; almost the whole assembly being in tears for a great part of sermon time. Mr. Whitefield's sermons were suitable to the circumstances of the town, containing just reproofs of our backslidings, and, in a most moving and affecting manner, making use of our great profession and great mercies as arguments with us to return to God, from whom we had departed.

Immediately after this, the minds of the people in general appeared more engaged in religion, showing a greater forwardness to make religion the subject of their conversation, and to meet frequently together for religious purposes, and to embrace all opportunities to hear the Word preached. The revival at first appeared chiefly among professors and those that had entertained the hope that they were in a state of grace, to whom Mr. Whitefield chiefly addressed himself. But in a very short time there appeared an awakening and deep concern among some young persons that looked upon themselves as in a Christless state; and there were some hopeful appearances of

conversion; and some professors were greatly revived.

In about a month or six weeks, there was a great alteration in the town, both as to the revivals of professors and awakenings of others. By the middle of December, a very considerable work of God appeared among those that were very young; and the revival of religion continued to increase; so that in the spring an engagedness of spirit about things of religion was become very general among young people and children, and religious subjects almost wholly took up their conversation when they were together.

In the month of May 1741, a sermon was preached to a company at a private house. Near the conclusion of the exercise, one or two persons that were professors were so greatly affected with a sense of the greatness and glory of divine things, and the infinite importance of the things of eternity, that they were not able to conceal it; the affection of their minds overcoming their strength, and having a very visible effect on their bodies. When the exercise was over, the young people that were present removed into the other room for religious conference; and particularly that they might have opportunity to inquire of those that were thus affected what apprehensions they had, and what things they were that thus deeply impressed their minds. And there soon appeared a very great effect of their conversation; the affection was quickly propagated through the room; many of the young people and children that were professors appeared to be overcome with a sense of the greatness and glory of divine things, and with admiration, love, joy and praise, and compassion to others that looked upon themselves as in a state of nature. And many others at the same time were overcome with distress about their sinful and miserable state and condition; so that the whole room was full of nothing but outcries, faintings, and suchlike.

Others soon heard of it, in several parts of the town, and came to them; and what they saw and heard there was greatly affecting to them; so that many of them were overpowered in like manner. And it continued thus for some hours, the time spent in prayer, singing, counseling, and conferring. There seemed to be a consequent happy effect of that meeting to several particular persons, and in the state of religion in the town in general. After this were meetings from time to time attended with like appearances.

But a little after it, at the conclusion of the public exercise on the Sabbath, I appointed the children that were under sixteen years of age to go from the meetinghouse to a neighbor house, that I there might further enforce what they had heard in public, and might give in some counsels proper for their age. The children were there very generally and greatly affected with the warnings and counsels that were given them, and many exceedingly overcome; and the room was filled with cries. And when they were dismissed, they, almost all of them, went home crying aloud through the streets, to all parts of the town. The like appearances attended several such meetings of children that were appointed.

But their affections appeared by what followed to be of a very different nature; in many they appeared to be indeed but childish affections, and in a day or two would leave them as they were before. Others were deeply impressed; their convictions took fast hold of them and abode by them. And there were some that from one meeting to another seemed extraordinarily affected for some time, to but little purpose, their affections presently vanishing, from time to time; but yet afterward were seized with abiding convictions, and their affections became durable.

About the middle of the summer, I called together the young people that were communicants, from sixteen to twenty-six years of age, to my house; which proved to be a most happy meeting. Many seemed to be very greatly and most agreeably affected with those views which excited humility, self-condemnation, self-abhorrence, love, and joy; many fainted under these affections. We had several meetings that summer of young people attended with like appearances. It was about that time that there first began to be cryings out in the meetinghouse; which several times occasioned many of the congregation to stay in the house, after the public exercise was over, to confer with those who seemed to be overcome with religious convictions and affections; which was found to tend much to the propagation of their impressions, with lasting effect upon many, conference being at these times commonly joined with prayer and singing. In the summer and fall, the children in various parts of the town had religious meetings by themselves for prayer, sometimes joined with fasting; wherein many of them seemed to be greatly and properly affected, and I hope some of them savingly wrought upon.

The months of August and September were the most remarkable of any this year, for appearances of conviction and conversion of sinners, and great revivings, quickenings, and comforts of professors, and for extraordinary external effects of these things. It was a very frequent thing to see a houseful of outcries, faintings, convulsions, and suchlike, both with distress and also with admiration and joy. It was not the manner here to hold meetings all night, as in some places, nor was it common to continue them until very late in the night; but it was pretty often so that there were some that were so affected, and their bodies so overcome, that they could not go home, but were obliged to stay all night at the house where they were. There was no difference that I know of here, with regard to these extraordinary effects, in meetings in the night and in the daytime. The meetings in which these effects appeared in the evening, being commonly begun, and their extraordinary effects, in the day, and continued in the evening; and some meetings have been very remarkable for such extraordinary effects that were both begun and finished in the daytime.

There was an appearance of a glorious progress of the work of God upon the hearts of sinners in conviction and conversion this summer and fall; and great numbers. I think we have reason to hope, were brought savingly home to Christ. But this was remarkable, the work of God in His influences of this nature seemed to be almost wholly upon a new generation; those that were not come to years of discretion in that wonderful season nine years ago, children, or those that were then children. Others that had enjoyed that former glorious opportunity without any appearance of saving benefit seemed now to be almost wholly passed over and let alone. But now we had the most wonderful work among children that ever was in Northampton. The former great outpouring of the spirit was remarkable for influences upon the minds of children, beyond all that had ever been before; but this far exceeded that.

Indeed, as to influences on the minds of professors, this work was by no means confined to a new generation. Many of all ages partook of it; but, yet, in this respect, it was more general on those that were of the younger sort. Many that had formerly been wrought upon, that in the times of our declension had fallen into decays, and had in a great measure left God and gone after the world, now passed under a very remarkable new work of the spirit of God, as if they had been the subjects of a second conversion. They were first led into the wilderness, and had a work of conviction, having much greater convictions of the sin of both nature and practice than ever before (though with some new circumstances, and something new in the kind of conviction) in some with great distress, beyond what they had felt before their first conversion.

Under these convictions they were excited to strive for salvation, and the Kingdom of Heaven suffered violence from some of them in a far more remarkable manner than before. And after great convictions and humblings and agonizings with God, they had Christ discovered to them anew, as an All-sufficient Savior, and in the glories of His grace, and in a far more clear manner than before; and with greater humility, self-emptiness, and brokenness of heart, and a purer and higher joy, and greater desires after holiness of life, but with greater self-diffidence and distrust of their treacherous hearts.

One circumstance wherein this work differed from that which had been in the town five or six years before was that conversions were frequently wrought more sensibly and visibly; the impressions stronger and more manifest by external effects of them; and the progress of the spirit of God in conviction, from step to step, more apparent; and the transition from one state to another more sensible and plain; so that it might, in many instances, be as it were seen by bystanders. The preceding season had been very remarkable on this account beyond what had been· before; but this more remarkable than that. And in this season these apparent or visible conversions (if I may so call them) were more frequently in the presence of others, at religious meetings, where the appearances of what was wrought on the heart fell under public observation. . . .

In the beginning of the summer 1742, there seemed to be some abatement of the liveliness of people's affections in religion; but yet many were often in a great height of them. And in the fall and winter following, there were at times extraordinary appearances. But in the general, people's engagedness in religion and the liveliness of their affections have been on the decline; and some of the young people, especially, have shamefully lost their liveliness and vigor in religion, and much of the seriousness and solemnity of their spirits. But there are many that walk as becomes saints; and, to this day, there are a considerable number in the town that seem to be near to God, and maintain much of the life of religion, and enjoy many of the sensible tokens and fruits of His gracious presence.

With respect to the late season of revival of religion among us for three or four years past, it has been observable that in the former part of it, in the years 1740 and 1741, the work seemed to be much more pure, having less of a corrupt mixture, than in the former great outpouring of the spirit in 1735 and 1736. Persons seemed to be sensible of their former errors, and had learned more of their own hearts, and experience had taught them more of the tendency and consequences of things. They were now better guarded, and their affections were not only greater but attended with greater solemnity, and greater humility and self-distrust, and greater engagedness after holy living and perseverance; and there were fewer errors in conduct.

But in the latter part of it, in the year 1742, it was otherwise. The work continued more pure, till we were infected from abroad. Our people, hearing and some of them seeing the work in other places where there was a greater visible commotion than here, and the outward appearances were more extraordinary, were ready to think that the work in those places far excelled what was among us; and their eyes were dazzled with the high profession and great show that some made who came hither from other places.

That those people went so far beyond them in raptures and violent emotions of the affections and a vehement zeal, and what they called boldness for Christ, our people were ready to think was owing to their far greater attainments in grace and intimacy with Heaven. They looked little in their own eyes in comparison of them, and were ready to submit themselves to them, and yield themselves up to their conduct, taking it for granted that everything was right that they said and did. These things had a strange influence on the people, and gave many of them a deep and unhappy tincture, that it was a hard and long labor to deliver them from and which some of them are not fully delivered from to this day.

The effects and consequences of things among us plainly shows the following things, viz.: that the degree of grace is by no means to be judged of by the degree of joy, or the degree of zeal; and that indeed we cannot at all determine by these things who are gracious and who are not; and that it is not the degree of religious affections but the nature of them that is chiefly to be looked at. Some that have had very great raptures of joy, and have been extraordinarily filled (as the vulgar phrase is), and have had their bodies overcome, and that very often have manifested far less of the temper of Christians in their conduct since than some others that have been still and have made no great outward show. But then again there are many others that have had extraordinary joys and emotions of mind, with frequent great effects on their bodies, that behave themselves steadfastly as humble, amiable, eminent Christians.

'Tis evident that there may be great religious affections that may, in show and appearance, imitate gracious affections, and have the same effects on their bodies, but are far from having the same effect in the temper of their minds and course of their lives. And likewise there is nothing more manifest by what appears among us than that the goodness of persons' state is not chiefly to be judged of by any exactness of steps and method of experiences in what is supposed to be the first conversion; but that we must judge more by the spirit that breathes, the effect wrought on the temper of the soul, in the time of the work, and remaining afterward.

Though there have been very few instances among professors among us of what is ordinarily called scandalous sin known to me, yet the temper that some of them show and the behavior they have been of, together with some things in the kind and circumstances of their experiences, make me much afraid lest there be a considerable number that have woefully deceived themselves. Though, on the other hand, there is a great number whose temper and conversation is such as justly confirms the charity of others toward them; and not a few in whose disposition and walk there are amiable appearances of eminent grace. And notwithstanding all the corrupt mixtures that have been in the late work here, there are not only many blessed fruits of it in particular persons that yet remain, but some good effects of it upon the town in general.

A party spirit has more ceased. I suppose there has been less appearance these three or four years past of that division of the town into two parties, that has long been our bane, than has been these thirty years. And the people have apparently had much more caution and a greater guard on their spirit and their tongues to avoid contention and unchristian heats in town meetings and on other occasions. And 'tis a thing greatly to be rejoiced in, that the people very lately have come to an agreement and final issue with respect to their grand controversy relating to their common lands; which has been above any other particular thing a source of mutual prejudices, jealousies, and debates for fifteen or sixteen years past.

The people are also generally of late in some respects considerably altered and meliorated in their notions of religion, particularly they seem to be much more sensible of the danger of resting in old experiences, or what they were subjects of at their supposed first conversion; and to be more fully convinced of the necessity of forgetting the things that are behind and pressing forward, and maintaining earnest labor, watchfulness, and prayerfulness as long as they live.

1745

102.

Regulations at Yale College

Yale College was granted a new charter in 1745, and a revision of the college laws was undertaken in the same year. The new regulations showed the influence of President Thomas Clap, who had strong views concerning the relations between school and students. Clap's conception of the college's function was spelled out in his Religious Constitution of Colleges, *published in 1754, but it is also reflected in the regulations of 1745. Those provisions of the regulations that bear on student life are reprinted below.*

Source: Franklin B. Dexter, *Biographical Sketches of the Graduates of Yale College with Annals of the College History,* New York, 1896, Vol. II, pp. 2-18.

CHAPTER I

Concerning Admission Into College.

1. That none may expect to be admitted into this college unless upon examination of the president and tutors, they shall be found able extempore to read, construe, and parse Tully, Virgil, and the Greek Testament; and to write true Latin in prose and to understand the rules of prosody and common arithmetic, and shall bring sufficient testimony of his blameless and inoffensive life.

2. That no person shall be admitted a freshman into this college who is more than twenty-one years old, unless by the special allowance of the president and fellows, or their committee.

3. That no person shall be admitted undergraduate in this college until his father, guardian, or some proper person has given a sufficient bond to the steward of the college, to pay the quarter bills of the said scholar allowed by the authority of college from time to time as long as he shall continue a member of said college; which bond the steward shall keep until such scholar has taken his second degree, unless he shall receive order from the president to deliver it up before. . . .

CHAPTER II

Of A Religious And Virtuous Life

1. All scholars shall live religious, godly, and blameless lives according to the rules of God's Word, diligently reading the Holy Scriptures, the fountain of light and truth; and constantly attend upon all the duties of religion, both in public and secret.

2. That the president, or in his absence one of the tutors, shall constantly pray in the college hall every morning and evening;

and shall read a chapter or suitable portion of the Holy Scriptures, unless there be some other theological discourse or religious exercise; and every member of the college, whether graduates or undergraduates, whether residing in the college or in the town of New Haven, shall seasonably attend upon penalty that every undergraduate who shall be absent (without sufficient excuse) shall be fined 1d.; for coming tardy after the introductory collect is made shall be fined ½d.

3. The president is hereby desired as he has time and opportunity to make and exhibit in the hall such a public exposition, sermon, or discourse as he shall think proper for the instruction of the scholars, and when he shall see cause so to do and give public notice thereof, every undergraduate shall be obliged to attend upon the same penalty as aforesaid. . . .

5. No student of this college shall attend upon any religious meetings, either public or private, on the Sabbath or any other day but such as are appointed by public authority or approved by the president upon penalty of a fine, public admonition, confession, or otherwise according to the nature or demerit of the offense.

6. That if any student shall profane the Sabbath by unnecessary business, diversion, walking abroad, or making any indecent noise or disorder on the said day, or on the evening before or after, or shall be guilty of any rude, profane, or indecent behavior in the time of public worship, or at prayer at any time in the college hall, he shall be punished, admonished, or otherwise according to the nature and demerit of his crime. . . .

CHAPTER III

Concerning Scholastical Exercises

1. Every student shall diligently apply himself to his studies in his chamber as well as attend upon all public exercises appointed by the president or tutors, and no student shall walk abroad, or be absent from his chamber, except half an hour after breakfast, and an hour and a half after dinner, and from prayers at night to nine o'clock without leave, upon penalty of 2d. or more to 6d. at the discretion of the president and tutors.

2. To this end the president or tutors shall, by turns, or as they conveniently can, visit students' chambers after nine o'clock, to see whether they are at their chambers, and apply themselves to their studies.

3. That the president and each of the tutors shall, according to the best of their discretion, instruct and bring forward their respective classes in the knowledge of the three learned languages, and in the liberal arts and sciences. In the first year they shall principally study the tongues and logic, and shall in some measure pursue the study of the tongues the two next years. In the second year they shall recite rhetoric, geometry, and geography. In the third year, natural philosophy, astronomy, and other parts of the mathematics. In the fourth year, metaphysics and ethics. And the respective classes shall recite such books, and in such a manner as has been accustomed, or such as the president upon the consultation with the tutors shall think proper; but every Saturday shall especially be allotted to the study of divinity, and the classes shall, during the whole term, recite the Westminster Confession of Faith received and approved by the churches in this colony, Wollebius, Ames Medulla, or any other system of divinity by the direction of the president and fellows. And on Friday, each undergraduate in his order, about six at a time, shall declaim in the hall in Latin, Greek, or Hebrew and in no other language without special leave from the president; and shall presently after deliver up his declamation to his tutor, fairly written and subscribed. And the two senior classes shall dispute in the fall twice a week; and if any undergraduate shall be absent from reciting or disputing

without sufficient reason, he shall be fined 2*d.;* and from declaiming, 6*d.* . . .

CHAPTER IV

Of Penal Laws

1. If any scholar shall be guilty of blasphemy, fornication, robbery, forgery, or any other such great and atrocious crime, he shall be expelled forthwith.

2. If any scholar shall deny the Holy Scriptures or any part of them to be the Word of God, or be guilty of heresy or any error directly tending to subvert the fundamentals of Christianity, and continuing obstinate therein after the first and second admonition, he shall be expelled.

3. If any scholar shall be guilty of profane swearing, cursing, vowing, any petty or implicit oath, profane or irreverent use of the names, attributes, ordinances or Word of God, disobedient or contumacious or refractory carriage toward his superiors, fighting, striking, quarreling, challenging, turbulent words or behavior, drunkenness, uncleanness, lascivious words or actions, wearing woman's apparel, defrauding, injustice, idleness, lying, defamation, talebearing, or any other suchlike immoralities, he shall be punished by fine, confession, admonition, or expulsion, as the nature and circumstances of the case may require.

4. If any person be guilty of stealing, he shall, besides the fine, pay triple damage and in all other cases of injustice shall make full restitution to the party injured.

5. If any scholar shall break open any other scholar's door or open it with a picklock or a false key, he shall be fined 1*s.* for the first offense; and 2*s.* for the second; and for the third, publicly admonished, degraded, or expelled.

6. If any scholar shall play at cards or dice at all, or at any lawful game upon a wager; or shall bring any quantity of rum, wine, brandy, or other strong liquor into college or into his chamber where he re-sides without liberty from the president or tutors, or shall go into any tavern within two miles of college and call for any strong liquor, or spend his time idly there unless with his parent or guardian, he shall for the first offense be fined 2*s.* 6*d.,* or be admonished; and for the second offense be fined 5*s.* and be degraded; and for the third offense be expelled. And if any scholar shall play at swords, files, or cudgels, he shall be fined not exceeding 1*s.*

7. That if any scholar shall do any damage to the college house, glass, fences, or any other things belonging to college, or shall jump out of college windows or over the board fences, he shall be fined not exceeding 1*s.* and pay all damages to be charged in his quarter bill.

8. That every student shall abstain from singing, loud talking and all other noises in studying time, on penalty of 4*d.,* and if any scholar shall at any time make any rout, disorder, or loud, indecent noises, screamings, or hollowing or shall call loud or hollow to any other scholar in the presence of the president or tutors, he shall be fined not exceeding 2*s.*

9. That if any scholar shall associate himself with any rude, idle, disorderly persons, or shall entertain companions at his chamber either in college or out after nine o'clock, or shall take any person who is not a near relation to lodge with him without liberty from the president or a tutor, he shall be fined not exceeding 2*s.*

10. That the president or either of the tutors may, when he sees cause, break open any college door to suppress any disorder; and if any scholar shall refuse to give the president or either of the tutors admittance into his chamber when demanded, or to assist in suppressing any disorder when required, or to come when he is sent for, or to give in evidence when he is called, he shall be fined 2*s.,* or be punished by admonition, confession, degradation, or expulsion as the nature of the case may require.

11. If any scholar shall behave himself

obstinately, refractorily, or contentiously toward the president or either of the tutors, he shall for the first offense be punished by fine, admonition, or confession, or being deprived of the liberty of sending freshmen for a certain time; for the second offense he shall be degraded or expelled.

12. That if any scholar shall write or publish any libel, or raise any false or scandalous report of the president or either of the fellows or tutors or the minister of the First Church of New Haven, or shall directly or indirectly say that either of them is a hypocrite, or carnal or unconverted, or use any such reproachful or reviling language concerning them, he shall for the first offense make a public confession in the hall; and for the second, be expelled.

13. If any scholar shall go out of the college yard without a hat, coat, or gown, except at his lawful diversion, he shall be fined 3d.; and if he shall wear any indecent apparel, he shall be punished not exceeding 2s.

14. If any scholar shall keep a gun or pistol, or fire one in the college yard or college, or shall go a-gunning, fishing, or sailing; or shall go more than two miles from college upon any occasion whatsoever; or shall be present at any court, election, town meeting, wedding, or meeting of young people for diversion or any suchlike meeting which may occasion misspending of precious time without liberty first obtained from the president or his tutor, in any of the cases abovesaid he shall be fined not exceeding 2s.

15. That all the scholars shall behave themselves inoffensively, blamelessly, and justly toward the people in New Haven; not unnecessarily frequenting their houses, or interesting themselves into any controversy among them. And upon complaint of any wrong done by any scholar to any of them, or any other scholar, the president shall order them to do justice and make restitution. And if any scholar shall refuse to do so, he shall be publicly admonished, and, if he continue obstinate, he shall be expelled and his bond put in sale if need be.

16. That every freshman shall be obliged to go any reasonable and proper . . . errand when he is sent by any student in any superior class; and if he shall refuse so to do he may be punished; provided that no graduate shall send a freshman out of the college yard, and no undergraduate shall send a freshman anywhere in studying time without liberty first had from the president or one of the tutors.

17. If any undergraduate shall tarry out of town longer than he has leave from the president or his tutor and shall send no excuse, he shall be punished 4d. a day for every day's absence. And if he shall not come nor send any excuse till the end of the quarter, and the fine be made up in the quarter bill, it shall not be taken out again upon any excuse or pretense whatsoever, unless it amount to more than 5s.

18. That when any scholar is ordered to make a public confession for any crime or breach of the laws of this college, and he refuse after admonition, he shall be expelled. And no scholar shall be readmitted or admitted to a degree unless he first make a public confession in the hall or meetinghouse.

19. If any scholar shall make an assault upon the person of the president or either of the tutors, or shall wound, bruise, or strike any of them, he shall forthwith be expelled.

20. That no scholar shall undertake to do or transact any matters or affairs of difficulty and importance, or which are anyways new or beside the common and approved customs and practices of the college, without first consulting with the president and obtaining his consent.

1747

103.

BENJAMIN FRANKLIN: The Speech of Polly Baker

As the editor of a newspaper with space to fill, and as a printer with time occasionally on his hands, Franklin wrote and published a variety of surreptitious pieces, pretending that their author was somebody else. The best known of these was a purported letter addressed to a friend, called Advice to a Young Man on the Choice of a Mistress *(1745). Only less famous, and widely circulated in its day, was* The Speech of Polly Baker, *reprinted here, which appeared at Philadelphia in 1747 and also in the same year in a London magazine. There was no such trial as the* Speech *records, of course, nor any woman named Polly Baker. If it comes to that, there was no law against bastardy in Connecticut. While Franklin may have intended a commentary on human affairs, he would only admit, many years later, to having sought the amusement of his readers.*

Source: *The Writings of Benjamin Franklin,* Albert H. Smyth, ed., New York, 1905, Vol. II, pp. 463-467.

The speech of Miss Polly Baker[1] before a Court of Judicature, at Connecticut near Boston in New England, where she was prosecuted the fifth time for having a bastard child.

"May it please the Honorable Bench to indulge me in a few words. I am a poor, unhappy woman, who have no money to fee lawyers to plead for me, being hard put to it to get a tolerable living. I shall not trouble Your Honors with long speeches; nor have I the presumption to expect that you may, by any means, be prevailed on to deviate in your sentence from the law in my favor. All I humbly hope is that Your Honors would charitably move the governor's goodness in my behalf, that my fine may be remitted.

"This is the fifth time, gentlemen, that I have been dragged before your Court on the same account; twice I have paid heavy fines, and twice have been brought to public punishment for want of money to pay these fines. This may have been agreeable to the laws, and I don't dispute it; but since laws are sometimes unreasonable in themselves, and therefore repealed, and others bear too hard on the subject in particular

1. Another account says her name was Sarah Oliter.

instances, and therefore there is left a power somewhere to dispense with the execution of them, I take the liberty to say that I think this law, by which I am punished, is both unreasonable in itself, and particularly severe with regard to me, who have always lived an inoffensive life in the neighborhood where I was born, and defy my enemies (if I have any) to say I ever wronged any man, woman, or child.

"Abstracted from the law, I cannot conceive (may it please Your Honors) what the nature of my offense is. I have brought five fine children into the world, at the risk of my life; I have maintained them well by my own industry, without burdening the township; and would have done it better if it had not been for the heavy charges and fines I have paid. Can it be a crime (in the nature of things, I mean) to add to the number of the King's subjects, in a new country that really wants people? I own it, I should think it a praiseworthy rather than a punishable action. I have debauched no other woman's husband, nor enticed any youth; these things I never was charged with; nor has anyone the least cause of complaint against me, unless, perhaps, the minister or justice, because I have had children without being married, by which they have missed a wedding fee. But can this be a fault of mine?

"I appeal to Your Honors. You are pleased to allow I don't want sense; but I must be stupefied to the last degree not to prefer the honorable state of wedlock to the condition I have lived in. I always was, and still am, willing to enter into it; and doubt not my behaving well in it, having all the industry, frugality, fertility, and skill in economy appertaining to a good wife's character. I defy any person to say I ever refused an offer of that sort. On the contrary, I readily consented to the only proposal of marriage that ever was made me, which was when I was a virgin; but, too easily confiding in the person's sincerity that made it, I unhappily lost my own honor by trusting to his; for he got me with child, and then forsook me.

"That very person you all know; he is now become a magistrate of this county; and I had hopes he would have appeared this day on the bench, and endeavored to moderate the Court in my favor; then I should have scorned to mention it; but I must now complain of it as unjust and unequal, that my betrayer and undoer, the first cause of all my faults and miscarriages (if they must be deemed such), should be advanced to honor and power in that government that punishes my misfortunes with stripes and infamy!

"I shall be told, 'tis like, that were there no act of Assembly in this case, the precepts of religion are violated by my transgressions. If mine is a religious offense, leave it to religious punishments. You have already excluded me from the comforts of your church communion. Is not that sufficient? You believe I have offended Heaven, and must suffer eternal fire. Will not that be sufficient? What need is there then of your additional fines and whipping? I own I do not think as you do, for, if I thought what you call a sin was really such, I would not presumptuously commit it. But how can it be believed that Heaven is angry at my having children, when to the little done by me toward it God has been pleased to add His divine skill and admirable workmanship in the formation of their bodies and crowned it by furnishing them with rational and immortal souls?

"Forgive me, gentlemen, if I talk a little extravagantly on these matters. I am no divine, but if you, gentlemen, must be making laws, do not turn natural and useful actions into crimes by your prohibitions; but take into your wise consideration the great and growing number of bachelors in the country, many of whom, from the mean fear of the expenses of a family, have never sincerely and honorably courted a woman in their lives; and, by their manner of living, leave unproduced (which is little better than murder) hundreds of their posterity to the thousandth generation. Is not this a greater offense against the public good than mine? Compel them, then, by law, either to marry, or to pay double the fine of fornication every year.

"What shall poor young women do, whom custom has forbid to solicit the men, and who cannot force themselves upon husbands, when the laws take no care to provide them any, and yet severely punish them if they do their duty without them — the duty of the first great command of nature and of nature's God, 'increase and multiply'; a duty from the steady performance of which nothing has been able to deter me. But for its sake I have hazarded the loss of the public esteem, and have frequently endured public disgrace; and therefore ought, in my humble opinion, instead of a whipping, to have a statue erected to my memory."

This judicious address influenced the Court to dispense with her punishment, and induced one of her judges to marry her the next day. She ever afterward supported an irreproachable character, and had fifteen children by her husband.

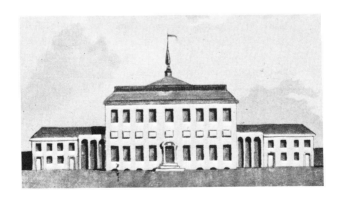

1748

104.

PETER KALM: A Trip to America

The Swedish naturalist Peter Kalm toured New York, New Jersey, and Pennsylvania from 1748 to 1751 under the sponsorship of the Swedish Academy of Science. His primary mission was to study the native flora and fauna, but he also recorded his impressions of the people he met. His account of his experiences, Travels into North America *(1753-1761), gained widespread popularity and subsequently was translated into German, Dutch, and English. The following selection, taken from an English translation made in 1770 by John R. Forster, includes some of Kalm's descriptions of America as it appeared to him in the last months of 1748.*

Source: *Travels into North America, etc., etc.,* translated by John R. Forster, Warrington [England], 1770, pp. 184-189, 222-261, 364-396.

AGRICULTURE was in a very bad state hereabouts. When a person had bought a piece of land, which perhaps had never been plowed since the creation, he cut down part of the wood, tore up the roots, plowed the ground, sowed corn on it, and the first time got a plentiful crop. But the same land being tilled for several years successively, without being manured, it at last must, of course, lose its fertility. Its possessor therefore leaves it fallow, and proceeds to another part of his ground, which he treats in the same manner. Thus he goes on till he has changed a great part of his possessions into cornfields, and by that means deprived the ground of its fertility. He then returns to the first field, which now is pretty well recovered; this he again tills as long as it will afford him a good crop, but when its fertility is exhausted, he leaves it fallow again, and proceeds to the rest as before.

It being customary here to let the cattle go about the fields and in the woods both day and night, the people cannot collect much dung for manure. But by leaving the land fallow for several years together, a great quantity of weeds spring up in it, and get such strength that it requires a considerable time to extirpate them. From hence it likewise comes that the corn is always so much mixed with weeds. The great richness of the soil, which the first European colonists found here, and which had never been plowed before, has given rise to this neglect of agriculture, which is still observed by many of the inhabitants. But they do not consider that, when the earth is quite exhausted, a great space of time and an infinite deal of labor is necessary to bring it again into good order; especially in these countries which are almost every summer so scorched up by the excessive heat and drought.

The soil of the cornfields consisted of a thin mold, greatly mixed with a brick-colored clay, and a quantity of small particles of glimmer. This latter came from the stones, which are here almost everywhere to be met with at the depth of a foot or thereabouts. These little pieces of glimmer made the ground sparkle when the sun shone upon it. . . .

The country through which we passed was for the greatest part level, though sometimes there were some long hills, some parts were covered with trees, but far the greater part of the country was without woods; on the other hand I never saw any place in America, the towns excepted, so well peopled. An old man who lived in this neighborhood and accompanied us for some part of the road, however, assured me that he could well remember the time when, between Trenton and New Brunswick, there were not above three farms, and he reckoned it was about fifty-and-some-odd years ago. During the greater part of the day we had very extensive cornfields on both sides of the road, and commonly toward the south the country had a great declivity.

Near almost every farm was a spacious orchard full of peaches and apple trees, and in some of them the fruit was fallen from the trees in such quantities as to cover nearly the whole surface. Part of it they left to rot, since they could not take it all in and consume it. Wherever we passed by, we were always welcome to go into the fine orchards and gather our hats and pockets full of the choicest fruit, without the possessor so much as looking after it. Cherry trees were planted near the farms, on the roads, etc.

The barns had a peculiar kind of construction hereabouts, which I will give a concise description of. The whole building was very great, so as almost to equal a small church. The roof was pretty high, covered with wooden shingles, declining on both sides, but not steep; the walls which support it were not much higher than a full-grown man. But, on the other hand, the breadth of the building was the more considerable; in the middle was the threshing floor, and above it, or in the loft or garret, they put the corn which was not yet threshed, the straw, or anything else, according to the season.

On one side were stables for the horses, and on the other for the cows. And the small cattle had likewise their particular stables or styes; on both ends of the buildings were great gates; so that one could come in with a cart and horses through one of them, and go out at the other. Here was, therefore, under one roof, the threshing floor, the barn, the stables, the hayloft, the coach house, etc. This kind of building is chiefly made use of by the Dutch and Germans; for it is to be observed that the country between Trenton and New York is inhabited by few Englishmen, but instead of them by Germans or Dutch, the latter of which especially are numerous.

Before I proceed, I find it necessary to remark one thing with regard to the Indians, or old Americans; for this account may perhaps meet with readers who, like many people of my acquaintance, may be of opinion that all North America was almost wholly inhabited by savage or heathen nations, and they may be astonished that I do not mention them more frequently in my account. Others may perhaps imagine that when I mention in my journal that the country is much cultivated, that in several places, houses of stone or wood are built, round which are cornfields, gardens, and orchards, that I am speaking of the property of the Indians. To undeceive them, I here give the following explication.

The country, especially all along the

coasts, in the English colonies, is inhabited by Europeans, who in some places are already so numerous that few parts of Europe are more populous. The Indians have sold the country to the Europeans, and have retired farther up; in most parts you may travel 20 Swedish miles, or about 120 English miles, from the seashore before you reach the first habitations of the Indians. And it is very possible for a person to have been at Philadelphia and other towns on the seashore for half a year together without so much as seeing an Indian. . . .

Besides the different sects of Christians, there are many Jews settled in New York, who possess great privileges. They have a synagogue and houses, and great country seats of their own property, and are allowed to keep shops in town. They have likewise several ships, which they freight and send out with their own goods. In fine, they enjoy all the privileges common to the other inhabitants of this town and province.

During my residence at New York, this time and in the two next years, I was frequently in company with Jews. I was informed among other things that these people never boiled any meat for themselves on Saturday, but that they always did it the day before; and that in winter they kept a fire during the whole Saturday. They commonly eat no pork; yet I have been told by several men of credit that many of them (especially among the young Jews) when traveling did not make the least difficulty about eating this or any other meat that was put before them; even though they were in company with Christians.

I was in their synagogue last evening for the first time, and this day at noon I visited it again, and each time I was put into a particular seat which was set apart for strangers or Christians. A young rabbi read the divine service, which was partly in Hebrew and partly in the rabbinical dialect. Both men and women were dressed entirely in the English fashion; the former had all of them their hats on, and did not once take them off during service. The galleries, I observed, were appropriated to the ladies, while the men sat below. During prayers, the men spread a white cloth over their heads; which perhaps is to represent sackcloth. But I observed that the wealthier sort of people had a much richer cloth than the poorer ones. Many of the men had Hebrew books, in which they sang and read alternately. The rabbi stood in the middle of the synagogue, and read with his face turned toward the east; he spoke, however, so fast, as to make it almost impossible for anyone to understand what he said.

New York, the capital of a province of the same name, is situated under 40°40′ north latitude and 47°4′ western longitude from London; and is about ninety-seven English miles distant from Philadelphia. The situation of it is extremely advantageous for trade; for the town stands upon a point which is formed by two bays, into one of which the River Hudson discharges itself, not far from the town. New York is therefore on three sides surrounded with water. The ground it is built on is level in some parts, and hilly in others; the place is generally reckoned very wholesome. . . .

The port is a good one; ships of the greatest burden can lie in it, quite close up to the bridge; but its water is very salty, as the sea continually comes in upon it, and therefore is never frozen, except in extraordinary cold weather. This is of great advantage to the city and its commerce; for many ships either come in or go out of the port at any time of the year, unless the winds be contrary. . . . It is secured from all violent hurricanes from the southeast by Long Island, which is situated just before the town; therefore only the storms from the southwest are dangerous to the ships which ride at anchor here. . . .

The entrance, however, has its faults; one of them is that no men-of-war can pass through it; for though the water is pretty deep, yet it is not sufficiently so for great ships. Sometimes even merchant ships of a large size have, by the rolling of the waves and by sinking down between them, slightly touched the bottom, though without any bad consequences. Besides this, the canal is narrow; and for this reason many ships have been lost here, because they may be easily cast upon a sand, if the ship is not well piloted. Some old people, who had constantly been upon this canal, assured me that it was neither deeper nor shallower at present than in their youth.

The common difference between high and low water at New York amounts to about six feet, English measure. But at a certain time in every month, when the tide flows more than commonly, the difference in the height of the water is seven feet.

New York probably carries on a more extensive commerce than any town in the English North American provinces; at least it may be said to equal them. Boston and Philadelphia, however, come very near up to it. The trade of New York extends to many places, and it is said they send more ships from thence to London than they do from Philadelphia. They export to that capital all the various sorts of skins which they buy of the Indians; sugar, logwood, and other dying woods, rum, mahogany, and many other goods which are the produce of the West Indies; together with all the specie which they get in the course of trade.

Every year they build several ships here, which are sent to London, and there sold; and of late years they have shipped a quantity of iron to England. In return for these, they import from London stuffs and every other article of English growth or manufacture, together with all sorts of foreign goods. England, and especially London, profits immensely by its trade with the American colonies; for not only New York but likewise all the other English towns on the continent, import so many articles from England that all their specie, together with

the goods which they get in other countries, must altogether go to Old England, in order to pay the amount to which they are however insufficient. From hence it appears how much a well-regulated colony contributes to the increase and welfare of its mother country. . . .

The goods with which the province of New York trades are not very numerous. They chiefly export the skins of animals, which are bought of the Indians about Oswego; great quantities of boards, coming for the most part from Albany; timber and ready-made lumber, from that part of the country which lies about the River Hudson; and, lastly, wheat, flour, barley, oats, and other kinds of corn, which are brought from New Jersey and the cultivated parts of this province. I have seen yachts from New Brunswick, laden with wheat which lay loose on board, and with flour packed up into tuns; and also with great quantities of linseed. New York likewise exports some flesh and other provisions out of its own province, but they are very few; nor is the quantity of peas which the people about Albany bring much greater. Iron, however, may be had more plentifully, as it is found in several parts of this province, and is of a considerable goodness; but all the other products of this country are of little account.

Most of the wine, which is drank here and in the other colonies, is brought from the Isle of Madeira, and is very strong and fiery.

No manufactures of note have as yet been established here; at present they get all manufactured goods, such as woolen and linen cloth, etc., from England, and especially from London.

The River Hudson is very convenient for the commerce of this city, as it is navigable for near 150 English miles up the country, and falls into the bay not far from the town, on its western side. During eight months of the year this river is full of yachts, and other greater and lesser vessels, either going to New York or returning from thence, laden either with inland or foreign goods.

I cannot make a just estimate of the ships that annually come to this town or sail from it. But I have found by the Pennsylvania gazettes that from the 1st of December in 1729 to the 5th of December in the next year, 211 ships entered the port of New York, and 222 cleared it; and since that time there has been a great increase of trade here.

The country people come to market in New York twice a week, much in the same manner as they do at Philadelphia; with this difference, that the markets are here kept in several places.

The governor of the province of New York resides here, and has a palace in the fort. . . .

An assembly of deputies from all the particular districts of the province of New York is held at New York once or twice every year. It may be looked upon as a parliament or diet in miniature. Everything relating to the good of the province is here debated. The governor calls the assembly, and dissolves it at pleasure. This is a power which he ought only to make use of, either when no further debates are necessary, or when the members are not so unanimous in the service of their King and country as is their duty. It frequently however happens, that, led aside by caprice or by interested views, he exerts it to the prejudice of the province.

The colony has sometimes had a governor whose quarrels with the inhabitants have induced their representatives, or the members of the assembly, through a spirit of revenge, to oppose indifferently everything he proposed, whether it was beneficial to the country or not. In such cases the governor has made use of his power, dissolving the assembly, and calling another soon after, which however he again dis-

solved upon the least mark of their ill humor. By this means he so much tired them, by the many expenses which they were forced to bear in so short a time, that they were at last glad to unite with him in his endeavors for the good of the province. But there have likewise been governors who have called assemblies and dissolved them soon after merely because the representatives did not act according to their whims, or would not give their assent to proposals which were perhaps dangerous or hurtful to the common welfare.

The King appoints the governor according to his royal pleasure; but the inhabitants of the province make up His Excellency's salary. Therefore, a man entrusted with this place has greater or lesser revenues according as he knows how to gain the confidence of the inhabitants. There are examples of governors in this and other provinces of North America who, by their dissensions with the inhabitants of their respective governments, have lost their whole salary, His Majesty having no power to make them pay it. If a governor had no other resource in these circumstances, he would be obliged either to resign his office, or to be content with an income too small for his dignity; or else to conform himself in everything to the inclinations of the inhabitants. . . .

No disease is more common here than that which the English call fever and ague, which is sometimes quotidian, tertian, or quartan. But it often happens that a person who has had a tertian ague, after losing it for a week or two, gets a quotidian ague in its stead, which after a while changes into a tertian. The fever commonly attacks the people at the end of August or beginning of September, and commonly continues during autumn and winter till toward spring, when it ceases entirely.

Strangers who arrive here commonly are attacked by the sickness the first or second year after their arrival; and it is more violent upon them than upon the natives, so that they sometimes die of it; but if they escape the first time, they have the advantage of not being visited again the next year, or perhaps never any more. It is commonly said here that strangers get the fever to accustom them to the climate. The natives of European offspring have annual fits of this ague in some parts of the country; some, however, are soon delivered from it; with others on the contrary it continues for six months together; and others are afflicted with it till they die. The Indians also suffer it, but not so violently as the Europeans. No age is secured against it. In those places where it rages annually, you see old men and women attacked with it; and even children in the cradle, sometimes not above three weeks old. It is likewise quotidian, tertian, or quartan with them.

This autumn the ague was more violent here than it commonly used to be. People who are afflicted with it look as pale as death, and are greatly weakened, but in general are not prevented from doing their work in the intervals. It is remarkable that every year there are great parts of the country where this fever rages, and others where scarce a single person has been taken ill. It likewise is worth notice that there are places where the people cannot remember that it formerly prevailed in their country, though at present it begins to grow more common; yet there was no other visible difference between the several places.

All the old Swedes, Englishmen, Germans, etc., unanimously asserted that the fever had never been so violent and of such continuance when they were boys as it is at present. They were likewise generally of the opinion that about the year 1680 there were not so many people afflicted with it as about this time. However, others, equally old, were of opinion that the fever was proportionably as common formerly as it is at present; but that it could not at that time be so sensibly perceived on account of the scarcity of inhabitants, and the great distance of their settlements from each other. It is therefore probable that the effects of the fever have at all times been equal. . . .

The servants which are made use of in the English American colonies are either free persons or slaves; and the former are again of two different sorts.

1. Those who are quite free serve by the year. They are not only allowed to leave their service at the expiration of their year but may leave it at any time when they do not agree with their masters. However, in that case, they are in danger of losing their wages, which are very considerable. A man servant who has some abilities gets between £15 and £20 in Pennsylvania currency, but those in the country do not get so much. A servant maid gets £8 or £10 a year. These servants have their food besides their wages, but must buy their own clothes, and what they get of these they must thank their master's goodness for.

2. The second kind of free servants consist of such persons as annually come from Germany, England, and other countries, in order to settle here. These newcomers are very numerous every year; there are old and young ones, and of both sexes; some of them have fled from oppression, under which they supposed themselves to have labored. Others have been driven from their country by persecution on account of religion; but most of them are poor, and have not money enough to pay their passage, which is between £6 and £8 sterling for each person; therefore they agree with the captain that they will suffer themselves to be sold for a few years, on their arrival. In that case, the person who buys them pays the freight for them. But frequently very old people come over who cannot pay their passage; they therefore sell their children so that they serve both for themselves and for their parents. There are likewise some who pay part of their passage, and they are sold only for a short time.

From these circumstances it appears that the price of the poor foreigners who come over to North America is not equal, and that some of them serve longer than others. When their time is expired, they get a new suit of clothes from their master, and some other things. He is likewise obliged to feed and clothe them during the years of their servitude. Many of the Germans who come hither bring money enough with them to pay their passage, but rather suffer themselves to be sold, with a view that during their servitude they may get some knowledge of the language and quality of the country, and the like, that they may be better able to consider what they shall do when they have got their liberty.

Such servants are taken preferable to all others, because they are not dear; for to buy a Negro or black slave requires too much money at once, and men or maids who get yearly wages are likewise too dear; but this kind of servants may be got for half the money, and even for less for they commonly pay £14, Pennsylvania currency, for a person who is to serve four years, and so on in proportion. Their wages, therefore, are not above £3, Pennsylvania currency, per annum. This kind of servants the English call servings. When a person has bought such a servant for a certain number of years, and has an intention to sell him again, he is at liberty to do so; but he is obliged, at the expiration of the term of the servitude, to provide the usual suit of clothes for the servant, unless he has made that part of the bargain with the purchaser.

The English and Irish commonly sell themselves for four years, but the Germans frequently agree with the captain before they set out to pay him a certain sum of money for a certain number of persons; as soon as they arrive in America, they go about and try to get a man who will pay the passage for them. In return they give, according to the circumstances, one or several of their children to serve a certain number of years; at last they make their bargain with the highest bidder.

3. The Negroes or blacks make the third kind. They are in a manner slaves; for, when a Negro is once bought, he is the purchaser's servant as long as he lives, unless he gives him to another, or makes him free. However, it is not in the power of the master to kill his Negro for a fault, but he must leave it to the magistrates to proceed according to the laws. Formerly the Negroes were brought over from Africa, and bought by almost everyone who could afford it. The Quakers alone scrupled to have slaves; but they are no longer so nice, and they have as many Negroes as other people. However, many people cannot conquer the idea of its being contrary to the laws of Christianity to keep slaves. There are likewise several free Negroes in town, who have been lucky enough to get a very zealous Quaker for their master, who gave them their liberty, after they had faithfully served him for some time.

At present they seldom bring over any Negroes to the English colonies, for those which were formerly brought thither have multiplied considerably. In regard to their marriage they proceed as follows: In case you have not only male but likewise female Negroes, they must intermarry, and then the children are all your slaves. But if you possess a male Negro only, and he has an inclination to marry a female belonging to a different master, you do not hinder your Negro in so delicate a point; but it is no advantage to you, for the children belong to the master of the female. It is therefore advantageous to have Negro women.

A man who kills his Negro must suffer death for it; there is not however an example here of a white man's having been executed on this account. A few years ago it happened that a master killed his slave; his friends, and even the magistrates, secretly advised him to leave the country, as otherwise they could not avoid taking him prisoner, and then he would be condemned to die according to the laws of the country, without any hopes of saving him. This lenity was employed toward him, that the Negroes might not have the satisfaction of seeing a master executed for killing his slave; for this would lead them to all sorts of dangerous designs against their masters, and to value themselves too much.

The Negroes were formerly brought from Africa, as I mentioned before; but now this seldom happens, for they are bought in the West Indies, or American Islands, whither they were originally brought from their own country; for it has been found that on transporting the Negroes from Africa immediately into these northern countries, they have not such a good state of health as when they gradually change places, and are first carried from Africa to the West Indies, and from thence to North America. It has frequently been found that the Negroes cannot stand the cold here so well as the Europeans or whites; for while the latter are not in the least affected by the cold, the toes and fingers of the former are frequently frozen.

There is likewise a material difference among them in this point; for those who come immediately from Africa cannot bear the cold so well as those who are either born in this country or have been here for a considerable time; for the frost easily hurts the hands or feet of the Negroes which come from Africa, or occasions violent pains in their whole body, or in some parts of it, though it does not at all affect those who have been here for some time. There are frequent examples that the Negroes on their passage from Africa, if it happens in winter, have some of their limbs destroyed by frost on board the ship, when the cold is but very inconsiderable and the sailors are scarce obliged to cover their hands. I was even assured that some Negroes have been seen here who have had an excessive pain in their legs, which afterwards broke in the middle, and dropped entirely from the body, together with the flesh on them. Thus it is the same case with men here, as with plants which are brought from the southern countries, and cannot accustom themselves to a colder climate.

The price of Negroes differs according to their age, health, and abilities. A full-grown Negro costs from £40 and upward to a £100 of Pennsylvania currency. There are even examples that a gentleman has paid £100 for a black slave at Philadelphia, and refused to sell him again for the same money. A Negro boy or girl, of two or three years old, can hardly be got for less than £8 or £14 in Pennsylvania currency.

Not only the Quakers but likewise several Christians of other denominations sometimes set their Negroes at liberty. This is done in the following manner: When a gentleman has a faithful Negro who has done him great services, he sometimes declares him independent at his death. This is, however, very expensive, for they are obliged to make a provision for the Negro thus set at liberty, to afford him subsistence when he is grown old, that he may not be driven by necessity to wicked actions, or that he may be at anybody's charge, for these free Negroes become very lazy and indolent afterward. But the children which the free Negro has begot during his servitude are all slaves, though their father be free. On the other hand, those Negro children are free whose parents are at liberty.

The Negroes in the North American colonies are treated more mildly and fed better than those in the West Indies. They have as good food as the rest of the servants, and they possess equal advantages in all things, except their being obliged to serve their whole lifetime, and get no other wages than what their master's goodness allows them. They are likewise clad at their master's expense. On the contrary, in the West Indies, and especially in the Spanish Islands they are treated very cruelly; therefore no threats make more impression upon a Negro here than that of sending him over to the West Indies, in case he would not reform. It has likewise been frequently found by experience that, when you show too much remissness to these Negroes, they grow so obstinated, that they will no longer do anything but of their own accord; therefore, a strict discipline is very necessary, if their master expects to be satisfied with their services.

In the year 1620, some Negroes were brought to North America in a Dutch ship, and in Virginia they bought twenty of them. These are said to have been the first that came hither. When the Indians, who were then more numerous in the country than at present, saw these black people for the first time, they thought they were a true breed of devils, and therefore they called them "Manitto" for a great while; this word in their language signified not only God, but likewise the devil. Some time before that, when they saw the first European ship on their coasts, they were perfectly persuaded that God himself was in the ship. This account I got from some Indians, who preserved it among them as a tradition which they had received from their ancestors; therefore the arrival of the Negroes seemed to them to have confused everything. But since that time, they have entertained less disagreeable notions of the Negroes, for at present many live among them, and they even sometimes intermarry, as I myself have seen.

105.

BENJAMIN FRANKLIN: Advice to a Young Tradesman

Franklin was among the first, as he was easily the most famous, of the type known as the self-made man. Particularly was this the case in financial matters, where he managed his affairs so as to acquire a fortune by the time he was forty-two, when he retired from business. His explanation of that accomplishment, along with his counsel to others who wished to emulate it, was given in various of his writings, but nowhere more concisely than in his Advice to a Young Tradesman *(1748). The candor of the* Advice *was typical of him, and the accuracy. In pointing out that money (rather than labor) begets money, and that the appearance of industry is for purposes of credit as good as the fact, he expressed as he liked to do the practice rather than the piety of success.*

Source: *Works*, III, pp. 463-466.

As YOU HAVE DESIRED it of me, I write the following hints, which have been of service to me, and may, if observed, be so to you.

Remember, that *time* is money. He that can earn ten shillings a day by his labor, and goes abroad, or sits idle, one-half of that day, though he spends but sixpence during his diversion or idleness, ought not to reckon *that* the only expense; he has really spent, or rather thrown away, five shillings besides.

Remember, that *credit* is money. If a man lets his money lie in my hands after it is due, he gives me the interest, or so much as

I can make of it during that time. This amounts to a considerable sum where a man has good and large credit and makes good use of it.

Remember, that money is of the prolific, generating nature. Money can beget money, and its offspring can beget more, and so on. Five shillings turned is six, turned again it is seven and threepence, and so on till it becomes a hundred pounds. The more there is of it, the more it produces every turning, so that the profits rise quicker and quicker. He that kills a breeding sow destroys all her offspring to the thousandth generation. He that murders a crown destroys all that it might have produced, even scores of pounds.

Remember, that six pounds a year is but a groat a day. For this little sum (which may be daily wasted either in time or expense unperceived) a man of credit may, on his own security, have the constant possession and use of a hundred pounds. So much in stock, briskly turned by an industrious man, produces great advantage.

Remember this saying, "The good paymaster is lord of another man's purse." He that is known to pay punctually and exactly to the time he promises may, at any time and on any occasion, raise all the money his friends can spare. This is sometimes of great use. After industry and frugality, nothing contributes more to the raising of a young man in the world than punctuality and justice in all his dealings; therefore, never keep borrowed money an hour beyond the time you promised, lest a disappointment shut up your friend's purse forever.

The most trifling actions that affect a man's credit are to be regarded. The sound of your hammer at five in the morning or nine at night, heard by a creditor, makes him easy six months longer; but if he sees you at a billiard table, or hears your voice at a tavern when you should be at work, he sends for his money the next day; demands it, before he can receive it, in a lump.

It shows, besides, that you are mindful of what you owe; it makes you appear a careful as well as an honest man, and that still increases your credit.

Beware of thinking all your own that you possess, and of living accordingly. It is a mistake that many people who have credit fall into. To prevent this, keep an exact account for some time, both of your expenses and your income. If you take the pains at first to mention particulars, it will have this good effect: you will discover how wonderfully small, trifling expenses mount up to large sums, and will discern what might have been, and may for the future be saved, without occasioning any great inconvenience.

In short, the way to wealth, if you desire it, is as plain as the way to market. It depends chiefly on two words, "industry" and "frugality"; that is, waste neither *time* nor *money*, but make the best use of both. Without industry and frugality nothing will do, and with them everything. He that gets all he can honestly and saves all he gets (necessary expenses excepted) will certainly become *rich*, if that Being who governs the world, to whom all should look for a blessing on their honest endeavors, does not, in His wise providence, otherwise determine.

AN OLD TRADESMAN

All would live long, but none would be old.

BENJAMIN FRANKLIN, *Poor Richard's Almanac*

1750

106.

Jonathan Mayhew: On Unlimited Submission to Rulers

Reverend Jonathan Mayhew, whom John Adams called a "transcendent genius,"
early parted company with his Puritan heritage. On the religious side, his ideas
changed gradually from Congregationalism to Unitarianism, and politically his
thought was sufficiently radical so that he supported the American Revolution. His
Discourse Concerning Unlimited Submission, *delivered as a sermon on*
January 30, 1750, marked the anniversary of the execution of Charles I of England
a century earlier. In it he argued against the divine right of kings and any form of
royal or ecclesiastical absolutism. The sermon, Adams' wrote to Hezekiah Niles
in 1818, "was read by everybody; celebrated by friends, and abused by enemies.
During the reigns of King George the First and King George the Second, the reigns
of the Stuarts — the two Jameses and the two Charleses — were in general disgrace
in England. In America they had always been held in abhorrence. The persecutions
and cruelties suffered by [the colonists'] ancestors under those reigns had been
transmitted by history and tradition, and Mayhew seemed to be raised up to revive
all their animosity against tyranny, in church and state, and at the same time to
destroy their bigotry, fanaticism, and inconsistency." Most of the discourse is
reprinted here.

Source: *A Discourse Concerning Unlimited Submission and Non-Resistance to*
the Higher Powers, etc., etc., Boston, 1750.

1. *Let every soul be subject unto the high-*
er powers. For there is no power but of
God: the powers that be are ordained of
God.
2. *Whosoever therefore resisteth the pow-*
er, resisteth the ordinance of God: and they
that resist shall receive to themselves dam-
nation.
3. *For rulers are not a terror to good*
works but to the evil. Wilt thou then not be
afraid of the power? Do that which is good,
and thou shalt have praise of the same.
4. *For he is the minister of God to thee*
for good. But if thou do that which is evil,
be afraid; for he beareth not the sword in
vain; for he is the minister of God, a re-
venger to execute wrath upon him that
doth evil.

5. *Wherefore ye must needs be subject, not only for wrath but also for conscience sake.*

6. *For, for this cause pay you tribute also; for they are God's ministers, attending continually upon this very thing.*

7. *Render therefore to all their dues: tribute to whom tribute is due; custom to whom custom; fear to whom fear; honor to whom honor.*

Romans 13:1-7

It is evident that the affair of civil government may properly fall under a *moral* and *religious* consideration, at least so far forth as it relates to the general nature and end of magistracy and to the grounds and extent of that submission which persons of a private character ought to yield to those who are vested with authority. This must be allowed by all who acknowledge the divine original of Christianity. For although there be a sense, and a very plain and important sense, in which Christ's *kingdom is not of this world,* His inspired apostles have, nevertheless, laid down some general principles concerning the office of civil rulers and the duty of subjects, together with the reason and obligation of that duty. And from hence it follows that it is proper for all who acknowledge the authority of Jesus Christ and the inspiration of His apostles to endeavor to understand what is in fact the doctrine which they have delivered concerning this matter.

It is the duty of *Christian* magistrates to inform themselves what it is which their religion teaches concerning the nature and design of their office. And it is equally the duty of all *Christian* people to inform themselves what it is which their religion teaches concerning that subjection which they owe to *the higher powers.* It is for these reasons that I have attempted to examine into the Scripture account of this matter, in order to lay it before you with the same *freedom* which I constantly use with relation to other doctrines and precepts of Christianity; not doubting but you will *judge* upon ev-

erything offered to your consideration with the same spirit of *freedom* and *liberty* with which it is *spoken.*

The passage read is the most full and express of any in the New Testament relating to rulers and subjects; and, therefore, I thought it proper to ground upon it what I had to propose to you with reference to the authority of the civil magistrate and the subjection which is due to him. . . .

The apostle's [St. Paul] doctrine . . . may be summed up in the following observations, viz.:

That the end of magistracy is the good of civil society, as such.

That civil rulers, as such, are the ordinance and ministers of God; it being by His permission and providence that any bear rule and agreeable to His will that there should be *some persons* vested with authority in society, for the well-being of it.

That which is here said concerning civil rulers extends to all of them in common; it relates indifferently to monarchical, republican, and aristocratical government, and to all other forms which truly answer the sole end of government, the happiness of society; and to all the different degrees of authority in any particular state, to inferior officers no less than to the supreme.

That disobedience to civil rulers in the due exercise of their authority is not merely a *political sin* but a heinous *offense against God and religion.*

That the true ground and reason of our obligation to be subject to the *higher powers* is the usefulness of magistracy (when properly exercised) to human society and its subserviency to the general welfare.

That obedience to civil rulers is here equally required under all forms of government which answer the sole end of all government, the good of society; and to every degree of authority in any state, whether supreme or subordinate. (From whence it follows that if unlimited obedience and nonresistance be here required as a duty under any one form of government, it is also required as a duty under all other forms and as a duty to subordinate rulers as well as to the supreme.)

And, lastly, that those civil rulers to whom the apostle enjoins subjection are the persons *in possession; the powers that be,* those who are *actually* vested with authority.

There is one very important and interesting point which remains to be inquired into; namely, the *extent* of that subjection *to the higher powers* which is here enjoined as a duty upon all Christians. Some have thought it warrantable and glorious to disobey the civil powers in certain circumstances and, in cases of very great and general oppression when humble remonstrances fail of having any effect and when the public welfare cannot be otherwise provided for and secured, to rise unanimously even against the sovereign himself in order to redress their grievances; to vindicate their natural and legal rights; to break the yoke of tyranny and free themselves and posterity from inglorious servitude and ruin. It is upon this principle that many royal oppressors have been driven from their thrones into banishment, and many slain by the hands of their subjects. . . .

Now there does not seem to be any necessity of supposing that an absolute, unlimited obedience, whether active or passive, is here enjoined merely for this reason, that the precept is delivered in *absolute terms,* without any *exception* or *limitation* expressly mentioned. We are enjoined . . . to be *subject to the higher powers,* and . . . to be *subject for conscience sake.* . . .

Were it known that those in opposition to whom the apostle wrote allowed of civil authority in general and only asserted that there were some cases in which obedience and nonresistance were not a duty, there would then, indeed, be reason for interpreting this passage as containing the doctrine of unlimited obedience and nonresistance, as

it must, in this case, be supposed to have been leveled against such as denied that doctrine. But since it is certain that there were persons who vainly imagined that civil government in general was not to be regarded by them, it is most reasonable to suppose that the apostle designed his discourse only against them. And agreeably to this supposition we find that he argues the usefulness of civil magistracy in general, its agreeableness to the will and purpose of God who is *over all,* and so deduces from hence the obligation of submission to it. But it will not follow that because civil government is, in general, a good institution and necessary to the peace and happiness of human society, therefore, there be no supposable cases in which resistance to it can be innocent. So that the duty of unlimited obedience, whether active or passive, can be argued neither from the manner of expression here used nor from the general scope and design of the passage.

And if we attend to the nature of the argument with which the apostle here enforces the duty of submission to *the higher powers,* we shall find it to be such a one as concludes not in favor of submission to all who bear the *title* of rulers in common but only to those who *actually* perform the duty of rulers by exercising a reasonable and just authority for the good of human society. This is a point which it will be proper to enlarge upon, because the question before us turns very much upon the truth or falsehood of this position. It is obvious then, in general, that the civil rulers whom the apostle here speaks of, and obedience to whom he presses upon Christians as a duty, are *good rulers,* such as are, in the exercise of their office and power, benefactors to society. . . .

And what reason is there for submitting to that government which does by no means answer the design of government? "Wherefore ye must needs be subject not only for wrath but also for conscience sake"

(Rom. 13:5). Here the apostle argues the duty of a cheerful and conscientious submission to civil government from the nature and end of magistracy as he had before laid it down, *i.e.,* as the design of it was to punish evildoers and to support and encourage such as do well, and as it must, if so exercised, be agreeable to the will of God. But how does what he here says prove the duty of a cheerful and conscientious subjection to those who forfeit the character of rulers? — to those who encourage the bad and discourage the good? The argument here used no more proves it to be a sin to resist such rulers than it does to *resist the devil,* that he may *flee from us.* For one is as truly the minister of God as the other. "For, for this cause pay you tribute also: for they are God's ministers, attending continually upon this very thing" (Rom. 13:6). Here the apostle argues the duty of paying taxes, from this consideration, that those who perform the duty of rulers are continually attending upon the public welfare.

But how does this argument conclude for paying taxes to such princes as are continually endeavoring to ruin the public? And especially when such payment would facilitate and promote this wicked design! "Render, therefore, to all their dues; tribute to whom tribute is due; custom to whom custom; fear to whom fear; honor to whom honor" (Rom. 13:7). Here the apostle sums up what he had been saying concerning the duty of subjects to rulers. And his argument stands thus: "Since magistrates who execute their office well are common benefactors to society and may, in that respect, be properly styled the ministers and ordinance of God, and since they are constantly employed in the service of the public, it becomes you to pay them tribute and custom and to reverence, honor, and submit to them in the execution of their respective offices." This is apparently good reasoning. But does this argument conclude for the duty of paying tribute, custom, reverence,

Courtesy, the American Congregational Association Collection; photo, Frick Art Reference Library

Rev. Jonathan Mayhew, portrait by John Greenwood

honor, and obedience to such persons as (although they bear the title of rulers) use all their power to hurt and injure the public? — such as are not *God's* ministers but *Satan's?* — such as do not take care of, and attend upon, the public interest, but their own, to the ruin of the public? — that is, in short, to such as have no natural and just claim at all to tribute, custom, reverence, honor, and obedience?

It is to be hoped that those who have any regard to the apostle's character as an inspired writer, or even as a man of common understanding, will not represent him as reasoning in such a loose, incoherent manner and drawing conclusions which have not the least relation to his premises. For what can be more absurd than an argument thus framed? — "Rulers are, by their office, bound to consult the public welfare and the good of society; therefore, you are bound to pay them tribute, to honor and to submit to them, even when they destroy the public welfare and are a common pest to society by acting in direct contradiction to the nature and end of their office."

Thus, upon a careful review of the apostle's reasoning in this passage, it appears that his arguments to enforce submission are of such a nature as to conclude only in favor of submission *to such rulers as he himself describes;* i.e., such as rule for the good of society, which is the only end of their institution. Common tyrants and public oppressors are not entitled to obedience from their subjects by virtue of anything here laid down by the inspired apostle.

I now add, further, that the apostle's argument is so far from proving it to be the duty of people to obey and submit to such rulers as act in contradiction to the public good, and so to the design of their office, that it proves *the direct contrary.* For, please to observe, that if the end of all civil government be the good of society, if this be the thing that is aimed at in constituting civil rulers, and if the motive and argument for submission to government be taken from the apparent usefulness of civil authority, it follows that when no such good end can be answered by submission there remains no argument or motive to enforce it; and if instead of this good end's being brought about by submission, a *contrary end* is brought about and the ruin and misery of society effected by it, here is a plain and positive reason against submission in all such cases, should they ever happen. And, therefore, in such cases, a regard to the public welfare ought to make us withhold from our rulers that obedience and subjection which it would, otherwise, be our duty to render to them.

If it be our duty, for example, to obey our king merely for this reason, that he rules for the public welfare (which is the only argument the apostle makes use of), it follows, by a parity of reason, that when he turns tyrant and makes his subjects his prey to devour and to destroy instead of his charge to defend and cherish, we are bound to throw off our allegiance to him and to resist, and that according to the tenor of the apostle's argument in this passage. Not to discontinue our allegiance, in this case, would be to join with the sovereign in promoting the slavery and misery of that society, the welfare of which we ourselves, as well as our sovereign, are indispensably obliged to secure and promote as far as in us lies. It is true the apostle puts no case of such a tyrannical prince; but, by his grounding his argument for submission wholly upon the good of civil society, it is plain he implicitly authorizes and even requires us to make resistance whenever this shall be necessary to the public safety and happiness. . . .

But it ought to be remembered that if the duty of universal obedience and nonresistance to our king or prince can be argued from this passage, the same unlimited submission under a republican or any other form of government, and even to all the subordinate powers in any particular state, can be proved by it as well; which is more than those who allege it for the mentioned purpose would be willing should be inferred from it. So that this passage does not answer their purpose but really overthrows and confutes it. This matter deserves to be more particularly considered.

The advocates for unlimited submission and passive obedience do, if I mistake not, always speak with reference to kingly or monarchical government, as distinguished from all other forms and with reference to submitting to the will of the king in distinction from all subordinate officers acting beyond their commission and the authority which they have received from the Crown. It is not pretended that any persons besides kings have a divine right to do what they please, so that no one may resist them without incurring the guilt of factiousness and rebellion. If any other supreme powers oppress the people, it is generally allowed that the people may get redress by resistance, if other methods prove ineffectual. And if any officers in a kingly government go beyond the limits of that power which they have derived from the Crown (the supposed original source of all power and authority in the state) and attempt, illegally, to take away the properties and lives of their fellow subjects, they may be *forcibly* resisted, at least till application be made to the Crown. But as to the sovereign himself, he may not be resisted in any case, nor any of his officers while they confine themselves within the bounds which he has prescribed to them. . . .

This is, I think, a true sketch of the principles of those who defend the doctrine of passive obedience and nonresistance. Now, there is nothing in Scripture which supports this scheme of political principles. As to the passage under consideration, the apostle here speaks of civil rulers in *general*, of all persons in *common*, vested with authority for the good of society, without any particular reference to one form of government more than to another, or to the supreme power in any particular state more than to subordinate powers. The apostle does not concern himself with the different forms of government. This he supposes is left entirely to human prudence and discretion. Now, the consequence of this is that unlimited and passive obedience is no more enjoined in this passage under monarchical government, or to the supreme power in any state, than under all other species of government which answer the end of government, or to all the subordinate degrees of civil authority, from the highest to the lowest. Those, therefore, who would from this passage infer the guilt of resisting kings in all cases whatever, though acting ever so contrary to the design of their office, must, if they will be consistent, go much farther and infer from it the guilt of resistance under all other forms of government and of resisting any petty officer in the state, though acting

beyond his commission, in the most arbitrary, illegal manner possible.

The argument holds equally strong in both cases. All civil rulers, as such, are the ordinance and ministers of God; and they are all, by the nature of their office and in their respective spheres and stations, bound to consult the public welfare. With the same reason, therefore, that any deny unlimited and passive obedience to be here enjoined under a republic or aristocracy or any other established form of civil government, or to subordinate powers acting in an illegal and oppressive manner, (with the same reason) others may deny that such obedience is enjoined to a king or monarch or any civil power whatever. For the apostle says nothing that is *peculiar to kings*; what he says extends equally to *all* other persons whatever, vested with any civil office. They are all, in exactly the same sense, the ordinance of God and the ministers of God; and obedience is equally enjoined to be paid to them all. For, as the apostle expresses it, there is *no power but of God*; and we are required to render to *all their dues*, and not *more* than their *dues*. And what these *dues* are, and to *whom* they are to be *rendered*, the apostle does not say, but leaves to the reason and consciences of men to determine.

Thus it appears that the common argument, grounded upon this passage in favor of universal and passive obedience, really overthrows itself by proving too much, if it proves anything at all; namely, that no civil officer is, in any case whatever, to be resisted, though acting in express contradiction to the design of his office; which no man in his senses ever did or can assert.

If we calmly consider the nature of the thing itself, nothing can well be imagined more directly contrary to common sense than to suppose that *millions* of people should be subjected to the arbitrary, precarious pleasure of *one single man* (who has *naturally* no superiority over them in point of authority) so that their estates, and everything that is valuable in life, and even their lives also, shall be absolutely at his disposal if he happens to be wanton and capricious enough to demand them. What unprejudiced man can think that God made *all* to be thus subservient to the lawless pleasure and frenzy of *one* so that it shall always be a sin to resist him! Nothing but the most plain and express revelation from Heaven could make a sober, impartial man believe such a monstrous, unaccountable doctrine; and, indeed, the thing itself appears so shocking, so out of all proportion, that it may be questioned whether all the miracles that ever were wrought could make it credible that this doctrine really came from God.

At present, there is not the least syllable in Scripture which gives any countenance to it. The hereditary, indefeasible divine right of kings, and the doctrine of nonresistance, which is built upon the supposition of such a right, are altogether as fabulous and chimerical as transubstantiation or any of the most absurd reveries of ancient or modern visionaries. These notions are fetched neither from divine revelation nor human reason; and if they are derived from neither of those sources, it is not much matter from whence they come, or whither they go. Only it is a pity that such doctrines should be propagated in society, to raise factions and rebellions, as we see they have, in fact, been, both in the *last* and in the *present reign.*

But, then, if unlimited submission and passive obedience to the *higher powers* in all possible cases be not a duty, it will be asked, "How far are we obliged to submit? If we may innocently disobey and resist in some cases, why not in all? Where shall we stop? What is the measure of our duty? This doctrine tends to the total dissolution of civil government and to introduce such scenes of wild anarchy and confusion as are more fatal to society than the worst of tyranny."

After this manner, some men object; and, indeed, this is the most plausible thing that can be said in favor of such an absolute submission as they plead for. But the worst (or rather the best) of it is that there is very little strength or solidity in it; for similar difficulties may be raised with respect to almost every duty of natural and revealed religion. To instance only in two, both of which are near akin and, indeed, exactly parallel to the case before us. It is unquestionably the duty of children to submit to their parents and of servants to their masters. But no one asserts that it is their duty to obey and submit to them in all supposable cases or universally a sin to resist them. Now does this tend to subvert the just authority of parents and masters? Or to introduce confusion and anarchy into private families? No. How then does the same principle tend to unhinge the government of that larger family, the body politic? We know, in general, that children and servants are obliged to obey their parents and masters respectively. We know, also, with equal certainty, that they are not obliged to submit to them in all things, without exception, but may, in some cases, reasonably and, therefore, innocently resist them. These principles are acknowledged upon all hands, whatever difficulty there may be in fixing the exact limits of submission.

Now, there is at least as much difficulty in stating the measure of duty in these two cases as in the case of rulers and subjects. So that this is really no objection, at least no reasonable one, against resistance to the *higher powers;* or, if it is one, it will hold equally against resistance in the other cases mentioned. It is indeed true that turbulent, vicious-minded men may take occasion from this principle, that their rulers may, in some cases, be lawfully resisted to raise factions and disturbances in the state and to make resistance where resistance is needless and, therefore, sinful. But is it not equally true that children and servants of turbulent, vicious minds may take occasion from this principle, that parents and masters may, in some cases, be lawfully resisted to resist when resistance is unnecessary and, therefore, criminal? Is the principle in either case false in itself merely because it may be abused and applied to legitimate disobedience and resistance in those instances to which it ought not to be applied? According to this way of arguing, there will be no true principles in the world, for there are none but what may be wrested and perverted to serve bad purposes, either through the weakness or wickedness of men.

A *people*, really oppressed to a great degree by their sovereign, cannot well be insensible when they are so oppressed. And such a people (if I may allude to an ancient fable) have, like the Hesperian fruit, a dragon for their protector and guardian; nor would they have any reason to mourn if some Hercules should appear to dispatch him. For a nation thus abused to arise unanimously and to resist their prince, even to the dethroning him, is not criminal but a reasonable way of vindicating their liberties and just rights; it is making use of the means, and the only means, which God has put into their power for mutual and self-defense. And it would be highly criminal in them not to make use of this means. It would be stupid tameness and unaccountable folly for whole nations to suffer *one* unreasonable, ambitious, and cruel man to

wanton and riot in their misery. And, in such a case, it would, of the two, be more rational to suppose that they did *not resist* than that they who did would *receive to themselves damnation.* . . .

To conclude, let us all learn to be *free* and to be *loyal.* Let us not profess ourselves vassals to the lawless pleasure of any man on earth. But let us remember, at the same time, government is *sacred* and not to be trifled with. It is our happiness to live under the government of a prince who is satisfied with ruling according to law, as every other good prince will. We enjoy under his administration all the liberty that is proper and expedient for us. It becomes us, therefore, to be contented and dutiful subjects. Let us prize our freedom but not *use our liberty for a cloak of maliciousness.* There are men who strike at liberty under the term licentiousness. There are others who aim at popularity under the disguise of patriotism. Be aware of both. *Extremes* are dangerous. There is at present amongst us, perhaps, more danger of the latter than of the former; for which reason I would exhort you to pay all due regard to the government over us, to the king and all in authority, and to lead a *quiet and peaceable life.* And while I am speaking of loyalty to our earthly prince, suffer me just to put you in mind to be loyal also to the Supreme Ruler of the universe, "by whom kings reign and princes decree justice" (Prov. 8:15). To which King eternal, immortal, invisible, even to the only wise God be all honor and praise, dominion and thanksgiving, through Jesus Christ our Lord. Amen.

1751

107.

Benjamin Franklin: On the Increase of Mankind

Franklin's "Observations Concerning the Increase of Mankind" were written in 1751 but were not published until four years later, when they were included in a tract by William Clarke on the colonizing activities of the French. In a preface to the work, Clarke explained that Franklin had been reluctant to let the "Observations" appear, but had been persuaded by "some of his friends, who thought the publication of them would be of general benefit and advantage." Franklin's reluctance evidently was thoroughly overcome, for he appended the "Observations" to two later publications of his own, a pamphlet of 1760 titled "The Interest of Great Britain Considered," and his famous report, reprinted in 1769, "Experiments and Observations on Electricity." In fact, Franklin had no need to be hesitant, for his little demographic study is one of the most significant contributions to the subject before the time of Malthus. The original or Clarke version of the essay concluded with two paragraphs dealing with the racial balance of the future population of America. These two paragraphs were omitted by Franklin in his subsequent reprintings, but they have been restored in the version that appears below.

Source: *The Writings of Benjamin Franklin*, Albert H. Smyth, ed., New York, 1905, Vol. III, pp. 63-73: "Observations Concerning the Increase of Mankind, Peopling of Countries, etc."

1. Tables of the proportion of marriages to births, of deaths to births, of marriages to the numbers of inhabitants, etc., formed on observations made upon the bills of mortality, christenings, etc., of populous cities, will not suit countries; nor will tables formed on observations made on full-settled old countries, as Europe, suit new countries, as America.

2. For people increase in proportion to the number of marriages, and that is greater in proportion to the ease and convenience of supporting a family. When families can be easily supported, more persons marry and earlier in life.

3. In cities, where all trades, occupations, and offices are full, many delay marrying till they can see how to bear the charges of a family; which charges are greater in cities, as luxury is more common. Many live single during life and continue servants to families, journeymen to trades, etc., hence cities do not by natural generation supply themselves with inhabitants; the deaths are more than the births.

4. In countries full settled, the case

must be nearly the same, all lands being occupied and improved to the height. Those who cannot get land must labor for others that have it; when laborers are plenty, their wages will be low; by low wages a family is supported with difficulty; this difficulty deters many from marriage, who therefore long continue servants and single. Only as the cities take supplies of people from the country, and thereby make a little more room in the country; marriage is a little more encouraged there, and the births exceed the deaths.

5. Europe is generally full settled with husbandmen, manufacturers, etc., and therefore cannot now much increase in people. America is chiefly occupied by Indians, who subsist mostly by hunting. But as the hunter, of all men, requires the greatest quantity of land from whence to draw his subsistence (the husbandman subsisting on much less, the gardener on still less, and the manufacturer requiring least of all), the Europeans found America as fully settled as it well could be by hunters. Yet these, having large tracks, were easily prevailed on to part with portions of territory to the newcomers, who did not much interfere with the natives in hunting, and furnished them with many things they wanted.

6. Land being thus plenty in America and so cheap as that a laboring man that understands husbandry can in a short time save money enough to purchase a piece of new land sufficient for a plantation, whereon he may subsist a family, such are not afraid to marry; for, if they even look far enough forward to consider how their children, when grown up, are to be provided for, they see that more land is to be had at rates equally easy, all circumstances considered.

7. Hence marriages in America are more general, and more generally early, than in Europe. And if it is reckoned there that there is but one marriage per annum among 100 persons, perhaps we may here reckon two; and if in Europe they have but four births to a marriage (many of their marriages being late), we may here reckon eight, of which if one-half grow up, and our marriages are made, reckoning one with another, at twenty years of age, our people must at least be doubled every twenty years.

8. But notwithstanding this increase, so vast is the territory of North America that it will require many ages to settle it fully; and, till it is fully settled, labor will never be cheap here, where no man continues long a laborer for others, but gets a plantation of his own; no man continues long a journeyman to a trade, but goes among those new settlers and sets up for himself; etc. Hence labor is no cheaper now in Pennsylvania than it was thirty years ago, though so many thousand laboring people have been imported.

9. The danger, therefore, of these colonies interfering with their mother country in trades that depend on labor, manufactures, etc., is too remote to require the attention of Great Britain.

10. But in proportion to the increase of the colonies, a vast demand is growing for British manufactures, a glorious market wholly in the power of Britain in which foreigners cannot interfere, which will increase in a short time even beyond her power of supplying, though her whole trade should be to her colonies; therefore Britain should not too much restrain manufactures in her colonies. A wise and good mother will not do it. To distress is to weaken, and weakening the children weakens the whole family.

11. Besides, if the manufactures of Britain (by reason of the American demands) should rise too high in price, foreigners who can sell cheaper will drive her merchants out of foreign markets; foreign manufactures will thereby be encouraged and increased, and, consequently, foreign nations, perhaps her rivals in power, grow more

populous and more powerful; while her own colonies, kept too low, are unable to assist her or add to her strength.

12. 'Tis an ill-grounded opinion that, by the labor of slaves, America may possibly vie in cheapness of manufactures with Britain. The labor of slaves can never be so cheap here as the labor of workingmen is in Britain. Anyone may compute it. Interest of money is in the colonies from 6 to 10 percent. Slaves, one with another, cost £30 sterling per head. Reckon then the interest of the first purchase of a slave, the insurance or risk on his life, his clothing and diet, expenses in his sickness and loss of time, loss by his neglect of business (neglect is natural to the man who is not to be benefited by his own care or diligence), expense of a driver to keep him at work, and his pilfering from time to time, almost every slave being *by nature* a thief, and compare the whole amount with the wages of a manufacturer of iron or wool in England, you will see that labor is much cheaper there than it ever can be by Negroes here. Why then will Americans purchase slaves? Because slaves may be kept as long as a *man* pleases, or has occasion for their labor; while hired men are continually leaving their masters (often in the midst of his business) and setting up for themselves.

13. As the increase of people depends on the encouragement of marriages, the following things must diminish a nation, viz.:

(a) *The Being Conquered.* For the conquerors will engross as many offices, and exact as much tribute or profit on the labor of the conquered, as will maintain them in their new establishment, and this diminishing the subsistence of the natives discourages their marriages, and so gradually diminishes them, while the foreigners increase.

(b) *Loss of Territory.* Thus, the Britons, being driven into Wales and crowded together in a barren country insufficient to support such great numbers, diminished until the people bore a proportion to the pro-

duce, while the Saxons increased on their abandoned lands; until the Island became full of English. And, were the English now driven into Wales by some foreign nation, there would in a few years be no more Englishmen in Britain, than there are now people in Wales.

(c) *Loss of Trade.* Manufactures exported draw subsistence from foreign countries for numbers, who are thereby enabled to marry and raise families. If the nation be deprived of any branch of trade, and no new employment is found for the people occupied in that branch, it will also be soon deprived of so many people.

(d) *Loss of Food.* Suppose a nation has a fishery, which not only employs great numbers but makes the food and subsistence of the people cheaper. If another nation becomes master of the seas and prevents the fishery, the people will diminish in proportion as the loss of employ and dearness of provision makes it more difficult to subsist a family.

(e) *Bad Government and Insecure Property.* People not only leave such a country, and settling abroad, incorporate with other nations, lose their native language, and become foreigners, but, the industry of those that remain being discouraged, the quantity of subsistence in the country is lessened, and the support of a family becomes more difficult; so heavy taxes tend to diminish a people.

(f) *The Introduction of Slaves.* The Negroes brought into the English sugar islands have greatly diminished the whites there. The poor are by this means deprived of employment, while a few families acquire vast estates, which they spend on foreign luxuries and educating their children in the habit of those luxuries. The same income is needed for the support of one that might have maintained 100. The whites who have slaves, not laboring, are enfeebled, and therefore not so generally prolific; the slaves being worked too hard and ill fed, their constitutions are broken, and the deaths among them are more than the births; so that a continual supply is needed from Africa. The northern colonies, having few slaves, increase in whites. Slaves also pejorate the families that use them; the white children become proud, disgusted with labor, and, being educated in idleness, are rendered unfit to get a living by industry.

14. Hence the prince that acquires new territory, if he finds it vacant or removes the natives to give his own people room; the legislator that makes effectual laws for promoting of trade, increasing employment, improving land by more or better tillage, providing more food by fisheries, securing property, etc.; and the man that invents new trades, arts, or manufactures, or new improvements in husbandry, may be properly called *fathers* of their nation, as they are the cause of the generation of multitudes by the encouragement they afford to marriage.

15. As to privileges granted to the married (such as the *Jus trium Liberorum* among the Romans), they may hasten the filling of a country that has been thinned by war or pestilence or that has otherwise vacant territory, but cannot increase a people beyond the means provided for their subsistence.

16. Foreign luxuries and needless manufactures, imported and used in a nation, do, by the same reasoning, increase the people of the nation that furnishes them and diminish the people of the nation that uses them. Laws, therefore, that prevent such importations, and on the contrary promote the exportation of manufactures to be consumed in foreign countries, may be called (with respect to the people that make them) *generative laws* as by increasing subsistence they encourage marriage. Such laws likewise strengthen a country doubly by increasing its own people and diminishing its neighbors.

17. Some European nations prudently refuse to consume the manufactures of East India. They should likewise forbid them to their colonies; for the gain to the merchant is not to be compared with the loss, by this means, of people to the nation.

18. Home luxury in the great increases the nation's manufacturers employed by it, who are many, and only tends to diminish the families that indulge in it, who are few. The greater the common fashionable expense of any rank of people, the more cautious they are of marriage. Therefore, luxury should never be suffered to become common.

19. The great increase of offspring in particular families is not always owing to greater fecundity of nature but sometimes to examples of industry in the heads and industrious education, by which the children are enabled to provide better for themselves; and their marrying early is encouraged from the prospect of good subsistence.

20. If there be a sect, therefore, in our nation, that regard frugality and industry as religious duties and educate their children therein more than others commonly do, such sect must consequently increase more by natural generation than any other sect in Britain.

21. The importation of foreigners into a country that has as many inhabitants as the present employments and provisions for subsistence will bear will be in the end no increase of people; unless the newcomers have more industry and frugality than the natives, and then they will provide more subsistence and increase in the country; but they will gradually eat the natives out. Nor is it necessary to bring in foreigners to fill up any occasional vacancy in a country; for such vacancy (if the laws are good . . .) will soon be filled by natural generation. Who can now find the vacancy made in Sweden, France, or other warlike nations, by the plague of heroism forty years ago — in France, by the expulsion of the Protestants; in England, by the settlement of her colonies; or in Guinea, by 100 years' expor-

tation of slaves that has blackened half America? The thinness of inhabitants in Spain is owing to national pride and idleness and other causes, rather than to the expulsion of the Moors or to the making of new settlements.

22. There is, in short, no bound to the prolific nature of plants or animals but what is made by their crowding and interfering with each other's means of subsistence. Was the face of the earth vacant of other plants, it might be gradually sowed and overspread with one kind only; as, for instance, with fennel; and were it empty of other inhabitants, it might in a few ages be replenished from one nation only; as, for instance, with Englishmen. Thus, there are supposed to be now upward of 1,000,000 English souls in North America (though 'tis thought scarce 80,000 have been brought over sea), and, yet, perhaps, there is not one the fewer in Britain, but rather many more, on account of the employment the colonies afford to manufacturers at home. This 1,000,000 doubling, suppose but once in twenty-five years, will, in another century, be more than the people of England, and the greatest number of Englishmen will be on this side the water.

What an accession of power to the British empire by sea as well as land! What increase of trade and navigation! What numbers of ships and seamen! We have been here but little more than 100 years, and yet the force of our privateers in the late war, united, was greater, both in men and guns, than that of the whole British Navy in Queen Elizabeth's time. How important an affair then to Britain is the present treaty for settling the bounds between her colonies and the French; and how careful should she be to secure room enough, since on the room depends so much the increase of her people.

23. In fine, a nation well regulated is like a polyp — take away a limb, its place is soon supplied; cut it in two, and each defi-cient part shall speedily grow out of the part remaining. Thus, if you have room and subsistence enough, as you may by dividing, make ten polyps out of one, you may of one make ten nations, equally populous and powerful; or rather increase a nation tenfold in numbers and strength.

And since detachments of English from Britain, sent to America, will have their places at home so soon supplied and increase so largely here, why should the Palatine boors be suffered to swarm into our settlements and, by herding together, establish their language and manners to the exclusion of ours? Why should Pennsylvania, founded by the English, become a colony of *aliens*, who will shortly be so numerous as to germanize us instead of our anglifying them, and will never adopt our language or customs any more than they can acquire our complexion?

24. Which leads me to add one remark, that the number of purely white people in the world is proportionably very small. All Africa is black or tawny; Asia chiefly tawny; America (exclusive of the newcomers), wholly so. And in Europe, the Spaniards, Italians, French, Russians, and Swedes are generally of what we call a swarthy complexion; as are the Germans also, the Saxons only excepted, who, with the English, make the principal body of white people on the face of the earth. I could wish their numbers were increased. And while we are, as I may call it, scouring our planet by clearing America of woods, and so making this side of our globe reflect a brighter light to the eyes of inhabitants in Mars or Venus, why should we, in the sight of superior beings, darken its people? Why increase the sons of Africa by planting them in America, where we have so fair an opportunity, by excluding all blacks and tawnies, of increasing the lovely white and red? But perhaps I am partial to the complexion of my country, for such kind of partiality is natural to mankind.

108.

Benjamin Franklin: Colonial Problems

A request by the printer for an appraisal of a manuscript by a certain James Parker, titled "The Importance of Gaining and Preserving the Friendship of the Indians to the British Interest Considered," brought forth the following reply by Franklin, written on March 20, 1751. Franklin's practical spirit and continuing concern for improved relations with the Indians led him to comment on matters ranging all the way from colonial trade policies and the need for political organization to Indian methods of warfare — the last reflecting contemporary concern over suspected alliances between the Indians and the hostile French. Franklin's ideas about colonial unity were soon made more explicit in his Albany Plan of Union. The letter appeared as an appendix to Parker's pamphlet, which was published in New York later in 1751.

Source: *The Writings of Benjamin Franklin,* Albert H. Smyth, ed., New York, 1905, Vol. III, pp. 40-45.

I HAVE, as you desire, read the manuscript you sent me, and am of opinion, with the public-spirited author, that securing the friendship of the Indians is of the greatest consequence to these colonies; and that the surest means of doing it are to regulate the Indian trade, so as to convince them, by experience, that they may have the best and cheapest goods and the fairest dealing from the English; and to unite the several governments, so as to form a strength that the Indians may depend on for protection in case of a rupture with the French; or apprehend great danger from, if they should break with us.

This union of the colonies, however necessary, I apprehend is not to be brought about by the means that have hitherto been used for that purpose. A governor of one colony, who happens from some circumstances in his own government to see the necessity of such a union, writes his sentiments of the matter to the other governors and desires them to recommend it to their respective assemblies. They accordingly lay the letters before those assemblies, and perhaps recommend the proposal in general words. But governors are often on ill terms with their assemblies and seldom are the men that have the most influence among them. And perhaps some governors, though they openly recommend the scheme, may privately throw cold water on it as thinking additional public charges will make their people less able or less willing to give to them. Or perhaps they do not clearly see the necessity of it and, therefore, do not very earnestly press the consideration of it; and no one being present that has the affair at heart to back it, to answer and remove objections, etc., 'tis easily dropped, and nothing is done.

Such a union is certainly necessary to us all, but more immediately so to your government. Now, if you were to pick out half a dozen men of good understanding and address and furnish them with a reasonable scheme and proper instructions and send them in the nature of ambassadors to the other colonies, where they might apply particularly to all the leading men, and by proper management get them to engage in promoting the scheme; where, by being present, they would have the opportunity of pressing the affair both in public and private, obviating difficulties as they arise, answering objections as soon as they are made, before they spread and gather strength in the minds of the people, etc., I imagine such a union might thereby be made and established; for reasonable, sensible men can always make a reasonable scheme appear such to other reasonable men if they take pains and have time and opportunity for it; unless from some circumstances their honesty and good intentions are suspected.

A voluntary union entered into by the colonies themselves, I think, would be preferable to one imposed by Parliament; for it would be perhaps not much more difficult to procure and more easy to alter and improve, as circumstances should require and experience direct. It would be a ·very strange thing, if Six Nations of ignorant savages should be capable of forming a scheme for such a union and be able to execute it in such a manner as that it has subsisted ages and appears indissoluble; and yet that a like union should be impracticable for ten or a dozen English colonies, to whom it is more necessary and must be more advantageous; and who cannot be supposed to want an equal understanding of their interests.

Were there a general council formed by all the colonies and a general governor appointed by the Crown to preside in that council or in some manner to concur with and confirm their acts and take care of the execution, everything relating to Indian affairs and the defense of the colonies might be properly put under their management. Each colony should be represented by as many members as it pays sums of __ __ hundred pounds into the common treasury for the common expense; which treasury would perhaps be best and most equitably supplied by an equal excise on strong liquors in all the colonies, the produce never to be applied to the private use of any colony but to the general service. Perhaps if the council were to meet successively at the capitals of the several colonies, they might thereby become better acquainted with the circumstances, interests, strength or weakness, etc., of all and thence be able to judge better of measures proposed from time to time. At least it might be more satisfactory to the colonies if this were proposed as a part of the scheme, for a preference might create jealousy and dislike.

I believe the place mentioned is a very suitable one to build a fort on. In times of peace, parties of the garrisons of all frontier forts might be allowed to go out on hunting expeditions, with or without Indians, and have the profit to themselves of the skins they get. By this means a number of wood-runners would be formed, well acquainted with the country, and of great use in wartime as guides of parties and scouts, etc. Every Indian is a hunter; and as their manner of making war, viz., by skulking, surprising, and killing particular persons and families, is just the same as their manner of hunting, only changing the object, every Indian is a disciplined soldier. Soldiers of this kind are always wanted in the colonies in an Indian war, for the European military discipline is of little use in these woods.

Public trading houses would certainly have a good effect toward regulating the private trade and preventing the impositions of the private traders; and therefore such should be established in suitable places all along the frontiers; and the superintendent of the trade, proposed by the author, would, I think, be a useful officer.

The observation concerning the importation of Germans in too great numbers into Pennsylvania is, I believe, a very just one. This will in a few years become a *German* colony; instead of their learning our language, we must learn theirs, or live as in a foreign country. Already the English begin to quit particular neighborhoods surrounded by Dutch, being made uneasy by the disagreeableness of dissonant manners; and, in time, numbers will probably quit the province for the same reason. Besides, the Dutch underlive and are thereby enabled to underwork and undersell the English; who are thereby extremely incommoded, and consequently disgusted, so that there can be no cordial affection or unity between the two nations.

How good subjects they may make, and how faithful to the British interest, is a question worth considering. And, in my opinion, equal numbers might have been spared from the British islands without being missed there, and on proper encouragement would have come over. I say without being missed; perhaps I might say without lessening the number of people at home. I question, indeed, whether there be a man the less in Britain for the establishment of the colonies.

An island can support but a certain number of people; when all employments are full, multitudes refrain marriage, till they can see how to maintain a family. The number of Englishmen in England cannot, by their present common increase, be doubled in a thousand years; but if half of them were taken away and planted in America, where there is room for them to increase and sufficient employment and subsistence, the number of Englishmen would be doubled in one hundred years; for those left at home would multiply in that time so as to fill up the vacancy, and those here would at least keep pace with them.

Everyone must approve the proposal of encouraging a number of sober, discreet smiths to reside among the Indians. They would doubtless be of great service. The whole subsistence of Indians depends on keeping their guns in order; and if they are obliged to make a journey of two or three hundred miles to an English settlement to get a lock mended, it may, besides the trouble, occasion the loss of their hunting season. They are people that think much of their temporal, but little of their spiritual, interests; and, therefore, as he would be a most useful and necessary man to them, a smith is more likely to influence them than a Jesuit; provided he has a good common understanding and is from time to time well instructed.

I wish I could offer anything for the improvement of the author's piece, but I have little knowledge and less experience in these matters. I think it ought to be printed; and should be glad there were a more general communication of the sentiments of judicious men on subjects so generally interesting. It would certainly produce good effects. Please to present my respects to the gentleman, and thank him for the perusal of his manuscript.

Proclaim liberty throughout the land unto all the inhabitants thereof.
Leviticus, 25:10; inscription on the Liberty Bell. The bell was ordered with these words by the Pennsylvania Provincial Assembly on Nov. 1, 1751. Twenty-five years later it tolled while the Declaration of Independence was signed.

1753

109.

Benjamin Franklin: The Futility of Educating the Indians

The relentless attempts of the early Puritan colonists to imbue the Indians with the white man's passion for work and moral regulation made few inroads into their tribal-centered life. Indian youths, educated at Harvard, received nothing but criticism from their elders upon returning to the wilderness, and found themselves unable to adapt to either society. To the red man, the white man's was an alien culture, dimly perceived to be superior, but fundamentally unsuited to his needs. The reluctance or inability of the Indian to be converted to the white man's way of life is pointedly illustrated in the following excerpt from a letter written by Benjamin Franklin to Peter Collinson, on May 9, 1753. Franklin, of course, had a theory of his own to explain the failure of the English to export their culture.

Source: Sparks, VII, pp. 68-73.

THE PRONENESS OF HUMAN NATURE to a life of ease, of freedom from care and labor, appears strongly in the little success that has hitherto attended every attempt to civilize our American Indians. In their present way of living, almost all their wants are supplied by the spontaneous productions of nature, with the addition of very little labor, if hunting and fishing may indeed be called labor, where game is so plenty. They visit us frequently and see the advantages that arts, sciences, and compact societies procure us. They are not deficient in natural understanding; and yet they have never shown any inclination to change their manner of life for ours or to learn any of our arts.

When an Indian child has been brought up among us, taught our language, and ha-bituated to our customs; yet, if he goes to see his relatives, and makes one Indian ramble with them, there is no persuading him ever to return. And that this is not natural to them merely as Indians, but as men, is plain from this, that when white persons, of either sex, have been taken prisoners by the Indians and lived awhile with them, though ransomed by their friends and treated with all imaginable tenderness to prevail with them to stay among the English; yet in a short time they become disgusted with our manner of life, and the care and pains that are necessary to support it, and take the first opportunity of escaping again into the woods, from whence there is no redeeming them. One instance I remember to have heard where the person was brought home

Courtesy, the Fogg Art Museum, Harvard University

Benjamin Franklin, portrait attributed to Robert Feke, 1748

to possess a good estate; but, finding some care necessary to keep it together, he relinquished it to a younger brother, reserving to himself nothing but a gun and a matchcoat, with which he took his way again into the wilderness.

So that I am apt to imagine that close societies, subsisting by labor and art, arose first, not from choice but from necessity, when numbers, being driven by war from their hunting grounds and prevented by seas, or by other nations, from obtaining other hunting grounds were crowded together into some narrow territories, which without labor could not afford them food. However, as matters now stand with us, care and industry seem absolutely necessary to our well-being. They should, therefore, have every encouragement we can invent, and not one motive to diligence be subtracted; and the support of the poor should not be by maintaining them in idleness but by employing them in some kind of labor suited to their abilities of body, as I am informed begins to be of late the practice in

many parts of England, where workhouses are erected for that purpose. If these were general, I should think the poor would be more careful and work voluntarily to lay up something for themselves against a rainy day, rather than run the risk of being obliged to work at the pleasure of others for a bare subsistence, and that too under confinement.

The little value Indians set on what we prize so highly, under the name of learning, appears from a pleasant passage that happened some years since, at a treaty between some colonies and the Six Nations. When everything had been settled to the satisfaction of both sides, and nothing remained but a mutual exchange of civilities, the English commissioners told the Indians that they had in their country a college for the instruction of youth, who were there taught various languages, arts, and sciences; that there was a particular foundation in favor of the Indians to defray the expense of the education of any of their sons who should desire to take the benefit of it; and said, if the Indians would accept the offer, the English would take half a dozen of their brightest lads and bring them up in the best manner.

The Indians, after consulting on the proposals, replied that it was remembered that some of their youths had formerly been educated at that college, but that it had been observed that for a long time after they returned to their friends, *they were absolutely good for nothing* — being neither acquainted with the true methods of killing deer, catching beavers, or surprising an enemy. The proposition they looked on, however, as a mark of kindness and goodwill of the English to the Indian nations, which merited a grateful return; and, therefore, if the English gentlemen would send a dozen or two of their children to Onondago, the Great Council would take care of their education, bring them up in what was really the best manner, and make men of them.

110.

Royal Instructions Concerning Land Grants

Land speculation was rife in eighteenth-century America, and by the middle of the century vast holdings were concentrated in the hands of a few in many of the royal colonies. The right to hold land, which legally still belonged to the King, was based on the payment of a quitrent that large landholders, for the most part, were able to evade. However, it was the policy of the Crown to encourage small landholders, and the following instructions were issued to the colonial governors sometime around 1753. The attempt to regulate the holding of land did not succeed, mainly because the governors and their councilors, by whom the land was in fact distributed, were themselves interested in speculation. Eventually, the Crown bypassed the governors; between 1764 and 1767 it granted over five million acres directly from England.

Source: *Royal Instructions to British Colonial Governors 1670-1776*, Leonard W. Labaree, ed., New York, 1935, Vol. II, pp. 527-528.

And whereas nothing can more effectually tend to the further improving and settling the said province, the security of the property of Our subjects, and the advancement of the revenue of quitrents than the establishing a regular and proper method of proceeding with respect to the passing of grants of land within the same; it is therefore Our will and pleasure that all and every person and persons who shall for the future apply to you for any grants of land shall previous to obtaining the same make it appear before you in council that they are in a condition to cultivate and improve the same by settling thereon in proportion to the quantity of acres a sufficient number of white persons or Negroes.

And in case you shall upon a consideration of the circumstances of the person applying for such grants think it advisable to pass the same, in such case you are to cause a warrant to be drawn up, directed to the surveyor general or other proper officer, empowering him or them to make a faithful and exact survey of the lands so petitioned for and to return the said warrant within six months at furthest from the date thereof with a plot or description of the land so surveyed thereunto annexed; provided that you do take care that before any such warrant is issued as aforesaid, a docket thereof be entered in the auditor's office; and when the warrant shall be returned by the said surveyor or other proper officer, the grant shall be made out in due form and the terms and conditions required by these Our instructions be particularly and expressly mentioned in the respective grants.

And it is Our further will and pleasure that the said grants shall be registered within six months from the date thereof in Our secretary's office there and a docket thereof be also entered in Our auditor's office there, or that in default thereof such grants shall be void, copies of all which entries shall be returned regularly by the proper officer to Our Commissioners of Our Treasury and to Our Commissioners for Trade and Plantations six months from the date thereof.

1753 - 1754

111.

Dispute Over a Sectarian Control of Colleges

The controversy about ecclesiastical control of higher education in the colonies was a persistent one and is reflected in the following selection, which includes three statements on the subject from different points of view. The first two reveal the widespread opposition to Anglican control of King's College (now Columbia University) in New York. William Livingston, a prominent Presbyterian, attempted to arouse opposition to such control through editorials in the Independent Reflector *in March 1753. He was joined by other New Yorkers, including James Alexander and William Smith, who addressed a protest to a member of the General Assembly on May 30 of the next year. When the charter of the college was granted, in 1754, it required that the president be an Anglican, but provided for an interdenominational board of trustees. For Thomas Clap, president of Yale, the issue was not religious control of colleges as such, but whether control should be exercised from within or from without. His views are revealed in the third part of the selection, an excerpt from his* Religious Constitution of Colleges, *published in 1754.*

Source: *Independent Reflector,* March 22, 29, 1753.
     The Querist: or, A Letter to a Member of the General Assembly of the Colony of New-York, etc., etc., 1754.
     Thomas Clap, *The Religious Constitution of Colleges, etc., etc.,* New London, 1754.

I.

WILLIAM LIVINGSTON:

Opposition to a Sectarian College

THE DESIGN OF ERECTING a college in this province is a matter of such grand and general importance that I have frequently made it the topic of my serious meditation. . . .

    To imagine that our legislature, by raising the present fund for the college, intended barely to have our children instructed in Greek and Latin, or the art of making exercises and verses, or disputing in mood and figure, were a supposition absurd and defamatory. For these branches of literature, however useful as preparatory to real and substantial knowledge, are in themselves perfectly idle and insignificant. The true use of education is to qualify men for the different employments of life to which it may please God to call them. It is to improve their hearts and understandings; to infuse a public spirit and love of their country; to inspire them with the principles of honor and probity, with a fervent zeal for liberty, and a diffusive benevolence for mankind; and, in a word, to make them the more extensively serviceable to the Commonwealth. . . .

This, therefore, I will venture to lay down for a capital maxim — that unless the education we propose be calculated to render our youth better members of society and useful to the public in proportion to its expense, we had better be without it. As the natural consequence of this proposition, it follows that the plan of education the most conducive to that end is to be chosen, and whatever has a tendency to obstruct or impede it ought carefully to be avoided. . . . I shall now proceed to offer a few arguments which I submit to the consideration of my countrymen to evince the necessity and importance of constituting *our* college upon a basis of the most catholic, generous, and free.

It is, in the first place, observable that, unless its constitution and government be such as will admit persons of all Protestant denominations upon a perfect parity as to privileges, it will itself be greatly prejudiced and prove a nursery of animosity, dissension, and disorder. The sincere men of all sects imagine their own profession, on the whole, more eligible and scriptural than any other. It is, therefore, very natural to suppose they will exert themselves to weaken and diminish all other divisions, the better to strengthen and enlarge their own. To this cause must in a great measure be ascribed that heat and opposition which animate the breasts of many men of religious distinctions, whose intemperate and misapplied zeal is the only blemish that can be thrown upon their characters.

Should our college, therefore, unhappily, through our own bad policy fall into the hands of any one religious sect in the province; should that sect, which is more than probable, establish its religion in the college, show favor to its votaries, and cast contempt upon others, it is easy to foresee that Christians of all other denominations among us, instead of encouraging its prosperity, will, from the same principles, rather conspire to oppose and oppress it. Besides English and Dutch Presbyterians, which perhaps exceed all our other religious professions put together, we have Episcopalians, Anabaptists, Lutherans, Quakers, and a growing church of Moravians, all equally zealous for their discriminating tenets. Whichsoever of these has the sole government of the college will kindle the jealousy of the rest, not only against the persuasion so preferred but the college itself. Nor can anything less be expected than a general discontent and tumult; which, affecting all ranks of people, will naturally tend to disturb the tranquillity and peace of the province. . . .

Another argument against so pernicious a scheme is that it will be dangerous to society. . . . And have we not reason to fear the worst effects of it where none but the principles of one persuasion are taught and all others depressed and discountenanced — where, instead of reason and argument of which the minds of the youth are not capable, they are early imbued with the doctrines of a party, enforced by the authority of a professor's chair and the combining aids of the president and all the other officers of the college?

That religious worship should be constantly maintained there, I am so far from opposing that I strongly recommend it, and do not believe any such kind of society can be kept under a regular and due discipline without it. But instructing the youth in any particular systems of divinity, or recommending and establishing any single method of worship or church government, I am convinced would be both useless and hurtful. Useless, because not one in a hundred of the pupils is capable of making a just examination and reasonable choice. Hurtful, because receiving impressions blindly on authority will corrupt their understandings and fetter them with prejudices which may everlastingly prevent a judicious freedom of thought and infect them all their lives with a contracted turn of mind.

A party college, in less than half a century, will put a new face upon the religion and, in consequence thereof, affect the politics of the country. Let us suppose what may, if the college should be entirely managed by one sect, probably be supposed. Would not all possible care be bestowed in tincturing the minds of the students with the doctrines and sentiments of that sect? Would not the students of the college, after the course of their education, exclusive of any others, fill all the offices of the government? Is it not highly reasonable to think that, in the execution of those offices, the spirit of the college would have a most prevailing influence, especially as that party would perpetually receive new strength, become more fashionable and numerous?

Can it be imagined that all other Christians would continue peaceable under, and unenvious of, the power of that church which was rising to so exalted a preeminence above them? Would they not, on the contrary, like all other parties, reflect upon, reluct at, and vilify such an odious ascendancy? Would not the church which had that ascendancy be thereby irritated to repeated acts of domination, and stretch their ecclesiastical rule to unwarrantable and unreasonable lengths?

Whatever others may, in their lethargy and supineness, think of the project of a party college, I am convinced that under the management of any particular persuasion it will necessarily prove destructive to the civil and religious rights of the people. And should any future House of Representatives become generally infected with the maxims of the college, nothing less can be

expected than an establishment of one denomination above all others, who may, perhaps, at the good pleasure of their superiors, be most graciously favored with a bare liberty of conscience while they faithfully continue their annual contributions, their tithes, and their Peter's pence.

A third argument against suffering the college to fall into the hands of a party may be deduced from the design of its erection and support by the public.

The legislature to whom it owes its origin, and under whose care the affair has hitherto been conducted, could never have intended it as an engine to be exercised for the purposes of a party. Such an insinuation would be false and scandalous. It would, therefore, be the height of insolence in any to pervert it to such mean, partial, and little designs. No, it was set on foot and, I hope, will be constituted for general use, for the public benefit, for the education of all who can afford such education. And to suppose it intended for any other less public-spirited uses is ungratefully to reflect upon all who have hitherto had any agency in an undertaking so glorious to the province, so necessary, so important and beneficial.

At present it is but in embryo, yet the money hitherto collected is public money; and, till it is able to support itself, the aids given to it will be public aids. When the community is taxed, it ought to be for the defense or emolument of the whole. Can it, therefore, be supposed that all shall contribute for the uses, the ignominious uses, of a few — nay, what is worse, to that which will be prejudicial to a vast majority? Shall the whole province be made to support what will raise and spread desperate feuds, discontent, and ill blood through the greatest part of the province? Shall the government of the college be delivered out of the hands of the public to a party?

They who wish it are enemies to their country; they who ask it have, besides this antipatriotism, a degree of impudence, arrogance, and assurance unparalleled. And all such as are active in so iniquitous a scheme deserve to be stigmatized with marks of everlasting ignominy and disgrace.

Let it, therefore, ever remain where it is — I mean under the power of the legislature. The influence, whether good or bad, we shall all of us feel and are, therefore, interested in it. It is, for that reason, highly fit that the people should always share in the power to enlarge or restrain it — that power they will have by their representatives in assembly. And no man who is a friend to liberty, his country, and religion will ever rejoice to see it wrested from them. . . .

Add to all this that, in a new country as ours, it is inconsistent with good policy to give any religious profession the ascendancy over others. The rising prosperity of Pennsylvania is the admiration of the continent; and, though disagreeing from them, I should always, for political reasons, exclude Papists from the common and equal benefits of society. Yet, I leave it to the reflections of my judicious readers whether the impartial aspect of their laws upon all professions has not, in a great degree, conduced to their vast importation of religious refugees, to their strength and their riches; and whether a like liberty among us, to all Protestants whatsoever, without any marks of distinction, would not be more commendable, advantageous, and politic.

II.

James Alexander and William Smith: A Protest Against a Sectarian College

Whereas a petition was on the 28th instant read in council. . . . *And whereas* that same petition was referred, by order, to a committee of His Majesty's council, or any five of them, who have this day made re-

port that they are of opinion that His Honor do grant to proper persons His Majesty's letters patent for incorporating the said college according to the purport and prayer of said petition; and that His Honor would be pleased to direct the attorney general to prepare a draft of the said charter to be laid before His Honor in council for the approbation of the board.

We, whose names are underwritten, being two of five of His Majesty's council for this province, who in the said committee dissented from the opinion then given by the Honorable Joseph Murray, Edward Holland, and John Chambers, Esqrs. We also having proposed that the said petition should remain for further consideration of the said committee before report should be made thereon, and the said committee having determined against our opinions in that point also, and carried the proposal in the negative, have therefore thought fit, for the justification of our loyal intention toward His Majesty's service, and our hearty concern for the best good of His Majesty's subjects in this province, and our true respect and deference to His Honor the Lieutenant Governor, and the Honorable Board of His Majesty's council, with all humility herein to set forth the grounds and reasons why we are of opinion that the said petition, with the exclusive clauses therein contained, ought not to have been granted.

Previous whereto we beg leave to declare that, in the political light in which we consider the intended college, it appears to us that any constitutional preferment by act of the government within this province of one denomination of Protestants exclusive of others, to any office that concerns the education of youth (a matter extremely interesting and important), will be injurious to the common rights of this people; naturally endanger the producing of factions and parties; tend to destroy that harmony which at present subsists among them; raise and maintain perpetual jealousies, feuds, animosities, divisions, and hatred among His Majesty's subjects within this province; put it in the power of the party preferred to oppress the rest; and tend to the advancement of particular interests and designs rather than the public good.

And although we are of opinion that the state of this province ought to have been fully considered in a time of more leisure than our preparation for His Majesty's service on the public affairs at Albany and our business on the circuit would admit of, yet we thought it our duty at this time, notwithstanding these disadvantages with regard to the present petition, to observe more particularly that it appears to us:

First, that the far greatest part (we suppose seven-eighths) of the freeholders and inhabitants of this province are Protestants of religious denominations different from those of the Church of England, established by law in South Britain, who are all zealously attached to the distinguishing characteristics of their own respective parties; and notwithstanding their different opinions in religion are all well affected to His Majesty's person and government and the Protestant succession of his royal house, and are good and profitable members of this community; and (at least) as to the far greatest part of them, have not hitherto been disqualified by any act of legislature for public service in any office, either civil, military, or literary within the government.

Second, that the free indulgence of liberty of conscience and an equal enjoyment of civil rights allowed to Protestants of all denominations, and the impartial distributing of offices of trust to Protestants of sufficient qualifications to discharge such offices within this province, has greatly tended to its present growth and prosperity; and that its future strength as a frontier province against the common enemy very much depends upon the preservation of those liberties and rights without the least violation or infringement.

Third, that the college established by the charter proposed, being evidently intended to draw to it the application of the public funds raised for the erecting a college or seminary of learning within this province, will contract the scheme of public education within narrower limits than appear to have been designed by the present public acts of legislation, and will prove a manifest infringement upon the rights of the people who are all equally interested in the money raised for that purpose.

Fourth, we conceive that a charter granted with such exclusive clauses will prove a public grievance, and tend to disoblige the far greatest part of the people of this province, who will be disposed to think that this government treats them unkindly in judging them unfit to be trusted in the education of their own youth in abridging their natural and civil rights and liberties, in an article of the highest importance; that it will tend to drive away the far greatest part of the youth of this province into the neighboring colonies for an education, and transfer a considerable part of our wealth to the support of foreign colleges; will tend to prevent strangers from settling among us; obstruct the increase of the value of our lands and His Majesty's revenues by quitrents; and, in the event, have an unhappy tendency to continue this province as a frontier against the French in a weak and defenseless state.

Wherefore, we are humbly of opinion against the grant of the present petition (among other reasons that may be collected from the premises) more particularly for that it appears to us:

First, as being unjust by any charter to exclude any Protestant denomination in this province from any offices in our college.

Second, as being inconsistent with religious liberty to impose any method of divine service unless it be formed for that purpose in such way as the legislature shall agree to.

Third, as tending to monopolize learning to a small party, and to drive the greatest part of the youth intended for an education to seek it out of this province.

Fourth, as subversive of the generous design of a public college, intended by the acts of legislature referred to in the petition, which do not exclude any denomination of Protestants from any office therein.

Fifth, as dangerous to the peace and prosperity of this province, by establishing in a minor party a constitutional right with an exclusive dominion over the far greatest part of the inhabitants thereof.

Sixth, as detrimental to His Majesty's interest, the honor of his government within this province, and the general good and welfare of the people that inhabit the same.

For these reasons we do enter our protestation against, and dissent from, the grant of the prayer of the said petition with such exclusive clauses as are contained in it; protesting further and declaring it to be our undoubted right and bounden duty for His Majesty's service and with regard to the civil and religious interests of the good people of this province, as occasion may require to publish this our protestation for the common good.

III.

Thomas Clap:
Defense of a Sectarian College

Colleges are religious societies of a superior nature to all others. For, whereas parishes are societies for training up the common people, colleges are societies of ministers for training up persons for the work of the ministry; and, therefore, all their religious instructions, worship, and ordinances are carried on within their own jurisdiction by their own officers and under their own regulation. . . .

Religious worship, preaching, and instruction on the Sabbath, being one of the most important parts of the education of ministers, it is more necessary that it should be under the conduct of the authority of the college than any other part of education. The preaching ought to be adapted to the superior capacity of those who are to be qualified to be instructors of others; and, upon all accounts, superior to that which is ordinarily to be expected, or indeed requisite, in a common parish.

There are many different principles in religion, and kinds of preaching, which, when they are in any degree faulty, cannot always be easily remedied by complaint to any other authority. And, therefore, every religious society naturally chooses, as far as may be, to have the nomination of their own minister. And this is much more necessary in a college where the preaching is of such general importance to a whole country; and such special care should be taken that it be, upon all accounts, of the *best kind*. And it cannot be reasonable nor safe that any particular parish, especially that which happens to be the nearest to a college, should appoint the minister for it. . . .

And where, as it generally happens, there are sundry places of worship in the city where a college is, if the students should disperse to all and every one of them, this would break up all order in the society and defeat the religious design and instructions of it. . . .

Yale College in New Haven does not come up to the perfection of the ancient established universities in Great Britain, yet would endeavor to imitate them in most things, as far as its present state will admit of.

It was founded A.D. 1701 by ten principal ministers in the colony of Connecticut, upon the desire of many other ministers and people in it, with the license and approbation of the General Assembly. Their main design in that foundation was to educate persons for the ministry of these churches, commonly called Presbyterian, or Congregational, according to their own doctrine, discipline, and mode of worship. . . .

The founders, at their first meeting in 1701, made a formal foundation of the college by an express declaration and giving a number of books for a library; and declared that "Their end and design in it is to propagate the blessed, reformed Protestant religion in the purity of its order and worship." And proceeded to give sundry rules and orders, particularly, "That the students should be well instructed in the principles of religion and grounded in polemical divinity," particularly prescribing what books of divinity they should recite, and no other but such as the trustees should order. And that special care should be taken in the education of the students, not to suffer them to be instructed in any different principles or doctrines; and that all proper measures should be taken to promote the power and purity of religion and the peace and best edification of those churches. And particularly order that the students should attend morning and evening prayers and other religious exercises; and especially the worship of God on the Lord's Day, on penalty not exceeding 6d. sterling.

The present governors of the college esteem themselves bound by law and the more sacred ties of conscience and fidelity to their trust, committed to them by their predecessors, to pursue and carry on the pious intention and design of the founders; and to improve all the college estate descended to them for that purpose. And, therefore, about seven years ago, began to lay a fund for the support of a professor of divinity in the college. And being, of late years, more sensible of the necessity of it, from the unhappy, divided circumstances of New Haven, and having received some large donations from the Honorable Mr. Livingston and Mr. Clarke for the purpose, and leased out some of the college lands, have determined to settle such a professor

as soon as, by leasing more of the said land or other ways, a competent support be obtained. . . .

The governors of the college cannot, consistent with the trust committed to them, give up the ordinary, public instruction of the students, especially in matters of divinity, to any but their own officers and substitutes; for they can have no sufficient security, as such governors, that others, who are not of their nomination and under their authority, will teach or instruct according to the design of the founders. And, if they should deviate from it, the governors could have no authority to prevent it. And, upon that account, it is more necessary that the governors of the college should nominate the preacher to it than any other officer or instructor.

Particularly, it cannot be reasonable that either of the three religious assemblies in New Haven should choose a minister for the college, or that the college should be obliged to attend upon such preaching as they, or either of them, should choose. They would not allow that the college should choose a minister for them, much less is it reasonable that they should choose a minister for the college, which is a religious society of a superior, more general, and more important nature.

This would be to subject the college to a jurisdiction out of itself in the most important point of its institution and design. And no society or body politic can be safe but only in its having a principle of self-preservation and a power of providing everything necessary for its own subsistence and defense.

Indeed, as the college receives its charter and part of its support from the government, it is necessarily dependent upon them and under their direction, and must choose such a minister as is agreeable to them, or otherwise they may withdraw their special protection and support. And it cannot reasonably be supposed that the General Assembly would neglect this part of their superintendency and suffer it to be exercised by any particular parish; for, by this means, it might easily happen that the college might be subjected to such preaching as would be contrary to the minds of the generality of the colony, as well as the design of the founders.

Some, indeed, have supposed that the only design of colleges was to teach the arts and sciences, and that religion is no part of a college education; and, therefore, there ought to be no religious worship upheld or enjoined by the laws of the college, but every student may worship where and how he pleases, or as his parents or guardian shall direct. But it is probable that there is not a college to be found upon earth upon such a constitution without any regard to religion. And we know that religion, and the religion of these churches in particular, both as to doctrine and discipline, was the main design of the founders of this college (agreeable to the minds of the body of the people), and this design their successors are bound in duty to pursue. And, indeed, religion is a matter of so great consequence and importance that the knowledge of the arts and sciences, how excellent soever in themselves, are comparatively worth but little without it.

It has been also supposed that every student might be obliged to attend upon some religious worship where he shall see cause, or where his parents may order or permit; and that a monitor may be appointed in each assembly in the town, with penalties for nonattendance. But to those who understand and consider the nature of college government, such a scheme plainly appears impractical. It is found by experience that no undergraduate monitor can be fully depended upon, and that it is absolutely necessary for the governors of the college to be present and strictly observe the attendance and behavior of the students with their own eyes. . . .

And, if parents have a right to order what worship their children shall attend at college, it would take the power wholly out of the hands of the authority of college as to matters of religion; and there may be as many kinds of religious worship at college as there are different opinions of parents. . . .

It has been said that liberty of conscience ought to be allowed to all to worship as they please; upon which, it has been considered that the college acts upon the principles of liberty of conscience in the *fullest sense.* And suppose that any man, under the limitations of the law, may found a college or school for such ends and purposes, and upon such conditions and limitations with respect to those who are allowed the benefit of it, as he in his conscience shall think best. And that his conscience, who has the property of a thing, or gives it upon conditions, ought to govern in all matters relating to the use of that thing, and not his conscience; who is allowed to take the benefit; who has no right to it but according to the will and conditions of the proprietor or donor. And liberty of conscience in him who is allowed to take the benefit extends no further than to determine whether he will accept it upon those conditions. And to challenge the benefit without complying with the conditions would be to rob the proprietor (or feoffee in trust) of his property and right of disposal. . . .

The governors of the college have always freely admitted Protestants of all denominations to enjoy the benefit of an education in it, they attending upon (as they always have done) our way of worship while they are there.

It has also been said that all the students ought to attend the worship of the Church of England, or so many of them as shall see cause, or as their parents shall order or permit; that the Church of England is the established religion of this colony and that those who do not conform to it are schismatics. Upon which it has been considered that the act of Parliament in the Common Prayer Book for the establishment of the Church of England is expressly limited to England and Wales and the town of Berwick-upon-Tweed. And it is a well-known maxim in the law that the statutes of England do not extend to the plantations unless they are expressly mentioned. . . .

It has also been said that Governor Yale and Bishop Berkeley, who were churchmen, made large donations to this college. Upon which it has been considered that, when any donation is given after the foundation is laid, the law presumes that it was the intention of the donors that their donations should be improved according to the design of the founders. The law presumes that every man knows the law in that thing wherein he acts. And, since, by law, the statutes of the founders cannot be altered, it presumes that the donor had not any design to do it. And there is not the least reason to suppose that the governor or bishop intended or expected that, upon their donations, any alteration should be made in the laws of the college or any deviation from the design of the founders toward the Church of England, or any other way.

If it was so, it seems as if they intended to buy the college rather than make a donation to it. And if there was evidence that they made their donations upon that condition, the college would resign them back again. . . .

It has been further said that there are a number of churchmen in this colony who, in the annual public taxes, contribute something toward the support of the college. Upon which it has been considered that, when a community are jointly at some public charge, it is equitable that the benefit of each individual should be consulted so far as it is consistent with the general design and good of the whole, or the majority. And though it is impossible that such a benefit should be mathematically proportioned to each individual, yet this college has educated as many Episcopal ministers and others as they desired or stood in need of, which has been a sufficient compensation for their paying about a halfpenny sterling per man in the annual support of the college.

And it may still continue to be as serviceable to the Church of England as it has been if they please, for the orders of it, remain in substance just the same.

It may further be considered that this college was founded, and in a good measure endowed, many years before there were any donations made by churchmen, or so much as one Episcopal minister in the colony. And if men's contributing something toward the support of the college gives them a right to order what worship their children shall attend upon while at college, it gives the same right to parents of all other denominations, which to admit . . . would defeat the design of the founders and destroy the religious order of the college, which ought, sacredly, to be observed.

Dost thou love life? Then do not squander time, for that is the stuff life is made of.

BENJAMIN FRANKLIN, *Poor Richard's Almanac*

Design to represent the beginning and completion of an American SETTLEMENT or FARM. | *Dessein qui represente la maniere d'etablir et de parachever une ...ou FERME AMERICAIN.*

Painted by Paul Sandby, from a Design made by his Excellency Governor Pownal. Engraved by James Peake.

London, Printed for John Bowles at N° 13, in Cornhill, Robert Sayer at N° 53, in Fleet Street, Tho.º Jefferys the Corner of S.º Martins Lane in the Strand, Carington Bowles at N° 69, in S.º Pauls Church Yard, and Henry Parker at N°.º 2, in Cornhill.

THE MIDDLE COLONIES

The colonial histories of New York and Pennsylvania contrast markedly in spite of similarities in climate and resources.

In New York the period of Dutch rule ended in 1664, 20 years before the settlement of Pennsylvania. At that time the colony was still thinly settled, New Amsterdam being the only settlement of note, although trading posts such as Fort Orange (Albany) had been set up along the Hudson. The practice of granting large tracts of land to individuals — the "patroon" system — contributed to the underdevelopment of the colony since it did not attract large numbers of smallholders, and hostile Indian relations precluded isolated estates.

The English inherited the Indian problem and adopted the land grant practices of the Dutch, so that, when a treaty was signed with the Iroquois in 1692, land speculation and the development of huge plantations characterized settlement of the Hudson Valley.

By contrast, the development of Pennsylvania was orderly from the start in spite of boundary disputes with neighboring colonies. Peace was assured by a treaty with the Indians, giving payment for lands. The Frame of Government, assuring a congenial political and religious atmosphere, and Penn's skillful management and propaganda attracted a steady immigration of small farmers, artisans, and craftsmen, particularly Germans, Quakers, and Scotch-Irish, who created a prosperous and variegated way of life.

A South-West View of the CITY of NEW YORK in North America.

New York

In New York both the Dutch and English granted large estates along the Hudson to favored individuals, thus creating an aristocracy of landowners. At the same time, New York's prospering commerce gave rise to merchants whose wealth brought them high social standing, and through intermarriage the landowners and merchants formed a single aristocracy in the colony. This aristocracy, jealous of their power and influence, often opposed the colonial governors who tried to limit their "home rule."

To the Honourable
RIP VAN DAM. Esqr
PRESIDENT of His Majesties Council for the PROVINCE of NEW YORK
This View of the New Dutch Church is most humbly
Dedicated by your Honours most Obedient Servt. Wm Burgis

(Opposite) A comfortable New York family; (below) the DePeyster mansion and a child of the De-Peyster family, merchants in New York, c. 1730

Self-portrait by Gerrit Duyckinck, freeman, glazer, painter, and alderman

(Left) Pieter Schuyler, colonial military leader and first mayor of Albany, helped gain and maintain alliance with the Iroquois; (above) mill near Poughkeepsie

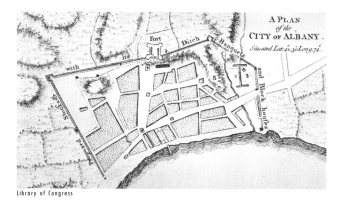

Dutch houses in Albany

(Above) "Christ and the Samaritan Woman," c. 1710, and (right) "Deborah Glen," c. 1739, each from a school of unidentified painters who catered to landowners of the upper colony. The "Christ" and others like it were copied from Dutch Bibles

(Above) Sir William Johnson, Indian agent who maintained friendly relations, enabling settlement of the Mohawk Valley; (below) Fort Johnson, scene of many Indian conferences

"An east prospect of the city of Philadelphia: taken by George Heap from the Jersey shore," 1754

Philadelphia

Although founded fifty years later than Boston and New York, Philadelphia was the largest American city by 1740, with a population of 13,000. Advertising abroad and a policy of religious toleration brought a rapid and diverse population growth, though William Penn's Quaker influence dominated the city for a long time.

Philadelphia and environs in 1706, showing the plan for the city and the public lands

SHORE, under the Direction of *NICHOLAS SKULL* Surveyor General of the PROVINCE of *PENNSYLVANIA*

A absolute Proprietors of the Province of Pennsylvania
Perspective View is humbly Dedicated by *Nicholas Skull*

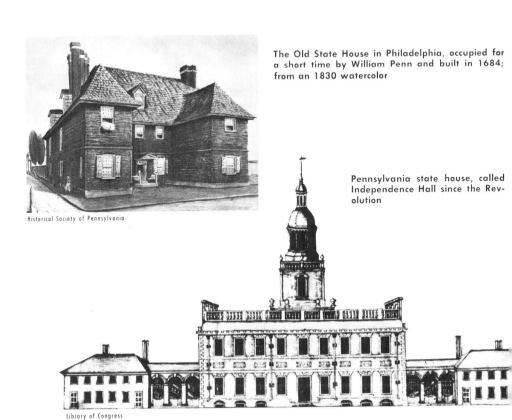

The Old State House in Philadelphia, occupied for a short time by William Penn and built in 1684; from an 1830 watercolor

Historical Society of Pennsylvania

Pennsylvania state house, called Independence Hall since the Revolution

Library of Congress

View of Bethlehem on the Delaware River, about 1768

Germantown and Bethlehem

German speaking Protestants from Moravia fled embattled Georgia where they had settled in 1735 and founded the town of Bethlehem about 1741. In the early years all land and labor in Bethlehem was communal.

German settlement in Pennsylvania had begun with the founding of Germantown in 1683 by Francis Daniel Pastorius at the head of a group of Quakers and Mennonites. Although most Germans coming to Pennsylvania went first to Germantown, the town itself did not become large and was later absorbed into Philadelphia.

King George II and Count Zinzendorf, the Moravian leader, before leaving for America

Germantown, north of Philadelphia city limits; detail from a 1740 map

Germans in several colonies were glassmakers

Governor Patrick Gordon, by Gustavus Hesselius

Hannah Penn, second wife of William Penn, painted by John Hesselius, son of Gustavus

Pennsylvania Portraits

A "walking treaty" with the Delaware Indians gave William Penn all the land he could walk in a day and a half. Later, in claiming the land, Thomas Penn hired an expert scout who greatly increased the distance covered. When Tishcohan (above, by Hesselius) and other chiefs protested, Penn hired Iroquois to drive the Delawares out

Self-portrait by Gustavus Hesselius, a Swede who came to Philadelphia in 1711. In addition to painting portraits and altar pieces Hesselius built organs, including one for the Moravians in Bethlehem

1754

112.

SAMUEL DAVIES AND GILBERT TENNENT: Reasons for
Founding Colleges in America

*The College of New Jersey (now Princeton University) was the first of several colonial
colleges that were established as a result of the Great Awakening. The charter of the
college, granted in 1746, prohibited the exclusion of any student on the basis of religion.
When Gilbert Tennent, a trustee, and Samuel Davies, later president, went to England in
1753 to solicit funds for the college, they found that this liberal provision in the charter
was a definite asset, and they were able to raise more than £3,000. Before leaving for
England, Davies and Tennent, both of whom had been active in the Great Awakening,
prepared a brochure describing the college, to be used in their fund-raising efforts. It
was first published in 1752, and then reissued in England in 1754, with some revisions.
The 1754 version of the brochure is reprinted here.*

Source: *A General Account of the Rise and State of the College, Lately Established
in the Province of New-Jersey, etc., etc.,* London, 1754.

NOTHING has a more direct tendency to advance the happiness and glory of a community than the founding of public schools and seminaries of learning for the education of youth, and adorning their minds with useful knowledge and virtue. Hereby, the rude and ignorant are civilized and rendered humane; persons who would otherwise be useless members of society are qualified to sustain with honor the offices they may be invested with for the public service; reverence of the Deity, filial piety, and obedience to the laws are inculcated and promoted.

The sciences have nowhere flourished with more success than in our mother country. The universities and seminaries of learning in England and Scotland are annually sending abroad into the Kingdom proficients in all kinds of literature; men of refined sentiments, solid judgments, and noble principles, who spread (if the expression may be allowed) a kind of literary glory over the British nation.

America remained, during a long period, in the thickest darkness of ignorance and barbarism, till Christianity, at the introduction of the Europeans, enlightened her hemisphere with the salutary beams of life and immortality. Science, her constant attendant, soon raised her depressed head, and the arts began to flourish. New England first felt her benign influences, whose sons she inspired with a generous emulation of erecting schools and colleges for the instruction of their youth, and instilling into the tender mind the principles of piety and learning. The southwestward colonies, except Virginia, continued a considerable number of years without any public institutions for the cultivation of the sciences.

At length, several gentlemen residing in and near the province of New Jersey, who were well-wishers to the felicity of their country and real friends of religion and learning, having observed the vast increase of those colonies, with the rudeness and ignorance of their inhabitants for want of the necessary means of improvement, first projected the scheme of a collegiate education in that province.

The immediate motives to this generous design were: the great number of Christian societies then lately formed in various parts of the country, where many thousands of the inhabitants, ardently desirous of the administration of religious ordinances, were entirely destitute of the necessary means of instruction and incapable of being relieved; the urgent applications that were annually made by those vacant congregations to the clergy in their collective bodies; complaining in the most moving manner of their unhappy circumstances in being deprived of the ordinary means of salvation and left to grope after happiness, almost in the obscurity of paganism, though the light of revelation shone on their surrounding neighbors; the great scarcity of candidates for the ministerial function to comply with these pious and Christian demands; the colleges of New England educating hardly a competent number for the service of its own churches — these considerations were the most urgent arguments for the immediate prosecution of the abovementioned scheme of education.

Accordingly, in the year 1747, a petition was presented to His Excellency Jonathan Belcher, Esq., governor of that province (a gentleman who has long signalized himself as a patron of religion and learning), praying His Majesty's grant of a charter for the establishment of a public seminary of literature in New Jersey. His Excellency, with the approbation of the council and attorney general of the said province, was pleased to comply with their request; and ordered a charter to pass the seals, incorporating sundry gentlemen, to the number of twenty-three, by the name of the Trustees of the College of New Jersey; and appointing the governor of New Jersey, for the time being, who is His Majesty's representative, to act as their president when convened. This charter places the society upon the most catholic foundation — all Protestants of every denomination who are loyal subjects to Our Most Gracious Sovereign (the happy effects of whose mild and equal administration the remotest colonies of the British empire sensibly experience and gratefully acknowledge) are admitted to the enjoyment of all its privileges and allowed the unlimited exercise of their religion.

The trustees, thus authorized with ample powers for the execution of this laudable design, in conformity to the plan of their charter, applied themselves with the utmost deliberation to form and enact such rules and orders for the regulation of the methods of instruction and conduct of the students as might tend to prevent the entrance of vice into the society, and the introduction of idleness, vanity, and extravagant expenses among its members. It would be repugnant to the design of a general narrative, as well as impertinent to the reader, to enter into a minute detail of these several private regulations. It will suffice to say that the two principal objects the trustees had in view were science and religion. Their first concern was to cultivate the minds of the pupils in all those branches of erudition which are generally taught in the universities abroad; and, to perfect their design, their next care was to rectify the heart by inculcating the great precepts of Christianity in order to make them good.

Upon these views this society was founded. Providence so far smiled upon the undertaking, in the first instance, as to point out a gentleman, possessed of every requisite endowment, to be placed at the head of such an academy. The Rev. Mr. Aaron Burr has been long known in these parts of America for his piety, affability, universal acquaintance with the arts and sciences, and his easy, familiar methods of instruction. Under his immediate tuition and government, this society has flourished far beyond the most raised and sanguine expectations. The number of students has increased, in the short space of five years, from eight or ten, to about sixty; besides near forty in the grammar school.

As no human institutions in a world of imperfection and error are so completely modeled as to exclude the possibility of further emendation, it may be said, without any intention of disparagement to other learned seminaries, that the governors of this college have endeavored to improve upon the commonly received plans of education. They proceed not so much in the method of a dogmatic institution, by prolix discourses on the different branches of the sciences, by burdening the memory and imposing heavy and disagreeable tasks, as in the Socratic way of free dialogue between teacher and pupil, or between the students themselves under the inspection of their tutors. In this manner, the attention is engaged, the mind entertained, and the scholar animated in the pursuit of knowledge. In fine, the arts and sciences are conveyed into the minds of youth in a method, the most easy, natural, and familiar.

But as religion ought to be the end of all instruction and gives it the last degree of perfection; as one of the primary views of this foundation was to educate young gentlemen for the sacred office of the ministry and fit them for the discharge of so no-

ble an employment; divinity, the mistress of the sciences, engages the peculiar attention of the governors of this society. Stated times are set apart for the study of the Holy Scriptures in the original languages, and stated hours daily consecrated to the service of religion. The utmost care is taken to discountenance vice and to encourage the practice of virtue and a manly, rational, and Christian behavior in the students. Enthusiasm, on the one hand, and profaneness, on the other, are equally guarded against and meet with the severest checks.

Under such management, this seminary, from the smallest beginnings, quickly drew the public attention, enlarged the number of her pupils, raised her reputation; and now, though in her infancy, almost rivals her ancient sisters upon the Continent.

Daily observation evinces that in proportion as learning makes its progress in a country, it softens the natural roughness, eradicates the prejudices, and transforms the genius and disposition of its inhabitants. New Jersey and the adjacent provinces already feel the happy effects of this useful institution. A general desire of knowledge seems to be spreading among the people. Parents are inspired with an emulation of cultivating the minds of their offspring; public stations are honorably filled by gentlemen who have received their education here; and, from hence, many Christian assemblies are furnished with men of distinguished talents for the discharge of the pastoral office. . . .

From the above representation of the ends for which this corporation was founded, the happy effects of its institution, and its present necessitous circumstances, it is hoped that the pious and benevolent in Great Britain, into whose hands these papers may fall, will extend their generous aids in the prosecution and completion of so excellent and useful a design. A Design! upon the success of which the happiness of multitudes in sundry colonies, and their numerous posterity, in the present and future ages far distant, in a great measure depends. A Design! which not only tends to promote the weal of the British inhabitants but also of the German emigrants; and to spread the gospel of salvation among the benighted Indian tribes and attach them to His Majesty's government. A Design! which is not calculated to promote the low purposes of a party, but in its views and consequences affects the Protestant interest in general, and Great Britain in particular, both in religious and civil respects; since, by this, the filial duty of her descendants will be inculcated, their manners reformed, and her trade increased; which is the basis of her empire, glory, and felicity.

The inhabitants of the infant colonies, dependent upon this seminary, unable to relieve themselves, are constrained to solicit and implore the assistance of others. And to whom shall they look but to their tender and powerful parent? To move her compassion, they plead their relation as children, as

fellow subjects, as Christian and Protestant brethren with her sons that still enjoy the advantages of residing in their native country. They plead the deplorable circumstances of the church, and the exigencies of the state, for want of such an institution brought to maturity. And they beg leave modestly to intimate their importance to their mother country, as they enlarge the British dominions upon a vast continent, whither the industrious poor may transplant themselves and find a comfortable subsistence, as they are a check upon the growth of the French power in America; engage the Indian natives to the British interest; furnish various assistances in time of war against the common enemy; and carry on sundry branches of trade advantageous to Great Britain, which will undoubtedly flourish more in proportion to their improvements in the liberal arts and sciences — for history and observation assure us that learning and trade mutually promote each other.

113.

BENJAMIN FRANKLIN: Albany Plan of Union

The problem of colonial defense on the eve of the French and Indian War led the English Board of Trade to call for a congress of the American colonies in June 1754. Seven colonies — Connecticut, Maryland, Massachusetts, New Hampshire, New York, Pennsylvania, and Rhode Island — sent delegates to Albany with instructions to work out plans for joint defense measures, for it was thought that without a collective effort they would be no match for the French. The delegates went a little further, and the so-called Albany Plan of Union, drawn up by one of the Pennsylvania delegates, Benjamin Franklin, provided for a loose confederation presided over by a president general and having a limited authority to levy taxes to be paid to a central treasury. Neither the Crown (jealous of its authority) nor any of the colonial assemblies (unwilling to sacrifice sovereignty) approved the plan, and the war was conducted under the old system. Despite the fact that the issue here was not independence, the Albany Plan was nonetheless a farsighted document, for it contained the seeds of the solution to colonial problems later adopted in the Articles of Confederation and in the Constitution.

Source: *Works*, III, pp. 8-29.

IT IS PROPOSED that humble application be made for an act of Parliament of Great Britain by virtue of which one general government may be formed in America, including all the said colonies, within and under which government each colony may retain its present constitution, except in the particulars wherein a change may be directed by the said act, as hereafter follows.

1. That the said general government be administered by a president general, to be appointed and supported by the Crown; and a Grand Council, to be chosen by the representatives of the people of the several colonies met in their respective assemblies.

2. That within ———— months after the passing such act, the House of Representatives that happen to be sitting within that time, or that shall be especially for that purpose convened, may and shall choose members for the Grand Council, in the following proportion, that is to say:

Massachusetts Bay 7
New Hampshire 2
Connecticut 5
Rhode Island 2
New York 4
New Jerseys 3
Pennsylvania 6
Maryland 4
Virginia 7
North Carolina 4
South Carolina 4
                                 ——
                                 48

3. ———— who shall meet for the first time at the city of Philadelphia, being called by the president general as soon as conveniently may be after his appointment.

4. That there shall be a new election of the members of the Grand Council every three years; and, on the death or resignation of any member, his place shall be supplied by a new choice at the next sitting of the Assembly of the colony he represented.

5. That after the first three years, when

JOIN, or DIE.

Courtesy, the Library of Congress

Wood engraving in the "Pennsylvania Gazette," 1754

the proportion of money arising out of each colony to the general treasury can be known, the number of members to be chosen for each colony shall, from time to time, in all ensuing elections, be regulated by that proportion, yet so as that the number to be chosen by any one province be not more than seven nor less than two.

6. That the Grand Council shall meet once in every year, and oftener if occasion require, at such time and place as they shall adjourn to at the last preceding meeting, or as they shall be called to meet at by the president general on any emergency; he having first obtained in writing the consent of seven of the members to such call and sent duly and timely notice to the whole.

7. That the Grand Council have power to choose their speaker; and shall neither be dissolved, prorogued, nor continued sitting longer than six weeks at one time, without their own consent or the special command of the Crown.

8. That the members of the Grand Council shall be allowed for their service 10s. sterling per diem, during their session and journey to and from the place of meet-

ing; twenty miles to be reckoned a day's journey.

9. That the assent of the president general be requisite to all acts of the Grand Council, and that it be his office and duty to cause them to be carried into execution.

10. That the president general, with the advice of the Grand Council, hold or direct all Indian treaties in which the general interest of the colonies may be concerned; and make peace or declare war with Indian nations.

11. That they make such laws as they judge necessary for regulating all Indian trade.

12. That they make all purchases from Indians, for the Crown, of lands not now within the bounds of particular colonies, or that shall not be within their bounds when some of them are reduced to more convenient dimensions.

13. That they make new settlements on such purchases by granting lands in the King's name, reserving a quitrent to the Crown for the use of the general treasury.

14. That they make laws for regulating and governing such new settlements, till the

Crown shall think fit to form them into particular governments.

15. That they raise and pay soldiers and build forts for the defense of any of the colonies and equip vessels of force to guard the coasts and protect the trade on the ocean, lakes, or great rivers; but they shall not impress men in any colony without the consent of the legislature.

16. That for these purposes they have power to make laws and lay and levy such general duties, imposts, or taxes as to them shall appear most equal and just (considering the ability and other circumstances of the inhabitants in the several colonies), and such as may be collected with the least inconvenience to the people; rather discouraging luxury than loading industry with unnecessary burdens.

17. That they may appoint a general treasurer and particular treasurer in each government when necessary; and, from time to time, may order the sums in the treasuries of each government into the general treasury; or draw on them for special payments, as they find most convenient.

18. Yet no money to issue but by joint orders of the president general and Grand Council; except where sums have been appropriated to particular purposes and the president general is previously empowered by an act to draw for such sums.

19. That the general accounts shall be yearly settled and reported to the several assemblies.

20. That a quorum of the Grand Council, empowered to act with the president general, do consist of twenty-five members, among whom shall be one or more from a majority of the colonies.

21. That the laws made by them for the purposes aforesaid shall not be repugnant but, as near as may be, agreeable to the laws of England and shall be transmitted to the King in Council for approbation as soon as may be after their passing; and if not disapproved within three years after presentation, to remain in force.

22. That in case of the death of the president general, the speaker of the Grand Council for the time being shall succeed and be vested with the same powers and authorities, to continue till the King's pleasure be known.

23. That all military commission officers, whether for land or sea service, to act under this general constitution, shall be nominated by the president general; but the approbation of the Grand Council is to be obtained before they receive their commissions. And all civil officers are to be nominated by the Grand Council and to receive the president general's approbation before they officiate.

24. But in case of vacancy by death or removal of any officer, civil or military, under this constitution, the governor of the province in which such vacancy happens may appoint, till the pleasure of the president general and Grand Council can be known.

25. That the particular military as well as civil establishments in each colony remain in their present state, the general constitution notwithstanding; and that on sudden emergencies any colony may defend itself and lay the accounts of expense thence arising before the president general and General Council, who may allow and order payment of the same, as far as they judge such accounts just and reasonable.

114.

BENJAMIN FRANKLIN: The Problems of Colonial Union

The year 1754 marked the outbreak of the French and Indian War. In an effort to obtain Indian support against the French as well as unity among the colonists, colonial representatives met at Albany in June. Franklin, a Pennsylvania delegate, presented his famed Albany Plan of Union, a scheme designed to unite the colonies. This plan was approved by the delegates, only to be afterwards rejected by the colonial assemblies as leaving too much power in royal hands, while at the same time it was disapproved in England as leaving too little. "The different and contrary reasons of dislike to my plan made me suspect that it was really the true medium," Franklin later wrote, "and I am still of the opinion it would have been happy for both sides of the water if it had been adopted." In the following letter, written in December, he set forth the merits of his proposed union to William Shirley, the royal governor of Massachusetts.

Source: *Works*, III, pp. 37-40.

On the subject of uniting the colonies more intimately with Great Britain by allowing them representatives in Parliament.

Dec. 22, 1754

Sir:

Since the conversation Your Excellency was pleased to honor me with, on the subject of *uniting the colonies* more intimately with Great Britain by allowing them *representatives in Parliament,* I have something further considered that matter and am of opinion that such a union would be very acceptable to the colonies, provided they had a reasonable number of representatives allowed them; and that all the old acts of Parliament restraining the trade or cramping the manufactures of the colonies be at the same time repealed; and the British subjects *on this side the water* put, in those respects, on the same footing with those in Great Britain, till the new Parliament, representing the whole, shall think it for the

interest of the whole to reenact some or all of them. It is not that I imagine so many representatives will be allowed the colonies as to have any great weight by their numbers, but I think there might be sufficient to occasion those laws to be better and more impartially considered, and perhaps to overcome the interest of a petty corporation, or of any particular set of artificers or traders in England who heretofore seem, in some instances, to have been more regarded than all the colonies or than was consistent with the general interest or best national good.

I think, too, that the government of the colonies by a Parliament in which they are fairly represented would be vastly more agreeable to the people than the method lately attempted to be introduced by royal instructions, as well as more agreeable to the nature of an English constitution and to English liberty; and that such laws as now seem to bear hard on the colonies would (when judged by such a Parliament for the best interest of the whole) be more cheerfully submitted to and more easily executed.

I should hope, too, that by such a union the people of Great Britain and the people of the colonies would learn to consider themselves as not belonging to a different community with different interests but to one community with one interest, which, I imagine, would contribute to strengthen the whole and greatly lessen the danger of future separations.

It is, I suppose, agreed to be the general interest of any state that its people be numerous and rich; men enough to fight in its defense, and enough to pay sufficient taxes to defray the charge; for these circumstances tend to the security of the state and its protection from foreign power. But it seems not of so much importance whether the fighting be done by John or Thomas, or the tax paid by William or Charles. The iron manufacture employs and enriches British subjects, but is it of any importance to the state whether the manufacturers live at Birmingham, or Sheffield, or both, since they are still within its bounds, and their wealth and persons still at its command?

Could the Goodwin Sands be laid dry by banks, and land equal to a large country thereby gained to England, and presently filled with English inhabitants, would it be right to deprive such inhabitants of the common privileges enjoyed by other Englishmen — the right of vending their produce in the same ports, or of making their own shoes, because a merchant or a shoemaker living on the old land might fancy it more for his advantage to trade or make shoes for them? Would this be right, even if the land were gained at the expense of the state? And would it not seem less right if the charge and labor of gaining the additional territory to Britain had been borne by the settlers themselves? And would not the hardship appear yet greater if the people of the new country should be allowed no representatives in the Parliament enacting such impositions?

Now, I look on the colonies as so many countries gained to Great Britain, and more advantageous to it than if they had been gained out of the seas around its coasts and joined to its land; for, being in different climates, they afford greater variety of produce; and being separated by the ocean, they increase much more its shipping and seamen; and since they are all included in the British empire, which has only extended itself by their means, and the strength and wealth of the parts are the strength and wealth of the whole, what imports it to the general state whether a merchant, a smith, or a hatter grow rich in Old or New England? And if, through increase of people, two smiths are wanted for one employed before, why may not the *new* smith be allowed to live and thrive in the *new* country, as well as the *old* in the *old*?

In fine, why should the countenance of a state be *partially* afforded to its people unless it be most in favor of those who have most merit? And if there be any difference, those who have most contributed to enlarge Britain's empire and commerce, increase her strength, her wealth, and the numbers of her people, at the risk of their own lives and private fortunes, in new and strange countries, methinks ought rather to expect some preference.

Index of Authors

*The numbers in brackets
indicate selection numbers
in this volume*

DOUGLASS, WILLIAM (c. 1691-Oct. 21, 1752), Boston physician and pamphleteer. Opposed smallpox vaccination. [83, 90]

DUDLEY, THOMAS (1576-July 31, 1653), colonial administrator. Governor of Massachusetts Bay Colony (1634, 1640, 1645, 1650) and thirteen times deputy governor; member of the committee (1637) on founding Harvard College; overseer of Harvard. [22]

DUMMER, JEREMIAH (c. 1679-May 19, 1739), Massachusetts and Connecticut agent in England. Benefactor of Yale College. [81]

EDWARDS, JONATHAN (Oct. 5, 1703-March 22, 1758), Congregational clergyman, philosopher, and theologian. Pastor (1729-50) of church at Northampton, Mass.; missionary to the Indians at Stockbridge, Mass. (1751-57); president (1757-58) of the College of New Jersey (Princeton); prolific treatise writer; wrote *Personal Narrative* (c. 1740), *Sinners in the Hands of an Angry God* (1741), *Freedom of the Will* (1754), *Original Sin* (1758). [96, 101]

ELIOT, JOHN (c. Aug. 5, 1604-May 21, 1690), clergyman and missionary, "Apostle to the Indians." Teacher (1632-90) of the church at Roxbury, Mass.; missionary to the Indians; author of *A Primer or Catechism in the Massachusetts Indian Language* (1653) and an Indian language translation of the Bible (1661), the first Bible printed in North America. [24, 36]

FRANKLIN, BENJAMIN (Jan. 17, 1706-April 17, 1790), printer, author, philanthropist, inventor, scientist, diplomat, and statesman. Born Boston, published *Poor Richard's Almanac* (1732-57); signed the Declaration of Independence; in France, 1776-85; member of the Constitutional Convention (1787); author of *Autobiography*. [88, 103, 105, 107, 108, 109, 113, 114] See also Author Index, Vols. 2, 3.

FRELINGHUYSEN, THEODORUS (1691-c. 1748), Dutch Reformed clergyman. Born in Germany. [82]

HIGGINSON, FRANCIS (c. Aug. 6, 1586-Aug. 6, 1630), Anglican clergyman. Drafted the confession of faith and covenant for the church at Salem, Mass. (c. 1629). [16]

HUBBARD, WILLIAM (c. 1621-Sept. 14, 1704), Congregational clergyman and historian. Pastor (1658-1702) of the church at Ipswich, Mass.; wrote *A General History of New England* (pub. 1815). [58]

JOHNSON, EDWARD (Sept. 1598-April 23, 1672), trader and author. Founder of Woburn, Mass. (1640); author of a history of New England. [47]

KALM, PETER (1715-Nov. 16, 1779), Swedish botanist. Toured North America (1748-51); wrote first scientific account of its natural history. [104]

LIVINGSTON, WILLIAM (Nov. 30, 1723-July 25, 1790), lawyer. Member (1774-76) of the Continental Congress; governor of New Jersey (1778-90); member of the Constitutional Convention (1787). [111]

MARVELL, ANDREW (March 31, 1621-Aug. 18, 1678), English poet, political satirist, and civil servant. [49]

MATHER, COTTON (Feb. 12, 1663-Feb. 13, 1728), Congregational clergyman. Assisted his father, Increase Mather, in pastorate of Second Church, Boston (1685-1723) and succeeded him (1723-28); supported witchcraft trials and executions (1692-93) but later withdrew that support; wrote *Wonders of the Invisible World* (1693), *Magnalia Christi Americana* (1702). [69, 75, 77]

MATHER, INCREASE (June 21, 1639-Aug. 23, 1723), Congregational clergyman. Father of Cotton Mather; pastor (1664-1723) of Second Church, Boston; president (1685-1701) of Harvard College; in England, secured new charter and new governor for Massachusetts (1688-92); wrote *Cases of Conscience Concerning Evil Spirits* (1693). [62, 68]

MAYHEW, JONATHAN (Oct. 8, 1720-July 9, 1766), Congregational clergyman. Pastor (1747-66) of West Church, Boston; noted for liberalism in religious doctrine. [106]

MICHAËLIUS, JONAS (b. 1584), clergyman. Founder of Dutch Reformed Church in New Amsterdam; Indian missionary. [15]

MORTON, THOMAS (c. 1590-c. 1647), early Massachusetts settler. Founded Merry Mount (Quincy); outraged Puritan leaders; was twice exiled from New England. [23]

MÜHLENBERG, HENRY MELCHIOR (Sept. 6, 1711-Oct. 7, 1787), Lutheran minister. Helped establish and spread Lutheranism in America. [98]

PASTORIUS, FRANCIS D. (Sept. 26, 1651-c. Jan. 1, 1720), founder of Germantown, Pa. Germantown official and educator; lawyer and author. [72]

PENN, WILLIAM (Oct. 14, 1644-July 30, 1718), Quaker, founder and proprietor of Pennsylvania. Born in London; political activist and tireless advocate of religious toleration; several times imprisoned for heterodoxy; prolific writer; author of *No Cross, No Crown* (in prison, 1669), *The Great Case of Liberty of Conscience* (1670), *Some Fruits of Solitude* (1693). [61, 70, 71]

PORY, JOHN (1572-Sept. 1635), English traveler, author, and geographer. Secretary of the Virginia Council at Jamestown (July 1619). [9]

ROBINSON, JOHN (c. 1575-March 1, 1625), English Separatist clergyman. Organizer of the Pilgrim emigration from Holland to America and effected their removal to Plymouth, England (1620). [11]

SEWALL, SAMUEL (March 28, 1652-Jan. 1, 1730), jurist. Member (1684-86, 1689-1725) of the Massachusetts Bay Colony Governor's Council; presided at Salem over witchcraft cases (1692); confessed error and guilt for his part in trials (1697); justice (1692-1718) and chief justice (1718-28) of the Massachusetts Superior Court. [73, 74]

SHUTE, SAMUEL (Jan. 12, 1662-April 15, 1742), colonial administrator. Governor (1716-27) of Massachusetts Bay and New Hampshire. [84]

SMITH, JOHN (c. Jan. 9, 1579/80-June 21, 1631), explorer and military adventurer. Member (c. 1607) of the governing council of Jamestown, Va.; led exploring expeditions up Potomac and Rappahannock rivers and around Chesapeake Bay; president (1608-09) of Jamestown Colony; wrote *A True Relation of . . . Virginia* (1608), *The Generall Historie of Virginia, New England, and the Summer Isles* (1624). [6, 8]

SMITH, WILLIAM (June 25, 1728-Dec. 3, 1793), jurist. Chief justice (1763) of New York; member (from 1767) of the New York Provincial Council; chief justice (1786-93) of Canada. [111]

SPARKE, JOHN (fl. 1564), passenger accompanying Admiral John Hawkins' expedition to West Indies (1564-65). [2]

SYMONDS, WILLIAM (fl. 1609), Anglican clergyman. [7]

TENNENT, GILBERT (Feb. 5, 1703-July 23, 1764), Presbyterian clergyman. Evangelist leader of Great Awakening; trustee of College of New Jersey (Princeton). [112]

TOMPSON, BENJAMIN (July 14, 1642- ? April 10, 1714), verse-writer, educator, and physician. [56]

URMSTONE, JOHN (fl. 1711), North Carolina missionary for the Society for Propagating the Gospel. [78]

VAN DER DONCK, ADRIAEN (May 7, 1620-c. 1655), Dutch lawyer. Emigrated to New Netherland as officer of justice for Kiliaen van Rensselaer, owner of large estate. [43]

WARD, NATHANIEL (c. 1578-Oct. 1652), Anglican clergyman. Dismissed from church for nonconformity; pastor at Ipswich, Mass.; wrote first Massachusetts legal code (1641); author of *The Simple Cobbler of Aggawam in America* (1647). [38]

WILLIAMS, ROGER (? 1603-c. March 1, 1683), Puritan clergyman. Advocated religious tolerance; banished from Massachusetts Bay Colony (Oct. 1635) for criticizing civil and religious authorities; with a few followers founded Providence (c. June 1636), the first settlement in Rhode Island; president (1654-57) of the colony. [46]

WINTHROP, JOHN (Jan. 22, 1588-April 5, 1649), lawyer and colonial leader. First governor (1629-34, 1637-40, 1642-44, 1646-49) of Massachusetts Bay Colony; organizer and first president (1643) of the Confederation of the United Colonies of New England; author of a *Journal* giving the history of New England. [20, 25, 28, 32]

WISE, JOHN (Aug. 1652-April 8, 1725), Congregational clergyman. Pastor (1680-1725) of the church at Ipswich, Mass.; opposed several of the convictions at the Salem witchcraft trials (1692). [79]